Plantation, Town, and County

edited by
Elinor Miller and Eugene D. Genovese

PLANTATION, TOWN, AND COUNTY

Essays on the Local History
of American Slave Society

UNIVERSITY OF ILLINOIS PRESS
Urbana   Chicago   London

For my parents
E. M.

In memory of Robert Starobin
E. D. G.

LIBRARY OF CONGRESS CATALOGING IN PUBLICATION DATA

Miller, Elinor, 1944–   comp.
  Plantation, town, and county.

  Includes bibliographical references.
  CONTENTS: Phillips, U. B. The slave labor
problem in the Charleston district.—Bonner, J. C.
Profile of a late antebellum community.—Hering, J.
Plantation economy in Leon County, 1830–40. [etc.]
    1. Slavery in the United States—Addresses,
essays, lectures. I. Genovese, Eugene D., 1930–
joint comp. II. Title.
E441.M63 1974   301.44'93   73-20359
ISBN 0-252-00390-X
ISBN 0-252-00412-4 (pbk.)

Contents

Introduction: New Perspectives
through Local History

The South, the Old and the New but especially the Old, has always been an enigma even to its participants, and to some extent it probably shall always remain so. The seemingly endless dualities that have gone into its making have resisted classification, much less transcendence. It is enough, for purposes of illustration, to juxtapose the undeniable cultural unity of southern Anglo-Americans and Afro-Americans—a unity that defines everything that we call "southern"—with that equally undeniable cultural separation which, among other manifestations, must provide the starting point for any attempt to understand black nationalism.

It is, however, the responsibility of historians to unravel enigmas, or at least to narrow their sphere; it is not their responsibility, although it is sometimes their practice, to wallow in paradoxes or surrender to elusiveness. For better or worse, the work goes on. In recent years our understanding of the South has been advanced by the intrusion of new viewpoints as well as by excellent work along older lines. In particular, the development of the comparative method has placed the Old South in a new light. As Frank Tannenbaum foresaw and C. Vann Woodward has demonstrated (see especially his recent book, *American Counterpoint*), the southern experience with slavery must be understood in the context of the worldwide experience with slavery, whether or not one focuses primarily on contrasts or on similarities.

This advance, together with those occasioned by the extension of psychological, econometric, and other methods of analysis, has its limits. Before long we find ourselves with the old questions, the old dilemmas, although, let us hope, on a higher level of sophistication and with a deeper and more enriched understanding of what is at issue. When used responsibly, models, analogies, and comparisons should help the historian do his job. But the job itself remains that of research, of empirical investigation—of getting at the story. We have quite possibly arrived at the point beyond which the theoretical quarrels—the sharp differences among talented and honest scholars over interpretation—cannot usefully be pursued without a massive introduction of new data.

Our understanding of the social history of the Old South and the slave regime remains severely circumscribed by the level of generalization on which we have been working. We know enough to differentiate Tidewater from Piedmont, upper South from lower, cotton belt from tobacco belt, yeoman farms from plantations, and so forth. But we hardly know enough about the differences in quality of life from one area or type of unit to another. Forced, as we generally are, to work with categories that are much cruder than they need be, we too often end with judgments more sweeping than we ourselves believe to be safe even as generalizations.

The extent of advance in the decades ahead would therefore seem to rest less on the introduction of new hypotheses, theories, or methods, although these must always be forthcoming, than on deeper research into the South's constituent parts. Perhaps it would be better to say that the time has come to apply and test our hypotheses, theories, and methods, old as well as new, in a more rigorous and specific way. Local history —that is, the discrete study of plantations, towns, and counties—is hardly new. Indeed, it may be a bit too old, for it has often been confused with antiquarianism by those whose definition of sophistication seems to include contempt for, or indifference to, those grubby details without which good history cannot be written.

Ulrich Bonnell Phillips, in his studies of Milledgeville, Georgia, and the Charleston district (the latter included in this volume), sets a good example early in the century. Our first great general historian of southern slavery did not find it beneath his dignity to build this history from the ground up. James Bonner's outstanding study of Hancock County, Georgia, has won him the admiration of specialists ever since its publication more than twenty-five years ago, but it has not yet generated the rash of parallel studies he might have hoped for. E. Merton Coulter has, for years now, filled the *Georgia Historical Quarterly* and his books with pioneering efforts in local history, but he has apparently had indifferent success in winning young followers. Edward Phifer's work on Burke County, North Carolina, has earned him the warm admiration of the historical profession, but again has inspired few followers.

In short, we have long had good men to show us how to transform local history into work of general significance. We have, however, been slow to learn. Still, there are signs of movement, as the recent studies by younger scholars in Louisiana suggest. We may yet get what we so clearly need: a large number of sensitive, in-depth studies of slavery in particular places—studies that can help us to refine, deepen, correct, and, if necessary, replace those generalizations about southern society which we are now quarreling over.

The studies presented in this volume are uneven; some, to be sure, are a good deal stronger and more useful than others. And they do not exhaust the literature. We present these selections in the hope that they bring together the most useful of such works, that they reveal the scope of research done so far, that they suggest the possibilities inherent in local studies, and, above all, that they stimulate further efforts by those for whom southern history remains so fascinating and so challenging.

PART ONE

The Slaveholding County

The first three essays in Part One focus on the slave economy, although they display careful attention to the social setting of that economy. Among the advantages of the contributions of Phillips and Bonner is careful attention to the temporal dimension of socio-economic change. Each in its own way provides a model for similar studies.

The contributions of Price, Phifer, Corlew, and Dorsett taken together touch on a surprising range of problems inherent in the slave regime. They illuminate the differences between farm and plantation life, as well as the specifics of slave hiring, control, resistance, and a host of other features of antebellum life.

Ulrich Bonnell Phillips

The Slave Labor Problem in the Charleston District

The Charleston district of South Carolina has long been a subject of deep interest to southern historians. Because it was the most radical, and because it was the earliest to proclaim its seccessionist sympathies, many historians have thought that it typified the ultimate dilemma of the entire South. Historians today are less likely to accept this thesis but are no less interested in the region. In this masterful essay, the late Ulrich Bonnell Phillips explores the complexities of a system which was the basis of an extensive labor system, a mode of racial control, and an intricate system of social organization which historians today recognize as the basis of Afro-American civilization.

For many years historians have neglected certain of Phillips's writings because they represented too closely the sympathies of an elite whose social order was clearly restrictive and repressive. Our antipathy to the social mores of that elite should not, however, obscure our recognition of its importance or blind us to its accomplishments. Judged upon its own terms, it was the architect of one of the most intriguing and stable cultures to exist in the Western world from the late eighteenth to the mid-nineteenth century. Phillips's deep sympathies to this social order allow a peculiar historical reconstruction which no amount of "objective data" can provide. Phillips perceives the ultimate ambiguities of a system predicated upon the slave who was both human and chattel, and he confronts us with the anguish of men, white and black, caught in a system which by 1860 had reached an impasse. For the slaveholding elite of the Charleston district, the Civil War was not a mere political conflict, but one which broached the end of a civilization.

The essential features and tendencies of a regime can best be analyzed in those instances in which it has been most fully developed and most persistently maintained. Isolated phases of American Negro slavery

Reprinted with permission from the *Political Science Quarterly*, XXII (September, 1907), 416–439.

may be studied with some success in many places and periods, but its complex working and far-reaching effects can perhaps be learned with relative completeness only from a study of some long-settled and very black portion of the southern black belts. The best example for our purpose is the low-lying coast region of South Carolina and Georgia, which had its focus at Charleston and may well be called the Charleston district. There as elsewhere the establishment of slavery was due entirely to the desire for a labor supply, and its patent effects were chiefly of an economic sort; but the system had also deep and inevitable influences and effects of a social character, and of course developed conspicuous outcroppings in national politics. For all these things the material which can be found for the Charleston district is eloquent.

The physical features of the district, so different from most other parts of North America, invited the early introduction of the plantation system, with Negro labor. The heat, dampness, and malaria retarded the growth of the white population and promoted the relative increase of the Negroes. The development of rice, indigo, and sea-island cotton as staples caused the firm establishment of plantations to utilize the fertile alluvial soil of the lowlands. The splendid harbor and the tongue of elevated and healthful land at Charleston caused the growth there of a genuine capital of the district. The regime thus promoted by the unchanging conditions of nature waxed strong and endured for generations, with far less change than is usual in American life. Lowland South Carolina began its successful career as a colony in the wilderness, producing staples by the use of Negro labor under white control on plantations, with its center and soul at Charleston. Thus it stands today, decadent it is true, but not revolutionized. It stands thus far, indeed, as a monument to the power of soil and climate in shaping and preserving systems of human activity, and to the effectiveness of race distinctions in resisting even cataclysmal attempts at alteration.

The colony was founded in 1670 by settlers who came to seek their fortune. At first they had no staple industry. They labored to produce most of the things they needed, and they exported only a small value in naval stores and peltry with which to buy a few European goods. About 1693 came the discovery of rice as a staple for export, and this gave an incentive for procuring a large labor supply and organizing it on the most effective system feasible. Negroes were found to be especially adapted to the climate, and the plantation system was borrowed from the West Indies, where it already flourished. A regime of plantation industrialism was instituted which was strong enough to dominate the situation. The Lords Proprietors, with their attempts at feudalism and arbitrary extraneous control, were brushed away; they were replaced after 1729 by a royal government, which was welcomed because it permitted a very large degree of self-government. The citizens worked out their own destiny, following the line of least resistance, which of course might or might not be the line of greatest permanent efficiency. There arose, then, a peculiar system of industry, commerce, and social life as the result of physiographic and ethnic influences. Its general features are too familiar to require description here. An important fact was the coordinate growth of the plantations to produce the staples and of the city of Charleston for commerce and incidental industry.

Indigo and long-staple cotton, as well as rice, were successively found to be producible with profit in the Carolina lowlands. The great demand of the world for these staples caused the growth of a strong local demand for labor, and especially for Negroes, who were known to be largely immune to malaria and unoppressed by the heat. Negro labor, of necessity unfree, furnished the chief supply in both country and city. Plantations were established wherever fertile land could be found in reach of navigation. These were scattered throughout the lowlands, mostly in isolation from one another, but all tending to have the same general features. It was found by experience that the best results in rice and indigo production were obtained from plantations with working forces of about thirty hands each, and the tendency was toward that size in the industrial unit.[1] The spread of a system like this, distributing one white family to every isolated group of from five to twenty or more Negro families, in a malarial region, resulted in a situation not fully duplicated elsewhere on the continent. The Africans were too numerous in the early stages for the whites to succeed nearly so well as did the Virginians and the men of the upland cotton belt in taming them to the ways of civilization. The field work was always done in the crudest manner; and the necessity of the master's moving away from his estate in the warm months, to escape the malaria, involved the adoption of some system of routine which would work with more or less automatic regularity without his own inspiring or impelling presence. Hence the system of tasks, by which the white overseer or Negro foreman (called a "driver") assigned a stated measure of land to be worked over by each laborer each day, varying in amount according to the laborer's classification as an able-bodied, prime or "full hand," a three-quarter hand, a half-hand, etc. When special work had to be done, like clearing land of

1. B. R. Carrol, *Historical Collections of South Carolina*, II, 202, and American Historical Association *Report* for 1903, I, 445.

its timber, the Negroes might be worked in gangs under the master's direction; but as a rule the task system was followed, as being more nearly automatic and requiring less active and vigilant supervision. Aside from field labor, there was need of such work as cooperage, blacksmithing, boating, and domestic service, to which chosen Negroes were assigned. In general it was recognized as useless to expect a high degree of efficiency in any branch of plantation labor or service, and there was a general contentment with moderate efficiency on the part of the Negroes and moderate profits from their unstrenuous labor. Zeal and growth in skill were encouraged; but, in view of the great numerical preponderance of the Negroes, to keep them docile was considered more important than to increase their labor value.

In the first stage of plantation and city development, the unskilled labor supply was made up almost wholly of Negro slaves, while the whites filled all other ranks, acting as artisans, foremen, farmers, planters, merchants, etc. A few of the whites were indentured servants, and a few white freemen were unskilled laborers, but only a few in either case, and the number was diminishing. It is safe to say that from about 1700 to 1720 there was fairly complete identity of racial, industrial, and legal classes. The Negroes were unskilled laborers and of slave status; the whites were skilled laborers and managers, and were freemen. The Negroes were employed in routine work; the whites filled all the versatile and responsible occupations. There was well-nigh complete subordination of Negroes to whites in every respect. Under this arrangement the economic and social needs, as the whites saw them, were harmonious.

But this simple relation could not long endure. Some of the Negroes proved relatively intelligent, acquired moderate skill in handicrafts, or proved their capacity for self-direction on a small scale in industry and commerce. These became foremen, boat captains (patroons), peddlers, custom blacksmiths, etc. The emergence of mulattoes, with far greater intelligence, hastened this development. Masters owning the labor of relatively high-grade workmen were naturally disposed to employ that labor to the best advantage—to encourage progress of their slaves in skill and thus to save themselves the expense of employing freemen for skilled tasks. The next step, following naturally, was for masters to secure instruction for their most capable youths through apprenticeship, and to set up some of the skilled slaves as craftsmen with shops for public patronage. The city, with its more rapidly growing complexity and specialization of industry, was of course the seat of the earliest and the fullest instances of this development.

The increasing competition of Negro slave artisans with the whites was of the greatest importance as regarded the relations of the races, because the colony depended mainly upon the outside world for its supply of manufactures, and the opportunities for craftsmen in the province were at the best very limited. Competition by the slaves tended to drive out a considerable proportion of the white freemen whose skilled labor would otherwise have been needed. Conditions were gradually becoming more complex: racial, legal, and industrial classes were ceasing to be so nearly coterminous as in the earlier time. A number of Negroes and mulattoes, indeed, were gradually coming to acquire legal status as freemen, exempt from slavery regulations, but in no wise recognized by the whites as their equals. The presence of these freedmen, of course, still further complicated the situation. The demand for labor was constantly growing, but mainly for unskilled labor. It was chiefly met by the slave trade and the natural increase of the Negro population. Skilled trades were entered more and more largely by exceptional Negroes and mulattoes. In times of depression, white mechanics were tempted to emigrate in search of better openings; but the persons of color, if slaves, could not migrate, and if legally free, had to stay in most cases because of the dearth of industrial opportunity for them in other quarters of America. Thus the proportion of Negroes increased in the trades as well as in the total population, city and country. This state of things aroused considerable apprehension.[2]

The importation of Negroes into America had been due, of course, to the economic motive of procuring a labor supply. The regulation of slavery had been instituted for their industrial control—to permit their

2. An act of the Assembly, adopted as early as 1714, declared that "the number of negroes do extremely increase in this Province, and through the afflicting providence of God, the whites do not proportionably multiply, by reason whereof, the safety of the said province is greatly endangered" (Thomas Cooper and D. J. McCord, *Statutes at Large of South Carolina*, VII, 367). The attitude of the public toward the labor and race problem in general is shown in the preamble to an act of 1712, "for the better ordering and governing of negroes and slaves." The preamble runs as follows: "Whereas, the plantations and estates of this Province cannot be well and sufficiently managed and brought into use without the labor and service of negroes and other slaves, and forasmuch as the said negroes and other slaves brought unto the people of this Province for that purpose, are of barbarous, wild, savage natures, and such as renders them wholly unqualified to be governed by the laws, customs and practices of this Province, but that it is absolutely necessary that such other constitutions, laws and orders, should in this Province be made and enacted, for the good regulating and ordering of them, as may restrain the disorders, rapines and inhumanity to which they are naturally prone and inclined; and may also tend to the safety and security of the people of this Province and their estates; . . . Be it therefore enacted," etc. (*ibid.*, 352).

"breaking in," their subjection to the rules of civilized labor. With the Negroes once on hand in large numbers, however, the enormous contrast between them and the whites in intelligence, standards, and institutions—in a word, in race character—brought up a social problem which overshadowed all economic issues. Slavery, originating as a system of labor control, was maintained as still more valuable in safeguarding the standards, institutions, and social well-being of the few whites against possible demoralization and overthrow by the numerous blacks. The Negroes were required by the system to abandon gradually the habits and points of view acquired in the African jungle, to accept and acquire as far as they could the ideas of the civilization into which they had been brought, and to abide by its rules of social conduct. Plantations and slavery made up a system of tutelage and police combined, providing education in civilized industry and life and at the same time preventing successful outbreaks of Negro revolt against white control.

The system showed its kindly or its harsh features, other things being equal, as the Negroes in a given case were relatively docile or fractious. Other things were not always equal: in some cases the mingling of the races in daily life was free and abundant, so that the Negroes had ample opportunity to use their imitative faculties and to acquire the white men's ways; in other cases the Negroes were isolated, their masters absent for long periods, white neighbors few and models for imitation not within reach. Under conditions of the latter sort, subjection in full would be required of the Negroes, little affection would be inspired, and little loyalty would be engendered to the system or to the society which it safeguarded.

The Carolina lowland plantations presented the less attractive of these sets of conditions. The acceptance of the situation was slow among the Negroes, and their adaptation to it was imperfect. Strict police control was necessary. This firm regulation, in turn, making against the intimate personal associations common in Virginia and the uplands, tended to preserve the race alienation which had called it into being. The Negroes of the South Carolina coast failed to acquire the English language in intelligible form; they clung to voodooism and other things African; and, in spite of their apparent and even oppressive sociability and friendliness, they remained largely foreign in spirit and in custom and subjects of mystery to their masters. The conditions in the Charleston district were always far more similar to those in the West Indies than to those in Virginia and the upland cotton belt.

Most of the South Carolina coast Negroes were unambitious; but some few, as we have seen, and especially the mulattoes, were eager to learn and with their masters' aid became artisans or otherwise largely self-directing in industry. The situation grew complex and in some ways embarrassing. In the divergence of economic interests and social needs, it became increasingly clear that the social needs were paramount. In frequent instances the financial interest of the master lay in giving his capable slaves as much industrial freedom as they could use; but it was a social necessity to keep under complete control every black who could possibly incite or take part in a servile insurrection or otherwise promote disorder. The situation was delicate, as all men knew; and the only sure safeguards against the outbreak of rapine and anarchy lay in watchfulness and masterfulness on the part of the whites.

It was recited in a legislative act as early as 1712 that

> several owners of slaves [are] used to suffer their said slaves to do what and go whither they will and work where they please, upon condition that their said slaves do bring their aforesaid masters so much money as between the said master and slave is agreed upon, for every day the said slave shall be so permitted to employ himself, which practice hath been observed to occasion such slaves to spend their time aforesaid, in looking for opportunities to steal, in order to raise money to pay their masters, as well as to maintain themselves, and other slaves their companions, in drunkenness and other evil courses.[3]

The competitive phase of the race-labor problem was touched upon by the grand jury of the province in its presentments in 1742: "We present as a grievance the want of a law to prevent the hiring out of negro tradesmen, to the great discouragement of the white workmen coming into this province." [4]

There thus appeared two interests favoring the restriction of Negro opportunity. The white laboring men wanted to keep the slaves out of the skilled trades as far as possible, and to that end opposed their being hired out under any circumstances for artisan's work. The men of the governing class opposed any broadening of Negroes' range of personal freedom as increasing the danger of demoralization and revolt. The white artisans, it seems, had not enough political strength to get their will enacted into law; [5] and the statutes prohibiting the hiring of their time by slaves were not sufficiently supported by public opinion to se-

3. Cooper and McCord, *Statutes at Large of South Carolina,* VII, 363.

4. Presentments of October 20, 1742, published in the *South Carolina Gazette,* November 8, 1742.

5. An exception to this is noted by Sir Charles Lyell, *A Second Visit to the United States* (New York, 1849), II, 78–83, in the case of a Georgia enactment of 1845, prohibiting the competition of Negroes as building contractors. Lyell gives a clear view of the conditions and the tendency which accompanied such legislation.

cure their enforcement. Like most other provisions of the slave code, this rule was generally disregarded when the interest or inclination of master and slave agreed in favor of its violation. In many cases the law, if enforced, would have seriously hampered industry and commerce. In the city, for example, stevedores, boat hands, messengers, carpenters, and day laborers in general were often needed for immediate service; and the employer could not submit to the delay and formality of seeking out and making contracts with the owners of the slaves whose labor he desired. For the sake of a flexible labor supply, some device like that of slaves hiring their own time was essential; and that being the case, the laws prohibiting this arrangement could not, of course, secure general observance. In quiet times, indeed, the citizens fell generally into easygoing practices, each following his own interest in managing his slaves (or letting them manage him) and thinking little of the provisions for public control. The discovery of Negro conspiracies in 1720 [6] and 1740 [7] spread alarm in the province and for the time stimulated public sentiment in favor of efficient police and other safeguards; but relaxation of control was not long in following each spasm of police reform.

From about 1740 to the outbreak of the war for American independence was the heyday of prosperity for the Carolina lowlands. Rice and indigo prices were excellent; the laboring force was rapidly enlarged; the cultivated area was extended, and the exports and imports increased. Merchants from many countries gathered at "Charles Town"; and many, acquiring wealth, adopted the Carolina standard of highest gentility and retired from commerce to enter planting careers. The city was beautified with handsome public buildings and private residences; the plantations were equipped with commodious mansions and substantial rice mills, smokehouses, Negro quarters, etc., many of which endure in more or less dilapidation to the present day. Carolina merchants and

6. Among the transcripts in the capitol at Columbia, S.C., from the British Public Record Office (B.P.R.O., S.C., B.T. 1, A2) is an official letter of 1720 from Charleston, unsigned, to Mr. Boone at London. It relates that a barbarous plot among the Negroes has lately been discovered, by which they purposed to take the town in full body. Some of the Negroes have been burnt, some banished. The leaders were slaves of Mr. Percival, who was absent in England. Percival is advised through Boone to sell his Negroes singly or else to provide strict management for them, for otherwise "they will come to little profit."

7. The revolt of 1740 is briefly described in an act of immunity which followed it (Cooper and McCord, *Statutes at Large*, VII, 416). Other conspiracies are listed and described in an anonymous pamphlet entitled, *A Refutation of the Calumnies Circulated against the Southern and Western States, Respecting . . . Slavery*, by a South Carolinian (Charleston, 1820; 88 pp.).

planters were in close touch through newspapers and correspondence with the whole world of commerce and affairs. Carolina youths were often educated in the colleges of England. Planters of a fine type of manhood, culture, and ability set a high standard in the commonwealth; and sons strove to fall nothing short of their fathers' attainments. In consequence, there was efficiency and thorough honesty in government; honor, candor, and cordiality in private relations; and kindly consideration, as a very general rule, toward all persons not obviously undeserving. The native slaves were encouraged to progress as far as circumstances could be made to permit; the imported Africans were broken into service as mildly as possible; all were well fed, adequately clothed and sheltered, and subjected to as mild a discipline as was compatible with public safety. On the whole, the province was as well ordered, prosperous, and happy in all its elements as could well be with such diverse racial components and so large a latent possibility for disorder and social revolution.

There were a few blemishes on the generally smooth surface of prosperity and contentment. The heavy volume of the slave trade caused a constant drain of capital to England and New England in payment to the traders; breaking in fresh and refractory Africans was, at the best, unpleasant business; the white mechanics disliked the competition of Negroes and mulattoes in their trades, and though the wages of the whites were higher, their number was relatively decreasing; the great and ever growing mass of half-savage Negroes, many of them embittered by harsh treatment, was a constant cause for disquiet; and the increasingly strained relations with the mother country were distressing from many points of view. But on the whole the people, flushed with their success in conquering the wilderness and their unchecked progress in wealth, were consciously happy and bravely optimistic.

When the war came, the situation was in several respects unique. South Carolina was the only colony that had to deal with large numbers of barbaric Africans. Among persons closely associated with these Coast Negroes there was little disposition to accept theories of human equality. The most influential citizens, whether patriot or loyalist, were determined to preserve the existing industrial and social order as a necessary condition of life in the district, no matter what system of government and allegiance should prevail. The conservatism of the people, in fact, saved the state from such an upheaval as afflicted Virginia in the Revolutionary period.

During the war, and for a while afterward, there was grave economic depression in the district. The closing of markets and the military depredations occasioned great though temporary damages, and the loss of the British bounty permanently killed indigo production. But the plantation system was not broken down. The planters in large number retained their lands and their slaves, and they tided over the lean years with hopes for the return of better times.

About 1786 it was discovered that long-staple cotton, with its high-priced silky fibre, was available as a staple to replace indigo and to supplement rice. Within a few years the new industry was widespread through the Georgia–Carolina lowlands, and planters were becoming serenely prosperous again.

At the close of the century, however, a wholly new factor was introduced, and in the first decades of the following century the economic situation was seriously modified. As a result of Whitney's invention of the gin for short-staple cotton in 1793, the whole interior of the Carolinas, of Georgia, and of the Southwest became capable of very profitable development by labor of any and every kind. In the relative scarcity of free labor for this vast region, an enormous demand was made by the upland and western cotton districts for slave labor, which after 1808 could be supplied, in the main, only from the old tobacco and rice districts. Slave prices rapidly mounted to unheard of figures; and with the planters of the Charleston district it became a serious question whether the lure of the golden West for their slaves and themselves could be permanently resisted. Many sold part of their Negroes to inland settlers; many moved west carrying with them such slaves as they had or could buy. In some years, as in war times and in periods of low cotton prices, the slave trade and the migration slackened; again it would wax so great in volume that only the most conservative could preserve immunity from the Georgia, Alabama, or Texas fever. The migration fever and the interior slave trade carried off nearly or quite all the increase from births, importation, and immigration in the Charleston lowlands, as is shown by the returns of the successive censuses.[8] In some decades there was positive shrinkage in districts in which before the Revolution the doubling of numbers within a decade had not been unusual.

8. Following are population statistics for the South Carolina Lowlands:

Charleston district (i.e. county)	*1790*	*1800*	*1810*	*1820*	*1830*	*1840*	*1850*	*1860*
White	11,801	14,374	16,011	19,376	20,804	20,921	25,208	29,136
Slave	24,071	41,945	45,385	57,221	61,902	58,539	54,775	37,290
Free colored	775	1,161	1,783	3,615	3,632	3,201	3,861	3,622

Charleston and all the surrounding country was seriously threatened with not only a relative but also an actual decline of population, white and black, of crops and earnings, and of political and social consequence. To save the situation, or even to mitigate the decline, it was necessary to improve the existing system of industry so as to make every resource tell to the utmost. Labor must be made more productive. This result could be attained in part through improvement in administration. Some of the coast planters, for example, developed such fine varieties of cotton and guarded their crops so well against careless picking, ginning and packing, that the output of their plantations commanded a heavy premium in the market.[9] But in its crux, the problem was, of course, to improve the quality and effectiveness of the labor itself. The system had to be made flexible by giving to every trustworthy slave who was capable of self-direction a personal incentive to increase his skill and assiduity. Under such conditions the laws which impeded industrial progress were increasingly disregarded and became dead letters. Slaves by hundreds hired their own time; whites and blacks, skilled and unskilled, worked side by side with little notice of the color line; trustworthy slaves were practically in a state of industrial freedom; and that *tertium quid*, the free person of color, always officially unwelcome, was now regarded in private life as a desirable resident of a neighborhood, provided he was a good workman. The liberalizing tendencies were fast relieving the hard and fast character of the regime, so far at least as concerned all work-

Colleton district	1790	1800	1810	1820	1830	1840	1850	1860
White	3,601	4,394	4,290	4,341	5,354	5,874	6,775	9,255
Slave	16,562	20,471	21,858	21,770	21,484	19,246	21,372	32,307
Free colored	175	38	211	293	418	428	319	354
Beaufort district								
White	4,364	4,199	4,792	4,679	5,664	5,650	5,947	6,714
Slave	14,236	16,031	20,914	27,339	30,861	29,692	32,279	32,530
Free colored	153	198	181	181	507	462	579	809
Georgetown district								
White			1,710	1,830	1,931	2,093	2,193	3,013
Slave			13,867	15,546	17,798	15,993	18,253	18,109
Free colored			102	227	214	188	201	183

Statistics for Georgetown prior to 1810 are omitted, because the district then had very different boundaries and area.

9. W. B. Seabrook, *Memoir on Cotton* (Charleston, 1844), 35, 36.

men who were capable of better things than gang and task labor.[10]

The great mass of the common Negroes, it is true, were regarded as suited only for the gangs and unfit for any self-direction in civilized industry; but even in this case a few thinking men saw vaguely from time to time that a less expensive method of control ought to be substituted for chattel slavery, involving as it did the heavy capitalization of lifetime labor as a commodity.[11] This period of economic liberalism produced that phenomenal generation of large-minded and powerful statesmen which included William Lowndes, Cheves, Calhoun, William Smith, and McDuffie, fitting successors to Rawlins Lowndes, Gadsden, Rutledge, Izard, Drayton, and the Pinckneys. No representatives of a perverse or reactionary commonwealth could have gained so decisive an in-

10. That the white laboring class was disposed to obstruct the growth of industrial opportunity for slaves, and was acquiring strength for this as years passed, is shown in a remarkable public letter written by L. W. Spratt of Charleston early in 1861, advocating the re-opening of the African slave trade. The letter, nominally addressed to John Perkins of Louisiana, was published in the *Charleston Mercury*, February 13, 1861. Its remarks upon free and slave labor relations are as follows:

"Within ten years past, as many as ten thousand slaves have been drawn away from Charleston by the attractive prices of the West, and laborers from abroad have come to take their places. These laborers have every disposition to work above the slave, and if there were opportunity would be glad to do so, but without such opportunity they come into competition with him; they are necessarily restive to the contact. Already there is disposition to exclude him from the trades, from public works, from drays, and the tables of hotels; he is even now excluded to a great extent. And . . . when . . . more laborers . . . shall come in greater numbers to the South, they will still more increase the tendency to exclusion; they will question the right of masters to employ their slaves in any works that they may wish for; they will invoke the aid of legislation; they will use the elective franchise to that end; they may acquire the power to determine municipal elections; they will inexorably use it; and thus the town of Charleston, at the very heart of slavery, may become a fortress of democratic power against it. As it is in Charleston, so also is it to a less extent in the interior towns. Nor is it only in the towns that the tendency appears. The slaves from lighter lands within the State have been drawn away for years by the higher prices in the West. They are now being drawn from rice culture. Thousands are sold from rice fields every year. None are brought to them. They have already been drawn from the culture of indigo and all manufacturing employments. They are as yet retained by cotton and the culture incident to cotton; but as almost every negro offered in our markets is bid for by the West, the drain is likely to continue; it is probable that more abundant pauper labor may pour in, and it is to be feared that even this State, the purest in its slave condition, democracy [i.e., industrial democracy or self-governing labor, as opposed to slave labor] may gain a foothold, and that here also the contest for existence may be waged between them."

11. Cf. "The Economic Cost of Slaveholding," *Political Science Quarterly*, XXII (September, 1907), 117.

fluence upon American affairs as was exercised by these statesmen in the second decade of the century.

To this progress of liberalism a single event gave a violent check. In the early summer of 1822 there was discovered in Charleston a widespread and well-matured conspiracy among the slaves and free Negroes for a servile revolt and the destruction of the whites. The leader was Denmark Vesey, and the headquarters of the conspiracy were in his blacksmith shop. Vesey was a native African of unusual ability who had bought his freedom in 1800 with part of the proceeds of a prize drawn in a lottery and had made himself a dominating person among the Negroes of the city. One of Vesey's right-hand men was Monday Gell, a Negro slave of talent, in charge of a harness shop, able to write fluently, and much indulged and trusted by his master. Monday, it was afterward reported, professed to be in correspondence with men of power in Africa and San Domingo who would give aid in the Carolina revolt. The chief organizer among the half-savage, lowest-grade Negroes was Gullah Jack, by inheritance a conjurer among the Angolas and reputed to lead a charmed life. Jack, himself little touched by civilization, was unable to plan, but was of great value in rousing the savage nature of his fellows to the desired pitch of frenzy. Another leader was Peter Poyas, who circulated the report that the whites had determined to thin out the Negroes and would begin a great killing on July 4. He urged the blacks to rise quickly and forestall the blow. These ringleaders had selected the points at which the Negroes in town and outside were to gather, upon a signal to be given at midnight of June 16, and had laid out a program for seizing the guardhouse and arsenal and sweeping the city with fire and sword.[12] An inkling of the conspiracy reached the police on May 30. The first Negroes arrested denied all knowledge of a plot; but after a week's solitary confinement they were ready to talk. Their admissions then led to other arrests and, after another season of tongue-loosening confinement, to still more alarming admissions and in turn to still more arrests. Finally, the evidence brought out at the formal trial of the prisoners laid bare the whole machinery and extent of the plot. The public thus learned the disquieting details in cumulative installments. The general effect of alarm and horror may be better imagined than described. There was apparently, however, no popular hysteria. A special constabulary was appointed for public safety, and a special court to try the Negroes under arrest. To its bench were appointed the most substantial,

12. *An Account of the Late Intended Insurrection among a Portion of the Blacks of This City*. Published by the authority of the Corporation of Charleston (Charleston, 1822; 48 pp.).

conservative, and respected citizens whom Charleston contained. Reputable attorneys were appointed for each side of every case; the trial of each slave was conducted in his owner's presence; and every other precaution was taken for fairness, justice, and security. During two months of unprecedented excitement in Charleston, while the trials were in progress, the Charleston corporation was "proud to say," in its official report, that "the laws, without even one violation, have ruled with uninterrupted sway—that no cruel, vindictive or barbarous modes of punishment have been resorted to—that justice has been blended with an enlightened humanity . . . to those who had meted out for us murder, rapine and conflagration in their most savage forms." As a result of the trials, thirty-five Negroes were sentenced to death and hanged before August 10; twelve were sentenced to death but respited with a view to commutation of sentence; twenty-two were sentenced to transportation; nine were acquitted with a suggestion to their masters that they be transported; and fifty-two were acquitted and discharged. Denmark Vesey's plot had passed into history with little noise in the great world outside, but with lasting impress upon the lowland community.

The effect of Vesey's plot upon public sentiment in the Charleston district is eloquently shown in a memorial presented by the citizens of Charleston to the South Carolina legislature in the fall of 1822.[13] It begins with a description of the position of the Negroes:

> Under the influence of mild and generous feelings, the owners of slaves in our state were rearing up a system which extended many privileges to our negroes; afforded them greater protection; relieved them from numerous restraints; enabled them to assemble without the presence of a white person, for the purpose of social intercourse, or religious worship; yielding to them the facilities for securing most of the comforts and many of the luxuries of improved society; and what is of more importance, affording them means of enlarging their minds and extending their information; a system whose establishment many persons could not reflect on without concern and whose rapid extension the experienced among us could not observe but "with fear and trembling," nevertheless, a system which won the approbation of by far the greater number of our citizens, who exulted in what they termed the progress of liberal

13. Memorial of the Citizens of Charleston to the Senate and House of Representatives of the State of South Carolina. Title page wanting, and list of signers not printed (12 pp.). This pamphlet, like most others concerning South Carolina in the period, is of extreme rarity. Its text will be reprinted shortly, with kindred material, in a volume of documents on plantation and frontier industrial society, to be edited by the present writer and published by the American Bureau of Industrial Research, Macmillan Company, New York. Cf. *American Historical Review*, XII, 207.

ideas upon the subject of slavery, while many good and pious persons fondly cherished the expectation that our negroes would be influenced in their conduct toward their owners by sentiments of affection and gratitude.

But, the document goes on to relate, a dreadful plot was forming which has now by providential means been discovered. It is the duty of the people and the state to provide preventives for such occurrences in force and hence this petition to the legislature. Constructive suggestions now follow:

After a careful inquiry into the existing evils of our slave system, and after mature reflection on the remedies to be adopted, [we] humbly recommend that laws be passed to the following effects:

1st. To send out of our state, never again to return, all free persons of color. . . . They form a third class in our society, enjoying more privileges than the slaves, and yet possessing few of the rights of the master; a class of persons having and exercising the right of moving unrestrained over every part of the state; of acquiring property, of amassing wealth to an unlimited extent, of procuring information on every subject, and of uniting themselves in associations of societies—yet, still a class, deprived of all political rights, subjected equally with the slaves to the police regulations for persons of color, and sensible that by no peaceable and legal methods can they render themselves other than a degraded class in your society. . . . Restraints are always irksome. . . . The free persons of color must be discontented with their situation. The hopes of the free negroes will increase with their numbers. . . .

The free persons of color will not emigrate, consequently the white people must; so that, as the free people of color are extending their lines, the whites are contracting theirs. This is not a mere speculation, but a fact sufficiently emphasized already. Every winter, considerable number of Germans, Swiss and Scotch arrive in Charleston, with the avowed intention of settling amongst us, but are soon induced to emigrate towards the West by perceiving most of the mechanical arts performed by free persons of color. Thus we learn, that the existence of this class among us is in the highest degree detrimental to our safety. . . .

The presence of free persons of color, the memorial continues, sets conditions before the eyes of the slaves which they cannot peaceably realize; it makes their labor irksome and offers many temptations; and the intimate association of these persons with the slaves permits at all times the dissemination of dangerous ideas and news items which the slaves would not otherwise learn. The memorialists admit that inconvenience would arise from the expulsion of the free persons of color, but urge that that must be tolerated for the general welfare. A stern policy, they assert, is necessary, "that we may extinguish at once every gleam of

hope which the slaves may indulge of ever becoming free—and that
we may proceed to govern them on the only principle that can maintain
slavery, the 'principle of fear.' "

They recommend, further, that the number of slaves to be hired out
should be limited by law, and no slave should be allowed to work as a
mechanic unless under the immediate control of his master. Most of
those who work out, they say, are largely released from control, to
work or idle or attend meetings and conspire without hindrance.

> But there is another consideration. The facility for obtaining work is
> not always the same. . . . Irregularity of habits is thus acquired; this ir-
> regularity produces restlessness of disposition, which delights in mischief
> and detests quiet. The same remarks will apply to the negro mechanics,
> who having a stated portion of labor to perform, are masters of the re-
> mainder of the day, when the work is ended.

The memorial closes with still other recommendations for the repression
of free persons of color and a more strict police over Negroes in general.
On the whole, an authoritative expression of more reactionary sentiment
would be hard to discover.

Two years prior to this excitement a pamphleteer had written: "We
regard our negroes as the 'Jacobins' of the country, against whom we
should always be upon our guard, and who, though we fear no permanent effects from any insurrectionary movement on their part, should be
watched with an eye of steady and unremitted attention." [14] In 1820 little heed seems to have been given to this writer; but when the terrible
discovery of the great plot had been made, his words were read as those
of a prophet.

The fright of 1822 soon passed. No important changes in the general
system were instituted, and the previous conditions of life and industry
were in the main restored. That period of excitement, however, was
epoch-making in that it checked the growth of liberalism and prepared the
community for its sensitive hostility to the Garrisonian agitation for
the overthrow of Negro slavery.

During the remainder of the antebellum period the industrial and social conditions of the Charleston district underwent little change. The
need for collective efficiency continued to be felt, and in most cases the
actual restrictions on labor were no more severe. Racial, industrial, and
legal classes were still by no means identical. That free persons of color
had a really excellent industrial opportunity in Charleston, and that

14. *A Refutation of the Calumnies, etc.,* 61.

many of them used it to advantage, is proved by the tax lists of the city. The list for 1860, which is available in print,[15] gives the names of 360 persons of color whose property was assessed in that year. The real estate owned by them was valued for taxation at $724,570. Of these 360 taxpayers, there were 130 who owned slaves aggregating 390 in number. The largest number of slaves held by a person of color was fourteen; the average number was three. In this list of persons of color, thirteen were classed as Indians; their real estate aggregated $73,300, and nine of them owned thirty-three slaves. It is quite probable, however, that most of these so-called Indians had a large infusion of Negro blood. This showing of the wealth and slaveholding of the free persons of color demonstrates that industrial opportunity was fairly free for them, and that a number of mulattoes, at least, made large use of their chance to earn money and save it.

By good fortune, we have a census of the city of Charleston for the year 1848,[16] which in its industrial tables gives complete data for a statistical view of the relation of racial, legal, and industrial classes in the later antebellum period. In summary it is here presented. It shows how large was the intermingling of the races and legal classes in nearly all the

INDUSTRIAL CENSUS OF CHARLESTON FOR 1848

	Whites		*Slaves*		*Free Colored*	
	Men	*Women*	*Men*	*Women*	*Men*	*Women*
Artisans						
Carpenters and joiners	120		110		27	
Masons and stone cutters	67		68		10	
Painters and plasterers	18		16		4	
Plumbers and gas fitters	9					
Wharf builders	2		10			
Boot and shoemakers	30		6		17	
Tailors and cap makers	68	6	36		42	6
Bleachers and dyers	5					
Hair braiders and wig makers	3	2				
Barbers and hairdressers		6	4	14		
Bakers	35	1	39		1	
Butchers	10		5		1	

15. List of the Tax Payers of the City of Charleston for 1860 (Charleston, 1861; 335 pp.).

16. J. L. Dawson and H. W. DeSaussure, Census of Charleston for 1848 (Charleston, 1849). Industrial tables, 31–36.

Industrial Census of Charleston for 1848 (Continued)

	Whites		Slaves		Free Colored	
	Men	Women	Men	Women	Men	Women
Artisans						
Blacksmiths	45		40		4	
Coopers	20		61		2	
Ship carpenters and joiners	52		51		6	
Riggers and sail makers	13					
Gun, copper, and locksmiths	14		1		1	
Cigar makers	10		5		1	
Cabinet makers	26		8			
Carvers, gilders, and upholsterers	16		1		1	
Tinners	10		3		1	
Millwrights	4				5	
Saddle and harness makers	29		2		1	
Wheelwrights	6				1	
Horseshoers	6					
Coach makers and trimmers	20		3			
Boilermakers	6					
Machinists	10					
Engineers	43					
Silversmiths and watchmakers	38					
Bookbinders	10		3			
Printers	65		5			
Organ and piano builders	4					
Other mechanics and journeymen	27		45		2	
Miscellaneous						
Seamstresses and mantua makers		125		24		196
Milliners		44				7
Market women and milk venders		9				
Pastry cooks and cooks		1	3	12		16
Laundresses				33		45
Midwives and nurses		5		2		10
Coachmen	2		15		4	
Draymen	13		67		11	
Omnibus drivers	7					
Wharfingers, stevedores, and porters	20		37		6	
Apprentices	56	5	43	8	14	7
Barkeepers	16					
Domestic servants	13	100	1888	3384	9	28
Laborers	192		838	378	19	2
Fishermen	10		11		14	
Superannuated			38	54	1	4

important industrial occupations.[17] Neither the public dread of disorder nor the class dislike of Negro competition could arrest the forces that urged the community toward the increase of its industrial efficiency.

The following table of slave prices is of value for study in many connections besides that in which it is here used. The prices quoted are the average prices, as well as can be ascertained, of prime fieldhands for the locality in the years stated. The averages for the Charleston district have been made from a great mass of manuscript bills of sale of slaves bought and sold in Charleston, recorded and now preserved among the archives in the state capitol at Columbia. The origin of the data for the

SLAVE PRICES IN THE CHARLESTON DISTRICT
AVERAGES FOR PRIME FIELD HANDS

Year	Price	Year	Price	Year	Price	Year	Price
1800	$ 500	1814	$ 450	1830	$ 450	1844	$ 500
1801	550	1815	500	1831	475	1845	550
1802	550	1816	600	1832	500	1846	650
1803	575	1817	650	1833	525	1847	750
1804	600	1819	850	1834	650	1848	700
1805	550	1820	725	1835	750	1849	650
1806	550	1822	650	1836	1100	1850	700
1807	525	1823	600	1837	1200	1851	750
1808	550	1824	500	1838	1000	1852	800
1809	500	1825	500	1839	1000	1853	900
1810	500	1826	475	1840	800	1855	900
1811	550	1827	475	1841	650	1858	950
1812	500	1828	450	1842	600	1859	1100
1813	450	1829	475	1843	500	1860	1200

SLAVE PRICES (FOR COMPARISON) IN MIDDLE GEORGIA

Year	Price	Year	Price	Year	Price	Year	Price
1800	$ 450	1821	$ 700	1839	$1000	1853	$1200
1805	550	1826	800	1840	700	1859	1650
1808	650	1828	700	1844	600	1860	1800
1813	450	1835	900	1848	900		
1818	1000	1837	1300	1851	1050		

17. Statistics of employments of the free persons of color in New Orleans and New York in 1850, valuable for comparison with that of Charleston, are printed in J. D. B. De Bow's Compendium of the Seventh Census of the United States (1850), 80, 81.

Georgia cotton belt, and the method of handling the figures, have been explained in my article on the economic cost of slaveholding.[18]

A comparison of these two local tables shows that slave prices at Charleston after about 1800 were practically never above those prevailing in the upland cotton belt; but that the interior usually offered a premium which often ranged from a hundred to several hundred dollars per head for prime fieldhands. The fact that in the face of this premium the planting families of the coast retained such a multitude of slaves in their district throughout the whole period shows that the spirit of the planters was not wholly commercial. It shows that the typical slaveholder of the coast deliberately and constantly preferred the career of the useful captain of industry to the life of the idle rich. Otherwise the temptation to sell his slaves west would have been irresistible. There is abundant unconscious evidence that the typical planter had a controlling distaste for selling slaves except in emergencies. The dominating consideration with masters and mistresses was not that of great profit, but that of comfortable living in pleasant surroundings, with a consciousness of important duties well performed. However radical they might by force of circumstances become in politics, the Carolina planters were beyond question careful, moderate, and intelligently conservative in matters of industry and social policy. But invincible powers, through largely misinformed sentiment, were being arrayed against them; and their unending task of race discipline was destined to most serious disturbance, if not, as it may prove, to permanent arrest.

With the great Civil War and its aftermath we are not now concerned. The killing off of the flower of Carolina manhood in the war time, the heartbreaking sorrow of the women and the old men who stayed at home, the black despair of the oncoming generation, the great upheaval and demoralization in the so-called Reconstruction period and the gradual return thereafter to moderately healthful conditions do not lie within the scope of this paper. It remains only to attempt a general resume of the situation in the later antebellum period.

In the slaveholding districts there was fully as much particularism and competition among the industrial units as anywhere else in America. A condition of the life of the system, in such a region as the Carolina lowlands, was efficiency; and the increasing competition of the West called for an increase of efficiency if the relative standards of prosperity and of comfort were to be maintained. This affected both city and country and was the direct concern of every member of the industrial and commer-

18. See "The Economic Cost of Slaveholding in the Cotton Belt," 117.

cial community. The struggle for increased efficiency tended to make every laborer who was capable of self-direction free to direct his own industrial efforts and to promote his full equipment by education for his work. It tended to cause Negroes, mulattoes, and whites to be put upon the same industrial footing, and to cause the capable slave to be given industrial freedom, under the system of hiring him to himself or otherwise securing to him rewards in some measure proportional to the value of the work done by him. This was the economic requirement of the times.

But the social requirement was largely in direct conflict with this. The community had always in contemplation the possibility of social death from Negro upheaval and control, as illustrated in San Domingo, and the milder fate of industrial stagnation and decay from premature emancipation, as illustrated in Jamaica.[19] To save their commonwealth from approaching either fate, the Carolinians contended with might and main against any abolition to be imposed from without, and in their local regulations they introduced every possible safeguard against successful conspiracy. Through laws enacted, reenacted, and fortified, they provided for strict patrol and general police, forbade the teaching of Negroes to read, forbade masters to hire to slaves their time, forbade Negroes to assemble without white persons being present, and restricted private emancipation. These laws were more or less observed or more or less disregarded according to the course of events and the play of public sentiment between the social and economic points of view.

From the social point of view all persons of color were of one class and regarded as all very possibly dangerous; from the economic point of view all capable Negroes and mulattoes were looked upon as the equals of the whites in their industrial class, and therefore meriting and requiring the same industrial freedom and incentive that the whites enjoyed. Public opinion oscillated between these two positions but inclined more generally to the restrictive point of view after Vesey's plot and during the Garrisonian agitation. Official policy in general inclined toward safeguarding society; but private policy was more controlled by eco-

19. Still another conceivable alternative would have been the fusion of the two races by interbreeding, the attempted blending of moral codes, and the consequent degradation of standards, which occurred in several of the Latin American states. That this development was impossible and little thought of in South Carolina was largely due to the English origin of the citizens. They were sturdy, proud, masterful, staunch. To recognize negroid morality and institutions as in any way entitled to equal footing with their own in the community was for them impossible. The tendency of the Garrisonian agitation in that direction was perhaps its most irritating feature.

nomic needs, and in that highly individualistic community private policy largely dominated. Society and industry in fact confronted an impasse, and politics were at a loss to find a way out of it unless by the
policy of drifting.

In 1860, failing to solve its part of the world's problem of equity in
human relationships, the commonwealth clashed with the dominant idea
of the period. In the championship of their system the planters and their
neighbors were defeated, and their system was shattered as far as it
could be by its victorious enemies encamped upon the field. But the
pendulum swings again. Facts of human nature and the law of civilized
social welfare are too stubborn for the theories of Negrophiles as well as
of Negrophobes. The slave labor problem has disappeared, but the
Negro problem remains.

James C. Bonner

Profile of a Late Antebellum Community

The central importance of the institution of Negro slavery has provided a dual focus for southern historians. The masters and the slaves have long been the subject of their attention. But though the majority of black Southerners were slaves, the majority of white Southerners were not slaveholders, and those who were held only one or two slaves. Those Southerners who owned land were farmers, not planters, and a significant group, the poor whites, owned neither land nor slaves.

Historians frequently cite the plight of the poor white as evidence of the crippling effect of Negro slavery. This is a likely cause, though not in itself a sufficient explanation for the existence of this group. For reasons which we are still better able to describe than explain, both education and literacy were less prevalent in the South than in any other region in antebellum America, and the attitudes and ideas which historians deem representative are in fact reflective of only one stratum of the population. The paucity of written materials such as diaries, memoirs, and letters make it difficult to gauge the sentiments of either the yeoman farmer or the poor white. Nonetheless, other records do exist, notably the federal census records, and it is from these that Bonner has reconstructed the social history of the yeoman farmer and poor white in Hancock County, Georgia.

The results of Bonner's study, though limited to one county, suggest an interpretation of southern history far different from Phillips's. Bonner detects the emergence of a socio-economic configuration similar to that which appeared after the demise of slavery. His conclusion corroborates the findings of many younger historians, both local and national, that the Civil War did not begin a new system of economic and social arrangements. It merely facilitated the development of changes which had begun before the war.

Reprinted with permission from the *American Historical Review*, XLIX (July, 1944), 663–680.

M ost historians agree that too little of the history of the Old South
has been written from the annals of the poor.[1] Yet that section had
its full share of landless white people in varying degrees of poverty. Just
above the very poor and the landless was another class which some historians have chosen to call "yeomen farmers." Partly because they were
too numerous, too commonplace, and too much like common folk
everywhere, these two classes have not inspired exhaustive studies commensurate to their numbers and to their importance in society. On the
other hand, the small upper class, the prima donna group of antebellum
southern life, has received notice far out of proportion to its numbers
and, it is sometimes suspected, its social and economic importance.

Significantly, the members of the upper class and of the group striving
for upper-class status have furnished nearly all of the written local accounts of the South's inarticulate masses. Too often the writer was a
haughty neighbor on whose land some poor white had squatted, and he
showed little sympathy for the lot of such men. Too much reliance has
also been placed in those contemporaries who wrote travel accounts.
Bumping over poor roads, for which the South was notorious, and eat-
ing food to which he was unaccustomed, the traveler was inclined to in-
ject his discomfort into a somewhat distorted description of the common
people whom he encountered. Sometimes a condescending visitor, such
as Frederick Law Olmsted, saw only what he came to see and, bent
upon obtaining his money's worth, recorded his observations in terms of
preconceived ideas, prejudice, and subjectivity. The limited scope of a
traveler's observations always precludes a complete picture of a section's
people. The queer customs and habits of the poor people of the Old
South, the unusual appearance of their habitations, or perhaps their pic-
turesque speech furnished the major topic for comment. Hence the
propertyless white, discovered long ago, is in great need of rediscovery.

Perhaps the most reliable data available for a comprehensive study of
the submerged half or two-thirds of the population are to be found in
the manuscript records of the federal census, particularly those of 1850
and 1860.[2] Indeed, tens of thousands of names of antebellum Southerners

1. This paper is a by-product of a longer study on "Agricultural Reform in the
Georgia Piedmont, 1820–60."

2. Beginning in 1850, three schedules were made up by the census enumerators
which form the principal documents on which this study is based. These are
Schedules I, II, and IV, that is, "Free Inhabitants," "Slave Inhabitants," and "Productions of Agriculture," respectively. Of these, the last is the most useful document. These records for the southern states are widely scattered, some being in the
National Archives, some in the various state archives, and some in university and
historical society collections. A few apparently have become lost. Of the Georgia

appear there, each with numerous facts recorded, and they are to be found nowhere else. Courthouses and local archives, even when the research historian has the patience to classify their resources, yield practically no data relative to those without property. Names on Schedules I, II, and IV of the seventh and eighth censuses, when alphabetized and collated into a single master file, result in a Domesday Book as rare as anything in Anglo-Saxon annals. While it is admitted that lives of people cannot be listed in columns and averaged, a master file such as this, to which all other available data are appended, will contain extensive and hitherto unused facts that can be made to yield an objective interpretation of the lives of the poor and illiterate. By using this device the written accounts of travelers and contemporaries can be checked and evaluated with great effectiveness.[3]

As an object lesson on what can be learned about the poorer masses of the Old South, a few of the less evident social and economic aspects of a single community are analyzed below in some detail. Hancock County, Georgia, selected for the study,[4] lies in the lower Piedmont, between

records, Duke University has the 1850 manuscripts of Schedule IV for the counties of Floyd through Murray. The D.A.R. library in Washington, D.C., has both the 1850 and the 1860 manuscripts of Schedule IV for the remaining Georgia counties. Schedules I and II, complete for all states, are in the National Archives. Unfortunately, the names of Negro slaves do not appear on any of these schedules. Such names would furnish a basis for a study of many aspects of the slavery regime. Only the age, sex, and color (black or mulatto) are recorded on the "Schedule of Slave Inhabitants."

3. For example, Charles Lanman visited Georgia's up-country in 1848 and spent the night in the cabin home of Adam Vandever, near Tallulah Falls. He described his host as about sixty years of age, crude, illiterate, and the reputed father of about thirty children. He tilled only a few acres around his cabin, and his livestock consisted of "a mule, some half dozen goats, together with a number of dogs." Charles Lanman, *Letters from the Alleghany Mountains* (New York, 1849), 31. The census records of 1850 tell a different story. According to these records, Vandever possessed horses, mules, cows, sheep, goats, and hogs. Products of his farm consisted of wheat, oats, rye, corn, peas, tobacco, honey, milk, butter, garden and orchard products, and home-manufactured goods. In 1860 he owned land, tools, and livestock worth $1,800. When Vandever died in 1877, he left a substantial estate, the records of which contradict the estimate of him given by his New England guest thirty years earlier. Minute Book I, Records of Habersham County, Clarksville, Georgia.

4. In preparing this study a card index was made that contained all names of people in Hancock County that appeared on Schedules I, II, and IV of the seventh and eighth censuses. A master list, containing these names with all available facts appended, was then prepared, including data from the various schedules and from other sources, such as the public records of the county, private collections, and newspaper accounts. For a description of the census manuscript records and a dis-

Milledgeville and Augusta, near the Pine Barrens. The conventional census tabulations qualify it as a somewhat representative community of the old plantation cotton belt. Most of its area is characterized by coarse sand and sandy loam, but there is some red clay in the northern part. Scrub oak and pine are not uncommon on the uplands, with gum, bay, and poplar in the swamps.[5] Despite the comparative poverty of its soil, this area was known throughout Georgia and neighboring states in 1860 for the progressiveness and culture of its people and for their optimistic enthusiasm for the agrarian way of life. The Hancock Planter's Club, one of the first successful agricultural societies of middle Georgia, furnished inspiration and guidance to southern planters for two decades before the Civil War. William Terrell, its first president, endowed a chair of agriculture at the University of Georgia; David W. Lewis, its first secretary, became the first executive secretary of the Southern Central Agricultural Society, a regional organization embracing Georgia and neighboring states.[6] Cotton strains, culture methods, and tools developed in Hancock County became well known wherever cotton was grown extensively.[7] Many significant agricultural, political, and intellectual movements in Georgia between 1830 and 1860 were identified with one or more of Hancock's prominent citizens. Even a superficial student of southern history will recognize on the list of this county's citizens many Southerners who had notable careers—governors, congressmen, jurists, and leaders in professional life.[8]

cussion of a technique in using them, see Frank L. and Harriett C. Owsley, "The Economic Basis of Society in the Late Ante-Bellum South," *Journal of Southern History*, 6 (1940), 24–26; also Blanche Henry Clark, *The Tennessee Yeomen, 1840–1860* (Nashville, 1942), xvii–xxii.

5. Roland M. Harper, "Development of Agriculture in Upper Georgia from 1850 to 1860," *Georgia Historical Quarterly*, 6 (1922), 14, 15; Zachary Taylor Johnson, "Geographic Factors in Georgia Politics in 1850," *Georgia Historical Quarterly*, 17 (1933), 28.

6. For a discussion of the contributions made by Hancock planters to the agricultural renascence of the lower South before 1860, see James C. Bonner, "Genesis of Agricultural Reform in the Cotton Belt," *Journal of Southern History*, 9 (1943), 475–500.

7. "[It] is the best cotton by two hundred fifty pounds per acre that I have ever planted," wrote a southwest Tennessean in 1860 of a cotton strain developed by David Dickson. *Southern Cultivator*, 18 (1860), 53.

8. For a discussion of the prominent citizens of Hancock County in the 1850's, when the community was at the zenith of its brilliant antebellum career, see George Gillman Smith, *The Story of Georgia and Georgia People* (Atlanta, 1900), 211; Lucian Lamar Knight, *Georgia's Landmarks, Memoirs, and Legends* (Atlanta, 1914), II, 544–645; Elizabeth Smith, "A History of Hancock County," unpublished manuscript in private possession.

Regardless of other attachments, nearly all of these leaders were engaged in farming or in planting. Observers in the 1850's invariably commented upon the agricultural progress which they were making. The fine breeds of livestock, improved tools, "neat, horizontal tillage," well-fed and happy slaves, and the genteel quality of its people were the county's well-known assets.[9] As an embellishment to its rural life, the county possessed "many country colleges,[10] white mansions, gardens and orchards, with all the unmistakable signs of taste, comfort, and plenty in evidence." [11] While climate, soil, and topography did not endow the community with unusual agricultural possibilities, there are perhaps few places in the cotton belt that have a greater claim to all the romantic traditions of the full life under the plantation slavery regime.

During the 1850's, when the new agricultural practices in the area were reaching a high degree of efficiency, there was a considerable movement of white people from the county. Many of these emigrants were landless farmers,[12] some were small landowners without slaves, and a few were small slaveholders. As the white population thus diminished, there was an increase in the number of slaves, a concentration of land-ownership, and a rise in land values.[13] This represents merely the familiar American phenomenon of a concentration of landholding, accompanied by an increase in the number of landless workers. The more affluent planters were buying up the land of small farmers, acquiring more slaves, and closing up the avenues by which landless farmers might acquire small holdings. Many small farmers, thus thwarted in their efforts to become planters, or even landowners, were moving to the newer counties in the northern and western parts of the state, or to the southwest. In addition, there is much evidence to support the theory that farm tenants who did not emigrate were being forced into a less favorable relationship to the land.

The superficial picture of the community at this time is one of high

9. *Soil of the South,* 5 (1855), 321; *South Countryman,* 1 (1859), 27; *Southern Cultivator,* 18 (1860), 262.

10. The reference here is to rural boarding schools offering instruction on the academy level.

11. *Southern Cultivator,* 18 (1860), 262.

12. The white population declined from 4,201 to 3,871, or 7.8 percent. At the same time the slave population increased from 7,306 to 8,137, or 11.37 percent.

13. The average value of holdings increased 46.6 percent, and the number of landowners declined 16 percent. The planters whose realty was valued at $10,000 and above in 1850 increased in number from 4 percent of the total to over 15 percent of the total in 1860. Planters comprising the upper 15 percent in 1860 owned more than half of the total land in the county.

agricultural prosperity for all classes, accompanied by the expansion of the plantation pattern.[14] This view, however, does not adequately characterize the whites in the lower economic group, who comprised approximately one-third of the total white population of the county. The idea that both the rich and the poor were becoming richer was given by agricultural commentators and observers of the upper economic class. Scant indeed are the records which originated from those who were forced off the land to become farm laborers, wage earners in the local textile mill, or emigrants to newer areas of better economic opportunity, real or fancied.[15] The actual situation was something like that observed in the South from 1930 to 1940, when federal subsidies brought a degree of prosperity to landowners in the cotton belt but forced tenants to become farm laborers or else encouraged them to seek urban employment.

14. David W. Lewis wrote in 1859 that property was as "equally distributed" among the people of the community as it was possible for it to be. *Southern Cultivator*, 17 (1859), 261–62. David Dickson in the following year boasted that the people of Hancock did not "have to hire out to get a living." *Southern Cultivator*, 18 (1860), 237. Apparently the white people who owned no land, like the Negro slaves, simply did not count in these evaluations of the county's social and economic welfare. The actual distribution of property in the county was such that a geographical representation produces a balanced, bell-shaped curve *among those who owned it*, but it was far from being equally distributed. The statements of Lewis, Dickson, and others, as illustrated above, are contradicted by the census returns as well as by statements of their contemporaries. For example, a visitor to Dickson's plantation in Hancock County in 1860 reported seeing from "fifty to one hundred white hirelings in almost constant employment" (*ibid.*, 203). Dickson admitted employing as laborers "three or four white men at a time," and they were not engaged on a yearly basis. *Southern Cultivator*, 17 (1859), 345; 18 (1860), 203, 237. That unequal distribution of land existed elsewhere in the South, despite its cheapness, is attested by Daniel Lee, editor of the *Southern Cultivator*. In 1856 he spoke of the "large number [of white men] at the South who have no legal right nor interest in the soil [and] no homes of their own." *Southern Cultivator*, 14 (1856), 282.

15. The little writing which these people may have done had bare chance of survival because of the transitory nature of their habitation. The proverb, "Three movings are equal to one burning," has significant implications for the historian here. The state and historical society collections of letters of soldiers written during the Civil War period are the only important source of extant writings by the common people of the Old South. Absence from home and army experience gave thousands of men their first incentive to write letters, and historical societies later encouraged their collection and preservation. While these letters deal largely with army life, they nevertheless give much insight into social and economic conditions at home. For a study of the common soldier in the Confederate Army, based largely upon these letters, see Bell I. Wiley, *The Life of Johnny Reb: The Common Soldier of the Confederacy* (Indianapolis, 1943).

The change had many of the characteristics of the enclosure movement in England at the beginning of the century.

A brief biography of an antebellum tenant farmer, while given largely through observations and comments of his aristocratic landlord, may furnish a typical example of what was actually taking place. Young David R. Ware, a landless farmer, came to Georgia from North Carolina around 1840. Married to a Hancock girl, he squatted on land near Granite Hill, abandoned to Bermuda grass. Having meager equipment, he could cultivate only a small plot. Around 1848, Andrew J. Lane purchased the place at two dollars an acre and joined it to his plantation at Granite Hill. "At the time of the purchase," wrote Lane, "[Ware] raised about half enough corn to feed himself, his wife, and a pack of dogs." By judicious management, however, the tenant prospered. When he first came to the place he had an old mare, a milch cow, a brood sow, and several pigs. His plan was to plow the mare during the morning and to let her graze on the Bermuda lot in the afternoon. He succeeded in growing good crops of corn and peas on the Bermuda lot, and he utilized all three of these to develop a simple but thriving livestock enterprise. By 1850 the census enumerator found that Ware owned five horses, a hundred pigs and hogs, and twenty-four head of cattle, seven of which were listed as milch cows. His landlord later affirmed that all of these animals were grown on the place. In addition, his field crop productions included 650 bushels of corn, 100 bushels of peas and beans, 400 bushels of sweet potatoes, three tons of hay, and three bales of cotton.[16]

In 1852 a spark from the chimney set fire to the house and Ware was forced, apparently by eviction, to leave the farm. Lane observed that "he parted from the place with many regrets and much reluctance," and one may safely infer that the landlord welcomed this opportunity to be rid of his prosperous tenant. Eight years later Ware was still in the county. "He [had] moved to another place where there was no pasture and his livestock [had] dwindled down to nothing," asserted his former landlord.[17] The census enumerator in 1860 listed him as a farm laborer.

16. David Lewis Phares, *The Farmer's Book of Grasses and Other Forage Plants for the Southern United States* (Starkville, 1881), 45; Charles Wallace Howard, *A Manual of the Cultivation of the Grasses* (Atlanta, 1881), 31; *Southern Cultivator*, 18 (1860), 265–66.

17. *Ibid.*, 266. It is interesting to note here the progress that Hancock farmers made in livestock and grasses from 1840 to 1860. Lane himself became a foremost advocate of Bermuda grass for the area. And while reciting to his neighbors the lessons he had learned from Ware, he unwittingly left to posterity many of the foregoing biographical facts on this antebellum tenant farmer. Bermuda played no

It is difficult to determine exact changes in the nature of the contracts between the landless farmer and the landlord which evolved during this period, for, like the postbellum sharecropper's contract, it was seldom in writing and hence remained informal and flexible. Enough data exist, however, for the formulation of a hypothesis of declining economic status. For example, the census enumerator for Hancock County in 1850 listed 210 men as farmers who owned no real estate, but the terms "farm laborer" and "tenant" were never used in designating the occupation of the individual. There is, however, occasional use of the word "renter." The enumerator in 1860 listed 198 "farm laborers" but made no use of the terms "renter" or "tenant." [18] While no very valid conclusions can be inferred from these facts alone, they do suggest that landless farmers throughout the county had dropped to the status of farm laborers, in keeping with the individual experience of David Ware. A system of tenancy had developed in the county before 1850 for the accommodation of landless farmers. But by 1860 such status in this plantation area had given way to the more popular methods of land operation, namely, wage labor and Negro slavery.[19] The transition to sharecropping, necessitated by events subsequent to Appomattox, was merely a new modifi-

---

small part in the new system of farming that made Hancock County famous. A planter in the county wrote in 1848: "With us everybody has learned how to use, how to keep under, and how to appreciate Bermuda grass." *Southern Cultivator*, 6 (1848), 180.

18. Obviously no instructions were given enumerators to guide them in making a classification. The systems used varied widely from one county to another and from one census year to the next. No valid conclusions relative to percentage of farm tenancy can be made from a study of a single schedule. In Floyd County in 1860, for example, the enumerator listed 335 farmers on the schedule of agricultural productions as "renters." For Henry County, 175 were listed as "tenants." These terms were not used by enumerators in either of these counties in 1850. Also, no landless farmers appear on the agricultural schedules of Gordon, Hall, and Hancock counties in 1860, yet Schedule I lists many "farmers" in those counties who owned no real estate. Hence, grossly erroneous conclusions might easily be drawn through failure to check all facts on Schedule IV with those on Schedules I and II. The necessity for these precautions and the lack of consistency in many of the records greatly try the patience of the investigator.

19. At the same time, small holdings manned by yeomen farmers were the prevailing pattern in certain of the newer counties in western Georgia. For example, Heard, Carroll, and Paulding counties, located in the upper Piedmont between the Chattahoochee River and the Alabama line, had very few slaves in 1860. Less than 1 percent of the farmers in this area could be classed as planters. This part of Georgia was opened to settlers after 1827, and they came largely from the old plantation counties of middle Georgia.

cation of an old system. Black freedmen were fitted into a tenant system previously devised, on a less servile basis, for white farmers without land.[20] As a rule, when large planters in the cotton belt have grown more prosperous, farm tenancy has given way to wage labor.

Not all of Hancock's landless farmers had become either emigrants or laborers by 1860. Fourteen actually advanced into the landowning group during the decade. Whether initiative and energy contributed more to their rise than marriage or inheritance or choice farm sites remains a question, but the latter explanation seems more probable.

A comparison of the agricultural productions of these fourteen farmers at the two census periods, one before and one after they made the transition to landownership, shows significant changes in crop emphasis and farming practices. For example, their livestock increased in value from an average of $242 to $1,164; their tools and implements advanced in value from an average of $15 to $182. The number of their milch cows alone rose 92 percent above the 1850 level. The variety and production of subsistence crops increased markedly. More significant still is the fact that cotton lost its position as the most emphasized crop and ranked far down the scale in the order of productivity.[21] Thus John Franks, a renter in 1850, produced sixteen bales of cotton; in 1860, as the owner of 200 acres of land, he raised only half as much cotton but ample livestock and subsistence crops. Home manufacturing disappeared almost entirely from the list of enterprises of the new landowners.[22] These facts indicate a remarkable similarity between land-use patterns of landless farmers of the lower South before 1860 and those of tenant farmers and croppers of the postbellum era. This addition to cash crops,

20. Many antebellum Southerners were acquainted with similar tenancy systems in 1860, such as those in England after the decline of feudalism and those of the Roman Republic in the days of Cato the Censor. The terminology associated with postbellum farm tenancy in the lower South was not new to Americans even in 1860. The term "cropper," for example, was used by an Illinois farmer in the 1850's when he wrote significantly that "absence from home . . . [compelled him] to depend . . . on 'annual croppers' who were accustomed to skim over the ground with the 'bar share' plow." Illinois Agricultural Society, *Transactions*, 3 (1857–58), 408.

21. There was evidently no appreciable difference in weather conditions for the two census years that might have influenced these changes. John T. Henderson, *The Commonwealth of Georgia* (Atlanta, 1884), 62–63; *Southern Cultivator*, 18 (1860), 285.

22. With the rising prosperity of planting enterprises throughout the decade, home manufacturing declined perceptibly among all classes. The decline was only slightly pronounced among small farmers and wage laborers.

the limited ownership of tools and livestock, and a supplementary income from odd jobs during the interval between crops have always been the lot of the landless farmer in the cotton belt.

A careful check of the names of non-landowners appearing on both the 1850 and the 1860 census schedules shows that many of them had changed their occupation completely. Like the Negro tenant who during the 1930's tended to disappear from the more mechanized agricultural areas of the South, the landless farmer of 1850 in Hancock County was sometimes found, ten years later, among the low-paid industrial workers of the vicinity, or occasionally trying his hand at a semi-skilled trade.[23]

In 1860 there were 198 white farm laborers in the county. Ninety-nine percent of them owned no real estate, and 91.6 percent owned no personal property. There were 96 textile workers, all of whom appeared to have an economic status even lower than that of the farm laborers. The 139 overseers had a much higher position than either of the other two groups, despite stereotyped views in which they are pictured as inferiors. For example, 20 percent of the overseers possessed personal property, and a few owned real estate. The factory workers, the landless farmers, and the overseers, together with their families, account for approximately 30 percent of the total white population of the county in 1860.[24] The farm laborers and the overseers, taken together, comprised more than 57 percent of the white agricultural population.

For purposes of detailed analysis the family heads and a few other individuals who were engaged in an occupation have been classified into seven occupational groups.[25] The landowning planters and farmers have been further classified into three subdivisions, based upon the value of individual real estate holdings.[26] By assigning the figures for property

23. Mechanization may have been a factor in causing this change in occupational status. An enthusiastic citizen in 1860 claimed that Hancock farmers had "more labor-saving machinery and agricultural implements, larger and better plows . . . than any people in the world." *Southern Cultivator*, 18 (1860), 341.

24. These three groups represented a total of 1,134 persons. The landowning agricultural population accounted for 1,695 people, or approximately 45 percent of the total white population.

25. It has been impossible to classify 7.2 percent of the families on the census schedules, even after checking all available data. It is safe to conclude that these unclassified families were in one of the lower economic categories.

26. This is perhaps the simplest and most valid criterion for the classification of landowners. False conclusions relative to the scale of agricultural operations of a planter may be drawn when reliance is placed in the number of slaves he owned, or in the number of acres under his control. The use of hired labor and tenants, the variation in the age and quality of slaves and in the fertility and condition of

TABLE I. ECONOMIC STATUS OF OCCUPATIONAL GROUPS, 1860

Occupational group	Number	Total in families	Percent owning realty	Percent owning slaves	Percent owning other personal property
Planters and farmers *					
$10,000 and above	56	267	100.0	100.0	100.0
$9,999 to $1,001	220	1,049	100.0	92.2	100.0
$1,000 and under	85	379	100.0	41.6	91.7
Professional class	48	195	62.4	54.1	77.1
Merchants	29	101	50.0	45.0	75.9
Tradesmen	116	414	13.7	7.7	26.9
Overseers	139	367	1.4	6.4	20.8
Farm laborers	198	610	1.2	0.016	8.4
Factory workers	96	157	0.9	0.0	0.0**
All others	110	276			

* While the lowest landowning agricultural subdivision (those whose land was valued at $1,000 and under) is placed third from the top in this table, it is evident that its position would be lower than this when measured by other criteria. For example, see the values of land and personalty assigned to the various groups in Table 2.

** The absence of personal property assigned to factory workers is explained by the failure of enumerators to list personal property evaluations of less than $100.

ownership to all groups, the various categories in Table 1 have been arranged to approximate a descending order of economic well-being.

Forty-eight professional people were enumerated in the county. This group occupied an economic position above that of any other nonplanter group and, as Table 2 indicates, above that of the small farmers. Part-time occupation in planting enterprises is responsible for their relatively high position. Sixteen of the professional men were physicians, and seven of these were also planters of considerable means. There were five Baptist ministers, all of whom were landowners. One of the four

the soil are factors of great importance not measured in slave or land ownership alone. A check of individual items on the "Schedule of Slave Inhabitants" for Hancock County shows that a planter sometimes owning fewer than ten slaves had more adult able-bodied laborers than a neighbor owning more than twenty. Similar instances were found on the agricultural schedules relative to acres of land. The total value of land and slaves is perhaps the best single index where comparisons are to be made between groups. Another index, which can be found only on the agricultural schedule, is the value of agricultural productions. The validity of this index for general use is somewhat questionable unless the factor of varying weather on crop conditions can be eliminated.

Methodist ministers was a planter, as was the Methodist bishop, George Foster Pierce, who owned eighteen slaves and 900 acres of land.[27] Other professional people included ten teachers, five lawyers, three druggists, two dentists, and a surgeon; some of these were also connected with planting interests.

The plantation life was the ideal to which all white men in the county seemed to aspire. The presence of this model is indicated in various ways other than its popularity among professional men. For example, there were progressively higher percentages of slave ownership on

TABLE 2. ECONOMIC STATUS OF OCCUPATIONAL GROUPS IN 1860

Occupational group	Average age of each group	Percent owning slaves	Average value of realty	Average value of personalty	Ratio of personalty to realty
Planters and farmers					
$10,000 and above	49.7	100	$21,786	$45,434	1.99
$9,999 to $1,001	45.8	92.2	4,268	12,904	3.02
$1,000 and under	44.9	41.6	719	2,348	3.26
Professional class	34.85	54.1	2,844	8,025	2.82
Merchants	33.5	45	1,862	5,848	3.14
Tradesmen	38.03	7.7	216	874	4.04
Overseers	28.8	6.4	72	1,524	21.16
Farm laborers	30.06	.01	15	44	2.87
Factory workers	24.09	0	4	0	0

the upper rungs of the economic and social ladder, and the more prosperous planters monopolized the higher age brackets. Also, in the middle and lower property-owning groups there was a high ratio of personalty to realty,[28] indicating that members of these groups, while striving for upper-class status, gave great importance to slave ownership. Figures supporting these conclusions are shown in Table 2.

In the occupations of individuals in all categories at the two census periods, there appears a decided tendency for lawyer, doctor, carpenter, merchant, and tailor to move into agriculture as fast as the accumulation

27. The itinerant nature of the Methodist ministry probably rendered him less disposed to own land than the Baptist minister.

28. That is, the ratio of slaves to land. This is taken as an indication that ownership of slaves by the middle and lower economic groups was of greater importance than ownership of land. The property of overseers, for example, consisted almost entirely of slaves. Planters in the uppermost economic subdivision were inclined to put more money into land and less into slaves.

of capital would permit. The complete abandonment of a trade or profession for agriculture may have been greatly stimulated by the increasing prosperity of the landowner, for the 1850's was a prosperous period in southern agriculture. The following letter, however, written by a middle Georgian in 1849, expresses the great ambition of a young man to engage in farming because it afforded him an ideal way of life: [29]

> I desire above all things to be a "Farmer" but I must first have the means. Then the question is, how am I to obtain these? My only resources are, a tolerably liberal education, a rather weak constitution, and a firm resolution to do something. . . . I wish to be a farmer because . . . it is the most honest, upright, and sure way of securing all the comforts of life. I never heard of a man who became bankrupt by farming. Farmers only become so by some kind of speculation. What can be more attractive than a well managed farm, with its fat hogs, horses, mules, and stock of all kinds? . . . I would say, nothing, unless it be the old farmers charming daughter who understands all about domestic things . . . and who has good taste enough to cultivate . . . a few flowers and floral vines about the door, to add beauty and loveliness to the scene. Oh! that I could win such a fair one as this. But, alas for me! wealth alone can win the fair one's heart, and gain the old man's consent these days, especially if he has a few "dimes" himself.[30]

This letter also suggests the difficulties involved in acquiring the land necessary for the ideal occupation. It was not an easy task to break into the landowning class in Hancock County in the 1850's,[31] and this was generally true of the plantation cotton belt. While the value of real estate owned by the average farmer in the third subdivision was only $719, the average value of personal property in this category was $2,348. Thus he needed more than $3,000 to join the landowning group, less than half of whose members possessed slaves and could lay claim to the plantation way of life. A study of the land values of individual farmers shows that the better and more productive arable lands were already in

29. "The pursuits of agriculture have become not a mere business of dollars and cents [with us] . . . but a business of pleasure," wrote a Hancock planter in 1846. *Southern Cultivator*, 4 (1846), 5.

30. *Southern Cultivator*, 7 (1849), 10.

31. This may account for the migration of many rural youths to towns and cities, a noticeable phenomenon of the 1850's. "A crying evil is the training of country boys for the law, encouraging them to leave home and seek in towns promotion," complained a Georgian in 1861. *Southern Cultivator*, 19 (1861), 78. "This itching of young men for the learned professions is a great evil in the land and should be discouraged by all who have an influence," said the *Savannah Republican*, quoted in *Southern Cultivator*, 17 (1859), 467. These professional men usually went into agriculture after they acquired sufficient capital.

the hands of wealthy owners who probably had no desire to part with them. In addition, the large planters had secured a great proportion of the unimproved land available in the community.[32] This is indicated in Table 3. Large planters in the 1850's were putting more money into

TABLE 3. STATUS OF LANDOWNING AGRICULTURAL SUBDIVISIONS

Planting subdivisions	Percent owning slaves	Average number of slaves to each planter	Average number of un-improved acres	Average number of improved acres	Average percent of un-improved land
$10,000 and above	100	55.1	1,983	910	68.5
$9,999 to $1,001	92.2	15.5	397	229	63.5
$1,000 and under	41.6	2.2	101	64	61.2

land and less into slaves.[33] In contrast, smaller planters were apparently demanding more slaves. This situation throughout the cotton belt was a major factor in the boom in slave prices during that decade. In 1860, for example, planters in the first subdivision owned one slave to 52.3 acres (improved and unimproved), while in the second subdivision the ratio was one to 40.4.[34] Many large planters were selling their surplus slaves

32. This was like buying an insurance policy against soil exhaustion and the necessity for moving westward. As Clark found in her study of the small farmer of Tennessee, the unimproved land was used for pasturage and brought into cultivation when older plots became exhausted. *Tennessee Yeoman, 1840–60* (Nashville, 1942), p. 9. It should be pointed out here that the prevailing low price of land was by no means an indication of its availability. Not only was land undervalued on the census returns and on the county tax books, but in some communities it was simply not for sale.

33. The plantation of David Dickson offers a typical example of conservatism in the use of slave labor by the larger planters. On his 13,000-acre plantation in Hancock County there were only fifty-five "full hands" in 1859. *Southern Cultivator,* 17, 345; 18 (1860), 203. Dickson used highly trained and efficient operatives and claimed thus to have obtained high production levels without excessive overhead costs in upkeep and supervision. George Frederick Hunnicutt, *David Dickson's and James M. Smith's Farming* (Atlanta, 1910), pp. 31 *et passim.* Out of a total of 144 slaves assigned to him by the 1860 census, only ten were over thirty-five years of age. Children and young adults abounded. Dickson wrote in 1859, "Double the number of slaves and the price [of land] will depreciate one-half." *Southern Cultivator,* 17, 255.

34. The ratio was one slave to 75.2 acres for farmers in the lowest subdivision, but less than half of the farmers in this subdivision owned no slaves.

to good advantage and keeping for their own use the younger and more efficient operatives, which is shown by a comparison of age brackets of slave families belonging to the different groups at the two census periods.

Of the 8,137 slaves in the county in 1860, over 96 percent were in the hands of agricultural groups, including nine overseers and two farm laborers. The 302 slaves belonging to the nonagricultural group were widely distributed in all categories of this group, the factory workers being the only class where no instance of slave ownership appeared. The nonagricultural slaveowners included eight merchants, three nonfarming physicians, two nonfarming attorneys, three teachers, two carpenters, a wagoner, tanner, coachmaker, blacksmith, clerk, druggist, and the county sheriff. Nancy Wadkins, a free Negro, owned two slaves.[35]

The number of slaves in the county was more than double that of the white population. This situation caused, and perhaps to a great extent determined, the robust program of diversification and subsistence farming recorded for the community in the late 1850's.[36] From the sprawling plantation of David Dickson to the twenty-five-acre farm of Shepherd Wilson there was a sound, self-sufficing economy, as indicated on the agricultural schedule. Measured by prices then current, the value of the subsistence crops was more than twice that of the cotton crop in most individual cases. In the county as a whole subsistence crops and livestock exceeded by more than four times the value of the cotton crop. The very large planters, however, were inclined to grow relatively more cotton than the small planters or farmers, but the big operators' failure to grow a great variety of subsistence crops was partly compensated for by their progress in the raising of livestock. The high average value of their animals indicates that they were taking advantage of improved breeds and probably slaughtering or selling off their inferior stock to less fortunate neighbors. Taken together, these facts point to a twofold purpose behind the practice of the large planters who were buying up the unimproved land: to provide fresh land for the future expansion of cotton-growing in the vicinity of the homestead, and to secure range for livestock. These purposes were interchangeable, in that livestock could

35. Apparently a legal technicality applying to members of her own family.

36. The Sandersville *Central Georgian* in 1855 made an observation that substantiates census data relative to diversification in the county. While criticizing the average Southern planter for growing cotton and buying subsistence products, the newspaper stated that "the most thrifty planters in Hancock, are those who raise their own pork and flour, at the risk of making less cotton." Quoted in *Southern Cultivator*, 13 (1855), 305.

be transferred from woodland pastures to abandoned farm land in the process of expansion.[37]

This concentration of landownership and the adaptation of the plantation to raising livestock undoubtedly had an adverse effect upon the fortunes of tenant farmers and squatters, many of whom were forced to seek employment as wage earners. As previously noted, the factory workers had an economic status lower than that of any other group. Only one of the ninety-six persons in this category is credited with possessing property of any kind. Indicative of low wages is the fact that often entire families—children, adults, males, and females—were factory workers. Only twenty-nine factory workers are known to have been heads of families, and some of these were widows. The average age of the worker was 24.09 years. The family size was 4.1.[38]

The economic status of the farm laborers was a little higher than that of the factory workers. Thirty-three of the farm laborers were unmarried and were sons of small farmers. In all probability they were working on their fathers' farms as unpaid members of the family. In addition, there were sons of small farmers who were not assigned an occupation

37. Soil exhaustion always tends to encourage the accumulation of large estates. When land becomes less fertile, new methods of farming require an outlay of capital and the acquisition of knowledge necessary for putting the new methods into practice. These added requirements cause small holdings to become marginal to their owners. Large planters in the 1850's not only had the capital or credit with which to purchase fertilizers, livestock, fences, and improved tools, but they also possessed some of the leisure and intellectual capacity essential to learning the new methods. The *Savannah Journal and Courier* observed in 1855: "No county in Georgia can produce more intelligence and refinement than Hancock, and its agricultural skill and energy are preeminent." Quoted in *Soil of the South*, 5 (1855), 321. These intelligent and skillful farmers were buying submarginal farms and converting them into profitable holdings.

38. A study of the unmarried factory workers reveals pertinent facts concerning social stratification. For example, the unmarried factory laborers lived generally with the families of farm laborers and tradesmen, and there was probably no social distinction between these three occupational groups. The overseer, although ranking below the tradesman in economic well-being, enjoyed a higher social status than the latter. The occupational origin of sixty-four of the ninety-six factory workers has been determined: twenty-nine were sons, daughters, or wives of factory workers; seventeen came from families whose head was engaged in carpentry; families of teamsters, farm laborers, shoemakers, and overseers contributed eight, five, four, and one, respectively. Thus the tradesman's family supplied most of the factory workers. Families of farm laborers contributed a small share. Only one representative of an overseer's family was found working in the factory. Farm laborers might associate freely with factory workers, but they showed a reluctance to send their children into this occupation.

by the enumerator and who, in all likelihood, were engaged as unpaid family workers. If the enumerator had listed the occupation of both the male and female members of the small-farmer family who worked in the fields, the total number of farm laborers would have been increased considerably. According to the enumerator's designations, however, there were only 198 farm laborers in the county in 1860. Of these, 107 were heads of families and the average family size was 4.9. Fourteen of the married farm laborers were born in other states and five in foreign countries. There were also five free colored laborers in the group. Most of the unmarried farm laborers were living in the homes of their parents, who were also farm laborers, overseers, or small farmers. Only three were sons of tradesmen.

Significantly, the agricultural families, regardless of their category, did not often send their sons into the trades.[39] While the tradesman was apparently more prosperous than the overseer and the agricultural laborer, there are no data indicating that sons of planters, small farmers, overseers, farm laborers, or even native factory workers entered any trade other than carpentry. Conversely, the tradesman's son rarely became an overseer or a farm laborer.

The tradesman group contained the highest percentage of bachelors and, except for an occasional seamstress, there were no females in this group. The average age of the unmarried tradesman was comparatively high, because this group had the largest percentage of immigrants from other states and from foreign countries. Thirteen came from Ireland alone, and they dominated the stonemason trade in the vicinity. The pursuit of a trade seemed to offer the greatest promise for the foreign-born who sought to acquire means necessary to enter the planting occupation. There are many records of such transitions in biographies of commonplace antebellum Southerners.[40] These ambitious immigrants

39. On the larger plantations the tradesman's work was often performed by skilled Negro slaves. This practice was frowned upon by those who sought to make the trades attractive to southern white men. "Confine the Negro to the soil thus to elevate and open the mechanic trades to the non-slaveholders around them," advised an agricultural reformer in 1861. *Southern Cultivator*, 19 (1861): 14.

40. Jarvis Van Buren came to Georgia from New York as a foundryman. He became an agriculturist and was largely responsible for the establishment of the commercial apple industry in northern Georgia before 1860. Charles A. Peabody, another Northerner, came to Columbus, Georgia, and set up a tailoring establishment. Later, as a prominent southern horticulturist, he helped edit the *Soil of the South* and the *American Cotton Planter;* he did much to develop truck farming in the gulf region. Richard Peters came to Georgia from Pennsylvania as an obscure engineer for the Georgia Railroad Company. Through judicious purchase of real

were not inclined to become tenant farmers, farm laborers, or factory workers, and they were not qualified as plantation overseers.

In the same way that the occupation of the tradesman was used by non-natives as a stepping stone to land ownership, the starting point of the ambitious native without training in a profession was the occupation of overseer. The overseer was far from the bottom of the social and economic ladder.[41] Of the 139 overseers enumerated, forty-two lived with the planter's family and probably enjoyed freely the society of his household. Twenty of these were sons of planters in whose homes they were recorded as living, which substantiates the well-known theory that planters often employed the oldest unmarried son as overseer. Some data relative to the occupational origin of the overseers may be found in Table 4. Apparently no farm laborers, factory workers, or tradesmen en-

TABLE 4. OCCUPATIONAL ORIGIN OF OVERSEERS, 1860

Overseers who were sons of overseers	22
Overseers who were sons of planters and farmers	20
Unmarried overseers living in home of planters (no kinship)	22
Unmarried overseers living in separate house from planter	30

tered the overseer class. Where their origin can be determined, they were recruited from the families of small planters and farmers.

Nine overseers owned a total of twenty-one slaves. Twenty others had personal property of various kinds, and only two possessed realty.

---

estate around the rapidly growing village of Marthasville (now Atlanta), he acquired a modest fortune and became one of the leading livestock farmers in the antebellum South. Robert Nelson, a Danish nurseryman and jack-of-all-trades, was instrumental in founding the commercial peach industry in middle Georgia before 1860. Many foreigners settled in Augusta and engaged in the nursery business. Most prominent of them was Prosper Jules Berckmans, who was the originator and disseminator of more worthy ornamental forms perhaps than any other southern horticulturist. He later acquired 1,100 acres of land in Hancock County, on which were planted peach and pecan orchards. Bonner, "Genesis of Agricultural Reform in the Cotton Belt," *Journal of Southern History*, 9 (1943), 492 *et passim;* Thomas Hubbard McHatton, "Gardening in Georgia," *Garden History of Georgia, 1733-1933*, ed. Loraine Meeks Cooney and Hattie C. Rainwater (Atlanta, 1933), 132; *Atlanta Constitution*, October 5, 1941.

41. Many contemporary documents attest the efficiency of Hancock's overseers. While reporting that the county had "splendid overseers," an observer in 1860 affirmed that Hancock planters no longer relied upon the judgment of their hired managers but "trusted less to them than any people in the world." *Southern Cultivator*, 18 (1860), 175.

None of the property-owning overseers was a son of the planter by whom he was employed, indicating that his property may not have been acquired through patrimony. The overseer group was the most indigenous of all: there were no foreign-born among them and only two were born outside the state. Fifty-four percent of the total were unmarried. Like the tradesmen, the percentage of elderly bachelors among them was large.

The factory wage-earners formed the lowest socio-economic group in the county and comprised nearly 10 percent of all the gainfully employed who were visited by the census enumerator. Since the entire family of the factory laborer often worked long hours at low wages, the group very likely did not supplement its income by other enterprises.[42] The absence of a home garden, for instance, probably lowered the standard of living more than any available data indicate.

These industrial wage-earners appear to have been the genuine poor whites in this particular community. The poor whites of historical tradition, however, were those who squatted on the land of others, dwelt in rude cabins, and eked out an existence by applying their wits to various enterprises, from hunting and fishing to subsistence farming. These poor whites, like David Ware, may have possessed more initiative and stubborn individualism than has ever been attributed to them. They might be understood better if it is remembered that they were by-products of a society wholly dominated by the agrarian philosophy. The contemporary observers who denounced them for their refusal to abandon the freedom of the fields and streams for stultifying labor in factory or workshop were passing judgment upon a rural agrarian phenomenon, and the standards of this judgment were those of a more urban industrial society.[43] In many southern communities there is still a feeling among landless farmers that one loses caste when he surrenders to the lure of the cotton mills, although he may gain materially in the process. This attitude must have been much more pronounced among landless farmers in the 1850's, when agriculture was accepted unquestionably as the ideal way of life.[44]

42. An excellent discussion of a southern mill village of this period, not far from Hancock County, appears in Broadus Mitchell, *William Gregg, Factory Master of the Old South* (Chapel Hill, 1928), 34 *et passim*.

43. The "Vanderbilt agrarians" have given some prominence to this idea in Twelve Southerners, *I'll Take My Stand* (New York, 1930).

44. By 1856 Daniel Lee, the northern-bred editor of the *Southern Cultivator*, had repudiated his earlier idea that free white labor would be available for manufacturing enterprises in the South. "What is unsteady, irresponsible hired labor worth, when the freeman often forsakes his plow to the ruin of a crop, to hunt wild tur-

Ulrich Bonnell Phillips, in his interpretation of southern history, emphasized the importance of the Negro aspect of the slave rather than the slave aspect of the Negro.[45] This interpretation explains the apparent solidarity of all classes of white men in the antebellum South. The stories of Richard Malcolm Johnston illustrate the unified character of southern life in his native Hancock in the decade before the Civil War.[46] This solidarity was more apparent than real, however, and owed what reality it had to the presence of large numbers of black men in a society dominated by whites. The foregoing data show that approximately one-third of all white families were both slaveless and landless and possessed only their labor with which to bargain in economic competition. Another third owned land but no slaves. The upper third possessed both land and slaves in varying proportions. This upper group had a strong vested interest in the institution of slavery. The middle group aspired to the same kind of life as the upper group, but only a few of its members were able to achieve it after 1850, when the flush conditions of the frontier in the cotton country had subsided. Members of the lowest group may have had similar aspirations, but their prime interest in slavery arose from the fact that it maintained a floor to their social and economic position. This floor was preserved through the legal sanction of a permanent, less privileged, servile class.

Although many of the muster rolls, church minutes, and courthouse records of earlier communities are still extant and offer abundant data for the genealogist, they fail to give many facts which the objective historian wishes to know. The most reliable and comprehensive logbook of any American community's social and economic life is to be found among the faded pages of the detailed census schedules. These schedules for Hancock County, when examined microscopically, tell a story of segregation, aversion to certain economic pursuits, and consequent social cleavages not greatly unlike those which prevail on opposite sides of

keys or visit groceries?" he wrote. "Without mental and moral training and a high standard of reliable, voluntary labor by the week, month, and year, are [sic] hardly to be expected in a mild climate." *Southern Cultivator*, 14 (1856), 282.

45. Phillips, *The Course of the South to Secession* (New York, 1939), 151–65.

46. Robert Cecil Beale, *The Development of the Short Story in the South* (Charlottesville, 1911), 53. For an example of these stories, see Richard Malcolm Johnston, *Old Times in Middle Georgia* (New York, 1897). Johnston's stories bear ample testimony to the presence in Hancock County of a large group of white people living on the borderline of privation on the one side and competence on the other. The unpolished speech, rough manners, and commonplace tenor of their lives are portrayed in such a manner that one feels the author has treated them with remarkable fidelity.

railroad tracks in modern industrial society. These admittedly represent some of the later aspects of antebellum southern life, evolving after the passage of the frontier in the eastern cotton belt.

Romantic and backward-looking Georgians of today, with a flair for genealogy in their blood, are wont to take great pride in a forebear who originated in Old Hancock. As in the case of F.F.V.'s, whose ancestors arrived in the Old Dominion by the grace of God and indentured servitude, the economic status of the ancestor makes very little difference to the Georgian, for time and distance lend undue enchantment. It is a sobering thought, however, to reflect that the successful planting aristocracy of Hancock County did not rest entirely upon the backs of its 8,-000 Negro slaves. A great mass of landless and slaveless white men occupied a broad socio-economic area between the slaves and their masters. The dynamic nature of the aristocratic, agrarian society of the plantation masters in this community cannot be denied, nor should their contribution to its economic and cultural development be minimized. Yet the fact remains that the social and economic organization which produced them was far from perfect when measured by the liberal standards of later generations—or by the more advanced standards of their own generation.

Julia Hering

Plantation Economy in Leon County, 1830-40

Julia Hering's article describes the growth of a slaveholding elite in one of the most interesting—and neglected—areas of the antebellum South. Unlike other states of the Old South, Florida's development was halting. Spanish, English, and finally American occupation, as well as decades of Indian warfare, distinguish it from more settled states such as Virginia and South Carolina. Planters from Georgia and South Carolina, where the institution of Negro slavery was already established though still to some degree fluid, settled in Middle Florida, of which Leon County is a part. Harassed by the depredations of hostile Indians who formed alliances with Negro slaves, planters here confronted problems peculiar to this region. The chief result of this warfare was that for many years Florida remained a frontier society. Typical of such societies in America were land speculation, wildcat banking, and a high incidence of upward mobility—elements characteristic not only of young societies but also of much of Jacksonian America.

Historians now recognize that the chief political impulse of Jacksonian democracy, its opposition to vested interests and popular involvement in the electoral process, significantly affected racial attitudes in the South. A less explored but no less important question is whether these changes also affected slaveholding and ultimately the lives of the slaves. Another question which we can only answer by comparative studies of slavery in other parts of the South is the extent to which the state's cultural and ethnic diversity affected the structure of the institution.

The area of cotton culture in Florida during the antebellum period was located mainly between the Apalachicola and Suwannee rivers, and in 1840 comprised the counties of Leon, Madison, Jefferson, Hamilton, and Gadsden. It is significant that this area constituted then more or less an island in northern Florida whose economy, social structure, and soil type differed from that in the remainder of the state. In this comparatively small and isolated region there came into being, between 1830

Reprinted with permission from the *Florida Historical Quarterly*, XXXIII (July, 1954), 32–47.

and 1840, a cotton economy which compared favorably with that of the Georgia Piedmont or the black belt of Alabama. The emphasis in this paper will be upon only one county in this island of cotton culture— Leon.

Leon County had gained a significant importance prior to the decade 1830–40 when it began to receive its first influx of planters from Virginia, the Carolinas, and Georgia. As in other parts of the lower South, this was a period of land speculation, and by 1839 there were, in the area of present Leon County, at least thirty planatations established well enough to use thirty to forty-five slaves. Most of these were located north and east of Tallahassee.

Even as early as 1773, William Bartram, while traveling through the area, wrote and described the region as being exceptionally fertile for the growing of cotton, rice, corn, and other agricultural products.[1] In 1835, Farquhar Macrae wrote about Leon County from his Wacissa planatation in Jefferson County, that "good lands are mostly all entered; the large tracts are still held by individuals in the market, at rates cheaper than any other land of similar quality in the southern country." Macrae further stated that the land was in no way inferior to the acreage that was selling in Alabama for twenty-five dollars an acre and could be bought in Florida for about ten dollars an acre, and the planters, "whether desirous of cultivating cotton, rice, tobacco, or grain, or breeding cattle, at once found before him, land . . . alluring in verdant pasturage, fertile forests and well furnished springs." [2]

Of the well-established plantations in Leon County by 1839, the average size appears to have been 1,500 to 2,500 acres, employing thirty to forty-five slaves.[3] Samuel Parkhill and Benjamin Chaires were among the larger landholders, and they appear to have been typical planters; for these reasons they have been selected for further mention.

Samuel Parkhill started buying land in Leon County in 1828 and by 1839 owned 4,400 acres and eighty slaves, which apparently comprised two separate plantations since about 3,400 acres were located northwest of Tallahassee touching Lake Jackson and the remaining 1,000 acres were northeast of the city.[4] Parkhill died in 1841, leaving his estate

1. *The Travels of William Bartram*, ed. Mark Van Doren (1928).

2. Farquhar Macrea, "Soils and Agricultural Advantages of the Floridas," *Farmers Register* (1835) 3: 516.

3. *Tax Book*, 1839, Leon County Courthouse. Probably more or less of this land was not cleared.

4. *Deed Record, Book* A, 271; Book D, 445; Book E, 265, 370, 624, 772; Book F, 314, 407; Leon County Courthouse.

heavily mortgaged and without having made a will. His widow, Martha Ann, petitioned the superior court of Leon County for one-third of the estate as a widow's dower. At the time of his death, the Union Bank of Florida in Tallahassee valued Parkhill's real estate holdings at $138,300; his personal property was valued at $4,400, which included furniture, livestock, farm equipment, and 2,020 bushels of corn. In addition, 383 bales of cotton were worth $14,000. Since Parkhill's acreage and slaves were mortgaged to the bank, the court allowed the widow to claim only one-third of the personal property, which gave her 127 bales of cotton stored in the warehouse of the "Railroad Depot near the City of Tallahassee." [5]

Parkhill also owned 1,383 shares of stock in the Union Bank. The bank filed suit against his estate on grounds that, by the provisions of its charter, each stockholder was entitled to a loan equal to two-thirds of the amount of his shares, provided that notes covering repayment with interest were renewed annually. Parkhill had made loans against the entire amount of his shares before his death, and he had never renewed his note or paid interest on it. Thus this planter played no small part in the ultimate failure of the bank, for it never could recover all that he owed. In the meantime, his unfortunate widow, Martha Ann, who actually realized very little from his estate, purchased, in 1843, a small piece of property southwest of the city, and later that year married Hiram Manly of Apalachicola.[6]

The financial story of Benjamin Chaires is somewhat different from that of Parkhill, even though Chaires followed the same general pattern in regard to buying land. The *Tax Book* for 1839 lists his estate as comprising 9,440 acres of land, eighty slaves, $800 worth of pleasure carriages, and as paying a territorial tax of $110 and a county tax of $86.

Chaires died in 1838, leaving his property to his wife and children. ". . . to my beloved wife Sarah Chaires . . . my mansion or dwelling house and 500 acres around it . . . my household furniture, carriage and horses and negro man Henry, the carriage driver; also one tenth part of all my personal estate." He had ten children, and five of them were still minors at the time of his death. Apparently Chaires felt no affection for his son-in-law, William Burgess, the husband of his daughter Mary Ann, for he did not include her in the one-tenth share but left her a sum of $10,000 to be paid her "whenever her husband . . . shall die, and

5. "Inventory of the Personal Estate of Samuel Parkhill, Deceased, Not Mortgaged but Set Apart as the Widow's Dower," *Court Record*, 1842, Leon County Courthouse.

6. "Petition of the Union Bank of Florida, Filed 5th April, 1845," *ibid*.

not before. . . . It being my express desire that said William Burgess shall not have any part of the same or enjoy any benefit whatsoever."

Chaires appointed his brother, Green Chaires, and his son, Joseph Chaires, as executors of his estate. Green and Joseph must have disapproved of Burgess, too, for they gave Mary Ann five female Negro slaves, and a horse and barouche with harness. However, it was distinctly understood that they would hold this property for the separate use of Mary Ann, free from the control of William.[7]

By 1845 the plantations of the Benjamin Chaires estate were still intact, and the county court authorized property division among the heirs. This included about 10,000 acres, numerous slaves, together with the crop of provisions at each of the plantations, livestock, including horses, mules, cattle, hogs, as well as plantation utensils of all kinds.[8]

Some other plantations of average size were those belonging to Hector Braden, Edward and Thomas Bradford, John Branch, William and John Craig, H. B. Croom, Alfred Gatlin, William Lester, Jeremiah Powell, John Shepard, Robert Williams, and others.

Since Alfred Gatlin and Jeremiah Powell were typical planters with average holdings, perhaps they should be mentioned. Gatlin is listed as having only about 1,000 acres in 1839 and thirty-five slaves, but by the time of his death in 1841 he had considerably increased his holdings. His widow Sarah Ann petitioned the court for one-third of his estate because she preferred the division made to her by law rather than the share left under her husband's will. In addition to his plantation and about seventy slaves, Gatlin had a house and property in Tallahassee. His personal property was reported as including two carriage horses, five mules, twenty-six head of hogs, twenty-one head of cattle, 514 bushels of corn, 3,000 pounds of fodder, as well as other items. Like so many of the other planters in Leon County, Gatlin's property was mortgaged to the Union Bank, which took fifty-three of his slaves in payment of his indebtedness.[9]

Jeremiah Powell came to Leon County about 1830 and started buying land. By the time of his death in 1839, he owned 2,700 acres and forty-five slaves. He had made his will in 1838, leaving his estate to his wife and six children. It was his wish that they should be maintained,

7. "Will of Benjamin Chaires, June 12, 1835," *Index to Estates, Book One,* File No. 31, Leon County Courthouse.

8. "The Petition of Mrs. Sarah Chaires, Widow and Legatee of Benjamin Chaires," *Court Record,* 1845, Leon County Courthouse.

9. "In the Matter of Assignment of Dower of Sarah A. Gatlin, Widow," Leon Superior Court, 1842.

clothed, supported, and well educated from the proceeds of his two plantations, which included his home plantation northeast of Tallahassee where he and his family lived. Powell kept most of his slaves at his lower plantation, known as "Pleasant Grove," which was located nearer the Jefferson County line. He also left an annual gift of $100 to the Methodist Episcopal Church of the Leon County circuit for ten years after his death.[10] For some time afterward the bank sued the Powell heirs and tried repeatedly to take possession of Pleasant Grove plantation.[11] It was supposedly a policy of the bank to make loans only on land which was secured by the additional collateral of slaves.

A good example of land speculation during this early period was the firm of Nuttall, Braden, and Craig. Many transactions made by this firm are recorded in the Leon County *Deed Records.* In 1833 the firm bought a whole township for $46,520, consisting of 23,040 acres, which was a grant made by the U. S. Government in 1825 [12] to General Lafayette. Nuttall, Braden, and Craig expected to make a profit of $60,000 on the transaction. Though the firm did sell off the land, most of their returns were promissory notes payable ten and twenty years later. The indenture for this transaction stipulated that the money was to be paid in full before January 1, 1844. However, in the late 1850's records show the Lafayette heirs were still trying to collect money due them.

John Gamble of Leon County played an important part in the cotton industry as planter and banker during this early period. Gamble was president of the Union Bank and was most anxious that planters borrow on cotton at home instead of abroad. He believed that they should have a more lenient system of credit than was the current practice. His argument was that southern bankers usually advanced the money that moved forward the whole crop on letters of credit. Bills of exchange were forwarded to the foreign market, often reaching their destination and maturing before the cotton arrived. Gamble claimed that this situation caused cotton to be force on the market in foreign ports whether or not the price realized for it was desirable. He thought the great southern staple was without protection and that the banks in southern seaports should arrange six-month loans at home so that cotton would not be sent to market accompanied by a bill of exchange which required an immediate sale, regardless of the condition of the market.[13]

Gamble, as president of the bank, was partly responsible for its failure

10. "Will of Jeremiah Powell," *Court Record*, 1838, Leon County Courthouse.

11. "Union Bank *v.* Powell Heirs," *ibid.*

12. *Deed Record*, Book K, 74.

13. "Cotton Convention," *Niles Weekly Register*, 57 (Baltimore, 1837) 185.

during the late 1840's. As in the case of Parkhill, previously mentioned, the bank did not observe the limitations of its charter, and money was frequently lent without the necessary security. When the effects of the financial crisis of 1837 began to be felt, mortgagors were unable to make their payments to the bank or renew their notes. At the same time, the territory itself was unable to pay interest to holders of the territorial bonds, popularly known as faith bonds. The territorial legislature demanded an investigation of the bank, but no signficant findings were ever reached. Actually, the bank was the political victim of its directors and stockholders, who were powerful members of the territorial government.[14]

As the financial condition of the bank went from bad to worse, Gamble began a series of lawsuits against persons owing the bank. The 1841–46 *Court Records* in Leon County show the astonishing amounts which were due the bank, and in most cases it held no collateral security. Some examples of these suits are those against Richard Call for $18,000, George Walker for $16,000, Robert Hackley for $19,000; but in Hackley's case $8,000 was recovered from the proceeds of the sale of Negroes.[15] At the same time, various persons filed suit against the bank for amounts they could not collect. To make matters worse, in some instances mortgaged slaves were taken out of the territory so that liens could not be made against them. One interesting complaint made by the Union Bank against B. A. Neal states that the "said negroes were removed, fraudulently and felonously . . . aided and abetted by others at present unknown." Another such complaint charges James Trotti with unlawfully removing his slaves from the territory in 1841, after he bought stock in the bank in 1838.[16]

During this early period St. Marks was a seaport for all middle Florida and lower Georgia. Ellen Call Long described the port as it was about 1830 as she traveled into the area on her way to Tallahassee as a "quaint little village, amphibious-like, consisting of a few dwelling houses, stores, etc., mostly built on stilts or piles, as if ready to launch when wind or tide prevailed."[17] Vessels came into Apalachee Bay from foreign ports and the northeast United States, bringing merchandise to supply the set-

14. Warren G. Fouraker, "The Administration of Robert Raymond Reid," thesis, Florida State University, 1949.

15. *Court Records*, 1841–46.

16. "Union Bank v. B. A. Neal, Running Off Negroes," 1843. "Union Bank v. James F. Trotti," 1841. *Court Records*.

17. Ellen Call Long, *Florida Breezes; or Florida New and Old* (Jacksonville, 1882), 35.

tlers. Before 1835, cotton and other agricultural products grown by the planters were usually taken down to St. Marks by wagon. Small boats lightered the cotton and other merchandise to and from the ships which were anchored out from shore. Cotton, tobacco, hides, syrup, brown sugar, molasses, and other products were taken to the port in exchange for flour, coffee, gunpowder, bolts of homespun, quinine, calomel, castor oil, and other needed items.[18]

Leon County planters and businessmen soon realized that a more practical means of transporting their cotton to St. Marks must be developed. The result was the Tallahassee Railroad Company, formed by a group of Leon County men including Green Chaires, Benjamin Chaires, R. K. Call, Sam Reid, Leigh Read, Samuel Duval, John Shepard, Samuel Parkhill, John Parkhill, and others. In 1834, 119 stockholders petitioned Congress for permission to construct the railroad, having already obtained a charter from the legislative council of Florida.[19] The old fort at St. Marks and the land adjoining it came into the possession of the United States by the Treaty of 1819. The petition stated that the fort, which was erected in 1759, was in a state of dilapidation and ruin, and was originally designed as a defense against the neighboring Indians but not to defend the bay and harbor of St. Marks from attacks by sea. The petitioners wanted 100 acres of land at St. Marks and a strip of land 100 feet wide from St. Marks to Tallahassee on which to construct the railroad. They presented a letter to Congress, written by Lieutenant George Long, artillery engineer, directed to General Richard Call, president of the Tallahassee Railroad Company, in which Long stated that "The only direction in which an enemy could ever arrive to disturb this section of the country . . . must be from the sea. The fort is of no consequence for the Government to retain for military purposes." [20]

In a letter dated April 19, 1835, to General Charles Gratiot, chief engineer of the U.S. Army, from Captain William A. Chase of Pensacola, Chase recommended that a railraod be constructed from Tallahassee to St. Marks "so that the business of trade as well as the customs could be transacted with every facility at Tallahassee." [21] The following year the line was built, and for several years loads of cotton were taken regularly from Tallahassee to St. Marks by this horse-drawn train.

18. W. T. Cash, "Newport as a Business Center," *Apalachee: The Publication of the Tallahassee Historical Society* (Tallahassee, 1944), 25.

19. "Memorial of the Tallahassee Railroad Company," *Senate Documents,* 23rd Cong., 2nd sess., vol. 2, 1834–35, doc. 267, no. 38, 1.

20. *Ibid.*

21. *William A. Chase Papers,* 1835, Leon County Courthouse.

Middle Florida exported 338 bales of cotton in 1827. From this meager beginning, the export grew to 15,870 bales in 1834. However, by 1840 this figure had increased to 32,000 bales, with the greater part coming from Leon County.[22]

It was soon discovered that the soil was especially suited for the growth of Sea Island cotton, which was superior to the short staple because of the length of its fiber. Although the Sea Island variety required more space per acre for cultivation, its market price per pound was about twice that of short staple. H. B. Croom wrote from his Lake Lafayette plantation in 1834 that an average of 600 pounds of long staple cotton was produced per acre and that it was not uncommon for 800 pounds to be realized. The short staple variety, under favorable conditions, yielded about 1,500 pounds to the acre.[23]

To quote Farquhar Macrae again:

> The cotton crop has never failed in Florida. The crop of the present year (1835) will, not withstanding the early and unprecedented frost, nearly double that of 1834. Most of our planters are reaping unusual returns . . . a planter working only forty servants can make and house in one crop 450,000 pounds of fine staple upland cotton, besides 3,000 bushels of corn, and some 20 barrels of sugar and syrup—leaving his crop of oats, rice, potatoes, untold!—and yet this is done in *Middle Florida* . . . the fortunate planter is my respected neighbor, Daniel Bird, Esq. of Jefferson County. The other gentleman is Col. Robert Gamble . . . who will this year realize from 65 acres of land, which have been for the last six years under continued cultivation of sugar cane (the most exhausting of crops) upward of 70 bags of cotton . . . minimum crops on our good and bad soil are never less than 600 pounds of cotton per acre.

Macrae also wrote that his fellow citizen Green Chaires sold $13,000 worth of cotton in 1835 made by twenty-two laborers.[24]

SLAVES

Prosperity in the culture of cotton was being reflected in high market prices which enhanced the value of slaves, especially good fieldhands. In 1835 Thomas Bradford paid $600 for a certain Negro boy named Mingo, aged about seventeen years.[25] In caring for slaves, planters were largely motivated by self-interest. However, it sometimes happened that

22. *Statistics of the United States of America, Collected and Returned by the Marshals of the Federal Districts* (Washington, 1841), 409.

23. H. B. Croom, "Some Accounts of Agricultural Soil and Products of Middle Florida in a Letter to the Editor," *Farmers Register*, 2 (June, 1834), 3.

24. Macrae, "Soils and Agricultural Advantages," 571.

25. *Deed Record*, Book D, 575.

through a feeling of genuine devotion slaveowners stipulated in their wills that their Negroes be freed. The will of William Oliphant, dated 1827, is unusual in this respect. Oliphant requested that his Negro man Monah and his four children be allowed all the privileges of free persons of color and that $250 was to be paid each of them to cover transportation costs to a free state of their choice.[26]

The law supposedly protected the slave from unduly harsh treatment. An interesting example is a case against Thomas Gaskins, overseer, for "unlawfully, willfully, knowingly and maliciously . . . with a heavy and large stick of wood cruelly beating the slave and breaking and fracturing the bone." It was not uncommon for slaves to be stolen. In 1831 William Wyatt, a planter in Leon County, sued John Pearce for stealing his Negro slave, Jack, worth $500. Pearce pleaded not guilty; but the verdict of the court was guilty, and he was sentenced to thirty-nine lashes. Another example of stealing slaves is the case against Aaron Dyer, a yeoman farmer, for stealing two Negro women worth $900 from Henry Thompson of Magnolia.[27]

Slaves were often hired to neighboring planters. In 1832 Gideon Green rented his three Negroes, Ester, Susan, and Henry, to Parson Hays and William Kerr for the sum of $85 for a year.[28] It was stipulated in this agreement that the slaves were to be furnished with two suits of clothes each, a hat and blanket and a pair of shoes apiece. To safeguard the health of Negroes on the plantation, it was highly important that their clothing be carefully looked after. Fieldhands were required to wear hats during the summer months and sleep in comfortable beds with sufficient cover on cold winter nights.

PLANTATION SUPPLIES

Apparently most of the supplies for the plantations in Leon County were furnished by several general merchandise stores located in Tallahassee. One such store was the firm of Gamble and Reid. The purchases made from this store by General Leigh Read in 1839 included 555 yards of bagging for $161, bolts of suiting and homespun, 932 pounds of rope for $140, nails, and osnaburg, a coarse cloth; also numerous smaller items such as whiskey, red flannel, brandy, Irish linen, paper flowers, ribbon, and shoes. Read's plantation must have been small, because his purchases for the entire year in 1838 amounted only to $941.[29] Payment

26. "Will of William Oliphant, 1927," *Leon County Court Record.*
27. "William Wyatt v. John Pearce," "Henry Thompson v. Aaron Dyer," *ibid.*
28. "Gideon Green v. Harp & Kerr, 1832," *ibid.*
29. *Account Book of Gamble and Reid,* Leon County Courthouse.

in cash seems to have been rare, but at the same time merchants always added their carrying charge to the planter's bill. In 1841 Gamble and Reid of Tallahassee sued Read for his past due account of $2,000, some of which was interest long overdue.

Another general merchandise store which catered to the planters was the firm of Parish and Byrd. An interesting list of purchases made by Frederick Smith from this store included a pair of pantaloons and one fine hat at $8.oo apiece, soap, olive oil, and almonds; also numerous cash notes paid out for Smith and cash paid to his Negroes in merchandise. As an example of such an entry: "Paid Asa in mds. 75 cents; this amt. lent him cash, $1.50; paid Edmund in mdse. 25 cents." [30]

Even though bagging, rope, pork, sugar, coffee, and molasses apparently were the most frequent plantation purchases, sundries of various kinds were nearly always included.

The firm of Laudeman and Sheffield in Tallahassee offered a variety of services in addition to general merchandise. Some of the accounts from this firm are: "to digging grave, furnishing plank, $10, to making coffin $30; to keeping mare 5 weeks for Jesse Hines, deceased, no charge." Jesse Willis, Turbut Betton, Robert Butler, and other well-known persons had accounts with Laudeman and Sheffield. Some of these accounts were not paid and had to be taken to court for collection. An interesting complaint against this firm made in 1831 states that the "small coffin and rough box that Laudeman charged $15 for was not worth 75 cents." [31] However, Laudeman and Sheffield had printed on their account book, "Never insult the unfortunate, especially when they implore relief or assistance. If you cannot grant their request, refuse them mildly and tenderly."

Nearly everything connected with the plantation was bought on credit. No matter what the price of cotton might be, the planter had to have his supplies. As a consequence, mortgages increased as debts mounted against him. Although the Leon County planter realized unusual returns from his crops during the period 1830–40, part of this was due to an overall prosperity in the cotton market, and to the fact that land was not yet exhausted. Also the prices of land and of slaves were less in Florida during this period than in other cotton areas of the South. Perhaps the profits in planting have in many instances been exaggerated, but there is no doubt that certain Leon County planters made much money in the production of cotton in this era.

30. *Ledger of Parish and Byrd*, 1839, Leon County Courthouse.
31. *Account Book of Laudeman and Sheffield*, 1831, Leon County Courthouse.

John Milton Price

Slavery in Winn Parish

The following article, though brief and concerned with a single parish in Louisiana, deals with one of the most important problems in southern history: conflict between different strata of slaveholders. This article corrects the all too prevalent error that only non-slaveholders opposed the slaveholding elite and secession. It also affords an introduction to the relation between slaveholding and social and political stability in the antebellum South.

Traditionally southern historians have depicted a tripartite class structure composed of planters, farmers, and poor whites. This is both erroneous and overly simplistic. Southern society was much more complex than this. The chief though not the only error in this interpretation is the neglect of the slaves and the intricate and frequently convoluted ways in which their presence mediated between each of these groups. Price here elaborates on this point and demonstrates that slaveowners could be opposed to both secession and the Confederacy. And what he describes in Winn Parish is true of other areas of the South. In such disparate southern states as Mississippi and South Carolina, antipathy to the large slaveholders who favored secession was significant. Sometimes skillful ideologues directed it into a virulent negrophobia much different from the subdued racism found in areas like the Charleston district. This occurred in Mississippi. In other areas, like the uplands of South Carolina, where slaveholdings were small, hostility to the planter elite was more direct, and the focus of the conflict was political.

The presence of such antipathy did not always mean opposition to the planters, secession, or the Confederacy. Economic and social fear of the Negro was always the most effective tool of the pro-secession ideologues, and these fears muted class antagonisms though they could never still them. It was only after the Civil War and Reconstruction that tendencies which had been localized and generally isolated came to the fore. The years of the farmers' protests and Populism were a peculiar though historically comprehensible admixture of rage against the Bourbons and the most virulent racism the South has ever known.

Reprinted with permission from *Louisiana History*, VIII, 2 (1967), 137–148.

F ew scholars will dispute the thesis of Frank Lawrence Owsley and his "Vanderbilt school" that the planter–poor white stereotype of southern antebellum society is so much bombast. But the historian who studies slavery in microcosm usually finds that scholars have been highly selective in their examination of sources, and specifically that they have neglected the hill country in the antebellum South. In generalizing about these isolated hill-country folk, historians have said that "they never had slaves," or that they possessed "relatively few slaves," and that slavery was "a way of life from which [they were] excluded." [1]

These generalizations have an element of truth in describing the slaveholding South as a whole, but they do not tell the complete story. Scholars have said that areas such as Winn Parish and north central Louisiana in general showed a strong antipathy for the plantation order. But a close study of slavery in this area sends such generalizations into a tailspin.

A majority of scholars, as well as Louisianians, would probably agree with the author of the following generalization about Winn Parish in the antebellum period. Its people are described as

> . . . out of touch with even provincial centers of civilization—lost souls in the folds of dismal, low hills . . . ignorant, superstititous, bigoted, inarticulate . . . they could not improve their lot or lift their swarms of progeny into the professional or business world. Their only outlets were sex, corn whiskey and religion . . . mostly Baptist . . . they were, like their obstinate red hills, their sunbaked fields and brittle corn stalks, severe, dry, uncompromising men, who took life seriously and lived by Puritan morals, shaken at intervals by dark storms of incest, sexual monstrosities, and social rebellion.

The account goes on to say ". . . the backwoods farmer had never had slaves. They tilled the sullen soil with their own sweaty, calloused hands and feared God." [2]

Such generalizations about a people and their way of life are dangerous, however, because such statements sometimes do not rest on a detailed analysis of the past. This is certainly the case with regard to slavery in Winn Parish. In 1860 that area contained a total of 1,352 slaves distributed among 205 masters—an average holding per master of 6.6 slaves. The total number of households in the parish was 587, of which 205 or about 35 percent were slaveholders. Slaves made up about one-

1. Carleton Beals, *The Story of Huey P. Long* (Philadelphia, 1935), 29; Frank Lawrence Owsley, *Plain Folk of the Old South* (Baton Rouge, 1949), 169; Perry Howard, *Political Tendencies in Louisiana, 1812–1952* (Baton Rouge, 1957), 64.
2. Beals, *The Story of Huey P. Long*, 28–29.

fourth of the total population of the parish in 1860. A closer look at population figures shows a total of 5,703 persons: 4,314 free whites, 1,352 slaves, and 37 free Negroes.[3] (See Tables I and II.)

How were these slaves distributed among the slaveholding population of the parish? Kenneth Stampp, in *The Peculiar Institution*, says that "in Louisiana about one-sixth of the slaves lived on units of less than ten. . . ."[4] While this ratio is true for the state as a whole, Winn Parish had almost half of its slaves in units of less than ten and about the same number in units of twenty or more. If "large slaveholder" means owning twenty or more slaves, then more than half the slaves were concentrated in numerous "small" holdings.

There were sixteen female slaveholders who owned an average of five slaves each. These women were not wives of slaveowners except in two cases. Three owned only one slave; the rest owned from two to twenty-six.[5] Slaves belonging to these women were in general younger than those of other slaveowners in Winn Parish. A study of the age of slaves on the whole showed that with few exceptions the oldest slaves were thirty to forty years of age.

In further characterizing Winn Parish slavery, one should consider violence among Negroes and between Negroes and whites. Unfortunately, this aspect cannot be gauged accurately, because all courthouse records for antebellum Winn Parish burned in 1868. However, Frederick Law Olmsted reported one incident which occurred in the parish:

> On Monday last, as James Allen (overseer on Prothro's plantation at St. Maurice) was punishing a negro boy named Jack, for stealing hogs, the boy ran off before the overseer had chastised him sufficiently for the offence. He was immediately pursued by the overseer, who succeeded in catching him, when the negro boy drew a knife and inflicted a terrible gash in his abdomen. The wounds of the overseer were dressed by Dr. Stephens, who pronounces it a very critical case, but still entertains hope of his recovery.[6]

Another case of violence involved a slave called Toney, who was given life imprisonment for "shooting to kill."[7]

Though several cases of miscegenation were related to the author while researching in Winn Parish, only one such case could be docu-

3. Based on United States Eighth Census, 1860.

4. Kenneth M. Stampp, *The Peculiar Institution*, (New York, 1956), 31.

5. Eighth Census, 1860.

6. Frederick Law Olmsted, *The Slave States* (New York, 1959), 272n.

7. *Annual Report of the Auditor of Public Accounts to the General Assembly of the State of Louisiana* (Baton Rouge, 1861), 107–8.

mented. The master was Thomas Woodward, who had been a brigadier general serving with Andrew Jackson during the Indian Wars of the early 1800's. Woodward had at least one child by a slave; the records show he emancipated the girl and provided quite well for her future. The old general had drawn up his will regarding the child and instructed his son and one T. O. Harrison to execute it. The terms of the will were contested upon Woodward's death, but the son carried out his father's wishes, as indicated by the following:

Succession of Thomas Woodward, Dec.

In the Name of God Amen

I Thomas Woodward of the Parish of Winn in the State of Louisiana, being of sound mind and discretion but mindful of the uncertainty of mortal life, Do make this my last Will and Testament.

From the love and respect I bear to the memory of my deceased Father Thomas S. Woodward, I give and bequeath to his natural child Sally Ann May born Slave for life but emancipated by my said Father under the laws of Arkansas in about 1854, the sum of Twenty Thousand Dollars ($20,000) to be paid her out of my Estate when she arrives at the age of majority or in the event of her marriage should she marry before majority.

I further give and bequeath to the said Sallie, for expenses of support and education the sum of Six Hundred Dollars ($600) annually to be paid her each and every year until she shall become of age or marry. I nominate and appoint Dr. Thomas O. Harrison of Montgomery in the Parish of Winn in the State of Louisiana as tutor of the said Sallie Ann to have the charge and guardianship of expenses and property and superintendance of her education.

In the event of the death of the said Sallie Ann May at any time without leaving heirs of her body, then the property hereinabove bequeathed to the said Sallie Ann shall revert to, vest in, and belong to my dearly beloved wife Louisa M. Woodward or her legal representatives.[8]

The father of Sallie Ann said this about Negroes in 1858: "Let me here remark one thing about negroes—particularly negroes who are raised in the slaveholding States of the United States. They are in general treated kind, and in early life are placed pretty much on an equality with the white children. They have but few cares, and they never fail to learn all the family names." [9]

In the northeastern section of Winn some slaveholders emancipated their slaves during the 1850's. The cemeteries in this area show ex-slaves buried in "white cemeteries" next to the family that owned them.[10]

8. Certified copy of Succession of Thomas Woodward, in author's possession.

9. Thomas Woodward, *Woodward's Reminiscences* (Montgomery, Ala., 1859), 108.

10. Gravestones observed in Ward 4, Winn Parish, La.

Much of the anti-secession sentiment came from this part of the parish.[11] By 1860 there were thirty-seven free Negroes in the parish; they were probably manumitted slaves.

Geographically, there is nothing very different about this section of north-central hill country from its neighboring parishes to the north, south, and east. Only on the western boundary is there a sharp contrast in topography—for Natchitoches Parish has an abundant amount of Red River soil that is rich and well suited for cotton production. Winn Parish contains 610,560 acres of land, and the soils, agricultural practices, and conditions encountered there are representative of those common over a considerable part of the hill section of antebellum Louisiana.

Winn is well supplied with streams and branches. The Red River is the southwest boundary. Drainage, for the most part, is provided not by Red River, but by the Dugdemona River, which crosses the parish diagonally from the northwest to the southeast corner. In colonial days of Louisiana the French made many settlements along the large water courses, and the area that later (1852) became Winn Parish attracted a number of French families along the Red River and Saline Bayou.

Some of the early military and immigrant trails to Mexico and Texas, such as the El Camino Real, crossed the parish. The immigrants came mainly from South Carolina, Kentucky, Tennessee, Georgia, Alabama, and Mississippi. In their westward journey across the country many were permanently attracted by the good fishing, hunting, and excellent range and pasture for hogs and cattle in what would later be Winn Parish.[12]

Dugdemona River was a greater obstacle than the Red River to east and west travel and commerce in the parish. "Practically all who lived north of Dugdemona River swamp went to the points of trade on the Ouachita, while those living south of the swamp went to the points of trade on the Red River, the difficulties of crossing the Dugdemona Swamp causing the division." [13] The Red River was navigable, but only during high-water time could even small boats ascend the Dugdemona, Saline, and Castor streams. Consequently, little farm produce was marketed by water.

This geographical setting of poor trade and travel routes encouraged the self-sufficient type of economy found on the smaller antebellum agricultural units. Cotton and sweet potatoes were the chief crops of all

11. Interview with H. B. Bozeman, Winnfield, La., January, 1966.
12. Thomas A. Caine, H. L. Belden, and L. L. Lee, *United States Department of Agriculture Soil Survey of Winn Parish, Louisiana* (Washington, 1907), 558.
13. *Ibid.*, 559.

slaveholders, with more emphasis on foodstuff production exhibited by smaller holdings than large operations. More sweet potatoes than corn were produced by smaller holdings, while large units raised little or no sweet potatoes but much corn.

The production record of Robert Eubanks deserves notice. He produced sixteen bales of cotton with five female slaves (of fieldhand age) and presumably hired labor. There is no record of the hired labor, but it is highly improbable that five fieldhands could do so well.[14] A chart of the production of the largest slaveholders in 1860 shows the following:

PRODUCTION OF LARGE SLAVEHOLDERS
(TAKEN FROM THE 1860 CENSUS)

Name	No. of slaves	Cash value of farm	Value of equip.	Value of livestock	Corn (bu.)	Cotton bale (400 lbs.)	Other
C. Wheeler	33	$ 4,000	$ 600	$1,650	2,000	74	
T. Woodward	100	13,000	1,200	3,170	4,000	104	350 bu. sweet potatoes
J. Strother	88	4,340	600	2,000	850	0	
W. A. Curry *	62	11,000	1,000	2,320	2,000	224	111 lb. wool
D. Boullt	129	150,000	4,000	7,500+	8,000	400	

* Curry produced this on the Liston Prudhomme plantation as overseer. He owned no slaves himself.

In 1860–61 when the question of secession enveloped Louisiana, how would Winn Parish react toward the idea of cutting off ties with the Union? The most recent explanation for the anti-secession feeling of the parish says, "The hill parishes, populated mostly by small farmers who held few if any slaves, displayed a conspicuous coolness toward secession throughout the secession crisis. . . . [Their] interests [were] inconsonant with the existence of slavery." [15]

Winn sent twenty-one-year-old David Pierson to the secession convention in 1861. The youngest delegate at the convention, Pierson was a non-slaveholding lawyer. He voted consistently against secession proposals and refused to sign the Ordinance of Secession after its pas-

14. Based on Eighth Census, 1860.
15. F. Wayne Binning, "Cooperation and Obstruction in the Louisiana Secession Crisis," (thesis, Louisiana State University, 1965), 51, 15.

sage.[16] In a letter to his father dated April 22, 1861, Pierson gave his reasons for opposing secession: "I was opposed to secession it is true, and it was because I thought it would lead to the present difficulties [Civil War] and that in my opinion there was room to hope for a pacific settlement of the difficulties between the two sections, that I voted and acted as I did on the secession question" [17] It seems plausible that a north-central hill parish delegate would be cool toward secession if the parish he represented had "few or no slaves," but David Pierson represented a parish with slaves accounting for almost one-fourth of its total population. The value of slaves in 1860 was $657,350, almost half the total value of property in the parish.[18] On the average, every slave was worth about $500.[19] Besides their property value, these slaves were largely responsible for the 2,965 bales of cotton and 129,781 bushels of corn produced in 1860.[20]

A comparison of Winn's record in the secession convention and her socio-economic situation in 1860 poses difficult questions for the historian. Pierson said anti-secession feeling existed because of fear of war. If his statement is taken at face value, the people of Winn Parish were not thinking so much about states' rights or state sovereignty as they were about the loss of valuable property—particularly slave property, as well as other losses. The people felt that the best protection for their property was in the Union, or they hoped at least for some solution short of war.

War came, but the firing on Fort Sumter did not cause the excitement in Winn that it caused elsewhere in the Confederacy, even though some troops were recruited from Winn early in the war. By September, 1862, however, the Confederacy sent General Richard Taylor with five companies into Winn and Jackson "to round up deserters, to arrest conscripts who failed to report, and to break up any jayhawking groups in the area." [21] These jayhawker groups continunued to plague the Confederacy until the end of the war.

Another problem causing discontent in Winn during the Civil War was the "tax in kind" act passed by the Confederate Congress in April,

16. Roger W. Shugg, *Origins of Class Struggle in Louisiana: A Social History of White Farmers and Laborers during Slavery and After, 1840–75* (Baton Rouge, 1939), 166–67.

17. David Pierson to William H. Pierson, April 22, 1861, David Pierson Letters (Archives, Louisiana State University, Baton Rouge).

18. *Annual Report of the Auditors, 1861*, 107–8.

19. *Ibid.*

20. *Ibid.*

21. John D. Winters, *The Civil War in Louisiana* (Baton Rouge, 1963), 306.

1863. This act stipulated that, starting with the crops of that year, every farmer was to deliver to the Confederate government fifty bushels of corn. The following year the farmers were to contribute one-tenth of their produce. In addition, one-tenth of their bacon and one-tenth of their livestock would be taken.[22]

Reaction to this tax in kind brought on another plague of jayhawking in Winn and surrounding areas. But jayhawking would not help the plight of the farmers, so a group of them decided to petition General U.S. Grant for help.[23] The following letter to Grant with seventy-two signatures was dated September 3, 1863:

State of Louisiana, Parish of Winn,

When, in consideration of the condition of our country and to make known our principles, it has obviously become necessary that we should embody ourselves for the protection of our homes, lives, and property: Therefore, we do adopt and publish the following resolutions:

Resolved, first, That we have undoubted evidence that the Confederate States are designed to be very aristocratic and exceedingly oppressive in its form of government.

Resolved, second, That we hold no further allegiance to the Confederate States except when overpowered and compelled by the sword.

Resolved, third, That we believe the United States is the most democratic and best form of government now in existence.

Resolved, fourth, That we are certain the State of Louisiana did not secede from the United States Government by a vote of the people.

Resolved, fifth, That we have only been kept from our loyalty to the United States by the force of arms and oppression.

Resolved, sixth, That we are willing to cordially welcome to our country the United States forces and flag of the Union.

Resolved, seventh, That we use all available means to preserve the Union.

Resolved eighth, That we hold ourselves in readiness as a home guard company to assist the United States troops at any time in the protection of our homes, lives, and property.

Resolved, ninth, That we send three men from this company as commissioners to the commander of the post at Monroe, or the nearest post, to make known these resolutions, to procure a United States flag, to procure arms and ammunition, and to make such other arrangements as the company may deem necessary for our defense.

22. *Ibid.,* 210.

23. To say that the only reason for these anti-Confederacy resolutions was the tax in kind would be untrue. The people of the area probably saw that the Confederacy would collapse, and they wanted to be in favor with the winning side. In 1863, Grant was in the Vicksburg area, which is not too far from Winn. Perhaps these people wanted to "put their house in order" just in case Grant crossed the Mississippi and came through or near Winn Parish.

Resolved, tenth. That we sign our names to these resolutions, and implore the blessing of Almightly God to rest upon us.

We and each of us do solemnly swear before Almighty God that we will faithfully maintain the above preamble and resolutions, and we further swear we will pledge our lives and property and our sacred honor in their support.

We further swear that we will receive this oath as legal and lawful.[24]

TABLE I *
(1860)

Total population	5,703
Free whites	4,314
Slaves	1,352
Free Negroes	37
(Almost 24% of the total population were slaves.)	
Value of total property	$1,597,720
Value of slaves	$ 657,350
Average value of each slave	$ 500
Number of householders	587
Number of slaveholders	205
(About 35% of the householders were slaveholders.)	
Average number of slaves per holding	6.6
Number of female slaveholders	16
Average slaveholding of females	5

Cotton production	2,965 bales on 6,722 acres	
Corn production	129,781 bushels on 9,378 acres	

Schools:
2 female academies
2 public schools with 700 pupils

Religion:
Baptist—9 churches
Catholic—1 church
Methodist—4 churches

Wages:

Average monthly wage from farm labor	$16.00
Average daily wage of laborer with board	.75
Average daily wage of carpenter without board	2.50
Weekly wage of female domestic with board	1.50
Board cost to laboring men for one week	2.50

* Based on *Annual Report of the Auditor of Public Accounts, to the General Assembly of the State of Louisiana* (Baton Rouge, 1861), 107–8, and *Eighth Census,* 1860, Schedules no. 1, 2, *Population* (Washington, 1864).

24. *The War of the Rebellion: A Compilation of the Official Records of the Union and Confederate Armies,* 70 vols. in 128 (Washington, 1880–1901), series I, vol. XXX, 732–33.

TABLE II

Miscellaneous Statistics:

* 19 physicians	1 miller
7 lawyers	2 bakers
9 schoolteachers	1 artist
10 mechanics	1 writer
1 merchant	1 clerk
6 blacksmiths	2 surveyors
3 bookkeepers	1 stockdriver
2 engineers	1 dentist
3 barkeepers	1 ginwright
3 wheelwrights	1 brickmason
13 clergymen	1 shoemaker
8 overseers	1 editor

* The author cannot account for the large number of physicians in the parish in 1860. With a white population of 4,313 there was one physician for every 227 persons.

Based on *Eighth Census*, Schedules no. 1, 2, *Population* (Washington, 1864).

Motivation for this coolness toward secession, the Civil War, and the Confederacy came perhaps from the realization by the people of that area that, despite their involvement with the peculiar institution, they were not in the mainstream of Louisiana's economic and social activity, but on the periphery. The postbellum heritage of the parish brings into sharper focus this disparity between the hill farmers of Winn and other parts of the state.

Even as Winn Parish populism of the 1890's and its socialism of the early twentieth century [25] would be forgotten, so would slavery in that

25. The center of Louisiana populism was Winn Parish. R. L. Tannehill, the only Populist candidate for governor, was from Winn, and the first Populist newspaper in the South was the *Winnfield Comrade*. This paper was edited by H. L. Brian and later by B. W. Bailey, two of the state's most outstanding Populist leaders. William Ivy Hair, "The Agrarian Protest in Louisiana, 1877–1900," (dissertation, Louisiana State University, 1962), 301.

In 1908, Eugene V. Debs spoke in Winnfield, where a Socialist party was already well organized. During the 1912 election Winn gave Debs a higher percentage of votes than any other parish. Socialists elected a school board member, a police juror, and Winnfield's entire slate of city officials. Grady McWhiney, "Louisiana Socialists in the Early Twentieth Century: A Study of Rustic Radicalism," *Journal of Southern History*, XX (August, 1954), 315–17; T. Harry Williams, "The Gentleman from Louisiana: Demagogue or Democrat," *Journal of Southern History*, XXVI (February, 1960), 11.

parish be forgotten, not only by Louisianians, but also by most scholars of the peculiar institution. Indeed, most historians neglect a very important facet of slavery when they neglect the isolated areas, the hill country, the piney woods regions that have been characterized in the past as "never having slaves," or having "few slaves if any." The existence of a substantial number of small and medium-size slaveholders in the Louisiana hill country is beyond dispute. Studies of other such regions in the South might force us to modify certain aspects of our view of antebellum slavery.

Edward W. Phifer

Slavery in Microcosm:
Burke County, North Carolina

Edward Phifer, the author of this article, is a resident of Morganton, North Carolina, a physician and a member of the American College of Surgeons. The recipient of many awards, among them the Southern Historical Association's annual prize for the best study in regional history, this article is a model of local history. In it Phifer ably employs sources available throughout the South. It can easily prove a guide for both the beginning student and the more advanced scholar. The thoroughness of this study and the care with which Phifer details the importance of geography, demography, economics, and ethnicity are an index to the diversity inherent in the system itself and the many factors which impinge upon it. Unlike many historians who emphasize the economic organization of the plantation and are concerned with structural changes in it, Phifer feels that the development of the institution was dependent upon the social and economic attitudes of the slaveholders themselves. If Phifer is correct, we must reconsider other issues in southern history. Among the most important is the question of change and diversity in the older regions of the South, for if the acceptance of slavery was determined by a rational assessment of its social and economic advantages, then Southerners were not the slaves of the system under which they lived. In other words, those Southerners who bought slaves and planted only cotton did so not because there were no other alternatives, but because those ends were the most profitable and feasible.

In affording us this glimpse of "the cellular structure of this sociopathological process," he reminds us that the subjects of this complex network of socio-economic arrangements deeply affected one another's lives. Nowhere—regardless of the differences of geography, incidence of slaveownership, or size of slaveholdings—did the institution fail to have this effect, and this alone is the one indisputable fact of antebellum southern history.

Reprinted with permission from the *Journal of Southern History*, XXVIII (1962), 137–165. Copyright 1962 by the Southern Historical Association. Reprinted by permission of the Managing Editor.

The local historian, casting about for an approach to a local historical situation which will enable him to make a contribution to general history—be it ever so trivial—finds himself in a particularly favorable position when he turns his attention to American Negro slavery. One would naturally suppose that the local and regional historian would exert his greatest efforts here, where his potential is particularly great. Such has not been the case. For example, most historians of counties and regions in western North Carolina who mention the institution of slavery at all are content to refer to it in an occasional oblique reference, as if such a condition hardly existed. Neither imagination nor intuition is brought into play in an attempt to fathom the attitudes and thoughts of slaves or slaveholders, nor does the historian use to best advantage the bits of local information he has accumulated, the relevant experiences he has undergone, the wicked old tales he has been told, or his knowledge of a thousand and one happenings that go to make up the personality of a community. The fact remains, however, that if the local historian is, in a manner of speaking, indigenous to the area which he is studying, if he springs from a curious admixture of all socio-economic groups, if he is cognizant of this admixture and has an awareness of the bad and good qualities of all and of the endless intermingling of families and family groups, then he is better able to attack the problem, objectively but without being wholly impersonal, than is the general historian.

Furthermore, the local historian of slavery is in a better position to develop the technique of dealing with minutiae than is the general historian, who likely lacks both the taste and the time for the study of a locality. Generalization is often the pitfall that traps the scholar trying to analyze the many facets of slavery, an area in which minute details can be particularly revealing. "We think in generalities," says Whitehead, "but we live in detail. To make the past live, we must perceive it in detail in addition to thinking of it in generalities." This then is the province of the local historian of slavery: to focus down upon a high-power field and examine the cellular structure of this sociopathological process, hoping that an understanding of slavery may be reached in this painstaking fashion after grosser methods have failed. The historian of locality, even if without formal training, may find himself uniquely qualified to detect nuances when information comes reticently and only through innuendo, to utilize familiarity for breaking down the barriers of the mind, and to exploit knowledge of family traits and idiosyncrasies in order to release his intuitive understanding. If this were not so, Wilbur J. Cash could not have written *The Mind of the South* and Faulkner could not have created Yoknapatawpha County. "You can't understand it," Quentin Compson says to his friend Shreve, who is puzzled by the South. "You would have to be born there."

The local historian who turns his attention to slavery cannot fail to note, after he has floundered about in the great mass of material scholars have marshaled on the institution, that, by and large, general historians have utilized source materials from restricted geographical areas much as if to say that these areas were representative of the entire slaveholding South. They have found it much easier to study the records of the great plantations than to search the crumbling annals of the small slaveholding farmer of the back country. Anyone thumbing through the much-used eyewitness accounts of travelers in the slave states will find the itineraries, more often than not, following the better traveled routes through Maryland, Virginia, and the Carolina tidewater, or up the Mississippi from New Orleans into the heart of the black belt of the New South—in other words, they tended to visit the areas that were more accessible, where they could see the most slavery with the least travel. Furthermore, those newspapers that continued to operate with any degree of permanency—and remain most available to scholars—were located in the larger coastal towns, not in the sparsely settled interior. In short, the critical analyses of the institution of slavery have not been derived, to any extent, from the study of regions occupied by the self-sufficing small slaveholding farmer but rather almost entirely from the study of the areas dominated by the rice, tobacco, and cotton planters, who, having large slaveholdings, farmed commerically—and this notwithstanding the fact that roughly half the slavery territory of the United States was the domain of small farmers, most of whom owned no slaves, many of whom owned only a few slaves, and none of whom for reasons largely geographical farmed commercially or grew a staple crop.[1] Here, obviously, is an area for study peculiarly suited to the talents of the local historian of slavery.

Admittedly slavery throughout the South had a certain uniformity, but it was far from complete. Certainly, slavery in the non-staple-producing areas—to which the county under study belongs—was not exactly the same as slavery in the staple-producing areas. Each of the two regions had certain general characteristics which served to set it apart

1. See particularly Ulrich Bonnell Phillips, *American Negro Slavery* (New York, 1918), and Kenneth M. Stampp, *The Peculiar Institution: Slavery in the Ante-Bellum South* (New York, 1956). See also Guion G. Johnson, *Ante-Bellum North Carolina: A Social History* (Chapel Hill, 1937), 468–612; Francis B. Simkins, *A History of the South* (New York, 1953), 116–152; and John S. Bassett, *Slavery in the State of North Carolina* (Baltimore, 1899).

from the other, as all the great historians of slavery have understood and duly emphasized. The non-staple regions were usually inland with poor farm-to-market transportation facilities. As the regions were broken by streams and mountains, with a markedly restricted amount of alluvial soil in the valleys, farms were, of necessity, small. Climate and soil conditions were unsuited to the cultivation of cotton or rice and usually poorly adapted to the cultivation of tobacco. The slave population was ordinarily less than 30 percent of the total population, and there were few large slaveholders. Treatment of the slaves was reputedly much less stringent than on the large cotton plantations of the black belt; the farmer lived in closer relationship to his "black family," often worked in the fields with them, and knew them intimately. The crops produced were not sold but were used to feed livestock, feed and clothe the slaves, and "keep body and soul together." Little money came in or went out. The small farmers lived on the farm and off the farm produce.

In summary, the history of slavery has been neglected by county historians; trivialities contribute to the story of slavery, and it falls to the local historian to present them; and, lastly, historians of slavery have not adequately studied the large areas where staples were not produced but where slavery nevertheless existed. Also the subject needs to be studied from an early nineteenth-century posture, rather than—as has been repeatedly done—from a twentieth-century moral position or from a position of "complete detachment."

Created from the western part of Rowan County, North Carolina, in the early days of the Revolution, Burke County initially encompassed a huge pie-shaped region lying entirely north of the Lord Granville line and including all of the present counties of Burke, Catawba, Mitchell, Madison, and Yancey; most of the present counties of Caldwell, Avery, and McDowell; large portions of the present counties of Buncombe, Haywood, and Alexander; and in addition small parts of the present counties of Lincoln, Cleveland, Rutherford, and Swain. First fragmented in 1791 to form Buncombe in the west, Burke by 1842 approximated its present size and shape, with an area of slightly more than 500 square miles.[2] (See Map.) Shaped like the upward-tilted head of a lonely wolf with her open mouth baying toward the northwest and the tip of her ear pointing in the direction of Old Salem, her nose and high, broad collar line are deeply corrugated by mountains. Her major stream, the Ca-

2. David L. Corbitt, *The Formation of the North Carolina Counties, 1663–1943* (Raleigh, N.C., 1950), 42–48.

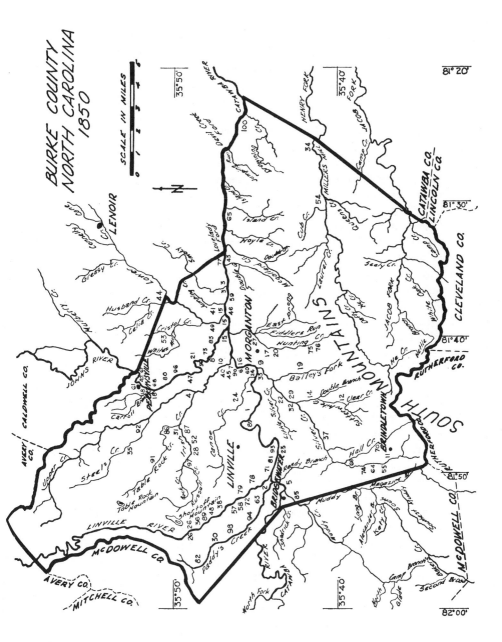

BURKE COUNTY
NORTH CAROLINA
1850

SCALE IN MILES
0 1 2 3 4 5 6

N

tawba River, flowing east, divides the county into two roughly equal parts, and the numerous tributaries create a herringbone pattern as they course down the slopes from the mountains. Significantly, the streams that feed into the Catawba from the north are more numerous and much larger than those that feed from the south. The northern mountains are higher and create a greater watershed than do the South Mountains; furthermore, the eastern end of these South Mountains drain into streams which flow south into Lincoln County to join the North Fork River, rather than north into the Catawba.

The map of the county makes it apparent why there was a very definite relationship, on one hand, between the stream pattern and size of these water courses and, on the other hand, the number of slaves owned by each slaveholder engaged in farming (as, of course, most were). The largest, flattest, richest land areas lay in the crotches between two or even three larger streams or up the broad river valleys which ordinarily existed for only a few miles above the mouths. The largest slaveholders had their plantations located on these rich alluvial deltas at the juncture between two major streams such as the junctures of Linville River, Johns River, Upper Creek, Lower Creek, Canoe Creek, Silver Creek, or Muddy Creek with the Catawba, or the juncture of Upper Creek with Irish Creek. Slaveowners with moderate holdings were also distributed along these major streams but not at the mouths, although most were situated at a point where a branch entered a major stream. Small slaveholders occupied the land along smaller streams, not at junctures, and the non-slaveholders had to be content with narrow bottoms high up on the creeks or with upland which was unsuited for serious farming. One might almost say, then, that the number of slaves stationed at a given point was directly proportional to the volume of water flowing by that point in a given period of time.

In 1860, 921 families in the county were engaged in farming, but only 548 persons were landowners, and only nine of these were listed as owning as many as 300 improved acres. Slaveholders, who held the best situated and most fertile land, comprised only 38 percent of the 548 landowners of the county, and 16 percent of these slaveholders owned but one slave. One farmer on the Linville River, Barnet H. Moore, owned seventeen slaves in 1860 but no land. He farmed the land of relatives and friends and was thus, if you like, a tenant-planter or slaveholding sharecropper. Apparently there was never a Negro slaveholder in Burke.[3] In 1860, sixty family heads owned ten or more slaves, but a large

3. See John Hope Franklin, *The Free Negro in North Carolina, 1790–1860* (Chapel Hill, 1943), 234–237.

segment of the population was almost untouched by slavery. This was particularly true in the southern and southeastern parts of the county, settled largely by Germans.

A number of questions immediately come to mind. What was the origin of the slave system in Burke County? How did it develop? Or, even, why did it develop at all if slavery was as unprofitable in the non-staple crop regions as many historians imply that it was? Very few of the early immigrants brought slaves with them when they moved into the county, and those that did brought only a few. These early slaveholders were almost all Scotch-Irish or English, not Germans, and they came to the county from regions where the slave system was well established, usually from Virginia or eastern North Carolina and not directly from Pennsylvania or other northern states. Once the germ of slavery had found its way into Burke County, the practice of slaveholding gradually spread through the purchase of slaves from other states and from North Carolina counties to the east.[4] Drovers or slave traders at intervals brought slaves through the county for sale, and inhabitants could attend slave sales customarily held in certain localities such as nearby Huntsville in southeastern Yadkin County.[5]

There is no evidence that the people of Burke resisted the development of slavery. Manumissions were few and far between. The only case of manumission recorded by the county court between 1796 and 1830 was on May 26, 1797, when one Ben was freed by Dr. Thomas Bouchelle, a native of Delaware, who at the time had probably been a resident of Burke County for less than a year.[6] The small number of free

4. See the following bills of sale: William Price to Henry Reid, September 12, 1793, in Austin-Reid Papers (Manuscript Department, Library, Duke University, Durham, N.C.); John McLean to Benjamin Burgin, February 27, 1798, and John James to Thomas McEntire, September 8, 1799, in Burke County Miscellaneous Papers (North Carolina State Department of Archives and History, Raleigh), Bills of Sale 1781-1815-1833 (C. R. 14.009); Hance Hamilton and others to Waightstill Avery, December 26, 1793, in Burke County Court Minutes (North Carolina State Department of Archives and History), July 1791–1834, January session, 1794; and Thomas Patton to Ben Smith, July, 1804, *ibid.*, July session, 1804.

5. See U.S. Census, 1850, North Carolina, Schedule 1 (National Archives), Surrey County (South Division); U.S. Census, 1860, North Carolina, Schedule 1 (National Archives), Yadkin County; and Yadkin County, Tax Lists, 1851–62 (office of Clerk, Superior Court, Yadkinville, N.C.). One resident of Burke County established himself as a slave trader in Charleston, S.C., about 1804 and apparently carried on a commerce in slaves in Burke County until 1808. Memoirs of Col. Thomas G. Walton (typescript, Southern Historical Collection, University of North Carolina, Chapel Hill), 10; County Court Minutes, October session, 1804.

6. *Ibid.*, July session, 1798.

Negroes in the county is further evidence of the reluctance of Burke slaveholders to free their slaves. Slavery gradually but steadily became more and more prevalent up to 1860. Although statistics are somewhat distorted by the population loss resulting from the formation of new counties (generally speaking, the territory ceded was to the west, where the proportionate number of slaves was smaller than in the territory which remained a permanent part of the county), a slave population of 26 percent in 1860 offers little support to the argument that the institution would have in the foreseeable future been abolished by local initiative, nor does it lend credence to the popular concept that this region exported large numbers of slaves to the Deep South in the decades before the Civil War.

Considerable insight into the attitude of the white inhabitants of Burke County toward the institution of slavery can be gained by the historian from the behavior and the tone of the personal correspondence of these people. One thing is certainly crystal clear: it never occurred to them to attempt to justify slavery on moral grounds. The valley of the Catawba was settled by two Protestant groups—the Scotch-Irish and the Germans. They had been molded for generations by almost identical historical experiences which had made them into hardened realists, the Scotch-Irish in particular. Having known only hard labor and grinding poverty and now engaged in the struggle to make their way on the frontier, they gave first priority to the acquisition of wealth. Property was paramount; they had a fanatical respect for it. Slavery appeared to them as a bonanza, and a pseudosalutary freedom from sentimentality permitted them to accept it as such. There was little time for contemplation in their lives, nor did abstractions tempt the unlettered mind. Besides, these comparatively recent arrivals had found slavery a well-established institution in America. As newcomers, who were they to express moral indignation?

The Scotch-Irish and German upcountrymen turned to legalism, already a component of their thought process, to justify the institution of slavery. The law and the law courts were at the center of their cultural and intellectual life. They looked forward to court week as the prime source of amusement. The lawyers were the actors of the day, and the courtroom their stage. Backwoodsman or yeoman farmer, the citizen of Burke was remarkably aware of his legal rights and was ready to go to court on the slightest provocation. The prosperous had no qualms about using the courts to drive a poverty-stricken debtor to the wall, and the leading men of the locality learned as justices of the county court the pompous ways and sententious language of the courtroom. In truth, all the white men of the county were exceedingly "courthouse conscious." For their purposes, legality was synonomous with morality. If the idea ever occurred to them that laws were human instruments and therefore imperfect, they rejected it. Slavery did not make them a guilt-ridden people.

Accepting slavery as the *fait accompli* that it most certainly was, and seeing it as providing relief from backbreaking labor and a means for gaining property and wealth or advancement in social status, they were not inclined to question the instrument of "progress." All of which is not to say that there were not among the Scotch-Irish and Germans of the county those who disapproved of slavery; [7] but the point is that the basis of disapproval was essentially *economic*, not moral.

A good indication of how little opprobrium was attached to slavery by the local citizenry is to be found in the identity of the slaveholders themselves. Professional people and church officers, as well as farmers and merchants, owned slaves. A Methodist minister on Paddy's Creek, William Fullwood, owned as many as nineteen slaves at one time, and the Presbyterian minister at Morganton and Quaker Meadows, John McKamie Wilson, Jr., had ten slaves in 1850. In fact, the slave census shows conclusively that among slaveholders were the most highly re-spected people in the community, the people who provided its moral and ethical leadership.

It appears, from a local coign of vantage, that one thing which has tended to lead scholars astray in their analyses of the economics of slav-ery has been their failure to probe the mind of the slaveholder.[8] What must be understood is that the slaveholder was not at heart an investor; he was a speculator. His primary interest was not in yearly income on

7. See Franklin, *Free Negro in North Carolina*, 8.

8. In his excellent summation of the historiography of the subject, Stanley M. Elkins directs attention to a new approach to the question of the profitability of slavery made by Alfred H. Conrad and John R. Meyer, who persuasively argue that conventional accounting methods applied to plantation records should be abandoned and replaced by "general economic theory." Elkins, *Slavery: A Problem in American Institutional and Intellectual Life* (Chicago, 1959), 231–237; Conrad and Meyer, "The Economics of Slavery in the Ante Bellum South," *Journal of Po-litical Economy*, LXVI (April, 1958), 95–130. For examples of the application of conventional accounting methods, see Thomas P. Govan, "Was Plantation Slavery Profitable?" *Journal of Southern History*, VIII (November, 1942), 513–535, and Rosser H. Taylor, *Slaveholding in North Carolina: An Economic View* (Chapel Hill, 1926), 98.

an investment; his primary interest was in appreciation. "The self-suffic-ing farmer was not seeking profits, but a living." [9] True, but through capital accumulation he hoped to endow his progeny for generations to come. The answer to the question of whether the man with capital and credit who was seeking to establish his family's fortunes believed that slaves were a good speculative risk is, of course, "Yes, he most certainly did." [10] Was he correct in this assumption? Were slaves a good specula-tive risk? The answer again is an unavoidable "Yes." Barring any radi-cal changes in the economic system, slaves were an excellent speculative risk, as the record shows. After 1800 the price of slaves generally rose steadily, except during the depression period of 1837–45. In 1799, John James of Brunswick County sold Thomas McEntire of Burke a twenty-year-old male for $400. Thirty-six years later W. A. Lenoir wrote his grandfather in Happy Valley, "I will just say to you and Fa-ther that $1,100.00 is about the lowest price for Negroe fellows in Mor-ganton and 8 or 900 for women. Some have sold for a good deal more." [11] By 1860 "Negroe fellows" were selling for not a great deal less than double this amount.[12] The slave had great mobility and therefore wide marketability, while natural increase provided a built-in growth component. Furthermore, the investment field was sharply limited for these provincial investors. Securities of canal and railroad companies did not perform well, and banking stocks—although stockholders, on the whole, fared better—were not popular in the western counties. Land, of course, was the commonest form of investment, but arable land was scarce in Burke County; and, as an investment, landholding was comple-mentary to slaveholding, for slaves provided the labor to make produc-tive the richer land of the county. During most of this period, the slave-holder in North Carolina also enjoyed a highly favored tax position. The slave tax as administered under the poll principle was smaller than if the ad valorem principle had been applied, as it was to real property.[13]

9. Lewis C. Gray, *History of Agriculture in the Southern United States to 1860* (Washington, 1933), I, 451.

10. See Isaac T. Avery to Isaac T. Lenoir, September 30, 1833, in Lenoir Family Papers (Southern Historical Collection, University of North Carolina).

11. See W. A. Lenoir to William Lenoir, September 1, 1836, *ibid.*

12. Phillips, *American Negro Slavery*, 370–371, insert.

13. The ad valorem principle was not applied to slaves until 1858. See George R. Woolfolk, "Taxes and Slavery in the Ante Bellum South," *Journal of Southern History*, XXVI (May, 1960), 180–200. In Burke County all land was taxed accord-ing to acreage until 1808, when town property was taxed ad valorem. In 1819 the ad valorem principle was applied to all real property; the tax rate on land was set at 18¢ per $100 valuation and the poll tax at 44¢. The rate gradually rose to 27½¢

The tax on slaves, furthermore, was confined to a highly productive age group, with exemptions allowable if the slave were, for physical or mental reasons, a burden on the owner.[14]

Few of the large slaveholders of Burke confined their activities to farming. Of the twenty leading slaveowners in the county in 1850, at least thirteen had occupations unassociated with agriculture. They were lawyers, physicians, merchants, ministers, innkeepers, building contractors, bankers, surveyors, postmasters, and county officeholders. Artisans, innkeepers, and manufacturers owned slaves and employed them in their shops; planters employed their slaves not only on their farms but also in household manufacturing, gold mining, public works such as road maintenance and river clearance, and, toward the end of the period, in railroad construction.[15] Slaveholders farmed as part of their way of life and in order to "make a living," but the fiscally sophisticated rarely depended on it for more than this. Cash and liquid assets were derived from other sources. "I am without an overseer," wrote a large slaveholder who was also a bank cashier, "and trying to farm, with a rather smaller force than usual, having some hands mining. Am afraid I shall not succeed very well, not having it in my power to devote as much of my personal attention to it as I could wish."[16]

Emphasis must be placed upon the unvarnished fact that slave breeding was what made slavery an attractive long-term investment. The subject, approached with diffidence by some and with self-righteous horror by others, has engendered much profitless and naïve debate. Again, it would seem that the key lies in the mind and conscience of the slaveowner. Fully realizing that active breeding was an indispensable requisite to successful slave ownership, the investor made certain, insofar as he was financially able, that the female of childbearing age was an integral part of his slave family and that the male slave in turn was a part of her environment. No additional planning or plotting was necessary; the

---

per $100 valuation on real property and 80¢ a poll in 1848. County Court Minutes, 1798–1834, 1844–48.

14. For examples, see exemption granted to John Erwin by the July, 1795, session of the county court and to George Corpening by the January, 1848, session. (County Court Minutes.) The slaveholder was not so favored in the capitation tax, which was levied only on free white males over twenty-one and under forty-five but on all slaves, male and female, over twelve and under fifty.

15. For example, Robert H. Erwin, a blacksmith, Joseph Hilton (Helton?), a saddler, William M. D. Howard, a tanner, and William S. Moore, a carriagemaker, each owned slaves to help in his shop. U.S. Census, 1850, North Carolina, Schedule 2 (National Archives), Burke County.

16. Isaac T. Avery to Selina L. Lenoir, March 16, 1833, in Lenoir Papers.

natural processes of reproduction went on without urging or prompting. Occasionally an owner would, in an unguarded moment, betray his true feelings on this matter, as in the optimistic phrase, "three Breeding Wenches and another wench nearly Grown," found in a private letter.[17]

It must be remembered that the class structure of Burke County was by no means entirely determined by slave ownership, nor was slave ownership a hallmark of nobility. *Noblesse oblige* did not hold then any more than it holds with the wealthy industrial and commercial classes today. The delineations of certain of the larger slaveholders in the county that filter down to us are disenchanting to say the least. A number, although clever enough to become financially successful, were uneducated and even illiterate.[18] Some have been portrayed as small, mean men—shrewd, tricky bargainers, greedy in the extreme, unscrupulous sharpers with a penchant for penury; a few as vulgar ruffians intermittently involved in drunkenness, lechery, or violence. On the whole, though, one gets the impression from the court records that the conduct of the slaveholders was superior to that of their non-slaveholding neighbors.

Strictly speaking there was never a real slaveholding or planter class in Burke County. Slavery flourished in it for little more than sixty years—about three generations. This is hardly sufficient time for the development of a stable aristocracy, even if other factors did not militate against it. A scrutiny of genealogical patterns goes a long way toward making clear why a slave aristocracy did not develop in Burke County. Without provisions for primogeniture and entail, the man seeking to found a slave dynasty had to assure that he lived a long time and that he left behind few children, preferably only one. It is as simple as that. For instance, five Greenlee brothers owned a total of 184 slaves in 1820; by 1850 there were no large slaveholders among the Greenlee heirs residing in Burke County. Of course, there was always the heir who, completely outstripping his brothers and sisters. built his own slave empire by ingenuity and energy, or by marriage, while the rest of his family ineluctably slipped into a lower stratum. More abruptly devastating to the incipient slave dynasty than frequent division of property was the failure of business ventures. For more than one Burke County slave-

17. Waightstill Avery to James Avery, January 23, 1816, in Waightstill Avery Papers (Southern Historical Collection, University of North Carolina).

18. Many small slaveholders were illiterate, but the largest Burke County slaveholder who could not read and write was Sara Van Horn, widow of John and owner of sixteen slaves in 1850. Burke County Records, Wills 1793–1905 (North Carolina State Department of Archives and History), II, 58.

holder, among the most disastrous of these ventures was investment in gold mines. John E. Butler, a victim of business reverses, owned fifty slaves in 1830 and was the seventh-largest holder in the county; in 1860 his widow did not own a single slave. All of this is to say that Burke County had a fluid society, and that what class stratification did develop was not necessarily based on slave wealth.

Slavery, as practiced in Burke County and elsewhere in the South, was grounded on a matriarchal system, a system rooted in the legal concept that the children of slaves were the property of the mother's owner, not the father's. In practice, the slave family unit was always designated by the name of the mother; for example, one would refer to "Viney's house" or "Viney's children." The point that has not been stressed, however, is that slavery, although matriarchal in this sense, was also a major component of a patriarchal system.[19] The peculiar twist here is that the slave husband was not the patriarch. The white master was. It is a gross understatement to say that this both denigrated the slave husband and tended to undermine the integrity of the slave family. Nevertheless, even though slave marriages had no legal status whatsoever, Christian marriage between slaves was widely practiced in Burke, and it was countenanced by the master and encouraged by the church. Nor was it uncommon for the slave husband and wife to have different masters who belonged to different churches.[20]

At this point in such a discussion the horrid specter, miscegenation, inevitably raises its head. In Burke County as elsewhere race mixing between male members of an owner's family and his female slaves did occur. In Burke the condition appears to have been just about as commonplace as one would expect, considering the intimate relationship that existed in the county between the slave and the slaveholding family.[21] The slave houses were in the yard of the slaveholder's dwelling, and younger male members of the owner's family in nearly every case played and worked in the fields year after year with slaves of their own age.[22] The attitude of the community toward race mixing was complex, but in Burke County a general pattern is discernible. If a bachelor slave-

19. See Keith F. McKean, "Southern Patriarch: A Portrait," *Virginia Quarterly Review,* XXXVI (Summer, 1960), 376–389.

20. Register of Grace Episcopal Church, Morganton, N.C., II, 113–114.

21. Illicit relations between the races were largely between white males and slave females. The writer knows of only two instances in which white women bore children by slaves, and in both the woman was unrelated to the master's family.

22. For example, see Diary of James Hervey Greenlee (in possession of J. Harvey Greenlee, Morganton; copy, Library, University of North Carolina), I, 51.

holder entered into an intimate relationship with a female slave and raised a family by her, but never became promiscuous, the situation did not become a topic of polite conversation, it is true; yet there is very little evidence that he was censured for his conduct or that he lost status in the community. Again, if a young boy of a slaveholding family had a child by a female slave, later married, and engaged in no further indiscretions, the incident was usually considered lightly and quickly forgotten. But the married slaveowner who promiscuously or openly consorted with his slaves became a social outcast, and he was never forgiven nor his actions forgotten so long as his name was remembered.

The close relationship that often existed between slave and slaveholding family was not always sordid in its implication. Both master and mistress ordinarily were conscientious about caring for the sick —even for the aged who no longer had commercial value.[23] Religion strengthened the bond between slave and free. Local churches, both rural and town, received slaves into membership, baptized their infants, and buried their dead in the plots reserved for their master's family. Although the slave customarily affiliated with the church of his master, on the whole he had considerable freedom of choice in his religious life. Furthermore, he was fairly treated by the church courts of conduct, which seem to have taken their work seriously during this period. At church gatherings slaves were expected to sit together, separate from the white members. Slave graves were poorly marked or not marked at all, but so frequently were white graves.[24] Twentieth-century segregation is not a by-product of slavery, but a reactionary aftermath to Reconstruction.

And yet in spite of all that has been said—that the slaveholder did not feel a sense of guilt, did not consider himself morally reprehensible; that close association between master and slave often promoted a feeling of reciprocal admiration and affection, just as it might, by the same token, promote a feeling of hatred or disdain; that treatment of slaves was less harsh and the institution itself more informal than in the areas of commercial farming—incidents did occur now and then which broke the seeming pastoral calm and created an atmosphere of tension.

23. See for example I. T. Avery to Thomas Lenoir, November 28, 1820, and Avery to Selina Lenoir, February 18, 1835, in Lenoir Papers.

24. Register of Grace Episcopal Church, II, 21, 83, 123; Minutes of Globe Church, Burke County (Southern Historical Collection, University of North Carolina), 1808, 1816, 1824, 1829–31, 1833, 1834, 1840; Morganton Presbyterian Church Sessional Book of Minutes, 1835–52, 11–12, 66, 70.

From the correspondence of Burke County people one senses that there ordinarily existed an atmosphere not of emotional tension but of slight restraint marked by a failure to express emotions that would otherwise have found free expression, a reticence born of circumspection. Perhaps the emotional tone of the community was set as much by the character and disposition of the inhabitants as by the presence of slavery, but a contemporary suggests otherwise when he speaks of "the unhappy excitement and the great sensitiveness of the community to everything connected with slavery." [25]

The underlying tension comes through to us in the reactions of the community to incidents of violence in the slave population and in the precautions it took to keep the slaves under strict surveillance. In the summer of 1813 a slave named Jerry, with the complicity of a female slave named Betsey, allegedly murdered his master, John W. Taggart, a small slaveholder from the eastern part of the county, south of Lovelady Ford. Tried together in the county court of pleas and quarter sessions before three justices of the peace and a jury of twelve men, most of whom were slaveholders, the two were found guilty and sentenced to be hanged. At the same term of court, a slave belonging to William McGimsey was found guilty of trespassing and was sentenced to stand one hour in the public pillory "thence to be taken down, confined to the public whipping post and there receive thirty-nine lashes on his bear back well laid on." Several years later Bolin Brantley, a free Negro, was required by the court to give bond in the amount of $300 with "two good Securities" or else be placed in custody by the sheriff because of his reputation as "a black man of bad fame." [26]

Perhaps prompted by the San Domingo revolt of 1791, patrolling was established in Burke County at least as early as mid-year 1792, and, contrary to reports of other localities, it was apparently performed faithfully and with vigor. The county court supported the patrols by administering very strictly the law that allowed a slave to carry a gun on his master's plantation only if his master posted bond and security.[27] When a slave belonging to a resident of neighboring Wilkes County failed to identify himself satisfactorily to the Burke patrol and was severely cowhided, the owner of the slave entered a complaint against the patrol, but the court ruled in 1821 that if a patroller punished with discretion,

25. Records of Morganton Presbytery, 1836–40 (Historical Foundation, Montreat, N.C.), 35 (3 sess., March 16–17, 1837).

26. County Court Minutes, July session, 1813, and October session, 1817.

27. *Ibid.*, July session, 1792; July session, 1818; January and April sessions, 1817.

he was not liable to the slave's master unless malice against the master was evident.[28] The Nat Turner revolt of late August, 1831, occurred in Southampton County, Virginia, only a short distance from those North Carolina border counties supplying slave labor for the gold mines of Burke and Rutherford counties. Repercussions in Burke County from this are described in this way:

> In consequence of letters, received last week from Rutherfordton stating that a Negro Preacher, and three or four other slaves had been examined and committed to Prison charged with meditating an insurrection in the neighborhood of the mines, the Community to some extent, but the Citizens of Morganton particularly, have been in a state of uncommon excitement for a few days past—the great number of Slaves employed about the mines, would render vigilance among Managers and Patrollers, proper at all times; but from the best information I can get, there is no Just ground for the Panic that has existed—the Negroes of the County are as orderly and submissive, as I ever knew them. . . .[29]

Several months later, one John Hay was arrested and lodged in the Burke County jail "under charge of exciting the negroes to insurrection." The community had hardly settled down from this episode when two slaves, Giles and Billy, were arrested on charges of conspiracy but were acquitted by jury trial. After this there apparently was no further panic in the county, but we do have occasional indications of continued slave unrest and white hypersensitivity. In early 1844 Isaac, a runaway slave belonging to James Upton, was said to be "lurking hid committing various and sundry depredations upon stock and other property." The county court issued a proclamation calling on him to surrender at once, warning that should he fail to do so he would be declared an outlaw, and "it shall be lawful for any person or persons to kill or destroy said slave Isaac by such ways and means as he or they shall think fit with out accusation or impeachment of any crime of the same." A second order states that Isaac "is suspected of being harboured by evil disposed persons" and therefore "that Daniel J. Forney and the patrollers in his neighborhood acting with him are permitted to search the house or houses of any person or persons whom they may have reason to suspect for harbouring said slave." [30]

28. Tate *v.* O'Neal in Helen T. Catterall, ed., *Judicial Cases Concerning American Slavery and the Negro* (Washington, 1926–37), II, 40, citing 8 N.C. 220 (1821).

29. Isaac T. Avery to Selina Lenoir, September 26, 1831, in Lenoir Papers. See also Johnson, *Ante-Bellum North Carolina*, 520.

30. County Court Minutes, January session, 1832; Burke County Superior Court Minutes, 1830–54 (North Carolina State Department of Archives and History), March 29, 1832; County Court Minutes, January session, 1844.

Other cases on record indicate that the court could be as lenient as it was sometimes harsh in dealing with a slave. In an action against Sam, a slave owned by David Greenlee, the indictment for petit larceny was quashed, and a vindictive white prosecutor was taxed with court costs. In 1827 a slave Abram was hailed into court on an unspecified charge, to which he submitted and prayed for benefit of clergy; it was "extended to him," the judgment of the court being that "the Defendant be taken to the public whiping post and there receive one stroke." [31] Early in the spring of 1830 two slaves belonging to William W. Erwin, the clerk of the superior court, were tried for murder. One was found not guilty, and the other, Solomon, being found guilty of manslaughter, prayed for and was given benefit of clergy, whereupon the court ordered that "Solomon be Branded with the letter M on the brawn of the left thumb . . . and that the owner of said slave pay the costs of the prosecution and the Prisoner be discharged." [32]

All of this makes one conclusion inescapable. When the crime of the slave threatened the institution of slavery or otherwise encroached on the economic welfare of the slaveholder, the punishment meted out was as harsh as the law allowed; but if, in contrast, the crime was of no economic consequence, or, if severe punishment would have been contrary to the economic interest of the slaveholder, mitigation was the rule. This is not to say that some particularly heinous crime, such as assault on a white female, would not have invoked the maximum penalty however it affected the interests of the slaveholder, but certainly property rights strongly influenced the courts of the county when dealing with slave crime. None of this contradicts the contention that "the master was more important than the law in determining the extent to which the activities of the slaves were curtailed." [33] The jeremiad of Mrs. E. C. Alexander of southwestern Burke County is in point: "The servants will not obey me. John ran away six weeks since. . . . Last week he returned and says he intends to leave again whenever he pleases." [34] While this

31. *Ibid.*, July session, 1819, and January session, 1827. Benefit of clergy had been extended to slaves as well as freemen in eighteenth-century Virginia, and North Carolina recognized the plea for some years after independence. See G. MacLaren Brydon, "Random Gleanings from the Virginia Gazette," *Historical Magazine of the Protestant Episcopal Church*, XVIII (December, 1949), 428, and *Cyclopedia of Law and Procedure* (New York, 1901–12), XII, 778n.

32. Superior Court Minutes, March 26, 1830. Whether the victim was white, free nonwhite, or slave cannot be determined.

33. Katherine Ann McGeachy, "The North Carolina Slave Code" (thesis, University of North Carolina, 1948).

34. Mrs. E. C. Alexander to W. L. Alexander, April 2, 1850, in Hoke Papers

may have been an uncommon situation, there is other evidence that slaves enjoyed considerable freedom of movement—occasionally to their own detriment, like Charles McDowell's Jerry, who "came by his death by a stab or stabbing with a knife from the hand of some other person than himself in an affray in Mr. Fleming's Island on Friday night last in which said Jerry and others were engaged." [35]

More productive for study at the county level than the legal aspects of slavery [36] is the problem of slave transfer, even though this has also received a great deal of attention from scholars. Slave transfer may, for our purposes, be divided into the three categories of sale, transfer through inheritance, and hiring. Slave sale or slave trading, "slave mongering," has generally been considered the most odious of the three. Yet it is certainly altogether possible that hiring or transfer by inheritance often created the greater hardship and grief for the slave. Slave sales in Burke County were infrequent in comparison with land sales. The county court records of deeds and bills of sale reveal approximately twenty land transactions to every slave transaction, and in one year when over 100 land deeds were recorded only two slave transactions were recorded.[37] Careful analysis of slave transactions, when the analysis is illuminated by some knowledge of the general characteristics of the persons involved in the sales, enables one to gain a very clear understanding of the prevailing ethics of slave trading. It becomes immediately apparent that there was no stigma attached to strictly local trades in which buyer and seller were both residents and intended to remain so. The local Presbyterian minister, John Silliman, for instance, did not hesitate to sell in 1831 a Negro boy to Samuel P. Carson, a resident of

---

(Southern Historical Collection, University of North Carolina), cited in Johnson, *Ante-Bellum North Carolina*, 496.

35. Burke County Miscellaneous Papers (North Carolina State Department of Archives and History), Coroner's Inquests, 1806–47 (C.R. 14.009), November 29, 1829.

36. For detailed treatments of the legal aspects of slavery in North Carolina, see Bassett, *Slavery in the State of North Carolina*, 10–28; Johnson, *Ante-Bellum North Carolina*, 493–521; Rosser H. Taylor, "Humanizing the Slave Code of North Carolina," *North Carolina Historical Review*, II (July, 1925), 323–331; Julius Yanuck, "Thomas Ruffin and North Carolina Slave Law," *Journal of Southern History*, XXI (November, 1955), 456–475; McGeachy, "North Carolina Slave Code"; and Ernest J. Clark, Jr., "Slave Cases before the North Carolina Supreme Court" (thesis, University of North Carolina, 1959).

37. County Court Minutes, April session, 1821. Possibly not all slave transactions were recorded, particularly where the chattel was removed from the county, but neither were all land titles recorded.

the area.[38] Also, it was considered all right for a local buyer to purchase
a slave from a seller who lived in another state, but a local seller who
sold slaves to a buyer from another state was often censured. The buyer,
unless he was a professional trader, was generally less subject to criticism
than the seller. One wonders whether the odium heaped upon the seller
stemmed more from the fact that the sale was a heartless act or from the
fact that it was evidence of his failure as a businessman, while the buyer
was admired as a symbol of aggressiveness and affluence. The most ob-
jectionable act was to sell to an itinerant trader or agent who obviously
intended to transfer the Negroes to a distant market;[39] but even the
most conservative of local slaveholders sometimes hankered to speculate
in the slave market, as indicated by a few lines that a Burke County
businessman-farmer scrawled covertly at the end of a letter to his brother-in-law, Thomas Lenoir:

> I will apprize you while I think of it of another circumstance. Negro
> property has taken a very considerable rise in Norfolk and every other
> place where purchases result in consequence of the number of purchas-
> ers for the Louisiana Market—this I learned at Raleigh and I mention
> it because you talked of selling property of that description[.] Women
> are quoted at $500.[40]

Some years later, however, Colonel Lenoir cautioned his son in Alabama
against selling "property of that description" unless the slave family was
kept together and was willing to be sold. He also strongly advised the
young trader to sell to a friend rather than to a stranger if at all possible.[41] It is easy to overlook the fact that sometimes the slave was not
only willing to be sold but wished to be sold, hoping, as it is one's nature to hope, that he might improve his lot, or knowing that at the very
least he would experience a change in scenery. Such apparently was the
case when a male slave belonging to Mrs. Thomas Espy, the widow of a
Presbyterian minister, accosted one Charles Stanlee, a nonresident who

38. *Ibid.*, October session, 1831. The purchaser, Samuel Price Carson
(1789–1838), son of John, was first secretary of state of the Republic of Texas.
Louis Wiltz Kemp, *The Signers of the Texas Declaration of Independence* (Houston, 1944), 45–56.

39. The only professional trader who made Morganton his headquarters was Z.
D. Lancaster, who operated in this area after 1850 and was undoubtedly an agent
for a larger trader from one of the commercial centers. U.S. Census, 1860, North
Carolina, Schedule 1, Burke County.

40. Isaac T. Avery to Thomas Lenoir, December 17, 1821, in Lenoir Papers.

41. Thomas and Selina Lenoir to William Lenoir, March 28, 1837, *ibid.*

happened to be in Morganton, and told the white man that he was anxious to be traded and requested that Stanlee buy him.[42]

Even from the standpoint of the slaveholder, slave trading did not present a pretty picture. Many individuals who prided themselves on being "smart" or "close" traders seemed to have derived satisfaction from "getting the best of the other fellow," from "driving a hard bargain." An example of a victim of such trickery and greed is William Alberto Erwin, who bought a Negro at a public sale after having accepted the statement of an interested party that the boy was intelligent, only to find that he was an idiot.[43] Fragmentation of slave families, common as the result of slave trades, can be easily illustrated from the slave records. For example, James Murphy, highly respected in the county, bought two small children from Richard Owens of Wilkes County without acquiring either parent.[44] Fragmentation of slave families was in fact inevitable, particularly in the transfer of slaves by inheritance. Wills were principally concerned with equitable distribution of property to rightful heirs, and administrators of estates were compelled by law to manage the affairs of the deceased in a manner which would produce the greatest revenue. Auction sales at the courthouse door—a necessary part of the institution—were unaffected by sentimental considerations.[45] Individual slaves went to the highest bidder. The law went so far as to provide even that "Negroes willed to be free" were to be sold "with the Stock and other property on hand" if necessary in order to pay the debts and settle the estate of the testator.[46]

A distasteful and tragic story of transfer by inheritance is that of the little slave girl Ony. Waightstill Avery, a large property owner of Burke County, provided in his will, in addition to large bequests to his children, that his niece, Margaret Avery, should receive "a likely negro slave of nine or ten years old or four hundred dollars in money" and made a bequest to his son-in-law, William B. Lenoir, contingent upon his payment of this legacy. When Colonel Avery died, Margaret Avery was the wife of John Murphy of Burke County, and Lenoir was living in Roane County, Tennessee. To comply with the terms of the will,

42. Charles Stanlee to J. E. Erwin, undated, in Burke County Miscellaneous Papers, Correspondence of the Clerk of the Court, 1812–68.

43. Erwin *v.* Greenlee in Catterall, *Judicial Cases,* II, 69, citing 18 N.C. 39 (1834).

44. County Court minutes, July session, 1803.

45. For example, see Rutherfordton, N.C., *Spectator,* August 6, 1830; Rutherfordton *North Carolina Spectator and Western Advertiser,* February 11, 1832; County Court Minutes, January session, 1832, 1833, and 1848.

46. See references to the will of William Probert (*i.e.,* Probit), *ibid.,* October session, 1811, and January session, 1812.

Lenoir had a relative conduct a young female slave, Ony, from Tennessee to North Carolina. When the little girl reached Murphy's plantation in Burke County, she was found to have acquired a limp. Because of this defect that apparently developed during her journey, Murphy refused to accept the girl as full payment of his wife's legacy. At his insistence, the question was submitted to a select committee of arbitration, which ruled that if the lameness had not disappeared within three months, Murphy would be entitled to an adjustment.[47] Once it is understood that Avery's bequest to his niece was obviously intended as an affectionate gesture, that Lenoir had a reputation for scupulous honesty, and that Murphy was a man of wealth and the sole heir of one of the largest slaveholders in the county, it becomes clear that this is a prime example of a reverence for the law which tended to blunt moral perception. Legalism did not provide for a sense of gratitude or of sympathy for a little ten-year-old girl who had been abruptly taken from her accustomed surroundings and transferred almost 200 miles over rough mountain trails only to find she was unwanted when she arrived at her destination.

Transfer by inheritance, although of necessity usually impersonal, was sometimes relieved of its harshness by the provisions of testators, most of whom tried to see that a mother and her smaller children were kept together. One expressed the "desire that my Servants, John and his wife Sally Should not be Sold if it can be avoided, especially to persons out of this County, and that they Should not be alloted to any Legatee who will take them out of the State unless they wish to go."[48] Another stipulated that his "servant Rufus and Alcy" be allowed to choose their owner from among his children or relatives at a value set by the executors should his wife die or marry again.[49] Still another required that to pay his debts his town lots be sold before any Negroes and that his wife should designate the order in which the slaves would be sold should this become necessary.[50] Jesse Moore arranged that a man and his wife were not to be sold but were to have the privilege of living with whichever of his children they chose.[51] Individual slaves were occasionally willed

47. Will of Waightstill Avery, February 20, 1819, a certified unfiled copy (office, Register of Deeds, Morganton), and in Burke County Records, Wills, 1793–1805, I (folio 15), 1–4; report of arbitrators, June 1, 1822, and Isaac T. Avery to William B. Lenoir, June 3, 1822, both in Lenoir Papers.

48. Item 6, will of Mary E. Patton, Burke County Records, Wills, 1793–1905, II (folio 4), 28.

49. Will of William W. Avery, *ibid.*, I (folio 3), 6.

50. Will of William L. McRee in Burke County Miscellaneous Papers, Wills, 1787–1900 (C.R. 14.103).

51. Will of Jesse Moore, *ibid.*

their freedom, but these bequests were always subject to the laws relating to manumission, strictly construed by the courts. Daniel Jones willed that his "negro girl Lizzie be set free on account of her good and faithful service to me and I give her my tract of land and my desire is that Dr. Jones should build her a house and see that she should be taken care of." [52] At her death Mary Probit, widow of John Probit, freed her slaves in accordance with her deceased husband's wishes, leaving one slave to a friend, Alexander Glass, to "have and enjoy . . . for 11 years," with the proviso that "at the end of said term" he was "to set her free." To four other slaves she bequeathed her plantation on Cain Creek, with furniture sufficient "that they may live comfortably." [53] In a very general way, it may be said that the small slaveholder more commonly made special provision in his will for his slaves than did the large slaveholder with multiple heirs, whose will was usually more impersonal in order to make it more easily administered.[54]

Slave hiring, the third form of slave transfer, was by definition a temporary arrangement. A common practice in Burke, the hiring out of slaves was conducted on a large-scale contractual basis during the gold rush of the early 1830's and during the railroad construction boom beginning in the late 1850's. Slaves were employed in railroad construction either by slaveholders entering into contracts themselves and using their own slave labor or by slaveholders hiring out their slaves to other contractors. In either case, the slaves were put under the immediate direction of an overseer who "followed the road" and was frequently a hard taskmaster.[55] Except in the cases of these big projects, Frederic Bancroft's generalization that it was "usually necessary" to hire out slaves "when slave property was in probate, or possessed by a life-tenant unable to employ it, or belonged to orphan children or other wards in chancery" holds true for Burke County.[56] For instance, when Samuel

52. Will of Daniel Jones, *ibid.*
53. Will of Mary Probat (*i.e.*, Probit), *ibid.*
54. For examples, see wills of William W. Erwin, Burke County Records, Wills, 1793–1905, I (folio 2), 44, and of Thomas Walton in William Carson Erwin Papers (Southern Historical Collection, University of North Carolina); partition report, estate of Margaret C. Tate, in County Court Minutes, October session, 1825.
55. For names of local slaveholders who employed slaves in railroad construction, see *Reports and Proceedings of Western North Carolina Railroad Company for 1858* (Raleigh, 1858). For a contemporary account of the treatment of slave railroad construction workers, see typewritten statement on inner back cover of a bound collection of Western North Carolina Railroad reports, 1855–66 (in possession of C. V. Walton, Morganton).
56. Frederic Bancroft, *Slave-Trading in the Old South* (Baltimore, 1931), 147.

Greenlee died intestate in 1848, leaving five minor children, a wife (who died three years later), and more than twenty slaves, a local lawyer who was appointed administrator managed to hire out the slaves belonging to the minor children to various individuals for periods of one year.[57]

The system of hiring to individuals seemed to work out more satisfactorily for all concerned than mass hiring for industrial purposes. One slaveholder noted, "Hands came Home from Mines several days ago—said they were mistreated." And on the following day he wrote that he had "declined sending the boys back to the mines." [58] Other holders were reluctant to hire out their slaves even to individuals, particularly to town residents. As one wrote ironically, "the largest boy is still in Morganton where his morals I suspect are not improving much." [59] Slaves themselves ordinarily did not object to being hired out to other citizens. One reason for this, perhaps, is that the practice sometimes gave a slave considerable independence and responsibility, as indicated by the diarist's remark, "Jerry came over from Burnsville and brought me $18.75 for his hire from M. Penland." [60] It must be stated in conclusion, however, that nothing in the records of slave hiring in Burke County supports Clement Eaton's thesis that this was a major step toward freedom for the slave. Apparently the slaveholders of Burke looked upon the practice simply as an important and profitable part of the system of slavery itself.[61]

"The more you press in toward the heart of a narrowly bounded historical problem," Arthur O. Lovejoy says, "the more likely you are to encounter in the problem itself a pressure which drives you outward beyond those bounds." Certainly this has been true in this study of slavery at the local level. What has been the residual impact of slavery upon the mind and character of the people of the county used in this study? What has been the effect of the legacy of slavery upon the freedman, the Negro? Upon the descendants of the non-slaveholding white yeoman? Upon the progeny of the slaveholder?

57. Five of Eph Greenelee's slaves were hired out in 1849 for a total of $149, four of Elizabeth's for $141, four of Alex's for $148.50, five of George's for $185.75, and seven of Emily's for $149.45. Sixteen persons hired one or more of these slaves. Record of accountability, estate of Samuel Greenlee, in Tod R. Caldwell Papers (Library, Duke University).

58. Greenlee Diary, I, 128–129.

59. Isaac T. Avery to William B. Lenoir, December 17, 1821, in Lenoir Papers.

60. Greenlee Diary, III, 88.

61. Clement Eaton, "Slave Hiring in the Upper South: A Step toward Freedom," *Mississippi Valley Historical Review*, XLVI (March, 1960), 663–678.

That the long enslavement of the Negro led to the retardation of the development of the Negro throughout the South is a notorious historical fact. But there can be no contradicting that the slave of Burke County had a distinct advantage over his brothers in the various black belts. If nothing else, his closer association with his master and his master's family permitted him to learn more about the white man's society in which he and his descendants were to live. But there remained the spiritual ignominy of slavery, the effect of which does not disappear in a day, and the local Negro's advancement has been slowed by his continued affiliation with the people of the old slaveholding class, most of whom were themselves held back by their inability to come to terms with the facts of postwar life. In fact, the effect of slavery upon the slaveholder and his progeny, if not so dramatic, was almost as disastrous as upon the Negro. Slavery created households of specialization in which the two diverse elements, whites and Negroes, became reciprocally dependent. As slaves developed in skill, mastering various crafts and manual arts, the slaveholder became more and more dependent upon the slave for goods and services. The classical disciplines were of no help to him in the new world where he found himself after Appomattox, and he failed to take the lead in the new age's industrialism. His descendants were left to nurture their pride and find justification in a pretense to nobility and high morality, while others did the work of the world.

It was the yeoman farmer who suffered least from the incubus of slavery, who might be said, in the end, positively to have profited from it. Not dependent upon slaves, he maintained the vigor, the independence, the mechanical resourcefulness, and the shrewd adaptability of the traditional frontiersman.[62] When the crutch of slavery was taken from his betters, the non-slaveholding yeoman was able to wrest economic, social, and cultural leadership from the soft and indolent victims of slavery.

A Burke County man, once a slaveholder, attempted to evaluate the peculiar institution this way in retrospect:

> I had over thirty slaves—all good and faithful. I would often leave things in their charge and they took good care. Some could read and write a tolerable legible hand, and keep ordinary accounts. Some were members of the church, and I would gather them togather on the Sabbath read to them and instruct them about the future and there responsibility to there Maker. Some were impressed, outhers seemed unmoved. In this part of the country slaves were well treated, fed, and clothed.

62. See Frank L. Owsley, *Plain Folk of the Old South* (Baton Rouge, 1949), and Robert R. Russell, "The Effects of Slavery upon Nonslaveholders in the Ante Bellum South," *Agricultural History*, XV (April, 1941), 112–126.

There was probably some rigid treatment where there were large numbers on a plantation, and where it required rigid treatment to keep all straight and in there places. I do not think emancipation has been such a boon for the colored race in this land. . . . I never was a great advocate of slavery, but I believe that the question of slavery, if justice an[d] righteousness had ruled, could have been more satisfactorily adjusted, without the loss of the thousands of precious lives and the millions of money.[63]

63. Ralph S. and Robert L. Greenlee, *Genealogy of the Greenlee Families* (Chicago, 1908), 249.

Robert E. Corlew

Some Aspects of Slavery in Dickson County

After the Revolutionary War, the state of North Carolina rewarded its veterans with western lands in an area which became Dickson County, Tennessee. Like many other newly settled regions of the United States during the early national period, Dickson County was a frontier area. When it officially became a part of Tennessee, slavery was already firmly established. In newly settled southern states slaves fulfilled the constant need for agricultural labor, particularly in regions where large plantations existed. Dickson County had neither large plantations nor large slaveholdings. The first great influx of slaves came to work in its iron furnaces. These slaves were a source of profit to their owners, who hired them to the county's nascent industrialists and to the factory owners themselves. The reciprocal benefit each of these groups enjoyed from their slaves reduced class friction and muted the hostility to industrialism found in other areas of the South.

Negro labor in industry or the skilled crafts was common throughout the South, but generally this was an urban phenomenon. As Phillips indicates in his article on the Charleston district, the appearance of skilled Negro craftsmen was an event fraught with serious consequences for the stability of the peculiar institution and the hegemony of the large slaveholders. Antipathy between white workers and slaves, whose market value accrued almost solely to their masters, angered white laborers, who found that black artisans worked for less than they did. This outrage was frequently directed against both the slaves and their masters. For this reason the economic potential of the slaves was frequently suppressed for fear of social uprising. It was the slave, particularly the very talented one whose skills and economic value demanded that he be allowed more sophisticated work than the fieldhand, who suffered most in this tangled web of social and political relationships.

Nat Turner offers a dramatic example of a slave of such extraordinary ability that a kind master allowed him privileges rare among the great mass of slaves. Turner's mind and a frenetic messianic religious fervor contributed to the rebellion of 1831. The years after

Reprinted with permission from the *Tennessee Historical Quarterly*, X (1951), 224–248, 344–365.

the uprising are those of great reaction against the enlightened liberalism of the South's revolutionary leaders. Stringent and repressive slave codes and a significant decline in manumission characterized these years. The implications of this situation are not difficult to gauge. For the masters and for the slaves, the contradiction between the slave as chattel and human meant that economic advantage often had to be sacrificed to political and social concerns. As long as racism and negrophobia forbade interaction between whites and blacks, Negroes could work as skilled artisans or factory workers. When they deprived white labor of economic opportunity, its resentment threatened the hegemony of the master class. This problem was particularly true in the older areas of the South, where social stratification occurred very early in a state's history and where the slaveholding elite was able to secure political power and maintain it throughout the antebellum period.

In other areas of the South such as the one Corlew describes, where antipathy to industrialization was not as intense as in Georgia or South Carolina, these problems did not exist. Rather, the chief purpose of slaveholding was economic; work in iron furnaces was a most remunerative outlet for slave labor. In Dickson County status was far more a function of economics than in other areas, where the opprobrium attached to industrial work often kept impoverished planters on eroded lands and made landless whites their tenants. Here as elsewhere in the South closeness to the soil was one of the most important forms of status. But here slaveholders hired out their slaves to work in the iron furnaces, and they used the profits from their slaves' labor to improve their land.

Dickson County is in Middle Tennessee, which was never a central part of the Deep South cotton belt. It is a region whose geography, demography, and social patterns suggested conflict and separation from the lower South. An important though necessarily theoretical question is how these differences might have affected its economic and political relations with the Deep South had not the Civil War intervened. The efficient and profitable use of slave labor in nonagricultural pursuits contradicted one of the chief tenets of pro-slavery thought: that slaves were uneducable children fit only for the most simple work.

Corlew remarks in his conclusion that the end of slavery prepared the way for social catastrophe. There is very little internal evidence to sustain this opinion. Rather, what one senses is the possibility for whites and blacks to live harmoniously (though certainly not equally) and a departure from the one-crop agriculture which stifled the South's development wherever it existed. Where prosperity existed and blacks did not threaten the economic position of whites but made social mobility among whites possible, racial tensions almost always lost their acerbic quality. If Reconstruction was a social catastrophe, it was not because of the demise of slavery but because the Civil War ended in this county the very slow and halting evolution toward a peaceful, prosperous biracial community.

N o G.I. Bill of Rights awaited Edward Dickson, Sterling Brewer,
John Johnston, and others who fought to make the Declaration of
Independence a reality. But the state of North Carolina did provide, in
1780, compensation for its veterans in the form of western lands located
in what was later to become Middle Tennessee. Dickson, Brewer, and
Johnston were among those given lands in the area later to become
Dickson County, and they became some of the county's first settlers.
While they yet shouldered muskets a few explorers had visited the new
West, but the territory later to become their homes remained little more
than a wild underbrush where animals and Indians hunted each other.

During the last quarter of the eighteenth century, however, the land
later to become Dickson County became accustomed to the white man's
rifle and axe. The Negro, and the mule he loved so well, made their appearance during this period.

Dickson County was officially created by act of the General Assembly of Tennessee in 1803.[1] Some twenty years earlier the Cumberland
country, of which Dickson was a part, was designated by no title other
than the rather ambiguous one of "the area west of the mountains."

On October 6, 1783, Davidson County was made a civil municipality
by act of the legislature of North Carolina.[2] The territory included in
that county embraced over three-fourths of Middle Tennessee, extending as far west as the Tennessee River, thus including what was later to

---

1. *Acts of Tennessee*, 1803–4, 1st sess., Ch. 66. The act was passed October 25,
1803. The following quoted portion stipulates the first boundaries: "Be it enacted
by the General Assembly of the State of Tennessee, That a new county by the
name of Dickson be, and hereby is erected and established out of that part of the
counties of Montgomery and Robertson, comprehended within the bounds following, to wit: Beginning on the south bank of Cumberland river, where the line
which separates the counties of Robertson and Davidson intersects the same, running thence down said river to a point, half mile below Fayetteville; thence south-
westwardly by a line which shall intersect Barton's creek, one half mile north of
the forge; thence due west to a stake or a point, one mile east of the east boundary line of Stewart county; thence east with said boundary to the Southwest corner of Williamson County, as established by an act of the last session of the General Assembly . . . thence north with the west boundary lines of the counties of
Williamson and Davidson to the beginning." The southern boundary of the state
continued to be the southern boundary of the county until 1807, at which time
Hickman county was established, and the present boundaries of Dickson and Hickman counties set.

2. W. Woodford Clayton, *History of Davidson County, Tennessee* (Philadelphia,
1880), 540. Clayton cites *State Records of North Carolina*, V. XXIV, Laws
1777–78, Ch. 52. Cited hereafter as Clayton, *Davidson County*.

become Dickson County. With the influx of Scotch-Irish and German settlers from the East, the population of Davidson grew exceptionally fast, so that in November, 1768, the General Assembly of North Carolina divided Davidson and the western portion became a new county by the name of Tennessee. This new county included all the territory now within the boundaries of Dickson, Montgomery, Robertson, and Houston, and parts of Hickman, Humphries, and Stewart. The county seat was located at Clarksville.

Tennessee County included Dickson until 1796, when the state was given the name of the county, and at the first session of the Tennessee General Assembly, on April 9, 1796, what had been Tennessee County was divided into the counties of Montgomery and Robertson. Dickson remained a part of these counties until 1803 when, as mentioned, it was created a county separate and distinct.[3]

Before Davidson County became a civil municipality, slavery was established in the Cumberland territory. Hale and Merritt, in their *History of Tennessee and Tennesseans*, make mention of a "negro fellow" who came with James Robertson when he and his party returned to the bluff on the Cumberland River in 1779.[4] The following year Colonel John Donelson and his group were accompanied by Negroes on their voyage from Fort Patrick Henry to the bluff.[5] By the time Dickson was created a separate county, slavery was firmly entrenched in Middle Tennessee.

Most of the early settlers of Dickson County were Revolutionary soldiers who had been given bounty lands in return for their military service, in accordance with a resolution passed in 1780 by the General Assembly of North Carolina.[6] By this act officers and enlisted men were given grants of land in proportion to their respective grades, the smallest grant consisting of 640 acres given to those discharged with the rank of private. According to the resolution, the lands on the Cumberland River were to be laid off and given to those North Carolina soldiers who served in the Revolutionary War and who were desirous of settling in

3. For a discussion of the early county formations in Middle Tennessee, see John Allison, "The Mero District," *American Historical Magazine* (Nashville, 1896–1904), I (1896), 115–24; John Allison, *Dropped Stitches in Tennessee History* (Nashville, 1897), 86.

4. Will T. Hale and Dixon Merritt, *A History of Tennessee and Tennesseans* (Chicago, 1913), II, 292–293.

5. *Ibid.*

6. Clayton, *Davidson County*, 45.

the new West. In 1786 John Hogg was given 640 acres in what is now Dickson County,[7] but it is doubtful if he came to take up his claim inasmuch as no evidence of his holdings can be found in the county records.

After that date families began to move in, and in the early 1790's James Robertson founded an iron furnace near the present town of Cumberland Furnace, which was later to become known as the Cumberland Iron Works—the first iron furnace in Middle Tennessee, and the second in the state.[8] Colonel King had founded the first one in Tennessee in 1794, which was known as King's Iron Works and was built near the mouth of Steele's Creek in Sullivan County.[9]

Shortly after Robertson established the furnace, William Blount secured the opening of a good wagon road to the Cumberland country; this greatly facilitated an increase in population.[10] For Robertson it meant more and cheaper labor, and a cheaper means of procuring necessary supplies. An observer traveling through the Cumberland country near the turn of the century wrote that on many parts of the road the immigrants could scarcely pass each other for the vast crowd. It was estimated that in the course of only two months over 26,000 people had crossed the Cumberland River at one place, and on another occasion, when the wagon road became too crowded, from 1,000 to 2,000 persons were traveling through the wilderness at the same time.[11]

It was the iron furnace which brought the first influx of slaves into Dickson County. Robertson did not operate the furnace on a very ex-

7. Goodspeed Publishing Company, *History of Tennessee from the Earliest Times to the Present, together with an Historical and Bibliographical Sketch of . . . Dickson . . . [and other] Counties* (Nashville, 1886), 992. Hereafter cited as Goodspeed, *History of Tennessee, Dickson County*.

8. The date of the establishment of this furnace varies with the historian, 1793 being the date generally accepted by residents of the county. Hale and Merritt state 1794, and Goodspeed's History "between 1790 and 1795." A. P. Foster, *Counties of Tennessee* (Nashville, 1923), 55, states the date as 1793, as does W. L. Cook, "Furances and Forges," *Tennessee Historical Magazine*, IX (1925), 190. Samuel C. Williams, "Early Iron Works in the Tennessee Country," *Tennessee Historical Quarterly*, VI (1947), 44, attempts to refute the early date, believing the establishment of the furance to have been several years later. J. B. Killebrew, *Introduction to the Resources of Tennessee* (Nashville, 1874), 705, sets the date at 1810.

9. Albert C. Holt, "The Economic and Social Beginnings of Tennessee," *Tennessee Historical Magazine*, VIII (1924), 36.

10. Thomas P. Abernethy, *From Frontier to Plantation in Tennessee* (Chapel Hill, 1932), 138.

11. *Ibid.* See also A. W. Putnam, *History of Middle Tennessee* (Nashville, 1889), 515–516; Margaret Kinard, "Frontier Development of Williamson County," *Tennessee Historical Quarterly*, VIII (1949), 10–11.

tensive scale, and he remained its proprietor only until 1802, at which time he sold it to a young Scotch-Irish trader from Pennsylvania who was destined to become one of the greatest iron developers in the South—Montgomery Bell. Bell brought slaves with him, hired others, and employed many whites in the development of the first iron furnace of the Cumberland country.[12]

The development of the iron furnaces in the first half of the nineteenth century, made possible largely through the use of slave labor, is one of the most important chapters in the history of Dickson County, and indeed of the Cumberland country. After Bell had gained some measure of success and had discovered that Dickson County was rich in iron ore, furnaces began to spring up throughout the Cumberland country. In Dickson County, besides the Cumberland Iron Works, there were Carroll Furnace, Steam Forge near Betsytown on Cumberland River, Upper Forge, Belleview Forge on Jones Creek, White Bluff Forge on Turnbull Creek, Valley Forge on Jones Creek, Piney Furnace on Piney River, and Worley [13] Furnace south of the present town of Dickson.[14] The latter furnace, owned and operated by Bell and named for a trusted slave, was the first furnace on the Cumberland River to use steam.[15]

Slave labor at the furnaces was recruited from slaves owned by the proprietors and those which could be hired from owners living in the vicinity. Occasionally the proprietors were forced to resort to advertisements in newspapers in order to recruit slave labor, as did Montgomery Bell in 1808, when he announced in the *Impartial Review and Cumber-*

12. Samuel C. Williams, "Early Iron Works in the Tennessee Country," 37, citing *Robertson's Letters*, vol. II, July 1, 1801.

13. This name is sometimes spelled Whorley. The furnace was named for Bell's slave James Whorley (or Worley), who came into Bell's possession when the latter was temporarily engaged in the hat-making business in Lexington, Kentucky, just prior to his coming into Middle Tennessee. The slave would take loads of iron to New Orleans and Cincinnati and sell them. The story usually goes that "he was never a dollar short." Merchants of New Orleans were said to have offered fabulous sums for the Negro, but Bell is alleged to have said in reply to one such offer, "I would not take all of New Orleans for him" (newspaper clipping among Leech Papers, n.d.). The Leech Papers, containing both printed and manuscript material relating to antebellum Dickson County, are in possession of Henry Collier Leech of Nashville.

14. W. L. Cook, "Furnaces and Forges," 192. This article appeared in the October, 1925, issue of the *Tennessee Historical Magazine* with no by-line. The following issue contained a note stating that the article was contributed by "our highly esteemed Hon. W. L. Cook. . . ."

15. Newspaper clipping among Leech Papers, n.d.

land Repository that he wanted "to hire eight or ten negro fellows by the year," for whose labor he promised to pay a "generous price."

Montgomery Bell was Dickson County's largest slaveholder and has been referred to as the greatest developer of the iron industry in Middle Tennessee. He was born in Chester County, Pennsylvania, in 1769,[16] and served a term as a tanning and currying apprentice.[17] Disliking this trade, he came to Lexington, Kentucky, and there engaged in the hatter's business for a short time. Here he did well financially and purchased a few slaves. From Lexington he came to Dickson County, bringing slaves with him.

One year after he bought the Cumberland Iron Works from Robertson, he increased the yearly output from less than 300 tons of iron to over 1,000 tons. Shortly after he acquired the furnace, he contracted with the U. S. Army to furnish it with cannonballs; the War of 1812 enabled Bell to make considerable money and to establish new furnaces and purchase new ore banks. It is common legend in the county that practically all the cannonballs used by American troops in the Battle of New Orleans were moulded at the Cumberland Iron Works.[18] The balls were said to have been hauled by wagon to the Cumberland River, a distance of approximately fifteen miles, and there put on flatboats and shipped by way of the Ohio and Mississippi rivers to New Orleans.

In Bell's later years he emancipated many of his slaves and gave money for the founding of an academy for boys. During his years at the forges and furnaces, however, he learned to drive hard and shrewd bargarins, to get the greatest amount of labor from the slave even if the whip was necessary, and to violate the law if such became necessary to accomplish his ends. For these reasons many lawsuits involving Bell came before the courts in Dickson County.

In 1840 Martha Dickson sued Bell for compensation for "work and labor done before the time by the hands of the said Martha in cutting cord wood at the special instance and request of said defendent in consideration thereof . . . [Bell] undertook and then and there faithfully promised to pay her . . . [but instead] craftily intended to deceive and

16. This is the date of birth carved on Bell's monument. He was buried at the narrows of the Harpeth River, near the site of his Patterson Iron Works, in Cheatham County near the Dickson-Cheatham line.

17. *Montgomery Bell Bulletin* (1901). No author or publisher listed. Leech Papers.

18. Goodspeed, *History of Tennessee, Dickson County*, 921. The author states, "It has been claimed, and has not been refuted, that all the cannon balls used by General Jackson at the battle of New Orleans, during the War of 1812 were cast by this furnace. . . ."

defraud said plff. . . ." The jury assessed the damages at $114.40.[19] Francis Prince has a similar experience with Bell. In 1807 he inserted the following announcement in the *Impartial Review and Cumberland Repository:* "All persons are forwarned from accepting a note drawn by me in favor of Montgomery Bell, for upwards of one thousand dollars, given last year, as I am determined not to pay up said note, on account of the said Bell not having fulfilled his contract therefor." [20]

Occasionally slaves would run away from Bell's ironworks. Bell would use every possible means to regain possession of them, as is indicated from his published announcement in an August, 1807, issue of the *Impartial Review and Cumberland Repository:*

2 0 0 D o l l a r s R e w a r d

Run-away on the 15th of the present instant from the subscriber at the Cumberland Furnace, Dickson County, state of Tennessee, a dark mulatto fellow, Called BILLEY, but will no doubt change his name, perhaps 34 or 5 years old, 5 feet 10 or 11 inches high, strong and actively formed, his countenance indicative of discontent, unless when he affects a smile, his features tolerably prominent without much flesh on his face, his clothing unknown, and will no doubt change them as he has an opportunity of pilfering others. He will I expect pass himself for a free man, has worked sometimes at the coaling business, his direction is uncertain, but it is supposed he will bend his course toward Louisiana, Indiana Territory, state of Ohio, or Lexington, Kentucky. It is not to be supposed he will acknowledge who he belongs to, he was guilty of crimes previous to his elopement, for which he expected punishment. Any person apprehending him will iron him in the most secure manner, paying no regard to any promises he may make, lodge him in jail and inform me of it so that I get him or if they bring him to me secured in irons shall have the above reward and reasonable expenses paid by Montgomery Bell.[21]

According to the census of 1820, Bell at that time owned 83 slaves; few other Dickson County owners held half as many.[22] In 1830 he held 97,[23] and by 1850 he had accumulated 332.[24] Bell carefully selected and trained his slaves in every capacity for operating an iron forge and fur-

19. Minutes, Circuit Court, Dickson County, (1839–45), 175. Since there are a great many citations to Dickson County records, it has seemed unnecessary to repeat "Dickson County" each time. Where records of counties other than Dickson are cited, that fact will be indicated. Absence of the county name will mean the records are of Dickson County.

20. May 16, 1807.

21. August 27, 1807.

22. U.S. Census, 1820—Dickson County, Tenn., Schedule I.

23. U.S. Census, 1830—Dickson County, Tenn., Schedule I.

24. U.S. Census, 1850—Davidson County, Tenn., Schedule I.

nace. Some became miners, some were colliers and moulders, and some could operate parts of Bell's furnace with little assistance.[25]

Buying and selling slaves began early in the county. It was required by law that bills of sale be filed with the county court, and the first recorded sale in the county was for "one Negro boy" sold December 20, 1804, by Ross Brewer to Sterling Brewer.[26] At the next meeting of the court in March, 1805, John Turner had sold to Nathan Nesbitt "a negro Man slave named Billy"[27] and Joseph Teas had sold to William Teas "a negro."[28] Thereafter, buying and selling slaves in the county took place not infrequently.

False representation as to the health and quality of a slave was an offense punishable by law just as was false representation of other property. At the October, 1840, term of circuit court John May was alleged to have sold two unhealthy slaves, a man and a woman, to Samuel Baker Alston. May was accused of "then and there falsely, fradulently warranteeing the said slaves to be sound and healthy and able bodied slaves and then and there sold the said slaves to the said plff . . . [for $1000, but] at the time [of the sale the slaves were] unsound and unhealthy and diseased and hath from thence hitherto remained and continued [so]. . . ."[29] Alston further alleged that he was put to great expense in buying medicine, clothes, and other necessities for them and that although the man was represented to him to be strong and healthy, in actuality he proved to be a "weak, feeble, and sickley man and greatly afflicted with disease. . . ." The jury assessed the damages at $324.95 and costs.[30]

There were many legal actions throughout the state in which the physical or mental condition of the slave was represented falsely. In the case of Cheatham *v.* Haley no warranty as to the health or condition of the slave was given, but later when it was "proved that she was a fool" and that the defendant knew it before making the sale, the plaintiff was given a verdict.[31]

25. W. McLain, *Journal of the Executive Committee, Report of the Expedition by the General Pierce* (n.d., n.p.). Typewritten copy among Leech Papers.

26. Minutes, County Court (1804–7), 39.

27. *Ibid.*, 68.

28. *Ibid.*, 147.

29. Minutes, Circuit Court (1839–44), 137–138.

30. *Ibid.*, 138.

31. Helen Tunnicliff Catterall (Mrs. Ralph C. H. Catterall), *Judicial Cases Concerning American Slavery and the Negro* (Washington, 1929) II, 483. 1 Overton 265. All cases involving slavery in Tennessee have been collected and digested, and may be found in Catterall, II, 482–601.

The practice of stealing slaves was not uncommon. The first case to come before a court in Dickson County which involved slave stealing was brought before the circuit court in 1837. In this case George Clark sued William Cox for damages and recovery of two slaves which Clark alleged Cox had stolen from him. The value of one slave was placed at $700, and the value of the other, a child, was placed at $200. The slaves were recovered and Cox was assessed damages amounting to $132.[32]

The value of slaves in the county fluctuated from time to time and depended upon the age, quality, skill, etc., of the Negro. The average assessed value of the slaves of Dickson County during the period 1838 to 1859 is shown in the following table. Values for the state are given for comparison.[33]

	Tennessee (Av. value)	Dickson County (Av. value)
1838	$540.00	$561
1840	543.00	571
1842	509.00	
1844	420.00	454
1846	413.72	448
1848	467.44	474
1850	506.93	477
1852	547.26	
1854	605.52	554
1856	689.00	720
1859	854.65	1100

The assessed valuation in Dickson County compared favorably with that of other counties in its area. In 1839 the average assessed value in Davidson County was $578, in Hickman $578, in Rutherford $598, and in Williamson $614. Cotton thrived in the rich farming land of West Tennessee, and there we find the highest assessed valuation. In Fayette County, for example, the value was placed at $634. The lowest of the state was found in Johnson County, in East Tennessee, the assessed valuation there being $368.[34]

Because of the many factors involved, it is next to impossible to arrive at an average price which slaves would bring. It seems, however, that there was a steady rise in the price after the mid-1840's. In 1831 Joel R.

32. Minutes, Circuit Court (1839–44), 27. Clark was a well-to-do farmer who owned more slaves than the average citizen.

33. *Report of the Comptroller of the Treasury of the State of Tennessee to the House of Representatives*, 1838, 1841, 1843, 1845, 1847, 1849, 1851, 1853, 1855, 1857, 1859.

34. *Ibid.*

Taylor of Davidson County sold to Joab Hardin of Dickson "a certain negro boy about twenty-one years old named Joe" for $450 in cash.[35] In 1843, the administrator of the estate of Joseph Larkins sold the Larkins' Negroes as follows: A "Boy named Sam," [36] $200; a "man named Jack," $275; a "woman named Ginsey," $300; and a "Boy named Bill," $300.[37] These prices seemed a bit low in comparison with prices which other slaves brought during the period.[38] If they were sold at auction, however, as they probably were, this partly explains the low price. Three years later, in 1846, the slaves of the estate of Rease Bowen were valued as follows: "Negro Boy Irmy valued at $600; . . . Negro Boy Tom valued at $625. . . ." [39]

Owing to the mediocrity of the soil, among various other factors, it is not to be expected that Negroes bought and sold in Dickson County —with the exception of some of those who worked at the iron forges and furnaces—would bring prices commensurate with those paid for slaves in Davidson and some of the West Tennessee counties where slavery was more profitable. However, as the above table indicates, the average value of slaves in Dickson County did range a bit higher than that for the state as a whole.

SMALL SLAVEHOLDING AND LANDHOLDINGS

A British author writing in 1862 described a slave society of "three classes, broadly distinguished from each other, and connected by no common interest—the slaves on whom devolves all the regular indus-

35. Bill of sale, Taylor to Hardin. Leech Papers.

36. Sam lived to be an old man and is remembered by some of the older citizens of the county. He is thought to have been the child of Jack and Ginsey, mentioned in the sale above. "Uncle Sam," as he was affectionately known to many in Charlotte, married Mary, the daughter of Dinah, who had belonged to the Dillahunty family. To this union was born Cora, who during the Reconstruction period married a Negro Yankee soldier named Lanier. Their children, McPherson, Gus, Emmett, and Charlie, are remembered especially for their respectful conduct when in the presence of white people. Gus, until his death in 1947, was a prosperous businessman in Dickson and was for many years a correspondent for the *Dickson County Herald*. Testimony of H. C. Leech, Lakeland, Fla.; Mrs. Ann Leech Corlew, Charlotte, Tenn.; and Mrs. Varrie Leech Neely, Nashville.

37. Administrator's report. Leech Papers.

38. Judge John Overton of Davidson County, for example, sold slaves during this period as follows: "Betty, $800; Wood, $600; Bob, $500; and Adam, $500." Overton, however, had the reputation of dealing only in superior slaves.

39. Administrator's Book (1846), 2.

try, the slave-holders who reap all its fruits, and an idle and lawless rabble who live dispersed over vast plains in a condition little removed from absolute barbarism." [40] Like the British author, northern and other foreign writers, travelers, and commentators had by 1861 drawn a stereotyped picture of the South, consisting of slaveholders, poor whites, and Negroes.[41] The poor white class was thought to be composed predominately of illiterate, drunken outcasts who could find no place for themselves in the complex social system. As with Lazarus and the rich man, it was thought that there was a great gulf fixed between the two classes which was not to be bridged by even the strongest and bravest of the poor whites.

On the basis of this classification, the people of antebellum Dickson County would come within the class of that "idle and lawless rabble" known as poor whites, since there were none except the iron manufacturers who owned either slaves or land on a scale comparable with the planter class. Only a cursory survey of the antebellum census records and county records will reveal, however, that the people of Dickson County were neither poor whites nor large slaveholders but were somewhere in between these two classes.

Most of the people were engaged in some form of agriculture, many owning small farms. Some of those who had farms also had slaves, but there were many who did not. Throughout the South, however, the mass of the farming population, whether slaveholding or non-slaveholding, was of neither the planter class nor poor white, but was of the middle or yeoman class, which enjoyed with the planter a high degree of economic and social security. John Corlew, for example, in 1860 owned only 80 acres of improved land, yet he had 50 hogs, seven mules, two horses, three cows, and for the previous year produced 1,000 bushels of corn, 30 bushels of wheat, and 10 bushels of rye.[42] Moses Parker in 1850 had only 100 acres of improved land, yet had two horses, one mule, six cows, 15 sheep, 70 hogs, and produced during the preceding year 100 bushels of oats, 75 bushels of corn, and 100 bushels of sweet potatoes.[43] Jacob Leech in 1860 owned only eight acres, yet had three

40. John E. Cairnes, *The Slave Power: Its Character, Career and Probable Designs* (London, 1862), 60. Quoted by Frank L. and Harriet C. Owsley, "The Economic Basis of Society in the Late Ante-Bellum South," *Journal of Southern History*, VI (1940), 25.

41. Owsley and Owsley, "Economic Basis of Society," 25.

42. U.S. Census, 1860—Dickson County, Tenn., Schedule IV.

43. U.S. Census, 1850—Dickson County, Tenn., Schedule IV.

horses, one mule, three cows, and 20 hogs, and produced for the preceding year 200 bushels of corn and 15 bushels of wheat.[44] Ben Corlew,
in the same year, held 65 acres of improved land, but had seven horses,
three cows, four oxen, nine sheep, 30 swine, and produced 150 bushels
of corn and 33 bushels of wheat. Virtually every farmer had horses, asses
and mules, milch cows, sheep, and swine, and produced an abundance of
wheat, corn, oats, Irish and sweet potatoes, and tobacco.[45] Men of these
means could not be placed among the "idle and lawless rabble" known
as poor whites, while none, of course, could pretend to be in the planter
class.[46] The county thus offered a home to many farmers whose land
and slaveholdings were by no means extensive.

The sizes of farms in Dickson County were a bit larger than might be
expected, when both improved and unimproved land is taken into consideration. When only improved land (that which has been cleared and
may be cultivated) is considered, however, the farms were comparatively small, none consisting of over 500 acres.[47]

Of those engaged in agriculture in 1850, more owned from one to
fifty acres than any other amount.[48] The same was true ten years later,
when, of 1,147 heads of families engaged in agriculture, 415 owned from
one to fifty acres. In the same year 132 owned from 51 to 100 acres, and
273 owned from 101 to 200 acres. There were very few large landholdings, and in 1860 only 65 owned 501 to 1,000 acres, and all of these
owned land on which there were less than 500 improved acres. As mentioned, in 1850 only Elias W. Napier and Anthony W. Vanleer owned
more than 5,000 acres, Napier holding 15,300 and Vanleer owning
12,500.[49] By 1860 Napier had died and his land had been divided. Only

44. U.S. Census, 1860—Dickson County, Tenn., Schedule IV.
45. *Ibid.*
46. The Owsleys have clearly shown that, throughout the South, "If the several
economic and social classes were graphically presented, the general appearance of
the chart would be a gentle curve where small farmer, middle-sized farmer, small
planter, middle-sized planter, and large planter touched each other without any
breaks." Owsley and Owsley, "Economic Basis of Society," 42. County and census
records indicate that on such a graph Dickson County farmers would range from
the small farmer into the middle-sized farmer group. Anthony Vanleer and the
Napier men (A. W., Elias W., Henry A. C., John W., Richard C., Charles W.,
and George) held land comparable in size to plantations, but they were engaged in
iron works of the county and did not farm extensively.
47. Anthony Vanleer held 500 improved acres in 1850. All other landowners held
improved acreage of much smaller size.
48. U.S. Census, 1850—Dickson County, Tenn., Schedule IV.
49. *Ibid.*

Vanleer remained as a large landowner, his holdings having mounted to 13,746 acres, of which 1,131 were improved.[50]

The majority of the people of Dickson County did not own slaves. In 1820 the number of non-slaveholding families was 433, while the number of families holding slaves was less than half that number—205.[51] The same approximate ratio held true ten years later. In 1830 the ratio of non-slaveholding to slaveholding families was 694 to 226,[52] and in 1840 it was 657 to 246.[53] In 1860 the white population of the county was 7,781 while the slave population was 2,201.[54] Throughout the entire slaveholding period, then, the non-slaveholding families outnumbered the slaveholding families.

Of the slaveowning families, more owned one slave than any other number. In 1820 and 1830 there were only eight who held more than twenty-five slaves, and they were all of the Montgomery Bell, Anthony Vanleer, Napier family class who were engaged in the manufacture of iron, and not primarily in agriculture. In 1820, of the 1,305 slaves in the county, 264, or about one-fifth, were held by six men connected with the iron furnaces and forges.[55] The same held true for 1830, and by 1840, with the entrance of William Fentress and a few others into the iron business and the increase in slaveholding on the part of the Napiers, the furnace men held approximately one-fourth of the slaves of Dickson County.[56]

These men did not use their slaves for labor at the furnaces exclusively, however, for most of them had large landholdings and used some of their Negroes on the land. The 12,300 acres owned in 1850 by Anthony W. Vanleer and the 15,500 owned by Napier have already been mentioned. In 1840, of the seventy slaves owned by Charles W. Napier, fifty worked at the furnace and ten were used in agriculture. Vanleer had fourteen slaves engaged in agriculture at the same time. Most of his slaves were of the "prime fieldhand" class, about 80 percent of them ranging in age from twenty to fifty-five.[57]

50. U.S. Census, 1860—Dickson County, Tenn., Schedule IV.
51. U.S. Census, 1820—Dickson County, Tenn., Schedule I.
52. U.S. Census, 1830—Dickson County, Tenn., Schedule I.
53. U.S. Census, 1840—Dickson County, Tenn., Schedule I.
54. U.S. Census, 1860—Dickson County, Tenn., Schedule I.
55. U.S. Census, 1820—Dickson County, Tenn., Schedule I. The six men were: Montgomery Bell, Anthony W. Vanleer, George Ross, R. C. Napier, George Napier, and James Goodrich.
56. U.S. Census, 1840—Dickson County, Tenn., Schedule I.
57. *Ibid.*

From the census records it is safe to deduce that the typical Dickson countian was one who had no slaves at all, or else owned one, two, three, or four slaves. The slave or slaves were used mostly for general duties of all kinds around the house and farm.

The small holdings may best be explained in economic terms: the soil and climate of the county were the deciding factors, and farming was not sufficiently profitable to encourage large slaveholdings. In Tennessee more than in any other state, the institution of slavery reflected the physiographic features of the state.[58] In East Tennessee, where much of the area was unsuitable for the growing of cotton and tobacco, slavery was unprofitable. With the exception of the valleys of the French Broad, the Watauga, and the Holston rivers, very little of the land was suitable for agriculture. In that part of the state the ratio of blacks to whites was one to twelve, and in two-thirds of that division the ratio was from one to twenty and over.[59] Consequently, the anti-slavery sentiment which was engendered in that section was not unexpected.

Middle Tennessee consists of long mountain slopes, plateaus, and undulating lands, and contains the rich central basin and fertile bottoms of parts of the Cumberland, Harpeth, and Tennessee rivers. Slavery was reasonably profitable there. It was most profitable, however, in the broad alluvial plains of West Tennessee, where cotton and tobacco could be remuneratively grown. In Middle Tennessee the ratio was one slave to three whites, while in the western section of the state the slave-white ratio was three to five.[60] So far as this ratio is concerned, Dickson County was a typical Middle Tennessee county, the ratio being very near one to three throughout the slaveholding period.

Dickson County contains a small portion of the rich bottom lands of the Cumberland and Harpeth rivers. It lies in the belt of the high dissected plateau known as the Highland Rim, which encircles the central basin. Its surface is chiefly high table land, predominately hilly, with many creek valleys. The ridge tops are smooth or gently rolling, especially in the northeastern area bordering Cheatham County.

Part of the soil of the county consists of Baxter silt loam. This soil is a brownish-gray silt loam, underlain by a yellowish-red clay loam. It is not extensive in the county, the largest and most typical areas being in the vicinity of Burns and Dickson in the south-central part of the

58. Caleb P. Patterson, *The Negro in Tennessee, 1790–1865* (Austin, Tex., 1922), 59.

59. Asa E. Martin, "Anti-Slavery Societies," *Tennessee Historical Magazine*, I (1915), 279.

60. *Ibid.*

county. It is also found on some of the ridges, especially between Dickson and Charlotte, and in places along the Harpeth Ridge in the northeastern parts of the county.[61]

More than 50 percent of the soil in the county consists of Baxter gravelly silt loam—a grayish-brown loam. Here both the soil and the subsoil consist of varying quantities of gravel and some of the hills are too stony for profitable cultivation. This type of soil occurs in all parts of the county, occupying all except the lower slopes and the river valleys already designated. Corn, wheat, and tobacco are grown with some degree of success on this soil.[62]

About 20 percent of the soil of the county consists of Dickson silt loam, which is ordinarily free from gravel. It is underlain at from six to eight inches by a silty clay loam which is non-porous, causing very poor drainage in some areas. The northern part of the Harpeth Ridge and the northern part of the ridge east of Sylvia consist of this type of soil. Approximately 50 percent of this soil had been cleared as late as 1923,[63] and considerably less was in use during slave days.

Approximately 10 percent of the soil is of the Hagerstown gravelly silt loam—a rather shallow soil, and found on the slopes in practically all parts of the county. It is underlain at eight to ten inches by a yellowish-brown clay loam, and on this soil, too, the water has a tendency to remain on the surface. Here corn is the principal grain crop and redtop the common grass.[64]

A small amount of the soil is of Hagerstown silt loam. This soil is quite similar to the Hagerstown gravelly silt loam, but is a bit more fertile. It is underlain at a depth of from eight to fourteen inches by a reddish-brown silty clay, which ordinarily extends to a depth of three feet or beyond. Limestone is often found at this depth. Crops thrive on the soil, and tobacco, corn, wheat, oats, and clover are the principal crops. The tobacco and corn yields are usually good, averaging over a period of years approximately 1,000 pounds per acre for tobacco and thirty to fifty bushels for corn.[65]

The climate is characterized by moderate temperatures in both sum-

---

61. John Alexander Kerr, W. J. Latimer, H. G. Lewis, and E. H. Bailey, *Soil Survey of Dickson County, Tennessee* (Washington, 1928), 321. Pamphlet published as an extract of *Soil Survey Report*, ser. 1923, no. 11, United States Department of Agriculture, Bureau of Chemistry and Soils.

62. *Ibid.*, 320.

63. *Ibid.*, 316–317.

64. *Ibid.*, 322.

65. *Ibid.*, 323.

mer and winter, the mean summer temperature being 76 degrees. The average frost-free season consists of only 188 days, and killing frosts have been recorded as early as October 2 and as late as May 2.[66]

From the foregoing facts concerning soil and climate, it is readily perceived that Dickson County is not an area conducive to extensive cotton-growing. J. A. Turner, in his *Cotton Planters' Manual* of 1865, states:

> It is now pretty universally conceded, that our best cotton lands are those which are of deep and soft mold, a sort of medium between the sandy and spongy, and those soils which are penetrated by the warming rays of the sun, inbibing readily the stimulating gasses of the atmosphere, and which allow the excess of rain water to settle so deep into the earth, as to lie at a harmless distance below the roots of the young plants. These are the properties of the soil so needful to the vigorous growth and early maturity of the cotton plant; and the knowledge of this fact is of great, and perhaps I may add, indispensable importance to its successful cultivation.[67]

Only a small portion of the Dickson County soil meets this test.

Despite the fact that Dickson County soil was not well suited to the growth of cotton, antebellum farmers of the county could not resist the temptation to attempt cotton planting in order to reap some of the huge profits which were to be made from that staple. The invention of the cotton gin served as an impetus to the growth of cotton, and by 1800 cotton was the chief crop in the Cumberland Basin, with tobacco second.[68] Gins were used in the Cumberland country as early as 1799,[69] and by 1807 Robert Jarmon had established a gin in Dickson County. In the summer of 1807 he announced through the *Impartial Review and Cumberland Repository* that he wished "to inform the public that he has erected a shop on Yellow Creek, 10 miles west of Dickson courthouse to make on a new plan, called the hollow neck teeth saw gins— The business will be carried on very extensively in the various branches. Gentlemen may be supplied at three shillings per saw." [70] Jarmon further explained that he was a stranger in the town, and in order to "show that his gins are superior to any now at work in this country," he submitted testimonials from James Robertson and Benjamin Joslin. Robertson testified that the gins were far superior to any he had ever

66. *Ibid.*, 309.
67. P. 12. Quoted in Chase C. Mooney, "Slavery in Davidson County, Tennessee" (thesis, Vanderbilt University, 1936), 10.
68. Abernethy, *Frontier to Plantation*, 200–201.
69. *Ibid.*, 201.
70. June 27, 1807.

seen before, and that from his personal observation he knew that Jarmon's gins would pick "near twice as much [as] the common gins in the country." Joslin stated that Jarmon had made fifty saws for him which "picked fifty pounds of seed cotton in five minutes." [71]

The chief ginning center of the Cumberland country was at Nashville, and by 1804 twenty-four gins had been established there, one of which was owned by Andrew Jackson. Before the establishment of Jarmon's gin in Dickson County, some would no doubt carry their cotton to the gins in Nashville.

The price offered by the average wholesale merchant in 1804 was $.15 per pound for loose cotton, and $.17 for baled lint. The price of cotton varied from time to time, and in 1807 the merchants of Nashville held a conclave and agreed to pay only $.12 and $.14, despite the vehement protests of the cotton growers, who used the *Impartial Review and Cumberland Repository* and other newspapers of the community as mediums through which to express their disgust at such low prices. By 1815, however, the price of cotton in Nashville had risen to $.20 and $.21 per pound,[72] and cotton was on its way toward a comfortable seat on a throne erected by, and to be constantly buttressed by, southern planters and northern and foreign markets.

Some of the cotton grown in Dickson County no doubt found market in Joseph Wingate's hatter's shop, which he established in Charlotte in 1808. At this time he advertised through a Nashville newspaper his desire for apprentices who would come well recommended to aid him in the hatter's shop which he was establishing at the county seat. He also advertised for journeymen who were offered the "highest prices for making hats." [73] Most of the marketable cotton, however, must have been sold outside the county.

Cotton did not prove profitable to any great extent in the county. By the beginning of the second quarter of the century production was beginning to decline, and by 1850 only nineteen 400 pound bales were produced in the entire county.[74]

In addition to those reasons given, there was at least one other reason for small slaveholdings. This was the presence of many children in virtually every family. The children of the white farmer proved a source of labor not generally taken into account by most writers on the sub-

71. *Ibid.*

72. For cotton prices at Nashville in the years mentioned, see John Wooldridge, ed., *History of Nashville, Tennessee* (Nashville, 1890), 243–244.

73. *Impartial Review and Cumberland Repository*, April 27, 1808.

74. U.S. Census, 1850—Dickson County, Tenn., Schedule IV.

ject. In the antebellum days children made their appearance early and
often in homes of both poor and the well to do. In 1820 John Sowel had
eighteen children, six of his sons being under ten years of age, and in the
same year Thomas Collier had eleven. Randolph Harris and Abraham
Harris had only seven each, but both had five sons under ten years of
age. The Harris families, like many others, thus had an ample labor supply for years to come. Willie Balthrop had fourteen children by 1820,
and Robert West had ten.[75] Benjamin Corlew, born in 1802, twenty
years later took to himself a sixteen-year-old bride and less than twelve
months later had the first of eighteen children. Every year or two thereafter a child was born to this family, fifteen of which lived past infancy.
Corlew's wife lived to be nearly sixty years old.[76] Life on the frontier
was extremely hard for women, however, and many of the men married
three and four times during their lifetimes.

TREATMENT OF SLAVES

With very few exceptions, slaveholders in Dickson County knew
their slaves well.[77] The average holding was small, which gave the
owner opportunity to know and work with his slaves.

The slaves in Dickson County were of the type which the English
traveler, James Stirling, described after his visit to the southern states
during the mid-1850's to observe the slave conditions. He spoke of the
lot of this type as being the best of all slaves. He pictured them as being
somewhere between the house servants and the plantation hands, and
neither spoiled nor abused. Not infrequently the slave lived with his

75. U.S. Census, 1820—Dickson County, Tenn., Schedule I.

76. Corlew Family Bible, in possession of Hubert Corlew, Charlotte, Tenn. The
fecundity of women was not confined to Dickson County or even to the South. In
Vermont families often had ten, twelve, and fifteen children, and in one community
of eight families there were one hundred and thirteen children, of whom ninety-
nine were attending the same school at the same time. In nearby Massachusetts,
Russell Sturgis had sixteen children. Virginia records reveal that families reached
the dozen level frequently and that not a few went beyond. An Iowa farm woman
during this period had twenty-three living children, which Craven states was
"probably exceptional but not unique." Avery Craven, *The Repressible Conflict*
(Baton Rouge, 1939), 44ff.

77. Montgomery Bell was one of the few exceptions. The story is told that Bell,
once seeing a Negro on the road with a fine pair of mules, and recognizing neither
the slave nor the team as his own, offered to buy the mules. The Negro, not
knowing his master, was quick to reply: "Nawsir, these hyar mules belongs to
Marse Bell." Newspaper clipping among Leech Papers, n.d.

master's family, Stirling observed, worked in the fields with him, took an interest in his affairs, and in return, became "objects of his regard." [78]

The will of Elias W. Napier indicates that virtually all his slaves were objects of his regard. The adequate manner in which he described his slave Ephragm indicates that he knew the man well, and the amount of property willed to him shows that Napier thought much of him. Napier stated in his will that he desired to emancipate his "negro man Ephragm who had one eye out . . . [and] in consequence of his faithfulness, honesty, and industry in attending to my business as a teamster" he is granted his freedom and given, together with a slave named Tom Keys, Napier's "best wagon and eight of . . . [his] best mules and Gear." [79] Napier emancipated over thirty slaves by his will, and he was as lavish in his praise and property with the other slaves as he was with Ephragm. To many he gave money. For the "yellow boy Soloman whom I have set free" Napier ordered his executors to provide him with "fifty dollars per annum for his schooling & etc., until he be put to some trade . . ." and to pay him upon his reaching twenty-one years of age "the Sum of Five Hundred Dollars to begin his trade on. . . ." [80]

The will of Joseph Dickson carried a provision typical of the manner in which most of the slaveholders of the county cared for their slaves. It provided that his "old Negro woman, Phillis, remain on the plantation with my wife until her [his wife's] death, after which she is to be supported by my sons Hugh, David, and Molton Dickson." His concern for the welfare and happiness of his slaves is further evidenced by the provision of his will giving his "old Negro fellow called Harry" his choice as to with which of Dickson's sons—Hugh, David, or Molton—he should live his remaining days. [81]

While the planters on some of the larger plantations of the South occasionally built separate churches for the slaves and provided separate ministers, such was not the case in Dickson County. The whites and blacks worshiped in the same church at the same time until late in the slaveholding period. In some of the churches there was a gallery, as in

78. James Stirling, *Letters from the Slave States*, (London, 1857), 291. Cited in Chase C. Mooney, "Slavery in Tennessee," 161.
79. Will Book A, 194.
80. *Ibid.*, 101–107. This will was probated June 12, 1848.
81. Will Book A, 1–2. Joseph Dickson was one of the earliest settlers of the county, and his will was the first to be recorded in the county. He was born and reared in Duplin County, N.C., and lived there until near the turn of the century, supposedly bringing his slaves with him when he came to Dickson County.

the Cumberland Presbyterian Church at Charlotte, but the usual case was an imaginary line draw somewhere in the church, with the Negroes in the rear.

Their position in the church did not prevent them from making the most of their day of rest, however. There was no question at all in their minds that "the Sabbath was made for man, and not man for the Sabbath." [82] Most of them went to great extremes and delighted in cleaning up, taking baths, and making preparations to attend the church services. They would put on their "Sunday best" and go singing to and from the place of worship. [83] Before departure, however, they would be sure to see that the white folks were in their carriage and safely on their way to church. Sarah Ann Hardin (whom the slaves affectionately referred to as "Miss Sar'n") was a particularly lovely Charlotte belle of the 1830's, and every Sunday the Hardin slaves would congregate outside her door and by her carriage to see her mount and ride away to the church. [84]

Many of the Negroes were instructed in religious matters in the home as well as in the church. This had been a custom adhered to from the early days, because of the scarcity of churches. [85] Most of the ministers, like Finis Ewing, [86] one of the founders of the Cumberland Presbyterian Church, preached in favor of teaching the slaves to read, and the *Revivalist*, a denominational paper of the Cumberland Presbyterians, published frequent editorials strongly advocating the same policy. [87] As late as 1850 Christopher Strong, an active member of the Associated Reformed Presbyterian Church, provided in his will that "my wife have those [slave] children, John Wesley and Tennessee, taught to read the Bible. . . ." [88]

On the plantations of the South, the tendency was to look upon the slave as a chattel, but in areas where the average holdings were one,

82. Quotation from Mark 2:27.

83. Bell Irvin Wiley, "Cotton and Slavery in the History of West Tennessee" (thesis, University of Kentucky, 1929), 69–70. Sarah Ann was the daughter of Joab Hardin, who owned more slaves than did the average county citizen. She later married Leonard Lane Leech.

84. Letter from Faustine James Kelly to Mrs. Varina Leech Neely (n.d.), Leech Papers.

85. James Ford Rhodes, *History of the United States from the Compromise of 1850 to the End of the Roosevelt Administration* (New York, 1928), I, 332.

86. An excerpt from one of Ewing's sermons appears below.

87. B. W. McDonnold, *History of the Cumberland Presbyterian Church* (Nashville, 1899), 413–415.

88. Will Book A, 220.

two, and three, as in Dickson County, the slave was given many more of his "natural rights." [89]

From the recorded wills it is evident that the Dickson County slave-owners made a special effort not to separate mother from child, to retain the slave within the family, to see that he or she had a comfortable old age, and to give the slave every consideration possible. If a man's estate was such that he felt that his family could not afford to continue to hold slaves, he sometimes provided that the slaves be given the right to select their new masters.

Occasionally, if a slave was old, the owner would provide for both emancipation and support in old age. Such was the case with John Humphries and many others. Humphries, a justice of the peace and owner of fifteen slaves, in 1826 provided in his will that "my old negro woman Amy . . . is to be permitted to live with which of my children she pleases but not as a slave, and which ever she chooses to live with shall be bound to maintain her as long as she lives but she shall be compelled to live with some of them." [90]

Four years later Moses Fussell provided that after the death of his wife, his "slave man Ben" should not be bound to serve any of his children, but was to have his freedom, and live free with any of his master's children. Provision for his upkeep was to be made from the estate, if such became necessary.[91] Nancy Woodard was another who provided that an old slave should be permitted to choose with which of her children he desired to live. Her "Negro man Moses" was to be permitted, upon her death, to choose which of the children he would serve, but his value should be taken out of that child's part of the estate. She further provided that if Moses did not want to live with any of her children, he was to be sold at public auction.[92]

Many owners took care to prevent the separation of a child from its mother, as did Henry Leek. In 1832 Leek provided in his will that all his Negroes were to be sold but that "those not over 10 [are] to be sold with their mothers." [93] George Tubb, unable to read or write, provided

---

89. Rhodes states that in the rich cotton districts the slave was treated poorly and that when death occurred the loss of property was the only thing bewailed. Slaves were treated best in the border states, he claims. Rhodes, *History of the United States*, I, 308.

90. Will Book A, 30–31.

91. *Ibid.*, 93.

92. Will Book B, 25.

93. Will Book A, 148.

in 1836 that his "negro woman Mary shall not be sold out of the family." [94]

In 1851 William Garrett thought it best to dispose of all of his slaves, but he provided in his will that they were to have the privilege of selecting their masters, and the executors were commanded "to allow them that privilege and to sell them at private sale . . ." [95] although it was quite evident that a much higher price could be gained if they were offered at a public sale.

The will of Joab Hardin, probated in 1852, is a masterpiece of humanity toward his slaves. Although Hardin held many, he is said to have known them all personally and to have held them in high regard. Five slaves, including a mother and infant daughter, were willed to Hardin's minor daughter, Sarah Ann. As guardian for this child he appointed E. E. Larkins, who was commanded not to hire out the five slaves indiscriminately, nor any others which might go to his ward through a division of the estate, but directed Larkins "as far as may be in his power, [to] hire them out at private hiring to humane and just persons, although in doing so he may receive a smaller amount of hire." He further stipulated that when Larkins hired out the slaves, he reserve the right to resume possession of them in case he should think the slaves mistreated. Finally, Larkins was directed to pay Hardin's "old man Sawney" seven dollars annually and also seven dollars to each of the other slaves. The daughter, Sarah Ann, was directed to continue these payments after she became of age. Two of Hardin's slaves were to be sold, and each was to receive five dollars upon sale. Item nine of Hardin's will appointed his father-in-law, Daniel Leech, guardian of his two youngest daughters, Faustina and Lorena, and directed that Leech be governed in hiring out their slaves by the same directions given Larkins. Each of the slaves was to be given five dollars, except those under age, and each daughter was directed to continue the practice upon her becoming of age. His wife was requested to give five dollars annually to each of the slaves willed her "during their natural lives." [96]

Elias W. Napier was another who is remembered for the kind manner in which he treated his slaves, and is mentioned in this respect earlier in this chapter. He was one of several brothers connected with the iron works of the county, and he owned many Negroes. In his will, probated in 1848, he directed that his slaves be given "certain sums of money which may be found in their possession" at his death, and his executors

94. *Ibid.*, 129.
95. *Ibid.*, 227–228.
96. *Ibid.*, 258–259.

were enjoined to protect the slaves in their possession. He emancipated more than thirty blacks through his will, and he provided that each should have money and "bacon, corn or meal, sugar, coffee and salt" sufficient to last him for a year after Napier's death.[97]

Christopher Strong is another who must be mentioned in this category. His character and his work at emancipation are discussed later in this study.[98]

It would be folly to conclude that all the slaves were at all times treated humanely. In the minds of some the slave was merely chattel and was to be considered as any other piece of property. The civil law considered him chattel, while the common law looked upon him as a person, and these two systems were interwoven in Tennessee so that the Negro had some of the restrictions, privileges, and immunities of both legal systems.[99] As chattel he was nothing more than personal property; he could not hold real or personal property, enjoy political rights, contract a civil marriage, control his time and labor or even his movements about the country.[100] He was subject to whippings and floggings, and this took place occasionally among Dickson County slaveowners. In the early history of the state the slave could sue for his freedom and could be held responsible for murder, arson, rape, and could be tried by jury. Tennessee was one of five states which allowed a slave to be tried by the twelve men good and true.

The first major trial involving a slave in Dickson County occurred in 1833. One Wiley had murdered William C. Bird, a slaveholder and a member of the patrol. Just what provoked Wiley to such wrathful conduct is not known, but justice was swift and sure. He was tried by a jury which, after hearing three days of argument, rendered a decision of guilty and recommended death by hanging. At this time few hangings, if any, had occurred within the county, and a set of uprights with a cross bar had to be hastily constructed. Wiley was executed on December 28, 1833, in a creek bottom area about one-half mile east of Charlotte.[101]

97. *Ibid.*, 191.

98. Dorsey L. Castleman, local historian, states that the reason for Strong's emancipation of his slaves was because of the intensity of the "deep-rooted sympathetic compassion that dwelled in his heart toward the many slaves he owned." Dorsey L. Castleman, "Story of Christopher Strong, Revolutionary Soldier, Citizen," *Dickson County Herald*, September 27, 1946.

99. Mary Wagner Highsaw, "A History of Zion Community in Maury County, 1808–60," *Tennessee Historical Quarterly*, V (1946), 132–133.

100. *Ibid.*, 132.

101. Goodspeed, *History of Tennessee, Dickson County*, 929–930.

Other trials in the county involving Negroes occurred occasionally thereafter. In 1838 Jacob Voorhies, a white man, was convicted of assault and battery upon the person of a slave named Daniel. The style of the indictment, representative of criminal indictments of the day, is of interest:

> . . . Jacob Voorhies . . . in the County of Dickson . . . with force and arms Maliciously and without any sufficient cause then and there did Commit an assault and Battery in and upon the body of a certain Negro slave the property of Elizabeth D. Collier, Lucy Ann Fletcher, Margaret Fletcher, Caroline Crawford, and Robert Collier, by Name Daniel, then and there ill treat him with fists, sticks, fist, whips, stones, staves, etc., and other wrongs and injuries to the said Daniel, then and there did to the great damage of the said Daniel Contrary to the statutes in such Cases Made and provided to the evil example of all Others in like cases offending and against the peace and dignity of the state.[102]

Voorhies was convicted and fined ten dollars.

Two years later, in another trial involving a slave, Mark Robertson was sued for four hundred dollars by Thomas Wynn, on a charge alleging Robertson to have shot and killed Wynn's "Black Man" and shooting and wounding another "Black Man" belonging to Wynn. A jury sustained a plea of not guilty.[103]

The slaves were at times mistreated, but some owners within the county felt an occasional flogging to be justifiable. John Eubank, for many years a member of the state legislature, in a letter written to Joab Hardin dated January 8, 1846, indicated that flogging of recalcitrant slaves was a practice not unknown to him: "On my return home yesterday Evening from Town to my astonishment your Boy Jack had left. his conduck had been such in the course of the day that he thout I would flog him when I got home. . . ."[104]

As has been pointed out, Montgomery Bell, the iron magnate, in 1807 offered a two-hundred-dollar reward for the apprehension of a runaway slave who ". . . expected punishment." [105]

Frequently the slaves were taught trades. In an advertisement in the *Impartial Review and Cumberland Repository* Thomas Overton indicated that he had in his possession several Negroes who had "skills" above that of common laborer, including "sawyers, a black smith, stone

---

102. Minutes, Circuit Court, (1830–38), 10. Much of the verbiage has been removed from modern criminal indictments.
103. Minutes, Circuit Court, (1839–45), 150–151.
104. Letter among Leech Papers.
105. See note 21.

mason, and a segar maker." [106] Of the semi-skilled laborers, perhaps that of blacksmith was most common. Many of the Negroes made exceptionally good blacksmiths, and such a skill was essential to a well-rounded plantation, iron forge, and furnace, or to a community. Slaves were not used to any great extent in the skilled occupations, white labor dominating this field. As a general rule, slaves were used chiefly for rough work.[107]

A frequent practice in Dickson County, as it was over the South, was that of hiring out slaves. Practically no occupation was omitted, and the price paid for the use of a Negro varied with the type work he did, the supply and demand of labor, and the price of the goods which the Negro helped produce. Generally, the slave when hired received treatment comparable to that which he received when worked by his master. While some owners would mistreat slaves as they would any other property, the thought that they had put up bond and were financially responsible for the health and welfare of the hired Negro was generally enough to strengthen sufficiently the restraining hand. The slave could not be hired lawfully without the consent of his master, and as a general rule the hirer was required to give bond and security for the slave while in his keeping. If the slave became sick and died, or ran away, the hirer was still under a legal duty to perform his part of the contract, unless the contract stipulated the contrary, even if the contract was for a year and the misfortune occurred the day after hiring.[108] State Representative John Eubank, who had rented a slave who showed an inclination to run away, no doubt had this in mind when he wrote the owner concerning the slave: "I think you had better Take him in Hand your Self as I think from his conduck that he does not want to Life with me. . . ." [109]

It was generally understood that those renting the slaves would provide them with the necessities of life such as food, clothing, and bedding. Occasionally such stipulations appeared in the contracts to rent. In 1839, when William Corlew rented out several slaves, he stipulated in the contract that the renters were to "further agree to furnish . . . [the slaves rented] . . . one summer and two winter suits of clothes, one

106. December 31, 1807.
107. Abernethy, *Frontier to Plantation*, 286.
108. Hicks *v.* Parham, 4 Tenn. 224. In this case the court stated in the opinion: the temporary owner "is substituted [for the time the Negro is hired] . . . in place of the absolute owner, and is subject to all the duties and to all the casualties which may happen in that time, so far as his interest reaches, unless there be stipulations in his favor to the contrary."
109. Letter from John Eubank to Joab Hardin, January 8, 1846, Leech Papers.

wool hat and blanket."[110] When hired to work at the iron furnaces in the county, the slaves fared even better, there receiving the usual provisions plus the services of a physician who was hired by the year to care for the health of the laborers.[111] The necessities given at the furnaces usually consisted of two or three suits of clothes, a hat, shoes, and blanket, with an overcoat being given the teamsters during the winter months. Work on Sunday and beyond the regular hours during the week generally brought to the slave additional remuneration. A weekly ration would consist of seven pounds of bacon, a peck of meal, and a quantity of molasses.[112] Often the slaves would trade their rations to white people living in the communities for produce of various sorts.[113]

The usual price in Tennessee for the labor of a slave for a year was eighty to a hundred dollars, in addition to the necessities provided the Negro.[114] The price, of course, varied considerably with the skill, age, and sex of the Negro. At the iron furnaces slave labor often brought more than this, due to the fact that the work was more difficult and often required a knowledge of certain skills and techniques. The furnaces in Dickson County paid from one to two hundred dollars at one period during the development of the iron works, and the labor of a few of the skilled workers brought even more.[115]

Quite often the slaveowner would advertise his slaves for hire in the newspapers, as would employers seeking to hire slaves. Thomas Overton, of Sailors' Rest, advertised in a Nashville newspaper in 1807 that he had "Negroes of several descriptions, to hire. . . ."[116] The following year Montgomery Bell, then at Cumberland Iron Works, inserted the following advertisement in the same paper: "Want to hire eight or ten negro fellows by the year for which I will give a generous price. . . ."[117]

Hiring out sometimes had its problems, slaveholders learned. William Corlew was forced in 1839 to sue certain operators of the Jackson Iron Works on Yellow Creek for his rent money.[118] The following October when the court again convened Richard Napier brought suit against

110. Minutes, Circuit Court (1839–45), 197–198.
111. Mockbee's statement, 1915, Cook Papers.
112. *Ibid.*
113. *Ibid.*
114. Abernethy, *Frontier to Plantation*, 286.
115. Mockbee's statement.
116. *Impartial Review and Cumberland Repository*, December 31, 1807.
117. *Ibid.*, March 10, 1808.
118. Minutes, Circuit Court, (1839–45), 197–198.

George F. Napier to recover fifty-one dollars "for the hire of Negro Man Jim . . . for one Month and four days." [119]

Many of the wills stipulated that certain slaves were to be hired out for specific purposes, not a few specifying that the money received was to be used for the education of the slaveowner's children. Such was the case with Joseph Dickson, who, in 1804, provided that his "young negro fellow called Virgil" be hired out for ten years, and the money received therefrom be used for educating and clothing Dickson's three sons.[120] In 1820 William Norris provided that his children were to be educated on the income received from his slaves.[121]

EARLIER ATTITUDES TOWARD SLAVERY, 1803–31 [122]

From the beginning of slavery in Tennessee, anti-slavery sentiment was to be found. It rested with a small minority, to be sure, but a determined one, while the great majority of the people did not take an active stand either way. Many (both slaveholders and non-slaveholders) desired emancipation, and as late as 1834 most of those who owned slaves hoped that some method of emancipation would be devised.[123]

Like the rest of the people of the South, Dickson Countians in these early years viewed slavery as a necessary evil, with church leaders being more zealous than others in advocating freedom for the blacks. Shortly after the establishment of the county, provision for emancipation began to appear in a few of the recorded wills. Those of Levin Dickson and Thomas Richardson are typical. Dickson, a slaveholder of moderate means and a clerk of the Turnbull Baptist Church session, in 1815 stipulated in his will that his "negro man Tom" was to be emancipated upon the death of his wife.[124] The following year Richardson, who owned four slaves, asked that the executors see that his "negro man be given up when his time . . . [expires]. . . ." [125] John Humphreys, in 1826, provided for his slave Amy to be emancipated in a qualified sense. He stipu-

---

119. *Ibid.*, 201.
120. Will Book A, 1–2.
121. *Ibid.*, 12.
122. In order that continuity in showing the change in denominational attitudes might be achieved, this chapter contains attitudes of the leading Protestant denominations in Dickson County from 1803 to the time of the Civil War.
123. Patterson, *Negro in Tennessee*, 176.
124. Will Book A, 18.
125. *Ibid.*, 25.

lated in his will that she "be permitted to live with which of. . . . [his] children she pleases, but not as a slave and which ever she chooses to live with shall be bound to maintain her as long as she lives. . . ." For her own protection Humphreys added, "but she shall be compelled to live with some of them." [126] A few others, not desiring to burden their heirs with blacks and being unwilling to emancipate, provided for the sale of their Negroes. Others provided for their sale upon the death of a stipulated heir. For example, Reaves Adams, who owned a small farm and one slave, provided that the slave should remain with his wife "during her [his wife's] natural life," but should be sold at her death rather than be bequeathed to his heirs.[127] The majority of the slaveholders of the county, however, tended to pass the slaves down to their heirs. Joseph Dickson, an uncle of Congressman William Dickson for whom the county was named, was one of them. He owned sixteen slaves, and in the first recorded will of the county he bequeathed all his blacks to his children.[128] Others followed suit. In 1821 William Hudson left "one negro girl . . . one Horse, and a cow and a calf . . ." to one daughter, and "one Negro girl named Elize and one Horse . . ." to another daughter.[129] Milton Loftis, a moderately prosperous farmer who owned four slaves in 1825,[130] Ann Marsh, who had four blacks in 1822,[131] and John Reynolds, who owned two slaves in 1825,[132] were typical small slaveholders who left Negroes to their wives and children. George Ross owned forty-seven blacks in 1828 [133] and James Goodrich had thirty at about the same time,[134] but neither made provision for sale or emancipation of any type.

While most of the owners stipulated that their slaves were to be sold, emancipated, or bequeathed to heirs, others used their wills to provide for the purchase of slaves. Early in 1822 John Hall, a farmer of moderate means, provided for the raising of five hundred dollars "which sum," he stipulated, is "to be appropriated to the purchase of a negro boy for the support of my wife and the raising [of] my youngest children." [135] In August of the same year Adam Wilson requested his executors "to

126. *Ibid.*, 56.
127. *Ibid.*, 28–29.
128. *Ibid.*, 1.
129. *Ibid.*, 35.
130. *Ibid.*, 78.
131. *Ibid.*, 74.
132. *Ibid.*, 80.
133. *Ibid.*, 88.
134. *Ibid.*, 45.
135. *Ibid.*, 42–43.

purchase a negro girl for the use of my wife Margaret with the money Thomas Parkes is due me when collected." [136]

An interesting point is the apparent effort toward equality of division which owners sought to achieve in bequeathing slaves to their children. Most of those who had children and slaves were careful to see that each child received at least one slave. John Humphreys, who bequeathed two slaves to his son Horatio and only one each to his other children, was careful to explain his action: "Now the reason of my gifting my son Horatio Humphreys with this negro girl China [in addition to another stipulated in another part of the will] is on account or consequence of his son, my little grandson, Benjamin Humphreys who measurably has but the use of one of his Arms, and in some measure his having so many children. . . ." [137]

The abolition attack which began in Tennessee in March, 1819, with the publication of Elihu Embree's Jonesboro *Manumission Intelligencer* seemingly had little or no effect upon slave sentiment in Dickson County until some fifteen years later. Anti-slavery feeling was reasonably strong before the 1830's, not only in Dickson County but also throughout the entire state. In 1823 there were in Tennessee twenty anti-slavery societies with a membership of 600, and between that year and 1830 a peak of twenty-five societies with 1,500 members was attained.[138] By the latter date, however, interest in such organizations was definitely waning, and by 1831 they had become practically nonexistent. The agitation caused by such societies, and by such periodicals as Embree's, which were filled with vituperative attacks against slavery in its every form; the Nat Turner insurrection, which implanted fear in the hearts of many; the shifting of the center of population in Tennessee to an area where slavery was more profitable; and a recognition of the necessity for a defense of the institution, which defense was already in a formative stage throughout slaveholding states—all were factors which tended to drive anti-slavery minds into pro-slavery camps in the South. These factors, and others rapidly becoming equal in importance, will be mentioned further on in connection with later attitudes toward slavery in Dickson County.

Throughout the land the churches took a conspicuous part on both sides of the slavery issue. For this reason it is necessary to examine briefly the denominational attitudes.

Church leaders in Dickson County were generally emancipationists.

136. *Ibid.*, 61.
137. *Ibid.*, 59.
138. Mooney, "Slavery in Davidson County," 68.

Many were at first quite ardent in their desire to "cease the traffic in human flesh and human souls," [139] but as the northern abolition crusade waxed warm, and as the clergy itself was vehemently attacked by Garrison and others, extreme emancipation feeling began to wane. This is best illustrated by an examination of the attitudes of the ministers and laymen of the Cumberland Presbyterian Church, a frontier denomination founded about seven miles south of Charlotte.

The Cumberland Presbyterian Church was an outgrowth of the Great Revival of 1800 and had sprung from a faction of the Presbyterian Church which felt that the traditional denomination was failing to meet the needs of the people.[140] This schism arose between those who advocated active participation in the revival and those who opposed it, and later questions of ministerial ordination, classical education for ministers, and doctrine developed to emphasize the divergence.[141] Dickson County was a part of the Cumberland country where the influence of the Great Revival was most felt, and Samuel McAdow,[142] a Presbyterian minister who favored active participation in the revival, resided in "an unpretending building [a log cabin] about seven miles from Charlotte." [143] It was in his home that the new denomination was officially formed.

McAdow was not a slaveholder, although he had spent all his life in slave states. He had several children, one of which filed a will in Dickson County court showing that he, like his father, did not hold slaves.[144]

McAdow did not enter the anti-slavery crusade with vigor, but his influence was felt in the movement.[145] When he saw that his family might

139. This was a statement of Finis Ewing, a Presbyterian minister and a founder of the Cumberland Presbyterian Church. Franceway Ranna Cossitt, *The Life and Times of Rev. Finis Ewing*, (Louisville, 1853), 273.

140. E. B. Crisman, *Origins and Doctrines of the Cumberland Presbyterian Church* (St. Louis, 1858), 21–22; Thomas B. Campbell, *Studies in Cumberland Presbyterian History*, (Nashville, 1944), 41.

141. Robert E. Corlew, "Birthplace of a Church," *Nashville Tennessean Magazine*, August 17, 1947, 22.

142. The name has been spelled both "McAdow" and "McAdoo." McDonnold and Campbell use the former spelling, while Patterson and others prefer "McAdoo." The family Bible, now in the vault at Bethel College, McKenzie, Tenn., carries entrances of both methods of spelling. The Will Book in which McAdow's son's will is filed spells it "McAdoo."

143. J. B. Logan, *History of the Cumberland Presbyterian Church in Illinois* (Alton, Ill., 1878), 170.

144. Will Book A, 22–24.

145. McDonnold, *Cumberland Presbyterian Church*, 411; Patterson, *Negro in Tennessee*, 132. Patterson exaggerates McAdow's activity when he speaks of McAdow as being "a most outspoken opponent of slavery."

become connected with slavery by marriage or inheritance, he hastily moved to Illinois. McDonnold speaks of McAdow as being "always charitable toward Southern . . . [slaveholders, although] he hesitated not to speak out against the institution which so long oppressed the country." [146]

Two others beside McAdow are given credit for assisting in the founding of the Cumberland Presbyterian Church. They are Finis Ewing and Samuel King, who were not residents of Dickson County but who spent much time in the county on visits to McAdow and in ministerial work. King was never a slaveholder, but Ewing was at the time of the founding of the new denomination. He hastily emancipated his slaves after his entrance into active ministry, and during his years of vigorously propagating the faith he preached boldly against the "traffic in human souls." [147] Ewing was to the young denomination what Jonathan Edwards was to the New England Revival of 1734, and what McGready was to the Great Revival of 1800. He preached in several states and was generally most eloquent on the matter of slavery. Following is an excerpt from one of his sermons in which he vigorously attacked slavery:

> But where shall we begin? O, is it indeed true that in this enlightened age, there are so many palpable evils in the church that it is difficult to know where to commence enumerating them? The first evil which I shall mention is a traffic in human flesh and human souls. It is true that many professors of religion, and, I fear, some of my Cumberland brethren, do not scruple to sell for life their fellow-beings, some of whom are brethren in the Lord. And what is worse, they are not scrupulous to whom they sell, provided they can obtain a better price. Sometimes husbands and wives, parents and children, are thus separated, and I doubt not their cries reach the ears of the Lord of Sabbath. . . . Others who constitute a part of the visible Church half feed, half clothe, and oppress the servants. Indeed, they seem by their conduct toward them, not to consider them fellow-beings. And it is to be feared that many of them are taking no pains at all to give their servants religious instruction of any kind, and especially are they making no efforts to teach them or cause them to be taught to read that Book which testifies of Jesus, whilst others permit, perhaps require, their servants to work, cook, etc., while the white people are praying around the family altar.[148]

This sermon received wide circulation. Later Ewing again lashed out against the institution, stating that he was "determined not to hold, nor

146. McDonnold, *Cumberland Presbyterian Church*, 411.
147. Patterson, *Negro in Tennessee*, 131.
148. Cossitt, *Life of Ewing*, 273. Quoted in McDonnold, *Cumberland Presbyterian Church*, 411, and Patterson, *Negro in Tennessee*, 131–132.

to give, nor to sell, nor to buy any slave for life." [149] Biblical authority was cited for his stand.[150]

Ewing's position on the slavery matter remained the orthodox position of the denomination until the mid-1830's, when a note of conservatism was struck. Fewer of the published sermons contained ideas on abolition, and the general assembly minutes became more tolerant in their attitude.

Within Dickson County many were hearers of the words of Ewing, but not all were doers. The Leech family, for example, were members of Ewing's church and had children named both Finis and Ewing, and the Hardin family were also members. Both families held slaves.[151]

The Reverend Robert Donnell was a Cumberland Presbyterian minister who owned slaves. He taught them from the Bible, called them to family prayer daily, "and spent a season in instructing them in spiritual things." [152] He later sought to emancipate his slaves but was unsuccessful. He then proposed to them that they be sent to Liberia, but they refused to go.[153]

Ephraim McLean, who was ordained in McAdow's cabin on the day following the organization of the Cumberland Presbyterian Church,[154] owned slaves and believed them incapable of carrying the responsibility of freedom. He is said to have emancipated them, only to have them sink into habits of drunkenness and idleness, and to later return and beg McLean to restore them to their former position.[155]

During the period 1830 to 1836 a denominational organ of the church, the *Revivalist*, fiercely attacked slavery. During the period this weekly paper published several editorials on the matter, one of which vigorously criticized the action of the legislature of South Carolina for enacting a law imposing a fine of not more than $100 and imprisonment of not more than six months upon any person who taught a slave to read or write. Although the denomination had no membership in South Car-

---

149. McDonnold, *Cumberland Presbyterian Church*, 411.

150. Ewing stated that he had taken his stand "mainly from the influence of that passage of God's word which says 'Masters give unto your servants that which is just and equal.'" McDonnold, *Cumberland Presbyterian Church*, 411, and Cossitt, *Life of Ewing*, 273. He was quoting from Paul's Epistle to the Colossians, 4:1. Many would have difficulty in stretching their imagination to include this verse in the anti-slavery argument. Also, apparently Ewing would ignore other letters of Paul which seemingly condone slavery.

151. Will Book A, 257–261; Leech Papers.

152. McDonnold, *Cumberland Presbyterian Church*, 412.

153. *Ibid.*

154. Campbell, *Cumberland Presbyterian History*, 84.

155. *Ibid.*

olina, the *Revivalist* exhorted Cumberland Presbyterians to "teach your slaves to read, and give them moral and religious instruction, and they will not only be better men but better servants. . . . If you would not provoke the God of heaven to entail upon us worse than Egyptian plagues, and lead out the oppressed by the hand of a second Moses, don't withhold from the African religious instruction." [156] If the *Revivalist* spoke for the denomination, this position represents a turning point in denominational attitude; a turning from an ardent advocate of emancipation to an acquiescence in a necessary evil. This acquiescence, however, was tempered by the injunction to give the slaves religious instruction and thus avoid a re-enactment of some of the horrors described in the Old Testament.

Many in Dickson County began to heed these instructions and to teach their slaves to read the Bible, although others in the South feared that teaching the blacks to read would be tantamount to exciting an insurrection. Daniel Leech owned a dozen or more slaves, and all were taught to read the Bible. [157] Christopher Strong, an active churchman, was another who believed in having his Negroes taught to read the Bible. [158]

By 1846 the Cumberland Presbyterian Church had expanded westward to the Pacific, [159] and in Dickson County several churches had been erected in addition to McAdow's home, which continued to serve as a place of meeting. Plans were being made at this time to build with slave labor a large brick church in Charlotte, and by the beginning of the Civil War it had been completed, principally by the labor of slaves owned by Leonard Lane Leech and others, and from bricks baked in a kiln near Charlotte operated by slave labor. By this time both the churched and the unchurched in the county were defending slavery.

Within the Cumberland Presbyterian Church the turn to a position of greater toleration of slavery was precipitated by the action of its Pennsylvania Synod, which in 1847 declared, "The system of slavery in the United States is contrary to the principles of the Gospel, hinders the progress thereof, and ought to be abolished." [160] At the next meeting of the general assembly of the church in Memphis in 1848 the denomination hastily disapproved of "any attempt by jurisdictions of the church

156. Quoted in McDonnold, *Cumberland Presbyterian Church*, 413–415.
157. Testimony of elderly citizens of the county. Daniel Leech in 1840 held twenty-three slaves. U.S. Census, 1840—Dickson County, Tenn., Schedule I.
158. Will Book A, 220.
159. McDonnold, *Cumberland Presbyterian Church*, 342.
160. *Ibid.*, 417.

to agitate the exciting subject of slavery," and felt that "the tendency to such resolutions, if persisted in, we believe is to gender strife, produce distraction in the church, and thereby hinder the progress of the Gospel." [161]

While the slavery issue was being debated pro and con on the denominational level, slaves were being accepted into full fellowship in the local churches. They were accepted as responsible human beings, for the salvation of whose souls the church was responsible. They participated in the early camp meetings and attended church with the whites. A special balcony was erected for the Negroes in the new brick church at Charlotte, and for years after Emancipation many of the ex-slaves would continue to attend services.

Negroes who felt the call to preach were ordained by the presbyteries in the same manner as were the whites, except the educational requirements were made more liberal. At the beginning of the Civil War it was estimated that about 20,000 Negroes held membership in the Cumberland Presbyterian Church.[162]

In 1851 the General Assembly adopted an attitude of greater tolerance for slavery by hiding behind the dove of peace. In answer to six memorials on slavery from Ohio and Pennsylvania signed by 150 people, the General Assembly adopted a resolution which became church policy until the Emancipation Proclamation:

> The church of God is a spiritual body, whose jurisdiction extends only to matters of faith and morals. She has no power to legislate upon subjects on which Christ and his apostles did not legislate . . . and we are fully persuaded that legislation on that subject [slavery], in any of the judicatories of the church, instead of mitigating the evils connected with slavery, will only have a tendency to alienate feeling between the brethren . . . instead of censure and proscription, we [should] cultivate a fraternal feeling one toward another.[163]

Thus the Cumberland Presbyterian Church, a product of the frontier and of Dickson County, was at first strongly anti-slavery, but as the abolition movement gained momentum in New England and in East Tennessee, as it appeared that there were many who would abolish slavery regardless of the cost, and since many of the members had now become

161. *General Assembly Minutes*, Cumberland Presbyterian Church (1848), 12–13.

162. Haskell M. Miller, "Institutional Behavior of the Cumberland Presbyterian Church: An American Protestant Religious Denomination (dissertation, New York University, 1940), 40.

163. *General Assembly Minutes*, Cumberland Presbyterian Church (1851), 56–57.

slaveholders, the denomination became more cautious and sought to rationalize on its anti-slavery stand. At all times the Church seemed to look toward ultimate emancipation, but in the interest of peace and brotherly love it sought to cushion the impact by diffusion.

Patterson has referred to the Cumberland Presbyterian Church as having taken "the most sensible position on the slavery question of any of the churches in Tennessee." [164] It recognized that slavery was an evil which had been forced upon the forefathers, and that a violent revolt would be imminent should an attempt be made to abolish the institution by one stroke of the legislative pen. [165]

The Baptist Church was the first religious group to organize a congregation in Dickson County. By 1800 the Baptists had pushed into the Cumberland country and established themselves, and by 1806 they had organized a church on Turnbull Creek about eight miles east of the present location of Dickson.

Although the Baptists as a denomination were anti-slavery, they admitted slaves to membership in their churches. The church on Turnbull Creek admitted slaves to membership on a basis equal with the whites. The records of the church frequently refer to Sister So-and-So, the slave of Brother So-and-So. [166]

There were two methods whereby one might be received into full fellowship of the denomination—by profession of faith (religious experience) and by transfer of letter. Negroes were admitted both ways, the same as whites. For example, in September, 1828, the session received one Carrel Milley "by the information of her master letting us no that she was a member in the state of Virginia and Baptised by a worthy Baptist" with the understanding that her letter would be forwarded from the Virginia church at the earliest possible date. [167] In May, 1844, the church baptized and received into membership "Elias Nappier [Napier's] negrow woman Liza by [religious] experience." [168]

The Negroes were subject to trial before the church session just as were the whites, and both whites and blacks were often cited to appear before the church court—the trial not infrequently resulting in ex-

---

164. Patterson, *Negro in Tennessee*, 136.
165. *Ibid*.
166. "Records of the Turnbull Primitive Baptist Church, 1806–1865," in possession of Henry J. Deal, Burns, Tenn., clerk of the church session. The pages of the record books are unnumbered, but each meeting of the session is dated. Hereafter cited as "Records of Turnbull Baptist Church."
167. *Ibid*., 1827.
168. *Ibid*., May, 1844.

communication. There seems to have been no discrimination, and an offense against God was one which must be punished regardless of who committed it. Members of the church sessions of the day had set themselves up as ordained of God to make sure that disobedience did not go unpunished, and that transgressors might be taught the way of the Lord. Although some churches might draw a color line, there was no segregation when the Lord administered justice through the church sessions. In June, 1816, at the regular meeting of the Turnbull Church session, "Minor Bibb's negro woman" was arraigned on two charges: one, of "Drinking two much and Dancing," and two, of "Keeping Bad hours." The session heard the case but gave no decision at the time, deciding to take the matter under advisement for a while and to render a decision at the July meeting. At the July meeting, however, Bibb was not present, and it was October of that year before the session rendered its decision and proclaimed to all that "the church then considers her no more with us." [169]

The Negroes and whites worshiped in the same building in the Turnbull Church, the front being used for the whites and the rear for the blacks. This practice continued with apparent success until the 1850's, when a slave by the name of Moriah Sellars bumped against Levi Tidwell's wife in an apparently avoidable accident. Friction resulted, the whites thinking the Negroes to be getting a bit too "uppity," and a separate building for the Negroes was erected in a nearby lot.[170]

One of the organizers of the church on Turnbull Creek, the Reverend Garner McConnico,[171] held slaves. McConnico's home was in William-

169. *Ibid.*, June, July, and October, 1816.

170. Henry J. Deal, seventy-five-year-old member, states that his mother witnessed the alleged "bumping."

171. McConnico came to Middle Tennessee from Lunenburg County, Va., leaving his native state in 1795 in an effort to "flee from the Lord." By 1797, however, he was actively ministering in the Cumberland country. He was to the early Middle Tennessee Baptists what the mythical Paul Bunyan was to the Canadian woodsmen. It was boasted among his followers that he could cast out devils and that he had a "voice like a trumpet." On one occasion he was said to have preached to his followers while standing on the opposite side of the roaring Harpeth, when he found that recent rains had swollen the river to a stage past fording. He was said to have preached "with perfect ease, every word being distinctly heard, although the waters of the Big Harpeth were roaring madly."

Although McConnico felt at ease with slave traders, he had little time for those who displayed an excessive amount of emotion at religious services. In his day the backwoodsmen were still feeling the effects of the Great Revival of 1800, from which emerged a religious exercise called the "jerks." McConnico had no sympathy for those who participated in such exercises, and when a "jerker" attended his ser-son County, but he did considerable work in Dickson County and was instrumental in keeping the church members together during the early years. Two bills of sale pertaining to McConnico's slaves are recorded in the Williamson County Minute Book for 1806. In April of that year he bought from Peter Edwards "one negro," and later in the same year he bought of William Pamplin one "Negro slave girl." [172]

Beside the Cumberland Presbyterian and the Baptist churches, the Methodist was the only other religious denomination to make a noticeable degree of progress in Dickson County during the early slaveholding period. As early as 1810 a small band of Methodists had established a log church about three miles south of Charlotte, called the Smyrna Methodist Church, and thereafter the growth of that denomination was quite rapid.[173] The attitudes of the Methodist toward slavery compare favorably with those of the Cumberland Presbyterian and Baptist, which have already been discussed. Unlike the Cumberland Presbyterians, however, the Methodists split in 1844 into the northern and southern branches. No record was left by the Methodist Church concerning attitudes toward slavery within Dickson County, although by 1830 churches had been established on Barton's Creek, Horse Branch, and Harpeth River, in addition to the one mentioned above. No record was found of a slaveholding Methodist minister in the county, but ministers of both the Cumberland Presbyterian and Baptist churches held slaves during the early period.

The attitudes of the people of Dickson County toward slavery were similar to those of the religious denominations. At first little attention was given to the problem of slaveholding. If a man wanted a slave, he bought one as he would other property, and if he desired to emancipate

---

vices and began his strange motions, McConnico was said to have "suddenly made a pause, and with a loud and solemn tone exclaimed, 'In the name of the Lord, I command all unclean spirits to leave this place.'" The jerker immediately became still and the report was spread abroad that McConnico had cast out devils.

The latter story is usually told in connection with McConnico's work in Middle Tennessee. It first appeared in David Benedict's *A General History of the Baptist Denomination in America, and Other Parts of the World* (Boston, 1813), II, 256. Also see "History Big Harpeth (McConnico's) Baptist Church, Williamson County," in Tennessee Miscellaneous Church Records, copied by WPA, in State Library, Nashville, 4; and W. Harrison Daniel, "Frontier Baptist Activities, 1780–1803, Being a Study of Some Aspects of Frontier Baptist Activities, 1780–1803" (thesis, Vanderbilt University, 1947), 55–56.

172. Minutes, County Court of Williamson County, 1800–1812, Vol. 1, Part 1, 191, 235 (WPA copies).

173. Goodspeed, *History of Tennessee, Dickson County*, 938.

or sell the slave, he did so with little thought of the possibility of his actions being subject to censure by others. By 1831, however, the people's attitude toward slavery began to change as they became conscious of the seriousness of the attack upon their way of life.

ATTITUDES TOWARD SLAVERY AFTER 1831

As previously observed, by the 1830's attitudes toward slavery had begun to change. The abolition attacks did much to alter the views of many who before had supported gradual emancipation. By this time Embree had passed away, and Benjamin Lundy, who for a few years published a paper in Greenville called *Genius of Emancipation*, had moved to Baltimore.[174] The influence of such agitators as William Lloyd Garrison, however, was felt during this period, and the caustic comments of Weld, Foster, Bourne, and others did not go unheeded. The bloody insurrection in Virginia, led by the mentally deranged agitator Nat Turner, occurred early in the 1830's and caused many to fear lest such be re-enacted within their own communities. Other factors which in the 1830's helped to drive anti-slavery minds into the folds of the pro-slavery group were: the strong belief in the constitutional guarantee of property rights; the rapid development of the old Southwest, where slave labor seemed necessary; the beginning of a rise in price of both cotton and slaves; and a growing belief that the world depended upon cotton, which, it was thought, could be grown profitably only under the slave system. Within the various communities there were other factors still which were peculiar to those communities alone.

Within Dickson County there were two events which took place in the early 1830's which perhaps did more than anything else to change public opinion and to prejudice local citizens against anything which smacked of incendiary literature and violence designed to influence the slave. One was the murder of a slaveholder and patrol by a black named Wiley.[175] Wiley was a recalcitrant Negro who no doubt had heard of the Nat Turner insurrection and the growing abolitionist activity; on November 25, 1833, he assaulted William Bird, beating him with a club until he died.[176] The slave was arrested shortly thereafter, tried, and sentenced to be hanged. The execution was carried out on December 28,

174. J. W. Patton, "Progress of Emancipation in Tennessee," *Journal of Negro History*, XVII (1932), 94.

175. Brief mention of this occurrence is made above.

176. Goodspeed, *History of Tennessee, Dickson County*, 929–930.

1833, with several thousand onlookers, many of whom were blacks.[177] The other local occurrence which influenced public opinion was the slave insurrection scare of 1835, which involved certain slaves at the iron furnaces in the county. This proposed insurrection is treated more fully later in connection with the insurrection scare of 1856.

Except for the few occurrences mentioned, the blacks seemed to have been quite tractable and obedient throughout the slaveholding period. Shortly after the abolition crusade got underway, however, provisions for the disposition and manner of handling refractory and disobedient slaves began to appear occasionally in the wills. William Morrison's will (written July 5, 1838) provided that if the two slaves which he bequeathed to his wife "should prove to be refractory or disobedient, my Executors are requested to sell such negroes . . . [and] to use their own discretion and make such disposition of a refractory or disobedient servant as they may think best for the benefit of my wife. . . ." [178] On July 10, 1846, Hartwell U. Slayden, a farmer and small slaveowner, wrote in his will that if "any of the negroes become contrary and ungovernable by my companion Jane or by any of my children . . . who are of age to govern and manage slaves, such of the negroes shall be put up and sold to the highest bidder." [179] Three years later, in 1849, William Adams wrote along the same line: "I authorize my Executor that in case my negro man Toby should become contrary or ungovernable to hire and sell him as he may think best. . . ." [180] These were the only wills which make reference to the refractory character of the blacks, and many of the wills indicate that the slaves conducted themselves properly and were loved by their masters.

Few attempts at emancipation were made after 1834. Elias W. Napier, Montgomery Bell, and Christopher Strong, all large slaveholders and wealthy citizens, in their wills provided for freedom for their blacks after that date. But on the part of the small slaveholder—and it is he with whom we are most concerned in a study of slavery in Dickson County—there were virtually no efforts at emancipation after that date.

As was mentioned above, from the early days of the county, emancipation by will was practiced not infrequently. This custom was continued into the early 1830's. Moses Fussell in 1830 provided in his will that

177. *Ibid.*, 930.
178. Will Book A, 66. With only one exception, no mention of refractory slaves had been mentioned in wills prior to this date.
179. *Ibid.*, 178.
180. Will Book B, 1.

"after the decease of my wife Lucy Fussell that my slave man Ben, shall not be bound to serve any of my children. . . ." [181] Fussell did not think the slave capable of shifting for himself, however, and provided that his (Fussell's) children were to take care of him.[182] In 1832 Ransom Ellis had one slave and would leave the question of emancipation for his wife, bequeathing to her "one negro woman named Milly with her future increase [to be] disposed of in such manner as she [his wife] may think proper. . . ." [183] Mary Yarrell in 1831 desired to free her slave, but she felt that out of fairness to her heirs the slave should pay her value in return for her emancipation. The will stipulated:

> I give and bequeath my negro woman named Matilda her freedom at my death when the said Matilda pays over to my Executors the sum of One Hundred Dollars for the express use of my adopted niece Rosanna Gilbert and my niece Tempy Edwards which will be fifty dollars each when the hundred dollars is divided equally between them. Then the said negro woman to be free the residue of her days.[184]

After the mid-1830's the wills indicate more and more a tendency of the slaveholder of the county to dispose of his holdings on the market, rather than to emancipate or bequeath them. Early in 1834 Richard C. Napier, who owned extensive property in both Dickson and Davidson counties, authorized the sale of his "Negro woman Mary, also Negro men, Charles, Speedley, Ivin, Tasberry, Stephen, Shelby, Daniel [and] Morehead. . . ." [185] Joshua White was not willing for his wife to retain his slave longer than two years after his death. He wrote: "I also desire that my Negro woman by the name of Rachel should be sold by my Executors within the limits of two years after my death. . . ." [186] At the October, 1841, term of the circuit court A. C. Hogins and William Phillips filed a petition to sell "a negro Man slave named Jim," [187] and on May 6, 1850, Epps Jackson wrote, "Sell my slaves. . . ." [188]

By 1850 emancipation sentiment resided in the minds of few, if any, so far as the small slaveholder was concerned, and the days of voluntary emancipation were at an end. As mentioned earlier, there were only three slaveholders who emancipated their slaves by will between 1849

181. Will Book A, 93.
182. *Ibid.*
183. *Ibid.*, 100.
184. *Ibid.*, 133–134.
185. *Ibid.*, 106.
186. *Ibid.*, 150.
187. Minutes of the Circuit Court (1839–45), 259.
188. Will Book A, 210.

and 1861. They were Elias Napier, Montgomery Bell, and Christopher Strong, the latter two making attempts at colonization in Liberia. These three men owned more slaves than all the rest of the people of the county together, Montgomery Bell alone owning 300 in 1850.[189] Strong and Bell transported many of their slaves to Liberia. Their attitude toward slavery seemed to be that gradual emancipation was best and that Negroes should be fully informed of the advantages and disadvantages of remaining in slavery in this country and of being free in a colony in Liberia.

Strong, who owned fewer slaves than Bell or Napier, provided in his will that all of his slaves should be informed of the advantages and disadvantages of going to a colony in Liberia, and that each should be given his choice of remaining in slavery or being sent to the colony.[190] He did not feel that they should remain in this country in a free status, and, too, the laws of Tennessee prevented the retention of free Negroes in the state unless a reliable white man would be security for them.[191] Strong further provided that his executor should place those who wished to be free in the hands of the American Colonization Society, which was to make immediate plans for sending them to Liberia. The following years Strong died; his executor did not place the slaves in the hands of the Society, but instead hired one Robert McNeilly, a prominent Dickson County lawyer, to accompany the blacks and assume the responsibility of placing them safely on the Liberian shores.[192] McNeilly, with his odd cargo, sailed from New Orleans the following year. Upon his arrival at Liberia he deposited the Negroes at a small colony with other freedmen, and thereupon he returned to Dickson County to resume law practice. After about three years, however, McNeilly began to receive the "most pitiful appeals" from the group pleading for goods and supplies, but most of all for McNeilly to come for them to take them back to the United States.[193] It was impossible to

189. U.S. Census, 1850—Davidson County, Tenn., Schedule I. Bell was at this time temporarily residing in Davidson County.

190. Will Book A, 220–221.

191. James H. McNeilly, *Religion and Slavery* (Nashville, 1911), 19; testimony of elderly citizens in the county.

192. Dorsey L. Castleman, "Story of Christopher Strong, Revolutionary Soldier, Citizen." Strong apparently invested a considerable sum of money in the project. Leonard Lane Leech, a young man at the time, before his death would bewail the fact that he was first offered the job at "a fee sufficient to retire upon," but declined, as he was afraid to embark upon what seemed to him to be a very perilous journey. Testimony of old citizens in the county.

193. McNeilly, *Religion and Slavery*, 19.

return for them, but from letters it was understood that two or three of the more intelligent ones had appropriated the entire colony, that many had died, and that most of them were on the verge of starvation. Shortly before the Civil War the letters ceased.[194]

Montgomery Bell, who had exploited slaves for their labor and Dickson County hills for its iron ore, two or three years before his death (1855) became imbued with a philanthropic spirit and offered freedom to all his slaves who wished to go to Liberia. At this time he owned more than 300 blacks, some of whom he knew personally. He proposed to them that if they desired to make the trip to Liberia he would pay their transportation and furnish them with enough provisions and food to last for six months.[195] About ninety slaves accepted the offer and assembled in the winter of 1853 in Nashville, where they were joined by other Negroes and transported to Savannah, Georgia. Here, on December 16, 1853, they boarded the brig *General Pierce* and sailed for Liberia. Seventy-three other blacks who were also making the venture departed on the same boat with Bell's Negroes.[196]

Aboard were some of Montgomery Bell's best slaves—some of whom had made cannon balls at Cumberland Furnace for the troops in the Battle of New Orleans. They apparently were quite thrilled with the prospect of freedom and a trip to Liberia. This is evidenced by the report made by the commander of the *General Pierce*, which is concluded with the words of an old Negro who had served Montgomery Bell all his life: "Do write a most loving letter to my old master, and tell him how much we love him, and will never stop thanking to the Lord for his goodness to us." [197]

Elias W. Napier, one of the pioneer settlers of the county, was the other large slaveholder to emancipate his slaves after most others had ceased. Napier had come to the county as a man of moderate means and had made a modest fortune from the iron industry in the county. He wrote his will in 1848 and made provision for the emancipation of thirty-one slaves.[198] He knew all of his slaves quite well and named their occupations within his will, as "Tom Keys my waggoner and overlooker

194. *Ibid.*
195. Old newspaper clipping among Leech Papers. Written by a reporter who had watched the Negroes assemble in front of the First Presbyterian Church, Nashville.
196. Statement by W. McLain in *Journal of the Executive Committee.* Typewritten copy among Leech Papers.
197. *Ibid.*
198. Will Book A, 183–197.

. . . Charity my old Female cook. . . ." [199] Napier was especially anxious to have the part of his will executed which pertained to emancipation.[200] The last item enjoins his executors to meticulously "carry out my views in regard to the several slaves that I have Emancipated in or out of the county of Dickson or state of Tennessee, as the circumstances may require." [201]

Turning now from the philanthropic ventures, let us examine one other factor of a sectional nature which had a profound effect upon southern attitudes toward slavery. This is the proposed slave insurrections of 1835 and, particularly, of 1856. Dickson County slaves played a part in both of them. As noted previously, as early as 1835 there had been rumors of a planned insurrection by the slaves at the Middle Tennessee furnaces, and at Clarksville the fear had become so great that weapons were procured from the armory at the state capitol in order that the feared revolt might be quashed in its incipience.[202] The following year the general assembly of Tennessee passed an act making it an offense punishable by law to circulate printed matter, to make addresses, or to preach sermons which fostered discontent or insubordination among slaves.[203] No violence occurred, and the event is of little significance except for the scare.

For some twenty years after the scare of 1835 the Negroes at the Middle Tennessee furnaces worked peaceably and without manifestations of revolutionary ideas. The year 1856, however, witnessed an event which acted as a catalyst in driving tolerant minds into pro-slavery tents. This was the proposed "Slave Insurrection of 1856," which caused a near panic among whites far and near. The slaves at Montgomery Bell's Cumberland Iron Works were active participants in the planned uprising.

The anticipated revolt was far greater in scope than the one of 1835; it embraced states from Delaware to Texas. It received considerable publicity in the southern press and in such northern newspapers as the *New York Journal*, the *New York Tribune*, and the *Evansville Journal*. Even the *Manchester* (England) *Guardian* gave the matter some public-

199. *Ibid.*, 183. The names of some of Napier's slaves are of interest: Thomas Benton, William Carroll, James Monroe, and Andrew Jackson.

200. In view of the state laws against emancipation mentioned above, question arises as to how Napier intended to accomplish his purpose. No mention of such is made in the will.

201. Will Book A, 193.

202. Ulrich Bonnell Phillips, *American Negro Slavery* (New York, 1918), 485–486.

203. *Acts of Tennessee*, 1836, ch. 44, sec. 2; Patterson, *Negro in Tennessee*, 49.

ity.[204] The entire iron district on the Cumberland and Tennessee rivers received a scare at this time, and one writer has referred to this area, particularly Montgomery and Stewart counties, as being "perhaps the most terror-stricken community of the entire South in 1856." [205]

The furnaces were several miles apart, and in some areas the Negro population greatly outnumbered the whites. At Louisa Furnace in Montgomery County a keg of powder was found under a church. Nearby a Negro named Britton was heard haranguing a group of blacks—presumably inciting them to insurrection—and upon his failure to obey an overseer's order to desist, he was shot.[206] According to a Nashville newspaper the slaves were being organized as "generals" and "captains" and were planning an insurrection on Christmas Day, at which time they were to march on Clarksville, capture the town, plunder its banks, and then flee to free territory in the North.[207] The patrol at Clarksville was strengthened, and it was reported that in every household there were ample arms and ammunition for any emergency.[208] Ironmasters throughout the vicinity were notified by the Clarksville city council on December 17 that no visiting slave would be permitted to remain in the town for more than two hours unless accompanied by a "responsible white person." In case this ordinance was violated, the slave was to be given twenty lashes.[209]

At nearby Dover the people were also in a state of panic and were reportedly well armed. Just north, in Christian County, Kentucky, a vigilance committee issued a Macedonian call, appealing to the "gentlemen from Hopkinsville" for aid and stating that "from reliable information we expect an attack from the negroes of the Iron works on our town tomorrow morning, perhaps tonight. Please come to our assistance." [210] The committee added that from "reliable information" it had been learned that the Negroes of "Eclipse, Clark, and Lagrange [these were iron furnaces] have united and are marching toward Dover and were within eight miles of that place when last heard from. Their intention is to relieve the negroes at Dover, then march to the Rolling Mill, then to

204. Harvey Wish, "The Slave Insurrection Panic of 1856," *Journal of Southern History* (1939), 206ff.

205. *Ibid.*, 210.

206. *Ibid.*

207. *Ibid.*; *Nashville Banner*, November 27, 1856, cited.

208. *Ibid.*

209. *Ibid.*, 211; *Baltimore Sun*, December 18, 1856, cited.

210. *Ibid.*, 213, quoting *Lexington Observer and Reporter*, December 10, 1856.

the Bellwood Furnace, then through Lafayette [in Christian County Kentucky] on to Hopkinsville and the Ohio River." [211]

In Nashville the city council found it necessary to increase the slave patrol for both night and day duty; Negro schools and churches were temporarily forbidden to operate, and all Negro assemblages after sundown were prohibited.[212]

The proposed uprising was ruthlessly brought to a close following a confession of a slave who had been employed at Montgomery Bell's Cumberland Iron Works and who had escaped from the furnace in order to avoid taking part in the conspiracy. His revelations were such as to cause the immediate arrest of nearly eighty blacks, "almost all of whom avowed their complicity in the plot and even gave the most precise details as to the execution of their project." [213] Jails of all the counties in Middle Tennessee were crowded, and nineteen slaves were eventually hanged at Dover.[214] In Dickson County at the Cumberland Iron Works some sixty slaves, some of whom belonged to Senator John Bell,[215] were implicated, and nine were hanged. Five of the nine were executed by a mob.[216]

The panic resulted in a serious financial loss for the furnace owners and operators, and twenty-five furnaces were forced to cease operation temporarily due to the widespread paralysis.[217]

The ruthless manner in which the proposed insurrection was put down well indicates the extent to which fear had gripped the hearts of the people. By 1857 the atmosphere was ripe for exaggerated tales of all kinds concerning slave uprisings, and there no longer could be doubt as to how people of Dickson County and Middle Tennessee felt about slavery.

While noting the change in attitude of the people of Dickson County, it is interesting to also examine briefly the attitude of the northern press on the matter of the proposed insurrection.[218]

211. *Ibid.*, 213–214; *Lexington Observer and Reporter*, December 10, 1856, cited.

212. *Ibid.*, 212.

213. *Ibid.*, 211; *Baltimore Sun*, December 13, 1856, cited.

214. *Ibid.*; *Baltimore Sun*, December 15, 1856, cited.

215. Bell was said to have lost some $10,000 in the insurrection panic.

216. Patterson, *Negro in Tennessee*, 50.

217. Wish, "Slave Insurrection Panic," 212.

218. Publications cited in this discussion of the insurrection have not been examined by the writer, and all of the material is taken from Wish's "The Slave Insurrection Panic of 1856."

The *New York Tribune* literally clapped its hands in glee at the proposed insurrection, thundering, "Let the South with her growing insurrection look to it. . . . The manacles of the slave must be stricken off." [219] The Boston *Liberator* stated that "revolution is the only hope of the slave; consequently the quicker it comes, the better." [220] The *New York Herald* was one of the few northern papers to express sorrow over the insurrection as it chided the *Tribune:* "It is painful to see the apparent gusto with which our nigger-worshipping contemporary of the *Tribune* gloats over the news of the projected Southern servile insurrection." It further expressed its disgust for Thurlow Weed's *Albany* (New York) *Journal,* which allegedly viewed the panic with "something of a chuckle of satisfaction." [221]

The *Maryville* (Tennessee) *Eagle* carried an article on November 1, 1856, in which it was stated that it would "rejoice in a successful slave insurrection which would teach slaveholders the wrong and danger involved in the act of slaveholding." [222]

SLAVEHOLDERS NO SOCIAL CLASS

As mentioned earlier, many antebellum writers and travelers to the South sought to leave the impression that there was a wide social gap between the slaveholder and the non-slaveholder which tended to foster a spirit of antagonism between the two groups. The questionnaires on social and cultural conditions of the South (usually referred to as the Moore Questionnaires) [223] collected by the late John Trotwood Moore reveal that there was little or no antagonism or distinction between the slaveholder and the non-slaveholder in Dickson County. Thirty Confederate veterans from Dickson County filled out the questionnaire forms,

219. December 13, 1856. Cited *ibid.,* 22.
220. March 13, 1857. Cited *ibid.*
221. December 11, 1856. Cited *ibid.*
222. Cited *ibid.*
223. In the early 1920's the late John Trotwood Moore, former Tennessee state librarian, sent a questionnaire to all veterans of the Civil War residing in Tennessee. The form included questions concerning ownership of property, general domestic conditions, and the relations between the slaveholder and the non-slaveholder, among others. Mr. Moore was attempting to obtain firsthand information as to what slavery in the antebellum South was actually like, and from this information he planned to write a social and cultural history of the antebellum South. Although these questionnaires, deposited in the State Library, Nashville, must be used with care since they were returned by old men some sixty to seventy-five years after the time of which they write, many writers have found them to be fairly reliable sources for the study of general conditions.

and what they reveal is the basis for the following discussion. In using this information one should bear in mind that the ratio of the slaveholding families to the non-slaveholding families was about one to four during the period covered in these recollections.

A feeling of superiority on the part of the slaveholder was not present in Dickson County; there seemed to be no line drawn between those who held slaves and those who did not. If a farmer had been reasonably successful and desired to spend his money for a few slaves, he made the purchase with no apparent thought of putting himself into another social class. The acquisition of a new slave seemed to be similar to purchasing a new mule or building a new barn; if any feeling of superiority existed, it was perhaps because of economic superiority rather than because of the mere fact that one had slaves and the other did not.

In reply to the query, "Did the men who owned slaves mingle freely with those who did not own slaves, or did slaveholders in any way show by their actions that they felt themselves better than respectable, honorable men who did not own slaves?" most gave an emphatic answer quite like that of Moses Garton, who replied, "There was no difference made between the men who owned slaves and those who did not." A few gave qualified answers; Elias N. Cathey replied: "In most cases slaveholders mingled freely with non-slaveholders but in rare instances a slaveholder seemed to think himself above a non-slaveholder." James K. Clifton, whose father owned one slave, replied: "None seemed to feel themselves better simply because they owned slaves."

To the question, "At the churches, at the schools, at public gatherings in general, did slaveholders and non-slaveholders mingle on a footing of equality?" all answered in the same vein as did G. H. Cline: "Slaveholders and non-slaveholders mingled freely. There was a general good feeling between non-slaveholders and slaveholders." A similar response was given in answer to the question, "Was there a friendly feeling between slaveholders and non-slaveholders in your community, or were they antagonistic to each other?" All of the replies indicate that if a candidate for public office in the county owned slaves, it made little or no difference one way or another so far as his vote-getting power was concerned.

The replies to the questionnaires indicate without exception that those who owned slaves aided and encouraged the young men of the time to work toward prosperity. Of the thirty men from Dickson County who replied to the questionnaires, none was over thirty years of age at the time of the war. Each replied that the opportunities in the community were good for a poor young man, who was honest and industrious, to save up enough to buy a farm or go into business for himself, and that young men, ambitious to make something of themselves, were encouraged by the slaveholders.

Those who held slaves worked by the side of the Negro, and everyone had to work for a living. To the question, "How was honest toil regarded in your community?" all replied that it was regarded as honorable. To the question, "To what extent were there white men in your community leading lives of idleness and having others do work for them?" most answered "none," while a few offered a brief explanation, as did James K. Clifton: "Then as now there were idlers, who expected others to work for them. These idlers were not confined entirely to slaveholders or non-slaveholders. There were some worthless nobodies in both classes, but none seemed to feel themselves better simply because they owned slaves."

Thus the questionnaires would indicate that there was little or no class distinction in Dickson County based solely on the ownership of slaves. This does not mean, of course, that there were no social distinctions among these people. Economic differences invariably cause social differences, and Dickson County was not immune to such custom. But the Moore Questionnaires do reveal that feelings of superiority were generally based upon economic ability and not upon ownership of slaves.

One historian has found that throughout the South there were occasional examples of antagonism between slaveholder and non-slaveholder.[224] She has traced this feeling to the poor non-slaveholder who, prompted by a feeling of inferiority, hesitated to approve in any way his wealthy neighbor who for economic reasons failed to share his interests.[225] This historian has further found that some of the worst snobs were owners of two or three slaves who, prompted by a sense of inferiority, sought to buy their way into what they felt to be a "slaveholding aristocracy." [226] However, this study on slavery in Dickson County has revealed no basis for a similar conclusion, despite the fact that of those who held slaves, more held one, two, or three than any other number.

The attitudes of citizens and church groups in the county were such as to admit that slavery was an evil, but to produce no panacea for its cure except through gradual and compensated emancipation and colonization outside the limits of the country wherever possible. Many felt

224. Blanche Henry Clark, *The Tennessee Yeoman, 1840–1860*, (Nashville, 1942), 12.
225. *Ibid.*
226. *Ibid.*

that the slave should be given his "natural rights" as rapidly as his evolution would permit, but first and foremost came the welfare of society as a whole.

By 1862 federal troops had occupied Dickson County and established "Camp Charlotte" at the county seat.[227] For all practical purposes the days of slavery were over, but they were not officially ended until 1865, since Tennessee was not a part of that territory covered by the Emancipation Proclamation. Before the ignorant blacks could learn what the long-promised millennium was, messiahs in the forms of crooks with carpetbags had descended like locusts upon them, and with more suaveness than a Dale Carnegie were instructing them in courses which might well have been termed "From Cannibalism to King in Five Short Generations." The superiority of the type of slavery from which he was emancipated to the type in which he subsequently found himself sent "Uncle" Carroll Leech and many others scurrying back to spend their remaining days with their former masters.

227. Goodspeed, *History of Tennessee, Dickson County*, 936.

Lyle Wesley Dorsett

Slaveholding in Jackson County, Missouri

Historians usually consider Missouri a border state and Jackson County (in its northwestern corner) a peripheral part of southern society. Nonetheless Jackson County's slaveholders were as zealous in their defense of the peculiar institution as were the most impassioned ideologues of the Deep South. Proximity to anti-slavery appears to have strengthened their commitment to it. The history of pro-slavery feeling in this county parallels that of other areas in the upper South. In the older parts of the upper South, where the institution was not as profitable as in Jackson County and where the community's commitment to it was not as profound, contact with abolitionists produced a similar response. In many cases this reaction was the decades-long legacy of fear of slave uprising. In other cases it was the result of racial bitterness which had little to do with the institution itself. In all cases it was the Negro, slave or free, who suffered. The "ultras," as contemporaries called extremists of either side, helped reverse social and political trends which would have made these areas more forthright in their defense of the Union and their opposition to secession. Jackson County was unique because it bordered the Kansas Territory, and its contact with anti-slavery zealots was almost continuous after 1854. But the tendency here for hostility to breed intransigence augured ill for efforts at moderation throughout the South.

Slaveholding in Jackson County determined class arrangements as it did elsewhere in the South, but it seemed to affect status and social etiquette far less. Southern paternalism was not merely an attitude towards one's slave but a social posture, and it is absent from Jackson County. Slaveholding deprived of paternalism emerges much more sharply as an economic venture, and the community appears as a more strikingly competitive one. The non-slaveholder who wrote to his brother in 1858 that the slaveholders of Jackson County were "some of the meanest people who ever trod this earth" perceived just this acerbity of the marketplace. Indiscriminate border warfare did nothing to make such men less mean. Men

Reprinted with permission from the *Missouri Historical Society Bulletin*, XX (1963), 25–37.

who fear the loss of their property seldom have time for social amenities.

The fertile valleys of the Kaw and Missouri rivers, as well as the wood-covered bluffs and hills surrounded by rich, rolling plains, all shared in attracting settlers to Jackson County, Missouri. Located on the border of the Kansas Territory in the northwest part of the state, Jackson County, during the four decades before the Civil War, served as a magnet for settlers from the east, and particularly from the slave states of Kentucky, Virginia, Tennessee, and North Carolina, which furnished the majority of the county's population born outside Missouri.[1]

Many of the migrants who came to the area brought not only their household goods and their livestock, but also their slaves. The new settlers succeeded in planting slavery so firmly into the soil of Jackson County that it was not to be uprooted, even in the face of uncommonly constant attacks, without the force of four years of war. The Jackson County slaveowners held tenaciously to their bondsmen because slavery was a thriving and profitable institution in that area of Missouri. Charles W. Ramsdell asserted that by 1860 slavery "was losing ground along its northern border,"[2] but it is clear that slavery was not losing ground in Jackson County. Indeed, by 1860 the slave population was greater than it had ever been previously, slave prices were at their highest level, and the slaveholders were more prosperous than their western Missouri forefathers had ever been. This point can be demonstrated through a discussion of the planting, growth, and ultimate demise of slavery in Jackson County.

Even prior to Missouri's statehood in 1821, Southerners were looking westward. The treasurer of the state of Virginia commented in 1816 that "with every intelligent person I have met, and many others, Missouri has been the subject of conversation. I find all have their minds turned that way. I have no doubt but it will be all the rage in two or three years, just like Ohio was ten years ago or less."[3] This Virginian's prediction was nearly accurate, for in just a short time the eastern portion of Missouri began growing rapidly.

1. Jackson County, Mo., *Census of 1850*, abstracted by Hattie E. Poppino (Kansas City: 1959), vii. (Hereafter referred to as *Jackson County, Census of 1850*.)

2. Charles W. Ramsdell, "The Natural Limits of Slavery Expansion," *Mississippi Valley Historical Review*, XVI (September, 1929), 171.

3. Quoted by Ulrich Bonnell Phillips, *Life and Labor in the Old South* (Boston: Little, Brown & Co., 1949), 86.

In contrast to eastern Missouri, the western part of the state did not experience much population growth until the 1830's. Jackson County by 1830 had a total population of only 2,822, with 193 of this total in bondage.[4] These 193 slaves were divided among 62 slaveholders in the county. The largest holder, one William Hudspeth, claimed 25 slaves. The majority of the early Jackson County slaveowners, however, held only two or three slaves.[5]

The 1820's provided little guidance in predicting Jackson County's growth in the following decade. By 1840 the county's total population had almost tripled, and the slaves numbered 1,361.[6] The number of slaveholders had increased to 330, with almost 30 possessing between 10 and 20 slaves. The largest slaveowner by this time, F. K. Cowherd, held 36 bondsmen.[7] Over 40 of the slaveholders by 1840 were pursuing livelihoods along non-agricultural lines, in such areas as the learned professions, manufactures, trades, and commerce. For the most part, however, those slaveowners who were not engaged in agriculture had only one or two slaves.[8]

This marked increase in Jackson County's slave population is understandable when one realizes that the migration of slaveholders into Missouri from the old Atlantic coast slave states did not really gain much momentum until 1830. Frederic Bancroft pointed out that the exhausted fields on the Atlantic seaboard began to take their toll by that date. Thus the lure of fertile land and higher slave prices, as well as the route to Missouri, which "was easy and nearly all by water," started a large migration.[9]

The presence of cheap, fertile land was undoubtedly the major impetus for migration to Missouri, but the high slave prices also played an important role. One student of the antebellum South says that slave prices in the western markets were usually substantially higher than

4. U.S. Department of State, *Fifth Census, A Schedule of the Whole Number of Persons within the Several Districts of the United States*, 1830 (Washington: Duff Green, 1832), 151. (Hereafter referred to as *Fifth Census.*)

5. Jackson County, Mo., *Census of 1830*, abstracted by Hattie E. Poppino (Kansas City: 1956), 26–27. (Hereafter referred to as *Jackson County, Census of 1830.*)

6. U.S. Department of State, *Compendium of the Sixth Census of the United States* (Washington: Thomas Allen, 1841), 90. (Hereafter referred to as *Sixth Census.*)

7. Jackson County, Mo., *Census of 1840*, abstracted by Hattie E. Poppino (Kansas City: 1956), 56–62. (Hereafter referred to as *Jackson County, Census of 1840.*)

8. Compiled from data in *Jackson County, Census of 1840.*

9. Frederic Bancroft, *Slave-Trading in the Old South* (Baltimore: J. H. Furst Co., 1931), 136, 401.

they were in the eastern markets.[10] The high price that Jackson County slaves were bringing in this period is well illustrated by a sale in 1836 of some of the Hambright family's slaves. A young male bondsman sold for $887, and his sister brought $796.[11] U. B. Phillips discovered that in Virginia by 1836 the average price of a prime fieldhand was only $800, and prime women usually sold for one-fourth or one-fifth less. Thus it is clear that at least some of the slaves in Jackson County were selling for a price well above the Virginia average.[12]

An increasing slave population in an environment of fertile land and high slave prices begins to leave one with an impression of Jackson County as the matrix of a slaveholder's utopia. This, however, is only part of the story. With the vast increase in the county's total population in the decade of the 1830's, some problems of great magnitude arose for the proponents of slavery.

One very early problem, a result of the increased migration from the northeastern United States into Missouri, came from the Mormon settlers in Jackson County. First appearing in small numbers in August, 1831, the Mormons numbered nearly 1,200 by 1833. In less than two years the zealous Mormons, who did not try to conceal their abolitionist sentiments, had successfully alienated a large portion of Jackson County's slaveholding population.[13] In July, 1833, there appeared in *The Evening and Morning Star*, a Mormon paper published in Independence, Missouri, an article entitled "Free People of Color." The article cited several clauses of the Missouri statutes which restricted free Negroes from entering the state unless they could produce evidence that they were citizens of one of the several states. The paper asserted that "so long as we have no special rule in the church, as to people of color, let prudence guide. . . ." [14] Many of the settlers interpreted this article as an invitation to free Negroes to enter the state. Considering such an invitation a threat to their slave property, some of the settlers in the county demanded immediate action against the Mormons.

On July 20, 1833, consequently, a group of about five hundred Jack-

10. Alfred G. Smith, Jr., *Economic Readjustment of an Old Cotton State: South Carolina, 1820–1860* (Columbia: University of South Carolina Press, 1958), 28.

11. Bill of sale of the slaves of James Hambright in 1836, in typescript, Box 1, Hambright MSS. Jackson County Historical Society.

12. U. B. Phillips, *American Negro Slavery* (New York: Appleton-Century Co., 1940), 370 and the chart opposite.

13. Louise D. Oliver, "The Mormons and Missouri, 1830–1839" (thesis, University of Kansas City, 1943), 29–36. (Hereafter referred to as Oliver, "Mormons.")

14. *The Evening and Morning Star*, July, 1833, vol. 11, no. 1. A reprint.

son County residents met at Independence to discuss their grievances against the Mormons. In a manifesto which was drawn up and adopted at the meeting, the article entitled "Free People of Color" was interpreted as part of a scheme for "inviting free negroes and mulattoes from other states to become Mormons, and remove and settle among us. . . . [This] would corrupt our blacks, and instigate them to bloodshed." The settlers further declared that for over a year "it was ascertained that they [the Mormons] had been tampering with our slaves, and endeavoring to rouse dissension and raise seditions among them." [15]

The meeting was climaxed by the signing of an ultimatum ordering the Mormons to leave the county immediately. After the ultimatum had been signed, the gathering, which had turned into a mob, marched to the nearby Mormon printing office and presented the document to the men working there. When the Mormons did not promise to leave Jackson County immediately, the shop and printing press were destroyed, and two Mormon men were tarred and feathered. Soon after that incident the Mormons abandoned the community. [16]

The Mormons were not the only spokesmen for human rights in the 1830's. Not long after the slaveholders had driven the Mormons from the vicinity, the fires of abolitionism broke out on another front. The Presbyterian Synod of Missouri in 1835 inaugurated a statewide movement condemning slavery and advocating emancipation with all possible haste. This blaze of abolitionism quickly spread from the Presbyterian to the secular realm, and an attempt was made to call a constitutional convention and abolish slavery in Missouri. The pro-slavery men quickly rallied to smother the anti-slavery flames. When the final vote had been counted, only Jefferson County had cast a majority of its votes for holding a constitutional convention. [17]

Reaction against abolition now set in throughout the state. By 1837 the sentiment had grown strong enough that the Missouri legislature passed an act "to prohibit the publication, circulation, and promulgation of abolition doctrines." [18] Undoubtedly due more to the temper of the times than to a fear of the new law, the anti-slavery impulse waned and

15. Quoted by Harrison A. Trexler, *Slavery in Missouri, 1804–1865* (Baltimore: Johns Hopkins Press, 1914), 122. (Hereafter referred to as Trexler, *Slavery in Missouri.*)

16. Oliver, "Mormons," 45–49.

17. Benjamin Merkel, "The Antislavery Movement in Missouri, 1819–1865" (dissertation, Washington University, St. Louis, 1939), 42–43. (Hereafter referred to as Merkel, "Antislavery in Missouri.")

18. *Laws of the State of Missouri* (City of Jefferson: Enquirer Office, 1840), 3.

did not become a significant force again until sectional controversy grew stronger in the late 1840's.

The dawning of the 1840's, in many respects, brought little change to the institution of slavery in Jackson County. A traveler in the 1830's or 1850's would have seen much the same thing that a traveler named Joel Palmer witnessed as he approached Independence in Jackson County during May, 1845. Palmer, an Indiana farmer, reported that he "traveled about twenty-eight miles, over a thinly-settled prairie county. The crops, cultivated generally by negroes, consisted of hemp, corn, oats, and a little wheat and tobacco." [19]

Throughout the antebellum period slavery in Jackson County, a contemporary reminisced, was always "much more a domestic than a commercial institution." [20] An examination of the Jackson County censuses for 1830, 1840, and 1850 bears out this statement, because these records show that only a small percentage of the slaveholding population held large numbers of Negroes, and a great many owned only one. The historian Harrison Trexler writes that in Missouri "the single slave held by so many persons was usually a cook or a personal servant, or perhaps a 'boy' for all-round work." This practice was prevalent because even if white help had been readily available, it was not congenial. Trexler also shows that Missouri was a state of small slaveholdings by adding that there were only 64 overseers in the entire state in 1850, and only 256 by 1860.[21]

On the basis of this evidence we can see that the plantation system was the exception rather than the rule in Jackson County. This point is well demonstrated by the words of a Kansan who lived near Jackson County, when he recalled that "slavery in western Missouri was like slavery in northern Kentucky. . . . Family servants constituted the bulk of ownership, and few white families owned more than one family of blacks. The social habits were those of the farm and not the plantation. The white owner, with his sons, labored in the same field with the negro, both old and young. The mistress guided the industries in the house in both colors." [22]

19. *Early Western Travels, 1748–1846*, xxx, "Palmer's Journal of Travels over the Rocky Mountains" (Cleveland: A. H. Clark Co., 1906), 33.

20. John G. Haskell, "The Passing of Slavery in Western Missouri," *Transactions of the Kansas State Historical Society*, VII (1902), 31. (Hereafter referred to as Haskell, "Slavery.")

21. Trexler, *Slavery in Missouri*, 18–19, 28.

22. Haskell, "Slavery," 31.

Since the majority of Jackson County slaveholders had so few slaves, the institution in many ways became more patriarchal there than it was in the Deep South. The bond between master and slave often became very close. A man from Independence remembered how his grandfather had written in his will that the slaves he held were to be kept in the family and never sold. His instructions were followed until the Civil War.[23] This strong bond between master and slave, however, did not exist in all cases. The continuous use of the threat of being "sold down South" to keep the slaves on their best behavior often became a reality rather than a mere threat.[24] An English traveler reported the heartbreaking story he heard from a young Missouri slave about how her master had sold her three daughters.[25] While travelers sometimes wrote what people wanted to read rather than what they actually saw, we know that many slaves were torn away from their families. After the death of J. K. Thompson in September, 1853, the Jackson County Court partitioned his twelve slaves among his several heirs, thereby completely breaking up the slave family.[26]

We have seen how some aspects of Jackson County slavery during the 1840's epitomized the years before and after that decade. The 1840's, however, did more than reflect the past and set the pattern for the future. The years just prior to 1850 ushered in some important changes. For one thing, there was a sharp increase in the slave population. Though numbering only 1,361 slaves ten years before, Jackson County's slave population had grown to 2,969 by 1850, while the total population had not even increased to twice its total of 1840.[27]

A marked change in personal wealth was experienced by many Jackson County slaveowners during this same period. A contemporary remembers that the "early western Missouri slaveholder was a poor man. His wealth at date of settlement consisting mainly in one small family of negro slaves, with limited equipment necessary to open up a farm in a new country."[28] Although the slaveholdings of Jackson County always

23. Trexler, *Slavery in Missouri*, 91.

24. *Ibid.*, 52.

25. Frederick Bremer, *The Homes of the New World* (London: Virtue & Co., 1853), II, 352.

26. Report of the Jackson County Court on the partition of the slaves of the J. K. Thompson estate, Misc. Papers on Slavery, Laura Lyons Papers, Jackson County Historical Society.

27. *Sixth Census*, 90; U.S. Department of State, *Compendium of the Seventh Census* (Washington: A. O. P. Nicholson, 1854), 266. (Hereafter referred to as *Seventh Census*.)

28. Haskell, "Slavery," 31.

remained small when compared to the holdings of many planters in the Deep South, they grew significantly in the late 1840's and into the 1850's. The average slaveholder of 1830 held only two or three slaves, but many slaveholders in the later period possessed between six and ten bondsmen. There were still many with only one slave, but the number of such people had dwindled in comparison with the earlier periods.[29]

Partly due to this increase in the slave population, Jackson County led the state in aggregate wealth by 1850.[30] A Jackson County resident who had moved there from the East looked upon wealth and slaveholding as almost synonymous during the 1850's.[31] A non-slaveholder in Independence wrote to his brother that the slaveholders in the area were "some of the meanest people who ever trod this earth," and went on to say that they had no respect for a man who did not own a sizable number of slaves and "a poor man, a mechanic, is looked upon as no better than a slave." [32]

Another important change that occurred in Jackson County during the 1840's and early 1850's helps explain some of the growth in the wealth and the slave population. It was during this decade that Jackson County, encompassing some of the fertile Missouri River Valley, became one of the principal hemp-producing counties in the state.[33] A rise in hemp production was usually accompanied by a growth in the slave population. The reason for this, according to Kenneth Stampp, was that "free labor avoided the strenuous, disagreeable labor required to prepare the crop for market." [34] Hemp seed was sown in the spring, usually in April or May, and then covered over with a harrow. During the growing season the crop required no cultivation, and the slaves were free to care for other crops. Later summer brought the cutting of the hemp crop, after which it was spread in the fields to dry. It was then tied into sheaves and stacked until November or December, when it was again spread on the fields for "dew rotting," which loosened the fibers. The

29. *Jackson County, Census of 1830; Jackson County, Census of 1850.*

30. Walter H. Ryle, *Missouri: Union or Secession* (Nashville: George Peabody College for Teachers, 1931), 45.

31. Calvin Davis, Independence, Mo., September 5, 1858, letter to brother William, folder: Letters of Iserman and Calvin Davis, Jackson County Historical Society.

32. J. C. Iserman, Independence, October 3, 1858, letter to William, *ibid.*

33. Miles W. Eaton, "The Deveopment and Later Decline of the Hemp Industry in Missouri," *Missouri Historical Review*, XLIII (July, 1949), 357. (Hereafter referred to as Eaton, "Hemp Industry in Mo.")

34. Kenneth M. Stampp, *The Peculiar Institution* (New York: Alfred A. Knopf, 1956), 49.

hemp was then gathered and, according to Stampp, "laboriously separated from the wood with a hand 'brake.' " [35]

Hemp production in Jackson County diminished somewhat in the decade before the Civil War. A student of Missouri's hemp industry states that Jackson County had become a second-rate producer by 1860.[36] The slave population, on the other hand, continued to rise, and by 1860 the bondsmen numbered barely under 4,000.[37]

The late 1840's and 1850's brought other changes which were much more momentous than an increasing slave population and fluctuations in the hemp production. Jackson County had always been surrounded by free territory. Iowa, which became a free state in 1846, was only about ninety miles from the northern boundary of Jackson County. Nebraska Territory was still closer. And Kansas, which was to become a hotbed of abolitionist sentiment by the 1850's, hovered immediately on the western border of the county. This free territory that almost engulfed Jackson County became increasingly hostile during the late 1840's and 1850's as free-soil settlers moved into the area in great numbers, with a resultant marked effect on Jackson County thralldom.

After 1845, and for quite a few years to follow, Iowa brought anti-slavery pressure to bear upon Jackson County and other parts of western Missouri. The Underground Railroad was making many successful runs from Missouri into Iowa. The little town of Tabor, Iowa, close to the Missouri and Nebraska borders, was the destination for many Negroes taken from Missouri.[38] The notorious John Brown and his little band hustled many Missouri slaves there, and one night he was almost caught in Jackson County. Brown managed to escape, but two of his followers were apprehended and jailed.[39]

Abolition activity in Jackson County reached a fever pitch after the passage of the Kansas-Nebraska Act in 1854. The Act, with its clause of "popular sovereignty," brought not only pro-slavery settlers to Kansas,

35. *Ibid.*

36. Eaton, "Hemp Industry in Mo.," 357.

37. U.S. Department of the Interior, *Eighth Census*, Vol. I, "Population" (Washington: Government Printing Office, 1864), 280–281. (Hereafter referred to as *Eighth Census.*)

38. Jacob Van Ek, "Underground Railroad in Iowa," *The Palimpsest*, II (May, 1921), 130.

39. Hildegarde R. Herklotz, "Jayhawkers in Missouri, 1858–1863," *Missouri Historical Review*, XVII (April, 1923), 278–279. (Hereafter referred to as Herklotz, "Jayhawkers in Mo.")

but also many free-soil settlers with their abolition designs.[40] According to one opinion, "the loss of slave-property in Missouri as a result of the increasing number of free-state settlers in Kansas was unbearable."[41]

By March, 1855, a Jackson County judge wrote in his diary that the antipathy on the Missouri-Kansas border was getting very grave. He reported that the abolitionists had so aroused the Missourians that they were holding mass meetings constantly to discuss the situation and make plans to deal with it.[42] Three months later, slaveholding representatives from the eighteen Missouri counties bordering Kansas met in Lexington, Missouri, for the Pro-Slavery Convention of Missouri. Only three counties sent more representatives than Jackson, which sent sixteen. At that meeting the representatives attacked the abolitionists in Kansas and cautioned the National Legislature not to allow Kansas to become a free state if it desired a perpetuation of the Union.[43]

The increasing loss of slave property in Jackson County forced the lawmakers of Kansas City in November, 1855, to revise the city ordinances regarding slaves, free Negroes, and mulattoes. No Negroes or mulattoes could hold assemblages of any kind at night. And all Negroes and mulattoes, whether slave or free, could not be on the streets between 10 P.M. and 4 A.M. without a pass from the mayor, if free, or from the master, if a slave.[44]

The threats offered by Pro-Slavery meetings and revised laws proved ineffective in abating slave theft in Jackson County. From 1855 to the beginning of the Civil War, local newspapers continually reported cases where slaves had been stolen. Not at all uncommon were incidents such as the one reported by the *Daily Western Journal of Commerce*. A Kansas City man heard his two slaves slip out of the house late one night. The slaves had a rendezvous with a group of white men who were going to hurry them over the border to freedom. The scheme was foiled, however, by the slaveowner's aim with his shotgun, which wounded one of the Underground Railroad workers.[45]

At times free Negroes took an active part in the slave-stealing activi-

---

40. Merkel, "Antislavery in Missouri," 172.
41. Herklotz, "Jayhawkers in Mo.," 268.
42. Merkel, "Antislavery in Missouri," 187.
43. "Address to the People of the United States Together with the Proceedings and Resolutions of the Pro-Slavery Convention of Missouri" (St. Louis: Republican Printing Office, 1855), 3–19.
44. *Kansas City Enterprise*, November 24, 1855, 2, col. 5.
45. *Daily Western Journal of Commerce*, July 11, 1860, 3, col. 1.

ties. On December 15, 1855, a free Negro was apprehended in Jackson County with four slaves in his company. According to the *Kansas City Enterprise*, the slaves "doubtless anticipated a hearty reception in the northern states, until their guide . . . was caught and incarcerated." [46] In some instances free Negroes worked with white abolitionists as decoys, to help entice the slaves from their masters. One free Negro in a Jackson County court told how he had worked for a long time with two white men in the slave stealing business.[47]

The activities of the free Negroes caused much alarm in Jackson County, but the potential threat was greatly exaggerated by the proslavery people. The census takers found only forty-one free Negroes in the county in 1850, and that number had grown to only seventy by 1860.[48] An article in a weekly Jackson County newspaper illustrates the unfounded apprehension over the presence of the free Negro. The article, entitled "Free Negroes," pointed out that the annual increase in the number of free Negroes was a problem of grave concern which must be immediately remedied. The free Negroes, according to the newspaper,

> exert an unhallowed influence over the minds of the slaves. Our slaves, seeing them riding about and enjoying the "sweets of liberty," as they term it, become discontented with servitude, and sigh to break asunder the ties which bind them to their owners. . . . They, together with the unprincipled abolitionists . . . succeed in decoying a great many from us.

This problem could be ameliorated, asserted the writer, if the Missouri legislature would only pass a law to have the free Negroes removed from the state.[49]

The free Negroes did not alone bear the blame for enticing away slaves. Free-state men in general were suspect at all times. A lady traveler in Kansas during 1856 was disgruntled with the way the Kansas Citians opened and inspected a large crate containing a piano before they let it cross the border.[50] A free-state man living in Independence wrote to his brother in the East that the slaveowners in Jackson County "hate a free-state man worse than they do the Devil." [51]

The widespread apprehension among the Jackson County slavehold-

46. *Kansas City Enterprise*, December 15, 1855, 2, col. 4.
47. *Daily Western Journal of Commerce*, October 30, 1860, 3, col. 1.
48. *Seventh Census*, 266; *Eighth Census*, 279.
49. *Western Journal of Commerce*, June 12, 1858, 2, col. 5.
50. By a Lady, *Six Months in Kansas* (Boston: J. P. Jewett & Co., 1856), 205.
51. Calvin Davis, Independence, Mo., September 5, 1858, letter to brother William.

ers, which was created by this prodigious increase in abolition sentiment and Negro stealing, did not retard the growth of the slave population to any great extent. As we have already seen, the number of slaves in the area continued to increase right up to 1860.[52]

The increasing vulnerability of slave property failed to hurl slave prices down as might have been expected. In fact, Harrison Trexler, in his study of Missouri slavery, discovered that "the golden age of slave values is the 'fifties.'"[53] Jackson County was no exception, for there slaves were selling at an all-time high. A young man twenty-two years old was sold for $1,000 in 1853, whereas a boy about the same age in the early 1840's was sold for only slightly over $700.[54] This 1853 price was more than $100 above the average price of prime fieldhands in Virginia at the same period.[55]

Slave hiring just prior to the Civil War reflected the great demand for slave labor that existed in Jackson County. A man in Westport, a town in Jackson County, ran a notice in a local newspaper stating that he would like to hire a Negro boy, about twelve or fifteen years old, by the month or year. This advertisement appeared constantly for about six weeks before the man either was successful or just gave up completely on finding a boy available in the area.[56] The scarcity of slave labor is also apparent in the terms that at least one Jackson County woman was willing to accept in order to hire two Negro boys. She not only made the usual agreement to feed and clothe the two slaves, but she agreed to pay the taxes on the two boys, and any medical expenses that might be incurred as well.[57]

Even though the slave population was increasing and slave prices were soaring, and there was an apparent demand for more human property in Jackson County during the 1850's, many slaveholders in the area refused to gamble. The increasing threat of one's slave property being carried off to freedom by the zealous abolitionists and free-soil settlers caused many Jackson County slaveowners to sell their Negroes. A steamboat captain commented on this trend in December, 1858, when he

52. *Sixth Census*, 90; *Seventh Census*, 266; *Eighth Census*, 280–281.

53. Trexler, *Slavery in Missouri*, 39.

54. See bills of sale for slaves, in Hambright MSS, Box 1, Folder 1854; Misc. Folder; Laura Lyons Papers, Misc. Papers on Slavery, Jackson County Historical Society.

55. Phillips, *American Negro Slavery*, 370 and the chart opposite.

56. The advertisement first appeared in the *Border Star*, December 3, 1859, 2, col. 5. It reappeared again and again until the February 11, 1860, edition.

57. Note signed by William Chrisman, January 16, 1860, Peake and Hudson Family Transactions, Box 43, Jackson County Historical Society.

was continually having slaves driven aboard his boat as he moved down the Missouri River.[58] A newspaper that circulated throughout Jackson County reported in November, 1859,

> An entire change has come over the State; an unholy coalition has been entered into by the Abolitionists and the slave driver. These two classes of men entered the State about the same time. The Abolitionist came persuading the negro away from his home, and started his newspapers and sent among the slave holders a warning notification that their slave property was not safe. The slave-holder became alarmed; the negro driver and buyer came to relieve him of his property at a good price.[59]

Whether or not slave drivers and some of the anti-slavery presses were working together cannot be established beyond uncertainty. There was, however, no lack of speculators in Jackson County to take advantage of the slaveholders' fears. At the time the county census was taken in 1850, the largest slaveholder, Jabez Smith, held 202 slaves. Smith was a speculator, not a farmer.[60] In May, 1859, Thompson McDaniels, another Jackson County slave dealer, was seen with four or five other men herding a group of about a hundred male slaves to the river to be put on a boat. Chained and handcuffed, those slaves had been bought in the Jackson County area and were going to be sold in the Deep South.[61]

Despite the precarious position of slave property in the 1850's, the institution of slavery was not destroyed in Jackson County. Instead of capitulating to the desires of the abolitionists and free soldiers, the majority of the Jackson County slaveholders fought their antagonists, rather than give up their bondsmen. The death and destruction spread by Jim Lane and his Jayhawk confederates along the Missouri border was soon spread into the Kansas Territory by pro-slavery men from Jackson and other border counties in Missouri.[62] Ultimately, of course, the archaic institution of slavery was brought to an end in Jackson County and elsewhere by the ravages of the Civil War.

The impact of the war was strongly felt in Jackson County throughout the summer and winter of 1861. Bands of Jayhawkers stormed into

58. Trexler, *Slavery in Missouri*, 205.
59. *Western Journal of Commerce*, October 20, 1859, 1, col. 3.
60. *Jackson County, Census of 1859*, 118.
61. *Kansas City Star*, August 15, 1897, 7, col. 3.
62. Merkel, "Antislavery in Missouri," 199–207. Merkel describes the organizing of several raids from Jackson and other border counties into Kansas. Also, by a Lady, *Six Months in Kansas*, 111, has a contemporary description of a raid into Lawrence, Kansas, by border Missourians. The Lady also describes the Missourians, their habits, and their horses.

Independence and Kansas City, confiscating slaves and plundering at will.[63] The Union commander in Missouri, General John C. Frémont, took the unauthorized liberty of issuing deeds of manumission to slaves of disloyal owners in the fall of 1861, much to the embarrassment of Abraham Lincoln. In spite of the fact that the President ordered an end to military proclamations which fixed the "permanent future condition" of slave property, [64] and the fact that some U.S. officers in Jackson County ordered the return of confiscated slaves to their rightful owners,[65] slavery was quickly disappearing in the area.

The *Western Journal of Commerce* reported in December, 1862, that Jackson County had lost hundreds of thousands of dollars worth of slaves, and the few that had not run away or been stolen or sold were "principally old broken down adults and useless children." [66] A traveler who came to Jackson County about eight months later found that "slavery in Missouri has run its race—nothing but shadows of the institution are observable." [67]

Throughout the next year and a half, it was apparent that the demise of slavery was imminent. The only question left was whether emancipation should be gradual or immediate. The conservatives were victorious in 1863 when a state convention was called in July, and gradual emancipation was adopted. The radicals, however, did not concede. By January 11, 1865, those who wanted immediate emancipation succeeded in persuading the state convention to adopt an ordinance to abolish slavery and involuntary servitude. That same day, Governor Thomas C. Fletcher issued a proclamation stating that "slavery is abolished in the State of Missouri," thus ending both slavery and the debate over gradual or immediate manumission.[68]

According to a student of Missouri slavery during the Civil War, the pros and cons of gradual and immediate emancipation could be argued

63. Albert Castel, "Kansas Jayhawking Raids into Missouri in 1861, "*Missouri Historical Review*, LIV (October, 1959), 2–7.

64. Roy P. Basler, ed., *The Collected Works of Abraham Lincoln* (New Brunswick, N.J.: Rutgers University Press, 1953), IV, 531–532.

65. U.S. War Department, *The War of the Rebellion: A Compilation of the Official Records of the Union and Confederate Armies*. Series I, Vol. 22, pt. 1 (Washington: Government Printing Office, 1888), 796–798, Brig. Gen. Richard C. Vaughan (U.S.A.), Lexington, Mo., December 1, 1862, to Col. William Wood, St. Louis, Mo.

66. Quoted by Merkel, "Antislavery in Missouri," 337.

67. Lela Barnes, ed., "An Editor Looks at Early-Day Kansas: The Letters of Charles Monroe Chase," *Kansas Historical Quarterly*, XXVI (Summer, 1960), 114.

68. Merkel, "Antislavery in Missouri," 414–415.

by the politicians, but due to the nearness of free territory and the chaos brought by the war, "the slaves themselves were deciding the question of immediate or gradual emancipation." [69] This was indeed an ironic yet extremely fitting end to slavery in western Missouri.

It can be seen on the basis of this survey of slavery in Jackson County that time wrought many changes in the county's peculiar institution. We have seen how in the late 1820's and 1830's Jackson County was an area of few, mostly poor farmers, who held only a small number of slaves. As the years passed, however, and lands became sterile in the old slave states, Jackson County's fertile river valleys became a strong impetus for men to enter her borders. By the 1840's and 1850's, Jackson County's entire population, both slave and free, had increased rapidly. With the increase in population came an increase in wealth to those who had settled, for the fertile valleys were paying dividends in rich harvests. By the time of the Civil War, slavery was anything but a decaying institution in Jackson County. Even in the face of uncommon attacks from abolitionists and free-soil settlers, who almost surrounded the western border county, slave prices were at their highest, the demand for slave labor was great, the slave population had reached its highest level, and most slaveholders were much wealthier than their early Jackson County forefathers. It is hard to believe that anything short of civil war could have persuaded those people to give up their bondsmen.

69. *Ibid.*, 270.

The Slave Plantation

The studies presented in Part Two attack their common subject differently. The opening selections by Wall and the Georgia Writers' Project of the WPA help us to understand the origins of the great plantations of the Southeast and the struggle that went into their growth and consolidation. The others treat various features of the plantation experience: the character of the planters, the nature of the big house, and the treatment of the slaves. Most clearly missing is the slave experience itself, analyzed locally and in depth. But the study of how slaves lived, in contradistinction to the study of how masters tried to make them live, is still at an early stage. Exploration of its local dimension lies ahead of us.

Bennett H. Wall

The Founding of the Pettigrew Plantations

During and after the American Revolution many Southerners argued that slavery was a burden and a curse. Thoughtful Southerners worried lest the increasing numbers of blacks might eventually overrun the South. Those who needed to found sufficient explanation in a conspiracy of northern and English merchants who grew rich at the peril of southern society. Nevertheless, Southerners continued to buy slaves, and a shrewd man like Charles Pettigrew with a keen eye to profit went so far as to fit out his own slave ship to bring Negroes directly from Africa to work on his plantation.

Charles Pettigrew and men like him used slave labor for profit and convenience. A minister, he was also a speculator for whom the value of slave labor constituted an important element in his economic calculations. Pettigrew, however, also exhibited those ambivalences about slavery which separate his generation of Southerners from those which were to follow. To understand those differences, it is necessary to distinguish racial, economic, and social attitudes. Pettigrew's generation thought the Negro inferior but felt that his position had been divinely ordained. The racial attitudes were far less virulent than those of antebellum Southerners. They also feared the Negro far less because they had not made him the mudsill of their civilization. Negro slavery had originated as part of indentured servitude, and though by the end of the eighteenth century race clearly constituted class, the system was not as rigid as it was to become. For the talented Negro opportunities still existed to learn a trade and to develop beyond the confines of plantation life. Fortunate slaves who worked hard and efficiently were able to buy themselves out of slavery or win manumission through life-long dedication to their masters. Finally, and most important, no one in the late eighteenth century thought slavery a positive good. It was a curse, though one which offered great profits. If the result was ambivalence or guilt, it accrued to the slave's advantage. When he became the cornerstone of southern society, slaveholders became more intransigent, the slave's life grew less flexible, and the possibilities for his social evolution diminished appreciably.

Reprinted with permission from the *North Carolina Historical Review*, XXVII (1950), 395–418.

During the post–Revolutionary War period the Reverend Charles
Pettigrew, famous Edenton, North Carolina, religious leader, found
it difficult to support his family on the income from his parish.[1] As a result he was forced to turn to planting as a means of support. Since he
had only a limited knowledge of agricultural methods, he learned by
trial and error. Just when he first became a landowner is not recorded,
nor is it known when he came into possession of his first farm. There is
reasonable doubt that he owned any land prior to his marriage to Mary
Blount on October 29, 1778. By this marriage he acquired slave property, some land in Tennessee, and some land near Edenton. After his
marriage he moved to a plantation near his wife's ancestral home, Mulberry Hill, and settled "on the north side of the road leading down the
Albemarle Sound and just across what was then Blount's Mill." [2] In 1779
he purchased lands in Tyrrell County, near Lake Phelps.

Three of Charles Pettigrew's parishioners, all leading citizens of
Edenton—Josiah Collins, Dr. Luther Dickinson, and Major Nathaniel
Allen—were land speculators; in order to develop one of their ventures in the region southeast of Edenton, they organized the Lake Company. The Lake Company's lands were along the shores of Lake Phelps,
which is in the peninsula, about sixty miles long and forty miles wide,
formed by Albemarle and Pamlico sounds in North Carolina. Four-
fifths of the region was an immense swamp.[3] The remainder was composed of narrow knolls of firm soil,[4] commonly known as "Chestnut
Oak Islands." [5] The principal characteristic of the soil around Lake
Phelps was its great fertility. The soil was a black loam or muck,[6] and
when under proper tillage "the drained swamp land is easy to plough,
and to manage and get in good order in all respects." [7]

1. A portion of the research on this study was made possible by a grant from
the University of Kentucky Research Fund Committee.

2. "Ebenezer Pettigrew Relates His Early Life," August 4, 1842, Pettigrew Manuscripts, Southern Historical Collection, University of North Carolina, Chapel Hill.
Hereafter cited as Pettigrew MSS.

3. See William Battle Cobb and William Anderson Davis, *Soil Survey of Tyrrell
County* (United States Government, 1924), 839–858. (A map is attached.) Hereafter cited as Cobb and Davis, *Soil Survey*.

4. Edmund Ruffin, "Jottings Down in the Swamps," in Edmund Ruffin, ed., *The
Farmer's Register* (1833–42), VII, 688–703. Hereafter cited as Ruffin, "Jottings
Down."

5. George C. Collins, "Discovering Lake Scuppernong (Phelps), North Carolina,"
Southern History Association Publications (Washington 1897–1907), VI, 21–27.
Hereafter cited as Collins, "Discovering Lake Scuppernong."

6. Cobb and Davis, *Soil Survey*, 839–858.

7. Ruffin, "Jottings Down," VII, 688.

Lake Phelps was discovered by Benjamin Tarkington, Josiah Phelps, and others in 1775. While hunting they became interested in learning why deer "when pursued usually ran off in a particular direction, from which the dogs soon returned as if baffled in their pursuit." After a search of two days they located the lake. Phelps publicized and has generally received credit for the discovery.

It was about twenty-five years later that Collins, Dickinson, and Allen formed the Lake Company. "They took up nearly all the surrounding swamp land by laying their own patents," [8] and they purchased a total of nearly 100,000 acres. They fitted out the slave ship *Guineaman* in Boston and sent it to Africa for Negroes. When the slaver arrived, the Negroes were set to work digging a canal from Lake Phelps to the Scuppernong River, a project of two years' duration. Lake Phelps had an elevation of eighteen feet above the Scuppernong River, and by the use of water wheels the declivity was utilized for power for saw, grist, and other mills.[9] The Lake Company began preparation of rice fields around the lake by draining the fields into the ditch or "Somerset Canal." By the use of flood gates on the ditches leading to the canal, and with the successive parallel slopes, ditches, and embankments formed by the leading ditches, "they were afforded great facilities for flooding the lands, and drawing off the water when desired, for rice culture." Flat boats capable of carrying fifty or sixty tierces of rice could come up the canal to the plantation, and small vessels of seventy-five tons or less received and discharged cargoes at the mouth of the canal. The canal was six miles long, twenty feet wide, and six feet deep.[10] In 1788 Charles Pettigrew moved to Lake Phelps to develop his property adjoining that of the Lake Company and to found a plantation regime of seventy-seven years' duration.

Before he moved to his Lake Phelps property, Pettigrew moved to Harvey's Neck in Perquimans County. His wife died shortly thereafter, leaving him an unrecorded amount of property, including several slaves. In 1788 he moved again. Ebenezer Pettigrew wrote a description of the new plantation:

> I lived at Hervey's neck until the fall of 1788 when my father took his effects in two small vessels & went over to the mouth of Scuppernong

8. The information about the discovery and early exploitation of Lake Phelps was obtained from the Ruffin and Collins sketches.

9. Charles Pettigrew to Henry Pattillo, January 9, 1789; Charles Pettigrew to the Lake Company, March 27, 1796, Pettigrew MSS.

10. Collins, "Discovering Lake Scuppernong," VI, 23; Ruffin, "Jottings Down," VII, 726–729.

river, where his things were taken out the vessels & put in the court
house which was on the plantation of Benjamin Spruill who then kept
the tavern for the court house . . . on the sunday evening after we had
arrived I suppose on the latter part of the week, my father with his sons
& the old lady who kept house for him, together with a few servants
with his effects in carts set out for a place which he had rented from
William Littlejohn of Edenton & about five miles from the mouth of
the River to take up our abode, but when we arrived, the house was
without a window shutter (glass it never had) and a thunder squall rising he thought best to turn back to a house for Shelter we had passed
nearest when we were coming.

The house of refuge was

an old high roofed house without even a window shutter, in the midst
of an old field without a fence around it, with a number of cattle feeding in it (for there was great range nearby) with their *bells* ringing together with the thunder at intervals and my axiety from fear of the
Squall, produced in me a feeling that no time can obliterate.[11]

This plantation was subsequently expanded to become part of one of the
key Pettigrew plantations, Bonarva. Charles Pettigrew proposed to build
a home at Lake Phelps, where in 1782 and in 1787 he added two small
farms to the property purchased in 1779. By 1789 he owned several
hundred acres of land, had built a home, and was ready to move to the
lake. He wrote his one-time teacher, the Reverend Henry Pattillo:

I am just about to settle some of my land on Lake Phelps in Tyrrell. I
can have no idea of more fertile soil. Since the year '79 I have been a
proprietor there, which has confined me to this part of the state. The
circumjacent Lands are possessed by three able Gentm in Co. namely
Messrs *Collins*, Dickinson & Allen. They have now completed a canal
near 6 miles being a communication between it & Scuppernong River,
which promises infinite advantages. They are erecting mills on it. It is
20 feet wide, & runs parallel with one tract of my Land within about
150 yards. They have generously given by *Deed of Gift*, every privilege
I could wish, *to me, my heirs & assigns forever*. This renders my Lands
of much greater value, although I have not expended a farthing, &
they perhaps thirty M pounds. An overseer whom they got from South
Carolina, says that it is equal in every respect, to the best plantations
there. . . . I think of moving over the ensuing Summer or fall, to live
at the Canal, as I Shall not only be more convenient to my Lands in cultivation, but that side of the Sound is found more healthy than this.[12]

The move was made in 1789. Since most of his labor force was busy
draining and clearing land, he was unable to plant a large crop of corn

11. "Ebenezer Pettigrew Relates His Early Life," August 4, 1842, Pettigrew MSS.
12. Charles Pettigrew to Henry Pattillo, January 9, 1789, Pettigrew MSS.

and rice. The work of reclamation proceeded with difficulty, and in June he wrote to his friend John Leigh, complaining that his health was endangered by the demands made upon him for supervision. He wrote descriptions of the lake and the surrounding country to his friends Leigh, Nathaniel Blount, and Charles L. Johnson. To Leigh he wrote:

> I write you from *Bonarva*—a name I have given my situation on the Lake. I sit under the shade of three beautiful Holleys. The surrounding Scene is truly romantic. On the one side, the prospect toward the water is very beautiful & extensive, while the gentle breezes play over the surface of the crystal fluid, and render the air grateful for respiration, and when the Sun sheds his warmest influence upon the earth—it being the meridian hour. On three angles of the improvement, ye woods are luxuriantly tall, & dressed in a foliage of the deepest verdure, while the cultivated field exhibits the utmost power of vegetative nature, and arrests my eye from every other object.[13]

All, however, was not right with his world. He complained:

> fertilizer renders it [the soil] equally productive of viscious weeds, to obstruct the growth of what is planted & to extract the Sweet which drops from the brow of Labor while he endeavours to erradicate them. . . . The Lake is not without its counterpart of inconveniences & although the soil is fertile though the Lake affords a beautiful prospect & is an unfailing source to overflow our rice lands, their being a declivity of several feet, perhaps not less than six in the distance of 90 poles back from the water, yet when warmed by the genial heat of the Sun in Summer it is rendered so prolific of flies and insects of every species, that it becomes intolerable to horses & horned cattle, the latter however, have the advantage, from a more copious sweep of tail for their defense.[14]

Pettigrew's holdings continued to grow in size as well as in improved cultivated land. In May, 1789, Pettigrew purchased an additional 110 acres of land.[15] He paid a tax of six pounds on his property in Tyrrell County in 1789.[16]

From 1789 until June, 1791, Charles Pettigrew followed a live-at-home farm program and exerted every effort toward preparing his lands for rice, corn, and wheat crops. Corn and wheat grew easily on any of the well-drained land, but the preparation and cultivation of rice fields was a tremendous undertaking. This work,

13. Charles Pettigrew to Dr. John Leigh, June 16, 1790, Pettigrew Papers, North Carolina Department of Archives and History, Raleigh. Hereafter cited as Pettigrew Papers.
14. Charles Pettigrew to Dr. John Leigh, June 20, 1790, Pettigrew MSS.
15. Land Patent, May 18, 1789; Receipt & Patent for Land bought by B. Tarkington, May 13, 1789, Pettigrew MSS.
16. Tax Receipt, 1789, Pettigrew MSS.

primitive and laborious, was accomplished by the task system. Ditches divided the field into "tasks" of a quarter of an acre. In March, hands prepared the fields with the hoe and dug trenches for the seeds. From that time until the harvest in September, they were busy alternately flooding the growing rice and clearing the fields of grass. In addition, there were ditches to be dug, trunks to be mended, flood gates to be kept in repair, a routine which kept the slaves for long hours in wet fields. . . .[17]

In 1791 Pettigrew returned to Edenton. He explained his move to his friend, the Reverend Henry Pattillo, as follows:

> I am returned from my farm at the Lake, a resident in Denton. They [the parishioners] have contributed an annual provision for my Life or During my stay among them. I would prefer the farmer's life but when on the farm, I found my attentions wholly engross'd,—So that it became necessary that I quit should either the farm or the Pulpit; For I found it impractible to Serve both God & Mamon.[18]

However, he did not give up his farming activities.

Pettigrew's move to Edenton shortened the distance to Mary Lockhart, daughter of James Lockhart and heir to considerable land and slaves, including the beautiful estate "Scotch Hall." [19] He was so interested in paying court to her that he confused the date of a state Episcopal convention.[20] On his return from the convention [?] he attempted to purchase some land worth 800 pounds for his fiancee, but he could not complete the negotiations.[21] Repeated accounts of his poor health were apparently unfounded, for in addition to preaching "two Sundays out of three" [22] at St. Paul's in Edenton, he carried on other ministerial duties,[23] paid calls at Scotch Hall,[24] and frequently visited his lake plantation. On one of visits to Bonarva he wrote his friend and neighbor,

17. Guion Griffis Johnson, *Ante-Bellum North Carolina* (Chapel Hill: University of South Carolina Press, 1937), 488–489. See also Duncan Clinch Heyward, *Seed From Madagascar* (Chapel Hill: University of North Carolina Press, 1937), 1–80; Lewis Cecil Gray, *History of Agriculture in the Southern United States to 1860* (Carnegie Institution of Washington, 1933) I, 277–290; John and Ebenezer Pettigrew to Charles Pettigrew, April 12, 1796, Pettigrew MSS.

18. Charles Pettigrew to Henry Pattillo, May 12, 1792, Pettigrew MSS.

19. "Genealogical." See also the wills of James Lockhart, 1753, and Elizabeth Lockhart, 1791, Pettigrew MSS.

20. Charles Pettigrew to Miss Mary Lockhart, October 3, 1793, and Solomon Halling to Charles Pettigrew, December 16, 1793, Pettigrew MSS.

21. Charles Pettigrew to Miss Mary Lockhart, October 3, 1793, Pettigrew MSS.

22. Salary Subscription List, 1791, Pettigrew MSS.

23. Sermons: Charles Pettigrew to Miss Mary Lockhart, October 3, 1793, Pettigrew MSS.

24. Ibid.

Major Nathaniel Allen: "I have been hitherto so closely confined to the overseeing Business . . . I thought to have seen town before this time, but I find it very disagreeable to leave everything to the management of careless negroes." [25]

Charles Pettigrew's friends noted as early as 1792 that he was planning to enter what he termed the "social State"—that is, to marry again. But it was not until June 12, 1795, that Pettigrew married Mary Lockhart. Immediately after the marriage Pettigrew moved his family to Scotch Hall, the home of his wife. Because of the distance from Scotch Hall to Bonarva plantation, he was forced to hire a part-time overseer. This overseer was probably a neighboring farmer engaged to visit the plantation and see after the Negroes and direct their works. In the absence of both the overseer and the planter, two Negroes, Charles and Pompey, directed the other slaves.[26]

In the early fall of 1795 a storm destoyed half of the corn in Bertie County and two-thirds of Charles Pettigrew's crop; but he reported to his sons at the University of North Carolina, "We shall, I hope have enough, as at my Lake plantation my corn was more forward, & out of the way to much injury." [27] He had every right to be concerned, because he had sold the last of the 1794 corn crop in August just before the storm. Later in September, 1795, he visited Bonarva to check his corn crop and to purchase some land. At Bonarva

> the Negroes had been cutting Rice almost all the week . . . & there is a good deal down which I must see put up in stacks before I leave them, which I expect we can have done by Saturday evening. Indeed if I could I would have the corn got into the crib before I Quit—But I purpose to leave the Lake on Sunday morning & to get up to Mr. Mackeys on Sunday evening so that you need not send over again before Monday, as I purpose to take ride with Mr. Lee over his land. I mean the Land that Mr. Pollock sold him some time ago. I flatter myself that I shall make a purchase, if he will sell what I shall think good and reasonable.

He found that the Negroes needed supervision, since they "had done just nothing from the time I had left them last. The fodder hangs all dead on the stalks except about a couple of cartloads of Blades. And they can offer very little excuse." He expressed the opinion that the indolence of his Negroes was partially due to visits of some of the Lake

25. Charles Pettigrew to Major Nathaniel Allen, May 19, 1792, Pettigrew MSS.

26. Thomas B. Littlejohn to Charles Pettigrew, December 18, 1794; Charles Pettigrew to Mrs. Mary Pettigrew, October, 1795, Pettigrew MSS.

27. Charles Pettigrew to John and Ebenezer Pettigrew, September 19, 1795, Pettigrew MSS.

Company's slaves. His Negroes had visited those on the adjoining plantation frequently enough to wear a trail to the lake.[28]

Throughout 1795 Pettigrew constantly worried about the title to the first land he purchased at the lake and which he later sold to the Lake Company.[29] He considered it so serious that he applied for the benefit of an act of assembly to rectify the error.[30] Finally in the spring of 1796 the situation became critical. The Lake Company brought matters to a head by denying to Pettigrew "the privilege of draining into the canal, after . . . shutting up haul creek, while but little water" was "vented thro the canal," whereby the lake was rendered so full to as to overflow, with its banks damaging Pettigrew's land and flooding his plantation. Then they ordered him to attend the public "processioning" of the disputed lands. Pettigrew admitted that he had sold them lands without clear title and that as a result he had lost half the acreage. His letter pleading his innocence of intent to defraud [31] must have convinced his ex-parishioners, for he continued to plant his Lake plantation and to purchase lands adjoining it. It may be assumed that an amicable settlement was made. Later he was allowed to use the Somerset Canal to flood and drain his rice fields.

Charles Pettigrew managed his lake property from Scotch Hall until January, 1797. At that time he moved to a farm that he purchased from James Dillon. "The tract consisted of sixty acres, forty cleared, for which he paid six hundred and forty dollars." He named his plantation Belgrade. His grandson wrote:

> My grandfather first came to Scuppernong on Sunday evening [1797]. He landed at the place now belonging to Gen. Bateman. At that time the corn house. The house he came to was situated in the back part of what is at present and old field grown up in pines . . . not a vestage of the house remains. . . . In the January of 1797, my grand Father moved into a house, formerly occupied by one of the old Settlers of the country named Alexander, situated on the Eastern ten foot ditch.[32]

There was great acitivity at Pettigrew's Bonarva plantation in the spring and summer of 1797. In addition to planting and caring for the crops of rice, corn, and wheat, the energies of all the inhabitants were di-

28. Charles Pettigrew to Mrs. Mary Pettigrew, October 1, 1795, Pettigrew MSS.

29. Charles Pettigrew to Lake Company, March 27, 1796, Pettigrew MSS.

30. Charles Pettigrew to Mrs. Mary Pettigrew, April 8, 1795. See Charles Pettigrew to the Lake Company, March 27, 1796, Pettigrew MSS.

31. *Ibid.*

32. "Genealogy," MSS. of ———? [either Charles Lockhart Pettigrew or William Shepard Pettigrew], 1838, Pettigrew MSS.

rected toward the construction of a dwelling house for the Belgrade plantation.[33] The frame was assembled in sections at Bonarva and moved by flat to Belgrade, where the house was completed.[34] His grandson noted that this house was more pretentious and more comfortable than any in which his father had previously lived.

In March, 1799, Pettigrew and his family moved into this new dwelling, and there he lived until his death.[35] Before moving to Belgrade he had erected four two-room slave houses.[36] In the following year he paid Joseph Alexander 100 pounds for fifty acres of land containing a dwelling house and outhouses located on the northwest side of the Scuppernong River.[37] This rounded out Belgrade plantation for several years.

Pettigrew's plantation demanded his close attention in 1799, and he could not leave to sell his crop. "Having no overseer at Home, I am constrained to give the more close attention, & particularly at this Season of the Year," [38] he wrote. His failure to market his crop left him with insufficient money for operating expenses.[39] His cash resources were further drained by expenditures on a farmhouse at Bonarva [40] and his expenditures on improvement at Belgrade. In spite of the economic pressure, he remained optimistic. Conditions did improve. He wrote to Dr. Andrew Knox as follows: "I have a fine crop in the ground & some time ago, Shipped for Lizbon 42 tierces of Rice & sold as many more on credit until nov'r. . . . I flatter myself, we will be able to shew you crops, equal to the best you can boast on the rich lands of Pasquot'k." [41]

By 1799, however, the work in the swampy region began to take toll of the Negroes at Bonarva. Malaria and respiratory diseases impaired the efficiency of his labor force and changed his outlook again.

In 1800 he received the grant and deed to his lands on the Tennessee River. These lands represented a portion of the property he inherited on the death of his wife. His lawyer, Major H. O. Tatum, stated that these lands were located within the Indian boundary and added that the grant could be moved. He advised against taking such action, however, since

33. *Ibid.*
34. *Ibid.*
35. Note in John Pettigrew's copy of the Laws and Regulations of the University of North Carolina, Pettigrew MSS.
36. Memorandum for Ebenezer Pettigrew, 1798, Pettigrew MSS.
37. Deed and Bill of Sale of Lands Bought of Joseph Alexander, Pettigrew MSS.
38. Charles Pettigrew to John Pettigrew, May 18, 1799, Pettigrew MSS.
39. Charles Pettigrew to Dr. Andrew Knox, August 20, 1799, Pettigrew MSS.
40. Charles Pettigrew to John Pettigrew, May 18, 1799, Pettigrew MSS.
41. Charles Pettigrew to Dr. Andrew Knox, August 20, 1799, Pettigrew MSS.

better lands were scarce.[42] Taxes were low on this land, but there were many difficulties involved in getting the money to the tax collector.

On several occasions Pettigrew sent money for the payment of taxes to both Tatum and Major George Weatherspoon. The money was sent by hand and was seldom delivered. On one such occasion Pettigrew wrote Major Tatum that any action that he took against the offenders would meet his approval, and he included in the letter the deposition of his son, Ebenezer, to the effect that he had sent a sum of money by a man named Smith.[43]

During these experimental years Pettigrew followed the example of the successful Lake Company proprietors and planted rice extensively, with corn and wheat the second-ranking crops. He made an effort to increase his income by increasing his production and spending as little as possible. He experimented with hemp, cotton, and other staple crops as possible income-producers. The development of a timber products industry utilizing timber from the land he was clearing was the major success he enjoyed. This also served to provide off-season work for the slaves. His approach to the problem of how to make his plantation pay was always realistic. He was incessantly checking on other planters, changing, building, and seeking ways to render his plantations efficient. Shortly before his death he and his son Ebenezer arrived at the conclusion that the difficulties in growing and marketing rice, coupled with the fluctuating price and the ill effects of the rice field work on the slaves, outweighed the value of the crop. Large-scale rice cultivation was soon abandoned, despite the heavy investment in ditches, gates, and machinery.

The problem of marketing crops and supplying the plantation was of major consequence to the success or failure of any plantation. In his efforts to market his crops Charles Pettigrew was much harassed by his inability to get boats to stop at "Port Scuppernong." Many times his crops were flatted to Edenton, where they were transshipped to northern ports or to foreign countries. In getting needed supplies delivered, the pattern was reversed. Ship captains refused cargoes, dictated freight rates, and in general irritated the peaceful planter. This phase of the plantation operation was a constant trial.

Charles Pettigrew utilized the service of a number of factors during his career as a planter. There were several prominent Edenton mer-

42. Major Howell Tatum to Charles Pettigrew, September 11, 1800, Pettigrew MSS.

43. Charles Pettigrew to Major Howell Tatum, September 12, 1803, Pettigrew MSS.

chants and factors who were long-established friends. Several of these were eager to help the "old Parson," as he was called, establish himself as a planter. Among these was John Little, who stated, "As to my services in this business I can assure you they are at yr. command, without any expectation of remuneration." [44]

Other Edenton factors with whom he dealt were John Cannon, Samuel Dickinson, Littlejohn and Bond, and the important vertical commission house of Josiah Collins. He also established connections with Kelly and Mollan, Tredwell and Thorne, Ballard and Diskin of New York, and Samuel Patrick of Baltimore.

Most of these factors charged standard commissions of 2.5 percent plus small service charges. They performed all types of services for the planter. They advised Pettigrew when and where to ship, procured boats for him, and arranged transshipment of cargoes. They filled his orders for supplies, superintended packaging, and secured transportation for the supplies to the plantation. This relationship of factor and planter was the key to the plantation system. It was only natural that Pettigrew was highly indignant when one of these factors dealt unfairly with him. In June, 1796, Thomas Trotter, agent for Pettigrew, sold eighteen casks of rice weighing 10,191 pounds to Samuel Dickinson. On the back of his invoice Pettigrew noted: "The Rice which Dr. Dickinson cheated us out of by cunning getting it for 3½$ when it was 7$ at N-York (Note) 18 Tierces of Rice I was cheated out of by Dr. S. D.—n. a #11119 *nett.*" [45] Another of the Edenton factors, John Cannon, had a chief clerk, Miller, whom Pettigrew thought too clever. On the back of a bill of sale for rice in 1802, he noted: "$66.87 the Sales but by deductions reduced to $47.41 cts. 4$ freight for 1 pr . . . [?] as allowed by Mr. Miller was too much. Therefore we want no more of Millers calculation in favor of his friends among whom I am afraid I am not considered one." [46] In 1802 he complained bitterly of being tricked by an unidentified Jewish factor who sold him 500 pounds of inferior iron at a price of two dollars per hundred more than the best quality was bringing.[47] In 1806 Charles Pettigrew began a long fight against the middle men and harbor authorities that was to be continued by his son, Ebenezer—a battle that was to last for over fifty years. The planter felt that harbormasters discriminated against small planters, thus subjecting their cargoes to unnecessarily risk spoilage. Furthermore, cargoes seldom measured ei-

44. John Little to Charles Pettigrew, March 12, 1799, Pettigrew MSS.
45. Invoice of rice sale, June 26, 1795, Pettigrew Papers.
46. John Cannon to Charles Pettigrew, January 9, 1802, Pettigrew MSS.
47. Charles Pettigrew to ———, 1806, Pettigrew Papers.

ther by weight or volume as much as in Edenton or on the plantation.[48] Such variations were the source of much irritation to all planters—and especially to Charles Pettigrew, who was careful to be exact in his measurements, whether of staves or of grain. The only recourse available to a planter, however, was to change factors. Despite these problems, he enjoyed good business relationships with most of his factors.

In 1793 Charles Pettigrew shipped his first rice crop, thirteen tierces, to St. Bartholomews; for it he received three dollars per tierce.[49] The only sale recorded between that year and 1799 was that previously mentioned to Dr. Dickinson. In 1799 he marketed seventy-two tierces of rice for an undisclosed price. The crop of 1801 was small and was sold to Watt Bell.[50] The 1802 crop averaged $22.30 per tierce, and the crop of 1803 averaged $29.84 per tierce, the highest recorded price for rice. The crop of 1805 was marketed through Littlejohn and Bond for five cents per pound.[51] His last rice crop was the least profitable one he raised. Captain Samuel Bateman took the rice crop to Baltimore, but it was so damaged in shipment that the factor reported: "I am sorry to informe you that the Rice is so much damaged from being Shiped or reshiped so offen that I have never been able to effect the Sale of it. . . . I shall have the Rice started and indevor to sepperate the good from bad as soon as posible." [52] Pettigrew wrote his son that "the Damp wheat which had stuck to the Tierces had moulded the Rice, which the man discovered by boring in a gimblet." [53] On his return Bateman reported that he had sold the rice for $3.50 per hundred pounds.[54]

Other crops sold for cash were wheat and corn. Wheat and corn did not figure prominently as cash crops before 1802. Apparently the plantation produced these two staples for consumption and for exchange with neighbors. Records show that some laborers in the Pettigrew ditching project of 1805 took payment in kind, principally rice, wheat, and corn.[55] In 1802 Charles Pettigrew mentioned to Ebenezer that he had attempted to bargain with a ship captain to take his lumber, staves, and corn to the West Indies.[56] By 1803 the wheat and corn crops planted

48. Charles Pettigrew to Ebenezer Pettigrew, November, 1806, Pettigrew MSS.
49. Invoice of Rice, 1793, Pettigrew MSS.
50. Watt Bell to Charles Pettigrew, June 30, 1801, Pettigrew MSS.
51. Charles Pettigrew to Ebenezer Pettigrew, June 9, 1805, Pettigrew MSS.
52. Samuel E. Patrick to Messrs. Charles Pettigrew & Son, December 2, 1806, Pettigrew MSS.
53. Charles Pettigrew to Ebenezer Pettigrew, November, 1806, Pettigrew MSS.
54. *Ibid.*
55. Charles Pettigrew to Ebenezer Pettigrew, October 3, 1804, Pettigrew MSS.
56. Charles Pettigrew to Ebenezer Pettigrew, December 21, 1802, Pettigrew MSS.

were more extensive than ever before. One reason given was "should it be War in Europe, rice and wheat will bear a good price." [57] The wheat crop of 1806, 7,026 bushels, was shipped to New York but was damaged in a storm. In 1807 Ebenezer Pettigrew noted in his account book that the sales of wheat, corn, and rice netted $1,100.76.[58] Since the records are scattered for these years, it is difficult to estimate total crop production. The only other crops marketed through factors were flaxseed, oats, clover, and peas.[59] Only small quantities of these were reported, and it is evident that many of these were traded for other products at the Pettigrew commissary. For example, in 1805 Ebenezer Pettigrew advertised wheat in exchange for beeswax.[60]

Factors engaged vessels to haul the steady supply of forest products turned out from the Pettigrew plantations. Lake Phelps was surrounded by excellent stands of poplar, pine, gum, and cypress trees. The canals and ditches provided an avenue for floating logs, and the sawmill was busy constantly. Eventually the riving of shingles and barrel staves by slaves and white farmers became a large-scale operation. The year 1807 seems to have been the peak production year for forest products. In that year Charles Pettigrew sold 32,500 twenty-two inch shingles,[61] 1,130 hogshead headings, 2,030 barrel staves, and 1,330 "Read" oak hogshead staves.[62] This forest products business was a burden to some of the factors, who found it difficult to dispose of shipments.[63] Proportionately the freight on such products, plus the charges for inspection and grading, were much higher than for other products. Ship captains did not like to haul such cargoes unless they could fit them piecemeal in with other cargoes. They found the charges for loading and unloading and transshipping too high. But Charles Pettigrew believed such income necessary, and the sale of timber products became an integral part of plantation production.

Pettigrew's factors also bought and shipped to his plantation all kinds of supplies. Just how much profit was made on such orders is not cer-

57. Charles Pettigrew to Ebenezer Pettigrew, May 22, 1803, Pettigrew MSS.

58. Ebenezer Pettigrew Account Book, 1807–15; Pettigrew MSS.

59. As an indication of the volume of some of these items, Ebenezer Pettigrew sold from Bonarva Plantation in 1806, ten and one-half bushels of flaxseed. John Popelston's Receipt, November 7, 1806, Pettigrew Papers.

60. Ebenezer Pettigrew Notice, June 10, 1805; Charles Pettigrew to Ebenezer Pettigrew, June 9, 1805, Pettigrew MSS.

61. John Popelston to Ebenezer Pettigrew, April 30, 1807, Pettigrew MSS.

62. Invoice, Captain Barnaby Etheridge, 1807, Pettigrew MSS.

63. Charles Pettigrew to Ebenezer Pettigrew, November, 1806; Samuel Patrick to Messrs. Charles Pettigrew & Son, December 2, 1806, Pettigrew MSS.

tain, for the purchase of the items for a detailed order entailed much patience, footwork, and packaging. It is difficult to determine just what portion of the supplies sent to Bonarva and Belgrade were for the Pettigrew family and slaves. Most of the white labor employed by the Pettigrews and many yeoman farmers of the region exchanged labor for such items as salt, leather, cloth, cooking utensils, dishes, nails, spikes, and similar articles. Thus it is not clear just who received such an order as that from Kelly and Mollan in 1805. This order was for "Linnen, Kersmuth, Blue Cloath, Buttons, silk velvet vest shape, 66 yds. Linnen, calico, green plaid, Fine India muslin, Blue Brd cloath, London cloath, paper pins 2 silk umbrellas . . . 25 spools thread, 14¾ lb. lump sugar." [64] Regardless of the eventual purchaser of such items, little difficulty was experienced in that phase of his factor relations.

Slave labor was not the only labor used on the Pettigrew plantations. After 1798 Charles Pettigrew operated on a pattern similar to that of a manor lord, but on a much smaller scale. (It is possible that this more nearly approximates the average in southern plantations than is generally pictured.) The Lake Company superintendent, Thomas Trotter, seldom employed local workmen, for Josiah Collins's vertical commission house had skilled carpenters, shipwrights, brick masons, and other artisans for hire. These men, when needed, could work directly on the Lake Company property, which by 1800 seems to have become in its entirety the property of Josiah Collins. Thus most of the local artisans and laborers turned for employment to Charles Pettigrew, and he came, after the fashion of a feudal lord, to feel responsible for their employment. Occasionally skilled artisans such as John Colston of Edenton were brought over to build machinehouses and install machines. But most of the work of skilled or semi-skilled nature was done by local artisans. Josiah Phelps, Cleophus Wiley, Jeremiah Frazier, Dempsey Spruill, and other craftsmen and farmer-craftsmen assisted Colston and other engineer-artisans. In addition they sawed lumber, erected outbuildings, and in general assisted on the plantation. Such individuals were necessary to the smooth operation of the two plantations, and the policy of using hired local semi-skilled laborers was so successful that it was continued by his sons and grandsons until the Civil War interrupted all plantation activities.

Negro slaves were the principal labor force on Charles Pettigrew's Bonarva and Belgrade plantations. It is difficult to determine exactly how many slaves Pettigrew owned at any given interval. In 1791 he

64. Kelly and Mollan Receipt, August 20, 1805, Pettigrew MSS.

noted on the back of an envelope that he had thirteen taxable Negroes.[65] In his will drawn in 1806 he left his wife fourteen slaves and the remainder to Ebenezer. The best available figure indicates that the remaining slaves numbered twenty-five.[66]

In his relations with his slaves Pettigrew was practical and at the same time sympathetic. He paid them bonuses for superior or extra work, rewarded them for good conduct with gifts, allowed them free time to hunt, fish, relax, and work on their own projects, and generally sought to be a good master. He was entirely aware of the weaknesses of the system of slave labor and sought to warn his sons:

> To manage *negroes* without the exercise of too much passion, is next to an impossibility, after our strongest endeavors to the contrary; I have found it so. . . . Let this consideration plead in their favor, and at all time mitigate your resentments. They are slaves for life. They are not stimulated to care and industry as white people are, who labor for themselves. They do not feel themselves *interested* in what they do, for arbitrary masters and mistresses; and their education is not such as can be expected to inspire them with sentiments of honor and gratitude. . . .[67]

Later he summed up his philosophy regarding slavery as follows: "It is a pity that agreeably to the nature of things, Slavery & tyranny must go together—and that there is no such thing as having an obedient & useful Slave, without the painful exercise of undue & tyrannical authority. I sincerely wish there was not a Slave in the world." [68]

Most of his slaves responded to his direction and care. Yet he was never able to trust completely even his slave drivers. He cautioned Ebenezer regarding the Negro driver, Fortune:

> In regard to your wheat, I am affraid it is too much exposed to the thievishness of the negroes. It is a very ready article of trade & *fortune* has his mercantile correspondents, who are ready at all times to receive him kindly. I observed the window at the back of the machine is not safe—nor did I see any way to confine down the Hatch, at either of the ends. Pray my Son be careful, & put no dependence in their honesty, for be assured their condition scarce admits of honesty, & they will improve opportunities of getting for themselves.[69]

65. Charles Pettigrew to ———, March 2, 1791, Pettigrew Papers.

66. Will of Charles Pettigrew, 1806, Pettigrew MSS.

67. "Last Advice of the Reverend Charles Pettigrew to His Sons" (printed), 1797, Pettigrew MSS.

68. Charles Pettigrew to Ebenezer Pettigrew, May 19, 1802, Pettigrew MSS.

69. Charles Pettigrew to Ebenezer Pettigrew, October 25, 1804, Pettigrew MSS. Fortune was a driver and one of the slaves most frequently mentioned.

After Ebenezer Pettigrew assumed the active management of Bonarva Plantation, his father frequently sent him jugs of wine, brandy, and rum by Negro slaves. That he feared the contents of the jugs would be sampled is established by the following note: "We have filled your jugg & tied a rag with 3 hard nots upon a Rag over the cork that the negroes may not take it." [70]

Several of Charles Pettigrew's slaves ran away; invariably they were the more important Negroes. Pettigrew wrote his wife to have the first of the runaways mentioned "put in the Stocks & kept securely." [71] The next runaway mentioned was Pompey, a much-trusted and valuable slave driver who was given great freedom of movement. Charles Pettigrew described Pompey's escape in a letter to Ebenezer:

> Last Monday morning Pompey ran away, while the others came to their Breakfasts, and we have not heard of him since. I am affraid he has gone for Edenton, & perhaps intends trying to get to a Brother whom Cambridge boasts of having a white wife somewhere northwards. I wish you therefore, to have secret inquiry made, as it is probable he may meet with sucour a few Days from his father, if in Town. I am sorry, I had occassion to take him to Town lately, as he had opportunity to hear of So many getting off so easily from there.[72]

Pompey's return was described in the same terse fashion:

> Mr Pomp came in on Sunday afternoon, expecting I suppose that it was sunday, he would escape with impunity, & So he did, until Monday morning, when I made George [another driver] give him a civil check for his impudence, & the loss of Just a week's work. The great affront was, I had made him wait upon us on Sunday to church . . . Cambridge had not come in from his going to feed the Hoggs in the morning— on Monday, I began to chide him for his behavior, on that Occasion, & he could not bear reproof without giving me so much impuance as made me threaten him, on which he put off. I have sent him to the Lake, & intend he Shall Stay there with fortune.[73]

The escape of other slaves occasioned little comment. If the Pettigrews grew excited about such events, they unemotionally concealed their excitement. For example, in 1806 Ebenezer noted in his memorandum book, "Sept. 19 Charles [a negro driver] ran away about 12 oclock" and on "october 6 Charles came in after being out 17 days." [74] On occasion Charles Pettigrew sought to forestall potential escapes by

70. Charles Pettigrew to Ebenezer Pettigrew (undated), Pettigrew MSS.
71. Charles Pettigrew to Mary Pettigrew, 1795, Pettigrew MSS.
72. Charles Pettigrew to Ebenezer Pettigrew, May 19, 1802, Pettigrew MSS.
73. Charles Pettigrew to Ebenezer Pettigrew, May 22, 1803, Pettigrew MSS.
74. Memorandum Book, 1805, Pettigrew Papers.

drastic action, such as clapping slaves in irons or having the slave drivers whip them. The problem of runaways, however, seldom complicated the operation of his plantations.

Perhaps Charles Pettigrew's attitude toward his slaves was colored by the fear of slave insurrection that was widespread in certain sections of the South. Rumors of slave uprisings often disturbed the well-ordered routine of a plantation and caused planters sleepless nights. Negro insurrections in Haiti and Santo Domingo "thoroughly alarmed the whites, not only of North Carolina, but of all the seaboard slave-holding states." [75] In 1802 the rumors of local insurrection became fact. Two Negroes were hanged for conspiracy in Camden County on May 15, and a week later two were hanged in Currituck County. The rumor reached Hertford County by June 1 and then spread to Bertie and Martin counties.[76] The ensuing contagion of fear spread into all the surrounding counties. In May, 1802, Charles Pettigrew wrote: "We had heard of the *negro plot*. I wish it may be properly Quelled—Linity will not do it—it will make them worse." [77] A month later he reported:

> We have had a rumpus in the upper end of this county with the negroes—whether there are any of the conspirators among us I know not—no Discovery had been made nor anyone implicated that we hear of. I wish that when the [y] enter upon the Tryal of the Edenton boys, The examiners would be very particular in regard to the negroes at the Lake whether any of them have joined for it is extraordinary if every other place abounds so with conspirators & there should be none among us.
>
> P. S. Mr. W. Trotter rec'd a Letter yesterday from Mr. Cator at Washington informing him of fifteen being found guilty there & 6 or 7 shot on the way to Williamston—*I Suppose for running.*[78]

After this date there is no mention of slave conspiracies or insurrections in his correspondence, nor is there any evidence that the threat of either or both ceased to worry him.

The work of the Pettigrew slaves was difficult and their tasks were varied. Most of the Negroes worked in gangs under the supervision of George, Charles, or Pompey. These gangs cleared new ground, rolled

75. Rosser Howard Taylor, "Slave Conspiracies in North Carolina," *North Carolina Historical Review*, V (1928), 21–26; Johnson, *Ante-Bellum North Carolina*, 510–521.

76. Johnson, *Ante-Bellum North Carolina*, 510–521.

77. Charles Pettigrew to Ebenezer Pettigrew, May 19, 1802, Pettigrew MSS.

78. Charles Pettigrew to Ebenezer Pettigrew, June 21, 1802 (italics mine), Pettigrew MSS.

logs into heaps, planted crops, hoed and ploughed them, and harvested, threshed, and loaded the crops on vessels. This labor of crop production was varied by such tasks as clearing vines and underbrush along the lake shore and canals, repairing ditches, building dikes, staking and filling in the lake shore to prevent flooding of the plantations, riving staves and shingles, and sawing trees. Such labor was monotonous but bearable. The worst task from the standpoint of slave health was that of cleaning the creek and canal. Pettigrew's Bonarva Canal and all his ditches constantly filled with refuse from his mills as well as from erosion. After the water level was lowered by use of sluice gates, slaves entered the canal with shovels and hoes and loaded the accumulated debris on flats. This constant, wearisome, and unhealthy task made both Charles and Ebenezer Pettigrew doubt the value of their agricultural system.

Besides routine labor, slaves were used on scores of other tasks, all of them important in the effective operation of the plantation. Glasgow was coachman [79] and houseman; Philis was cook; [80] George, Pompey, and Anthony were drivers of foremen, and they directed the work at Bonarva when neither master nor overseer was present; [81] Cambridge was the herdsman for the hogs and cattle; [82] Frank was the assistant blacksmith; [83] Lester and Pompey were errand boys or messengers.[84] Women fieldhands hoed rice and corn with the men during the routine of planting and housing crops. Cloth was issued to them which they made into clothes during the winter months.[85] Some of the women worked in the house spinning flax into linen thread and cotton into yarn. Several of the Negro women were excellent nurses, and on one occasion Charles Pettigrew risked the life of one of the female slaves by sending her to nurse neighbors "ill of a dreadfully putrid fever; So that those who either visited or attended them generally took it, until I was obliged to Send a negro wench to nurse them." [86] All slaves both young and old, male and female, had the task of keeping the hordes of tiny "rice-

79. John and Ebenezer Pettigrew to Charles Pettigrew, April 12, 1796; February 23, 1797; Pettigrew MSS.

80. John and Ebenezer Pettigrew to Charles Pettigrew, October 3, 1795, Pettigrew MSS.

81. Charles Pettigrew to Mrs. Mary Pettigrew, October 1, 1795; Charles Pettigrew to Mrs. Rebecca Tunstall, June 22, 1803, Pettigrew MSS.

82. Charles Pettigrew to Ebenezer Pettigrew, May 22, 1803, Pettigrew MSS.

83. Charles and Ebenezer Pettigrew Manuscript Book, Pettigrew MSS.

84. Correspondence, 1796–1807, *passim*, Pettigrew MSS.

85. Charles and Ebenezer Pettigrew Manuscript Book, Pettigrew MSS.

86. Charles Pettigrew to Major Howell Tatum, September 12, 1803, Pettigrew MSS.

birds" and pigeons from the rice fields. On one occasion Charles Pettigrew wrote Ebenezer that "the Birds are as bad at the Lake as ever. I
have almost all our force there at present, to assist in replanting, keeping
out the Birds & going over the Corn with the Hoe. . . . Anthony being
out in the field keeping the Birds off the rice." [87] The Pettigrews, both
father and son, demanded that slaves work efficiently; both supervised in
person as many of the tasks as they could.

Yet there were opportunities for the slaves to relax and to perform
labor more directly related to their own comfort. Records reveal that
the slaves hunted for 'possum and coon, sought bee trees, fished along
the canal and on the lake shore, had their individual garden plots, and
were permitted to make shingles and staves in the swamp on their own
time. They sold or traded to the plantation commissary beeswax, coon-
skins, rice, corn, flax, wheat, shingles, staves, and fence rails. Undoubtedly Charles Pettigrew engaged in these transactions for purposes of
morale rather than gain, for the policy of paying top Edenton prices for
such items was standard. The Negroes who had relatives in Edenton
were allowed to visit their kinsmen occasionally, although as a policy
this practice was gradually discontinued. If there was any widespread
grumbling or discontent among the slaves, neither father nor son recorded it.

On the Pettigrew plantation adequate food and shelter were provided
for slaves. Fish, meats, rice, meal, and flour produced on the plantations
were slave staples. There were plenty of grapes and nuts in the fall.[88] Il-
lustrative of the most important item in slave diet is this note from
Charles Pettigrew to Ebenezer: "I shall send you three Barrels now of
packed Herrings—one whole fish, & the other two cut—and for
present use, some, perhaps 300 of smoke dried . . . as it might be inju-
rious to open one of the Barrels so soon after packing." [89] Slave cabins
may not have been comfortable, but they were repaired along with the
rest of the plantation's buildings. Every effort was made to insure the
health of the slaves. The distance from physicians forced Charles Pettigrew to become a "Quack," as he termed it, and frequently he exhausted himself fighting epidemics among his slaves. Several of his slaves
died from either pneumonia or tuberculosis, and others were victims of
what he called "fever." The worst fever year was 1799. He wrote Dr.
Andrew Knox at Nixonton, near what is now Elizabeth City:

87. Charles Pettigrew to Ebenezer Pettigrew, May 22, 1803, Pettigrew MSS.
88. Charles Pettigrew to Dr. Andrew Knox, August 20, 1799, Pettigrew MSS.
89. Charles Pettigrew to Ebenezer Pettigrew, n.d., Pettigrew MSS.

We have had on this side the most mortal fever, ever known Since the Settlement of the place (many fatalities). . . . It Seems however to spread, for one of our negroes has it. It is the slow nervous fever, & in the advanced stage. . . . I expended almost all my Little Stock of physic on them, & did everything I could as a Quack. . . . Cyder & Water, I think has as good an effect to raise the pulse as either *wine* or *french Brandy*. . . . It is happy for the poor who can cheaply command it.[90]

All of his Negroes recovered from that epidemic but his son John, who caught the fever while on a visit to his home, died.

Like many southern planters, Charles Pettigrew considered the necessity of employing an overseer one of the worst features of the plantation system. In his "Last advice to his Sons" he expressed his opinion of overseers:

It will be necessary that you keep an *overseer:* and this will be attended with so much *expense* that it will require you to be very cautious. . . . This will make it necessary that you keep exact accounts of *profit* and *loss;* also that you pay a close attention to the man into whose hands you entrust the management of your plantation affairs. Overseers are too generally very unfaithful in the discharge of the trust reposed in them. . . .[91]

All of his references to overseers indicate that this was a considered opinion. In 1790 he wrote: "Two heavy crosses I have, are a poor crazy constitution and a miserable clump of an overseer, whom I have to oversee." [92] He expressed the following opinion of the Collins's overseer: "Allen & Dickinson have a Quarter of negroes below them on the Lake & an overseer, which seems to be as much of a negro in principle as e'ra one of them." [93] In 1800 he wrote his friend Nathaniel Blount that he had taken to riding to a plantation which

I have on a Lake about 9 miles off once & sometimes twice a week, which I find greatly conducive to health. This I am under the necessity of doing, from the fullest conviction that overseers require little less oversight than their employers *fidelity*, there is not so much *Difference* between *white* & *black* as our natural partiality for the former would persuade us.[94]

By 1803 he was completely convinced of the inadequacy of overseers and expressed this opinion: "We have no Overseer, choosing rather to

90. Charles Pettigrew to Dr. Andrew Knox, August 20, 1799, Pettigrew MSS.
91. "Last Advice of the Reverend Charles Pettigrew to His Sons," 1797 (printed), Pettigrew MSS.
92. Charles Pettigrew to Nathaniel Blount, June 16, 1790, Pettigrew MSS.
93. Charles Pettigrew to Mrs. Mary Pettigrew, October 1, 1795, Pettigrew MSS.
94. Charles Pettigrew to Nathaniel Blount, May, 1802, Pettigrew Papers.

oversee the negroes, than an Overseer & them to, without which Employers generally go to leeward. The negroes at the Lake plantation have commonly done better by themselves with a little direction than with such Overseers, as we have had." [95]

In his effort to become self-sufficient, Charles Pettigrew placed all kinds of livestock on his plantations. Horses were unable to give effective work in the hot, damp climate, and Ebenezer was cautioned not to "distress" them.[96] It was necessary, however, that horses be kept for riding and for travel by chair. Virtually all of the heavy hauling was done by ox teams. Care had to be exercised with oxen. Charles warned Ebenezer: "As you intend to plough the Oxen, be very cautious in respect of the heat of the Day, as they are easily killed, & now the sun shines intensely hot—you had better have them ploughed only Early in the morning & late in the afternoon, as you are Sensible how careless the negroes are." [97]

Sheep were kept for wool and for food. Hogs in great numbers ranged the woods until fall, when they were penned and fattened. Charles Pettigrew warned Ebenezer that if a change should take place with regard to slavery, it would be better to "have fewer hogs, that much corn may not be necessary." [98] The plantation was well supplied with all kinds of domestic fowl as well as game and fish. In the winter season at least one of the slaves hunted to provide game for the table.

The Pettigrews planted a variety of vegetables and fruits. Lake Phelps originally was known as "Scuppernong," and "grape time" [99] at Lake Scuppernong was famous throughout the Edenton region. Minor crops such as flax, oats, barley, rye, and peas also played a role on the plantation. Salt, spices, and condiments were purchased, but most of the other foodstuffs were produced on the plantation. From the mills wheat flour was obtained, rice was plentiful, wine from the indigenous scuppernong was renown, and cider was made at the press. Certainly there was no shortage of food or drink for either the Pettigrews or their slaves.

On the third of November, 1803, Ebenezer Pettigrew returned from the Edenton Academy and assumed direction of Bonarva Plantation.[100]

95. Charles Pettigrew to Mrs. Rebecca Tunstall, June 22, 1803, Pettigrew MSS.
96. Charles Pettigrew to Ebenezer Pettigrew, October 25, 1804, Pettigrew MSS.
97. Charles Pettigrew to Ebenezer Pettigrew, August 7, 1804 (1801?); Charles Pettigrew to Ebenezer Pettigrew, n.d., Pettigrew MSS.
98. "Last Advice of the Reverend Charles Pettigrew to His Sons" (printed), 1797, Pettigrew MSS.
99. Charles Pettigrew to Dr. Andrew Knox, August 20, 1799, Pettigrew MSS.
100. Manuscript of William Shepard Pettigrew, Pettigrew MSS.

Charles Pettigrew retired to what he termed the "mannor" plantation,
Belgrade. From Belgrade he instructed Ebenezer to the details of plantation management by the use of notes carried by messenger. Both plantations were so well integrated that the labor force was interchangeable.
Hence, while the bulk of the machinery was located at Bonarva, the
Belgrade products were "flatted" to the machinery and processed. An
important feature of the plantation system of Charles Pettigrew was the
fact that he sought to use machinery wherever possible. By 1807 he had
at his Bonarva Plantation a sawmill, grist mill, rice-threshing machine,
rice-husking machine, grain separator, wheat-threshing machine, and
hydraulic ram. These rendered his plantations more efficient and allowed greater mobility of his labor supply.

When Charles Pettigrew died on April 8, 1807, he left his lands to his
wife, Mary Lockhart Pettigrew, and to his son, Ebenezer Pettigrew. To
his wife he left "the full possession of my house and mannor plantation
[Belgrade] together with every other house & convenience thereto belonging or in any wise appertaining." She was to have the continued
and uninterrupted use of this plantation throughout her life. He also left
her the stored meat and grain as well as all his stock of cattle, two-thirds
of his hogs, half his sheep, three horses (Fox, Peacock, and Fancy) and a
horse cart, a riding chair, and a yoke of oxen. He left her fourteen Negroes, "Namely: Thelma, Philis, Edith, Jack, Pompey, Charles, Cambridge, Cloe, Airy, Claressa, Judith, Gillsy, Lewis & Lucy." To Ebenezer he left "the plantation & Houses which he is now in possession of,
on the Lake, Known by the name of Bonarva, all my land in Mall
Creek, the Land & plantation which I bought of Joseph Alexander, the
mannor plantation & the lands, thereto belonging . . . also my lands in
the State of Tennessee," and all the remaining property not left to his
wife. In his will Charles Pettigrew made provision for abitrating any
difficulty between his wife and his son.[101]

By hard work and careful management Charles Pettigrew founded an
efficient plantation system. He was possessed of a tremendous land hun-
ger, and he constantly added all the adjoining lands that he could purchase. He also acquired lands by both his marriages. Thirty years after
the death of Charles Pettigrew, Edmund Ruffin, the famous agricultural
reformer, visited the two plantations, Belgrade and Bonarva, then under
the direction of Ebenezer Pettigrew. His judgement of the life work of
Charles Pettigrew is the appraisal of a careful observer. "Mr. Pettigrew,
the elder commenced his labors . . . under all the disadvantages of his

101. Will of Charles Pettigrew, 1806, Pettigrew MSS.

neighboring proprietor, and with the great additional ones of very limited capital and a small and weak laboring force. Under such circumstances, the extent and value of his drainage, clearing and cultivated land and other improvements, are wonderful." [102] The plantation system Charles Pettigrew established was to survive successive economic disasters until the Civil War destroyed the labor supply.

102. Ruffin, "Jottings Down," VII, 729.

Drakies Plantation

The history of Drakies Plantation demonstrates that the successful plantation was a well-organized and efficient operation. Throughout most of its history Drakies was not. A series of natural calamities coupled with bad management contributed to its frequent sale. Natural calamity, of course, is something one cannot predict; today it contributes to the erratic character of the agricultural economy. Nonetheless, the more efficient the plantation, the more able it was to weather disaster. Prosperity also contributed to durability, and affluence allowed a measure of political influence. In Georgia this was registered in the end of the prohibition against slave labor and reflected the strength of those more interested in profit than in philanthropy. Groups which become entrenched through political and economic power frequently rise to elite status. When the society is an open one, as it appears to have been in Georgia in the late eighteenth and early nineteenth century, economic decline did not necessarily suppose the end of an elite. All Southerners aspired to be planters and so widely esteemed their social stature that many a wealthy widow felt little embarrassment about marriage to an impoverished planter. Similarly, the respectability afforded by the name of an old plantation family made its poorly dowered daughters attractive to new men whose social position was based largely on wealth.

The plantation was above all a business venture, and it rose and fell by the efficient management of its owners. This is an important fact to remember, because Southerners tended to romanticize plantation life and to depict it as a venture distinct from either industry or commercial agriculture. The social attitudes produced and the lifestyle which its very wealthiest members exhibited clearly distinguish it from other modes of economic organization. But, like them, it produced goods for a world market and was susceptible to its fluctuations. In this crucial respect the plantation and the goods it created resembled all other economic activities in the antebellum period.

Reprinted with permission from the *Georgia Historical Quarterly*, XXIV (1940), 207–235.

D rakies Plantation, approximately ten miles northwest of Savannah, is one of the few Savannah River plantations of early settlement days that have escaped the enveloping influence of industry. Its acres are still under cultivation, though on a diminishing scale, after 200 years of varied agricultural development.

In early colonial days the approach to Drakies was by water, but today the old Augusta Road passes the entrance of the plantation. A number of antiquated one-room huts face the plantation road itself, and one in particular is noticeable. Leaning slightly, as if to leave its stick and mud chimney, this hut of wide vertical boards has taken on a soft green hue from age, and the old shingled roof is covered with ivy.

The narrow plantation road leads through Drakies for approximately two miles to arrive at the present-day house, a frame bungalow set well back from the river. A short distance northwest is the site of the house of one of the original grantees, Sir Francis Bathurst, who built on the bluff overlooking the river and marshlands. Other plantation dwellings were probably erected near this same spot on the bluff after the colonial owner, George Cuthbert, named the plantation Drakies and lived there; but the only evidences of these settlements are a number of odd-sized bricks with traces of tabby mortar embedded in the earth. It is likely, however, that further excavations might reveal the foundation of one of these earlier houses. A short distance to the east on the bluff, the remains of an old rice mill chimney are a reminder of a later period when Drakies was one of the outstanding rice plantations in this vicinity.

When allotments were made to the Georgia colonists for tracts along the Savannah River, the acreage that was eventually to become known as Drakies under George Cuthbert lay between two creeks, Augustine and River Ness, later called Black Creek. This land was made up of three river tracts which, because of their ready transportation facilities, were considered highly desirable. Nevertheless, the first three owners of these tracts were followed by ill fortune and disaster, and the doleful story of each portrays struggles that existed throughout the Colony.

Although most of the colonists were primarily interested in gaining a livelihood from the soil, there were some persons who followed other equally important occupations. Among these was Walter Augustine, earliest of the first three settlers on the later Drakies land, who apparently regarded agriculture as secondary to the sawmill industry with which he planned to meet the demands of the Savannah lumber market.

It may be conjectured that Augustine carefully investigated various available lands suitable to his industry before he selected the 500-acre tract north of a creek which flowed into the Savannah River, about ten

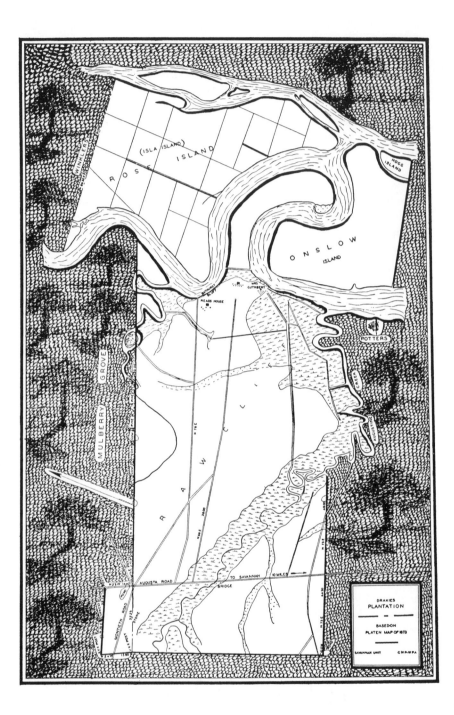

DRAKIES
PLANTATION

BASED ON
PLATEN MAP OF 1873

SAVANNAH UNIT   G.W.P.A.-W.P.A.

miles above the town. This particular section of the later Drakies acreage abounded in pine, and the ready access to the creek, down which the lumber might easily be conveyed to the city, doubled the value of the tract to Augustine. He petitioned for the 500 acres and received his allotment in 1734,[1] after which the creek forming his southern boundary [2] became known as Augustine Creek.

Some distance from the Savannah River, "higher up that creek . . ." Augustine built his sawmill, at a cost of £800.[3] He doubtless regarded his prospects as decidedly favorable, and they might have proved so but for unforeseen difficulties. The mill "wch was judged to be well built . . ." turned out to be a source of expense, anxiety, and even danger, for it was reported that "by not laying a Proper foundation it has been Severall times blown up. . . ." [4] These repeated disasters, accompanied by the heavy expense of necessary repairs, were a constant setback to Augustine, who had a family of six to maintain.[5] In spite of his adversities, however, it is probable that during the first year he was optimistic, foreseeing that with the growth of the Colony and the increase in the demand for lumber his business would expand and eventually become well established.

At this time, 1734, when Walter Augustine was attempting to make a success of his lumber business, the 200 acres adjoining his land on the north were allotted to Sir Francis Bathurst, "of the County of Gloucester Baronet." [6] Unlike Augustine, Sir Francis seems to have expected the agricultural products of his land to provide a livelihood for himself and family of twelve,[7] and he set about establishing a permanent plantation home in the colony. In selecting his land he had acted wisely and chosen a tract which consisted of both high and low land. The marsh acreage formed a small peninsula, extending into the Savannah River, while the highland on which the house was built terminated in a bluff at the water's edge. To the north of the bluff the river makes a decided curve inland where the land is visibly affected by its flood tides. It would seem that Sir Francis built his house upon the bluff not only because it was the most desirable and healthful site, but also on account of

---

1. A. D. Candler, ed., *Colonial Records of the State of Georgia* (Atlanta, 1904–16), II, 123. Referred to hereafter as *C. R., Ga.*
2. *Ibid.*, IV, 163.
3. *Ibid.*, V, 529.
4. *Ibid.*, XXI, 272.
5. *Ibid.*, V, 529.
6. *Ibid.*, II, 66, 70.
7. *Ibid.*, V, 529.

its accessibility to the river, which was the easiest means of transporting both persons and supplies.

Almost from the start Sir Francis was set upon by misfortune greater than that which befell Augustine. Naming his plantation Bathurst Bluff, he had a part of the land fenced in and planted corn. He failed, however, to build his fence strong enough, for the Trustees' horses, which were allowed to roam at large, broke into the field and destroyed the entire crop.[8] When Sir Francis's son Robert "went to complain of it" to Chief Magistrate Thomas Causton "because there was no body else to complain to . . . he laugh'd at it and Said he'd not be troubled about it. . . ."[9] The loss of this first year's crop was only the harbinger of other ill luck to come.

The following year Sir Francis, undaunted by his previous loss, planted his field in corn for a second time. It appears that he had profited little from his costly experience, for he took no precaution in building a more secure fence around the field. Consequently, his new corn crop was destroyed by "the Post Man Mr. Elberts horses. . . ."[10] Again Sir Francis approached Causton, hoping to receive some compensation, and again Causton treated the report with indifference.[11] The total loss of two successive crops was a decided blow to Sir Francis. Besides this, he "reced great Losses by his Servants Death and Sickness,"[12] for his indentured help, unacclimated to heavy field work in the low coastal region, were fatally striken with "fevers and fluxes."

While Augustine was struggling against odds to recover from the disasters to his sawmill, and Sir Francis was undergoing his equestrian troubles, the third Drakies settler came to add his trials to those of his luckless neighbors. The land adjoining Bathurst Bluff on the north lay within the limits of Joseph's Town, a district in which no allotments had hitherto been given. The year 1735 found a number of requests being made for land in this section, and the 500 acres adjacent to and north of Bathurst Bluff passed into the hands of George Dunbar.[13]

Dunbar, a Scotsman of good family and education, was captain of the ship *Prince of Wales*,[14] which gave invaluable service to the colony by transporting supplies and mail down the coast as well as plying to and

8. *Ibid.*, XXII, Part I, 6.
9. *Ibid.*
10. *Ibid.*
11. *Ibid.*
12. *Ibid.*, XXI, 272.
13. *Ibid.*, VIII, 705.
14. *Ibid.*, I, 190–191, 221; II, 132.

from England with passengers and cargo. He had a sister Priscilla who a few years later married Patrick Houstoun, prominent in colonial affairs.[15] It may be that Priscilla Dunbar stayed with her brother for a time at his Joseph's Town plantation, just as Ann Cuthbert kept house on neighboring Mulberry Grove for her brother John.[16] No record remains, however, of the site Dunbar selected for building a hut or cottage for himself or quarters for his indentured servants.

Of these three tracts that later formed Drakies, Dunbar's was less adapted to successful cultivation than either Bathurst's or Augustine's. Black Creek ran through his plantation, and the land was subject to the overflow of this large creek as well as to the flood tides of the Savannah River. Dunbar probably endeavored to raise garden crops, mulberry plants, and perhaps indigo or grapes, only to find his plantings washed out. Because of the prohibition of slaves in Georgia, until 1749 he was unable to attempt rice culture, for which the land was ideal; therefore he early discovered that he had on his hands a tract large in size but not adapted to practical uses.

In 1736 almost unheard of difficulties were presented at Bathurst Bluff, while on either side Augustine and Dunbar persisted in their futile efforts to surmount their problems. Augustine's sawmill seems to have been constantly in need of repairs, and the expenditures of cash necessary to maintain it in running order kept him in a continuously impoverished state. "In this work, the loweness of his Circumstances brought upon him some Difficultys," and it became necessary for him to exchange "Sawed work" for provisions in order to tide his family over the trying times.[17]

Serious as were the problems of Augustine and Dunbar, they appeared relatively small when compared to the tragedies that beset Sir Francis Bathurst during this year. By this time the Bathurst family was virtually impoverished. Apparently Sir Francis was not easily discouraged, for again he planted corn, probably in the expectation that at least this, his third year's crop, would come to fruition. In the spring Lady Bathurst, a delicate gentlewoman unaccustomed to the hardships of pioneering, was taken ill, and the family's circumstances were so reduced that Robert Bathurst later wrote, "when my dear Mother lay on her death bed, we had no boat to go down to Savannah to get necessarys for her, and I wrote to my Sister to . . . see Mr. Causton to get Something for my Mother, but he would let her have nothing but One bottle of Madera

15. *Ibid.*, 442.
16. *Ibid.*, IV, 454.
17. *Ibid.*, XXI, 272.

wine, which . . . was poor comfort for a woman on her death bed." [18]

On April 20 Robert Bathurst wrote to another sister in London to inform her of their mother's death "of the 2d Instant wch is a Great Grief and Loss to us all. . . ." [19] This sad occurrence was followed by a third economic disaster. The Indians whom, according to Robert Bathurst, "Causton encouraged to do me all the mischief . . . possible . . . destroyed my corn & hoggs," [20] thus leaving the family in dire want.

At the time of Lady Bathurst's death there was a widow, Mrs. Perber, "an Old Gentlewoman of kin to the Duke of Chandois," [21] living in Savannah. Rumors that she was possessed of a large fortune "and such other falsifieties" [22] had reached Sir Francis at Bathurst Bluff. Hardly two months after his first wife's death, he married Mrs. Perber. It is evident that he took this step in desperation to save his family from further privations, for at the time his son "lay ill" and "had nothing to eat or drink or to take but bread & water." [23] John Wesley performed the marriage ceremony at Mrs. Perber's house at 10 A.M. on July 18, 1736.[24] Shortly afterward it was discovered that the reports concerning the wealth of the second Lady Bathurst were entirely erroneous.[25] She lived only three months after her marriage, and upon her death it was found that, instead of owning any property whatsoever, she had accumulated debts for which Sir Francis was held responsible.[26] As if these tribulations were not too great for one man to endure, on September 23, 1736, Sir Francis' youngest daughter was accidentally drowned in the river at the plantation.[27] This tragedy doubtless hastened the death of the unfortunate baronet, which occurred in December of the same year.

To young Robert Bathurst, with both parents dead, servants gone, crops destroyed, and his stepmother's debts left to him and his "brother in law Piercy" the aspect must indeed have looked hopeless. "I really

18. *Ibid.*, XXII, Part I, 5.
19. *Ibid.*, XXI, 148.
20. *Ibid.*, XXII, Part I, 6.
21. *Ibid.*, 5.
22. *Ibid.*
23. *Ibid.*, 8.
24. Nehemiah Curnock, ed., *The Journal of the Rev. John Wesley* (London, 1909), 247. Wesley's diary records the marriage of Sir Francis Bathurst to a Mrs. Pember, but Robert Bathurst refers to her as Mrs. Perber.
25. C. R., *Ga.*, XXII, Part I, 5.
26. *Ibid.*
27. *Ibid.*, XXI, 272.

believe," wrote Robert, "my Father and Mother both died for want of proper necessaries." [28]

The following year, 1737, found conditions becoming worse not only on the Drakies tracts but for the colonists in general. Very soon after the founding of Georgia there had arisen a feeling of discontent among many of the settlers; they resented the restrictions on slaves and land tenures in Georgia which made it impossible for them to attain the degree of prosperity reached by slaveholding South Carolina planters with unlimited acreage. Added to these persons were planters who, like Augustine, Bathurst, and Dunbar, had tried to succeed, but because of adverse circumstances had failed, and who by this time had become discouraged. In 1739 the feeling of unrest and dissatisfaction in Georgia reached a dangerous point, and there was a general exodus that actually theatened the survival of the colony.

Naturally, there was no demand for lumber when people were skeptical about the colony's very existence. Walter Augustine could no longer hope for his sawmill to provide an income, and, greatly discouraged, he was among the first of the Savannah River settlers to leave his land in order to seek his fortune elsewhere.

Robert Bathurst, also planning to leave the colony, was completely without funds. To obtain enough money to carry out his plans, he tried to dispose of his household goods and servants; but when Thomas Causton heard of this, he claimed that all of the property belonged to the trustees in payment of the debts incurred by the elder Bathurst. Young Bathurst, fearing that should he oppose Causton he might lay himself liable to being held in Georgia, relinquished his rights to all of his personal property. In 1737, greatly embittered, he moved to "Charles Town" with his brother-in-law "& Sister Piercy," lamenting the fact that he was "leaving a good plantation . . . in Georgea, with no body to take care of it. . . ." [29]

In 1738, when William Stephens made a tour of the Savannah River plantations, both Augustine's land and Bathurst Bluff were deserted. In his journal Stephens wrote, "We now walked through the Land that had been occupied by Sir Francis Bathurst, where little had been done during his Life, and since it was wholly neglected; thence we continued our Walk through that Land which Augustin had possessed, but very little of it had been cultivated, and it was all deserted by him, as well as

28. *Ibid.*, XXII, Part I, 8.
29. *Ibid.*

the Saw-Mill, which he attempted to make some Distance higher up that Creek. . . ." [30]

George Dunbar was still making an attempt to operate his plantation when William Stephens and others made their tour of the Savannah River later that year. At this time the deserted plantations of Augustine and Bathurst were being used by Captain Patrick Mackay, Scotsman and malcontent, who had placed a number of servants in ". . . What Houses or Huts they found to live in . . ." and the servants were tending a large number of cattle that Mackay had placed upon these two tracts. [31] In 1741 Dunbar, too, despaired of accomplishing anything under existing conditions and moved to Frederica. [32]

It is probable that he was not actively engaged in planting while at Frederica. At that time the colonists were having trouble with the Spanish and French, and on April 20, 1741, Dunbar returned to Savannah under orders from Oglethorpe "to go into the Indian nations to commune with the head Men among them, and keep them steady in our Interest at this important Juncture; when the *French*, as well as *Spaniards*, are busy" [33] with hostile preparations.

It was not until 1748 that Dunbar finally relinquished all rights to his Savannah River tract and asked for the privilege of exchanging it for acreage elsewhere. He gave as his reason for wanting to do so that he was unable to occupy his plantation since it was constantly overflowed by the "Rivers Savannah and Ness. . . ." [34]

Meantime, the tracts of Augustine and Bathurst had remained unoccupied, and, when Dunbar at last gave up his land, there were some 1,200 idle acres on these three plantations.

Several years passed before the Georgia restrictions on slavery and land were abolished and it became feasible to cultivate large acreages in rice. Subsequently there followed numerous requests for grants along the Savannah River, and the early 1750's found long-unused land again being settled and cultivated.

It was at about this time that Daniel Cuthbert, of whom nothing is known save that he was a Scot and in all likelihood related to John and Ann Cuthbert of Mulberrry Grove, settled south of the Joseph's Town estate on George Dunbar's tract. There is no record of an allotment to him of the 500 acres, but when Ann Cuthbert, then Mrs. Patrick Gra-

30. *Ibid.*, IV, 163–164.
31. *Ibid.*, XXII, Part I, 72.
32. *Ibid.*, Supplement to IV, 127.
33. *Ibid.*
34. *Ibid.*, II, 502–503.

ham, received a grant to her brother's plantation in 1752, her land was described as bounded "on the South by Land of Daniel Cuthbert." [35] It is almost certain that Cuthbert planted rice, thus bringing to Drakies its first Negro slaves to toil at the gigantic task of ditching the expanse of lowland. Somewhere slave huts must have been built, but whether or not Cuthbert lived on the plantation is not established.

Daniel Cuthbert was still in possession of this acreage in 1759 [36] when Patrick Houstoun, later fifth baronet, set up a plantation on the adjoining tract once owned by Sir Francis Bathurst. Houstoun, "quiet modest Landholder" since the founding of the colony, was then living at his plantation, Rose Dhu, on the Forest River.[37] He had married Priscilla, sister of George Dunbar,[38] and probably was well acquainted with both the advantages and disadvantages of the Joseph's Town acreage and the vicinity southward. Evidently with an eye to the general prosperity brought about by large-scale rice planting, he applied for and received on October 2, 1759, a grant for the 200 acres of Bathurst Bluff.[39] At the same time he also received 481 acres on "Ilay" Island opposite the mainland grant.[40] As he had previously spent "a good deal of money Labour & time" [41] in establishing Rose Dhu, it is hardly likely that he ever lived at either of these Savannah River plantations.

In the meantime Walter Augustine's deserted tract with its sawmill was still idle, for the Augustines did not return from Charles Town to struggle in the Georgia colony. After the death of Augustine, his son Frederick came into possession of the property but did not establish a legal claim under the new land regulations resulting from Georgia's being made a Royal Province until he received a grant to the acreage [42] in 1760. Augustine Creek in colonial days had been an asset as a means of conveying lumber to the Savannah River. It now enhanced the property value by providing a means of irrigation for rice fields. Young Augustine, however, who was established in Charles Town, made no effort to clear or cultivate the tract but offered it for sale.

There was living in Georgia at this time a Scot, George Cuthbert,

35. Register of Grants, Book A, 366, in Office of Sec. of State (Atlanta). See *Mulberry Grove Appendix.*
36. Register of Grants, Book B, 273 App. 1.
37. *C. R., Ga.,* II, 42; V, 499, 500.
38. *Ibid.,* V, 442.
39. Register of Grants, Book B, 273, App. 1.
40. *Ibid.,* 274, App. 2.
41. *C. R., Ga.,* XXVI, 249.
42. Register of Grants, Book G, 145, App. 3.

presumably a relative of Daniel Cuthbert. George Cuthbert had arrived in the province in 1753 and had already acquired 650 acres of land and twenty-nine slaves [43] by 1763. Apparently Daniel Cuthbert left Georgia or died before 1763, and his plantation fell into the hands of George Cuthbert either through sale or inheritance; for in January of that year the latter received a grant to "that tract of Land containing Six hundred acres" south of Mulberry Grove.[44] To the original owner, George Dunbar, the tract surveyed as 500 acres had been far more land than he could possibly have cultivated with his white servants; to Cuthbert, with slave labor available, it served as the nucleus for the large working unit that he was planning to develop on the river.

In May, 1765, Cuthbert purchased for £1,000 the 500 acres belonging to Frederick Augustine.[45] Cuthbert's two tracts, containing a total of 1,100 acres, were separated by the 200-acre holding of Sir Patrick Houstoun, now "Baronet." Apparently an exchange of this acreage for 200 acres of the Dunbar tract [46] was effected, though no conveyance from the baronet to Cuthbert is available.[47] Cuthbert was now in possession of 1,100 acres in adjoining lands, consisting of three plantations that had comprised the lands of George Dunbar, Sir Francis Bathurst, and Walter Augustine, with the exception of the 200 acres conveyed to Sir Patrick. Adjacent to the original Dunbar tract lay 250 acres that Mathias West had acquired by grant in 1760 and which Cuthbert purchased from West.[48] Cuthbert also incorporated into Drakies Plantation certain lands that he had been allotted at earlier dates. These lands included 100 acres adjoining the original Bathurst tract,[49] approximately 250 acres of another 500-acre tract formerly belonging to Watler Augustine, and 100 acres that lay two miles from the river.[50] Thus it was that the aggregate acreage in the plantation was 1,800 acres during Cuthbert's ownership. It was probably upon the consolidation of all these tracts that the estate

43. *C. R., Ga.*, VII, 338.

44. Register of Grants, Book D, 267, App. 4.

45. Conveyance Book C, II, 1141, App. 5, in Dept. of Archives and History, Rhodes Memorial Library, Atlanta. No record of the lease can be found.

46. Conveyance Book X, I, 254, App. 6a; 255, App. 6b.

47. Deed Book Q, 424, App. 19, in Record Room: Superior Court, Chatham County Courthouse, Savannah.

48. Register of Grants, Book B, 399, App. 7. No record can be found of the conveyance from West to Cuthbert.

49. *C. R., Ga.*, VII, 338–339; Register of Grants, Book A, 381, App. 8.

50. *C. R., Ga.*, VII, 417. No record can be found of the conveyances of these tracts to Cuthbert.

was called Drakies from "Droggie or Drakies," part of the barony of Castle Hill, ancestral home of the Cuthberts in Scotland.[51]

General conditions were prosperous. Cuthbert probably expected to follow the example of many other owners of rice plantations who annually invested large profits in the acquisition of additional slaves, making it possible to cultivate greater acreages in rice and to realize even greater profits. Undoubtedly, Cuthbert's intention was to place Drakies among the foremost of the Savannah River rice estates in order that he might share generously in these profits, but he had succeeded only partially in his plans when he suddenly decided to leave Georgia.

In view of the effort Cuthbert had made to consolidate the valuable tracts of Drakies, it is strange that in 1768 he should have published the following notice: "The subscriber intending soon to leave this province gives notice, that he is ready to appear to answer, and give bail in any suit or action that may be brought against him, agreeable to an Act of the General Assembly of this province called the Attachment Act." [52] Whatever were the reasons motivating Cuthbert's desire to leave Georgia, they will probably never be known, for a month after this notice the paper stated briefly: "Died. In Savannah, George Cuthbert, Esq. . . ." [53]

Activities at Drakies were temporarily brought to a standstill until a settlement of Cuthbert's estate could be made. His will, drawn a year before his death, made provision for an annuity of £300 to his wife Mary, an annuity of £50 to a cousin, James Chapman, and a £12 annuity to a "Woman slave." [54] Dr. James Cuthbert, a brother, and Alexander Ingles were appointed executors.[55] The will named Joseph and George Cuthbert, sons of Dr. James Cuthbert, beneficiaries of the real and personal estate. It was stipulated that Joseph, upon coming of age, was to receive half of the estate and upon reaching the age of thirty was to receive the other moiety. A proviso stated that "in case the said Joseph Cuthbert shall have squandered or made an ill use of the former moiety hereby bequeathed him, then upon trust that the moiety or half part

51. *Historical Collections of the Joseph Habersham Chapter*, Daughters of the American Revolution (Savannah, 1902), II, 238; James Gaston Baillie Bulloch, *The Cuthberts, Barons of Castle Hill and Their Descendants in Carolina and Georgia* (Washington, 1908), 19–20.

52. *Georgia Gazette* (Savannah), March 9, 1768.

53. *Ibid.*, April 20, 1768.

54. File Box C, 20, App. 9, in Record Room: Court of Ordinary, Chatham County Courthouse, Savannah.

55. *Ibid.*

last hereby bequeathed to him shall be delivered up to George Cuthbert. . . ."

The will further requested that after the yearly bequests were paid to those named, Dr. James Cuthbert should "possess and enjoy" the whole estate and receive all surplus profits until such time as the estate should be delivered to either Joseph or George Cuthbert. In the event the annuities could not be met from the profits, the administrators were to sell a part of the real estate to meet the bequests.

Drakies at this period was in excellent condition, but it was operated on a small scale. A Campbell map of 1778 shows the Cuthbert settlement on the Augustine Creek side of the plantation.[56] Nearby were erected outhouses, barns, stables, and even a blacksmith shop, where in 1766 John Hyatt, a "Blacksmith from Pennsylvania," was executing all kinds of "mill work, shipwork, edge tools . . . plough irons . . . or any other branch of country work whatsoever. . . ."[57]

Pursuant to his brother's will, Dr. James Cuthbert, a prominent physician and a plantation owner in his own right, assumed the management of Drakies. The large annuities which were to be paid from the production of the plantation no doubt caused him much concern, for the Drakies had not been developed to such a degree that large profits could be expected. However, it may be assumed that, inasmuch as Dr. Cuthbert was entitled to all profits over those to be paid in annuities, he made unusual efforts in behalf of his own interests. Whatever success he made is not known, but in view of later developments, when the plantation was sold under execution to satisfy the payment of the accumulated annuity of George Cuthbert's cousin James Chapman, it is believed that Dr. Cuthbert's progress on Drakies was negligible. No doubt he managed Drakies until the Revolutionary War throttled all economic activities in Chatham County. At the close of the war he was left sole manager when Alexander Ingles, the other executor, was banished as a loyalist.[58]

However true it may be that the struggle for freedom left Drakies in a sad state of affairs, postwar demands for products raised in Chatham County made the undertaking of its rehabilitation feasible. Consequently, it is probable that Dr. Cuthbert expended much earnest effort in reclaiming the tillable lands and restocking it with Negroes. Beyond the rehabilitation of Drakies and the evident appreciable agricultural

56. Archibald Campbell Map, 1778, showing Savannah River plantations, in R. R.: U.S. District Court, Chatham County, Ga., Division.

57. *Georgia Gazette*, July 9, 1766.

58. File Box C, 20, App. 10.

progress of his postwar efforts, it is doubtful whether he succeeded in satisfying the encumbrances on the estate.

Dr. Cuthbert died sometime prior to 1786.[59] Joseph Cuthbert, his son and next administrator of the estate of George Cuthbert, returned an inventory and appraisement listing more than eighty slaves.[60] The fact that neither Joseph nor George Cuthbert the younger, during the eighteen years of their father's administration, advanced a claim of the interest devised to them under the will of their uncle has a direct bearing on the economic development of Drakies. It will be remembered that under George Cuthbert's will the special legacies provided by him for his wife and his cousin James Chapman were secured by the whole estate "both real and personal." Therefore, with the inability of Dr. Cuthbert to pay the legacies as they fell due,[61] the encumbrances on the estate became heavier and heavier. With these conditions aggravated by the dismal aftermath of the war, it is believed that Joseph Cuthbert, the chief beneficiary, refused to concern himself with an interest so heavily bound. Rather, he appears to have centered his activities on Colerain, a few miles below Drakies, where he operated a large rice plantation.

Upon his fathers' death, Joseph Cuthbert, who never claimed the encumbered Drakies as his inheritance, was appointed to complete the administration of the estate of his uncle, George Cuthbert.[62] His first act was to make an inventory of the personal property which at that time was valued at £2,402.10s, most of which was in slaves.[63] During the following six years profits shrank considerably, and in 1791 it became necessary to sell twenty-three slaves at a price of £997.[64] There is little doubt that the value of Drakies was commensurate with this low price received for the slaves.

Joseph Cuthbert died intestate about 1792, and Lewis Cuthbert, probably his brother, became administrator of Drakies,[65] which now belonged to George Cuthbert, brother of Joseph, under the will of their uncle. An appraisement listing "A broken Set of Blacksmith Tools," "Old saws," "8 Head of Oxen," and other meager items is indicative of conditions on Drakies. The 146 acres of tide swamp and 1,660 acres of pine land were unvalued, while 57 "Negroes great & small" were ap-

59. *Ibid.*
60. *Ibid.*, 22, App. 11.
61. *Ibid.*, 7, 1051, App. 18.
62. *Ibid.*, 20, App. 10.
63. *Ibid.*, 22, App. 11.
64. Deed Book H, 727, App. 12.
65. *Georgia Gazette*, January 10, 1793; James Gaston Baillie Bulloch, *History and Genealogy of the Habersham Family* (Columbia, S.C., 1901), 197.

praised at £1,735.[66] It is interesting to note, from the following list, the comparative value of slaves at that time:

Cuffie (Driver)	£50.
Andrew (Sickly)	£20.
June	£60.
July (Carpenter)	£80.
Marcus (Old)	£10.
Little Cuffie	£55.
Faust (Blacksmith)	£60.
Old Drusilla (Superannuated)	
Little Elvira	£10.
Judy (very sick)	

It is apparent that both George and Lewis Cuthbert died leaving the administration of Drakies to Mrs. Ann Cuthbert, widow, probably of Dr. James Cuthbert, and mother of Joseph, George, and Lewis. Mrs. Cuthbert's tenure was fraught with legal battles resulting from claims against the estate, among them the claim of David Adams, who recovered a judgment against the estate for the sum of £1,872.[67] In June, 1796, an execution was issued upon this judgment, and all that tract of land lying on Black Creek was sold to Thomas Gibbons for the paltry sum of $900.[68]

Perhaps if there had been no other debt against the estate, it would have been comparatively easy to effect this payment. However, just before this Chapman had died and his executors obtained a judgment against Mrs. Cuthbert, administratrix of the estate of George Cuthbert, who was unable to meet the annuity payments.[69] The last of the lands belonging to the Cuthbert estate was sold at auction on February 8, 1797, for £2,610. 4s. 8d.[70] The sale included the 146 acres of tide swamp and the 1,660 acres of pine land.

The purchaser was Jacob Read, South Carolina statesman and one of the most outstanding planters of his time, who was already in possession of acreage bounding Drakies. In 1781 he had purchased for $1,060 from the executor of Andrew Lord's estate [71] what was thought to be 750 acres west of Drakies but later turned out to be 1,145 acres.[72] This par-

---

66. File Box C, 20, App. 13.
67. *Ibid.*, 6, 932, App. 14; 15a; 15b.
68. Deed Book Q, 83, App. 16.
69. File Box 7, 1051, App. 17a; 17b; 18.
70. Deed Book Q, 424, App. 19.
71. *Ibid.*, W, 296, App. 20.
72. *Ibid.*, Z, 292, App. 21.

ticular acreage had been granted in 1760 to the Reverend John Joachim Zubly,[73] Tory clergyman, who had sold it in 1771 to Andrew Lord.[74] Following his purchase from Lord, Read in 1783 had purchased from the Commissioners of Confiscated Estates for £7,689 a 560-acre tract on the southern part of Isla Island and 200 acres known as the Red House tract "on the Main." [75]

The Isla Island acreage acquired by Read was the tract on the southern point of the island which had been granted to George Dunbar in 1759 [76] and which upon his death had been inherited by his sister Priscilla Houstoun,[77] who had conveyed it to her son Sir Patrick Houstoun.[78] The Red House acreage was the tract which the elder Sir Patrick had purchased from George Cuthbert and which, upon his death in 1762, had been left to Lady Houstoun along with the residue of his estate.[79] The younger Sir Patrick had evidently acquired this acreage from her,[80] for in 1774 he had sold it, together with approximately 500 acres on Isla Island and additional acreage, to William Greenwood and William Higginson for £300.[81] As the confiscated property of Greenwood and Higginson, the two tracts had finally been sold to Jacob Read.

Jacob Read's consolidation of these holdings with Drakies brought the plantation acreage to 3,700. Although the various tracts were at times distinguished by their separate names (Drakies, Red House, Isla Island, and Creek Field), the aggregate acreage was operated as one unit and generally known as Drakies Plantation. Two hundred and eight Negroes, an adequate number to cultivate his large holdings, were placed on the land. Since Read continued to live in Charleston and practice law there, it is evident that the house he built on Drakies and called "Read House" [82] was frequented only at intervals by himself and family. The plantation was placed in charge of an overseer procured through an ad-

73. Reg. of Grants, Book B, 377, App. 22; D, 311, App. 23.
74. Deed Book Z, 306, App. 24a; 307, App. 24b.
75. *Ibid.*, U, 210, App. 25.
76. Reg. of Grants, Book B, 275, App. 26.
77. Will Book AA, 83, App. 27.
78. Conveyance Book X, I, 257, App. 28a; 258, App. 28b.
79. Will Book AA, 83, App. 27.
80. No record can be found of a conveyance from Lady Houstoun to her son, Sir Patrick Houstoun.
81. Conveyance Book CC, I, 128, App. 29a; 129, App. 29b.
82. John McKinnon Map, September 5, 1816, showing Savannah River plantations, in County Engineer's Office, Chatham County Courthouse.

vertisement in the daily newspaper for "an overseer of good character, and who is thoroughly acquainted with the culture of Rice. . . ." [83]

Drakies became so well established under Read's ownership that it was apparently unaffected by general adverse conditions. Even when the rice embargo of 1806 was in effect, occasioning a slump in the market which proved detrimental to many rice planters in this vicinity, Drakies rice was being advertised and handled by a number of Savannah factors. In 1809 this notice appeared in the newspaper:

SEED RICE

Of a very superior quality, and warranted free of red rice, deliverable either in town, or any where else on the river Savannah on application to

F. D. PETIT DE VILLERS

at whose ware house, Rice of a Superior Quality, pounded at Gen. Read's Mill, at Drakies, may be had.[84]

Three days later Marquand, Paulding and Company offered for sale fifty tierces of superior quality rice from "Drakies Mill." [85] Similar advertisements continued to appear throughout the year and tend to show that during this trying time, although the market was overloaded and the embargo still effective, Jacob Read had no thought of abandoning rice culture. In fact, so great was his success at Drakies that he was actively engaged in modernizing his rice mills. By August, 1810, the renovation was complete and an announcement was made to this effect:

The Pounding Machine at Drakies Plantation, having undergone a thorough repair, and all the wooden Machinery having been removed, and replaced with Iron Castings, viz. Iron Wheels and Iron Segments and Coggs, will continue to work through the summer and Autumn. The stores are large and safe, and the Miller is ready to receive Rice to be pounded on Toll, in any quantities that can be sent, which will be pounded with care and expeditons and it is hoped without any of those vexatious delays that attend the operations of works in wood.[86]

It is reasonable to assume that Drakies was not immune to general conditions brought on by the War of 1812. Savannah's proximity to the sea was the cause of much concern due to the possibility of assault by the enemy. Consequently, there was a general feeling of fear and unrest which prevented the planters from carrying on their usual agricultural

83. *Columbian Museum and Savannah Advertiser*, March 29, 1806.
84. *Ibid.*, March 6, 1809.
85. *Ibid.*, March 9, 1809.
86. *Ibid.*, August 2, 1810.

activities. Apparently Read met with losses during this conflict, for in 1816 he added a second codicil to his will that gave his executors, Mrs. Read, their son Jacob, and Thomas Winstanly, power to dispose of any of his estate at public or private sale for the purpose of paying his debts.[87] Read's will, made in 1801, bequeathed his Georgia holdings to his wife and four children, Jacob, Jr., William George, Catherine, Ann Louisa, and Cornelia Annabella, share and share alike.[88]

One month after the second codicil was added to Read's will, he died, leaving on Drakies 265 slaves, $2,720 in livestock, "A bulk of rough-rice that will yield about Seven hundred Tierces, & valued at the rate of Twenty Five Dollars per Tierce ..." or $24,500, implements, boats, and flats valued at $550, and household furniture worth $240.[89] This was at the opening of an economic boom that was to last until 1830.

The management of Read's estate with the payment of his debts was taken over by Jacob Read, Jr., who during the ensuing general prosperity was unfortunate enough to meet with major financial reverses. Consequently, on May 11, 1823, he borrowed $5,159.31 from the Planters Bank, securing this loan with his interest in Drakies and the slaves at the plantation.[90] This amount was insufficient to meet his needs, and in March he borrowed $18,411.55 from John Williamson.[91] Two months later he sold eighty acres of the plantation for $1,182.50 to James Wallace, who owned Mulberry Grove, the adjoining plantation on the north.[92] This acreage, situated at the confluence of Black Creek and the Savannah River, had been in colonial days a portion of George Dunbar's plantation. With the exception of this sale, Drakies for nearly two score years continued as 3,600 acres.

The Williamson loan did little toward placing the plantation on a sound basis. In 1829 John P. Williamson brought an equity suit for payment,[93] and by 1831 Jacob Read, Jr., was unable to hold Drakies longer. The plantation was seized and sold at auction to William Wightman of Charleston, who paid $112,500 for the acreage, 208 slaves, the mills, "also two Plantations Flats, two rowing boats—five small ferry boats —four Plantation horses—Seventeen Mules, Sixty-nine head of Cattle

87. File Box R, 75, App. 30.
88. *Ibid.*
89. *Ibid.*, App. 31.
90. Deed Book 2M, 135, App. 32.
91. *Ibid.*, 2Q, 359, App. 34.
92. *Ibid.*, 2M, 327, App. 33.
93. *Ibid.*, 2P, 54, App. 35.

... Plantation Tools and Furniture." [94] The estate was described as including the tracts "called Drakies, Red House, Creek Field and Isla Island."

Wightman, since 1787 a "Goldsmith, Jeweller and Hair Worker,/ at the Sign of the Golden Hart, No. 236 Meeting Street," Charleston, appears to have been a man of some means and integrity.[95] Under his ownership for the next few years conditions at Drakies gradually improved, and there is every reason to believe that the plantation took on a semblance of its former [96] prosperity. This era reached a sudden close in 1837, when a general panic followed a market crash.

Wightman had died two years previously and had requested in his will that his plantation in Georgia, as well as his South Carolina property, be sold by his executors, Thomas Purse and Edward North, in order to pay any debts left by him and also for the purpose of meeting his legacies.[97] An inventory shows that in 1836 there were 177 Negroes on Drakies and that the fields were planted not only in rice but also to a certain extent in cotton and corn. Negroes, livestock, farming implements, vehicles, lumber, crops on hand, the Drakies acreage, and a tract on the Ogeechee River were valued at $151,129.21.[98] Wrightman's will was probated in 1836, and the following year market values dropped. The executors, who probably expected land values to depreciate further, sold Drakies and 168 slaves on January 1, 1838, for $100,000 to John A. Fraser, another South Carolinian.[99]

Apparently Fraser placed an overseer in charge of Drakies and continued to live in Charleston. It is not likely that he realized any great benefits from the plantation during the subsequent five years, as the general depression lasted until 1843. There followed a period of partial recovery, and land values rose slightly. When Fraser sold it to Dr. William Coffee Daniell in 1846, Drakies containing 3,417 acres and 154 slaves brought $95,000.[100] This $5,000 loss was comparatively small when consideration is given to the fact that for about six years real estate had been exchanging hands at greatly reduced rates. The deed of sale included "the Crop

94. *Ibid.*, 2Q, 359, App. 34. The acreage in Drakies was not stipulated in this conveyance, but apparently the sale included the plantation in its entirety of 3,600 acres.

95. *Gazette of the State of Georgia* (Savannah), March 15, 1787.

96. *South Carolina Historical & Genealogical Magazine* (Charleston, 1909), X, 106–107.

97. File Box W, 168, App. 36.

98. *Ibid.*, App. 37.

99. Deed Book 2V, 491, App. 38.

100. Deed Book 3D, 409, App.39.

of Rice and provisions," the cattle, stock, utensils, and "everything . . . with the exception of the Books, pictures, Plate and Linen in the Drakies House." These last items give evidence that though Fraser resided in Charleston, he has used his Savannah estate for occasional visits.

Dr. Daniell, the new owner of Drakies, born in Greene County in 1792, was one of the most distinguished physicians in Georgia. Possessing a knowledge of malarial remedies unknown to the majority of the medical profession at that time, he was author of a work, *Observations upon the Autumnal Fevers of Savannah, Ga.* Twenty years before purchasing Drakies, from 1824 to 1826, he had been mayor of Savannah.[101]

Soon after Dr. Daniell acquired Drakies, general economic conditions improved, and the proceeds from the plantation doubtless provided fair profits for a number of years. But another panic occurred in 1857 which caused a drastic drop in land values, and Daniell, instead of waiting for a revival of prosperity, sold the eastern part of Drakies on the mainland and the Isla Island tract to John F. Tucker [102] for $25,000. Two years later and probably still affected by the depression, Daniell disposed of the western half of the plantation to John P. Keller,[103] who paid only $15,000 for approximately 1,700 acres. From this time the section owned by John Keller was never again combined with the eastern half, which had been part of Drakies since the time of George Cuthbert.

John Keller sold the western half of Drakies in 1864 to Elizabeth and James Ulmer and William Norris for $20,000.[104] After the Civil War this was divided and sold off in small lots. Since this western half was never again a part of the plantation itself, from this point on the text will deal only with the 1,900 acres comprising that part of Drakies which was originally granted to Cuthbert, Augustine, Bathurst, and Dunbar, and which Tucker purchased in 1857.

In December of the same year Tucker gave Henry L. Toomer a mortgage on the plantation to secure a debt of $53,650.[105] This debt may have been incurred by Tucker in order to purchase Negroes, for he was alleged to have been actively engaged in illegal slave trading and, in 1859, was brought to trial along with others as an accomplice in aiding and abetting the importation of Negroes from Africa.[106] It was

101. *Memoirs of Georgia* (Atlanta, 1895), I, 188–190.

102. Deed Book 3Q, 231, App. 40; 233, App. 41; 246, App. 42. In spite of intensive research, no record can be found of the deed of sale other than that contained in the deed to secure debt.

103. *Ibid.*, 3S, 498, App. 43; 531, App. 44.

104. *Ibid.*, 3W, 133, App. 45.

105. *Ibid.*, 3R, 3, App. 46.

106. *Daily Morning News* (Savannah), November 17, 1859.

charged that those brought to trial had carried a boatload of 400 slaves from Jekyll Island and landed them in South Carolina. These slaves were purported to be from the *Wanderer*, the last ship known to have unloaded a human cargo on Georgia soil. When the case was brought to trial, the United States was represented by District Attorney Henry R. Jackson, who later was to become owner of Drakies for a short time.[107] Insufficient evidence against Captain Tucker and the other defendants resulted in their exoneration.[108]

In 1866, when the close of the Civil War found southern planters in destitute circumstances, Toomer foreclosed his mortgage against Tucker and took over Drakies.[109] The plantation mansion had been burned, and the rice fields, unplanted and overflowed, were ruined for immediate cultivation, so that Drakies yielded no profit to Toomer. In 1871 George H. Walter & Company obtained a judgment against him, and the plantation was sold at a sheriff's sale for $4,000 to Henry R. Jackson,[110] a leading lawyer of Savannah. Jackson sold the following month at a profit of $1,500 to George A. Keller,[111] who had long been an experienced planter and in the annual fairs of Chatham and Effingham counties had won many prizes.[112]

When George Keller acquired Drakies, planters had changed their methods of operating plantations. Subsequent to the Civil War hired labor was introduced to replace slaves, and it was usually to the advantage of both the planters and employees that the laborers live on the plantation in tenant houses furnished by the owner. The laborers, relieved of the expense of rent and often given garden plots and after crops, were in a position to work for nominal wages, sometimes as little as forty cents a day. Since George Keller was financially able to carry on extensive farming interests, it is probable that the plantation was a source of profit, although there are no contemporary estate accounts available.

In the 1890's several severe storms wrought havoc to successive Chatham County crops with disastrous results to the financial status of Savannah River planters. These catastrophes, added to the competition of middle southwestern rice planters, finally brought about the abandonment of rice culture in this vicinity. On a small scale, however, rice con-

---

107. *Ibid.*
108. *Ibid.*, May 5, 1860.
109. File Box 418, 9742, App. 47a; 47b.
110. Deed Book 4L, 332, App. 48.
111. *Ibid.*, 195, App. 49.
112. *Savannah Morning News*, November 2, 1857.

tinued to be planted on Drakies and on Keller's Isla Island property until 1900, when it was given up because of the increasing difficulty of controlling the flow over the rice fields after the deepening of the Savannah River channel by the federal government.[113]

Around 1890 truck farming had already begun to take its place on Drakies as the chief source of income. The highland was particularly adapted to the growth of Irish potatoes, beans, watermelons, corn, cabbage, and any number of other garden products. A crop of 2,000 barrels of potatoes was not unusual.

In 1898, two years before his death, Keller conveyed Drakies to his ten children by his first wife: George, Lamar, W. W., Paul, I. W., and Georgia Keller, Adarene Ulmer, Ella Oliver, Iola Gilbert, Mattie B. Wells; and his grandson, Gordon Saussy.[114] Drakies at this time was estimated at 1,690 acres, although Keller had sold forty acres in 1881 to Harry Roberts for $500, two acres in 1887 to W. W. Keller for $200, and "ten hundred acres more or less" in 1894 to I. W. Keller for $1,200.[115]

In March, 1898, George A. Keller, Jr., and his brother, I. W. Keller, bought for $1,200 the 9/11 interest in 1,000 acres from the other Keller heirs.[116] The part of Drakies purchased included the northernmost 450 acres on the mainland, once George Dunbar's, and the 550 acres on Isla Island.

Of the remaining 690 acres of Drakies, in August, 1898, the Keller heirs sold to Paul Keller 184 acres for $1,500 [117] and to W. W. Keller 410 acres for $2,400, together with a 92-acre marsh island near by.[118] A tract of 8¼ acres remained in the hands of all the heirs and was later subdivided into eleven equal lots, one for each heir.[119]

George A. and I. W. Keller in 1904 agreed to a division of their jointly owned mainland acreage [120] and continued truck farming. Paul and W. W. Keller also engaged in this type of planting, and to the present day Drakies on the mainland has continued to produce truck crops under the ownership of the four brothers or their heirs.

In 1931, for the construction of a canal "to be known as McCoombs

113. For information on Drakies of contemporary times acknowledgment is made to Judge Gordon Saussy, Savannah, grandson of George Keller.

114. Will Book R, 81, App. 53; Deed Book 7Y, 105, App. 54.

115. Deed Book 6E, 371, App. 50; 6B, 17, App. 51; 7K, 178, App. 52.

116. *Ibid.*, 7Y, 106, App. 55.

117. *Ibid.*, 109, App. 56.

118. *Ibid.*, 111, App. 57.

119. *Ibid.*, 9W, 427, App. 58.

120. *Ibid.*, 8T, 349, App. 59.

Cut," the Drakies heirs gave to the city of Savannah easements on a strip of land on Isla Island to be conveyed to the federal government "in consideration of the mutual benefits to be derived." [121]

No doubt the abandoned rice fields on the island had become a natural feeding ground for migratory fowl, for the government decided to add this island to the Savannah River Wild Life Refuge. Upon securing an option on the property, the government found that the titles were not in order. Friendly condemnation proceedings were instituted, and on May 9, 1938, the owners of Isla Island sold their interests at $5.00 an acre, or a total of $7,308.[122] The southern part, 607.02 acres belonging to Drakies, brought $3,038.10. By a late resurvey the island has been found to contain in the aggregate 1,461.60 acres.

A recent agreement among the several owners of Drakies and Mulberry Grove once again fixed the boundary line between the two estates.[123] On Drakies two cottages and farm buildings are still in use, but on Mulberry Grove no house remains. Unless the trend shifts, Drakies will soon present the deserted aspect of its neighbor. The past several years have found its planting slowly diminishing. In 1939 Paul Keller was the only Drakies owner to harvest a crop, and his farming activities were limited to a small area of truck products largely for his personal use.

It is probable that in the future, with Savannah's steady growth and ideal shipping facilities, industrial interests will locate on Drakies. Railroad spurs, whirring machinery, and the hiss of steam will replace agriculture. All traces of the old rice fields will disappear, and Drakies as an outstanding plantation will become a memory.

121. *Ibid.*, 32N, 438 App. 60.
122. Common Law, No. 2439, App. 62A; 62B; Deed Book 32W, 141, App. 62C; 33D, 249, App. 63.
123. *Ibid.*, 30B, 232, App. 61.

Herschel Gower

Belle Meade: Queen of Tennessee Plantations

Much has been written about what the great plantation represented to Southerners of the antebellum period. Though relatively few in number, they did exist. One of the most beautiful is Belle Meade, near Nashville, Tennessee. A great deal of nostalgia surrounds these plantations, and too frequently we think of them as typical of antebellum southern society. Only its wealthiest members lived this way.

The propensity toward conspicuous consumption was a common one among the South's elites during this period. Gracious living may well have been sufficient reason for the establishment of Belle Meade, but frequently such extravagance had a deliberate social purpose. As long as this lifestyle offered proof of the superior gentility of southern life, other Southerners (often impoverished as a result) could accept the rationale for its existence. None of the brash competitiveness of the Yankee merchants intruded into these idyllic circumstances. They sustained deferential patterns which actually bore little relation to the true interests of the yeoman farmer or the poor white. Distance from the real patricians of southern society only strengthened the elite's position. It also obscured the economic origins of its graciousness and gentility. At Belle Meade extravagance was possible because the first members of the Harding family were successful and astute businessmen; postwar decline followed because their successors were not.

The arguments of the apologists of the old regime focused upon its lack of competitiveness. Calhoun described antebellum southern society as a Greek democracy dedicated to the cultivation of all white members of society and dependent upon the labor of Negro slaves. James Hammond, another South Carolina ideologue, was less erudite than Calhoun, but more direct. Negro slaves were the mud-

Reprinted with permission of the author from *Tennessee Historical Quarterly*, XXII (September, 1963), 203–222. The author is especially indebted in writing the Belle Meade story to Miss Margaret Lindsley Warden for permission to quote from her article in the *Nashville Tennessean Magazine* (1950); to Albert F. Ganier for his extensive notes and research on the early period; to Stanley F. Horn for the Civil War period; and to Mrs. Frank L. Owsley, Mrs. Finley W. Harbison, Mrs. William M. Blackie, Sr., and the Board of Governors of Belle Meade Mansion.

sill of southern society. Families such as the Hardings and plantations such as Belle Meade indicated what was possible for all white
members of the South if its peculiar institution were left unimpeded.
Clearly this argument is false and masks the racial supremacist arguments which muted class antagonisms. Considered either a lie or a
myth, the promise it proferred was sufficient to blunt racial and
class conflict. It was an ideal which stimulated few to purposeful
and innovative endeavor. If anything, it did the reverse. Esteem for
the great planters became part of a neurotic compensation which afflicted black and white alike. In the words of the late Wilbur Cash,
it divorced pride from accomplishment, and made race the mark of
a man's status.

B elle Meade has been properly christened "Queen of Tennessee Plantations." The reasons for its renown are numerous, and the regal title
is richly deserved. Its large-scale farming operations from the 1840's
through the 1880's were very likely the most successful in the Mid-
South during half a century. Its stable was recognized as the most famous nursery of thoroughbred racing stock west of the Appalachians.
Its porticoed mansion, standing in cool grandeur near the banks of Richland Creek, was the scene of social events seldom paralleled in the history of Nashville.

Under the ownership and guidance of William Giles Harding
(1808–86), the estate of 3,500 acres—with its twenty miles of stone
fences—acquired a reputation for wise husbandry, gracious living, and
social splendor which has captured the imagination of awestruck visitors
ever since.

The scale on which the Hardings entertained is no mere rumor, for
on February 26, 1857, Randal W. McGavock noted in his diary: "In the
evening I attended the largest party I ever saw in Tennessee at General
Harding's, given to his son John who has recently married the widow
Owen." Other references over five decades express the delight of eminent visitors—among them Grover Cleveland, Theodore Roosevelt,
William H. Taft, Admiral Dewey, Thomas Nelson Page, and Joel
Chandler Harris—after inspecting the paddocks and fine stock, the
acres of wheat and clover and fruit trees, or the game preserve of 400
acres known as "General Harding's Park." One part of this area provided a home for the herd of buffalo and the 300 deer in which General
Harding took a special interest. The designation "Deer Park" is still retained in street names in the present city of Belle Meade.

In brief, then, the Belle Meade of William Giles Harding (and of his
son-in-law and successor, William H. Jackson) is the Belle Meade most

frequently celebrated by writers and visitors of later years. As popular and compelling as this image of grandeur may be, it represents only a part of the total history of a century and a half of this renowned estate.

The earliest chapter begins with the arrival in 1780 of the pioneering white man, who claimed the rich soil of Middle Tennessee for his own and took up the dark timberlands along the Cumberland. With the building of Fort Nashborough, James Robertson and his intrepid colony of first settlers established a toehold for civilization in the midst of the red man's ancient hunting ground. At some time during 1780 or 1781, Daniel Dunham, a member of John Donelson's party, ventured seven miles westward into the primeval forest—following either the waters of what is now Richland Creek or the path of the buffalo and Indian trail later known as the Natchez Trace—to choose for his settler's claim those fertile and promising acres which years later were to be known as Belle Meade, "the beautiful meadow."

In a small clearing convenient to a spring and close to Richland Creek, Daniel Dunham built a small log cabin as testimony of his rugged determination. His 640 acres were known as Dunham's Station, and he was given a pre-emption claim to them by the Register's Office in Davidson County (at that time part of North Carolina) in 1786. Because his station was erected on the Chickasaw Trail which connected the Mississippi country with the French Lick at Nashborough, Daniel Dunham's presence was a particular source of irritation to marauding bands of Indians. After much harassment during the next few years, the hopeful Dunham was massacred there in the spring of 1789. But the Dunham heirs held their ground. Even though the Indians burned the original cabin in 1792, a son, Daniel A. Dunham, went to work to build a second, more commodious dwelling. The west room was erected first, then the east. This is the double log cabin, with its connecting dog-trot, which presently stands at the edge of the Belle Meade lawn and symbolizes the early era of the hard-pressed but valiant Dunhams.

As long as the white man could hold on, there was an obvious need for Dunham's Station as an outpost for Nashville. Then a few years later, after James Robertson had negotiated treaties with the Indians, there was a further need, for by now the Chickasaw Trail was renamed the Natchez Trace, and travelers liked to stop there to clean up, refresh themselves, take a hearty meal, and recuperate from their arduous 550-mile journey from Natchez before traveling the last few miles to Nashville. For those leaving Nashville and going south, the double cabin on the Dunham property was conspicuously located: the Natchez Trace left the Nashville Public Square by way of present Charlotte Avenue, passed Cockrill Spring (in Centennial Park), and proceeded out Richland (now Harding) Pike. It went past Dunham's cabin and crossed Richland Creek about a hundred feet upstream from the present bridge at Leake Avenue. On these early stone abutments once rested a much-traveled covered bridge, at the west end of which the Hardings maintained a well-equipped blacksmith shop. A few hundred yards upstream they erected a stone dam across the creek to furnish power to run a mill.

The era of the early Trace was colorful—not only in Tennessee, but in the entire Southwest as well. As early as 1784 a group of white explorers from Natchez came overland along the Trace to join the settlers at Nashville. From that time on, hardy flat-boatmen, unkempt and hungry, returning on foot from Natchez, trudged by the Dunham cabin en route to their homesteads in upper Tennessee or to their points of embarkation along the Ohio River. Indian traders, highwaymen, mail carriers on horseback, and preachers with their Bibles in their saddlebags rode back and forth, using the Trace for reasons both pious and pragmatic. The parade that passed the double cabin in buckskin or homespun or clerical broadcloth had penetrated the wilderness and would soon bring it under the domination of the white man.

In 1801, at the beginning of a new century and a new era, the federal government voted funds and negotiated contracts for clearing and widening the Natchez Trace so that mail services could be conducted with regularity and wagons could be driven, for commerce and profit, toward the Southwest. From about 1795 to 1800 Colonel Benjamin Joslin, pioneer and Indian fighter, operated Dunham's Station—presumably on a lease or rental basis. Francis Bailey arrived there with a party from Natchez in 1797 and mentioned Joslin as his host at that time. Records show that in 1801 Joslin was formally awarded a federal contract for providing the mail services to Natchez—a service which he had privately initiated earlier—and it is known that his riders were dispatched weekly from Nashville with their leather mail pouches bulging. In order to maintain this weekly schedule between the two distant points, Colonel Joslin employed at least five horsemen for the 1,100-mile round trip. Therefore, he must have kept a number of horses for their use—a deduction that points to the Belle Meade property as a center for grazing and maintaining horses almost from the beginning of its history.

Despite hardships, bloodshed, and the loss of countless lives, the work of the first settlers had finally been effective: Tennessee became a state with its own government in 1796. Now the lands along the Cumberland would be relatively safe for ambitious newcomers with a keen eye for opportunities in the new country. Tradesmen, farmers, businessmen, and land developers moved west, bringing their families with them with less fear of Indian massacre or frontier deprivation.

Among the group of hardy, enterprising farmers were Thomas and Giles Harding of Goochland County, Virginia, who arrived in Middle Tennessee in 1798 and bought adjoining tracts of land, about five hundred acres in all, east of the Harpeth River and north of the Little Harpeth. (This is now part of the Ed Hicks farm southwest of Nashville on Highway 100.) Having sold their established holdings in Virginia because of soil depletion or because their instinct for better lands pointed to Tennessee, the Harding brothers, cash in hand, purchased their initial tracts of fine soil from Nashville's early settlers or their luckless widows and children who had been left with too much land, too little cash, and too few hands to transform their holdings into profitable operations. A sufficient amount of ready money or credit, a family of strapping boys and girls, a few slaves, and boundless energy were the requisites for success in the Tennessee of 1800. It seems clear that Thomas and Giles Harding were able to meet most of these requirements from the beginning. And though Thomas died in 1805 and Giles in 1807, they lived long enough to see their sons modestly established on productive lands in the new state.

John Harding (1777–1865), son of Giles, was thirty years old in 1807 at the time of his father's death. That year he bought the 250 acres of land from Daniel A. Dunham which lay "on the east side of Richland Creek, including old Dunham's Station." However modest at the time, this purchase was to be the foundation of Belle Meade, for John Harding, a resourceful and industrious young man, moved into the double log cabin with his new bride Susannah Shute and established the Harding dynasty with the birth of their son William Giles Harding in 1808. From this initial purchase John Harding systematically added to his Richland Creek lands in tracts varying from 10 to 469 acres through 1842, when more than 3,500 acres had been accumulated in twenty-nine transactions.

The industry and achievements of John Harding were tangible evidence in his own time of his intelligent handling of his resources. Added to the revenue he realized from competent management of the Belle Meade domain in the 1830's was the considerable profit he made from the sale of a cotton plantation which he had acquired earlier in Louisiana. After clearing three large farms in Tennessee and this one in Louisiana, John Harding, years later at the age of sixty-three, took eight Negro slaves and cleared another in Arkansas near Plum Point Bend.

This valuable cotton plantation was given to his grandson, John Harding McGavock.

Besides farming, from as early as 1815 (according to the yellowed pages of the Belle Meade account books) John Harding was engaged in the lucrative business of boarding and breeding horses for a large clientele in the vicinity of Nashville. A typical entry from the well-filled ledgers shows that "Samuel Houston sent two ponys" to Harding to board on March 2, 1819, and then a bay horse during the Christmas season of the same year, and paid up his account in full the following April. That same leather-bound volume reveals that Ralph E. W. Earl, the itinerant portrait painter and friend of Andrew and Rachel Jackson, boarded his "brown poney" with Harding from October 21, 1818, to January 30, 1819—before settling at the Hermitage for a residence of seventeen years.

Other ventures, such as supplying hay and fodder for Nashville stables, the raising of beef, the growing of fruit, and the production of cotton, made John Harding a rich and respected citizen by the time his son William Giles came of age. But in spite of their wealth, John and Susannah Harding and their children are said to have lived simple and unostentatious lives, devoid of pretension and show. In all, Harding's life was exemplary of the success reflected in a steady will combined with the wise handling of land resources, labor, and family.

John Harding brought his son William to manhood not only as his heir, but also as his capable successor. The boy was born in 1808 in the now-famous double cabin; he grew up in the larger Harding house constructed soon thereafter on the site of the present mansion. As a youth of fourteen, William Giles entered the University of Nashville while Dr. Philip Lindsley was president. Possessing a serious and scholarly turn of mind, he grew impatient with the atmosphere he found at the struggling little university. So he set out from home at the age of sixteen and visited Middletown, Connecticut, where the Military and Scientific Academy, presided over by Captain Aiden Partridge, a former superintendent of West Point, was located. Here he was graduated in 1829.

Instead of a literary or legal or ecclesiastical calling, Cadet Harding possessed an interest in the sciences. In the pursuit of his studies at the academy in Connecticut he found a proper climate for work in the scientific disciplines which were compatible with his inclinations and which would prepare him for a career in agriculture and horse breeding at home. His father's foresight in allowing William to study in New England was to yield enormous dividends in the next five decades of Tennessee agriculture.

Married first in 1829 to Mary Selene McNairy, William G. Harding began his career as a farmer on a sizable tract of land which his father owned east of Nashville on Stone's River. Ten years later, his business abilities proven to his father's satisfaction, William was given the full management of Belle Meade when John Harding turned over the reins of the flourishing establishment to his son. The confidence and trust of John Harding in his son is a telling memorial to both men.

Having lost his first wife in 1837, William G. Harding was married for a second time to Miss Elizabeth Irwin McGavock in 1840. The daughter of Randal McGavock, owner of Carnton near Franklin, the new Mrs. Harding was mistress of Belle Meade for twenty-seven years during its zenith. It was she who suffered the raging flames which destroyed the Harding's older home in 1851, during which two of the children, Selene (born 1846) and Mary Elizabeth (born 1850), were hastily pitched out of a second-story window onto a feather bed. It was she who helped her husband sketch the plans and see to completion in 1853–54 the present Belle Meade mansion. Family tradition has it that Harding had learned enough civil engineering to supervise the construction of the fabled edifice from his own drawings. It has also been suggested that William Strickland of Philadelphia, architect of the Tennessee State Capitol, drew the plans for Belle Meade and Harding executed them. Yet it was Elizabeth McGavock Harding, wife, mother, and gracious hostess, whose genuine executive ability was responsible for running the large household and providing the ease of living and comfortable entertainment for scores of visitors for over a quarter of a century.

It was also Elizabeth McGavock Harding who took her stand valiantly during the anxieties of the Civil War—after Union Troops triumphed at Fort Donelson in February, 1862, and overran the city of Nashville. Her husband, a general in the state militia before 1861, was arrested in Nashville as a political prisoner in April, 1862, and detained first at the state penitentiary and then sent to the federal prison at Fort Mackinac Island. As an "ardent secessionist" William Giles Harding at the age of fifty-three had contributed half a million dollars, it was believed, to the arming of Tennessee troops and the defense of the state from Union invaders. Upon his arrest and detention Mrs. Harding assumed the management of Belle Meade, and the lush estate became a particular target for officers and unscrupulous foragers of the federal commissary. The abundant fields of spring crops which Harding himself had planted, the beef, pork, and wild deer, and the famous stables were all but depleted to supply the needs of the Union Army in Nashville.

The letters which Mrs. Harding wrote from Belle Meade to her hus-

band in the Michigan prison provide readers with many details of the
plantation and the raising of crops in wartime:

> I took a long ride over the place yesterday, examined the wheat, oats,
> clover, etc; the former does not look so well, has rust, but Mr. Beasley
> [the overseer] does not think the grain formed injured, but it has not a
> heavy thick appearance like good wheat to me, & I don't think it will
> yield much; the oats look fine & I think will bear a heavy harvest; the
> clover, at Johns' & the well field, looks splendid, the best in the neigh-
> borhood it is said, & it was so rich & fine, particularly the latter. Mr. B.
> says the corn in the Johns field is better than he ever saw it there be-
> fore, & it is certainly very clean & in growing condition; but the nicest,
> greenest and largest corn is in the "red house field," & it was a beautiful
> sight to see the ploughs *splitting the middles* & leaving not a weed
> behind—& who do you suppose were the plowers? Cloe's Dick, Edy,
> Nancy, Alfred, Ellen Isabel, Coley, & Thornton—about the youngest
> set of plowers I ever saw; they were as merry as if it was a perfect
> frolic, & seemed much gratified that I went out to see them. Jeff was at
> the head, & when they all got to the turn row, I stopped them, told
> them I had just received a letter from you and that I intended answer-
> ing it and tell you who I saw plowing so nicely; *every one* stood out &
> begged not to be forgotten, & "Tell Master howdy for me," & Jeff said
> "Tell Master I am trying to make as good a crop as if he was here."
> And Mr. B. says he is.

A few weeks later Mrs. Harding wrote of her journey into Nashville
to see Andrew Johnson, military governor of Tennessee, to arrange permission to visit her husband if he were to be held indefinitely in Michigan. In the same letter she gave further news of Belle Meade, reporting
that the "cherries, plums & apples [are] now in perfection." She also reported a humorous incident in the household, related obviously to provide the general with a chuckle:

> Susanna [her personal maid] received your letter yesterday, & I have
> never seen her so gratified and proud—not only of the letter itself but
> your commendation & appreciation of her fidelity and devotion to
> yourself. I was amused at her this morning; she was looking at your
> photograph & remarked, "Master looks as if he was about to say to you,
> 'Wife, I want *big Lou, little Lou, & Kingston* [house servants] to save
> hay. It looks like rain, & we must push ahead.'" Singularly enough, then
> Mr. Beasley stepped in & said, "Mrs. Harding, I have *a great deal of
> hay down,* & it looks very threatening. Can't you spare me a few
> hands?"

Prisoner Harding would have enjoyed the humor of the incident, for
Mrs. Harding had chided him more than once about how as soon as she
was in the midst of feverish preparations for company he would take her
household servants off to the fields "to save hay."

The same letter bears testimony of the times in which it was written:

I wish you could ride over the "red house field" & see the rich, deep green sea of verdure, high as my head, waving in the bright sunshine; it is so suggestive of "peace & plenty" one can scarcely realize that stern war, in all its sad reality, is around and about us. . . . Your Father [John Harding] spent today with us, is in fine health & as much pleased to read Susanna's letter as though addressed to himself; says it matters not who your letters are directed to, so he hears *you are well, cheerful & hopeful.* Some one said to him, "Now that Cousin Frank [McGavock] has been arrested, your time may come next." He very quickly replied, "Well, I shall not take any oath." [An oath to disavow the Confederate cause.] I could not but be amused at his prompt manner, quite unlike a man of 85 years. Since the servants heard I would certainly visit you, there has been no end to their offers of assistance; hearing gold was very difficult to get, many proffered their 5 & 10 dollar pieces, & *one* told me he could lend me $85. I feel very grateful, for they *know* how much you wish me to go. I read portions of every letter to them. When they hear I have one, they congregate & ask to hear what Master says. The mention of their names is followed by a general show of ivory, & messages that would fill my next sheet, if I were to attempt to write them.

Still another letter from Mrs. Harding to her husband points out the vulnerable position of their plantation and the almost constant harassment she was forced to endure:

It is a happy thing these days to be obscure, and a man's safety now depends on his insignificance; how I envy such quiet and seclusion as is to be found in the hills and hollows of "Sam's Creek," [a secluded sulphur spring and wooded area several miles north of Belle Meade in Cheatham County, at one time a summer resort with hotel] and if I could, you would find, on your return, Belle Meade and all its appurtenances occupying as unfindable a place as possible; the "Park" in particular I would place where it never could be found by stragglers and visitors in general.

Several months later, a Union observer, writing a report to Washington on "Nashville as a Type of the Rebellion," contributed in his survey the following remarks on General Harding and the pillaging at Belle Meade:

A portion of our army was quartered on or near his place during many weeks. There was grand hunting after those deer and buffalo. The goats were ruthlessly taken "in the wool." The stables were confiscated— what was left of the stud, the rebels having taken the best of the serviceable nags. Hundreds of tons of his hay and thousands of bushels of his grain were hauled into our camps. Miles of his fencing were burned. His men negroes kept company with his departed stock.

After his release from the island prison, General Harding was allowed to return to Nashville in September, 1862. The next year he filed a claim against the federal government for the damages his property had suffered during the first year of Union occupation. The record book of the Federal Board of Claims has been recently acquired by the Tennessee State Library and Archives and it reveals, under claim #439, that William Giles Harding estimated his losses at $32,000 during these first months of the war in Tennessee. The Board duly investigated the claim and the claimant, and made an award to him in the amount of $27,617. (There is no record, however, that this sum was ever actually paid.) It is of further interest that the notation under "Remarks" in the same official ledger categorizes General Harding as "Chairman of the Rebel Military Board at Nashville which voted $5,000,000 to arm the State."

Other records bring to light the levying of special taxes against the property of southern landowners as a consequence of the war. On February 27, 1865, Harding's 3,500 acres were valued at $165,000, on which, federal tax receipts show, the owner paid $577.50 under "An Act for the Collection of Direct Taxes in Insurrectionary Districts within the United States." In the same period the government collected further revenue on the assessed value of Harding's carriages, silver plate, and other holdings.

Late in 1864, when General John Bell Hood led his Confederate Army into Middle Tennessee to fight and lose the two-day Battle of Nashville, the Confederates brought a wagon train looking for sorely needed supplies to General Harding's park for safety, stationing the wagons in the secluded area at the Belle Meade racetrack. Late in the afternoon of December 15, Lieutenant James Dinkins of Chalmers' Division was dispatched with an escort company from headquarters to bring the supply train to the Confederate main line on the Hillsboro Road. Stanley F. Horn has described the scene in *The Decisive Battle of Nashville:*

> When Dinkins and his company arrived at Belle Meade just before dark, they found that the wagons had been captured and burned and that there was a force of Federal soldiers, some mounted and some on foot, in the grounds around the mansion. Undismayed, Dinkins and his company moved around behind the big barn and formed for a charge. Dashing through the yard, yelling and firing as they went, they stampeded the surprised Federals but in pursuing them encountered another body of bluecoats who quickly turned the tables on them and sent them scurrying back through the Belle Meade grounds.

The next action, recounted many years later by James Dinkins himself in his *Personal Recollections and Experiences*, brings the skirmish into focus:

The enemy opened a hot fire, and as the boys returned through the yard the bullets were clipping the shrubbery and striking the house. [The stone columns of the porch still bear testimony today.] Nine of the enemy were killed or wounded and some fifteen captured. As we rode back, we saw Miss Selene Harding standing on the stone arm of the front steps waving her handkerchief. The bullets were falling thick and fast about her, but she had no fear in her heart. She looked like a goddess. She was the gamest little human being in all the crowd. I passed and caught her handkerchief and urged her to go into the house, but she would not until the boys had disappeared behind the barn. They fell back and awaited the coming of General Chalmers, who soon arrived.

The terrible costs of the Civil War—the losses of crops, cattle, fences, racing stock, about 140 slaves, and a considerable personal fortune—did not defeat Elizabeth and William Harding or dispossess them of their holdings. Unlike other plantations which had flourished in the grand manner in the halcyon days of the Old South and which could never again regain their former prominence in the cotton economy or renew the lost grandeur of an older age, Belle Meade came back with style and vigor during the next two decades. As long as the land was there and General Harding to oversee it, no outside forces seemed bold enough to destroy the great domain. Harding's unwillingness to accept defeat and his total dedication to the agrarian principles of the good husbandman are undoubtedly reflected in the philosophical statement of another Tennessee agrarian of the 1880's. "The basis of all wealth is the soil of the land. Prosperous cities, towns and huge manufactories seem to spring up and flourish as if by magic and without reference to the agricultural advantages of the country; but such growth will be but temporary unless sustained by a country possessing agricultural wealth. It may almost be reduced to a mathematical problem in which it may be said that the soil and climate equal the wealth of the country." In spite of the fact that Harding's capital and labor were greatly depleted by the four-year conflict, the master of Belle Meade held on to his vast holdings and managed, through skill and patience, to effect an admirable recovery by the time of his death in 1886.

At the General's right hand during most of this postwar period was his capable and colorful son-in-law, William Hicks Jackson, the husband of Selene Harding. A resident of Jackson, Tennessee, and a West Point graduate of 1856, William H. Jackson served in the U.S. Army on the frontiers of New Mexico and Texas until the time of the Civil War. As a Confederate officer he first served as a captain of artillery under Generals Pillow and Polk. Then he was transferred to cavalry, was wounded

at Belmont, and was promoted to the rank of brigadier general for his
gallant conduct in the capture of Holly Springs, Mississippi. Later,
while his division was under the command of Nathan Bedford Forrest,
Jackson helped cover the retreat of General Hood's army from Tennessee after the Confederates lost the Battle of Nashville.

When the war ended General William H. Jackson returned briefly to
West Tennessee to manage his father's cotton interests. Soon thereafter
he was hired by General Harding to assist in the management of Belle
Meade. Before many months had passed, he proved himself as efficient
an organizer of farm laborers as of military units. He became acquainted
with the Harding family through a shared interest in agricultural science and membership in the Methodist Episcopal Church. In 1868 he
joined the household by marriage to General Harding's older daughter
Selene, who had become mistress of the mansion at her mother's death in
1867.

Nor were the claims on Nashville of the Jacksons from West Tennessee to stop there. On one of his trips to call on Selene Harding, General
Jackson was accompanied by his older brother, Howell; the two were
treated to the sight of the younger Harding sister playing in the creek as
they drove onto the Belle Meade grounds. Seven years later Howell, a
widower with three children, married Mary Elizabeth Harding. His additional purchases for the building site of his 1886 mansion, West
Meade, brought the total Harding-Jackson holdings to 5,300 acres of
contiguous property.

According to an eminent biographer of Belle Meade, Miss Margaret
Lindsley Warden, the two Jackson brothers were very different in appearance and personality:

> William was blue-eyed, auburn-haired, bushy-browed, ruddy-faced and
> powerfully built like a wrestler. He stood only a few inches above five
> feet and weighed about 225 pounds. Very erect in bearing, he once
> heard a small colored boy advise one of his fellows to "rear back and
> throw out yer chist like the ginral." His brother Howell was small and of
> refined features and slender build. He was a studious, serious-minded
> lawyer, quiet and reserved, but genial among his intimates. He was re-
> spected for accurate learning, sound judgment, and strict integrity.

Howell and Mary Elizabeth Jackson eventually inherited 2,000 acres
of the general's property on the northwest side of the Harding Road.
Adjacent to this they bought 350 acres and built there, in 1886–87,
the large red brick, timber-trimmed Victorian residence West Meade.
The remainder of Mary E. Jackson's inheritance from her father, some

997 acres, lay on the southeast side of the Harding Road and was known in the family as the High Pasture because it was there that the cows were grazed. This High Pasture became the first half of Percy Warner Park many years later as the city moved westward and the Howell Jackson heirs gradually sold their holdings at their own convenience.

But if the Harding connections, with their double first cousins, are still sometimes subject to confusion, it is even more difficult to deal adequately, in short space, with the bloodlines and offspring of the Belle Meade thoroughbreds and racing stock. The horse industry which John Harding began in the early decades of the nineteenth century—and which gained momentum and international recognition under William G. Harding and William H. Jackson—commands the space of a full chronicle in the annals of horsebreeding. Again it is convenient to quote from Miss Warden's account in the *Nashville Tennessean Magazine:*

> The Thoroughbred stud of Belle Meade, called at the time of its dispersal in 1902 the nation's "oldest and greatest," may be considered to date back as far as 1816, when John Harding owned or "stood" the imported English stallion Boaster "on the old Natchez Road." Six years later another English sire, Eagle, was located at John Harding's but advertised as if owned by Montgomery Bell. In 1823 the founder of Belle Meade headed a company of Nashville men who paid $8,000 for the imported Arabian stallion, Bagdad.
>
> William G. Harding stated in *The American Turf Register* of August, 1839, that the first foal bred by him was the filly Alpha, by imported Leviathan out of Juliet by Kosciusko, born in 1836. He wrote, "This, I suppose, is the acknowledged center of the racehorse region. Blood stock here is all the go. To be without it is to be out of fashion, and destitute of taste. So I too have procured a little bit of the real grit, which by-and-by I hope to increase. . . . Since it is a custom to bespeak names in your valuable journal, I will claim for all mine at once, the Greek Alphabet, from Alpha to Omega, inclusive." (The most famous of these alphabet horses was the gray mare, Gamma.)
>
> Priam, winner of the English Derby of 1830, was one of the first stallions owned by William G. Harding, and he joined the stud in the early '40's. Other pre-Civil War sires included Childe Harold and Vandal, while Jack Malone and John Morgan, both dating from 1858, were there during the war years. The famous Bonnie Scotland, possibly the greatest sire at Belle Meade, came in 1872 to replace Vandal and Jack Malone, which had died that year. In the late '70's came Great Tom, also from England, and the Kentucky-bred Enquirer. In the early '80's two noted stallions added were Bramble and Luke Blackburn, while in 1886 at the Pierre Lorillard dispersal, $20,000 was given for Iroquois, the American-bred horse that had won the English Derby and had been champion of his year in England in 1881.

But General Harding, promoter of the turf and devotee of the
blooded horse, breeder and advocate of thoroughbreds, not once during
his long life succumbed to the "evils of the racetrack." He staunchly de-
fended the industry but "resolved never to bet a cent on the result of
any contest of speed or any game of chance."

Thus we have characterized for us the tone of Belle Meade under
William G. Harding. The next two decades following his death saw the
decline, fall, and dissolution of Tennessee's queen of plantations. If the
brass knuckles of fate in the form of a civil war had failed to crush the
Hardings, the unhappy events at the end of the century broke their descendants' grip and dispersed them from their holdings. Tragedy, waiting in the wings and biding its time for an entrance, strode at last to the
center of the stage.

The causes most frequently given for the decline and dispersal are numerous and complex. Here they can be outlined but briefly. The general
opinion has it that Belle Meade crumbled from within. Character
amounted to fate, in one sense, and the third and fourth generations
were not equal to the vicissitudes of the times, which embraced the
panic of 1893 and the changing economy in the New South. Yet the
lavish way of life was still maintained in the halls of the mansion and on
the racetrack long past the time that prudence would have sanctioned it.
The physical strength of William H. Jackson was failing by the turn of
the century, and the death of his only son, William Harding Jackson,
from typhoid at the age of twenty-nine left the estate proper without a
strong hand to guide it.

The old order gave way in 1902, when there was a "complete dispersal sale" of the Belle Meade stud. In 1904 the contents of the proud
mansion were sold on the auction block. The deer herd presented some
special problems for the hands of the receivers, for these sleek, graceful
animals were too wild to be captured without maiming. Finally they
were bought by a subscription raised by kind-hearted nostalgic Nash-
villians and allowed their freedom in the woods nearby, with the gentlemen's agreement among hunters that they were not to be molested for a
specified period of time. For years after this, older residents still recall,
the deer were seen furtively crossing the Harding Road at twilight in
the vicinity of their old enclosure.

Again we are indebted to Margaret Linsley Warden for the final
chapter on the stables:

> To the horse lovers of the nation the saddest part of the dissolution of
> Belle Meade was the end of Luke Blackburn. Annie D. Richardson Jack-
> son [widow of William Harding Jackson] kept the old hero and a small

band of Thoroughbreds as long as there was any hope of maintaining the place. But everything had to go. Even Uncle Bob's saddle horse was auctioned but bid in for him by white friends. [Uncle Bob was stallion groom for many years.] Walter Parmer bought The Commoner and what mares he wanted.

Luke Blackburn, old and useless, had outlived the fortunes of his people, and a single bid, $20, took the once great champion of the American turf. Mrs. Jackson had the old blanket of his sire, Bonnie Scotland, thrown over his swayed back as he went down the road beyond Belleview to South Harpeth. There in a small log stable fixed up by his purchaser, William H. Allison, farmer and stockman, Luke Blackburn lived for three years until a goitre choked him to death at 29. From his paddock on the river bank it was noticed that he would always stand facing east, looking toward Belle Meade, the erstwhile "oldest and greatest" Thoroughbred nursery in America.

The hammer of the auctioneer splintered the domain into a number of parcels, and from time to time these were divided and sold by a succession of real estate companies and private investors. Among them were Luke Lea, James E. Caldwell, Jacob McGavock Dickinson, and the Bransford Realty Company. Dickinson, who was secretary of war under President Taft and also a kinsman of the Hardings, bought the mansion and 400 acres in 1906. It was during his tenure that President Taft was entertained there in the summer of 1909. Subsequent owners were J. O. Leake and Walter O. Parmer, until Meredith Caldwell and his family acquired the house and fifty acres from Parmer's estate in 1936. The Caldwells were the last private family to reside at Belle Meade, selling it and the twenty-four acres in the present lawn to the State of Tennessee in 1953.

This final transaction in the long history of Belle Meade was urged and supported by a group of farsighted citizens with a keen sense of the heritage symbolized by the fabled estate. Leading this group—at a time when there was every indication the house would be razed—was a committee from the Nashville Chapter of the Association for the Preservation of Tennessee Antiquities. Particularly zealous was the late Mrs. Guilford Dudley, Sr., who solicited the support of the governor and the Tennessee legislature. By legislative action the necessary funds were appropriated for the purchase of the property in 1953, with the understanding that it would be opened to visitors throughout the year.

Since that time, under the capable management of a board of governors appointed by the A.P.T.A., the house has been refurbished and restored. The grounds have been embellished by the planting of over 300 young trees, creating an arboreteum of 130 varieties.

Other structures at Belle Meade, in addition to the manor house, have
been made attractive for visitors. After we enter the main drive from
Harding Road and cross the small bridge over Richland Creek, we pause
by the heart-shaped pool which reflects the white columns of the mansion. Here we find a symbol, in the shape of the pool, of the heart and
center of the old plantation. Turning right we look down the spacious
lawn to the early log cabin, steeped in history and carefully restored.

Behind the mansion, convenient to the old kitchen, stands one of the
largest brick smokehouses in America. Here, in one season 20,000
pounds of hog meat were cured and stored for the use of the farm hands
and for the family banquet table. This magnificent smokehouse still pre-
serves some of the mouth-watering aromas of the salt, hickory smoke,
country hams, and cured bacon which hung from the beams and caused
visitors in the dining room to keep asking for more.

No visit to Belle Meade should be too hurried to enjoy the enchant-
ing vistas along the gravel walk leading to the gardener's house and the
family mausoleum. Then at the rear of the house there is the fine barn,
with its carriages, spacious stalls, and great loft to command the attention of visitors from an age oriented to high-speed transportation. The
outstanding carriage collection includes four vehicles originally belonging to Belle Meade's owners, along with more than twenty carriages of
different body styles which illustrate the great variety to be seen on
American roads before the turn of the present century.

In the house itself the fine furniture, antebellum fittings, and many excellent portraits are the valued gifts from several donors who would not
willingly let pass from memory the queenly grandeur that was once
Belle Meade.

Ralph B. Flanders

Two Plantations and a County of Antebellum Georgia

The end of the antebellum period interrupted a decade of prosperity and change. The relation between the two phenomena was direct and explicit. When one-crop agriculture became unprofitable, diversification frequently resulted. When one-crop agriculture thrived, other changes occurred. The following article describes the Everett and Tooke plantations near Houston and what was Peach County, Georgia.

Plantation life in this area represents the quintessence of antebellum southern civilization. Prosperous and efficient, these plantations offered their slaves a modicum of independence and a well-defined social life. Here at least slavery was no prison and southern paternalism no mere ideal. Many historians believe that life in this part of the South represented the most refined and final stage of plantation society and that the newer areas of the South would eventually duplicate its social patterns. If this is true, then the peculiar institution might have promised some prospect of improvement or acculturation for its slaves. The generous master who allowed his slaves religious instruction provided a means of spiritual sustenance. Slave marriages established a basis for a more stable social life, and individual farming the means of improvement and perhaps the money necessary to buy his or her freedom. In this region at least the well-being of the slaves depended upon the prosperity of the plantation.

Of equal importance, however, is the fact that the prosperity of the county and lands surrounding the plantations did not parallel each other. The critical moment in this change came in 1844, when slaveholding among nonplanters began to decline. The price of cotton reached its nadir in 1844, and economic decline affected farmers and planters alike. Unlike other regions of the South, where planters reinvested in land and slaves, surplus capital here helped finance manufacturing which utilized the labor of landless whites.

Throughout the antebellum period, agriculture was far more important than manufacturing. The tendency for ownership of land

Reprinted with permission from *The Georgia Historical Quarterly*, XII (March, 1928), 1–24.

and slaves to concentrate in fewer hands was the result of significant changes in the economic organization of this region. Though essentially an agricultural phenomenon, it demanded a solution beyond the traditional confines of the South's economy. During the postbellum period interest and activity in manufacturing increased greatly. The promoters of industrialism addressed themselves to whites who could not compete with black agricultural labor and who therefore represented a significant social threat. In this region efforts to resolve these potential disruptions began before the Civil War.

B etween the Ocmulgee River and Echeconnee Creek, just a few miles south of Macon, lies one of the fairest counties of Georgia.[1] On either side of the Dixie Highway fertile fields of waving corn dotted with stacks of hay merge into broad acres of cotton, with groves of pines to relieve the monotony. Peach orchards grace the countryside, and their pink, feathery blanket charms the traveler in the spring. In general the land is a level, sandy loam, with a clay subsoil. A larger part of the county lies in the pine woods belt, and a goodly portion in the rotten limestone region which was known in antebellum days as "the black lands." The southern part is very fertile, and formerly the larger plantations were located here. This section of the state, and Houston county in particular,[2] is famous as the home of the "Georgia Peach," and the success attending the cultivation of this fruit has attracted national attention.[3] Cotton, corn, hay, and peas are grown, in addition to peaches, pecans, and apples, and all kinds of stock are raised. There is scarcely a better county, agriculturally speaking, in that state.

In the antebellum period this section was especially attractive to the planters of the old cotton belt, whose lands were being exhausted, and it is barely possible that the Treaty of Indian Springs, made in 1821, whereby this territory was acquired from the Creek Indians,[4] was the result of pressure brought to bear upon the state officials by this class of society. Whatever may have been the motive, the fact remains that no time was lost in settling the newly acquired lands. Shortly after the treaty negotiations, in the same year, Houston county was created,

1. This paper was awarded the prize of $250 offered by the Georgia Historical Society for the best article within the field of Georgia history.

2. This reference includes Peach County, which was a part of Houston until recently.

3. *Georgia, Historical and Industrial*, by the Department of Agriculture, Atlanta, Georgia, (1901), 712–716.

4. Ulrich Bonnell Phillips, *Georgia and State Rights*, 53. See map, 40.

named in honor of the distinguished governor by that name. The oak and hickory lands necessary for the cultivation of cotton were plentiful, long-leaf pine uplands were abundant, and the presence of a very small acreage of swamp land added to its attractiveness. The red hills and rolling land in the north made the county a desirable place of residence from the standpoint of health.[5]

The southern part of the county, while very fertile, was unhealthy for the whites, but not so for the Negroes. Therefore we find the larger plantations located in this region, operated under overseers or superintendents, while the proprietors in many instances resided in the towns of Fort Valley and Perry or in adjoining counties.[6] "Much of this pine belt was productive and the valley of the Flint River adjoined it, and it soon had a settlement of excellent people, who formed a village called Fort Valley, probably because of its having been the site of one of the early Indian forts. The land about the village lay well and was quite productive, and when the railroad reached it the section was thickly settled." [7] It is in this section that the two plantations described below were located.

It is the purpose of this essay to present two plantations, each representative of a type, and in a general way to describe the county of Houston. In its preparation recourse has been made to the local archives of the county, which are now preserved in the courthouse at Perry, and the records there extant have been carefully examined. The scarcity of material has necessitated the reliance upon oral tradition in many instances, but proper weight has been given this type of information.[8]

THE TOOKE PLANTATION

In the southeastern part of Houston county, in and about the little village of Hayneville, were located the plantations of Allen and Joseph

5. *U. S. Census*, 1880, vol. VI. *Cotton Production*, 227.

6. A notable example of this type of planter was Colonel Joseph Bond, who owned six plantations, extending from Bibb to Newton counties, but whose home was in Macon.

7. George G. Smith, *Story of Georgia and Georgia People*, 372.

8. The interest of the writer in this particular study was aroused by Warren Grice of Macon, Georgia, who was born and reared in Houston County, and whose father was a slaveowner in that locality. The writer wishes to express his appreciation for the many favors extended by Mr. Grice. The title for the essay was suggested by Dr. Louis Martin Sears, visiting professor at Duke University, Durham, North Carolina.

Tooke.[9] The name of Joseph Tooke stands out in the annals of the county, for he was a prominent citizen, a successful planter, and a true gentleman of the Old South. His name was identified with many worthwhile enterprises.[10] In addition to his own affairs he acted as executor of the estate of his brother Allen, and he demonstrated his ability in this capacity. An appraisement of the estate of Allen Tooke, made at the time when the executor assumed control, shows he owned the following property: [11]

1 wagon, 6 mules, and a boar	$900.00
1 bay filly	50.00
1 black mare	50.00
1 small horse	80.00
1 black colt	10.00
90 head stock of hogs at $3.00	270.00
1 lot plows and stocks	70.00
1 lot carpenter's tools	15.00
1 40 saw cotton gin	110.00
1 threshing machine	30.00
1 lot books	8.00
35 head stock of cattle at $5.00	175.00
Book case, soda, bofat, medicine chest, mahogany furniture, 5 bedsteads and furniture.	
38 slaves, ranging in price from $200 to $1,000.	
2 mules	200.00
Amount of joint property:	
11 slaves, $1,000 to $1,500.	
1 yoke steers and cart	$ 80.00
1 cow and calf	12.00
1 gin	100.00
50 head stock of hogs at $4.00	200.00

The exact amount of land owned cannot be ascertained, but 1,908 acres were returned as taxable in 1835.[12] The following table shows the number of slaves and acres owned or controlled by Joseph Tooke from 1835 to 1864.[13]

9. The two estates are treated as one, inasmuch as much of the property was held in common, and Joseph Tooke acted as the executor of the Allen Tooke estate after 1837.

10. Joseph Tooke was a stockholder in the Hayneville Academy, chartered in 1838 (*Acts of Georgia Assembly of Georgia*, 1838, 12). In 1852 his two-year-old bay filly was awarded a silver cup at the Southern Cultivators Agricultural Association fair.

11. Houston, Appraisements A.

12. Houston County *Tax Digest* 1835. Hereafter referred to as *Tax Digest*.

13. Table compiled from tax digests for years indicated.

1835	Allen and Joseph Tooke	74 slaves	3,966	acres
1839	Joseph Tooke	61 slaves	1,780	acres
1844	Joseph Tooke	166 slaves	3,867½	acres
1848	Joseph Tooke	168 slaves	5,012	acres
1853	Joseph Tooke	172 slaves	5,510	acres
1859	Joseph Tooke	123 slaves	2,800	acres
1864	Joseph Tooke	129 slaves	2,800	acres

The decrease in the number of slaves and acres from those of 1853 to the number listed in 1859 may be accounted for by the fact that between these dates a final settlement of the Allen Tooke estate was made. However, this does not account for the small increase between 1859 and 1864. It is probable that Mr. Tooke sold a number of his slaves. Financial statements lead us to believe that Joseph Tooke was an able administrator. Under his management a plantation operated with slave labor was profitable, but it is still open to question whether, if the same capital had been invested in stocks and bonds, the returns would have been larger.

About eight miles from Perry, the county seat, was located the plantation of Joseph Tooke.[14] The big white house, fronted with large columns, stood some distance from the road and was approached by an avenue of oak and cedar trees. Flower gardens, climbing roses, and vines added to the beauty and comfort of the place. The main body of the house contained eight rooms which were connected by an ell, with a five-room section containing the dining room, kitchen, and pantries. A little distance from the back yard were outhouses of various kinds, including a concrete smokehouse [15] and numerous cribs. Across the road, facing the Tooke Home, the overseer's house was located. This was a simple frame dwelling with five or six rooms. To the rear of this house were the slave quarters. The drawing below indicates the relative position of the several buildings, as described by the daughter of Mr. Tooke.

The quarters were composed of about forty houses, arranged in rows of eight or ten each, neatly whitewashed and elevated so as to insure sanitation. The cabins were small frame structures with two main rooms and one or two shed rooms, depending upon the size of the family. A

14. The general description of the plantation is based upon an account given the writer by the youngest daughter of Joseph Tooke, who was sixteen at the outbreak of the Civil War. Although well advanced in age, Mrs. Elizabeth Daniel is young and vivacious in spirit, and her story rings true. Naturally her account is biased, but in general her statements tally with the evidence.

15. Pennsylvania-Dixie Cement Corporation, producer of large quantities of cement, is located on the old Tooke place. According to Mrs. Daniel, the deposits were used in contructing walls, foundations, etc.

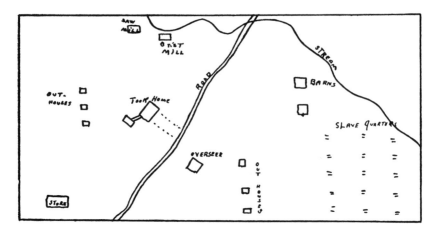

vegetable garden, a henhouse, and perhaps a dog completed the scene. It was the duty of the overseer to see that all premises were kept clean and sanitary. By working on holidays, overtime, at night, at any odd moment, industrious Negroes might raise small crops or poultry which they were permitted to sell, either in town or to their masters. The money derived from this source would be spent for such luxuries as tobacco and gay cloth.

It was not the custom on the Tooke plantation for any meals to be prepared in the cabins, for all food was cooked in a common kitchen located in the yard, where five women busied themselves all day at this task. A large brick oven and a hundred-gallon kettle constituted the main equipment. Vegetables and meat, with corn pone, were cooked and sent to the Negroes in the fields, each receiving his share in a tin bucket provided for that purpose. Breakfast was eaten before going to work, and supper after returning from the field. Occasionally molasses varied the diet, and on Sundays and holidays a more elaborate menu was provided.

A nursery with two slave women in charge cared for the children whose mothers worked in the fields, and the proper diet for them, prepared in the main kitchen, was here served. The sick were placed in an infirmary, where they received every attention. In ordinary cases Mr. Tooke would prescribe, but if the ailment were of a serious nature a physician was called.

The interests of Joseph Tooke were quite extensive, and his larger and more important enterprises probably overshadowed plantation affairs. Two or three miles from Perry, Mr. Tooke owned and operated a cotton factory known as Houston Factory,[16] run by white labor under the direction of a Mr. Doolittle, a northern machinist. It is quite possible that many of the slaveowners obtained their Negro hats and osnaburgs from Houston Factory.[17] In addition to this, "Joseph Tooke and Son & Company" manufactured buggies, wagons, and some furniture; [18] in contrast with the cotton factory where no slaves worked, Negro labor was used here. In 1857 Austin, a smith, was hired for six months for $673; Dave, six months for $150; and Tom, a wood workman, four months for $104.[19] A store selling general merchandise served as an outlet for the products of the factories. A lime kiln, a grist and saw mill completed the plantation enterprises. In order to market his products, both industrial and agricultural, Mr. Tooke purchased a steamboat called "The Oak" which plied between Macon and Savannah.

In many respects the plantation was a self-sustaining unit, the main expense being clothing for the slaves. The vouchers listed in the annual returns of the estate show very few entries for groceries. In 1838 $43.89½ was spent for Negro cloth and $26.42 for 22 pairs of negro shoes at $1.18¾ per pair. Later in the same year $8.00 worth of wool hats and $37.10 for more shoes was spent. Blankets also were purchased from time to time; the same bill noted contained an entry of $37.96 for blankets.[20] Osnaburg, linsey, and woolen cloth were purchased to be made into clothes for the slaves. The following table of expenditures for the year 1843 may be considered typical: [21]

To cotton osnaburg 7.10—46 yds. $11.75	$ 11.75
85 lbs. sugar @ 10c 8.50. 4 sacks salt 12.00	20.50
55 lbs. coffee 11c 5.55. 21 pr. negro shoes 26.25	31.70
12 blankets 12.00, 9 blankets 84c 7.56	19.56
47 yds. osnaburg 4.70. 60 yds. lincey 18¾ c11.25	15.95
30 yds. woolen cloth 28c 8.45. Pd. Tax 26.40	34.85
Clks. fee 1.12½. School bill 6.37½ act. 200.00	207.50
Pd. children board 150.00. 44 yds. woolen cloth	164.37½
24 yds. woolen cloth 23c 5.55.33 yds. osnaburg 3.33	8.88

16. Remains of this factory may be seen today at the place still known as Houston Factory. The original building was destroyed by fire but was rebuilt by Mr. Tooke after the war.

17. James A. Everett made purchases from Tooke Factory. (Houston County *Annual Returns* K, voucher No. 110.) Hereafter referred to as *Returns.*

18. In 1857 $5,493.92 worth of buggies were sold to one man. *Proceedings Houston Superior Court,* 1857, 147ff.

19. *Ibid.,* 147.

20. *Returns* A.

21. *Ibid.,* B, 289.

Cash for cotton 9.00, Pd. overseer 242.00		251.00
Shop a/c 65.00. Bagging, rope, twine, 87.40		151.40
Cash for salt 7.50. Joint acct. J. & A. Tooke		7.50
For overseeing and co, ½		345.84
(This entry is for the joint plantation account, total $691.68¼.)		
	Total	$1276.29

The upkeep of the equipment and the wages of the overseer were important items in the annual expense. Apparently food was furnished the overseer in addition to the annual stipend.[22] In 1842 the overseer was paid $242.00, but the following year he received only $172.00. In 1847 Augustus Jeter was paid $250.00 for his services. As a general rule the overseers were recruited from the poor white class, and it is probable that the majority were inefficent, thereby necessitating frequent change. In addition to the overseer's wages new cabins were built and old ones repaired; cotton gins needed constant attention, and new equipment must be purchased. Bagging, twine, rope, hardware of various sorts, and plantation tools figure in all the vouchers.[23]

As a general rule three suits of clothes were issued to each slave during a year, but more often, especially on the smaller plantations, as they were needed. The work clothes were made of osnaburg, with heavier material for the cold months. Joseph Tooke was proud of the appearance of his slaves and desired that they make the best showing possible.

Slaves properly clothed and fed needed little medical attention. Mr. Tooke, although not a doctor of medicine, was something of a physician and adminstered epsom salt, Cook's pills, or applied liniment when necessary; the more serious ailments were treated by competent doctors, but from the records it appears that the Negroes were unusually healthy. In 1850 Dr. Cumming visited and prescribed for two Negro women and extracted the tooth of "Levi, a man," all for six dollars. The following year one of the male slaves was treated for gonorrhea, but just how prevalent this disease was it is not possible to determine. This is the only case recorded.[24] According to Mrs. Daniel, during pregnancy and for three or four weeks following childbirth women were not required to work. It was also affirmed that Joseph Tooke never sold a slave, but a glance at the first table in this article contradicts this assertion. Since from 1844 to 1864 there was no appreciable increase in the number of slaves, either a baby died every time one was born, which seems incredi-

22. *Returns*, 1838.
23. *Ibid.*, B, 263.
24. *Returns* D, 113.

ble after an examination of the medical bills, or many slaves were sold. The latter seems the more tenable theory.

All able-bodied men and women above twelve years worked in the fields, either in gangs or separately, according to the nature of the work. Aged, infirm, or crippled slaves wove baskets, mended or made clothes, or were assigned light tasks about the place. The old women often canned fruit and cared for the children. An experienced bricklayer, painter, wheelwright, and blacksmith were kept on the plantation. The household servants consisted of two cooks, a maid for each of the five girls, a Negro woman cleaner, and a carriage driver. Any or all of these were liable to be pressed into service when an emergency arose.

Into the dark life of the slave some light did come. On the Tooke plantation all of Saturday was given as a holiday, during which time the slaves could cultivate their own patches or wash and mend clothes. Sunday, of course, was strictly observed, and no one was allowed to work. After breakfast the Negroes would gather on the back porch, where they would be taught the Bible by some member of the Tooke family. Those who were members of the church were permitted to attend; sometimes religious services were held on the plantation and some slaves might preach to the Negroes. Preaching by free Negroes or slaves from other plantations was discouraged, for often wolves lurked in sheep's clothing, and the danger from the doctrines of the abolitionists must be guarded against.

The Fourth of July was a high-water mark with the Negroes, for it meant a plantation barbecue. The night before six or seven hogs and some sheep would be prepared, and until dawn the fragrant odors of burning oak and roasting pork and mutton would fill the air. At noon the tables would be spread in a grove and white and black would partake of the same food. After dinner the "little niggers" would dance and sing to the accompaniment of the guitar and banjo, much to the delight of the audience.[25]

Weddings always called for elaborate celebrations, regardless of the color of the contracting parties. Mr. Tooke encouraged marriage among his own slaves, for should a male slave marry the slave of another, the issue went to the owner of the female. However, if a slave fell in love

25. *Albany Patriot*, August 11, 1854. The editor describes a plantation barbecue, given the Negroes on the plantation of B. O. Keaton, in vivid terms. "The tables were loaded down with a profusion of the choicest eatables. . . . All the negroes were dressed in a neat and cleanly manner, and it was impossible to divine which of them seemed the happiest, so joyous and contented did they all appear." Another such barbecue is recorded in the *Albany Patriot*, February 3, 1859.

with and married one on another plantation, he was permitted to visit his wife.

The red letter day on the calendar was Christmas. When Mr. Tooke carried his cotton to New Orleans or Savannah, he brought back presents for all the Negroes on the place. The children in the white house took keen delight in filling the stockings on Christmas Eve and distributing them the next morning. No one was forgotten. At noon the slaves assembled in the yard, where tables were spread, and feasted on turkey and fruit. It was a rule that no child should be whipped during Christmas week, nor was any work required.

The writer is aware that the foregoing is a very rosy picture of the institution of slavery, and the attention of the reader must be called to the fact that only one side of the picture is presented. Undoubtedly Joseph Tooke was a model slaveowner and his slaves were well treated, but it was a matter of economic necessity that one do this; otherwise the value of the property in slaves would decrease. It must be remembered that the motive behind the whole institution was economic and not humanitarian. No one doubts but that the lot of the Negroes was far better in America than in Africa, but their value as a supply of labor led men to buy them. The picture of the plantation of Joseph Tooke is drawn from the records indicated and reflects no bias of the writer.

THE EVERETT PLANTATION

Another of Houston's prominent citizens was James Abington Everett, who lived in Fort Valley. Unfortunately, it has been impossible to obtain any information relative to the Everett Plantation prior to 1848, but after that date, over a period of twenty years, a fairly consecutive story may be gotten from the annual returns of the executor of the estate. Everett was one of the first settlers of the county and identified himself with various phases of civic life. His name appears among the trustees of the old Fort Valley Female Seminary which was chartered in 1838; [26] he was a trustee of the Wesley Manual Labor School, which had as its directors such men as James O. Andrew, Ignatius Few, Lovick Pierce, Samuel Anthony, and Joel Walker. In fact, it was through the generosity of Everett that the school was made possible: "James Abington Everett of Houston County hath made a donation of $25,000, designed as a permanent fund. . . ." [27]

26. Lucian Lamar Knight, *Georgia Landmarks*, II, 798. The seminary was rechartered in 1852. *Acts of General Assembly of Georgia*, 1852–53, 326.
27. *Acts of General Assembly*, 1837, 19ff.

Everett was very successful as a planter. The tax returns for 1839 show that he owned 156 slaves and 11,096½ acres of land; five years later these holdings had increased to 213 slaves and 12,139½ acres of land.[28] In 1848, at the time of his death, Everett owned 242 slaves, 12,144½ acres of land lying in Houston, Crawford, and Coweta counties, and an entire estate appraised at $500,000.[29] It is easy to believe that he was one of the wealthiest men in the entire state of Georgia. M. L. Green, his executor, proved to be an excellent administrator, and the estate flourished under his control.

The piety and benevolence of Everett is clearly shown by his will. The following items are interesting in this connection: [30]

> Item Tenth. I give to the Revd. Reuben H. Luckey, the sum of one thousand dollars.
> Item Sixteenth: I give and bequeath the sum of two thousand dollars for the benefit of the Mission established by the Methodist Episcopal Church South in the Creek Nation said sum to be paid to the Revd. Bishop James O. Andrew and Joshua Soule and to be by them [applied] to the use above specified. Said sum to be paid in four annual installments; if Bishop Andrew deems otherwise, in two annual installments.
> Item Seventeenth: I give and bequeath to my old friend the Revd. James Dunwoody the sum of $500.00 . . . to be expended by my executors in the purchase of a negro man or boy for him.
> Item Eighteenth: To my old friend Revd. John Fullwood . . . $500.00 to buy a negro man for him.
> Item Twenty-one: To the Foreign Missionary Society of the Methodist Episcopal Church South, $150.00 annually until the last heir is of age.
> Item Twenty-Two: To the Domestick Missionary Society of the Methodist Episcopal Church South $150.00 annually until the estate is settled.

That Everett was a staunch advocate and believer in the plantation regime supported by slave labor is indicated in his will. He left the sum of $15,000 to his "Beloved wife Mary Beaufort" with instructions to the executors to "lay [it] out in the purchase of Negroes for her." [31] The Negroes and lands were to be kept together and more added from time to time at the discretion of the executors.[32]

M. L. Green, one of the executors, devoted his entire time to the management of the Everett estate; the three plantations (the Home Place,

---

28. *Tax Digest*, 1839, 1844.

29. *Ibid.*, 1848; Houston County *Appraisements and Sales A*, 397ff. To the tax-burdened individual of 1927 it does not engender happiness to note that in 1848 Everett paid only $116.32 for taxes on an estate valued at $500,000. Cf. Appendix C.

30. Houston County *Wills A*, 220ff.

31. *Ibid.*

32. *Ibid.*, item 26.

Hog Crawl, and River Place) were left under the care of overseers. The credit vouchers for the salary of these men throws a light upon this interesting class in antebellum society. J. C. Ashburn received for his services on the Hog Crawl place $682 in 1852,[33] but his successor, J. W. Hill, drew only $550.[34] Isaac Thompson and N. C. Greer received $400 and $500, respectively, as overseers on the other plantations.[35] John D. Thompson was paid $600 for his services on the Hog Crawl place in 1860.[36] Others were employed but evidently did not give satisfaction. For example, S. L. Murry was at the River Place for only a little over a month, receiving $51,[37] and E. B. Towman was discharged after nine days.[38] Some years later, in 1864, E. B. Thompson was again employed.[39] The conclusion may be drawn that the overseer was a source of constant worry to the planter and competent overseers were hard to find.

However unsatisfactory some of the overseers may have been, some efficient ones undoubtedly were employed who assumed their responsibility and faithfully discharged their duties. Otherwise the plantations would not have been so successfully operated. Every care was taken that the slaves be kept in good physical condition, and the large sums of money spent each year for drugs and medical attention support this assumption. Whether it was "a visit and medicine for Peg" [40] or "a surgical operation for Floyd," [41] no expense was spared. Sometimes a physician signed a contract to treat the slaves on the plantation,[42] or he might call on the individuals as needed. The names of Doctors William J. Green, John D. Wade, and W. H. Hollinshead appear in the various returns, and Mathews & Green, a Fort Valley firm, supplied the drugs. No serious illnesses were noted in the itemized medical bills, but constant attention was required. In 1852 $550.75 was the sum of one bill,[43] and in 1860 the account was $648.36.[44] "Cupping and scurryfying negro

---

33. *Returns* D, 341ff.

34. *Ibid.*, E, 577ff. Voucher no. 84. The number hereafter referred to in citing the returns applies to the voucher numbers.

35. *Ibid.*, K, no. 113, 143.

36. *Ibid.*, M, no. 90.

37. *Ibid.*, no. 118.

38. *Ibid.*, no. 87.

39. *Ibid.*, P, no. 46.

40. *Ibid.*, C, 393ff. The charges were $2.50.

41. *Ibid.*, 304. The operation cost was $15.00.

42. *Ibid.*

43. *Ibid.*, E, 585.

44. *Ibid.*, M, no. 90.

man $1.00, setting fractured finger and dressing Gabriel's hand $3.00," [45] "attention to boy servant—gravel—$6.00," [46] "removing tumor from Dely (River Place) $5.00," [47] "visit to Tom and reducing hernia —$6.00," [48] are typical entries. Large quantities of chalk mixture, tincture of iodine, Seidlitz powders, epsom salts, Cook's pills, liniment, vermifuge, blue mass, quinine, laudanum, paregoric, and cherry pectoral were bought.[49] From the standpoint of the Negro's health it may be concluded the institution of slavery was beneficial to him; whether the motive be economic or humanitarian, the result was the same.

The Everett plantations were generally self-sustaining, as far as food supplies were concerned, for little in the way of groceries was purchased; molasses and sugar, with an occasional lot of bacon sides, seem to have been the only commodities not produced on the plantations. In 1854 three hogsheads of molasses, costing $113.40, four hogsheads of bacon sides, and 400 pounds of sugar were purchased.[50] Usually sufficient quantities of bacon and ham were produced to supply the slaves and leave a surplus for marketing.[51] Corn, a little wheat, potatoes, yams, and all varieties of vegetables, together with pork, beef, and mutton, were raised on the plantations. Watermelons and fruits served to vary the diet.

The items in the personal grocery bill of the Everett family indicate that they were quite aristocratic in their taste, and we may visualize a table groaning with delicacies. All kinds of crackers, pickles, apples, grapes, almonds, pecans, Brazil nuts, candies, cheese, fig paste, wines, and liquors appeared on their accounts.[52] Dress goods purchased by the ladies in the family lead us to believe that they moved in the highest circles of society. One of the boys attended the University of North Carolina, and a girl was enrolled in the seminary at Winston-Salem. The Everetts were representatives of the old southern aristocracy.

In addition to the staple groceries that must be supplied, the next item in the expense was clothing. In October, 1852, 86 pairs of shoes costing $95.75, 136 blankets valued at $152.23, and 54 hats costing $40.50 were purchased. The returns for 1858 show that 787½ yards of kerseys worth

45. *Ibid.*, K, nos. 120, 123, 129.
46. *Ibid.*, C, 424.
47. *Ibid.*, M, no. 78.
48. *Ibid.*, no. 144.
49. *Ibid.*, K, nos. 120, 123, 129, 140.
50. *Ibid.*, F, 87ff.
51. *Ibid.*, passim.
52. *Ibid.*, K, no. 140.

$128.30 and 68 hats at $1.00 per hat were bought from "Joseph Tooke and Son & Co."[53] The largest shoe bill appeared in the financial statement of 1859:[54]

39 pairs men's shoes (Russett) for River Place	$ 62.40
8 pairs boys' shoes (Russett) for River Place	9.20
77 pairs men's shoes (Russett) for Hog Crawl	123.20
11 pairs boys' shoes (Russett) for Hog Crawl	12.65
87 pairs men's shoes (Russett) for Home Place	139.20
34 pairs boys' shoes (Russett) for Home Place	39.10
1 pair shoes by Simon of River Place	1.60
257 pairs shoes	$387.35

At various times during the year, when the necessity arose, shoes were bought for the slaves, as the last item in the above table indicates. No mention is ever made of a difference between shoes supplied men and women; probably they both wore the same kind. The sum of $61.00 was spent for 24 men's wool hats and 25 boys' hats the previous year.[55]

Constant repairing and building went on under the plantation regime. In 1854 twenty houses were built on the estate and several were repaired,[56] a smokehouse costing $50.00 was constructed, and lumber to the sum of $2,480.90 was bought for the plantations.[57] The following year wells were dug, ditches excavated, and a pond near the Negro quarters of the Home Place drained, costing $350.78. In this connection it is interesting to note that men not in the plantation were employed to do this work, probably because of the danger involved.[58] In 1853 fifteen spinning wheels "for use on the plantation" were purchased for $46.50.[59]

As was the custom, slaves on the Everett plantations were accorded the privilege of raising small crops of their own or of performing odd jobs outside their regular working hours in order to earn money. Making shingles and dressing lumber was a profitable occupation of this sort. In 1854 Ralph earned $12.50 by cutting shingles, Robbin $5.00, and Daniel $20.00. "The boy Aaron" by dressing lumber at night made $10.25, Mark $3.66, and Dick $3.40. West attained the heights of a capitalist among his fellows when he received $150.00 for making 336 barrels. Hauling coal at five cents a bushel was not very profitable, but

53. *Ibid.*, D, 341ff.
54. *Ibid.*, K, nos. 70, 108, 110.
55. *Ibid.*, M, 85ff. cf. K, no. 168.
56. *Ibid.*, F, 87ff.
57. *Ibid.*, G, 81ff.
58. *Ibid.*, E, 585.
59. *Ibid.*, F, nos. 48, 49.

many boys engaged in this work. The "boy Ephrom," Sam, and Little Sam worked in the brick kiln at night. The corn crops made by the slaves were not large, but some money was made in this manner.[60]

M. L. Green obeyed the instructions of James A. Everett to invest in more Negroes. A few slaves were sold from the estate. For example, in 1850 seven Negroes, six men and one girl, were sold for $4,000; five more were sold for $4,825 and one boy, Solomon, for $950.[61] As each heir became of age the proper share of the estate was awarded. This accounts for the decrease in the number of slaves held by Green for the heirs. Eighteen Negroes were given to Mrs. Mary B. Mathews in 1852 as her share of the estate.[62] The first sum expended for slaves was in 1853, when $12,450 went for that purpose.[63] The next year $12,000 more was invested, and on the eve of the war $26,975 was expended for slaves.[64] It is probable that too many slaves were bought, as many were hired out. Several instances appear in the records where carpenters and blacksmiths were hired out.[65]

The staple crop raised on the plantations was cotton. The table shows the increase in the number of bales produced: [66]

		value crop
1848	(at the time of Everett's death)	$11,239.33
1852	346 bales (part crop 1851)	10,156.32
1853	339 bales	14,367.51
1854	362 bales	14,050.15
1855	1003 bales	31,696.64
1856	275 bales	13,754.28
1858	523 bales	15,161.38
1860	484 bales	18,094.46

In 1855, the banner year in the history of the estate, disconnected lands were sold for $37,640.82. The sale included lands in Jones, Crawford, Dooly, Campbell, Sumter, Stewart, Macon, and Pulaski counties.[67] The drop from 1,003 bales of cotton produced in 1855 to 275 in 1856

60. *Ibid.*, G, 81ff. The Negroes at the Home Place raised 80½ bushels of corn, receiving $40.25; those at the River Place raised 101 bushels for $50.50. In 1860 Paul, a boy, sold 12 chickens "for the party" for $1.80 and 10 dozen eggs for $1.00. (*Returns* M, 742.)

61. *Ibid.*, C, 424.

62. *Ibid.*, D, 341.

63. *Ibid.*, E, no. 109.

64. *Ibid.*, F, no. 9; *ibid.*, M, nos. 93, 127, 140, 147, *ibid.*, 171.

65. *Ibid.*, H, 361; *ibid.*, K, nos. 111, 118; *ibid.*, C, 474.

66. Compiled from annual returns of estate. Various volumes.

67. *Ibid.*, G, 73.

may be partly explained by the fact that one-sixth of the estate went to I. R. Flewellen as provided by the will. This part, including 62 Negroes, was appraised at $64,459.18.[68] Hardeman and Sparks, a Macon firm, handled most of the cotton for the estate.

Plantation life on the Everett places probably resembled that of other sections of the South. Little information is available on this point. It is interesting to note, however, that missionaries were employed to instruct the slaves in the principles of the Christian religion. T. C. Coleman received $450.00 for six months' work in this capacity, and in 1864 James Dunwoody was paid $150.00.[69] The slaves were doubtless well treated. In one instance a Negro man was sold in order to prevent separation from his wife,[70] but the steel beneath the velvet is felt when the following item is read: "May, 1852, Taking off Irons from negro, $2.00; Ironing a negro, $3.50." [71]

THE COUNTY

The plantations described may be considered more or less typical of the county. That not all the planters were as successful as Tooke and Greene [72] may well be believed. The county itself resembled others of the lower cotton belt and in many respects was better. After the acquisition of the Creek lands in 1821, the section was rapidly settled. Planters from the older counties moved in, cleared the land, and erected their first homes. Gradually the log houses gave way to more pretentious ones and well-ordered plantations emerged from wild forest land. From an average slaveholding of 5.9 in 1829, the growth was fairly rapid; in 1864 it had grown to 18.01. The number of individuals owning from one to five slaves increased until 1844, but after that date a decline is noted, while the larger holdings increase. The small landowner probably could not afford to pay the high prices for fieldhands.

The court records show that the slaves were quiet and peaceable, for only twenty-six cases appear from the founding of the county until after the war. Petty crimes were probably dealt with summarily by the master or overseer, but those of a more serious nature which did reach the courts indicate no unusual violence on the part of the Negro. Twelve of

68. *Ibid.*, F, 87ff.
69. *Ibid.*, C, 474; *ibid.*, P, 520ff.
70. *Ibid.*, E, 577.
71. *Ibid.*, D, 341ff.
72. M. L. Green, the executor of the Everett estate, may be considered as a planter.

the total number of cases involved misdemeanors, such as gambling with Negroes, selling spirituous liquors to slaves, or trading with a slave without a ticket. Twelve were capital offenses: in these cases the Negroes were convicted of murder, rape, arson, and three for assault with intent to murder. The culprits were hanged. Three cases were recorded where the master murdered the slave. In the case of State *v.* Columbus Thompson, for killing a slave, a true bill was returned, "but from circumstances we recommend him to mercy before the proper tribunal." [73] It was unnecessary for the court to bestow that mercy, for Columbus Thompson escaped the country.[74] John E. Bartlett murdered his own slave Ellen with a "sharp blunt weapon, unlawfully, feloniously, willfully and with malice aforethought," beating her and fracturing the skull, but he was found "Not guilty." [75] In like manner Solomon Haddock killed his female slave Chaney with a stick, tied a rope about her neck, but could not be convicted.[76] It would have been a benefit to society to have executed him, as two years later he attempted to murder one William Knight.[77] One case of cruelty to a slave appears. Williamson Mims, a leading citizen of the county, permitted proper food and sustenance to be withheld from four slaves but failed of conviction.[78]

The single case of rape on record is worthy of a hasty glance. Stephen, a slave, assaulted one Mary Daniel, a white girl, in a cotton field while her father was absent at a "house-raising," but he did not accomplish his purpose. After conviction in the inferior court the case was appealed to the superior court, which affirmed the decision of the lower court, and Stephen was hanged.[79] The grand jury failed to return a true bill in the case of State *v.* Charles, accused of arson. Excitement waxed high in 1858 when an old Negro woman and a servant girl on Major Belvins plantation assaulted a Mrs. Bryant, the wife of the overseer, hitting her about the head and shoulders with an ax, wounding her to such an extent that death resulted. Mobs threatened to lynch the slaves, who were jailed at Perry. The old woman was said to have been "a very bad character." [80]

In spite of the few crimes committed, the inhabitants of the county

73. *Minutes of Houston Superior Court, 1840–43.* Hereafter cited as *Min. Sup. Ct.*
74. *Ibid.,* 1845.
75. *Ibid.,* 1846–51. Pages of records are numbered and fully indexed.
76. *Ibid.,* 1851–54. Cf. April term, 1855.
77. *Ibid.*
78. *Ibid.,* 1854–56.
79. *Min. Sup. Ct.,* 1851–54. State *v.* Stephen.
80. *Georgia Journal and Messenger,* April 14, 1858.

were constantly afraid of the Negroes. From the beginning of the county the grand juries periodically presented as a grievance, a danger, the failure on the part of the authorities to enforce the patrol law. "We have reason to believe that the Patrol Laws are almost entirely neglected," said the grand jury in 1851.[81] Two years later this body recommended that the existing law be amended "as at present the slave population roves at large when and where they please unless the overseers prevent." [82] If this condition were present, the masters must have had confidence in their slaves to permit it.

Another source of constant worry to the grand juries was the presence of a free Negro element in the county. It would be enlightening to know the reason for such a fear, if any, for there were only two Negroes of this class in the county in 1848 and only six in 1853. Moreover, in none of the wills examined were Negroes manumitted.[83] The tax digest for 1853 states that there were no Negroes who were "nominally slaves." [84] However, the digests also say that no Negroes hired their time, but a glance at the annual returns will reveal the error in the statement. In 1849 the following presentment by the grand jury appeared:

> The frequency with which large crowds of negroes are permitted to assemble, ostensibly for the purpose of religious worship, and more especially the practice of permitting these crowds to be addressed by Negro Preachers or Exhorters. . . . the white persons, who have the agency and supervision of such meetings should have an eye single to the interest, peace and security of the citizens, and should therefore permit them to be held but seldom and never without an efficient Patrol being in attendance. . . . Our experience and acquaintance with the character of the slave population, teach us that professions of religion are too frequently used by them, as a cloak to rascality.[85]

The arraignment goes on for some length and the lack of enforcement of the Patrol Law is again scored. "The streets and corners of the village [Perry] are thronged, at all hours, from Saturday night till Monday morning with negroes."

The planter class of the county carefully guarded the institution of slavery; their sentiment was probably expressed by Howell Cobb,[86] a prominent lawyer of Perry who embodied his ideas in a book entitled *A*

81. *Min. Sup. Ct.*, 1851–54.
82. *Ibid.*
83. The act of 1818, rendering all manumission by deed or will void was repealed a few years later; in 1859 the 1818 law was reenacted.
84. *Tax Digest*, 1853. Also see digest for other years.
85. *Min. Sup. Ct.*, 1846–51.
86. Not to be confused with Howell Cobb of Athens, Ga.

Scriptural Examination of Slavery. According to his belief, African slavery was a punishment inflicted upon the enslaved for their wickedness, and slavery, as it existed in the United States, was a providently arranged means whereby the African was to be lifted from his deep degradation to a state of civil and religious liberty. Like Toombs, however, he believed that the condition of the slave was not permanent, but that voluntary manumission would be the ultimate result. Nevertheless, Cobb held that "we who are connected with the institution at this day are to regard it as permanent—perpetual." [87]

Houston county contained a large number of wealthy planters [88] and the inhabitants view the history of their county with pardonable pride. Swift's Mill, Houston Factory, and Houser's Lake still draw their share of pleasure-seekers as they did of old, when the Dennards, McGehees, Belvins, Toomers, Housers, Lawsons, Tookes, and Everetts assembled for a fish fry or a party. A few of the old homes are left as a monument to the old regime.

87. Howell Cobb, *A Scriptural Examination of Slavery* (1856) 24.
88. See Appendix D.

Charles H. Moffat

Charles Tait, Planter, Politician, and Scientist of the Old South

Biography is one of the most interesting and important forms of historical literature. It details day-to-day existence and gives us a sense of an era too frequently missed in topical studies. The subject of much biographical literature has been the politically powerful —notably, those who have held high public office. When this type of study is well done, we are able to study the bases of power, gauge the changing relation of the electorate to its public representatives, and view the impress of local issues—a particularly important subject in areas where newspapers and other means of communication such as good roads are few, and where discussion of national topics is therefore sharply minimized. This type of analysis is therefore crucial for our understanding of antebellum southern history. For, despite the attention historians have given its political leadership, we still know far less than we should about how these men came to power, how they defined themselves politically, and what meaning if any party identification had on the local level.

We do know from this and other studies that, as the Era of Good Feeling came to an end, politics began to emerge as a significant social force. The erratic and factional political associations of the past decade disappeared. In this short biography, Charles Moffat describes how acerbic local politics could be. Moffat correctly believes that we must know more about men like Tait, influential though little-known individuals. Politically he belonged to the generation of Southerners who came to power with Calhoun and Cheeves during the War of 1812. And like these men he was a strong nationalist, vitally interested in national defense. Intellectually and culturally he more closely resembled the men of the Revolution and the early national period—men who, like Jefferson, considered themselves part of a trans-Atlantic intellectual community. Tait may therefore not be as typical as Moffat thinks. Men of such varied interests are rare anywhere. We are left to wonder whether men like Tait are

From the *Journal of Southern History*, XIV (1948), 206–233. Copyright 1948 by the Southern Historical Association. Reprinted by permission of the Managing Editor.

individuals of superior abilities or whether they are products of a specific milieu. He conforms to the social ideal of southern society.

That ideal remained a model of socially acceptable behavior throughout the antebellum period, and there were men throughout the region who embodied it. The exact nature of their influence is more difficult to gauge. It is one of the curiosities of southern history that, while that ideal became instilled in southern life, the men who represented it were accorded less and less esteem as the antebellum period progressed. Admiration for learning and the life of the mind declined, and the social ideal of the planter who was also a gentleman and scholar became stylized and devoid of content. In this context it is interesting to note how fashionable dueling became in quarrels of honor between "gentlemen," and how popular the works of Sir Walter Scott were among the South's readers. For some this gave the South a dream-like quality. For the more astute it demonstrated how arcane if not antiquated much of southern chivalry really was.

Tait died in 1835, during the period when the ambivalences of the South's founding fathers toward slavery were finally resolved in its favor. With the close of the debate on slavery all other intellectual activity diminished in vigor. Attention of Southerners focused more and more on the protection of slavery and on ideas hostile to their peculiar institution. Political crises exacerbated the South's fears, and what began as a selective hostility to ideas subversive of slavery concluded as a pervasive anti-intellectualism. In such a milieu men like Charles Tait, who might have provided the measure of moderation necessary to prevent the Civil War, appeared less and less frequently. By 1860 those who remained proved powerless to stay the secession of the South.

The lives of military and political leaders are often studied in minute detail, while lesser, more typical men are neglected. Perhaps this has been especially true of the study of the history of the United States in the nineteenth century, a period of great economic and social change and bitter political controversy. While the importance of these biographical studies of men of influence and power in the political and military affairs of the time should not be minimized, the historian may also find in the lives of such men as Charles Tait, educator, scientist, pioneer planter, jurist, and member of Congress, many facts which contribute to a fuller understanding of the period in which he lived.

Tait first entered public life as an educator, and after a brief term as head of Richmond Academy, Augusta, Georgia, he became, successively, a member of the state legislature, judge of the state supreme court, and senator from Georgia. Following ten years of service in the Senate, he was appointed judge of the federal court for the Alabama district. But his interests were wider than the legislative hall and the judicial bench. He was also a successful planter, a member of the American Philosophical Society, and an important figure in American paleontology.

Although Tait's contribution to his time was largely made in Georgia and Alabama, he was born in Louisa County, Virginia, on February 1, 1768, of Scotch ancestry. He was the oldest of the ten children of James Tait and his wife Rebecca Hudson Tait, a cousin of Elizabeth Hudson, the mother of Henry Clay.[1] His early boyhood was spent on his father's tobacco farm in Virginia, but when decreasing yields and rising costs of production made tobacco culture less profitable to the Virginia farmers, James Tait in 1783 joined the southwestward migration to the fresh soil of the Georgia Piedmont. Through the generosity of a friend, Governor George Mathews of Georgia, James Tait was granted under the headright system more than 3,000 acres of land in Wilkes, Elbert, and Franklin counties.[2] The elder Tait was one of the first purchasers of lots in Petersburg, where he and his fellow Virginians formed the nucleus of a well-known and prosperous settlement on the Broad and Savannah rivers.

After receiving his basic education in Virginia, Charles Tait moved in 1785 to his father's new residence on the Savannah River. Most of James Tait's land was devoted to the cultivation of tobacco, and Charles evidently assisted his father and brothers in caring for the crop. At some time during his youth in Georgia, while hauling tobacco to market, he was thrown from a horse, severely injuring his leg. Infection developed, the leg was amputated, and he wore a wooden stump for the remainder of his life.

At the age of eighteen Tait enrolled as a member of the first class at Wilkes Academy in Washington, Georgia, in 1786. Here he studied for two years the traditional classical course offered by that early institution and established acquaintanceship with a number of people who were to be important as either friends or opponents in his later career.[3] During this period he also came under the influence of Bishop Francis Asbury,

1. Brief biographical data on Charles Tait may be found in Allen Johnson and Dumas Malone, eds., *Dictionary of American Biography* (New York, 1928–37), XVIII, 274–275, in Thomas M. Owen, ed., *History of Alabama and Dictionary of Alabama Biography* (Chicago, 1921), IV, 1640, and in Alma C. Tompkins, *Charles Tait* (Auburn, Ala., 1910).

2. Information furnished the author on January 7, 1946, by John B. Wilson, Secretary of State of Georgia.

3. Charles Tait's Diary, 1826–27, in possession of Mrs. Felicia B. Moore, Washington, D. C.

who had converted James and Rebecca Tait to Methodism before they left Virginia and who in 1788 organized the first Methodist conference in Georgia in their home in Petersburg.[4] This close association with the Methodist bishop led Charles Tait to enter Cokesbury College, Abingdon, Maryland, in May, 1788; and after only a few months' study he was appointed to the faculty of the college, serving as professor of French and as instructor of the "charity students." [5]

While in Abingdon Tait married Mrs. Anne Lucas Simson of Baltimore, to whom two sons were born—James Asbury in 1791, and Charles Jefferson in 1794.[6] By 1792 the elder Tait was urging his son to return to Georgia, and in 1794, having become dissatisfied with his position at Cokesbury College, Charles resigned and returned to Elbert County.[7] His interest in education had not diminished, however, and in April, 1795, he was inaugurated as the fifth rector of Richmond Academy at Augusta.[8] This Academy, chartered by the Georgia legislature in 1783 and still operating as an academy and junior college, is the oldest institution of learning in the state, and undoubtedly the rectorship was the choice educational position in Georgia at that time.

In 1796 William H. Crawford became the head of the English department at the Academy. In light of future events, Tait's association with Crawford was the most important connection that he made while in Augusta. The two young men were deeply interested in political affairs, and shortly after Crawford came to Augusta he and Tait organized a public debating society, of which Cowles Mead, Major George Watkins, and other prominent Augustans were members.[9] But by 1797 the finances of Richmond Academy had become involved as a result of mismanagement on the part of the board of trust. When the trustees curtailed expenses by reducing faculty salaries, Tait resigned the rectorship

4. James A. Tait's Memorandum Book, 1850, in possession of Albert Tait, Camden, Ala. See also John H. McIntosh, *The Official History of Elbert County, 1790–1935* (Athens, Ga., 1940), 69.

5. George W. Archer, *An Authentic History of Cokesbury College* (Bel Air, Md., 1894), 14; Bernard C. Steiner, *History of Education in Maryland* (Washington, 1849), 240. Cokesbury, the first Methodist college in the world, had been chartered by the Methodist Conference in 1784 and dedicated by Bishop Asbury in the following year.

6. Owen, ed., *Dictionary of Alabama Biography*, IV, 1640. Charles Jefferson lived less than a month.

7. James A. Tait's Memorandum Book, 1844.

8. Charles G. Cordle, "An Ante-Bellum Academy: The Academy of Richmond County, 1783–1863" (thesis, University of Georgia, 1935), 17, 57.

9. *Savannah Georgian*, May 28, 1823.

and was succeeded by Crawford, who served for a year in the dual capacity of rector and English teacher.[10]

James Tait died in 1798, and Charles inherited from his father several slaves and half of the land on which his father had lived.[11] For the next twenty years he maintained his home on this Georgia plantation, which he called the "Retreat." Entrusting the management of his property to an overseer, Tait now devoted the larger part of his time to law and politics.[12]

The Virginia planters who settled in the Broad River section were contemptuous of their neighbors who lived on the pineland stretches in the lower part of Wilkes County. The residents of the southern portion of Wilkes County were former residents of North Carolina, whose social and economic views were not in accord with those of their somewhat better educated Virginia-born neighbors to the north. It was largely the North Carolina element, led by General Elisha Clark, who formed an alliance with several influential Federalists and succeeded in inducing the Georgia legislature to enact the notorious Yazoo Act, by which several million acres of the public domain were sold to several companies of speculators at an extremely low price. The Virginians of the Broad River settlement, being men of property and therefore more conservative in financial matters, were not slow in condemning the participants in the Yazoo transactions. The "Yazoo Fraud" furnished the issue on which Georgia's first political parties were based. James Jackson resigned his seat in the Senate and was elected to the Georgia legislature, where he was instrumental in securing the repeal of the Yazoo law. The Jackson party, made up largely of the Virginia planter and professional group, included among its leaders such men as Charles Tait, William H. Crawford, William W. Bibb, and David B. Mitchell. These men embraced the principles of Thomas Jefferson and declared themselves to be the Republican party in Georgia, thus forcing the North Carolinians to align themselves with the Federalists for a time. The odium of "Yazooism" discredited the Federalists in Georgia, however, and by 1800 the North Carolinians joined John Clark's faction of the Republican party. The Jackson-Crawford party continued to appeal to the Virginia or planter-professional groups, while the Clark faction claimed to represent the small farmers and frontiersmen. There was in reality no difference in

10. Cordle, "An Ante-Bellum Academy," 18–19.

11. James Tait's Will, probated January 30, 1798, in Ordinary Records, 1791–1803, Will Book B (Ordinary's Office, Elbert County Courthouse, Elberton, Ga.).

12. James A. Tait's Memorandum Book, 1850.

principle between the two, the distinction being largely based on personalities rather than principles.[13]

Tait was strongly Jeffersonian in his philosophy and supported the Republican party in national and local politics. His connection with Richmond Academy had given him a certain amount of prestige, and in 1799 he was elected to the state senate from Elbert County. While in the senate he was chiefly interested in the improvement of transportation facilities in the Broad River country, and he was responsible for an act which made provisions for the improvement of navigation on the Broad and Savannah rivers between Elbert County and Augusta. As chairman of the senate committee on university affairs, Tait reported on February 4, 1799, that his committee had enrolled an act authorizing the board of visitors to decide on a proper location for the University of Georgia.[14]

After serving one term in the state senate, Tait returned to Elbert County, where for the next four years he engaged in the practice of law. During the period Tait and his friend Crawford were in partnership for a brief time, although Crawford's office was in Lexington, Georgia. Tait had received no formal legal training but had "read Blackstone" while at Cokesbury College. His contemporaries considered him a strong and astute lawyer and a person of "far more than ordinary ability." [15] Although, according to his son, he "had his foibles," he seems not to have become involved in the illegal land transactions so common at this time. Most of his legal cases dealt with wills, land titles, and money claims, and his memoranda indicate that his practice was financially successful.[16]

In the spring of 1803 Thomas P. Carnes resigned his position as superior court judge of the western circuit. The office was a stepping-stone to political preferment, and though Tait hoped to be appointed to the

13. See Charles H. Haskins, "The Yazoo Land Companies," in *Papers of the American Historical Association* (New York, 1886–91), V (1891), 395–437. A convenient brief account is in E. Merton Coulter, *A Short History of Georgia* (Chapel Hill, N.C., 1933), 187–192.

14. Georgia Legislature, *Senate Journal* (1799), 11, 34.

15. Lucian L. Knight, *Georgia's Landmarks, Memorials, and Legends* (Atlanta, 1913), II, 16; William F. Northen, ed., *Men of Mark in Georgia* (Atlanta, 1907), II, 263; John E. D. Shipp, *Giant Days, or the Life and Times of William H. Crawford* (Americus, Ga., 1909), 50.

16. James A. Tait to Albert J. Pickett, n.d., in Pickett Papers (Alabama Department of Archives and History, Montgomery); William H. Crawford to Charles Tait, November 7, 1819, in Tait Papers (Alabama Department of Archives and History); Charles Tait's Memorandum Book, 1800–1802, in possession of Mrs. A. B. Howard, Montgomery, Ala.

post, Governor John Milledge granted an *ad interim* appointment to John Griffin, a brother-in-law of John Clark. When the legislature convened in November, 1803, Tait was elected over Griffin to fill the unexpired term. The Western Circuit, over which Tait presided, embraced all of upper Georgia. The Oconee River was the frontier line until 1804, and Tait was the first judge to hold court on the west side of that river.[17]

Since the superior court was the state's highest tribunal, the judges possessed great authority, and their duties were so varied and complex that the office required a veritable "legal Hercules." [18] Tait possessed, however, certain qualities which especially fitted him for the office. He was a man of tremendous industry, perseverance, and energy, and he throve on work, his favorite maxim being, "The busiest man is the happiest man." He deplored miscarriages of justice and was especially sympathetic toward those whom he felt to be the falsely accused victims of private passion.[19] Fully conscious of the powers vested in him and doubtless sobered by the responsibility, he seems to have been generally known for his magnanimity and moderation in the administration of justice.

In such a period of intra-party strife, no politician was immune from bitter personal attack by his enemies within the party. Tait's election to the bench over Judge Griffin brought down upon him all the bitterness of the Clark faction in Georgia. Shortly after Tait assumed office John Clark circulated an acrimonious indictment in which he charged that the Judge was ill tempered, immoral, corrupt and dishonest, and generally incompetent. While in the senate, according to Clark, Tait had attempted to secure the passage of a law setting aside a court decision in order to benefit one of his clients. Clark also asserted that Tait, in his judicial capacity, had been influenced by his friendship with Crawford to the extent that he had rendered decisions favorable to Crawford's clients, and claimed that because of his partiality people who had cases to be tried in the Western Circuit considered it to their advantage to secure Crawford as their lawyer.[20]

17. Georgia Legislature, *House Journal*, November 19, 1803; James A. Tait's Memorandum Book, 1838.

18. Warren Grice, *The Georgia Bench and Bar* (Macon, Ga., 1931), , 266.

19. James A. Tait to Pickett, n.d., in Pickett Papers; James A. Tait's Memorandum Book, 1850; Franklin County, Ga., Superior Court, Minutes of the January Term, 1805 (Georgia Department of Archives and History, Atlanta).

20. Clark's statement was later expanded and published in pamphlet form in connection with an attack on Crawford. See John Clark, *Considerations on the Purity of the Principles of William H. Crawford, Esq. Deducible from his Conduct*

The attack was renewed in 1806, when Clark learned that Tait in his judicial capacity had come into possession of an affidavit in which one Robert Clary, a fugitive from justice in North Carolina, charged that Clark had accepted $20,000 in counterfeit money for the sale of 1,100 acres of land and had then exchanged these funds with his brother-in-law, the state treasurer, for sound money. Despite the fact that Tait declined to take action because of the unreliable character of the deponent, Clark claimed that Tait and Crawford were conspiring against him and petitioned the legislature to impeach Tait on charges of having participated in a foul conspiracy. In the proceedings which followed Tait was vigorously defended by Crawford and, after the examination of twenty-eight witnesses whose names Clark had suggested, was exonerated by a vote of 57 to 3, despite the presence in the legislature of a number of Clark men.[21]

Frustrated in his attempt to oust Tait from the judgeship, Clark now challenged Crawford to a duel. Clark came through this encounter unscathed, but Crawford's wrist was badly shattered; when he refused to accept a renewal of the challenge after his recovery, Clark concluded that the only way left for him to obtain satisfaction was to settle accounts with Tait. Instead of resorting to a duel, however, Clark felt that it would be more insulting to Tait's dignity to give him a public horsewhipping. Consequently, as Tait was driving along a Milledgeville street in the summer of 1807, Clark, on horseback, accosted him and with a cowhide lash applied thirty or more strokes upon his back. As a result of this assault upon a judge of the high court, Clark was fined $2,000 and was required to post a bond for good behavior for a period of five years, but Governor Jared Irwin, a member of the Clark faction, remitted the court sentence.[22]

By 1809 Tait, weary of the local political broils and anxious to extend his sphere of influence, decided to enter national politics. When John Milledge resigned his seat in the Senate in 1809, Tait became a candidate for the vacant post. His opponent was Major Elisha Clark, the solicitor-general of the Ocmulgee district and a brother of John Clark. After a spirited contest in the legislature, Tait was elected on the third ballot by

---

in Connexion with Charles Tait, Esq. towards the Author of this Publication (Augusta, Ga., 1819).

21. *Augusta Chronicle,* December 13, 1806; Shipp, *Giant Days,* 69–72.

22. For Clark's version, see Clark, *Considerations on Principles,* 105–110; for contemporary comments on the governor's action, see *Athens* (Ga.) *Express,* May 27, 1809, and Bolling Hall to David B. Mitchell, May 26, 1809, in *Georgia Historical Quarterly,* XXI (1937), 383–384.

a majority of one vote.[23] He took the oath of office as a senator on December 28, 1809, to serve the remainder of Milledge's unexpired term, and in 1813 he was re-elected for the full term ending in 1819.

During his entire senatorial career he was active and influential and frequently showed an independence of party control. He broke with his party, for example, in supporting the bill to re-establish the United States Bank in 1811, and when this bill was defeated he championed the recommendation of Secretary of the Treasury Albert Gallatin for the adoption of a system of internal taxation. Tait voted for Senator William B. Giles' Army Bill, and he condemned the inconsistency of those Republicans who voted for that measure and at the same time refused to vote for taxes with which to finance an increased military organization. "He must have been either a fool or a Rascal," he said, "who voted for the Troops . . . and who will not now vote for the money & the means of raising . . . the Army. . . . War, Army & Taxes are inseparably connected." [24]

The members of the Georgia delegation in Congress were War Hawks from the beginning of the quarrel with Great Britain. As early as 1810 Representative William W. Bibb had declared: "If all the states were as ready for war as Georgia is, I should be ready and willing to encounter the enemy." [25] Crawford, who was Georgia's senior senator at that time, saw no alternative save war, nor would Tait pursue any middle ground so long as the British persisted in enforcing their Orders in Council. In February, 1812, he wrote Governor David B. Mitchell, "If the O[rders] in C[ouncil] are not repealed War ought and I hope will be declared." [26]

With the declaration of war against Great Britain in June, 1812, Tait realized that the United States was becoming involved in a conflict with the leading naval power of the world, and as a member of the Senate Naval Affairs Committee he sought to strengthen that arm of the service. On December 14, 1812, he obtained an amendment to a Senate bill in order to provide for the building of ships of not less than seventy-four guns, and the amended measure was passed by the Senate. Passage by the House was delayed for a few days because of opposition to Tait's amendment by members of his own party, but in the end his point of

23. Savannah *Columbian Museum and Advertiser*, December 7, 1809.

24. Charles Tait to David B. Mitchell, February 20, 1812, in *Georgia Historical Quarterly*, XXI, 385.

25. Amanda Johnson, *Georgia as a Colony and State* (Atlanta, 1938), 204.

26. Tait to Mitchell, February 20, 1812, in *Georgia Historical Quarterly*.

view prevailed.[27] During the remainder of the war Tait kept the cause of the Navy before Congress by offering resolutions of appreciation to individual heroes of naval engagements; and in answering the opponents of such a resolution for Commodore Oliver H. Perry in December, 1813, he showed that he had a clear perception of the significance of the victory on Lake Erie. "The victory on the lake was decisive in every particular," he said. "It transported our land forces to the enemy's shores to conquer and redeem; it dispersed the savage, quieted the fears of our fellow citizens on the western frontier, and gave peace to a land which repeated massacres had stained with the blood of its people." [28]

In contrast with his admiration for the heroes of the naval warfare, Tait had little respect for the generals who were conducting the war on land. He expressed his feeling that the Army seemed "not to have any good officers," and he considered it especially unfortunate that General Henry Dearborn had been retained in command. "No man," he said, "has any confidence in his capacity to conduct an army; he appears to be an obstinate and ignorant old man." [29] And lack of respect gave way to contempt when his attention was turned to the attitude of the Federalists in refusing to support the prosecution of the war. He scornfully recorded in his diary in 1813 that "No Federal gentleman was present" among the 250 guests at a dinner which he had attended in honor of the naval heroes. "Such is the rancor of party spirit," he added, "that the two parties cannot join in the celebration of the most glorious events in the history of this country! What will posterity think of the present times? On the subject of the navy, there should be no division of opinion." [30]

Tait's most distinguished work in the Senate was rendered in connection with the enlargement and reorganization of the Navy. In 1814 he was made chairman of the Naval Affairs Committee, a position which he held until the expiration of his term in 1819. Believing that "the true remedy against maritime wrongs is maritime force," he declared that a strong Navy cannot fail "to procure respect from abroad and safety at home." [31] His conviction that "a strong Navy is not only the most effi-

27. *Annals of Congress*, 12 cong., 2 sess., 31–33 (December 14, 1812). For the debate in the House of Representatives, see *ibid.*, 404–450 (December 16–23, 1812).

28. *Augusta Chronicle*, January 24, 1814, quoting from Tait's speech of December 29, 1813, in the Senate.

29. Charles Tait's Diary, May–July, 1813.

30. *Ibid*. See also Tompkins, *Charles Tait*, 8–9.

31. *Annals of Congress*, 13 cong., 3 sess., 113 (November 28, 1814).

cient and appropriate but also the cheapest defense for this country" led him to originate and sponsor the Naval Appropriation Act of 1816, which provided for an annual naval appropriation of $1 million to extend over a period of eight years. The bill passed the Senate under his sponsorship on April 26, 1816, and became law three days later. An integral part of the reorganized naval establishment was the Navy Board, which Tait also conceived in an effort to render the "civil administration of the navy as complete as the nature of the institution will admit." [32] This Board was to be composed of naval officers who were to collaborate with the Navy Department and to give it the benefit of their practical observation and experience.

His interest in improvement of the efficiency and morale of the Navy was also shown in such minor matters as the obtaining of larger appropriations for the Navy pension fund in 1816, and his insistence that this fund be protected "from the hands of rapacity, negligence and fraud." [33] As early as 1814 he had recommended that Congress create the rank of admiral in order to encourage greater attainments among the ranking officers by opening the way for further promotion, and in 1815 his program visualized a national academy for the training of naval officers.[34] In time, of course, these efforts began to receive favorable recognition, and many leading officers of the Navy began to urge that he be appointed Secretary of the Navy. In support of this suggestion, the *Baltimore Patriot* stated in 1817 that he deserved the position not only because of "his long and honorable service," but also because "the firmness and talents of this gentleman, his extensive knowledge of all matters connected with the navy, and his close application to business will qualify him to discharge the duties of the office; while his correct, dignified, and gentlemanly deportment justly render him a favorite with the people and with the officers of the Navy." [35] Although the appointment

32. *Ibid.*, 14 cong., 1 sess., 363 (April 26, 1816), and Appendix, 1886 (April 29, 1816); Tait to Benjamin W. Crowninshield, December 27, 1816, in *American State Papers, Naval Affairs* (Washington, 1834–61), I, 444.

33. Tait to Crowninshield, February 13, 1816, in War Records Archives, Navy Department, Miscellaneous Letters (National Archives), II, 32.

34. Tait to Crowninshield, January 9, 1815, *ibid.*, I, 81; *Annals of Congress*, 13 cong., 3 sess., 114 (November 28, 1814).

35. Quoted in Savannah *Columbian Museum and Gazette*, September 16, 1817. The Savannah paper also published statements from Commodores Oliver H. Perry, John Rodgers, and Stephen Decatur in support of Tait. Rodgers wrote directly to Tait that he would "consider it a most fortunate circumstance if such a gentleman as you were to be appointed—one to whom the Navy could at all times look to with confidence . . . no one I am sure, would be more acceptable to the nation

was given to another, Tait continued his work in behalf of the Navy, and after the close of his term in the Senate he was described by a former colleague as "the most zealous and most efficient supporter of the navy in Congress." [36]

Second only to his activities in connection with naval affairs during his senatorial career was Tait's interest in the advance of the southern frontier and the subsequent admission of new states into the Union. As chairman of special committees of the Senate, he participated directly in the formulation of the enabling legislation that admitted Louisiana, Mississippi, and Alabama to statehood. On January 18, 1811, he was made chairman of a select committee to consider a bill which had originated in the House of Representatives "to enable the people of the Territory of Orleans to form a constitution . . . preliminary to admission . . . into the Union," and a week later he reported a recommendation from that committee for changes in the proposed boundary.[37] His amendment was modified and accepted by both houses, and the approval of the measure by the President on February 20 marked the end of an extended debate in which eastern Federalists had displayed strong sectional prejudice in their attempts to prevent its adoption.

In the case of Mississippi, both intersectional and internal rivalry played important parts in delaying statehood. Within the territory the development of a strong movement for division into two states brought conflict between the residents of the Natchez district and those of the Alabama-Tombigbee region; and when the question of admission came before Congress in 1811, the northern opponents of the federal three-fifths ratio managed to postpone action on the ground that in ceding its western lands to the national government in 1802 Georgia had stipulated that the territory should be admitted as a single state.[38] Tait, who was particularly interested in creating two states, exerted his influence with

---

—and none so much so to the officers of the Navy." Rodgers to Tait, September 3, 1817, in John Rodgers Papers (Division of Manuscripts, Library of Congress).

36. James Barbour to Tait, January 7, 1821, in Tait Papers.

37. *Annals of Congress*, 11 cong., 3 sess., 98 (January 18, 1811), 103 (January 25, 1811). See Everett S. Brown, *Constitutional History of the Louisiana Purchase* (Berkeley, 1920), 170–187, for an account of the debate on this bill prior to its passage.

38. For the question of division, see Thomas P. Abernethy, *The Formative Period in Alabama, 1815–1828* (Montgomery, 1922), 33–40, and Franklin L. Riley, "Location of the Boundaries of Mississippi," in *Publications of the Mississippi Historical Society*, III (1900), 167–184. For the larger question of opposition to the three-fifths ratio, see Albert F. Simpson, "The Political Significance of Slave Representation, 1787–1821," in *Journal of Southern History*, VII (1941), 315–342.

his Georgia friends, and on January 4, 1813, he reported to the Senate
that Georgia had agreed to a division.[39] Problems connected with the
conduct of the War of 1812 caused further delay, and it was not until
1817 that Tait, as chairman of the Senate committee to which the question had been referred, obtained the passage of a bill to enable the people of the western part of the Mississippi Territory to form a state government, together with a second measure providing for the organization
of the eastern part as Alabama Territory.[40]

Tait's interest in obtaining statehood for Alabama was both personal
and political. The territorial governor was William W. Bibb, who had
recently been his colleague as senator from Georgia, and among the new
settlers who flocked into the territory following the opening of Indian
lands were many of his Georgia friends and political associates. His own
son, James A. Tait, had served in the Creek War in Alabama and had
returned to the region early in 1817 for the purpose of locating desirable
lands to which the entire family might move. Since Tait himself was expected to join this group on the expiration of his term in the Senate,
they naturally depended upon him to assist them in obtaining permission
to set up a state government. "Your work is still incomplete," one of
them wrote after the creation of the territory. "I think you ought to
crown your other labors of love . . . by procuring the act of admission
to the Union." [41] Thus it was to him that the petition of the territorial
legislature asking for statehood was sent in November, 1818; and when
he presented that petition to the Senate on December 11, he was immediately made chairman of a committee to prepare an enabling act.[42] So
rapidly did this committee proceed with its work that on March 2,
1819—two days before the end of his senatorial career—Tait had
the satisfaction of seeing President Monroe sign the measure authorizing
the framing of a state constitution for Alabama. And by the time the
constitution was sent to Congress for the final act of admission the following December, he had moved to Alabama and had unsuccessfully
sought election as one of the first senators from the new state.[43]

39. *Annals of Congress*, 12 cong., 2 sess., 38 (January 4, 1813).
40. *Ibid.*, 14 cong., 2 sess., 71 (January 17, 1817), 91 (January 31, 1817), 139 (February 21, 1817).
41. John W. Walker to Tait, September 22, 1818, in Tait Papers. For the plans
of the Tait family, see Tait to James A. Tait, January 29, 1817, *ibid*.
42. Walker to Tait, November 11, 1818, *ibid.; Annals of Congress*, 15 cong., 2
sess., 66 (December 11, 1818).
43. William W. Bibb to Tait, July 14, 1819; Walker to Tait, August 7, 1819; and
William H. Crawford to Tait, November 7, 1819, in Tait Papers; Tait to Walker,

Before his retirement from the Senate, Tait had also taken an active part in the early stages of the debate over the admission of Missouri to statehood. He understood that the Missouri question was primarily a struggle for political advantage, but he expressed a hope that the wisdom of his work in framing the legislation which admitted Louisiana, Mississippi, and Alabama into the Union would be demonstrated during "the progress of this great question." [44] He was made chairman of the Senate committee to which the Missouri question was referred in February, 1819, and it was on his recommendation that the Senate struck out the Tallmadge amendment,[45] which would have prohibited slavery in Missouri. Tait believed, however, that Senator Rufus King of New York, rather than Representative James Tallmadge, was the arch-conspirator who had "raised this tempest merely to ride into power." He regarded King as a "plausible, insidious, and insincere politician," and considered DeWitt Clinton, whom he called King's ally in fomenting the agitation, a man without principle. "All that wicked ambition can suggest he is capable of," he declared.[46] He dismissed them both with the statement: "They are New York politicians and the whole of them may go to the devil." [47]

It is evident that the Missouri question shook Tait's nationalism. As the controversy progressed, he feared that it was no longer a question merely of political power but had become a threat to the Union. "Everything is now at stake," he wrote in 1820 to Representative Thomas Cobb of Georgia, "not only political power but domestic tranquility and social repose." He realized that it was impossible not to connect this issue with "the momentous one of emancipation of slaves," but, he said, "If Congress pursues this question with a view to affect our right to own slaves . . . the slaveholding states must . . . form a separate Confederacy." [48]

Tait's decision not to allow his name to go before the Georgia legislature for re-election in 1819 was based in part upon his knowledge of the

---

October 8 and 9, 1819, in John W. Walker Papers (Alabama Department of Archives and History).

44. Tait to Walker, January 5, 1820, in Walker Papers.

45. *Annals of Congress*, 15 cong., 2 sess., 251 (February 22, 1819), 272–273 (February 27, 1819).

46. Tait to Walker, January 1, February 11, 1820, and Tait to Thomas Cobb, February 29, 1820, in Walker Papers.

47. Tait to Walker, April 11, 1821, *ibid*.

48. Tait to Cobb, February 29, 1820, *ibid*.

strong resentment within the state against all members of Congress who had voted for an increase in their pay in 1816, but it is also clear that he expected his efforts in behalf of statehood for Alabama to be rewarded with a senatorship from the new state. His plans to leave Georgia were begun as early as January, 1817, when he instructed his son to make a tour of the Alabama country in search of a desirable location for a future home. The place to be selected, he said, should unite fertility, salubrity, and navigation, and must have "a stream near at hand for a mill and machinery," an elevated site "on the summit of which a mansion house can be built in due time," a good spring, an extensive range for livestock, and other desirable land nearby, "where will settle a number of good neighbors." [49] Before the end of the year the younger Tait had established himself as a squatter on a tract of public land on the lower Alabama River, where he had built a cabin and made plans to raise a crop preparatory to the removal of his family from Georgia. By the beginning of 1819 the entire Tait family had completed the migration to Alabama, and immediately after the adjournment of Congress in March, Tait himself proceeded directly to the new location without going back to Georgia.[50]

From the time of his arrival in Alabama in April, 1819, Tait found himself deeply involved in the political activities of the new state. Together with William W. Bibb and John W. Walker, both new arrivals from Georgia, he was recognized as one of the leaders of the faction which sought to bring over the influence of the Crawford machine from Georgia to Alabama. Opposed to this group was a less formal coalition of newcomers from Tennessee and North Carolina who eventually became the supporters of Andrew Jackson, but whose original stand was merely anti-Georgia rather than pro-Jackson. Crawford and Tait were accused of considering Alabama as their own creation and of hoping to make it a pocket borough. Thus when Tait let it be known that while he did not intend to solicit public office he felt that "it is now time for the legislature to think of my service and to act as it may deem

49. Tait to James A. Tait, January 20, 1817, in Tait Papers. See also Frank L. Owsley, "The Pattern of Migration and Settlement on the Southern Frontier," *Journal Southern History*, XI (1945), 173–174.

50. James A. Tait to Charles Tait, January 1, 1818; Mrs. James A. Tait to Charles Tait, January 20, 1819; and Charles Tait to James A. Tait, February 13, 1819, in Tait Papers. In his letter to his son, Tait explained that his route would be planned to include visits with former Presidents Jefferson and Madison in Virginia and Judge John Overton in Tennessee.

proper," [51] his ambition ran into unexpected complications. In the first election under the new state constitution Bibb won the governorship, and the Georgia faction then gave its support to Walker and Tait as candidates for the two positions as senators. Walker, a resident of North Alabama, seems to have met with little opposition, but in the southern part of the state the anti-Georgia group put forward William R. King, a former congressman from North Carolina, as a candidate against Tait. An attempt by Crawford to remove King from the contest by offering him an appointment as receiver of the General Land Office was branded as outside interference, and the growing resentment against the Georgians led Tait to withdraw his candidacy. "I came to bring peace, not a sword," he wrote. "If I cannot be taken into the state without a struggle, I enjoin my friends not to mention my name in relation to any other appointment . . . in the gift of the legislature." [52]

But this renunciation did not necessarily imply withdrawal from political life. Tait desired public office as a mark of prestige and position, which to him were more important than material wealth,[53] and with many powerful friends in Washington his thoughts turned to the possibility of an appointive post in the federal government. An opportunity soon developed with the creation of the federal judicial district of Alabama in April, 1820. Within a month President Monroe had accepted the recommendation of Crawford and Walker that the appointment as district judge be given to Tait, and the nomination was unanimously confirmed by the Senate on May 13, 1820.[54] After considerable delay in completing the organization of the court, Tait took the oath of office in February, 1821, and for the next five years he served as the only federal judge in the state. Despite the handicaps of inclement weather, disease, and poor transportation facilities, he was regular in fulfilling his appointments and was generally known for his punctuality.[55] He also established a reputation for vigorous and fearless administration of justice in

51. Tait to Walker, October 8, 1819, in Walker Papers. See also Abernethy, *Formative Period in Alabama*, 45–49, 102–109, for a discussion of the political rivalries.

52. Tait to Walker, October 9, 1819, in Walker Papers. Crawford's efforts in behalf of Tait are described in Crawford to Tait, November 7, 1819, in Tait Papers.

53. Writing of his son in 1820, for example, he said: "James, who has never yet risen higher than a militia captain . . . will I dare say get rich; but what is this miserable trash without consideration." Tait to Walker, January 5, 1820, in Walker Papers.

54. Walker to Tait, May 14, 1820, in Tait Papers.

55. *Mobile Commercial Register*, January 28, 1824.

spite of repeated efforts of political foes or disgruntled lawyers to bring about his removal from office.[56]

Sessions of the district court were held at Cahawba, in the central part of the state, and at Huntsville, in North Alabama, but the major part of Tait's work was done at Mobile, where most of the cases involved such offenses as smuggling of merchandise, the illicit slave trade, and piracy. Here his earlier service as chairman of the Senate Naval Affairs Committee undoubtedly provided a background that was to aid him now in grappling with the manifold intricacies growing out of admiralty law. Perhaps the most significant and certainly the most complex case to come before his court was one which grew out of the efforts of the government to bring about a more effective enforcement of the laws prohibiting the importation of slaves into the United States. Violations of the federal act of 1808 had been notorious, with the Gulf of Mexico as the principal scene of the smuggling activities, but it was not until after the close of the War of 1812 that the federal authorities were able to give the problem the attention which it required. A revenue cutter was finally assigned to duty in the Gulf in 1818, and in June of that year three American schooners carrying 107 African Negroes were captured and brought into the port of Mobile. Instead of condemning the cargo, as a new federal law of April 20, 1818, had provided, the Alabama territorial court permitted the Negroes to be placed in the hands of the persons to whom they were being shipped, and within a short time 38 of them disappeared; but no further action was taken in the case by the territorial authorities.

When Tait assumed his duties as district judge, therefore, he inherited this unfinished problem in which the federal authorities were deeply concerned because of its significance in their efforts to stop the slave trade. At the request of the United States marshal, he reopened the case in the first session of his court. Summoning the remaining 69 Negroes before the court, he condemned all three vessels and their cargoes as forfeited to the United States and denied the claim of the state of Alabama to jurisdiction in the matter. After further litigation over numerous minor technicalities, the claimants of the cargoes and the owners of the

56. In 1822, when a lawyer who had been refused a license to practice in the district court petitioned the House of Representatives to bring impeachment charges against Tait, the House Committee on Judiciary reported that it had found "no irregular or illegal proceedings," but that on the contrary Judge Tait deserved commendation for refusing to relax the rules of the court in the face of denunciation and the threat of persecution. *Annals of Congress*, 17 cong., 2 sess., 463–467 (December 29, 1822), 715–718 (January 28, 1823).

ships appealed to the U.S. Supreme Court for restitution, and that tribunal upheld Tait's decisions on all the main points in the issue.[57] In dealing with this case he not only won the praise of the Mobile press for "the patient, liberal and dignified manner" in which he presided;[58] but he also displayed vigor and initiative which helped to establish a precedent for the handling of other cases in the government's campaign to prosecute smugglers of African Negroes.

In cases involving piracy and the smuggling of merchandise he was equally vigorous and fearless. During his term of service thousands of dollars worth of contraband merchandise, ranging from molasses and straw hats to firearms and whiskey, were condemned and forefeited to the federal government by action of his court. Much more serious, however, was the upsurge of piratical activities in the Gulf of Mexico following the War of 1812, and in his early charges to grand juries Tait urged that special attention be given to the prosecution of cases of piracy. Interspersed throughout the records of his court from 1822 to 1824 are charges of piracy against schooners, brigs, and sloops, but the final settlement of most of these cases is left in tantalizing obscurity. But by 1824 he was able to report that, because of the vigilance of the Navy, the integrity of the mercantile class, and the action of the courts, "criminal prosecutions on account of piracy are not common." [59]

Meanwhile the responsibilities of his judicial office had not absorbed Tait's entire attention. From the time of his arrival in Alabama in 1819, he had maintained his interest in the possibility of establishing himself and his sons as planters in the new region to which they had moved. Seeking a soil similar in content to that which they had known in the Georgia Piedmont, they were not attracted by the black, sticky soil of the prairie but chose the light, sandy loam of the Alabama River bottom. Here in 1819 and 1820 they bought 2,600 acres of land in Monroe County, along both the east and west banks of the Alabama River, at prices ranging as high as twenty dollars per acre. But the effects of the

57. *House Documents*, 19 cong., 1 sess., no. 121 (Serial no. 136), 53–70; *House Reports*, 19 cong., 1 sess., no. 231 (Serial no. 142). A brief note on the case is in Helen T. Catterall, ed., *Judicial Cases Concerning American Slavery and the Negro* (Washington, 1926–37), III, 132.

58. *Mobile Commercial Register*, January 21, February 7, 1822, and January 14, 1824.

59. For examples of Tait's charges to the grand jury, see *ibid.*, June 6, 1822, and January 14, 1824. The only extant records of the court for this period are in District Court of Alabama, Ledger Book, 1821–24 (Office of Clerk, District of Southern Alabama, Mobile), a small manuscript volume which is obviously not complete.

panic of 1819 and the abolition of the credit system for the sale of public lands forced them to relinquish to the government all of their holdings except 952 acres.[60]

Nor was forfeiture of lands their only disappointment, for disease ravaged the Tait household, and death took a heavy toll of their slaves. For a time Tait contemplated shifting his establishment to the pine barrens of the interior, and in 1821 he was considering a move to the Tennessee Valley. The fertility of the soil in the lowlands appealed to him, however, and despite the unhealthfulness of the region, no change was made. He and James made eighty-eight bales of cotton their second year, which was twice as much as they had produced in Georgia with the same labor force.[61] His first wife had died in 1818, before the family left Georgia, and in 1822 he remarried and established his home at Claiborne, a thriving town on the Alabama River in Monroe County.[62] During the succeeding years he gradually increased his holdings by the purchase of desirable tracts in both Monroe and Wilcox counties, and as early as 1825 he became interested in making a study of extensive fossiliferous deposits which he had found in the vicinity of Claiborne.

With the development of this new scientific interest and the necessity of giving more attention to his rapidly growing landholdings, it was perhaps natural that Tait should begin to place less emphasis upon the prestige of official position. By 1826 he had definitely decided to end his political career, and in April of that year he resigned from his office as district judge. His plans had already been made for an extended tour of the United States, and on April 25 he and Mrs. Tait left Claiborne for a trip which took them up the Mississippi and the Ohio to Pittsburgh and by way of the Erie Canal and the Hudson to New York and New England before they settled down in Philadelphia in September, 1826, for the winter. A detailed diary which he kept during the course of this journey reveals him as a close observer who seemed to possess an insatiable desire for information.[63] While he recorded his impressions of manners and customs, travel conditions, comparative prices, and public works, the attention which he gave to educational institutions and mu-

---

60. Tait Land Tables, 1821–23, in possession of Albert Tait, Camden, Ala.

61. Tait to Walker, March 5, November 16, 1821, in Walker Papers; James A. Tait to Tait, February 5, 1822, in Tait Papers; James A. Tait's Memorandum Book, 1850.

62. Tait's second wife was the widow of Judge John Griffin, whom he had twice defeated for the superior court judgeship in Georgia.

63. This diary, covering the period from April 25, 1826, to October 27, 1827, is now in the possession of Mrs. Felicia B. Moore, Washington, D.C.

seums and to distinguished scientists whom he met indicated the depth
of his interest in cultural and scientific activities.

To some extent, perhaps this new scientific interest was a survival
from his early experience at Cokesbury and at Richmond Academy,
where he had taught the rudiments of the known sciences of the time,
but it had undoubtedly been stimulated by his curiosity concerning the
unusual deposits in his Alabama environment. It is also possible that he
was motivated by practical considerations connected with his agricultural interests, for it was not uncommon at that time for planters to
study both chemistry and stratigraphy in the hope of finding ways to
improve the condition of their soil. Whatever the cause, he became so
enthusiastic over the possibility of becoming a scientist that shortly after
his arrival in Philadelphia in the fall of 1826 he registered for courses in
geology and chemistry at the University of Pennsylvania. Though he
was now fifty-eight and, as he said, "on the downhill of life," he found
these subjects to be a "fountain of pleasure" which he hoped "to draw
on hereafter." His chemistry instructor was the noted Dr. Robert Hare,
and he studied geology and mineralory under Solomon Conrad, one of
the most distinguished naturalists of that period.[64]

While in Philadelphia Tait visited the Philadelphia Academy of Natural Sciences, where he became acquainted with such eminent scientists as
Isaac Lea, conchologist and paleontologist, Charles A. Poulson, natural-
ist, and Samuel G. Morton, anthropologist, and where he added to his
own scientific knowledge by reading extensively from various books on
conchology and botany and by examining all the specimens available to
him.[65] In the spring of 1827 he was elected to membership in the American Philosophical Society, and in acknowledging this honor he wrote:
"It will be a matter of great consolation and of just pride to reflect that
my name is enrolled in the same catalogue with that of . . . Franklin,
Jefferson, and Rittenhouse." [66]

In the fall of 1827 Tait returned to his frontier home at Claiborne,
where he was to devote the remainder of his life to his geological and
agricultural interests. Here he had the good fortune of immediate access to an area which a contemporary scientist was soon to describe as

64. Tait to James A. Tait, December 16, 1826, in Tait Papers.
65. Tait to James A. Tait, November 1, 1826, *ibid*.
66. George Ord to Tait, April 20, 1827, *ibid.;* Tait to Ord, April 23, 1827, in
American Philosophical Society Archives, Philadelphia. Tait's pride in this honor
would undoubtedly have been greater if he could have known that he had received
a recognition which came to no other resident of either Georgia or Alabama
within his own or the succeeding generation.

offering "more charms for the fancy of a geologist than any spot probably in America." [67] Along the bluffs of the Alabama River at Claiborne
and on Tait's plantation were vast desposits of shells, fossils, corals, and
bones that no scientist had ever seen. Tait hoped to make these deposits
known and thus to make his contribution to scientific knowledge. He
now began shifting bones and shells from these great fossiliferous beds,
and he collected a large number of specimens, wrote elaborate descriptions of his findings, and painted accurate plates of the various fossils.
But his chief discouragement lay in the difficulty of classifying and in-
terpreting his data. He was in the strictest sense a pioneer in the study
of Alabama geology, for nothing whatever had been done on this subject before 1827.[68]

Since scientific clearing houses were not available, such investigations
were then pursued largely in isolation. Tait, understanding that fact and
realizing his own limitations, called upon the scientists whom he had
known at the Philadelphia Academy for assistance in identifying and
classifying the fossils which he found. On the basis of his specimens and
descriptions it soon became apparent to the Philadelphia scientists that
the Claiborne beds represented the most notable and prolific tertiary formation that had thus far been found in America. In a report on new
specimens which Isaac Lea presented before the American Philosophical
Society in March, 1832, he referred to Tait as one "to whom science is
greatly indebted for his exertions in making known the natural history
of his vicinity," [69] and before the end of that year Tait was notified of
his election as a corresponding member of the Philadelphia Academy of
Natural Sciences.[70] And in the following year Lea dedicated to Tait his
new book, *Contributions to Geology*, which included an extended section on the Claiborne deposits based entirely upon information and materials which Tait himself had furnished.[71] Anxious to obtain more direct advice and assistance, however, Tait asked the Philadelphia
Academy to send one of its specialists in the field of tertiary fossils to
Claiborne, and in 1833 Timothy A. Conrad, the son of the man under

67. Timothy A. Conrad to Tait, July 19, 1834, in Tait Papers.

68. Michael Tuomey, *First Bennial Report on the Geology of Alabama* (Tusca-
loosa, Ala., 1850), x. Isaac Lea, to whom Tait sent some of his plates, wrote that
they were done in "a very superior and correct manner." Lea to Tait, September
30, 1829, in Tait Papers.

69. *Transactions of the American Philosophical Society*, n.s., V (1832–37), 40.

70. Tait to Samuel G. Morton, October 16, 1832, in Archives of the Philadelphia
Academy of Natural Sciences.

71. Isaac Lea, *Contributions to Geology* (Philadelphia, 1833), 1–186, especially
the dedicatory note and p. 28.

whom Tait had studied geology at the University of Pennsylvania, responded to this request. Conrad had published in 1832 the first two parts of his famous *Fossil Shells of the Tertiary Formations of North America*, and after a year of residence as a guest in the Tait home at Claiborne, during which he and Tait made a careful examination of the deposits, he was able to complete his book on a scale which established his reputation as the leader in systematic research on the tertiary period of geological history.[72]

Although the greater part of Tait's life had been spent in public service, he apparently never lost the attachment for the soil which had been acquired through his boyhood experience in Virginia and Georgia, and during these later years when he was making his contribution toward the beginning of serious work in the study of tertiary geology, he was also deeply involved in the supervision of his extensive agricultural interests. As a planter in the Georgia Piedmont, he had turned from tobacco to cotton as his principal crop, and his decision to move to Alabama had been dictated in part by the better opportunities for cotton culture which the new region seemed to offer. It was with the expectation of becoming planters on a more expansive scale, therefore, that he and his son planned their move, selected their locations, and began the purchase of land in the Alabama River valley. Proceeding cautiously but persistently after the forfeitures of 1820, they gradually increased their holdings to approximately 4,000 acres, which were divided into three plantations—Medina, in Monroe County, and Springfield and Weldon, farther up the river in Wilcox County.

To provide the labor supply for this establishment, Tait had brought with him from his Georgia plantation twenty-five working hands, and as the needs increased more slaves were added by purchase, until at the time of his death in 1835 he was one of the largest slaveholders in the state, with a total of 115 slaves.[73] No record has been found to indicate that he ever sold any of his Negroes, and his memorandum book for the year of his death shows that there were five generations of slaves in his possession, one of whom had been in the family for seventy-eight years. Believing that it was better to have "the character of a good master than

---

72. For a good account of Conrad's work in collaboration with Tait, see Harry E. Wheeler, "Timothy Abbott Conrad, with Particular Reference to His Work in Alabama One Hundred Years Ago," in *Bulletins of American Paleontology*, XXIII (1935–37), 1–157.

73. Charles Tait's Memorandum Book, 1835, in possession of Mrs. A. B. Howard, Montgomery, Ala. Of this total, 39 had been purchased in April, 1835, at a cost of $22,545. Bills of Sale, 1835, in possession of Albert Tait, Camden, Ala.

a rich one,"[74] Tait fed and clothed his Negroes well, made it possible for some of them to learn to read and write, and provided them with the same quality of medical attention that the members of his own family received. He believed that with care his slaves would multiply rapidly, and he gave "a full share of attention to this end of the business."[75] He frequently purchased Negro girls of twelve to fifteen years of age, paying as much as $50 more for them than for boys of the same age. In 1835 he bought eight such girls at an average price of approximately $625 each. So successful was Tait in managing "this end of the business" that between 1819 and 1834 fifty-eight Negroes were born on his plantations.[76] He was also mindful of the spiritual needs of his Negroes, for he bequeathed to his heirs "forever in trust" a chapel which he had built in Wilcox County so that his "black people . . . might have an opportunity for religious instruction."[77]

Like many other planters, Tait depended upon overseers to operate his plantations. And, like others, he found the selection and retention of satisfactory overseers to be a major problem. Writing from Philadelphia in 1826 concerning the employment of a new overseer, he said: "If he 's honest, industrious, experienced, and a good manager, I shall not grudge him a good salary."[78] But he found few who possessed all these qualifications, and his unfortunate experiences with overseers were typical of the time and place in which he lived. One overseer permitted Negroes from another plantation to spread whooping cough among Tait's slaves, thus resulting in the death of two children; another lost his authority over the slaves; and still another, through carelessness, allowed the gin house to burn. His experiences led him to the conclusion that "few overseers will act as they ought to."[79]

Tait's plantations were both agricultural and industrial establishments, with an important part of the finished goods used on them being fashioned at home by his slaves. In addition to cobblers, tanners, blacksmiths, and seamstresses, there were Kiah the millwright, Smith the gunsmith, and Hezekiah, an unusually versatile carpenter who made

74. Tait to James A. Tait, February 15, 1827, in Tait Papers.
75. Tait to James A. Tait, January 27, 1827, *ibid.*
76. Charles Tait's Memorandum Book, 1835. On the other hand, the son estimated in 1850 that he had lost nearly 300 Negroes by death during the past thirty years. James A. Tait's Memorandum Book, 1850.
77. Charles Tait's Will, copy in possession of Judge Robert E. Tait, Mobile, Ala.
78. Tait to James A. Tait, November 1, 1826, in Tait Papers.
79. James A. Tait to Tait, September 22, 1824, and January 7, 1834, and Tait to James A. Tait, November 1, 1826, *ibid.,*; also James A. Tait's Memorandum Book, 1826.

everything from cotton scales to gears for the gin machinery, including a new device for removing trash and yellow flakes from the cotton fiber. Although the plantations were not self-sufficient agricultural units, Tait insisted that corn must be grown, not only because he considered it "the mainstay of life," but also because it was essential for raising enough hogs to provide his Negroes with "as much pork as they can eat." [80] Occasionally he raised a surplus of corn, but just as often he found it necessary to buy in order to meet the needs of his own establishment. From time to time he purchased cattle, sheep, and other livestock, and, partly to provide forage but partly also for their beneficial effect on the soil, he sometimes planted leguminous crops.[81] He found the growing of wheat to be impracticable because of the lack of flour mills in the region, but he encouraged his slaves to raise all kinds of vegetables in patches of their own, and he experimented intermittently in horticulture.

But despite these manifestations of an interest in diversification, his chief crop was cotton, most of his land and resources being devoted to the production of this staple. Having come from a section of Georgia where cotton was the principal agricultural product, he had learned to give special attention to the quality of his crop and to its preparation for market. Consequently he usually received a high price for his cotton, which he shipped to Mobile aboard Alabama River steamers, at a cost of about a dollar per bale.[82] Conforming to the mercantile policy of his day, he sold his cotton and bought his supplies through a factor, his accounts for most of the period of his operations in Alabama being handled by Jeremiah Austill, a well-known Mobile commission merchant and cotton agent. Tait's profits from cotton were small in the early years, but from 1824 to his death in 1835 his cotton planting became increasingly lucrative. In 1831, his largest crop year, he produced 350 bales, which Austill sold for him at about nine cents per pound, or a total of about $11,000. This was about the same as the returns from a smaller crop in 1825, which had sold at fifteen cents, and in 1834 Tait sent Austill 209 bales, which the factor sold at more than eighteen cents per pound, the entire crop bringing approximately $15,000.[83]

80. Tait to John W. Walker, November 19, 1819, in Walker Papers; Tait to James A. Tait, February 15, 1827, in Tait Papers.

81. A letter from the overseer of "Weldon" describes the results of an experiment with peas on that plantation in 1832. Daniel McLeod to Tait, October 27, 1832, in Tait Papers.

82. Jeremiah Austill to Tait, June 10, 1832, and miscellaneous shippers' receipts, *ibid.*

83. Austill to Tait, March 26, 1832, and May 2, 1835, *ibid.*; James A. Tait's Memorandum Book, 1826.

Most of Tait's supplies were also handled by Austill, although he maintained accounts with various Mobile and Philadelphia firms from which he purchased paints, groceries, cut glass, wines, jewelry, clothing and cloth, and other items. His financial operations were carried on through the Mobile branch of the United States Bank, where his excellent standing is shown by the fact that in 1835 he was offered a loan of $50,000.[84] This offer was apparently not accepted, but at about the same time he seems to have incurred an indebtedness of $10,000 to the estate which Mrs. Tait had inherited from her first husband for eighteen slaves who were being transferred to his ownership.[85] The meticulous care with which this transaction was recorded suggests that it may have been a part of the process of clarifying the interrelations between the two estates in order that legal entanglements might be avoided in case of the death of either Mrs. Tait or himself. If this was the purpose, the action was timely, because Tait's health failed rapidly during the summer of 1835, and on October 7 he died at his son's home in Wilcox County.[86]

As he recorded in the epitaph which he prepared for use on his tombstone, Tait had, "in the course of his pilgrimage through life, enjoyed much of public favor and patronage,"[87] and in addition to the prestige of public office, which he held in high esteem, he had also acquired that material wealth which he once characterized as "miserable trash."[88] The diversity of his interests seemingly gave him rare powers of adaptation which enabled him to be equally at home among statesmen in Washington, scholars in Philadelphia, lawyers and teachers in Georgia, and pioneer planters in the bottomlands of Alabama. For that reason he could hardly be classified as a typical southern planter. His interest in science alone would have differentiated him from his fellow planters, although many of them also were men of varied interests and diverse abilities. His career was more nearly that of the southern man of affairs who aspired to eminence in many fields. Such individuals, in the pattern of William Byrd and Thomas Jefferson, were doubtless more numerous in the South (as well as elsewhere) in the seventeenth and eighteenth centuries than in later periods, but Tait's life demonstrates the extension of the pattern into the nineteenth century. Further, a study of the attitudes,

84. Tait to James A. Tait, April 29, 1835, in possession of Albert Tait, Camden, Ala.

85. Articles of Agreement between Charles Tait and Sarah Griffin Tait, April 11, 1835, *ibid.*

86. *Selma* (Ala.) *Free Press*, October 24, 1835.

87. Tompkins, *Charles Tait*, 29.

88. See note 53, above.

interests, and experiences of such a man sheds some light on the economic, social, and political life of Georgia and Alabama during the early years of the nineteenth century, and it contributes to our knowledge of the general cultural pattern of the time. It is significant that even though the regions in which he lived were all in the frontier stage during most of his life, a man of Tait's caliber could find congenial companions and a pleasant, satisfying life as a political leader, lawyer, scientist, and planter, and could leave his impact on the life of his state and his country.

Mack Swearingen

Thirty Years of a Mississippi Plantation: Charles Whitmore of Montpelier

Too much nostalgia, imprecise language, and a distinctly anti-agrarian bias have portrayed the South's economy as a mixture of inefficiency, waste, and simple backwardness. Those searching for a cause have laid the blame on Negro slavery. This is too simple an answer and one which ignores the history of southern agriculture and Negro slavery. Slavery provided the South's planters with a relatively cheap labor force, whose chief characteristic Northerners argued was its laziness and inefficiency. No one who has read the accounts of the cultivation of any of the South's staples could concur in this assessment. If the slaves were inefficient, it is less the result of intrinsic qualities of slave labor than the product of the men who directed it. Complaints of planters against inefficient and disinterested overseers confirm this belief. Nevertheless, other factors are equally important, among them the attitude of the planter himself.

Though the word "ecology" is a rather recent addition to our public vocabulary, its central concern, the preservation of the land against predatory individuals interested only in profit, had many advocates in the antebellum South. The emigration from east to west early in the South's history told a tale of worn, eroded lands. And as the antebellum period progressed, the agricultural techniques which depleted the Old South reappeared in the New South. This was the result not of slave labor but of the men who guided it. Our confusion about the possibilities of growth, innovation, and change in the antebellum South derives from an implicit belief that agriculture is always inferior to manufacturing and industry. In the South the highest profits and the largest gains in capital investment went to agriculturists. Their adherence to the land did not make them backward or "feudal;" if anything, the reverse. The South's failure to industrialize should not be interpreted to mean backwardness or shortsightedness. The social stigma attached to industrial labor no doubt inhibited its growth, but the central factor was an economic one. The most remunerative of all economic ventures in the antebellum South was agriculture. To understand the antebellum South we must focus upon that sphere of its economic activity.

Many historians have argued that significant change was underway before the Civil War. Agricultural societies and their journals urged the use of new techniques to revitalize old areas and preserve new ones. This study of Montpelier Plantation shows that rational and efficient organization could be applied to agriculture. Whitmore's success indicates that the historical argument which explains secession as an imperative need to expand ought to be carefully reexamined. Propounded by the South's political leadership in the decade before the Civil War, it may lack factual substance. Expansion is not equivalent to growth, and the addition of new lands to an independent South may have been an important stimulus to continue its regressive and ruinous agricultural techniques. Closer study of other individuals like Whitmore (whose names could easily be gleaned from agricultural journals) and analysis of their social and political attitudes, as well as the social status afforded them, could help us gauge the direction of this predominantly agricultural society in the decade before the Civil War.

The value of plantation diaries and journals for the study of the economic and social history of the South has been recognized by students of history since the turn of the century.[1] A few such records have been published in documentary form; many others have been reduced to monographic status. It is the purpose of this study to analyze the daybook of a transplanted Englishman who established Montpelier Plantation three miles from Natchez a decade after the admission of Mississippi into the Union.

Charles Whitmore, master of Montpelier, was born on December 20, 1789, apparently in Gloucestershire, the old Marcher county on the Welsh border. The Whitmores were a "county family," manorial landlords, lusty members of the British squirearchy in the golden age of squires before the Reform Bill. The head of the family, Thomas Charleton Whitmore, was younger than Charles by nine years, and it was he who occupied Apley Park, the ancestral home at Stockton village in the neighboring county of Salop. The hall at Apley was a huge, massive structure which frowned on the countryside in the same forbidding fashion as did most of the gloomy manorial castles in which the pride of England then lived.

1. A paper read before the history division of the Southwestern Social Science Association, Oklahoma City, April 19, 1935.

Charles seems to have spent much of his time at Apley, but he was a member of the cadet branch of the family and their seat was near Cheltenham in Gloucestershire. Though members of this junior branch owned extensive property, they apparently could not boast of a gloomy and impressive manor house in which they could billet whole generations of the clan. At any rate, Charles, who was a younger son, left Gloucestershire in 1818 and went to Liverpool, where he entered the service of Thomas B. Barclay and Company as a clerk. There on September 1, 1826, he married Miss Elizabeth Lyon, who was connected with a very old and honored family in England, one of whom is now the Duchess of York.

It must have been about this time that the head of the junior Whitmores died and the Gloucestershire property was divided among the heirs. Charles Whitmore used the profits from his share for his migration to and settlement in America. Just when he came over he nowhere says, but he does give the date of his settlement at Montpelier as April 7, 1828. In the winter of 1834 he began to keep an accurate record of activities on his plantation. This record, which he calls his "Agricultural Journal and General Memorandum," continues until 1864.[2] In many respects it is much like all other such documents. It seems to have been written originally on separate sheets and then bound and rebound from time to time to include the latest records. This is apparent from the fact that the type of paper changes every now and again, and that odd sheets are bound in all through the book. The binding is of ordinary boards, and the paper is of regular foolscap size, eight by thirteen. A few pages were stitched in before the title page and on these are a few newspaper clippings, a drawing of an eclipse, and a list of correspondence from May 30, 1853, to December 21, 1854. Immediately following the title page are three which were originally left blank but which now contain tax returns for the years 1848 and 1854–62, and also a list of abnormal temperatures and other climatic phenomena from November 20, 1841, to July 3, 1863. The book is enlivened throughout by drawings of eclipses, comets, members of the family, animals, farm implements, and the like. Plots, plans, and diagrams are often used to clarify what is written.

The first proper plantation entry in chronological order is "The Distribution of Winter Clothing for 1834," and the last entry is dated June 6, 1864. Between these dates the only part missing is a small section cut

2. This plantation journal was presented to the writer by one of his students at Tulane University, Miss Mary Pendleton Febiger, a great granddaughter of Charles Whitmore.

out by a female descendant to prove her right to membership in the United Daughters of the Confederacy. The deleted section destroys the entries from November 27, 1862, to December 22 of the same year, and from January 25 to 27, 1863.[3]

Any such record of plantation life would be important for historians today because there is still much to learn about southern plantation economy, but there are several points of especial interest about Charles Whitmore and Montpelier. To begin with, he was by birth and training a member of the English landed gentry after whose style of life southerners consciously modeled their own. As a gentleman born and bred, he did not have to work up to his position in the top social stratum of southern society. Members of his family were manorial aristocrats and landlords in England; in Mississippi, therefore, he was spared the arduous struggle by which his neighbors had raised themselves from upcountry farmers to the level of feudal lords. He was furthermore an educated man who went at the business of farming with intelligence. This is a fact of significance, and with it this study is especially concerned.

It has been repeated *ad nauseam* that the old agricultural economy of the South was backward and unscientific. Of recent years it has become steadily more apparent that this accusation is unjust. That the bulk of southern farmers were unlettered and cultivated their land wastefully and stupidly is probably true, but there were many leaders among the agriculturists of the South who were not guilty of unenlightened methods or attitudes. These leaders realized the importance of agriculture to the South and applied themselves to its study with energy and good sense. While many farmers in the cotton country were wallowing in ignorance and probably destroying the birthright of their children, there were others who made contributions to agricultural science that were in all likelihood equal to similar contributions made by agriculturists of the other sections. Among these one thinks of George Washington, Thomas Jefferson, Edmund Ruffin, Thomas Affleck, and B. L. C. Wailes.

In addition to these leaders—experimenters and innovators—there were also many planters who were intelligent and businesslike even though they did not blaze new trails. It is to this class, rather than to that of the great leaders, that Whitmore belongs. He made no startling contributions or discoveries and his name was not known far and wide, but his methods were scientific, businesslike, and successful. He belongs to the important and probably large group of practicing agriculturists

3. Apparently there was only one entry between January 25 and 27, and this was the account of enlistment. It is impossible to determine how many entries were on the reverse side in the period from November 27 to December 22.

who are clearly slandered when the charge of backwardness is hurled. Any historian of the South has available for study plantation journals or diaries carefully edited and printed. It is fair to assume that only the best planters kept journals and diaries and that these do not therefore give any true picture of the average or mean type, but it is nevertheless worth emphasizing that no one can read any number of such documents and still believe that waste, stupidity, and medievalism were the chief characteristics of southern agriculture.

It is in order to examine Whitmore as a typical specimen of "planter sapiens." His plantation, however, was much smaller than the average. It was just over 300 acres in size, varying slightly from year to year as a result of occasional sales and purchases. It lay compactly along two creeks and had doubtless been cultivated for fifty years before he acquired it, for all the land near Natchez had been continuously occupied since the Revolutionary War. Like all the soil in that area, it is a loessal deposit and generally fertile, although subject to disastrous washing. In 1841 he bought a thousand-acre tract on the Tensas river in Louisiana, but this he rented out, and it is rarely alluded to in his journal. His slaves in 1834 numbered twenty, but after a few years he had a complement averaging thirty-five, including children born on the place.

With the exception of one year, cotton was his chief crop, but he also produced for sale a large variety of other products among which corn was the most significant. There was never a year in which he depended exclusively on cotton, and once in disgust he raised none at all. Nevertheless, as his most important interest it deserves consideration first.

Whitmore began his preparations shortly after the turn of the year. His first step was to send hands into the fields to knock down stalks. This done, he broke out the old middles and threw up new ridges, for which job he used double plows. He then harrowed the ridges and was ready to begin planting. Usually he planted early in April, but on one occasion he had his crop out of the ground by March 27. Only once or twice did he have to replant on account of starting too early. He planted his seed in a drill which was opened by a small horse-drawn implement designed for that purpose and called an "opener." It is hard to tell from his phraseology whether he used a mechanical planter for placing seed in the drill, but from his manner of alluding to the process and from the speed with which it was completed, the impression is left that he early abandoned the practice of seeding by hand and used one of the various mechanical planters then on the market. He nowhere makes reference to his manner of covering the seed. Several methods were in use at that time, and the only possible conclusion from his journal is that if he possessed a mechanical planter, this implement very likely completed the covering operation also.

Shortly after the crop came up the process of barring off began. This was done by a scraper, a plow type of recent invention. One scraper on the market was designed especially for cotton cultivation, and this was the kind used by Whitmore. It threw the dirt from the plant and greatly reduced the amount of hoeing necessary by uprooting the grass and weeds in the ridges. Immediately after this operation Whitmore began moulding, that is, throwing the dirt back to the plant. In some years he was compelled to bar off without moulding, or vice versa, when abnormal weather made his crop too backward or too advanced.

When the moulding process was completed, hoe gangs went over the crop as a rule three times, thinning to a stand and incidentally removing grass and weeds. Checking grass and weeds was done as much as possible, however, by horse-drawn implements instead of by hand. For example, the barring off operation described above was done with a scraper; after the moulding was finished, the war on enemy vegetation was carried on principally with the sweep, another new kind of plow. The sweeps alternated with the hoe gangs and kept the rows as clean as possible. The crop was not laid by until the plows had gone the fifth time over and the hoes the third time. This usually was not until the middle of July, and the first picking was practically always begun by August 1. Picking continued until January, and the whole routine then started over again.

Several comments on this procedure are necessary before any reference is made to seed selection, fertilizing, rotation, and crop yields. The first point is that this method is not materially different from the one employed now. Another obvious comment is that there was no innovation or pioneering in this kind of cotton culture. From an examination of his routine, it was evident that Whitmore could not be called a leader. But it is a point of considerable importance that his methods were not backward, wasteful, or stupid. He followed in every detail the recommendations and methods that were suggested by the most scientific agriculturists of the day. He was abreast of the times in every practice, and it is hardly fair to call a man backward or stupid when any mistake that he makes is not his error but that of the most reliable authorities in his field. The point is that Whitmore's agriculture was intelligent and up to the minute, whether it was bad or good. It is unreasonable to condemn a planter for bad agriculture when even the best know no better and when he is alert and sensible in carrying out the best practices of his time. Whitmore's routine followed to the letter the recommendations laid down in Mississippi's agricultural bible—the report of B. L.C. Wailes on the agriculture and geology of Mississippi.

That Whitmore had a truly scientific attitude toward planting is even better demonstrated by his interest in seed strains. On occasion he conducted his own experiments and carefully recorded in what fields he placed what types. One can be sure he noted and used the results of these experiments, although for some curious reason he did not record these results in his book. He bought seed from many of his neighbors and also tried several varieties of Mexican seed.[4] In 1839 Whitmore made a careful experiment, apparently designed to determine whether it was worthwhile to buy an expensive fine grade variety. He put several qualities in four different fields and out of the crop saved 3,500 pounds of cotton for seed for the next planting. This was a good year for him to save his own seed, because his cotton had grown seven feet high and he had made ninety-five bales on a hundred acres. It is exasperating that he did not note the results of this experiment, but it is worth something to observe that next year he made only seventy-five bales. In 1846 he planted a Mexican type in his garden and noted that he got 62 seeds from one boll which weighed 235 grains—75 grains staple and 160 grains seed. The following year he planted another row of this in his garden but did not bother to record what happened. In 1853 he tried another variety called "Pomegranate," which he noted with obvious awe cost three dollars a bushel. In the same year he commented that seed to be safe must be dry.

Similarly intelligent was his use of the various methods of preserving or enriching the soil. It has already been noted that he knocked down and plowed under the old stalks, which was and is good sense. He likewise made frequent use of all the "home-made" fertilizers such as rotten leaves, manure, cotton seed, and ashes. In 1844 he mentioned the use of a commercial fertilizer, but he recorded no further information about it. His crop that year was nineteen bales larger than the year before. In 1845, as the guano mania began to sweep the country, he wrote to Ringgold Ferriday and Company in New Orleans asking the price of it and the manner in which it was shipped. Apparently dismayed at the exhorbitant rate, he did not buy any for ten years, but in 1855 he pur-

---

4. It should be noted that practically all cotton at this time was of Mexican origin, although domesticated. When Whitmore especially mentioned some kind of Mexican seed it must therefore have been a recent importation. The first Mexican cotton to be tried in this country was carefully bred around Petit Gulf about 1820, and from these experiments most of the domestic strains were produced, almost entirely eliminating the use of Tennessee green seed.

chased thirty-four sacks weighing 4,754 pounds, which cost him $131.25 delivered in Natchez. This was probably motivated by desperation, because he had engaged a worthless overseer who brought the crop down from 105 bales in 1852 to 39 bales in 1854. Something was necessary to increase production after dismissal of the overseer.

Whitmore's experiments with guano were cautious. He used only nine bags in 1855, carefully noting in which fields it was put and using part of it for a garden experiment. In this latter operation he planted a few rows of okra in ashes and manure and a few in guano. As usual, he did not record what happened, but his cotton crop went up to fifty-five bales. In 1856 he used twelve and a half sacks, and his crop went up to sixty-seven bales. In 1857 he used the remaining twelve and a half sacks, and his crop dropped to forty-eight bales. As acreage figures are not available for this period, it cannot be determined how much of the increase resulted from the use of fertilizer. He did conclude, however, that guano caused his oats to ripen earlier and also doubled their size. In applying guano to his fields Whitmore used several methods, sometimes sprinkling his seed with it and sometimes mixing it with black soil and cotton seed. His results were obviously gratifying though not at all spectacular. Apparently he was not greatly impressed and ordered no more guano.

Aside from the use of various fertilizers, he also tried other means of improving and saving his soil. Every year or so he put one of his cotton fields in peas, of which he noted two varieties—ordinary field peas and "Oregon peas." In 1841 he carried out a complete rotation schedule, putting all his good cotton lands in corn and peas and his poor cotton lands in oats. His cotton crop that year he put down in new lands. He regularly switched fields from cotton to corn and back again every year or so, but as usual he made no comment on the results of these operations.

In picking his crop he showed an increasing efficiency which was characteristic of the whole South. In the first decades of the century an adult slave as a rule picked no more than fifty or sixty pounds a day, but as the years passed planters developed and used a cotton whose bolls opened wider and from which it was easier to pick the lint. Also slaves acquired more skill through long practice. The result was that in later decades adult hands could pick on the average about two hundred pounds a day. This progress can be traced on Whitmore's plantation. He set down the daily weights picked by each slave only for the first crop recorded in the journal, but every year he totaled the amount picked each day during the season. In 1835 the largest amount picked in one day by one hand was 142 pounds, and few hands averaged as much as 100 pounds. The largest day's picking in 1835 was 1,500 pounds. By 1850 a good day's work ran up to 2,500 pounds, and a total for one day of over 3,000 pounds was several times recorded. These figures almost exactly double those of the 1830's, whereas the hands available for cotton picking were not double the earlier number, although there was an increase. One can therefore say that efficiency in crop gathering resulted in an increase which was apparently equal to that of other well-managed establishments.

Whitmore also had his share of trouble with pests. He first noted one in 1844 and called it the "cut worm," but this was the year in which he first used compost, and his crop was nineteen bales larger than the year before in spite of the pest. This enemy returned in 1846 with a friend, the "boring worm," and reduced the yield to thirty-one bales. Two years later he returned with another gangster, this time the "army worm." Lugubriously Whitmore moaned that half his crop was destroyed, but he made eighty-two bales, which makes a liar out of him! Next year the worms were worse and the yield went down to sixty-one bales. In this year Whitmore made a careful note of the pest's life history: "The Cotton Worm has eaten up nearly all the leaves, Blossons, & young bowls, and are increasing rapidly—the moth very thick and Crysalis hanging on every stalk—The first appearance 1 Sept by a Yellow Butterfly; afterwards a green worm then the regular moth & black striped army worm." This is probably a garbled biography in which the lives of two separate villains are telescoped. In 1852 there appeared both rot and rust, but the damage they caused could not have been serious, because the yield this year was 105 bales, which is second-highest for the whole period. The principal interest attaching to the rot is that it coincides almost identically with the developments that are observed when the boll weevil gets to work. Wailes attributed rot to an insect that laid its eggs in the boll, and there are reasons for believing that the boll weevil made at least two invasions before the devastating visitation that began about 1890.

About the yield on Montpelier Plantation there is little satisfactory information, as complete statistics are rarely given in the journal. Every year Whitmore recorded either the total bales made, the total pounds gross, or the total pounds net (lint), but he rarely gave all three.[5] Simi-

5. In arriving at the totals in the following chart the figures for 1840 were omitted except in the case of the bales. The figures for gross and net in 1840 are somehow erroneous, for which Whitmore held his overseer responsible. Whitmore was in Europe when the crop was picked. The defective bookkeeping in 1861, 1862, and

larly, he recorded the number of acres planted in only five years. Naturally from these figures one can derive nothing with precision, but by combining them and using a statistical process which no one would defend, the following estimates have been made in which little faith is placed. An annual planting of 100 acres averaged 63 bales a year. The average weight of the bales was 407 pounds, and the average yield per acre about 250. The ratio of lint to gross was approximately 27 percent.[6]

1863 was of course the result of the war. Whitmore was at that time very old, ill, and depressed, and obviously lost interest.

Years	Acres	Pounds gross	Pounds net (lint)	Bales
1835	73	65,000		47
1836	88½	63,130		47
1837		76,440		52
1838		68,100		48
1839	100	135,700		95
1840		123,734(?)	31,331(?)	75
1841	95	85,222		56
1842		181,556	46,715	116
1843		102,494		63
1844		133,300		82
1845	No Crop			
1846		43,600		31
1847		125,975		78
1848		133,585	33,852	82
1849		99,400	24,833	61
1850	126	76,850	26,004	67
1851		140,000	37,800	73
1852		155,000		105
1853		66,200	19,144	45
1854		53,500	15,731	39
1855		72,200	23,004	55
1856		98,020	27,582	67(69?)
1857		76,095		48
1858		76,450		48
1859		83,200		52
1860		20,270		
1861		77,775		
1862				
1863				26
Totals	482.5	2,309,062	254,665	1578

6. If the average net per bale for the nine recorded years (407) is divided by the average gross per bale for the twenty-three years (1,413), the ratio of lint to gross becomes 28.8%. Using this percentage for the five years in which the acreage is recorded, one gets 257.3 pounds lint per acre (28.8% of 882). By one computation,

This is not impressive production, but it is definitely good for land on which commercial fertilizers were rarely used and which had probably been in cultivation for at least fifty years before he planted his first crop.

From the very outset Whitmore owned his own gin and press. Sometimes he ginned his neighbors' cotton as well as his own, and when he did so he charged them at first one-eleventh and in later years one-tenth. He usually packed a couple of bales of "trash" cotton every year, by which he must have meant the gin sweepings which are now called linters. In 1841 he spent $125 building a single screw press, and he must also have made some improvements on his gin, as he increased its rate to seventy pounds every ten minutes. In 1848 he installed a new cylindrical gin brush which he said was much better than the old fan brush, and in 1854 he built a new sixty-four-saw gin stand.

After having completed on his own place the entire process of producing cotton for the market, Whitmore then undertook to market his crop with as little reliance on middle-men as possible. Instead of dealing on a commission basis through some regular cotton factor, he sent his crop directly to his old Liverpool firm, Thomas B. Barclay and Company. The only profits that accrued to the great dealers in Natchez and New Orleans were trifling matters of freight, insurance, and drayage. It is further worth noting that in all the thirty years for which he left a record, he did not once borrow money with which to put down his crop.

then, the yield per acre is 243.7 and by another 257.3, but neither is determined by an entirely sound statistical method. The best one can do is to guess from these estimates that the yield was probably around 250 pounds on an average. It is worth noting that in 1839 Whitmore got 95 bales from 100 acres, while in 1850 he got only 67 bales from 126 acres. There is no telling what this means. Although his bales increased considerably in weight between those two years, they did not increase enough to absorb this difference. The following statistics on the cotton yield are pertinent:

Highest yield (1842)—181,556 pounds gross, or 116 bales.
Lowest yield (1860—drought)—20,270 pounds gross, or about 14 bales.
Average pounds gross per year (25 years)—92,363.
Average bales per year (25 years)—63.
Average pounds gross per bale (23 years)—1,413.
Average pounds net (lint) per year (9 years)—28,296.
Average pounds net per bale (9 years)—407.
Ratio of lint to gross (9 years)—27.6%.
Average acres in cotton (5 years)—96.5.
Average pounds gross per acre (5 years)—882.
Average bales per year (5 years)—62.4.
Average bales to acre (5 years)—0.64.
Average pounds gross per bale (5 years)—1,365.
Average pounds net per acre (5 years)—27.6% of 882, or 243.4.

There were probably inefficient and unbusinesslike planters around Natchez, but Charles Whitmore was not one of them.

Next in importance came the corn crop. Whitmore took as many pains with this as with his cotton. He noted where he got his seed and what kind it was, mentioning for example Golden Flint and White Flint. In the front of his journal is pasted a clipping from an agricultural periodical listing what not to do in corn cultivation. In other places are his own comments on his methods, such as the following:

> 27 February 1845—Commenced planting Corn, distance 18 inches for single stand, and 4 feet apart in Row.

> 23 April 1853—Corn ridges to be thrown up high in winter, and just before planting two wide furrows thrown back, then opened for planting.

He always pulled the succors off his corn and always pulled the leaves for fodder. The fodder he pressed into bales, apparently using for this his cotton press. He also had his own grist mill and did his own grinding. He noted his acreage in corn only twice—in 1839 he planted forty acres, and in 1841 he planted thirty-eight. The total yield is likewise recorded only twice; in 1835 it was over 877 bushels, and in the following year it was 1,270 bushels. These were the first two crops and thereafter the totals must have been much larger, or at any rate it would seem so from his annual allusions to the time spent in gathering, hauling, and grinding. A few times he had to buy corn for use on the place, but more often he sold a surplus. Sometimes he disposed of it by the wagonload from the field as it was being gathered. The grinding was usually done on rainy days, and it was always noted how much meal a given quantity of corn had made.

Whitmore seldom bought hay. Besides his corn fodder he had oats and other grass crops which he denominated as "hay," leaving us in the dark as to what kind. Much hay was baled, and some was sold. He used also an imported straw cutter for some purpose, but for what is not apparent. Its use certainly impressed his neighbors, because he ordered several from England for them—making, by the way, a little commission on the transaction. He also planted peas, turnips, and peanuts, all of which could be used as forage. He harvested sixteen wagonloads of peas in 1844.

Various miscellaneous crops are mentioned frequently. Whitmore seemed especially interested in his potatoes, both white and sweet, giving in considerable detail his various methods of producing them and commenting on which procedure was best. Usually when it was entered

in the book that potatoes had been planted there was added the comment, "in the dark of the moon." The following are typical items from
his journal:

> 17 March 1853—planted Sweet potatoes on the poplar cut by opening
> the cotton ridges with a cotton opener, then putting the cuttings in the
> line 1 foot apart, and hawling the soil up afterwards. The operation was
> rapid and easy.

> 24 March 1853—The hoes working *Irish* potatoes, which are very
> defective owing to being planted in the water furrow & the heavy rains
> overwhelming them.

> 26 March 1853—Digging awhile in the orchard in consequence of the
> Irish potatoes having rotted (the better way is hereafter to plant on the
> surface and cover over with manure & Earth).

Whitmore had a vegetable garden which the women worked, an orchard in which he took great pride, a vineyard of Madeira grapes, and a
variety of flowering plants. He imported a shipment of dahlias from England. He tried sugarcane only once. In his orchard were not only the
customary peaches and melons but also apples, which were unusual in
the South. The apple trees were produced by grafting and were known
locally as "Whitmore's Monthly."

The same painstaking care which all this production indicates was
likewise shown even in the selection of hedges. In a long letter to an English friend he presented an elaborate analysis of the various shrubs
available as hedges, such as holly, hawthorne, Cherokee rose, and something that he calls "pirocanthus." He concluded that on his place he
would use crepe myrtle.

It is to be expected that he was equally careful to insist upon only the
best in livestock. He imported cattle, swine, and even poultry from England. His pigs were in great demand and were sold as far away as
Vicksburg and New Orleans. His neighbors would sometimes borrow
his English boar. In 1860, however, he decided to raise no more pigs,
because the Negroes killed so many that he was compelled to inflict
more punishment than he was willing to mete out. He said there was
nothing wrong with fine Cincinnati meat anyhow.

To all this could be added countless other details about his business
methods, his personal hobbies, his family life, his slaves, and all the other
phases of plantation life, but the picture of Charles Whitmore, planter, is
already sufficiently clear. We see in him a gentleman born, a practical
farmer, a successful man of affairs. That he was intelligent, or scientific,
in managing his place there can be little doubt. How many more like

him there were in Mississippi cannot be said, but one can be reasonably sure that there must have been at least some others. In any case, to the charge of stupid agriculture in the cotton kingdom the journal of Charles Whitmore shouts from every page an emphatic denial.

J. Carlyle Sitterson

The McCollams: A Planter Family of the Old and New South

By all measurements sugar cultivation was the most strenuous and expensive southern agricultural pursuit. Geographically it was confined to parts of Texas and Louisiana. It was only in Louisiana, however, that sugar cultivation was completely successful. The innovative planter who cultivated sugar differed from planters elsewhere in the size and type of investment he made. Whereas the majority of planters gauged their capital investment through the market value of their slaves and the fertility of their land, a third factor entered the calculations of these planters: the value of their machinery. As the price of slaves spiraled in the 1850's, planters elsewhere made special efforts to protect their investment. In the sugar belt of Louisiana the situation was otherwise. Though the life of the slave was always dependent upon the kindness of his master and mistress—and the McCollams were especially kind— nowhere else did slaves work as hard as they did here. The introduction of time-saving machinery meant that slaves were even more expendable here than in other parts of the South.

The South's cotton growers competed in a world market. Their economic relation to the North was a dependent one. Though the secessionist southern Democrats were ultimately incorrect when they argued that cotton production alone was capable of sustaining a Confederacy, the 1850's supplied much proof to support their contentions. No such evidence existed to lure the Louisiana sugar growers into their ranks. A national tariff protected them against foreign competition; and even had the Confederacy made comparable concessions, its desire to expand south, particularly into Cuba, would have made the position of Louisiana's sugar growers difficult if not untenable. They therefore voted for the Whig party, and long after it had become a victim of the divisive effects of slavery they adhered to its principles. That party encouraged business activity, a system of transportation to facilitate shipment of goods from one part of the country to another, and a high tariff to protect

From the *Journal of Southern History*, VI (1940), 347–367. Copyright 1940 by the Southern Historical Association. Reprinted by permission of the Managing Editor.

nascent industries. While the Whig party never enjoyed the political success of the opposition Democrats, it was the more progressive of the two. It derived from Henry Clay's "American System" and was national in the political and economic alignments it proposed. The principles it represented, when enacted into legislation during and after the Civil War, revolutionized the economy and class structure of the nation. In the North many old Whigs became Republicans; in the South, Democrats, but the most progressive and business-oriented members of the party. Political distinctions aside, their origins lay in antebellum Whiggery. Though the McCollams were agriculturists, their economic outlook reflected these antecedents.

The following article portrays the history of the McCollam family during the antebellum and postbellum periods. Sitterson's fascinating account of sugar cultivation also details the history of the kind of men who were able to overcome the havoc wrought by the war. Astute businessmen, they saw that though Emancipation had made the Negro legally free, economic necessity provided a large and malleable work force ignorant of its rights and in many ways more fettered than before the war.

Louisiana and its sugar belt are not typical of the entire South. Though the Civil War wrecked its sugar industry and forced the planters to begin anew, it ravaged this area far less than the eastern seaboard. In a more general way it is typical of many slaveholding societies, where mechanization brought a new class to power whose commitment to slavery was less profound than that of the old slaveholding elite. These men saw that slavery was unprofitable and aligned themselves with the forces of abolition. Emancipation ended the institution and the expense of life-long care of the slave. Of course, it did nothing to alter racial attitudes which contributed to the new bondage in which the ex-slave found himself. In the antebellum South, members of this class would have been, like McCollam, Whigs and opposed to secession. Secession purported to defend the South's most valuable property, its slaves; and though popularized as a democratic act, it was in effect the last and most desperate act of a moribund class. It is therefore not surprising that when Andrew McCollam, a representative of the class which was to dominate the postwar South, finally signed the ordinance of secession, he wrote his wife, "It was the bitterest pill that I ever took."

In the early 1830's thousands of Americans were moving from their homes in the East into the Midwest and the Southwest.[1] Cheap, virgin land and the promise of social and political advancement in a rapidly de-

1. Unless otherwise stated, the material in this paper was taken from the McCollam Papers which are in the Southern Historical Collection in the University of North Carolina Library. The papers consist of family letters, business papers, Mrs.

veloping new region were the forces that lured them westward. Among
the many families that left New York were the McCollams of Cherry
Valley. Most of the family settled near La Porte, Indiana, in December,
1835. One member, Andrew, turned southward, and 1838 found him
settled at Red River Landing, Louisiana. This settlement, however, did
not prove to be a permanent one, for the year 1839 found him in Donaldsonville married to Ellen Slattery, niece of the well-to-do Edmund
Slattery. By this date John McCollam had joined his brother in Louisiana and was assisting him in the occupation of surveying in Assumption and neighboring parishes. At this time Andrew's financial status
gives little indication of the wealth he was to accumulate. In 1843 he
listed for taxes in the parish only eight acres of land and four slaves.

On Bayou Lafourche a few miles from Donaldsonville was a small
plantation which Slattery had purchased from Raphael Mollier. It was
on this planatation that Andrew and Ellen went to live in January, 1843.
McCollam lost no time in getting his new place ready for the cultivation
of sugar. He purchased seed cane from a neighboring planter, and by
February the planting was under way. The following year or so found
him constructing such necessary farm buildings as a smokehouse, a back-
house, and a sugarhouse. In spite of these activities he found sufficient
time to raise much-needed capital by continuing his surveying.

Andrew McCollam was fortunate in having married into a well-con-
nected family whose relatives and friends bestowed many favors upon
the young couple. Hardly a week passed in the years 1843–45 that some
food was not sent to them by the Slatterys, the Rightors, the Maurins,
or other friends. A neighbor lent them a cow, and Ellen helped to keep
the family supplied with meat by raising chickens and turkeys.

Sugar planting was an expensive undertaking requiring a considerable
outlay of capital for machinery and labor—indeed, much too expensive an occupation for a young man without money. Here again Andrew's relatives and friends served him well. His wife's uncle had provided land for him, and in 1845 a friend, Dr. E. E. Kittredge, endorsed
his note for $1,000 to assist him in building a sugar mill. In 1847 Slattery
purchased 80 acres of land adjoining the plantation at $10 an acre,
thereby increasing the size of the place to over 600 acres. With field
hands selling from $500 to $1,000 each, the problem of obtaining labor
was no easy one. In this respect Andrew was fortunate in 1844 in inter-

---

Andrew McCollam's plantation diary covering the years 1843–50, and Andrew
McCollam's diary of a trip to Brazil in 1866. The collection covers the years
1835–1900 and contains material on social, political, and economic life in Louisiana during that period.

esting a Mississippi planter, Green by name, in supplying the plantation with slaves in return for a portion of the profits. By January, 1846, Green had placed twenty-six Negroes on the McCollam place. In December, 1847, Edmund Slattery and Mrs. Sarah Green (probably the wife of the Mississippi planter mentioned above) entered into a four-year partnership in sugar production on the plantation occupied by the McCollams. Each party was to contribute property valued at $15,670. Slattery's part of the capital included 640 acres of land valued at $12,-830; four Negroes valued at $2,600; two horses, one mule, and a yoke of oxen at $200; and blacksmith tools and plows worth $40. Mrs. Green's capital consisted of 34 slaves (24 working hands and 10 children) valued at $15,200, and 10 mules and farming utensils worth $470. Andrew McCollam was hired to oversee and manage the plantation, for which he was to receive $700 and a dwelling house the first year.

McCollam proved to be a capable slave master and plantation manager. Clothing was distributed among the Negroes in the spring and fall of that year. When a slave was taken ill, he was attended by the family physician. The small number of Negroes made for a close relationship between master and slave. Death of a Negro was felt as a real loss. Although the work of the hands on a sugar plantation was heavy, especially during cultivation in the spring and grinding in the fall, in slack seasons they were allowed time for entertainment. Each year in the summer after the crop had been laid by, they were allowed a few holidays at which time they usually had a dinner and a ball. Again in December at the end of the grinding season they were given several holidays which were enlivened by a barbecue.

Under the influence of abolitionism in western New York, Andrew's mother solicitously wrote her son on March 19, 1844:

> My dear son allow me to say to you do treat them [the slaves] kindly. I think there is a great responsibility on every man that has slaves under their care. It is wicked to abuse a beast and more so to abuse our fellow men. They are rational beings and ought to be treated as such but I have great confidence in your humanity. I think and hope if you err it will be on the side of mercy.

Being in closer contact with Negroes than his mother, Andrew knew that they were more like children than rational beings and had to be cared for as a father cared for his children. As long as they performed their tasks and gave no trouble, disciplinary measures were unnecessary. However, when a Negro ran away, the usual punishment was a whipping. Mrs. McCollam recorded in her plantation diary for October 26,

1844, that McCollam gave her Negro woman Prissilla "a good whipping" for running away. In April, 1845, he gave her another whipping and sent her into the field "for bad conduct." Kit, a fieldhand, had to be whipped occasionally for refusing to work as directed by the driver, Big Isaac. On one occasion McCollam gave him "a severe whipping and put him in the Stocks for a week." Alfred was whipped "very severely" October 3, 1845, for stealing chickens. Mrs. McCollam had to put a chain around the ankle of a house servant, Esther, to keep her from "running about at night." On the whole, however, there were few disciplinary problems among the Negroes on the place.

McCollam occasionally hired white laborers to perform specific tasks on the plantation. In May, 1845, he hired two Irishmen to ditch at $15 an acre. In August, 1846, "Mr. Adolphe a carpenter" was hired at $30 a month to build a storehouse, a workhouse, and Negro cabins. In 1848 a blacksmith was hired at $3 a day. In January, 1847, one Daley began work at $45 a month as a carpenter. He wanted to learn to become an overseer, and he received no pay for the time devoted to overseeing. In January, 1849, Daley became McCollam's overseer at $600 a year. In August, however, Daley and Edmund Slattery quarreled, and Daley was discharged for striking the old man.

As Andrew was short of capital, he realized that the plantation must maintain itself as completely as possible. Consequently, in addition to sugarcane he planted corn, Irish potatoes, sweet potatoes, beets, green peas, onions, tomatoes, cabbages, and turnips, and he grew oranges and peaches. Pigs and chickens provided most of the meat consumed on the place. Clothes for the slaves were to a large extent made at home. Thus McCollam's purchases for plantation supplies consisted mainly of such products as butter, cheese, coffee, and flour. The plantation was heavily wooded, and some revenue was derived from the sale of wood to steamboats at $2.50 to $3.00 a cord. With a large part of the arable land devoted to food crops, the acreage in cane was necessarily limited, averaging from 75 to 100 acres. From this McCollam made on an average about 150 hogsheads of 1,200 pounds each a year. Occasionally he sold his sugar at the plantation, and in 1846 he shipped some by boat to New York, but usually it was marketed in New Orleans.

Green and McCollam had an interesting way of dividing the profits of the business. After enough sugar and molasses had been sold to pay the current expenses of the plantation, the remainder of the crop was divided between the two and each was to dispose of his share as he saw fit. In 1848–49, for example, out of a crop of 163 hogsheads of sugar, the proceeds from the sale of 43 were sufficient to pay the running expenses for the year. There remained 60 hogsheads of sugar and 118 fifty-gallon barrels of molasses for each of the partners. McCollam's sugar, sold at the plantation for four cents a pound, yielded about $2,880 and his molasses about $1,770, giving him a total return of $4,650. Not including depreciation and his salary for managing the plantation, the crop netted him a return of 31 percent on his $15,000 investment. This was the partners' best year. In 1846, when they made only 55 hogsheads, it is doubtful if the crop much more than paid for itself. How much of Slattery's share of the profits actually went to McCollam is uncertain; the intimacy of the two families and McCollam's rapid advancement to the position of a prominent and prosperous planter would lead us to think that Slattery allowed his nephew to retain a large part, if not all, of the profits.

In February, 1850, McCollam and Green decided to terminate their partnership. They agreed that the one who offered the other the highest price for his half of the plantation should become sole owner. Accordingly, Green bought McCollam's interest in the plantation for $30,000. Although a $1,700 sugar mill and several hundred dollars worth of livestock had been added to the plantation since the beginning of the partnership in 1847, a $30,000 valuation on half the property was almost double the amount Edmund Slattery had invested in the place. Nevertheless, McCollam was reluctant to sell. The plantation had become endeared to both Andrew and Ellen because it was near Donaldsonville, where there were many friends and relatives. More than this, they had raised their family there. In the years 1840–50 Ellen had borne her husband eight sons, of whom only three, Andrew, Edmund Slattery, and Henry, were living in 1850.

In August, 1850, the McCollams rented a place three miles up Bayou Lafourche for twelve dollars a month so that they could have a garden and a place to keep their livestock. They stayed there only a few months, for in February, 1851, it was sold. They then rented another house a few miles away, "the dirtiest most wretched house" Ellen had ever seen. Meanwhile, Andrew and his brother John were on the lookout for a good sugar plantation. They looked at several plantations near Baton Rouge, several on Bayou Black, some in Assumption and Pointe Coupée parishes, and others below New Orleans. In December, 1850, Andrew almost purchased the Herring place, located on the railroad nine miles below New Orleans. It was in good order and possessed a labor force of fifty-four Negroes. The price was $72,000, to be paid in four years. Thinking the land too hard and too expensive to cultivate, he decided against buying it. Finding the prices of plantations too high for his capital, Andrew regretted having sold the Bayou Lafourche place. He remarked that he had "just thrown away thirty thousand dollars," for in four years his share of the Bayou Lafourche plantation would have been worth $60,000. In April, 1851, he looked at the Tanner plantation on Bayou Black in Terrebonne Parish and was well pleased with it, declaring it to be "the first place yet offered" him upon which any money could be made. When his wife decided she could be content to live on Bayou Black "if the mosquitoes don't nearly eat me up," he purchased the plantation. This plantation, owned by J. N. Tanner and R. D. Jordan, had twenty-six mortgages on it totaling $50,000. It contained about 1,700 acres of land with a frontage of 45 acres on each side of the bayou. It was bounded above by land of James Hanna and Mrs. Sarah York and below by land of William A. Shaffer. The plantation embraced sugar machinery, fifteen slaves, five oxen, two mule carts, an oxcart, a wagon, a bagasse cart, and a large number of plows and other farming utensils. It was purchased by John McCollam for $50,000.[2] How little actual cash was involved may be seen by the following account of the arrangements. He assumed a mortgage of $12,611.12 for the cash payment and agreed to pay the balance of $37,388.88 in four annual installments of $9,347.22, 1852 to 1855, with interest at 8 percent. P. Haven and Company of New York through their New Orleans agent paid $7,102.50 on the cash payment, and received as security a first mortgage on the plantation amounting to $7,700. In 1853, in order to secure cash for the payments on the plantation, Andrew McCollam gave Haven and Company notes for $16,000 to be paid in 1854. As security he put up his growing sugar crop and a note of $6,905.56 on Sarah Green of Assumption Parish, payable to Edmund Slattery and carrying 8 percent interest from 1850.

In the spring of 1851 the McCollam brothers began sugar planting on their new place, Ellendale (named for Andrew's wife), a few miles from Houma. In the eleven years from 1851 until the disruption produced by the war in 1861, their annual crop averaged 391 hogsheads. In 1860–61 they produced their largest prewar crop of 500 hogsheads. In only one year after 1852 did their crop fall below 350 hogsheads. In 1856, when a cold, wet season and severe floods injured the sugarcane throughout Louisiana, they made only 111 hogsheads. The increasing size of operations at Ellendale is clearly indicated by the following table of sugar production:

2. Just why John rather than Andrew purchased the plantation in his name is not revealed in the family papers. Perhaps there was some personal or legal reason for having the property placed in John's name.

Year	Sugar (hhds. of 1,100 lbs.)	Average price per lb.
1851	108	3–4c
1852	260	2¾–4¼c
1853	438	3–5½c
1854	352	3–6¼c
1855	350	5–8c
1856	111	6–10⅛c
1857	390	4–6½c
1858	645	4½–6½c
1859	430	4¾–6½c
1860	500	3½–5c
1861	720	

The annual net return from the sale of the crop averaged in round numbers $18,000 to $20,000. In 1852–53, for instance, 428 barrels of molasses and 251 hogsheads of sugar brought $13,021.61. In 1856–57 from a crop of only 111 hogsheads of sugar and 252 barrels of molasses they received $16,500. These were the two smallest crops produced on the plantation from 1852 to 1861. Of course the high return for the small crop of 1856–57 is explained by the unusually high prices of sugar that year, from 6 to 10 cents per pound. On the average the McCollams' sugar sold at prices from 2¾ to 5½ cents per pound.

In order to farm so large a plantation and produce so much sugar, a larger labor force than the fifteen Negroes found on the place in 1851 was necessary. Accordingly, slaves were purchased frequently in New Orleans. In March, 1853, Andrew bought several slaves for which his factor made the cash payment. In 1858 the McCollam brothers purchased three Negro men from John B. Smith of New Orleans for $4,100. By 1860 the number of slaves on the place had increased to eighty-seven, of whom thirty-eight were men, twenty-two were women, and twenty-seven were children under twelve. Also during this period the size of the plantation was increased by the purchase of 200 acres from William A. Shaffer, whose plantation adjoined Ellendale.

Andrew and John McCollam were both able and enterprising planters. Besides increasing their operations from year to year, they enlarged the plantation equipment and improved the sugar machinery. In January, 1860, they sold their sugar engine to a certain Gatewood on Bayou Dularge for $3,000 and placed an order with Leeds and Company of New Orleans for a new engine and mill for $10,000—"the largest and best mill in the Parish." As Ellen McCollam wrote, "This is one ten thousand dollars lost to the North oweing to the Abolitionist."

The McCollams sold their sugar and purchased their supplies from their New Orleans factor, William G. Hewes, who was connected with the New York brokerage house of P. Haven and Company. In the spring of 1855 the McCollams shipped 104 hogsheads of sugar and 502 barrels of molasses by schooner from New Orleans to be sold in New York, hoping that higher prices there would yield them a larger profit. The sugar sold at 5¾ to 6¼ cents a pound for a gross return of $6,-887.56 and the molasses at 17 to 25 cents a gallon for a gross return of $3,016.02. Marketing charges, however, were excessive. These included freight at $6 per hogshead on sugar and $5 for each 110 gallons of molasses, insurance at 10½ percent on molasses and 2½ percent on sugar, a selling commission of 5 percent, brokerage of ½ percent, and additional drayage, weighing, cooperage, and labor charges. The total cost of marketing was $1,530.05 for the molasses and $1,543.44 for the sugar; in other words 50 percent of the gross return from the molasses and 22 percent from that of the sugar was taken in the marketing charges. Apparently the McCollams found shipping their produce directly to New York unprofitable, since there are no other records of sales there. Marketing costs were no small item even when the sugar was sold on the New Orleans market. In 1852–53, for example, when 251 hogsheads of sugar and 428 barrels of molasses sold for a gross amount of $14,252.17, the cost of marketing, including the factor's selling commission of 2½ percent, freight, insurance, weighing, and cooperage, totaled $1,230.52 or 8⅗ percent of the gross return. In addition, the McCollams carried river and railroad insurance at ⅜ percent on their sugar and molasses while it was in transit, making the total cost of marketing approximately 9 percent of the gross sale.

The McCollams prospered during the prewar decade. As is usually the case for antebellum plantations, there is no complete record available of profits and losses at Ellendale. The business papers contain sufficient information, however, to assure us that the business of sugar planting was a profitable one for them. In 1852 they were in debt to their factor to the sum of $12,000, whereas in June, 1861, they had a credit balance of $3,020.70. Further evidence that their operations were profitable is the increase in the value of the plantation. In 1860, when John deeded two-thirds of the plantation with two-thirds of all the slaves and equipment to Andrew, the plantation was valued at $150,000.

Life in the Louisiana sugar region was not characterized by the loneliness which was often associated with southern rural life. The McCollam Papers show that hardly a month passed without several overnight guests at Ellendale, and weeks in which there were not visitors for meals were rarities. Among these overnight guests were the Slatterys, the Connellys, the Rightors, the Maurins, the Lawes, Dr. Kittredge, and other friends from Donaldsonville. Likewise their new neighbors, the Minors and Shaffers, visited them frequently. Holidays were usually the occasion for a celebration of one sort or another, especially July 4. At this time there was speaking in the day and dining and dancing in the evening. The Christmas season was always enlivened by balls and dinners in the neighborhood. In 1843, when there was only one guest for Christmas dinner, Ellen found the day "a very dull one." The beginning of the new year brought the celebration of the Grand Military Ball at Houma, which the McCollams usually attended. For the children, then as now, the great day was circus day. In March, 1860, Andrew junior attended the Louisiana State Fair at Baton Rouge and found it "highly exciting especially when the blood horses were brought in and trials of speed took place."

For a good southern Whig the occasion of a lifetime was a visit from Henry Clay. Ellen McCollam wrote in her diary January 16, 1844, of his visit to Donaldsonville:

I can say as Sir Walter Scott did, when he received the Duke of Wellington at his house that he considered it one of the proudest of his life —for I have this day been presented to Henry Clay not in a rabble crowd, but in a small circle when I could see him, and hear him converse and converse with him, he arrived from the Bayou about 5 o'clock in the afternoon, in the Steamboat Music—he was received by a number of gentlemen at the landing, who had a Carriage ready to take him to Mr. Rightor's house—where in the absence of Mrs. Rightor my Aunt did the honours of the house—when the Carriage came to the door—My Uncle and Mr Lafort met him at the steps Aunt and myself received at the hall door and was then presented to him, many gentlemen called to see him the Ladies could not call on him the weather was so bad. They could not walk out—After a short time I had an opportunity of chatting a little with him—he makes every one feel perfectly at their ease, and certainly is one of the most delightful old gentlemen I ever met—he took up Andrew several times in his arms and tried to make friends with him. About 8 o'clock a handsome supper was served furnished by my Uncle Cousins and Winchester Lawes and superintended by my Aunt. Twenty-five persons supperᵈ with him, after supper they went to the ball which was got up for the occasion he was then presented to all the ladies in the room—about ten o'clock Aunt and myself went to the ball we found Henry Clay laughing chatting with the ladies as gaily as a young man of twenty five, I again had several opportunities of speaking with him he invited me to take gumbo with him—which I did, and leaving the supperroom with him he asked me to prominade with him, which I did at the risk of nearly tiring the old gentleman out, although he bears fatigue admirably well—on leaving the ball I bid him farewell (I fear) forever—although I expressed a hope to him that we should meet again ere long—a hope however that I can sincerely cherish for he has nearly lived the time alloted to man—What a pity such a man should ever die.

Trips to New Orleans were frequent, and occasionally longer trips were made, as in the fall of 1843 when John McCollam visited his mother in Indiana, or in July, 1850, when Ellen accompanied friends on a trip up the river to Vicksburg for ten days, or in May, 1859, when Andrew made a trip to New York.

Both Andrew and Ellen McCollam were determined that no expense or inconvenience should interfere with the education of their children. In January, 1848, Andrew junior "commenced going to school to Mr. Sawyer," and the following year Edmund, at the age of four and a half, began school. After moving to Terrebonne Parish, the parents sent Andrew junior to boarding school in Donaldsonville. In 1855 both Andrew junior and Edmund enrolled at Centenary College, Jackson, Louisiana. Even the financial stringency of the war did not prevent the McCollam children from continuing their education, for in January, 1864, Nellie entered Ursuline Convent in New Orleans, and in the following fall Henry was sent to the Louisiana State Seminary at Alexandria.

With the McCollams as with most southern planter families, the works of Byron and Scott were favorites. In January, 1848, Ellen McCollam was delighted to receive "a beautiful copy of Byron." In January, 1860, she wrote Andrew junior:

> [Your father has purchased] all of Walter Scott's novels 28 vol. . . . You and Edmund can indulge yourselves to the fullest extent in Scottish lore. I suppose you have read many of them, but they will bear reading more than once, for the history and fine descriptions of Scottish character.

> Your father purchased another fine work called "The Wonder of Our Age" by Von Humbolt. "Cosmos a Physical description of the Universe" in five vols. Your father is reading . . . now, I think you will like the work although learned as it is.

Andrew McCollam was prominent in the Whig party of Louisiana and in 1849 was a delegate to the conventions that nominated the Whig candidates for governor and senator. When the issue of secession was presented in 1860, Andrew, being a Union Whig, thought that the South should remain in the Union until Lincoln committed "some overt act." When South Carolina began taking steps toward a dissolution of the Union, he commented in disgust that "she always was a 'damphool' State, and deserves to be whipped into the traces." He was elected as a delegate to the Louisiana secession convention in January, 1861, and there "tried all the means known to parliamentary tactics to procure co-operation of the Southern states, but all to no effect. The majority were determined on doing the act." He signed the ordinance of secession, but wrote his wife on January 27, 1861, "When I assure you it was the bitterest pill that I ever took you will appreciate the pain it gave me to do it." When Mrs. McCollam first learned the news of the passing of the ordinance, she "felt a perfect heart sinking" and prayed that God would arrange everything "with truth and justess for the welfare of our own as well as future generations."

The excitement following the attack on Fort Sumter and Lincoln's call for troops spread rapidly throughout the South, engulfing the youth of the section. Andrew junior wrote his parents from Centenary College on May 1, 1861, that the college was "almost disorganized" with only thirty boys left there and those intending to leave as soon as money arrived from home. All the rest had left and joined military companies. He thought it "clearly and unmistakably" his duty to join the army immediately because "it would be very disagreeable for me to go with those companies which would be formed afterwards as they would be composed of the dregs of the parish, and very mortifying not only to me, but to the whole family to have me drafted into the militia." Both Andrew and Edmund joined the Confederate Army in 1861 and survived the war without serious injury.

Life in the Louisiana sugar region was seriously disrupted during the war. The capture of New Orleans and much of Louisiana by the Federals in 1862 placed the sugar plantations under strict military supervision. An order issued by General Benjamin F. Butler in 1862 declared all property of disloyal persons in Louisiana west of the Mississippi (except in the parishes of Jefferson and Plaquemines) subject to confiscation and sale at auction. Loyal persons (those who had not taken up arms against the United States since the occupation of New Orleans) were allowed to work their plantations with white and Negro labor under contract. A permit of December 10, 1862, allowed the McCollam brothers to sell their sugar and molasses to any loyal citizens of the United States. The presence of Union soldiers was particularly disagreeable to the inhabitants, who reported that they stole "chickens, hogs, and everything they can get or carry off." When not allowed to visit Ellendale, A. F. Rightor of Lafourche Parish wrote Andrew McCollam on December 3, 1864, "I pray God we will have no necessity . . . [in the spring] to have a pass that an unlettered dog of a soldier must spell out the gracious permit to a free citizen to visit his friends."

As early as the spring of 1862 Ellendale was beginning to feel the effects of the war. Andrew McCollam described the situation as follows: "Our condition is becoming criticle our negroes have no pork and the present stock of shoes and negroes clothing is so low that if no importation takes place within the coming year our slaves will some of them be in rags, and others, I fear will be even worse off. We have not the means of makeing them ourselves." In February, 1863, he complained that his Negroes had stolen some of his mules. The burden upon the sugar planters was made heavier in many cases by the shiftlessness of the hired overseers. In August, 1863, William J. Minor, owner of the South Down plantation in Terrebonne Parish, requested Andrew McCollam to discharge his overseer, who was "a great rascal and not to be depended upon in any way." The real conditions at Ellendale were described vividly in Andrew's letter of March 26, 1863, to his son:

> The negroes are some of them at home but the most of them are off and appear to have no wish to return. We are trying to make a crop of cane and some corn. We do not feel much hopes of doing much. . . . 18 of our men enlisted in the negroes Federal army & I do not much expect that we shall ever get them 11 have died mostly children. Mrs. Connelly & family are well and making a crop have most of the hands at home for a wonder. Ours have acted more vilianously than any others in the parish. . . . Mr. Kessee is here overseeing. We have about 16 hands enough to make seed cane & corn for another year. We hope to keep the place up so that if the troubles are settled by another year we can go on and make a crop. Your Uncle John is in New Orleans trying to get the negroes to come home. He may get some more perhaps.[3]

Real suffering and anguish lay beneath Ellen McCollam's comment in March, 1863, "God grant this war may be brought to an end soon. You cannot imagine all I have suffered this winter."

Hopes that the end of the war would bring relief from suffering and a return to normalcy in the Louisiana sugar region were doomed to disappointment. By the summer of 1865 the house servants had left Ellendale to swell the tide of roaming free Negroes in the South. In December the Freedmen's Bureau at New Orleans issued a series of regulations controlling the relations between employers and freedmen. Planters were

3. It is difficult to generalize about the behavior of Negroes on southern plantations during the Civil War. In some instances they remained at home and worked as usual. In other cases they seized the first opportunity to leave the plantation and roam about the country or join the federal army. For examples of the variations in the behavior of slaves on Louisiana sugar plantations, see the Lewis Thompson Papers in the University of North Carolina Library and an article by the present writer, "Magnolia Plantation," in *Mississippi Valley Historical Review*, XXV (1938), 197–210.

required to make written contracts with their laborers, pay wages which the Bureau considered just compensation for a specified amount of work, and provide rations, quarters, clothing, medical attention, and opportunity for the instruction of children. In addition to the burden that the payment of money wages placed upon an impoverished planter class were added heavy taxes on the sale of sugar. In April, 1866, Andrew McCollam sold six hogsheads of sugar at 13¼ cents per pound for a gross return of $815.07. On this sale the following taxes were paid: an internal revenue tax of 2⅖ cents per pound, a U.S. government tax of ⅛ percent, and a Louisiana state tax of ¼ percent, making a total of $152.60, or approximately 18 percent of the gross sale.

Prospects for a return of economic prosperity and social and political order in the sugar region seemed remote indeed in the spring of 1866. Accordingly, the McCollam brothers decided to join a group of southern planters on a trip to Brazil to investigate the possibilities of settling there permanently. Leaving his sons Andrew junior and Edmund to manage the plantation, Andrew, accompanied by his brother John, embarked in May, 1866, upon "the great enterprise" of his life which was "destined to be either a complete failure or one fraught with more for weal or woe to me and mine than any I have ever attempted." Andrew was greatly disappointed with Brazil. He wrote in his diary of the trip, July 17, 1866, "With a people who do not speak my language or with whom I can not talk and in a country where everything is going to decay I must now confess to myself I have not the courage to settle." A few days later he wrote that he had "seen more idlers and idleness" in the few weeks that he had been in Brazil than in all his life in the United States. Even "once happy but now downtroden U. S. A." seemed preferable to Brazil.

In the spring of 1867 Andrew and his wife made a trip to Cuba, which he found to be "the most butiful country" that he had ever seen. He declared that only "the doubt that hangs over the future of this fine island" prevented him from settling there.

By this time the difficulty of adjusting the plantation to the free labor system was somewhat lessened. On this subject Edmund wrote his father March 9, 1867:

> Everything is moving in a manner that I think would please you if you were here; the Negroes all appear to be sattisfied, and are working well, although there has been a[n] unusual number of conjugal jars, and consequent separations of bed and board; but those slight ripples on the surface seldom disturb the even current of plantation life you know.

After the war the labor system at Ellendale took two forms, hired labor and farming on shares. A considerable number of Negro laborers worked for cash wages, which in 1869 were fifteen dollars a month with rations. During the grinding season, when laborers worked all day and half the night, wages were forty dollars per month. Toward the end of the century it became more common to hire laborers by the day at a rate which usually ranged from fifty to seventy-five cents and occasionally higher. In December, 1873, a contract was made with twenty-two Negroes for the cultivation of portions of the plantation. The following is a summary of the terms of the contract between the planter and his tenants: (1) owner agreed to furnish land and seed cane and houseroom free of rent; (2) owner agreed to grind the cane and to furnish carts and wagons to haul it; (3) owner agreed to keep the sugarhouse and machinery in repair; the tenants were to keep the wagons in repair; (4) owner agreed to furnish one half of the hogsheads and barrels, the tenants to furnish the other half; (5) owner agreed to advance provisions and supplies and to receive in return a lien on the sugar crops of the tenants until repaid; (6) owner agreed to furnish one-third of the wood to take off the crop, the tenant the other two-thirds. As a fair compensation for the use of the land, sugarhouse, and seed cane, the tenants agreed to cultivate the land faithfully; to furnish labor, teams, and implements; to furnish seed corn; to furnish their labor during the grinding season at market rates; to pay half of the expenses of grinding the cane made on land that they cultivated; and to turn over to the owner one-third of the corn and half of the sugar and molasses made on the land.

Difficult problems of labor control and discipline occasionally arose at Ellendale under the free-labor system. For example, in February, 1873, Evans, the overseer, shot and stabbed a Negro boy who refused to pile cane because he did not feel well. The Negroes on the place were "highly incensed" and might have mobbed the overseer had he not shut himself up in the house. That the McCollams did not approve of his action is indicated by the fact that he was immediately discharged.

In the early years after the war the lack of ready capital necessitated a "live-at-home" and diversified production program at Ellendale. Melons, vegetables, butter, eggs, beef, and chickens were raised on the place. As the sugar region recovered somewhat from its depression, Edmund and Alex, then in control of Ellendale, began again to resort to large-scale specialized production of sugar and the purchase of a large part of their supplies. For instance, in 1889, $6,574.52 was expended for the following supplies: 30 pounds of tobacco, 34½ barrels of mess pork, 17 sacks of corn, 4 carloads of oats, 93½ pounds of flour, 275 pounds of coffee, 3 barrels of grits, 65 pounds of lard, 97 sacks of peas, 6 sacks of salt, 2 sacks of bran, 34 boxes of shoulders, 85 barrels and 7½ tons of cornmeal, and $1,351.70 worth of hardware and farm implements.

Upon the death of his parents in 1873 (his Uncle John McCollam had died in 1867), Edmund became manager of Ellendale and administrator of the McCollam estate which in 1870 had been assessed for taxation in Terrebonne at a valuation of $55,000. Edmund could hardly have chosen a more inauspicious time to begin management of the estate. On December 30, 1872, his sister Nellie described conditions as follows: "We have failed to make expenses on this place. . . . I tell you it is disheartening work to see around me daily the absolute signs of decay which the planting interests exhibit—Everyone is terribly blue the condition of affairs in Louisiana is positively terrible." That the McCollams were in financial straits at this time is indicated by Nellie's statement in March, 1873, "If we fail to make a good crop this year we are lost." Apparently the next few years were none too good financially, for in 1878 Edmund petitioned the court to allow him to mortgage Ellendale in order to raise sufficient capital to cultivate the land. His petition was granted, and he mortgaged the plantation for $20,000 to Clapp and Brothers, commission merchants of New Orleans.

Edmund bent all his energies to the task of making Ellendale a "going concern." He maintained the equipment of the plantation in as good order and repair as possible. In 1881 repairs were made on the sugarhouse. Again in 1883, $2,800 was spent upon repairs on the sugar machinery. In 1900, $2,000 was spent to change the sugar mill from a two- to a three-roller mill. In production Ellendale maintained approximately the same scale of operations in the period 1880–1900 as in the 1850's, from 350 to 700 hogsheads and over. The fact that this plantation has remained in the McCollam family and is still a profitable sugar estate attests Edmund's energy and ability in the face of obstacles that destroyed many weaker and less capable planters.

Alex McCollam, a younger brother of Edmund, began the production of sugar in 1880 on Argyle, a plantation in Terrebonne. Gaps in the records at this point make it impossible to state the source of his acquisition of Argyle or its exact size. Beginning with a small crop in 1881–82 (58 hogsheads of sugar and 66 barrels of molasses which sold for $5,629.49), he expanded his production rapidly in the 1880's. In the summer of 1883 he had a sugar mill constructed at a cost of $6,000. Until 1884 he marketed his sugar in the form of yellow sugar in hogsheads, as was the practice in the prewar period. From 1884 to 1888, however, he paid one cent a pound to have the sugar granulated either at a nearby refinery or in New Orleans. The following table shows the annual production and sale at Argyle:

Year	Sugar		Molasses		Receipts
1881	58 hhds.	(200 lbs. each)	66 bbls.	(50 gal. each)	$ 5,629.44
1882	176 hhds.	(200 lbs. each)			10,130.27
1883	961 bbls.	(340 lbs. each)	245 bbls.	(50 gal. each)	c. 14,500.00
1884	944 bbls.	(340 lbs. each)	231 bbls.	(50 gal. each)	
1885	749 bbls.	(340 lbs. each)	219 bbls.	(50 gal. each)	12,311.97
1886	695 bbls.	(340 lbs. each)			
1887	1059 bbls.	(340 lbs. each)			
1888	231 hhds.	(340 lbs. each)	286 bbls.	(50 gal. each)	c. 11,600.00
1889					
1890	206 hhds.	(340 lbs. each)	311 bbls.	(50 gal. each)	c. 10,200.00

In order to expand operations and keep the plantation properly equipped, Alex, being short of capital, was forced to borrow heavily from his New Orleans factor, at first Gidiere, Day, and Company, and later Ermann and Cahn. In January, 1891, the latter firm pointed out that his debit balance was $6,000 and requested him to draw upon them as little as possible until his account was reduced. By this time losses for several years and lack of capital forced Alex to sell Argyle and join Edmund in the management of Ellendale. A letter of March 15, 1891, from a close friend reveals the tragedy of financial bankruptcy to the southern planter.

> It is, believe me, with genuine, unavailing regret, that I learn of the sale of Argyle & the downfall of the ambitious hopes centered in it. It seems as if we, of the old regime, are destined to a swift destruction—a descent from the ambitious heights we once saw the great world from. Yet not one of us with a desire to desert our ancestral acres for new *yet not* greener fields—After five years of exile, the pain of yielding up our homes to Vandals is one that time's touch fails to heal—no other place seems like home to us. It was a long struggle with us, as with you, to hold on till a clear harbor should be seen in the sea—we missed the harbor—& you miss it—& are left drifting rudderless with the onsweeping tide—It seems such a little while since you came from abroad—so hopeful of the future, so willing to make an honest effort to succeed—in seeing you lose Argyle, I feel as if I were seeing my own brothers fail again, despite their endeavors. . . . I have hoped against hope, that in the general upheaval, you all would stand—you have been always, the best friends we ever had & I sincerely regret it has been so utterly out of our power to extend the helping hand to you, you alone held out to us.

Social life in the Louisiana sugar region was not appreciably different in the period 1865–1900 from the immediate prewar years. As before the war some member of the McCollam family made an occasional trip to the North, usually Washington and New York. In 1868 Andrew junior and his father traveled into the Northeast and went into Canada. Andrew McCollam even managed to send Alex to Europe. There was a continual round of visiting of several days' duration among the younger members of the McCollam, Connelly, Minor, and Cage families. Visits to New Orleans were more frequent but perhaps less prolonged than in the 1850's. In 1873 Nellie, Henry, and Edmund attended the Mardi Gras festivities. Henry met many of his college friends there, and both he and Edmund "were both the worse for too much . . . beer."

Until his death in 1873 Andrew McCollam gave his children every advantage that his means permitted. Even the lean years immediately following the war were not allowed to interrupt their education. Henry, who had entered the Louisiana State Seminary at Alexandria in the fall of 1865, remained there until 1869, when he entered the University of Virginia, where he studied for three years. His younger brother Willie entered Louisiana State Seminary in the fall of 1870, and Alex joined Henry at the University of Virginia in 1871. From Henry's letters home one gathers that college boys then were little if any different from those of today. The Friday night "hops" and the "society of the ladys" were matters of major interest. That life at school was not allowed to become too well ordered and refined is indicated by Henry's letter of December 3, 1865: "I verily believe that we have the most mischievous set of boys here that ever collected together . . . they will come into your room with a blackening-brush, and black your face, or beat you pretty near to death with a pillar or a clothes bag."

In most instances the advantages and opportunities that the McCollams gave their children were well repaid in the form of able and respected citizens. In the case of Andrew junior, however, his father experienced a bitter disappointment. After receiving a law degree from the University of Louisiana (later Tulane University) in 1868, he began the practice of his profession in New Orleans. In order to shift some of the heavy burden of plantation management from his shoulders, Andrew McCollam entrusted the control of his finances to his son. Andrew junior proved to be an incapable bookkeeper, and by December, 1872, he had his father's financial affairs "in a dreadful condition." He was by this time becoming a heavy drinker. Whether this had any influence upon his mismanagement is uncertain. At any rate his sister wrote December 30, 1872, "I don't think Pa will ever have anything more to do with Andrew." What became of Andrew, the writer has been unable to discover. His name never again appeared in any of the McCollam Papers.

Though Andrew junior failed to attain the prominence which might reasonably have been expected of him, Edmund had an honorable and useful career. He interested himself especially in flood control on the Mississippi River, a problem of particular importance to the sugar region. In 1878 Governor Francis T. Nicholls appointed him to membership on the Board of Levee Commissioners for his district with the duty of supervising flood control in Terrebonne and adjacent parishes. In 1881–82 he repeatedly urged his friend Randall L. Gibson, member of the House of Representatives from Louisiana, to secure federal appropriations to strengthen the levees and to deepen and make navigable the streams in Terrebonne. He was instrumental in the construction in the parish of a canal that lowered freight rates to and from New Orleans. In 1877 Governor Nicholls appointed him a member of the Board of Control of the Louisiana State University and Agricultural and Mechanical College in which he took a vital interest. He was prominent in the state Democratic party, serving in the legislature, in the Louisiana constitutional convention of 1898, and representing his state at several national Democratic conventions.

Thus ends the recorded chronicle of the McCollams, a planter family of the Old and New South. In many respects the family typified the characteristics commonly associated with the planter class of the lower South. Ambitious, energetic, and able, the elder Andrew McCollam settled in 1838 in the sugar region, that El Dorado of the South. There he prospered and grew rich with the country until the Civil War wrecked the Louisiana sugar industry, seemingly beyond repair. Wealth and comfort, however, did not destroy the indomitable energies of all the younger McCollams. Whereas many of their friends and neighbors, deficient in endurance and adaptability or perhaps simply less fortunate, succumbed to the destruction of more than ten years of economic and social collapse, the McCollams survived. Upon the ruins of an antebellum fortune they built a postbellum fortune. Nor did life for them in the New South change substantially from its pattern in the Old South. Planters in the best sense of the word before the war, the McCollams remained planters after the war.

Abigail Curlee

The History of a Texas Slave Plantation, 1831-63

We know less about slaveholding and plantation life in Texas than in any other southern state. One reason is because there are so few records: the only extant ones are for the plantation described below. This article is therefore intrinsically important and also offers a means of comparison between a relatively new region and an older—and more studied—area of the South. A careful reading will show that the owners of the plantation Curlee studies were men of keen administrative talents. In this regard they were not unique. Nevertheless, the reader will notice in this history of the plantation an increasing tendency toward efficiency and rational organization as the years pass. It should be obvious both from Curlee's remarks and from the journals she quotes that these men were primarily businessmen and the plantation a business venture. The cotton and tobacco plantations of the older South were also business ventures, but their owners were men of strikingly different demeanor. Whether this difference is merely one of regional variation or whether the Texas plantation owners were products of a new economic and social milieu are questions which only further comparative study can answer.

One fact which should be clear from this study, however, is that Negro slavery was not the barrier to economic success that many historians have thought it to be. Nor does it appear to be an impediment to efficiency and innovation. In this regard there is scattered evidence to corroborate these points. Though no one will consider the cultivation of rice in South Carolina and Georgia efficient, it was highly remunerative. In Louisiana the cultivation and processing of sugar employed slave labor and utilized sophisticated and expensive machinery. Here too profits were large. Where labor was most tedious and undiversified, the opportunities for the acculturation and socialization of blacks declined significantly. In areas of the older South where labor was less tedious and relations between blacks and whites more open, the threat of sale to the New South

From the *Southwestern Historical Quarterly*, XXVI (October, 1922), 79–114. Reprinted by permission of the Texas State Historical Association.

and not merely to Louisiana was often sufficient to quell the most intransigent slave. In distinction to the plantation slave, the existence of non-plantation slaves appears very much like the lives of slaves who lived in similar circumstances throughout the South.

From highly incomplete evidence, then, it appears that Ulrich Bonnell Phillips was correct when he said that our understanding of the South must come from intensive study of its plantations. Detractors have argued that the majority of slaves and slaveholders did not live on plantations. Nonetheless, evidence of growth and change appear here first. And it was the planter, not the farmer, who controlled the political and social life of the antebellum South. Comparative studies of plantations in different regions of the South, established at different moments in the antebellum period, should therefore be our starting point. From the information garnered here, we may well be able to ask whether the social history of the South is everywhere the same and begin the far more difficult study of whether differences in plantation development, structure, and organization affected the lives of the slaves.

JAMES F. PERRY'S REMOVAL TO TEXAS FROM MISSOURI AND SETTLEMENT AT PEACH POINT, 1831

In May, 1824, Stephen Fuller Austin and James E. Brown Austin were making plans to move their mother, the widow of Moses Austin, and their widowed sister, Mrs. Emily Margaret B. Bryan, from Missouri to Texas. Stephen drew up minute and definite instructions for James E. B., who was to go to Missouri and conduct them to Texas. He wrote:

> Be very particular to collect all the little property that Emily has and provide well for them on the journey, bring all their beds and bedding and pot kettle and crockery ware &c that are of light carriage, and bring all kinds of garden seeds and roots, particularly nectarenes Peach, Pairs Grapes &c &c—Currants—Gooseberry—Rose Roots. . . . I am most in favor of your coming by land—bring the family of negroes that Emily has at all hazards and I will settle with Bryan for them—if you can get Luck and Babtiste and Pool without paying too much money do so and not without
>
> You must bring a good sett of blacksmith tools—Some homemade cloth for me for summer and winter clothing. I wish all the family to wear nothing else—.
>
> . . . have a good tent provided for the road and bring as much furniture as you think a light wagon can haul from Natchitoches— [1]

1. Memorandum for my brother, May 4, 1824. Austin Papers, Miscellaneous.

Although the plan of the Austin brothers did not materialize, this is the beginning of the Perry interest in Texas. For the next trace of Mrs. Bryan is a letter [2] from Solomon R. Bolin, telling of her marriage to James Franklin Perry at Hazel Run on September 23, 1824.[3] Mrs. Moses Austin died before she could make her trip to Texas.

Stephen Austin still desired that his sister should make her home in Texas. This desire increased after he became accustomed to her marriage and saw the opportunity for wealth in Texas. He was unwilling for them to make the move, however, until Mr. Perry had inspected the country for himself. By 1827 he was advising a visit to Texas, saying, "I shall expect you in October next without fail." [4] Perry did not make the tour of inspection, and Austin became more urgent as he saw the assured future for Texas. At the end of 1829 he wrote that he had petitioned "the Govt. of the State for eleven leagues of land for you on Galveston Bay, within Six or Seven Miles of Galveston harbor, if the half of that is granted it will be a fortune."

> There is a fine opportunity here for a good Merchant, and a regular trading schooner to ship produce such as corn, lard, etc. to Tampico and Vera Cruz would make money rapidly— There is considerable cotton made and some sugar— Beef Tallow, pork, Lard, Mules, etc.
>
> The 11 Leagues I have petitioned for will cost you about $1000 including everything, and you will be allowed, 4, 5, and 6 years to pay a part of that in and the balance can be settled by me easily.. . . . Try and bring some of the breeds of English cattle, nature never made a better place for stock than the land I have asked for you—oysters and fish and fowls at your door etc the latitude is about 29°—10'—it is about 80 miles from this place [San Felipe de Austin]. . . . Bring all your capital.[5]

In this same letter Austin instructed Perry to indenture his servants by hire or contract before a judge or clerk, and to bring furniture enough to be comfortable. He mentioned twice in this one letter that Perry was to bring seeds. He had asked, he said, that Perry might have two years within which to occupy the land. Apparently Austin had not yet convinced Perry of the future of Texas, for he continued to advise him to come. Later he wrote, "Bring bedding and furniture. . . . We are beginning to get *up* in this country and decent and fine cloths have taken the

2. Solomon R. Bolin to Stephen F. Austin, December 5, 1824.
3. Moses Austin's Record.
4. S. F. Austin to J. F. Perry, May 26, 1827.
5. S. F. Austin to J. F. and E. Perry, December 12, 1829.

place of buckskin." [6] Within a few days he wrote, "The fall is the best time to remove on a/c of health." [7] On receipt of the grant which he had petitioned for, Austin wrote as follows:

> I now have the pleasure to inform you that I yesterday received the grant from the Governor. he has had the goodness to grant to James F. Perry and to his wife Emily Margarita Austin Eleven Leagues of land to be selected on any vacant lands in Austin's colony and he has issued all the necessary orders to the General land Commissioner to give a patent in due form as the colonization law requires. . . .
> The grant is subject to the condition that you remove and settle here with your family within two years from the first day of last January. [8]

But before this letter of March 28 was written, James F. Perry was on his way to Texas. His notebook kept on the tour of Texas indicates that he left Potosi, Missouri, on Sunday, March 21, 1830, "for the purpose of viewing Austins Colony in Texas. arrived at Herculanium on the same evening there I had to remain the 22d and 23d waiting for a passage to New Orleans. . . . March 31st Wednesday Land at New Orleans until friday the 10th day of April, at 12 o'clock saild in the Schooner Pocahontas for the port of Brazoria in Texas—" Mr. Perry continues his day-to-day account with details of the trip, landing, tour of Texas to find Austin, and the hospitality extended him by the Texans. He thus described his impressions of the country:

> The country from the mouth of Brasos for five or six miles is all a praA araria near the sea shore sandy then low and marchey. gradually rises a little untill the timber commences is generally a clay land. and looks poor much appearances of craw fish. although the land looks unproductive there is emence coats of fine Grass growing on it and affords emence pasture for Stock of all kind. from where the Timber commences on the Brasos the Bottom[s] of the Brassos are heavily timbered as far up as I have yet been say for one to six and eight miles on each side of the river and in some places wider the timber consists of live oak Large quantities of it black oak Red Oak post oak white oak pecan ash mulberry Ellam cottonwood and sundry other not recollected the undergrowth is wild peach [and] sasafras. [9]

Austin wrote Mrs. Perry on May 15 that Mr. Perry liked the location. [10] Perry evidently made arrangements with Austin to superintend the preparations of the new home. Austin was anxious and willing to prepare his sister's home, because of his desire to have her and her chil-

---

6. S. F. Austin to J. F. and Emily Perry, January 3, 1830.
7. S. F. Austin to J. F. Perry, January 16, 1830.
8. S. F. Austin to J. F. and E. Perry, March 28, 1830.
9. Perry's notebook, March 21, 1830, to April 8, 1830.
10. S. F. Austin to Emily Perry, May 16, 1830.

dren near him. Austin wrote that they should get passports from James W. Breedlove, Vice-Consul for Mexico at New Orleans. In the same letter he reported the Steam Saw Mill in successful operation.[11] On July 4, 1830, Austin wrote, "I have engaged bricks and shingles etc to put a house in this place for you to winter in and will have it ready, and a store room—"[12] But the building plans for the Perry home did not go smoothly. Austin wrote in September:

> I have no house up nor under way— . . . The Steam Mill did not get under way as soon as was expected and has broken down several times and done but little— I am now contracting with a carpenter to put up a frame store in this place and will try to have it ready by the time Hunter arrives—[13] . . . the place where I originally intended to settle all my family is at peach point below Brazoria, on the Sea Shore prairie at the edge of the timber 6 miles from sea beach—
>
> I am expecting instructions as to the introduction of negroes, and as I have now no hope of seeing you this fall there will be time enough to send them to you before I leave here for Saltillo.[14]

James Perry and William W. Hunter established a store at San Felipe de Austin before Mr. Perry moved his family to Texas. Austin wrote in December, 1830:

> Your goods by the Nelson arrived safe John Austin came up yesterday and has stored them all up in good order— Nothing will be opened until Hunter arrives—I shall have to use some of the nails to finish the store house— . . . The frame is up so that the building will be all ready by the time Hunter arrives he can get the goods up—[15]

Hunter reached San Felipe on January 12, 1831, and began the business. The next day after his arrival, Hunter wrote to a merchant in New Orleans:

> This will inform you of my arrival in this place on yesterday The country I am as well pleased with as I Calculated on being I think the prospect pretty good for trade here there are but few goods at this time they appear to bring a tolerable profit. I have been somewhat disappointed in Consequence of my not being able to get a house. I will not be able to get to Making Sales So Soon on a/c of it, and Of course will not be able to do quite as well as if I could have opened immediately.[16]

11. S. F. Austin to Jas. F. Perry, June 15, 1830.

12. Austin to Perry, July 4, 1830.

13. A reference to William W. Hunter, Perry's commercial partner.

14. Austin to Perry, September 22, 1830. Austin was a member of the state congress, which met at Saltillo.

15. Austin to Perry, December 9, 1830.

16. Hunter to—[Merchant in New Orleans], January 13, 1831. Perry and Hunter's Letter Book.

According to Austin records, James F. Perry and his family left Potosi, Missouri, on June 7, 1831, for Texas and arrived at San Felipe de Austin on August 14.[17] The family consisted of Mrs. Perry, her six children—William Joel, Moses Austin, Guy M., and Mary Bryan, and Stephen and Eliza Perry—and Perry's niece Lavinia. Evidently they did not remain in San Felipe long, for a note in the *Texas Planter* of November 16, 1853, says that they moved in the winter of 1831 to Chocolate Bayou in Brazoria County, and in 1832 removed to Peach Point, ten miles below Brazoria.[18] It was late in 1832 when Perry moved to Peach Point, for he said in September, "I am now living near the west end of Galveston Bay Near the head of the tide on a small stream called Chocolate about 8 miles from the bay. a verry pleasant situation and an excellent situation for Raising Stock." He was undecided at this time where to move, for he continued, "We are situated to[o] far from a neighbourhood and can therefore have no school since I brought Hunter out it will be necessary to move either to San Felipe where the goods now are or to Brazoria where we will have the advantages of a good school." [19] Austin wrote later, "After much perplexity I have finally closed the division of the Peach point tract and taken the lower half you will therefore chuse your situation below the division line which Borden will run—I shall divide the point into two tracts and you will take the upper one adjoining the division line." [20] In his autobiography Guy M. Bryan briefly outlined the coming to Texas and final settlement at Peach Point:

In the Spring of 1831, I came with my step-father and Mother to Texas. We, our family and negroes, travelled by land, having two horse wagons and carriage. I riding a mule all the way from Missouri to San Felipe, Texas, reaching there on the 15th day of August; where Mother and children remained until the Spring of 1832 at which time we moved to our homestead prepared by Mr. Perry on Pleasant Bayou, a branch of Chocolate Bayou now in Brazoria County, where Mr. Perry established a ranch.

In December 1832, Mr. Perry moved to Peach Point, ten miles below Brazoria, West of the Brazos, where he established our permanent home.[21]

17. Moses Austin's Record.
18. Clipping from *Texas Planter*, Brazoria, November 16, 1853.
19. Perry to McGready, September 12, 1832.
20. Austin to Perry, November 4, 1832.
21. Autobiographical sketch of Guy M. Bryan (1896). Copy in Archives, University of Texas.

As Bryan stated, Peach Point continued to be the home of James F. Perry until his death of yellow fever at Biloxi, Mississippi, in 1853, when his son Stephen S. Perry inherited the plantation. It will be noted that Bryan's account varies from the Austin record in the date of arrival and also from the *Planter* in the date assigned for the move to Chocolate Bayou.

Perry's grant, as Austin wrote in 1829, was for eleven leagues; however, he received twelve. The title to the five leagues located on "Chocolate Bayou" was given on August 25, 1831, as was that for the two leagues situated on the east side of Dickinson's Creek, and the one league on "Clear Creek one league from the mouth." [22] Under "Concessions and Augmentations," Perry was granted on October 28, 1831, one league situated "Between San Bernado and Bay Prairie and is N 25° The above league was first granted to Benj. Linsey." On November 3, 1831, he was granted two leagues—"South of Yeagua and Joins N. Clary." [23] Perry was granted on December 6, 1832, one league, situated on "Yegua Davidson's Creek and is known as N 6." [24] Of this land granted to Perry, there were 45 labors of farming land and 255 labors of grazing land, making a total of 12 leagues.

GENERAL DESCRIPTION OF AGRICULTURE
IN TEXAS, 1831–36

When Perry came to Texas, the country was sparsely settled from Bexar to the Sabine River. West of Bexar and extending to the Rio Grande, the country was unsettled.[25] He found the agricultural methods crude and good implements scarce. The people were, as a rule, living in log houses and cultivating the river bottom land. The bottom lands had to be cleared of timber or of cane. Mrs. Holley said that this cane land was prized, because it was rich alluvial soil. The cane brakes could be cleared by burning the dead reeds. If the cane land was not cultivated, the cane was valuable as food for cattle and horses in winter, being young and tender when the grass was dead.[26] The prairie lands were

22. List of Titles to settle 300 Families within the Ten Border Leagues on the Gulf of Mexico, Coast Contract no. 3, p. 42 of Title Book. Austin Papers.

23. Title Book, Contract no. 2, p. 34.

24. Title Book. Titles made under settling 500 families, 1827, 1828, 1831, 1832, 1833; p. 33.

25. Colonel J. N. Almonte's "Statistical Notice" in Kennedy's *Texas: The Rise, Progress and Prospects of the Republic of Texas*, II, 72.

26. Holley, *Texas* (1836), 87.

generally considered more suitable for grazing than for farming. As late as 1850 it was the belief that the timbered portions of Texas were best adapted to agriculture. The vast prairies were regarded as valueless except for grazing and stock raising. Also it was an axiom that farming could not succeed west of the Brazos.[27] Abundant pasturage was afforded on the thin and sandy coastland for stock of all varieties.

In 1834 the country was divided into the three political departments of Bexar, Brazos, and Nacogdoches. The Bexar Department was largely peopled by Mexicans. Almonte says there were no Negro laborers here. All the provisions raised by the inhabitants were consumed in the district. The wild horse, when caught, was cheap. Cattle were cheap, a cow and calf being considered equal to ten dollars. This was the condition all over the colony. Mrs. Harris said that there was little money in Texas. Her father received cattle and hogs in lieu of money for his practice as a physician, a cow and a calf passing as ten dollars.[28] In the Bexar region there were only five thousand or so head of sheep. They exported from eight to ten thousand skins of various kinds, and imported a few articles from New Orleans.

The Department of the Brazos was the section that Perry was interested in, for it was here that Austin's Colony was located. San Felipe, Columbia, Matagorda, Gonzales, and Mina were the five municipalities of this department, and in addition there were considerable towns at Brazoria, Harrisburg, Velasco, and Bolivar. Almonte estimated the population of the department at 8,000, of which he thought 1,000 were slaves.

Almonte said that around 2,000 bales of cotton had been exported from the Brazos in 1833,[29] while Austin, who left Texas for Mexico City in April, 1833, had estimated that the crop for that year would be 7,500 bales.[30] But there had been a big overflow in 1833 which had cut down the crop. Almonte said that 5,000 bales had been exported in 1832. The maize crop in 1833 was over, 50,000 barrels, but none was exported. The cattle of the department Almonte set down at about 25,000 head. The market cattle were driven to Natchitoches for sale. The cotton of the Brazos was exported to New Orleans and returned from

27. Wood, "Reminiscences of Texas and Texans Fifty Years Ago," *The Quarterly of the Texas State Historical Association*, V, 115.

28. "Reminiscences of Mrs. Dilue Harris," *Quarterly of Texas State Historical Association*, IV, 123.

29. Almonte, "Statistical Observations," in Kennedy's *Texas*, II, 75.

30. Austin's "Statistics of Texas" (1833) in Johnson-Barker, *A History of Texas and Texans*, I, 174–176.

10 to 10½ cents per pound after paying 2½ percent duty in New Orleans. No sheep were raised here, but there were probably 50,000 hogs in the district.

Almonte calculated that the trade of the department had reached $600,000 based on the production of 1832. The 5,000 bales of cotton would bring in $225,000, and 50,000 skins would be $50,000, totaling $275,000, while the sale of cattle and hogs would bring the total to this figure, $600,000. This report estimated the imports at $325,000.[31] Austin's report gave this district a large number of gins and mills, setting down in the municipalities of Austin and Brazoria thirty cotton gins, two steam sawmills and grist mills, six water-power mills and many run by oxen and horses. There was one water-power mill for sawing lumber and running machinery in Gonzales.[32]

The Department of Nacogdoches contained four municipalities, Nacogdoches, San Augustine, Liberty, and Jonesboro, with a population of 9,000, 1,000 of this number being Negroes. Besides the municipalities there were four other towns in this district: Anahuac, Bevil, Teran, and Teneha. This section was not as well developed as it should have been, Almonte thought. He somewhat unfairly attributed its backwardness to neglect and indifference of the impresarios. As a matter of fact, it was primarily due to restrictions of the federal government.

The trade of Nacogdoches was estimated by Almonte to be $470,000. The exports were estimated at 2,000 bales of cotton, 90,000 skins of deer, otter, and beaver, and 5,000 head of cattle, equal in value of $205,000. There was an excess of $60,000 of imports over exports for the year, which fact Almonte accounted by for the stock in the stores of the dealers.

There were twice as many cattle in this department as in that of the Brazos, but the price of cattle per head was the same. There were, 60,000 head of swine, which would soon furnish an article of export.[33]

Almonte and Austin are both indefinite as to the number of gins and mills in this section. Austin said, "The municipalities of Liberty and Nacogdoches are very well provided with mills and gins, and there is great progress in this industry in all parts of Texas." [34]

As to transportation of their products, Austin mentioned a steamboat

31. Almonte's "Statistical Notice," in Kennedy's *Texas,* II, 75–76. Juan N. Almonte was commissioned by the Mexican government in 1834 to inspect and report on Texas.

32. Austin, "Statistics of Texas," in Johnson-Barker, *Texas and Texans,* I, 174.

33. Almonte's "Statistical Notice," in Kennedy's *Texas,* II, 77.

34. Austin, "Statistics of Texas," in Johnson-Barker, *Texas and Texans,* I, 174.

in the Bay of Galveston. He also indicated that a company had been formed to bring one to the Brazos River.[35] Apparently this plan was realized, for the next year Almonte reported a steamboat plying on the Brazos and two others expected for the Neches and Trinity rivers.[36] An item in the *Telegraph* in 1836 reported that another steamboat, the *Yellow Stone*, had arrived to run on the Brazos.[37] Plans for bettering the roads were going forward with rapidity, although the roads were described as fairly good as they were.

The statistics of both Almonte and Austin are open to question. Almonte's two months' tour was too brief for a comprehensive understanding of conditions, and Austin, although better informed than Almonte, may have exaggerated in the effort to make a strong case for Texas in its application for statehood.[38]

The labor on Texas farms was done by the farmer and his slaves, if he owned any.[39] The Texans were slaveholders, but not on an extensive scale. Large plantations with a hundred or more Negroes did not gain the foothold in Texas that they had in the Old South. One Negro family was more often the rule than a crew of fifty slaves. The farmer ordinarily worked side by side with his slaves. Colonel Jared E. Groce had about a hundred Negroes, the largest number owned by one man in Texas prior to the Revolution.[40] It was estimated in 1836 that there were 5,000 Negroes in Texas, 30,000 Anglo-Americans, 3,470 Mexicans, and 14,200 Indians.[41] The estimate of 5,000 Negroes is a rather large increase over the 2,000 in Almonte's report, although there had been a rapid immigration in the latter part of 1834 and throughout 1835. Absentee ownership did not exist in Texas, nor was there much free labor. At this early date land was so cheap and so easily obtained that even the poor man had an opportunity to obtain a farm where he could make a living with a minimum amount of labor. It was the custom for neighbors to exchange labor. The work was often long and hard; and the returns, as now, were not always commensurate with the labor. Crude methods of cultivation, overflows, and droughts were the principal causes of poor yields.

35. *Ibid.*, I, 175.
36. Almonte's "Statistical Notice," in Kennedy's *Texas*, II, 78.
37. *Telegraph and Texas Register*, January 24, 1836.
38. E. C. Barker, in Johnson-Barker, *Texas and Texans*, I, 175.
39. Bugbee's "Slavery in Texas," in *Political Science Quarterly*, XIII, 662–663.
40. Register of Land Titles, General Land Office, Austin, Texas, Translation, I, 264, 265.
41. Morfit to Forsyth, August 27, 1836, in Yoakum, *History of Texas*, II, 197.

All authorities agreed that cotton was the most extensively cultivated crop and the best adapted to the soil. The statistics of Almonte and Austin bear this out. Mrs. Holley's information seems to be inaccurate in her statement that Texas "has for some years, produced as much as 10,000 bales, with the prospect of 60,000 bales in 1836." [42] When it is recalled that 1836 was the year of the "runaway scrape" and that the men were in the army, this seems exaggerated, but she may have written this earlier.[43]

Cotton was planted late in February or early in March and it was ready for the first picking by the last of July or the middle of August, according to the season. Frequently they were picking as late as December.

Indian corn or maize was the staple food for man and beast. As late as 1856 Frederick Law Olmsted complained of the steady diet of cornbread and bacon which was set before him in his journey over Texas.[44] Two crops of corn were sometimes planted and harvested. The first one was planted about the middle of February, after there was little danger of a freeze, and harvested in the summer; the second crop was planted in June for fall harvesting. Mrs. Holley stated that seventy-five bushels to the acre had been gathered, but that this was not the rule, as the farmers did not put enough labor on the corn crop to produce that amount. Most of the crop was required for home consumption.[45] The *Texas Gazette* of May 22, 1830, republished a chapter of a book which stated that the "produce of last season consisted of 1000 bales of cotton, 150,000 bushels of corn, and 140 hogsheads of sugar." The cotton was mostly shipped to New Orleans, and the surplus corn and other products to Matamoros, Tampico, and Vera Cruz.[46] This article declared that wheat, rye, oats, and barley were grown to some extent in the undulating districts, where they yielded abundantly, but that the scarcity of mills and the low price discouraged their production. Austin, on the contrary, reported, "The sowing of wheat has not progressed so much, because the climate is not suitable for this grain in the settled region near the coast." [47]

If the farmer had sufficient force and suitable land, he usually tried his

42. Holley, Texas (1836), 61.

43. *Telegraph and Texas Register*, September 2, 1837.

44. Olmsted, *A Journey through Texas* (1857), 15, 116.

45. Holley, *Texas* (1836), 62–63.

46. *Texas Gazette*, May 22, 1830, "From the American Quarterly Review, XIII, March, 1830—G. F. Hopkins and Son: 1829."

47. Austin, "Statistics of Texas," in Johnson-Barker, *Texas and Texans*, I, 175.

hand at raising sugarcane and manufacturing sugar and molasses. According to Mrs. Holley, sugarcane was beginning to be cultivated extensively in 1836. She described Texas cane as superior to that of both Arkansas and Louisiana.[48] In 1849 the *State Gazette* reported the average
yield on a Brazos plantation to be half a hogshead to the acre, estimating
1,000 pounds to the hogshead. The system of cultivation was not so advanced as in Louisiana.[49]

Tobacco and indigo were indigenous plants, but under Mexican law
the tobacco trade was a state monopoly and production was restricted.
Indigo was little cultivated. It was manufactured in families for domestic
use, and was preferred to the imported indigo.[50]

Sweet potatoes were extensively cultivated upon the drier prairies.
Melons abounded everywhere. Beans, peas, Irish potatoes, and a variety
of vegetables were grown in the gardens. The Texans usually had a fall
and winter garden as well as a spring and summer one. In 1830 James
Hope, "gardner and seedsman," was advertising his Connecticut garden
seed and his fruit trees at San Felipe.[51] Fruit trees produced abundant
crops.

Stock raising was commonly considered to bring the largest returns
with the least expenditure of time and effort. Austin did not attempt to
estimate the number of cattle in his report of 1833. An editorial in a
contemporary newspaper summed up the whole matter in this comparison:

> Corn, sweet potatoes, butter, honey, and every article of subsistence
> are in demand at this place and bring a good price. Corn is worth $1.50
> per bushel, and butter 25 cents per lb. The farmer or planter without
> the resources for acquiring a strong force (say 50 hands) to engage in
> sugar making may turn beneficially his attention to the planting of cot-
> ton with from 5 to 20 hands; and we know several who successfully un-
> dertake this branch of agriculture with no other aid than the white indi-
> viduals of their own family; if, however, he prefer a more easy mode of
> living, he may raise horses, mules, horned cattle, or hogs.[52]

Mrs. Holley at the same time discussed stock raising as follows:

> The extensive natural pastures found in the prairies furnish peculiar
> facilities for rearing horses, black cattle, hogs, sheep and goats. They re-
> quire no attention but to be branded and prevented from straying too
> far from home and becoming wild. Large quantities of mules are raised

48. Holley, *Texas* (1836), 61–62.
49. *State Gazette*, September 8, 1849.
50. Holley, *Texas* (1836), 63–64.
51. *Texas Gazette*, May 29, 1830.
52. *Telegraph and Texas Register*, Columbia, September 13, 1836.

annually, many of which are carried to the United States; and it proves a very lucrative business, inasmuch as the labor and expense in rearing them are trifling and the price they command good. . . . In many parts of Texas, hogs may be raised in large numbers on the native mast. Acorns, pecans, hickory-nuts &c. with a variety of nutritious grasses and many kinds of roots, afford them ample sustenance during the year.[53]

Beef, hides, milk, butter, pork, lard, poultry, and lumber were some of the products of Texas besides the products of the soil. An article in the *Telegraph* says in 1835 that many of the settlers counted their herds by the hundred, and that great numbers of cattle were annually purchased and driven to New Orleans by drovers who visited the country for that purpose.[54]

On the whole the people seem to have lived on what they and their slaves produced. Land was so cheap and fertile that they made no effort to conserve the soil, but planted the same crops on the same land year after year.

LIFE ON THE PLANTATION[55]

The Peach Point Plantation was opened in December, 1832, west of the Brazos river, ten miles below Brazoria. The conditions the first year were unhappy. Cholera and malaria scourged the settlements in 1833, and a letter from Perry to Austin describes their effects:

Our family has not been entirely clear of sickness since June and part of the time scarcely enough well of either servants or whites to wait on the sick and at the worst of our sickness there was not a Physician could be had or a neighbour to call to see us.

With regard to our crops and improvements we have done very little since the middle of June as the Blacks were all sick as well as ourselves —we made a good crop of corn and pumpkins about 8 or 900 bushels of corn and plenty of pumpkins. We planted 13 acres of cotton the last week in June which bid fair to do pretty well but the early frost has injured it much as it had not commenced opening we do not expect much of a crop Cotton is now a fine price in N. O. from 16 to 18 cts. There is fine crops in this neighborhood and I am told all over the colony where the overflow did not injure it.[56]

53. Holley, *Texas* (1836), 66–67.

54. *Telegraph and Texas Register*, October 31, 1835.

55. Based upon Record Book from 1838 to 1851 and a Plantation Day Book, 1837–63. These volumes were given to the University of Texas by Mrs. James F. Perry II and her son and daughter-in-law, Mr. and Mrs. Stephen S. Perry of Freeport. They still own the Peach Point Plantation.

56. Perry to Austin, October 26, 1833.

Since the Day Book did not begin until 1837, and the first crop recorded in the Record Book is that of 1838, there is an interval of four years to be bridged over. This gap can only be spanned by Perry's correspondence. His expectations of good crops for 1834 as forecast in a letter to Austin did not come true.[57] In January, 1835, he reported that the cotton crop had been very small. This was due partly to small acreage incident to opening the plantation, and partly to ravages of cotton worms, which destroyed about one-third of the crop. Such cotton as he harvested Perry shipped to New Orleans and sold for sixteen cents a pound. To his factors he wrote, "The cotton crop in this country was verry fine with the exception of some 5 or 6 plantations in my neighborhood which was destroyed by the worms." [58]

It will be recalled that Perry had settled at Chocolate Bayou before moving to Peach Point. Evidently there was some question as to the advisability of closing out the establishment there, for Austin wrote Perry, "I am greatly in favor of keeping up the Chocolate bayou stock farm, and intend to spend some of my time there—the place is of no value except for stock, but is good for that purpose." [59] That he was guided by Austin's wishes and retained the Chocolate Bayou ranch is indicated by occasional entries in the Day Book.

A letter from Perry to Austin in May, 1835, indicates the progress made in the plantation. He wrote,

> I have made arrangements to settle our Dickenson and clear Creek lands and within the summer have the others settle[d] we have about 65 or 70 acres in cotton this year but the season since the 1st Mar has been so dry that prospects for crops are bad so far.[60]

In November of the same year Moses Austin Bryan, Perry's stepson, wrote, "Am rejoiced to hear that you are all in good health and getting along so well in the way of picking out cotton etc." [61]

The next year the country was in turmoil and confusion incident to the Revolution. Early in the year Perry was advised to take his family to a place of safety because of possible uprising of Negroes and dangers from Indians.[62] Three days after this letter was written, Perry wrote that he was at Lynch's Ferry and that he had not gotten the "waggon across the San Jacinto." At the time he was undecided whether to take

57. Perry to Austin, May 13, 1834.
58. Perry to Messrs. Lastraps and Desmare, January 15, 1835.
59. Austin to Perry, November 6, 1834.
60. Perry to Austin, May 5, 1835.
61. Bryan to Perry, November 18, 1835.
62. Henry Austin to Perry, April 5, 1836.

his Negroes any further or not.[63] This move was part of the so-called Runaway Scrape. Perry decided to leave his family on San Jacinto Bay. Together with several of his Negro men, he joined James Morgan on Galveston Bay, where he assisted in the building of fortifications to keep communications open to New Orleans.[64] As a consequence of this absence from home during the planting season, the crops for 1836 were short and hardly adequate for food and seed for the next year. Perry contracted with the Schooner *Colonel Fannin* to carry his crop of twenty-two bales to Messrs. John A. Merle & Co. of New Orleans. In the letter notifying this company of shipment he inquired whether he could obtain a loan of two or three thousand dollars for April or May, 1837, if the crop prospects were good at that time.[65] The twenty-two bales did not go by the *Colonel Fannin*, as is seen from the following letter.

> Enclosed you will also receive a Bill of Lading pr Schooner Julias Ceiser for twenty two Bales of Cotton, the whole amount of my crop, which I hope you will receive in good order and get a good price for it as I need all I can get and more too.[66]

There is no record of the 1837 crop. Conditions could not have been prosperous, for Perry was borrowing money, as is seen from the following letter from his factor.

> Money is very scare here [New Orleans]. If we can possibly advance the $500.—you speak of we will enclose it to Mrs. Perry.
> New cotton begins to come in July and ranges from 10 to 12c in price we fear Cotton will not go above 10c this season.[67]

Peach Point in its beginning was primarily a cotton plantation, with corn and other products to supply the plantation needs. It is not until the 1850's that sugarcane becomes the leading crop. Beginning with 1838 there is a fairly comprehensive record of the cotton crop through 1849, giving the records of the pickers by name, the total weight of the crop, the number of bales, the price of the crop, a partial account of the outlay for the crop, and observations on the weather. While a few references were made to the planting of the corn, it was not until 1846 and 1847 that a full record was given of the yield. The records for this crop were never as complete as were those for cotton. The records for cane

---

63. Perry to Austin, April 8, 1836.
64. *Texas Planter*, November 16, 1853.
65. Perry to John A. Merle & Co., New Orleans, January 29, 1837.
66. Perry to John A. Merle & Co., February 6, 1837.
67. James Reed & Co. to Perry, October 5, 1837.

and its products began in 1848. The daily routine of the plantation is most fully illustrated in the farm journal for 1848 kept from day to day by Stephen S. Perry, the eldest son of James F. Perry. This journal began on January 16. The last entry was for November 24; but there are no entries for July and September, only two for August, and one entry for October. This journal recorded labor routine, delinquencies of the slaves, and weather conditions, presenting in brief a picture of labor conditions on the plantation.

When the journal began, the ginning of the 1847 crop was still going on; and, indeed, the last bale was not ginned until March 17, 1848, by which time some of the early cotton for 1848 was coming up, though part of the 1848 crop was not yet planted. The preparation of the ground began on February 8 with the pulling of the cotton stalks, and on March 9 they were still breaking up cotton stalks. In the meantime the ploughs were throwing up cotton ridges so that the cotton planting started on March 1. The year before the planting had started eleven days later. The cotton planted early was coming up before all of the cotton land was prepared for the seed. By March 31 the first ploughing of the cotton had begun and was finished by April 12; on May 1 the second ploughing started, the hoes were going at the same time as the second ploughing. On the first of May the cotton in the prairie field was replanted because a third of it was missing. Mr. Perry noted by the middle of June that the crop was fine, being nearly as high as his head. All the middles had been ploughed out by June 20, and the hoeing was finished within a week, thus "laying by the cotton." The Negroes were free for other crops and work until cotton picking began on July 31. The total crop of 154,188 pounds in the seed had been picked by October 11.

Besides attending to the cultivation of the other crops of corn, potatoes, and cane, the hands were occupied in splitting rails, getting board timber and basket timber, tearing down and rebuilding fences, making and cleaning out ditches, shelling corn, killing hogs, minding the birds from the corn, hauling wood, working on the roads, building Ben's chimney, killing a beef, and attending to brood sows and their litters. No work was done on Sunday.

Turning to the annual statistics, the 1838 cotton crop was gathered between September 4 and some time in December—"the date knot nown precisely"—by fifteen pickers, among whom were Ben, Peter, Bill, Doctor, Sam, Dick, John, Beck, Mary, Chaney, George, and Ned. The fifteenth hand picked one day. The gang picked 667 pounds a day near the beginning of the season and 3,214 pounds as the season advanced. The 1838 crop for the entire plantation was 127 bales, of which number Dick, Sam, and Bill owned one and one-half bales.

The next year there were twenty pickers with Betcey, Caroline, Margaret, Bob, Clenen, Allin, Frank, Tom, Sam, and Simon in the crew in addition to those of the previous year. The crop lacked 21 bales of being as large as that of 1838, being 106 bales. The average weight of the bales was 545 pounds, and netted 6½c per pound. This crop had been hauled to the river by January 16.

The plantation was apparently divided into three fields for cotton. These are designated in the record for 1840 as "Prairie field," "Field by the Gin," and "Field by the House." The crop of 106 bales was gathered by twenty-five pickers. Bill and Peter were expert pickers, Bill picking 325 pounds on August 26 and Peter 334 pounds on the same day. The average of the other twenty-two pickers for this day was 196 pounds. The yield for this year was classified as 40 "first rate" bales, 59 "good" bales, and 4 "not so good." All of the crop was in by October 26. The shortness of the season may be explained by a note under date of September 1 that the worms had destroyed the cotton.

Each year the number of bales decreased, only 89 being ginned in 1841. In this year the pickers numbered nineteen; however, George picked only two days. Peter and Bill kept the lead, with Caroline and Bob close followers. Turner, Prunell, Simon, and Allin were the poorest pickers, gathering in one week 780, 575, 510, and 580 pounds respectively. This was the same week that Peter had 1,470 pounds to his credit. This year's crop bore out Perry's statement that "the prospects for crops are rather bad," and that the blacks had been sick.[68]

The picking in 1842 must have been very scattering, because it took nineteen Negroes from July 1 to October 20 to pick 50 bales. The largest amount gathered in one day by any picker was 293 pounds.

By May 26 the 1843 crop was blooming, and on August 15 picking had begun. Peter picked a total of 8,131 pounds for the season; Caroline, 7,632; Bill, 6,725; Bob, 6,992; Ben, 5,975; Betcey, 6,534; Beckey, 5,436; Chaney, 5,241; Dock, 5,443; George, 5,086; John, 5,764; Ned, 5,815; Turner, 2,783; Purnell, 4,569; Allin, 3,786; Mary, 809; Westley, 1,899; Sam, 456; Jim, 3,468; L. Ben, 3,398; thus making a grand total of 101,403 pounds of seed cotton. The 61 bales delievered at Aycock's warehouse weighed 29,328 pounds. A letter from Guy M. Bryan to his friend Rutherford B. Hayes explains the short crop of this and the previous year:

68. Perry to Somervell, June 18, 1841.

. . . we have had for the last two months the most unprecedented rains. The whole country has been under water. The Brazos River has again overflowed its banks. The crops which were most promising have been cut off one fourth. My father who had a most promising crop will not make more than 60 bales of cotton. Our lands which cost three thousand dollars annual tax, bring us in scarce a farthing. We are thus dependent upon our cotton crop for our active means, & that having failed for this year, I fear we will be unable to pay expenses. I however hope to obtain of a large cotton planter, who has made a tolerable crop, & owes us 15 or 1600$ & is an *honest man* a sufficient sum to answer my purposes & enable me to go to the U. S. . . . . The crops of the country have nearly failed for three years in succession.[69]

Despite worms in the gin house field by September 4, and their spread to the other cotton fields, the 1844 crop amounted to 118 bales averaging 537 pounds each, or a total of 63,326 pounds of lint cotton. Of this crop 40 bales made up the better cotton, while there were three ordinary bales and three stained ones. In addition to the workers of 1843, Silvy, Dave, Elish, Charlot, Big George, Jill, Lowey, and L. John picked part of the time, numbering twenty-eight hands in all—Turner was not on the roll. Peter, Bill, Betcey, Caroline, and George were leading the field in the amount picked. This crop had to be replanted in May, while the first cotton planted was blooming on May 22. The net proceeds were 4⅓ cents a pound.

The banner year of the plantation was 1845, when the yield was 130 bales. The twenty-two hands gathered 77,233 pounds of seed cotton from the Prairie field, of which 53,699 pounds was classed as "fine" cotton, and 90,412 pounds in the Timber field. The hands were irregular in their picking—Allin, Bob, Betcey, and Caroline lost from the field 4 days each; Charlot and Mary, 2 days each; Purnell, 3 days; Bill and John Jack, 5 days; Ben, 39; Beckey and Westley, 14; Clenen, 34; Chaney, 11; John, 12; George and Silvey, 7 each; Lowey, 9; Ned, 33; and Robert, 33 days. Sam picked three days.

The cotton crop of 1846 was very short. There were 10 bales, two of which were silk cotton. The lint total of these 10 bales amounted to 4,660 pounds. How poor the picking was may be judged by the fact that those hands who could pick around 400 pounds per day picked from 51 to 116 pounds per day.

In 1847 the cotton planting started on March 11, and the hands went into the field on August 10 to begin gathering the white staple. On August 20 the cotton worm made its first appearance. Mary Ann, Simon, Neece, Jerry, a Negro belonging to Mrs. Jack, Gustus, Morris, Lucy,

69. Bryan to Hayes, December 21, 1843. *The Quarterly*, XXV, 108.

Dick, yellow Simon, and Tom were new hands on the record book. By November 8 the twenty-seven hands had picked 193,000 pounds. By November 8, Hill the overseer had baled eight bales, and the last of the 105 was not ginned until March 17, 1848. The 105 bales came to 55,262 pounds.

The planting of the 1848 cotton was described above. Twenty-three hands, starting on August 1, had gathered the crop by October 20, although they did not finish baling until February 8, 1849. The 82 bales weighed 42,108 pounds. There were 3,057 pounds of seed cotton classified as "fine."

The following year nineteen hands (Allin, Bill, Ben, Bob, Betcey, Beckey, Clenen, Caroline, Chaney, George, John, Ned, Mary, Peter, Robert, Sam, Silvey, Westley, and Simon) began picking on August 9 and by October 8 were picking the last of the thin cotton, when none of the hands picked over 100 pounds per day. The 39 bales of the 1849 crop, weighing 18,221 pounds, averaged 467 pounds each. There was no record of the 1850 crop in either of the books.

The first picking of the 1851 crop yielded 20 bales of good quality, weighing 10,339 pounds. The nine bales of the second picking came to 4,457 pounds. The last picking brought the total to 38 bales. This is the last record of a cotton crop on the plantation in either the Record Book or the Day Book.

Corn was the staple food of the South; indeed, in one form or another it was the main dependence in Texas. The records show that very little flour was bought. As early as 1833 Perry wrote that they had raised "8 or 900 bushels of corn and plenty of pumpkins." [70]

The journal for Perry's plantation is most satisfactory for 1848, and that year is, therefore, taken to illustrate the routine of corn cultivation. Rotation of crops was practiced to some extent at Peach Point, unlike many of the plantations, as is evidenced by this entry of April 18: "Commenced ploughing corn hilling it up and ploughing out the middles. Corn looks well indeed wants rain very much. good stand in all of it except the cotton ground replant not all come up." The first step in the planting of the corn was the clearing of the ground. The corn planting began on February 17 and was finished on the morning of February 25. The corn came up slowly that year, necessitating the minding of the birds from February 26, when the corn began coming up, through March 10, at which time all the corn was not yet up. The ploughs started in the corn on March 23 and the hoes began the next day and

70. Perry to Austin, October 26, 1833.

continued for a week. Stephen Perry under March 24 made this note, "We did not harrow our corn this year, I do not think we did right we smothed down the ridges with the hoes." By April 7 both corn and cotton needed rain; the corn, however, as was natural, was suffering most. On April 18 they commenced ploughing the corn a second time, to hill it up, and plough out the middles. The stand of corn in 1848 was good except in the bottom field, which had been replanted. Seven ploughs were running in the corn with the hoes on April 19. The third ploughing started on May 12 and was finished on May 18, but the hoeing continued. A corn crop furnished plenty of labor after it was laid by, for it had to be gathered and there was the shucking and shelling as occupations for rainy days. It was not unusual in Texas to plant two crops of corn a year, but there is nothing to indicate that this was done on the Perry plantation. They did plant potatoes in the corn.

As a rule, there was more corn raised on the plantation than was consumed there. In 1838 the Record Book showed that 15 bushels of corn and 11 bushels of corn in the shuck were sold; in 1839 a surplus of 31 bushels of corn, 54 bushels unshucked corn, and 23 bushels of corn meal were sold; in 1841, out of 73 loads, 10 bushels of corn, 9 of meal, and $1.25 worth of "hommoney" were sold; in 1842, 1 bushel of seed corn and 30 bushels of meal; in 1843, 10 bushels of corn and 83 bushels of meal. In 1844, they sold 150 bushels of corn, contracting to grind 20 of it into meal, 57 barrels of unshucked corn, 5 bales of fodder, and 80 bushels of meal. The following year the plantation disposed of 228 bushels of corn, 20 bushels in the shuck and 30 bushels of meal. The crop of 1846 amounted to 3,800 bushels and was gathered in September. Of this amount, 123 bushels and 116 sacks of corn, 11 barrels of corn in the shuck, and 17 bushels of meal were sold. In 1847 the crop, which was planted between March 2 and 6, yielded 92 loads, estimated at 2,300 bushels. They record as sold 24 bales of fodder, 110 bushels and 114 sacks of corn, 42 barrels of corn in the shuck, and 8 bushels of meal. Of the 1848 yield of 144 loads (about 3,600 bushels), 60 bushels were sold. From the crop of 1850, the memorandum shows as sold 583 bales of fodder and 58 barrels of corn. From this time until 1863 there are no records of any sales except 176 bushels in 1858. In 1863 the overseer, Mr. Ayers, sold 1,162 bushels of corn and 23,973 pounds of fodder to the government, and 25 bushels of meal to various civilians. The price varied from seventy-five cents to a dollar per bushel. Apparently the plantation never had to buy corn or meal, but always had sufficient to supply their needs. The custom was to charge toll in kind for grinding corn at the mill. All this corn may not have been raised on the Perry land.

Part of it may have come from the mill, no doubt some of the meal did.

The crop which was apparently taking the place of cotton in the 1850's was sugarcane. Phillips, quoting from P. A. Champonier's *Statement of the Sugar Crop*, says, "Outside of Louisiana the industry took no grip except on the Brazos River in Texas, where in 1858 thirty-seven plantations produced about six thousand hogsheads." [71] The Day Book showed that Mr. Perry was buying over two barrels of sugar a year after 1843, and in 1847 he bought 1,125 pounds. He sold Andrew Churchill a barrel (of 234 pounds) of sugar in 1847. This large purchase in 1847 may have been due to his buying in large quantities to get it cheaper for himself and neighbors. In 1846 he paid Major James P. Caldwell, from whom he usually bought his sugar supply, $12 for a barrel of molasses. It is uncertain when Perry commenced raising cane. In the journal for 1848 under date of April 15, Stephen entered this statement, "Ploughing cane and hoing cotton. First time the cane has been ploughed this year." There is nothing to indicate that this was the first cane crop on the plantation. A heavy frost on November 4, the day on which the cutting had begun, killed the cane. By November 10 the cane was cut. These are the only facts known about the crop, except that there is no record of their having bought any sugar in that year or in 1849. In November, 1849, the purchase of 180 yards by 39 yards of sugarcane for seed was made from James P. Caldwell. This was 143/100 acres at $40.00 and amounted to $57.20. James Hext, overseer for Perry, and a man by the name of Dillon measured the cane.

The sugar mill was not installed on the plantation until 1850. In May of that year the sugarhouse was built, and Close & Adams installed the mill and engine in October. The sugar-making began on December 12, 1850. A few days before this a severe freeze had spoiled "the most of the seed cane which was put up in malay" [matlay].[72] The breaking of the jack chain delayed the sugar-making for a day and a half. On January 1 the cane had been rolled, but it became too sour to work up. The 1850 crop produced 165 barrels of molasses, of which four barrels were reserved for home use, two for W. J. Bryan, and one for M. A. Bryan. In June 45 barrels of sugar were shipped in the *General Hamer* to T. Crosby. William N. Payne charged $354.80 for 100 molasses barrels of

---

71. Ulrich Bonnell Phillips, *American Negro Slavery*, 168.

72. Seed cane was stored in "matlay" for the winter. Phillips (*American Negro Slavery*, 244) describes the process as the laying of the stalks in their leaves with the tops turned to the south to keep out the north wind, with the leaves of each layer covering the butts of that below, and with dirt over the last butts in the mat. Perry bought by the yard as the cane lay on the ground.

mixed sizes, 68 large barrels, 2 meat barrels, 2 molasses barrels, 8 sugar buckets, and 52 hogsheads, while Horace Chadwick (apparently the same name sometimes spelled Shattuck) charged $63 for 42 molasses barrels to pack sugar in. Out of the crop of 1851, 202 barrels of molasses and 60 hogsheads of sugar were shipped; 2 barrels of sugar being sent to Rosanah P. Brown, Delaware, Ohio. The expenses for the sugar crop of 1851 included: $25 for work done on the furnace of the sugar house; $192 to Jesse Munson for making 96 hogsheads of sugar; $50 to W. N. Payne for making 50 "hogsheads"; and $433.92 to Horace Chadwick for making 321 barrels and 5 hogsheads; besides the hire for extra slaves.

There were several interruptions and hindrances to the sugar-making of 1852. At first the pump refused to work; then the furnace mouth gave way and there was a delay until a mason could come to rebuild it. On November 13 they were interrupted by the burning of the corn house and stables with over 3,000 bushels of corn and most of the ploughs, harrows, and carts. They saved about 150 bushels of corn. The uncut cane was injured by hard frost and ice in the early part of January. They had begun cutting and hauling the cane on October 23, and on January 10 they finished boiling the last of the crop. The extra expense for hired help, including $93.33 to Cash for overseeing, was $646.60. The warehouse bill from Crosby showed that 450 barrels of molasses and 71 hogsheads of sugar from this crop had been stored; there were then, on March 23, 75 barrels of molasses and one barrel of sugar. On August 15 there was an entry that 72 barrels had been shipped to W. Hendly & Co. of Galveston in two shipments. Shattuck's bill for making and repairing barrels for the 1852 and 1853 crops was $651.23. Munson charged $420 for boiling the sugar and serving as engineer for the 1852 crop. The records for 1852 are meager.

The 1854 sugar crop was finished by December 27, and a good crop was made. The net proceeds on 53 barrels after paying storage, expense to Galveston, and expenses after leaving Galveston, which included freight, wharfage, auction charges, cooperage, interest, commission, and guaranteeing, were $5,364.49. After deducting $2,579.63 for expenses, the net proceeds of the 1855 crop were $6,781.13. The 180 barrels and 140 hogsheads were marketed in Baltimore, Galveston, and New York. The price for sugar from 1851 on varied from five cents to six cents per pound. During the Civil War it was higher. In 1863 Mr. Ayers, in Stephen S. Perry's absence, sole $415 worth of sugar at fifty cents a pound.

Potatoes, like corn, were a staple food on the plantation. In 1837 the current expenses were charged with $5.50 for potatoes. This may have been for seed, as this is the year they were so abundant. This is the last record of potatoes purchased until 1847, when three barrels were bought. On the contrary, several barrels were sold every season. In 1845 some 200 bushels of sweet potatoes and 18 bushels of Irish potatoes were sold. After 1853 there are no records of sales except five bushels in 1857.

Tobacco was a minor product of the plantation. In 1846 Perry sent R. and D. G. Mills of Brazoria 2,526 pounds at six cents per pound, with the understanding that they should give him half of the profits above that amount. This is the only record of transactions in tobacco.

The record contains various entries of miscellaneous products sold. These included eggs, sometimes by the keg, chickens, muscova ducks, turkeys, geese, butter, pecans, tallow, hominy, and hard soap. The sales were not in large quantities, nor were they made regularly.

There is no record of how many hogs they had or how they raised them, except in the 1848 farm journal. Between January 27 and February 1, 47 hogs were killed. This was probably only a small part of the number killed that winter, for Texas farmers believed that old saw that meat killed before Christmas kept better, and they would hardly have gone that late in the season without fresh meat. On January 31 the entry reads, "Tearing down and rebuilding fences. Hunting sowes and pigs, put nine sowes with about forty young pigs in the Prairy field." From 1839 to 1849 there was a gradual increase in the amounts of pork and lard sold, after which time the sales fell off abruptly. In 1848 they sold 12 hogs, 1,744 pounds of bacon at eight cents, and 334 pounds of lard at nine cents per pound. In 1843 and the two following years the sales of pickled pork averaged about 300 pounds at eight cents per pound.

The Chocolate Bayou stock farm was kept as Austin desired, but there were few entries made in regard to it save two pages under "Pleasant Bayou Ranch," giving the accounts from 1856 through 1859. There was exchange of labor to some extent between Peach Point and Pleasant Bayou, as is seen in the journal of Stephen Perry. This is shown in the entry of April 17: "Need left this morning for Chocolate Bayou (Sam coming in his place)"; on April 19 this additional statement was entered, "Robert left for Choclet on the 17 of April with Need carryed two mules with him."

From the beginning this place had been considered ranching land. In 1834 Austin instructed Perry to "collect all the stock you can in claims due me and put them on your farm at Chocolate Bayou, in your own brand." [73] From Peach Point they shipped out on an average of 13 hides a year at 7 and 8 cents. In one year they received $27 for 15 hides. Very

73. Austin to Perry, January 14, 1834.

few beefs were sold from the plantation. In 1839 they received $240 for cows; in 1840, $182; in 1845, $100 and a note for three cows at $10 each; in 1846, $40. There were no records of the sale of hides from Chocolate. They bought corn in small quantities occasionally. In 1847 and again in 1848, about 2,000 pounds of corn was shipped Aycock for the use of Judge Low in payment of loans of corn from him.

Edward Austin took charge of the Pleasant Bayou stock in 1846 at the salary of $200 per annum with the provision that he make his wages out of the stock. N. S. (?) Davis had charge from 1856 until as late as February, 1859. He sold 233 beefs and five stags for $5,532. The expense account totaled $1,307.98, including articles purchased for the ranch and $200 for Davis's services. In 1842 Edmund Andrews was charged with $300 worth of timber from Chocolate, and Hopkins is charged with $500 for "timber taken away and destroyed on my land on Chocolate Bayou." It cannot be determined from these inadequate accounts whether the ranch was a financial success or not.

In the sketch of Perry's life in the *Planter*, 1853, he is described as "one of the best planters and masters in the State." [74] When he came to Texas in 1831 Perry brought his slaves with him, but their number and qualities are unknown. There is no complete list of Perry's slaves. The daily record of the cotton picking which was kept by name is the nearest to a list of the slaves. There are no records of purchase or sale of Negroes except in two cases. In 1832, Austin wrote Perry as follows:

> I am sending you Simon & wish you to keep him close at work untill I return. He has been idle for so long that he will require a tight rein—he is in the habit of gambling—but he is a useful hand on a farm if he is kept close to his business.[75]

This would seem to indicate that Austin already had a Negro by the name of Simon, while in 1836 he wrote to his brother-in-law:

> McKinstre has a very likely negro 27 years of age, healthy and a good field hand—he has ran away owing to a terrible whipping Mc. gave him the other day, but I believe has no very bad habits—he asks twelve hundred dollars cash—I have an idea of buying him—what do you think of the price—if I take him will send him to you untill I need him.[76]

Whether Perry advised it or not, Austin did pay $1,200 for another slave by the name of Simon, who is described as of a "dark complexion,

74. Clipping from the *Texas Planter*, 1853. Austin Papers.
75. Austin to Perry, March 3, 1832.
76. Austin to Perry, November 11, 1836.

aged about 27 years and in good health." [77] This Simon is probably the one by that name on the records. In April, 1842, William Joel Bryan is debited on the Record Book with $1,000 paid to Hopkins for "negress Ann and child" and with $3,000 paid to Dr. Smith for "negress Tamar, negroes Donor & George." On the same day Joel is again debited with $1,000 to Emily M. Perry for boy Frank. A note to the side of the page reads: "Entered in Mrs. E. M. Perry's Book." In 1834 John R. Jones, who was selling out to go into the mercantile business, offered Perry his Missouri Negroes in payment of a debt. In 1841 and again in 1848 Hamilton White offered to settle a debt for land with Negroes.[78] Before this, in 1837, George Hammeken had written Perry from New Orleans of an opportunity to buy one Gouverneur's slaves.[79] Whether or not Perry closed with any of these proposals is not apparent. The list of field-hands in the record is supposedly complete, but there is nothing to indicate the number of domestic slaves.

There is scarcely anything in the records to indicate how the Negroes lived. No punishments for the Negroes are recorded. They seem to have been on the whole fairly healthy. The record for 1841 is probably a representative year. In this year Ben was out of the field on account of a snake bite. George was sick all of the cotton-picking season of 1841. John and Beckey were out a few days. Mary was away from the field 26 days, 17 of these following the birth of a son on October 11. This is the only record of the birth of a child to any of the slaves on the plantation; in fact, there are no records of there being any children, unless this is implied in the labor of driving the birds away from the young corn. This sort of work would probably be done by children or infirm Negroes. In 1848 Allin was sick practically all the spring, Westley for part of May, and Mary during the fall. Stephen Perry, in his synopsis of the months of January, February and March, said, "The atmosphere has become so impure, which has produced sickness among the negroes, they complain principally of pains in the breast and sides, sores, and rumatisms &c &c." As far as the farm journal carried the record in 1848, the Negroes lost from the field 115 days from sickness. The only record of any of Perry's slaves running off was in an entry of May 30, 1848. Tom ran away and was gone until June 7. No reason was assigned for his running away. Nothing is shown as to the Negroes' social life. There is an entry in November, 1839, that they had a half day's picking and that Sam was married that day.

77. Receipt from George B. McKinstry to Austin, Columbia, November 25, 1836.
78. White to Perry, September 16, 1841, and January 20, 1848.
79. Hammeken to Perry, July 26, 1837.

Perry hired out his own slaves and, in turn, employed the slaves of others as need arose. He frequently had to hire additional labor in the sugar-making of the 1850's. Such emergencies were met by mutual accommodation of neighbors, and not by hiring from a slave gang. In 1834 Edmund Andrews wrote asking, "Have you none among those of Westall's [slaves] that you will hire me for a cook." [80] John P. Borden in 1837 wrote to hire either Clara or Milly as a cook.[81] In 1844 W. J. Bryan hired Frank, George, Clenen, Bob, Mary, and Silvy to assist with his cotton. The next year he hired Sam, Allin, Purnell, Westley, Ben, John, Ned, and Bill a total of sixty-two days to gin and bale his cotton. In June, 1855, Perry let Mr. Shattuck have a Negro woman at $15 per month. The records indicate that Perry hired outside help more often than he let his slaves out. In 1843 he hired Ben and Jim at $10 per month from Dr. Leonard. From 1844 to 1850 he hired Jerry, Tom, and George from Mrs. Laura H. Jack. Beginning with 1850 his expense account for hired slave labor was high during the season of sugar-making, which required a large force to work day and night. He paid from $20 a month to a dollar per day in the sugar season when the work was hard. He had hired nine slaves in 1851 from Mrs. Bell of Bernardo and from Edmund Arrington. This number was increased to eleven in 1852.

If the slaves worked on Sunday, which they frequently had to do in sugar-making, they received the dollar themselves. The expense account for the sugar crop of 1852 included $45 "for some hands." This may have been for their Sunday labor. In 1853 at least fifteen Negroes were hired from Major Caldwell, Major Lewis, W. & J. Hopkins, Derant, and Guy M. Bryan; and ten for 1853. Perry had considerable trouble on account of hired Negroes running away for a few days at a time— probably to see their families. Guy's Negroes, Henry, Sam, Simon, Bill, Nathan, and little John, ran away at various times during 1852 for a day or so at a time. Perry boarded the hired Negroes, but he evidently charged their clothing to their masters. In 1853 he charged Major Lewis with six pairs of shoes and one blanket. In 1854 Estes was charged with one pair of shoes, which was deducted from Estes's bill of $60. In 1855 Captain Black was charged with $15 for ten pairs of shoes for his Negroes. In 1853 Perry paid for Negro hire $638.80. Of this amount, $28.50 was for Sunday work and $45 for the home hands. The one item of Lewis's hire for 1854 was $800.

There was some work which the slaves and overseers could not do, so

---

80. Andrews to Perry, October 26, 1834.
81. Borden to Austin, August 13, 1837.

white labor was called in. Most of the work done by white labor was shopwork, stocking ploughs, carpentering, installing the sugar mill, making barrels, papering the pantry, and engineering work on the sugar house and furnace. This would point to the inference that the Negroes on the plantation were fieldhands unskilled in any trade. Apparently they worked in gangs, for Bill had charge of a gang in 1848.

Over the Negroes there passed a constant stream of overseers, beginning with William Joel Bryan, who was credited with $800 for service in "1837 & 1836" and 1838 & 1839. The salaries for the overseers varied from $20 a month to $650 a year. It is uncertain how long Joseph M. Trimble served in 1838 after he was employed on January 2. There were three overseers in 1839: one Ramsey, K. K. Koontz, and David H. Love. Ramsey and Love were both discharged. M. M. Aycock served throughout the year of 1840. In 1841 J. J. Harwell was employed as overseer, but it was not indicated how long he remained in Perry's employment. Denman contracted to serve from December 18, 1841, to January, 1843. He became ill and left after a week's service. Denman had a horse, and the agreement was that if the horse were kept on the plantation it was to be used for its keep. On January 6, 1842, John Kellen began to serve as overseer. The two following overseers served for two years each: John Handcock for 1843 and 1844, and Chapman White, whose family lived in Mississippi, for 1845 and 1846. William L. Hill agreed on March 22 to serve as overseer for $25 per month, provided Perry was satisfied. He and Perry made a settlement on November 27 of that year. Joseph Hext, who was overseer throughout 1849 and 1850, came for $20 a month with a contract to receive $25 if 110 bales were made and sold at seven cents. They made 39 bales of cotton in 1849. Jesse Munson, who was skilled in sugar-making and who had made up the 1851 sugar crop, was overseer from January 1 to October 19, when he began to make up the sugar crop of 1852. H. J. B. Cash took Munson's place as overseer on October 19, 1852, and with the exception of short intervals he continued in Perry's employ until January 1, 1855. A man who is called at various times Seiers, Sayer, and Seayer began overseeing on December 13, 1856, at the rate of $600 a year. He served one year and began on another, but it is not recorded whether he worked the full two years or not. Hull, the last one of whom there is an account, was to receive $50 per month, and Perry agreed to furnish him beef, meal, molasses, and a servant to assist his wife and to cook and wash.

The Negroes were allowed small patches of their own in which they raised cotton, corn, and vegetables. In the calculations made about 1852 of the size of the various fields, the measurements of the prairie field were fifty-six acres after four acres had been taken out for garden and lot; the timber field was 187 acres after a deduction of one acre for each of the nine "boys," Simon, Sam, Ned, Ben, Bill, Peter, John, Clenen, and Bob. African Bill and Sam each received $38.87 for their 1839 cotton crop; Bill and Peter were each credited with $55.02 for their 1840 and 1841 crop; Ned, $30.72 for his 1841 cotton; Simon, $41.34 for his crop. On December 25, 1845, Clenen was debited to Ben for balance of $2.32 due him for rent of ground for 1845. The crops of Simon and Peter were short in 1846, being 73 pounds and 115 pounds respectively. On November 27, 1847, this entry was made, "Bill African By 2,220 lb. Seed Cotten Crop of this year suppose to be worh 1½c but to[be] paid at what my crop sells for—$16.05." In 1854 the total crop for seven "boys" was 11,036 pounds. When one slave picked another slave's cotton, he was credited on the Day Book with the money for the picking. The Negroes raised corn as well as cotton. Ben sent sixteen and Simon six barrels of corn to Brazoria in 1848. In 1850 Bill was credited with 585 pounds of fodder at one cent a pound, and sixteen barrels of corn at $8.00. In 1855 Purnell is credited with 20½ bushels of corn. The Negroes must have raised hogs, for Clenen sent fifty pounds of bacon worth $10 to M. B. Williamson in 1847, and Ned sent sixty-one pounds to Canon.

There is no record of clothing and supplies being issued to the Negroes. On the other hand, the Negroes are charged with shoes, tobacco, and merchandise from Mills and Bennett, Stringfellow and Aharns, and other firms. This may have been to keep account of what was spent on each slave, but the shoes and other articles are only charged against those Negroes who are shown to have had a patch of ground, except George, who is charged with one pair of shoes in 1850. The "coars" shoes and "Russett Brogans" ranged in price from $1.25 to Sam's $3.50 boots in 1849. These merchandise orders may have come from the proceeds of their crop to supplement their regular clothing allowance. The merchandise included combs, flannel, five-dollar dress patterns, sugar, padlocks, net and cambric for two or three mosquito bars, buckets, and straw hats. Between 1839 and 1851 there are recorded thirteen pairs of shoes against Bill and three pairs being for Betcy; Sam had a pair for each year from 1839 to 1842; Ben, Peter, Simon, and Ned had five pairs each for the four years, one pair of those bought for Peter was for Silvey; three of John African's twelve pairs were for Becky; Allin and Clenen had two pairs each between 1839 and 1842, and George had one pair. Sam is charged with twenty-three plugs of tobacco, Ben with seven, and Ned with fourteen plugs.

Although the plantation was located on the Brazos, the products had to be hauled to Aycock's in Brazoria, which was nine miles from the plantation, or to Crosby's Landing. There is no record of a landing at Peach Point. If there was no immediate market or no boat to transport the goods, they were stored in the warehouse at the shipping point. Both Aycock and Crosby often acted as agents to dispose of the farm products. Frequently one of the various schooners (*Alamo, Josephine, John G. McNeel, Hamer, Oscar, Washington, S. M. Williams*, or the *Rein Deer*) plying on the river was at the landing and received the goods at the end of the haul, and thus shipment was made directly to William H. Hendley & Co. of Galveston, who disposed of the shipment in New Orleans, Baltimore, or New York. Perry did some banking business with the firm of R. Mills & Co. of Brazoria, with its successor, R. & D. G. Mills, and with James Reed & Company of New Orleans. These firms sold the crops on different occasions, but William Hendley & Co. did most of this work. Perry settled Crosby's bill for storage and ferriage on March 23, 1853, for $118.75. This bill went back far enough to include $25.50 for storage of 408 barrels of molasses of the crop to 1850 and 1851 at 6¼ cents. Many of the supplies for the plantation came from James Reed & Company, R. & D. G. Mills, and William Hendley & Company. Smaller items came from Mills and Bennett, Stringfellow & Aharns of Brazoria, Smith and Pilgrim, Blackwell and Schlecht, E. Purcell and Company, and Canfield and Slater of Galveston. It was not indicated where all of these firms were located.

The 106 bales of the 1839 cotton crop netted $3,744 after deducting $297 for the cost of the bagging and rope for baling. This year and the years immediately following were hard in Texas, because of the panic in the United States and the declining value of Texas currency due to the unsound finances. The currency depreciated steadily until it was worth about one-third of its face value. The prices, according to the *Telegraph*, were unreasonably high; pork was eighty cents per pound; a beef, from $70 to $80; corn meal $6 to $8; coffee per pound, 50 to 60 cents; butter, from $1.25 to $1.50 per pound.[82] Mills & Bennett shipped the 1840 crop of 103 bales, and the net proceeds were $4,561.73, after deducting cost of bagging, rope, charges to and at San Luis, and the balance of the interest. This is about two cents per pound more than the year before. R. & D. G. Mills handled the 89 bales of the 1841 crop and returned a net price of $4,338.58. The sum of $1,306.14 was the net price of the 50 bales of the next year, while the 61 bales of 1843 yielded $2,700.78 after the usual expenses incident to baling were paid. Perry

82. *Telegraph and Texas Register*, October 2, 1839.

ginned J. T. Hawkins's 1843 crop also. He was to receive one-tenth of the net proceeds after R. & D. G. Mills had sold the crop, plus a dollar per bale for packing. The extremely low price of three cents in 1844 brought the net proceeds of the 118 bales to $3,133.45, or $174 as the net yield per slave for each of the eighteen fieldhands. The largest cotton crop of the whole period, 130 bales, brought in only $4,644.55. It is a big jump from 130 bales to the ten-bale crop of 1846. This brought $46 per bale, and $700 would cover the amount brought in by corn, meat, and lard as set down in the record. Thirty-six bales of the 105 bales of the 1847 crop brought $1,217.46. It was not recorded how much the 159 bales of the 1848, 1849, and 1851 crops amounted to. The sale of sugarcane products for 1852 through 1856 added to that of 1863 both retail and wholesale as recorded was $14,236.29, but this is not likely to be a complete record.

Perry wrote in 1833 that for the past several years farmers had raised cotton with great success, averaging "from 7 to 8 bales to the hand weighing from 540 to 560 each besides corn and everything ells for the support of their farms." But the 1838 crop was the only one with which Perry was ever able to equal this record. The crop that year averaged nine bales to each of the fourteen hands. The crop of 1845 averaged six bales to the hand, and the 1839 one averaged five bales. The average for 1846 was one-half bale. The average per hand for the twelve years from 1838 through 1849 was 4⅙ bales.

For brief glimpses of the life and environment of the family who owned and made Peach Point their home, we are dependent on fragmentary sources. From the first Austin, who had visions of a splendid, comfortable life on the plantation, had urged his brother-in-law to plant fruit trees and raise a garden. In fact, Austin himself was always gathering new varieties of peaches, plums, grapes, figs, and other fruits and trees to send home, even from Mexico. In 1839 one Holsteine was employed as "gaurdner from 1st Feby to 10th Sept." He was paid $140 for his 7⅓ months of service. On December 16, 1840, a "sparrigrass" (asparagus) bed was planted, as well as varieties of fruits. In this year it was planned to have a row of fruit trees on each side of the road from the house to the gate. Gage and damson plums, peaches, apricots, figs, and pears were already growing, and Perry indicated from which trees he wished sprouts taken for the new orchard. In 1843 Guy M. Bryan wrote of the garden,

> It has been perfectly green throughout the whole of the winter. It is pleasant to a *sore-eyed man* to wander in the *dead of winter* through walks embowered with roses & fragrant shrubs of every kind & colour,

to meet at every turn the orange the vine the fig & pomegranate, all of which abound in my mother's yard, the products of our genial clime & mother's guardian care.[83]

The place then presented a great contrast to that described by Austin in 1836 as "still in the primitive log cabbins and wild shrubbery of the forest." [84]

Mrs. Perry, the mistress of this pleasant home, was a woman of culture and education, trained at "The Hermitage," a fashionable school for young ladies in New York. Her husband was a man of strong intelligence and public spirit, a factor in the economic progress of Texas from his arrival in 1831 to his death in 1853. Her son, Guy M. Bryan, was a graduate of Kenyon College at Gambier, Ohio, where his brother Stephen Perry was also a student. Henry Perry, the youngest brother, was a graduate of Trinity College at Hartford, Connecticut. In 1848 Rutherford B. Hayes, Bryan's classmate and bosom friend, visited the plantation, and through extracts from his diary and comments of his biographer we can see how it impressed him:

> The House was beautifully situated on the edge of the timber, looking out upon a prairie on the south, extending five or eight miles to the Gulf, with a large and beautiful flower garden in front.
> Social life here afforded no end of entertainment—balls and parties rapidly followed one another, the guests riding ten, fifteen, and even twenty miles, arriving early in the afternoon, and remaining for nearly twenty-four hours, the great plantation house supplying room for all. "An exceedingly, agreeable, gay, and polished company . . . merriment and dancing until 4:30 a. m.—like similar scenes elsewhere. Gentlemen breakfast from 10 till 11:30; all off by 12 o'clock."
> January 25 [1849].
> Ride with Uncle and Guy over Gulf Prairie to the mouth of the Bernard, to fish and eat oysters. A glorious day. Deer, cattle, cranes, wild geese, brant, ducks, plover, prairie hens, and the Lord knows what else, often in sight at the same time. The roar of the Gulf is heard for miles, like the noise of Niagara. Staked out horses with "lariats," eat old Sailor Tom's oysters, picked up shells, fished and shot snipe until 5 P. M., then rode home through clouds of mosquitoes, thicker than the lice or locusts of Egypt—like the hair on a dog's back. Notice the eagle's nest on the lone tree in the prairie and reach home glad to get away from the mosquitoes.
> Tuesday, January 30.—Ride with Mr. Perry over to Sterling McNeal's plantation. A shrewd, intelligent, cynical old bachelor, full of "wise saws and modern instances"; very fond of telling his own experience and talking of his own affairs. Living alone he has come

83. Bryan to Hayes, January 21, 1843. *The Quarterly*, XXV, 104.
84. Austin to Ficklin, October 30, 1836.

to think he is the "be all" and "end all" here. The haughty and imperious part of a man develops rapidly on one of these lonely sugar plantations, where the owner rarely meets with any except his slaves and minions. Sugar hogsheads vary from 1100 to 1800 lbs. White and black mechanics all work together. White men generally dissolute and intemperate. Returned, found Uncle Birchard returned from Oyster Creek, with the trophy of a successful onslaught upon a tiger cat. Glorious weather. One little shower.

Monday, February 5.—Cold and clear. Forenoon spent with Stephen and the ladies—music and flirting. Afternoon rode up to Major Lewis's. Three agreeable young ladies; music, singing, and dancing—city refinement and amusement in a log cabin on the banks of the Brazos, where only yesterday the steam whistle of a steamboat was mistaken for a panther.[85]

It was in 1848, probably in preparation for the visit of this guest who was later to be President of the United States, that Mrs. Perry ordered silverware "not to cost over $400," with Austin's seal to be engraved on each article. The service included coffee pot, teapot, sugar bowl, cream pot, slop bowl, four ivory salt spoons, and one dozen each of teaspoons, dessertspoons, dining forks, and dessert forks.[86]

Finally a word needs to be said of the two old volumes which form the principal source of this study. They are mildewed, blurred, and faded, so that the task of deciphering them is, in many places, extremely difficult. The memoranda which they contain were written for the use of the planter, without thought of the historian. Many aspects of life on the plantation which we should like to see in a day-to-day commonplace record are lacking, simply because to the writer they were commonplace. As it is, however, this is the only known contemporary record of an antebellum Texas plantation. There may be others—even more complete ones—in neglected family archives, but they are not available. One likes to believe, as in some respects was probably the fact, that Peach Point was a typical Texas slave plantation. It was self-sustaining. There was around it an atmosphere of culture and contentment. The Negroes remained long in the family, were apparently treated with consideration, and there is every indication that they were comfortable and happy.

85. Williams, *Life of Rutherford B. Hayes*, I, 50–51.
86. Perry to Hammeken, June 9, 1848. Mrs. Perry sent to New Orleans her mother's service (Mrs. Moses Austin's, that is) to Hyde and Goodrich with coin and silver, and it was converted and made larger. The original service had been smaller and plainer.—Note by Mrs. Hally Bryan Perry.

Slavery in Towns and Cities

The study of urban slavery—and, more broadly, non-rural slavery —is still in its infancy. Richard C. Wade's *Slavery in the Cities* forcefully opened the discussion, but progress has been slow. In Part Three we present one of E. Merton Coulter's many contributions to the local history of Georgia. It is followed by three essays on Louisiana; they provide a contrast between the incomparable New Orleans and two much smaller urban settlements. Finally for a different kind of contrast, we offer two studies from a northern state. But Hershberg's study of Philadelphia requires special attention, for it represents a major step forward in its methods and use of census data. It may well serve as a model for the study of slavery, at least in its economic and demographic aspects, in southern as well as in northern cities.

—

E. Merton Coulter

Slavery and Freedom in Athens, Georgia, 1860 - 66

"Slavery and Freedom in Athens, Georgia, 1860–66," is a frequently amusing account of racial interaction in one of the older regions of the South. Coulter's attitude toward Athens's irascible blacks derives from the accounts of John H. Christy, editor of the *Southern Watchman*, whose jeremiads against youth and its lack of respect remind us that the strictures of an older generation against a younger one are not a recent phenomenon.

Coulter says that patterns of slavery varied throughout Georgia, and his description of Athens depicts one of many. A more complete historical analysis replete with demographic and economic information will tell us whether the patterns of racial interaction here and in the rest of the state varied in response to economic changes and fluctuations in the world market which produced agricultural diversification, biracial emigration, and industrialization, or whether differences in various parts of the state were merely sequences in a historically continuous pattern.

Since this article deals with the antebellum and postbellum periods, it is important to emphasize that what conservative Athenians like Christy considered rambunctiousness is merely one of several possible interpretations of slave behavior here. If Christy is correct, then a significant breakdown in the institution was underway before the war, which simply accelerated it. However, other factors more difficult to demonstrate but equally important should not be ignored. Among the most important of these are the forms of regional etiquette and status which constituted the South's unwritten patterns of social behavior, or more simply, its tradition.

The South's tradition was a combination of social patterns of the eighteenth-century patricians and those planters who through wealth or status deserved the title "gentlemen." With the exception of Louisiana and parts of Florida, these patterns were Anglo-Saxon and specifically English in origin. Clearly they are both historically and socially unrepresentative of the great majority of Southerners.

Reprinted with permission from the *Georgia Historical Quarterly*, XLIX (September, 1965), 264–293.

Nevertheless, as ideal types and social models they have received a great deal of attention. An extensive contemporary literature informed slaveholders of proper and responsible conduct. Those who mistreated their slaves often were themselves socially ostracized.

Though it was the slaveholding elite which formulated these canons and in whose support they functioned, they touched every member of southern society. For though the South's tradition was a function of class, at its core was status defined by race. Central to the South's social arrangements were the superiority of the white man and the inferiority of the black. Though the Negro slave was inferior to the poorest white, he was also more valuable and therefore less likely to be sacrificed to dangerous labor. This meant that, though the poor white might hate the slave for depriving him of work, he did not feel totally emasculated because of his poverty. Obviously it was in the interest of the slaveholding elite to keep the poor whites ignorant and impoverished. Otherwise they would have detected that the blacks were not their enemies but their most convenient allies, and the coherence in outlook necessary for class consciousness would have been established. Though there were isolated examples of just this tendency throughout the antebellum period, particularly where the slaveholding elite was most entrenched, it was not until well after the war, when agricultural depression worsened the lot of black and white farmers, that class action became a prominent part of southern political life.

Before the Civil War it was racial identification and the status which that lent to the poorest white which formed the basis of southern society. It is within this context that "Slavery and Freedom in Athens, Georgia" must be read. Editor Christy's strictures against boisterous slaves should not be misinterpreted to mean the collapse of the system. That would have involved the rearrangement of the class structure. Christy was a conservative moralist who understood that minor infractions could be tolerated as long as tradition did not impair racial status. A mode of racial control formulated by the South's ruling class, identification by race was more important than the difference between master and slave. It established the basis of a primary form of social organization, the community, withstood the South's military defeat, and survived the North's reconstruction policy. Durable though this mode of identification was, it was neither inflexible nor untouched by historical change. To what degree the passage of time altered it is a question which can only be answered by careful scrutiny of Athens, Georgia, throughout the entire antebellum era.

Slavery was a harsh-sounding word; but in Athens, Georgia, servitude was not as harsh as the word sounded, and, indeed, in Georgia as a whole, this lot of the colored man varied from hard labor to virtual freedom from it. Some of the laws relating to slavery were severe on their face; others guaranteed the slave protection against cruel punishment. In either case, the law might, and often did, operate as a dead letter, depending for enforcement on the attitude of the master or the sentiment in the community.

The slave, though a person, was still property, and being such, he could not own property. Anything the slave possessed belonged to his master; even a gift to a slave became the property of his master. A slave should not be taught to read or to write or to act as a clerk, whereby he might learn to do so. Nor could he work in a printing office in any capacity where reading and writing were necessary; but he might turn the crank on a printing press. It was against the law to sell to a slave writing paper or ink or any other writing materials for his own use. No white person might play cards or otherwise gamble with a slave. A slave might not work in a liquor shop where he would have access to strong drink; and no one might sell or give to a slave any spirituous liquors, except that a master might furnish his slave such beverages whenever he thought it would be to the benefit of the slave.[1]

Frequent references in the various laws relating to slavery (often referred to as the slave code) indicated how lightly slavery rested on some classes of Negroes, and in some cases on all Negroes. There were such expressions as these: "each negro or person of color nominally a slave," "nominal slave," and "nominal slaves, or slaves who have purchased themselves."[2] Now and then a slave might hire himself out to a person not his master, until he was legally prohibited from doing so without a permit from his master. And in 1850 a law was passed prohibiting a master from allowing his slaves to run around hunting someone to whom he might hire himself, unless he paid a fee of $100 for such a privilege.[3]

According to Georgia law the normal condition of a Negro was slavery, and therefore any Negro claiming to be a free person of color (often abbreviated fpc) must be able to prove himself to be so; and a Negro was defined as anyone with one-eighth Negro blood. This fact, of course, placed a severe handicap on such Negroes, and led unscrupulous white men to seize and sell such people as being slaves. A law passed in 1835 declared that since free persons of color were "liable to be taken and held fraudulently and illegally in a state of slavery, by

1. R. H. Clark, T. R. R. Cobb, and D. Irwin, *The Code of the State of Georgia* (Atlanta, 1861), 319, 877, 878, 879, 880, 881.

2. *Acts of the State of Georgia, 1849–50* (Milledgeville, 1850), 377; *Athens* (Ga.) *Southern Watchman*, July 6 (3, 3); December 6 (3, 4), 1864. The first number in the parentheses indicates the page; subsequent numbers indicate the columns.

3. *Georgia Acts, 1849–50*, p. 377; Clark *et al.*, *Code of Georgia*, 878.

wicked white men, and be secretly removed whenever an effort may be made to redress their grievances, so that due inquiry cannot be made into the circumstances of their detention and their right to freedom," it would now be the right and duty for the Justices of the Inferior Courts to take jurisdiction in such cases and make proper inquiry into the true facts.[4] And it became the duty of the Ordinary in every county to appoint guardians for all free persons of color who might reside in the county. As there was actually little distinction between a slave and a free person of color, except as to enforced labor, most laws relating to slaves applied also to the latter. Frequently the expression "free persons of color" would appear in the slave laws, and where not, it was to be assumed that the application was there unless by the nature of the law it would not be logical.[5]

In 1860 there were in Clarke County (Athens being the principal town, though not the county seat) 11,218 inhabitants. Of these, 5,539 were white, 5,660 were slaves, and 19 were free persons of color. Of the last-named Negroes, 13 were black and 6 were mulattoes. More than a third of the people in Clarke County lived in Athens, which had a total population of 3,848. Of these, 1,955 were white, 1,892 were slaves, and only one free person of color.[6] But these numbers were to be greatly changed during the war years, for there was a considerable increase of the slave population by planters allowing their servants to come to Athens, and very likely a majority of the free persons of color moved into Athens. Thus it appears that in 1860 Clarke County as a whole had more slaves than white people, but that Athens had a slight majority of whites.

Before the Civil War broke out, Athens had developed the reputation of being a sort of "nigger heaven," for the slave seemed to have had little hindrance from running around over town as he pleased, and war conditions were to greatly intensify this situation. Sometimes Athens slaves were referred to as "Free Slaves," as was the heading to a protest written by "Justice" for the Athens *Southern Watchman* (one of the two town newspapers) and published two years before the war. Said "Justice," "There are more free negroes manufactured and made virtually free in the town of Athens in two months, than there are bona fide free negroes in Clarke and any ten of the surrounding counties."

4. *Acts of the General Assembly of the State of Georgia . . . November and December, 1835* (Milledgeville, 1836), 101–103; Clark *et al., Code of Georgia*, 319.

5. Clark *et al., Code of Georgia*, 321, 322.

6. *Population of the United States in 1860; Eighth Census* (Washington, 1864), 58–59, 62–63, 66–67, 74.

And all of this came about by the very best citizens of the town hiring to their slaves their time and letting them run loose seeking employment—all against the state law and the ordinances of the town. But the Negro thus set free "in nine cases out of ten, idles away half his time, or gambles away what he does make, and then relies upon his ingenuity in stealing to meet the demands pay day inevitably brings forth, and this is the way in which our towns are converted into dens of rogues and thieves." If the laws could not be enforced, then, this indignant correspondent advocated their repeal "and let every one who suffers from the depradations from these drones upon the honest portion of the community, be prepared at all times, to free himself from their encroachments by a judicious use of powder and lead." [7]

The election of Abraham Lincoln as President of the United States in November, 1860, threw a chill of fear into the hearts of Athenians and of Georgians throughout the state. Negroes knew something about the meaning of Lincoln's election, and white people now felt that their slave population was ripe for abolition emissaries to stir up a servile insurrection. A week after the election a mass meeting was called in Athens, which resolved that an efficient police force be organized to patrol the town and that in addition there be organized volunteer policemen to patrol every ward in the town. It resolved also that the patrol system in the county, which had largely fallen into disuse, be brought to life, and that its activities be stepped up beyond what had been the custom when the system first had been inaugurated throughout Georgia. The most practical work of this mass meeting, extralegal to say the least, was to set up a detective force called a vigilance committee "to examine into all alleged attempts at insurrection among the slaves." [8]

As expressed by John H. Christy, the editor of the *Southern Watchman*, "Our object is not to spread needless alarm—far from it; but with the lights before us, we should be recreant to duty if we failed to warn the people everywhere to be on their guard."

"It is needless—indeed would be imprudent—to publish the facts on which we base our opinions; but they are of such a nature as to demand the exercise of prudent foresight in the prevention of any attempts at insubordination." Christy wanted it to be understood that the work of vigilance committees was not to terrorize the slave population, but on the contrary, "Humanity to the slaves, no less than the safety of the whites, demands the utmost vigilance." [9]

7. *Southern Watchman*, April 28 (2, 5), 1859.
8. *Athens* (Ga.) *Southern Banner*, November 15 (3, 3), 1860.
9. *Southern Watchman*, June 26 (2, 3), 1861.

The constituted authorities were not asleep to the supposed dangers. The grand jury of Clarke County in its presentments in 1861 recognized that there had been much "delinquency" in the patrols, and it warned them "to use great vigilance and care," to keep an eye on all strangers, and to watch over the movements of slaves.[10] The next year the grand jury observed that justices of the inferior courts, justices of the peace, "and others charged with the duty of trying slaves for misdemeanors and crimes" had been too lax in the performance of their tasks, and it recommended the appointment of "patrol commissioners" in the several militia districts, apparently either to engage in patrolling or to direct the work of those who already had been appointed.[11]

Athens had been incorporated as a town in 1806, and it was to be governed by three commissioners; [12] in 1815 the number was increased to five; [13] and seven years later two more were added.[14] In 1847 the government of the town was completely changed. Now an intendant (mayor) and wardens (councilmen) should rule over Athens. There were to be three divisions, called wards, with two wardens elected from each, except for Ward One, which should elect three. The intendant was elected by a city-wide vote.[15] The other town officials were a marshal, a deputy marshal, and a clerk for the city council, which had the right to pass ordinances not in conflict with state laws and the constitution. On the touchy subject of slave control, the commissioners back in 1831 had been given the right to pass all ordinances and rules "necessary for the government of slaves and free persons of color." [16] Under the rule of the intendant and council the intendant was given the power to try all cases involving the city ordinances and the "good order and peace" of the city.[17]

As the town grew larger more wards were added, and on special oc-

10. Minutes of the Superior Court, August, 1860, pp. 132–133. Manuscript ledger in Office of the Clerk of the Court, Athens, Clarke County.

11. *Southern Watchman*, February 19 (3, 5), 1862.

12. Augustin Smith Clayton, *A Compilation of the Laws of the State of Georgia, 1800, to the Year 1810, Inclusive* (Augusta, 1812), 329–330.

13. Lucius Q. C. Lamar, *A Compilation of the Laws of the State of Georgia, Since the year 1810 to 1819, Inclusive* (Augusta, 1821), 1006–1007.

14. William C. Dawson, *A Compilation of the Laws of the State of Georgia, Since the Year 1819 to the Year 1829, Inclusive* (Milledgeville, 1831), 442.

15. *Acts of the State of Georgia, 1847* (Milledgeville, 1848), 26–28.

16. *Acts of the General Assembly of the State of Georgia, November and December, 1831* (Milledgeville, 1832), 243.

17. *Acts of the General Assembly of the State of Georgia, November, December, January, February & March, 1855–56* (Milledgeville, 1856), 400–401.

casions additional marshals or policemen were provided. Starting out with modest boundaries, Athens in 1842 was extended two miles in every direction from point zero, which was the chapel on the campus of the state university.[18] (The university had been founded in 1801, and the town had grown up around it.) The town hall was the seat of government. It was a two-story building, with the city market on the first floor, flanked by the calaboose, and on the second floor were the town hall and offices.[19]

The services provided by the city were elementary, but sufficient for that day and generation and the attitude of mind of its citizens, who believed that the Lord helped those who helped themselves. The streets were lighted by gas lamps; and to take care of them there was a lamplighter appointed by the council, which generally awarded him a salary of $75 a year.[20] The streets were unpaved, of course, muddy in wet weather, and dusty in dry. To keep them in a passable condition, the city owned a mule, a cart, and a few necessary tools. To operate this establishment the council hired annually a slave from some citizen slaveowner, at a cost of $130—more, nearer the end of the war, when Confederate money became less valuable. In 1862 the council hired General Thomas R. R. Cobb's boy Joe "to work the streets, drive and take care of the town mule—he, the said Cobb, is to board and clothe said boy, and pay all physician's bills, if any."[21] Cobb was killed in December, 1862, at the Battle of Fredericksburg, but this boy Joe continued to work the streets in 1863, at least for a short time; but for most of this year a boy Lige was in charge of the mule and the streets. Boy Lige in January, 1865, was voted by the Council a reward of $50 "for his general faithfulness."[22] (It was customary to call any Negro "boy" who was not old enough and respectable enough to be dubbed affectionately "uncle.") As the city did not own a stable, it rented one for the mule, generally paying $12 annually.[23]

To protect the city against fires there was a volunteer fire department ("Hook and Ladder" company) to which the city made some small ap-

18. *Acts of the General Assembly of the State of Georgia, November and December, 1842* (Milledgeville, 1843), 97–97.

19. Augustus Longstreet Hull, *Annals of Athens, Georgia, 1801–1901* (Athens, 1906), 127.

20. *Southern Watchman*, January 23 (3, 5), 1861; January 22 (3, 3), 1862.

21. *Ibid.*, January 22 (3, 3), 1862.

22. *Ibid.*, January 11 (3, 3), 1865. See also *ibid.*, January 14 (3, 3), 1863; January 5 (3, 3), 1864.

23. *Ibid.*, January 22 (3, 3), 1862.

propriations. There being no water works during the war years, the city depended on cisterns privately owned and several which apparently the city owned—one being under Broad Street opposite the university campus. In those halcyon days of economy and simplicity, the total cost of the city government did not reach $5,000. The cost for 1863 was $4,200.[24]

Since there were few industries in Athens in which slaves might be employed, it was a problem for owners to find work for their slaves, and for the guardians of free persons of color to be responsible for their welfare. This was indeed a problem when it is remembered that there were almost 2,000 slaves in Athens in 1860. Of course, the great majority of them were used as household servants, yard boys, gardeners, carriage drivers, and in other capacities in keeping with city dwellers. For instance the Hull family, prominent in Athens from the beginning, subsisted four slave families on their lot. From these families the Hulls recruited a cook, a laundress, a nurse, a seamstress, a housemaid, a carriage driver, a gardener, and a few general utility hands. They had a plantation nearby which could absorb some of their city slaves.[25]

To take care of some of the surplus Athens slaves, the city council every year, in violation of their own ordinances and of state law according to the critics, allowed Athens slaveowners to pay a certain fee (generally referred to as a tax) and thereby let their slaves live away from the owners' lots. This dispensation also was allowed to the guardians of free persons of color. But any slave or free person of color who did not live on the lot of his owner or guardian and for whom the fee was not paid was required immediately to move beyond the city limits. It was the intention of the law that such persons must live on the lots of those who employed them, but evasions seem never to have been widely punished. Also it was possible for the employer, instead of the owner or guardian, to pay the fee. Naturally the guardian expected to be repaid, and so did the owner.

The fee varied with the individual slave or free person of color, depending on whether man or woman, on the ability of the person to perform labor (and hence on age), and with the progression of the war years. In 1861 Dr. Alonzo Church, former president of the University of Georgia, paid $10 each for his women slaves Caroline and Ann to live off his lot; and the council (or board, as it generally denominated itself) tolled off at its February meeting in addition the following

24. *Ibid.*, December 4 (3, 4), 1861; January 13 (3, 3), 1864.
25. Hull, *Annals of Athens*, 283–284.

free persons of color, and also . . . . the slaves living separate and apart from their owner's, employer's or guardian's lot . . . Isaac Walker, free person of color, $25; Willis Parks, free person of color, $25; T M Daniel's girl, Caroline, $10; Billy Nance, free boy of color, $25; Milledge Nance, free boy of color, $20; T F Cooper's girl, Arra, $25; D H Alexander's girl Matilda, $25; Jonas Cochran, free boy of color, $25; Dr H C Billups' old woman, Dalla, $5; J I Carlton's Caesar and wife, $10; R D B Taylor's old woman, Venis, $5; M E McWhorter's boy Jim and Wife, each, $15; M J Claney's girl, Julia, $10; J M Barnell's girl, Eve, $10; Athens Manufacturing Co.'s slaves, $50 [made cotton goods]; Wm M Morton's woman Dolla, $10; do do boy Jim, $20; George Morton, free boy of color, $25; L C Matthews' woman, $10.[26]

Thus, it is seen that the fees ran from $5 to $25. During the year a few other slaves and free persons of color were allowed to live off the lots of their owners or guardians,[27] making about thirty or forty all told.

The next year the fees per person were doubled;[28] for the year 1863 the fees for free persons of color amounted to $1,000;[29] in 1864 at least fifty-six slaves and free persons of color were allowed to live apart from owners and guardians, and the fees ran as high as $100 each.[30] During 1865 as long as the war lasted the dispensation was still going on, and the fees ranged as high as $500 per person.[31]

As this licensing system worked itself out, it set free to roam around over town with little hindrance from thirty to fifty or sixty slaves and free persons of color, looking for something to do for wages or to steal enough to pay their owners or guardians the license fees. Editor Christy made opposition to this system the recurring theme for editorials from the beginning of the war to its end. It was the cause of widespread thievery:

26. *Southern Watchman*, February 27 (3, 3), 1861; March 19 (3, 5), 1862; *Southern Banner*, September 18 (3, 4), 1861; *Proceedings* of City Council, II, 57. These minutes of the City Council are in the City Hall in Athens. Since these minutes were published in the two Athens newspapers, the newspaper source has been used in most cases as being much more accessible. Also there is a microfilm of the minutes in the University of Georgia Library.

27. *Southern Watchman*, March 13 (3, 5); April 17 (3, 5); July 17 (3, 6), 1861.

28. *Ibid.*, January 22 (3, 4), 1862. See also *ibid.*, February 5 (3, 3); April 2 (3, 4), 1862.

29. *Ibid.*, January 13 (3, 3), 1864. See also *Southern Banner*, February 18 (3, 5), 1863.

30. *Southern Watchman*, January 13 (3, 4); January 15 (3, 5); March 15 (3, 3), 1864.

31. *Ibid.*, January 25 (3, 4); February 8 (3, 4); April 12 (3, 4), 1865.

No man's property is secure so long as such numbers of lazy, rascally buck negroes are permitted to live off their master's premises.

We venture the opinion that there is not another community of the same extent in the Confederacy where there is so much petty thieving as in Athens. No wonder a member of the Legislature from this place said a few years ago that this town had been converted by the negroes into a 'den of thieves.' [32]

From every standpoint the system was bad. It was not only against the law, but also it had a bad effect on the other slave population which did not enjoy this liberty. "Everybody knows," he declared, "that negroes who are nominally slaves, but really free, will not work so long as they can find any thing to steal, and the dens established by the license system of the Council afford the best hiding places imaginable. The negroes are obliged to have something to eat—their inherent love of idleness prevents them from working, and stealing becomes a necessity." During the first half of the year 1864 Christy had lost through theft 100 pounds of bacon, beef worth $600, and two hogs worth $500 each— all because the city council allowed "a lot of worthless negroes the glorious liberty of violating the laws." It was high time that a stop be put to granting these indulgences. [33]

Christy would grant this much: "We do not say that these pets do all the stealing—but we do say that the whole system tends to encourage theft, insubordination and other crimes among our negroes—and everybody knows this to be true." [34]

As the year 1865 came in, the council again sold for a fee the right of Negroes to live off the lots of their owners, guardians, and employers; and Christy again attacked this group of lawmakers for violating their own laws and the laws of the state. As a final resort he offered this advice: "Let us petition for a repeal of the Town charter—let Athens become simply '216th District G. M.'—let the patrol laws of the state be enforced, and then let us see if buck negroes cannot be whipped back to their owner's or their hirer's lots." The council seemed to have been prevailed upon year after year in granting these indulgences, by Athens slaveowners who found some of their slaves a nuisance on their own lots, and by slaveowners out in the county who found that they could make more out of their slaves by sending them into Athens than they

---

32. *Ibid.*, January 13 (2, 1), 1864.

33. *Ibid.*, June 15 (3, 1), 1864. Christy said that Negroes could "be seen perambulating your streets all hours of the day. There are crowds of them idle, or doing such work as might be easily despensed with." He said there were 500 to 1,000 who could be spared for a year or so. *Ibid.*, November 4 (2, 2), 1863.

34. *Ibid.*, March 8 (2, 3), 1865.

could by leaving them on their plantations. White men could not violate a law of Athens with impunity, said Christy, yet a "gentleman or lady of 'de African scent' can buy an indulgence to violate it openly three hundred and sixty five days in succession at from ten to fifty dollars hitherto." At this time Christy explained it cost a little more because of inflation.[35]

Besides stealing, what other occupations were slaves and free persons of color engaging in? By now the "Four Horsemen of the Apocalypse" were appearing over the horizon of Athens—certainly at least three of them, before the end of the first year of the war—the variety that was to be a plague for the next four years, Speculation, Inflation, Scarcity. And slaves and free persons of color were to have places in the picture. Before the end of 1861 Editor Christy raised the spectre:

It seems that the people have determined to destroy one another. Everybody is raising the price of everything, because salt, coffee, and a few other articles happen to be high! We fear the end of all this will be terrible! These exhorbitant prices are already doing greater damage to the country than old Abe's army can ever do. Our people are ruining the country. We have no fear of the Federalists. Their armies may be driven from the field; but the greedy, rapacious bloodsuckers in our midst, shielding themselves behind the letter of the laws which they daily violate in spirit, are determined to pursue a course which leads to inevitable ruin. Can nothing arrest them? Public opinion cannot, because the great mass of our people being guilty of some sort of extortion, are ready to tolerate it in others.[36]

These off-the-lot Negroes found ready employment in buying and selling foods and other products of farms and gardens. P. E. Moore, one of the wardens, in a board meeting raised the cry against this evil as well as others besetting the town:

The general demoralization of the town, from the unrestrained excesses of youth, and the night brawls of riotous adults, having increased to such a degree as to be a subject of general remark, and the stealing, trading and trafficking between negroes and trifling white people have become such an intolerable burthen upon the middle classes in town, and the surrounding farmers, that it is the emperative duty of this Council, to use every lawful means in their power to put a stop to it.

He recommended that two policemen be employed to assist the marshal and his deputy in preserving order.[37]

In fact in November, 1861, the council had sought to curb this traf-

35. *Ibid.*, January 18 (2, 1–2), 1865.
36. *Ibid.*, December 11 (2, 5), 1861.
37. *Ibid.*, January 22 (3, 3), 1862.

ficking by Negroes, declaring that no slave or free person of color might purchase or sell within the town or outside any flour, meal, corn, oats, butter, lard, chickens, turkeys, ducks "or any other fowls," eggs, apples (dried or green), sweet potatoes, or yams. Anyone found guilty after a trial before the intendant should be fined $20 "or whipped or imprisoned." The fine should be paid by the owner or guardian, regardless of whether such person had given permission for such trafficking.[38] Later the council amended this ordinance by adding "peas, beef, pork, bacon, cotton yarn, wool, jeans, cloth, or any other article or thing, except such articles as are usually made by slaves and vended for their own use only." The fine was now raised to as much as $100, and anyone informing on such trafficking should be allowed half of the fine.[39]

Since much of the trafficking was being carried on at the instance of white traders and merchants, the council about this time made it a fine of from $10 to $300 for any such person to send slaves or free persons of color out into the town to drum up any kind of country produce; and the marshal was directed to "whip all such slaves, or free persons of color, found drumming in violation of this Ordinance."[40] If a Negro might not drum for a merchant or other trader, then might he not set up a little business of his own? Apparently some were doing that, for near the end of 1863 the council forbade any "slave, nominal slave or free person of color" to keep any store or grocery or to act as a clerk in any such establishment belonging to his master, his guardian, or anyone else. Any white person permitting this activity should be fined from $20 to $100; slaves should be whipped, and free persons of color and nominal slaves might be imprisoned for not more than one month.[41] Also the council declared "that any white man engaged in buying or selling with a slave or free person of color, directly or indirectly, any beef, mutton, lamb, or any other article, at the market or in the town of Athens, be fined in a sum of not less than fifty dollars, to be collected as other fines."[42] This ordinance must not have been interpreted as forbidding free persons of color (at least) to buy from the keeper of the market or from merchants in the town; otherwise it is difficult to see how a free person of color could keep from starving to death, unless he lived by stealing.

Despite the very essence of the slave code that property could not

38. *Ibid.*, November 6 (3, 4), 1861.
39. *Ibid.*, April 8 (3, 3), 1863.
40. *Ibid.*, April 2 (3, 4), 1862.
41. *Ibid.*, October 7 (3, 4), 1863.
42. *Ibid.*, September 16 (3, 3), 1863.

own property, and therefore that a slave could not own anything, it seems that slaves acquired in some way vehicles and draught animals; and by so doing they came into competition with the white draymen of the town. At this time the Georgia Railroad (the only railroad reaching Athens) stopped on the east side of the Oconee River, not desiring to go to the expense of building a bridge and come closer to the heart of town. Therefore, quite a business grew up in hauling freight and passengers to and from the depot. To keep slaves and free persons of color from engaging in this activity, the council enacted an ordinance stating that any such person operating for his own use or account a dray drawn by one and not more than two mules, horses, "or other animals" should be fined $50 and given twenty lashes, unless permission had been granted by the intendant. If the dray were drawn by three or more animals, the fine should be $100 and thirty lashes.[43] This ordinance did not forbid Negroes from engaging in other transportation activities; but to discourage any hauling of freight or passengers in Athens, the council in January, 1865, declared that any slave or free person of color "owning horses, mules, wagons, hacks, buggies or any other vehicles" should be taxed $100 each for every animal, $50 each for every two-horse wagon and buggy, and $100 each for hacks and carriages.[44]

The many rules and town ordinances would make it appear that the Negro population was well controlled, but seeping through all these regulations was the fact that the Negroes largely had their own way, for there were few policemen to enforce the rules. After 9:00 P.M. no Negro was allowed on the streets unless he carried a pass; nevertheless, Negroes frequently might be found wandering around at almost any time of night. And of course Editor Christy, who carried the burden of complaining about conditions, had something to say on this subject, using this headline, "Are the juvenile 'Buck Niggers' to govern Athens?" He answered in this way:

As a voter and tax-payer, we want the question settled whether the respectable law-abiding tax-payers or the irresponsible juvenile negroes are to govern this town.

These little miscreants gather in bands at the street corners and elsewhere on Sundays, and by their loud laughing, singing and boisterous talking, annoy quiet citizens. We have laid this matter before the proper authorities—an attempt has been made to abate this nuisance —but the police force is so small and the territory so large, that while these sable juvenile riots are being suppressed in one locality, they are in full blast in another! Nor do these imps of Satan confine themselves

43. *Ibid.*, March 15 (3, 3), 1864.
44. *Ibid.*, January 25 (3, 4), 1865.

to noisy demonstrations in the street. They throw stones at hogs, cows and dogs, and even into the enclosures of quiet citizens, endangering the lives of their children.

Now, this nuisance can be very readily abated, without the interference of the police, if the owners of these juvenile savages will see that they don't leave their lots on Sunday, except to attend church or Sunday-school. Will not our good citizens try the experiment? [45]

Instead of complaining to the council as Christy often did in his editorials, Athenians soon began to take their woes to Christy. When the war was far along and most of the eligible citizens were in the Confederate army, Christy noted: "A very respectable lady asked us the other day if the few white men left here had determined to permit the negroes to do as they pleased in the streets—remarking, that she had been frequently compelled to walk around crowds of these odorous gentry on the street corners, who showed no disposition to make way for her." [46]

Christmas times were especially vociferous occasions for the Negroes; a few extra policemen might be hired, and on other occasions as many as seven helped to patrol the town.[47] The Christmas of 1862 passed off quietly, but the " 'servile descendants of Ham' were, however, rather numerous for a day or two. It rained all day Saturday and this was a damper on the spirits of Sambo and Dinah." [48]

Negroes, like white boys, went swimming in the Oconee River; but neither blacks nor whites were allowed to swim in daytime in the river where it flowed through the main part of town (this being in the pre-bathing-suit era) or in Trail Creek, a small water flowing into the Oconee in the middle of town. Violation of this ordinance carried a fine of $10 for whites, and the penalty for Negroes was twenty lashes.[49]

Negroes on Sundays were not permitted to hire any horse, buggy, carriage, hack, or other vehicle or to drive vehicles other than their owners' or guardians', and any Negro so bold as to do otherwise would subject himself to thirty-nine lashes and imprisonment in the guard house until called for by his owner or guardian. Any white person hiring a horse or vehicle to "or driving any slave or free person of color" on Sunday should be fined not less than $50.[50]

But to make up for the prohibition against enjoying themselves riding

45. *Ibid.*, June 5 (2, 1), 1861.
46. *Ibid.*, June 16 (3, 1), 1864.
47. *Ibid.*, February 11 (3, 4), 1863; April 6 (3, 4), 1864.
48. *Ibid.*, December 31 (2, 5), 1862.
49. *Ibid.*, June 15 (3, 5), 1864.
50. *Ibid.*, September 16 (3, 3), 1863.

around on Sundays, the Negroes seem to have taken advantage on week-days of the opportunity of riding down to the depot to see the Georgia Railroad train come in and to ride back up the hill. Christy was indignant at this situation: "We are told that idle boys and buck negroes ride in vehicles from the depot, while wounded soldiers who have lost their limbs fighting for their country have to hobble over on crutches. We mention this thing thus plainly, not to offend any one, but simply to call attention to an evil which can be easily cured, and which, moreover, is a reproach to our town." [51]

Most of the Negroes in Athens were either Methodists or Baptists, with some Episcopalians (and all worshiping in their special ways). They had their own churches, with the exception of the Episcopalians, who used the town hall on "Sunday evenings" (probably meaning afternoons), conducted by white members.[52] The meeting nights for the Negroes were originally on Wednesdays; but in 1863 the council changed the time to Thursday nights.[53]

Negroes were allowed other forms of entertainment besides going to their funeral and burial exercises. In 1864 the Negro musician prodigy Blind Tom was brought by his master to Athens to give performances. After playing the piano to white audiences, in which, of course, no colored people were allowed, on his last appearance he performed "exclusively for servants"—no white people being allowed to attend.[54]

There were two serious disturbances in Athens in 1862 in which Negroes were the centers: one was a large gathering of them which might easily have led to a riot, and the other was a lynching. In January a group, estimated at fifty to a hundred, gathered and showed their great joy at the defeat of one of the candidates for the marshalship "by throwing up their caps and hurrahing at the very top of their lungs." Even without this demonstration their assembling was against the town ordinances and was "outrageous; but we further give it as our opinion [said Christy], for negroes to be suffered to assemble by hundreds to make a public demonstration of their approval or disapproval of the election of an officer, is not only wrong in itself, conducive to insolence and insurrection, but that they should be permitted to do so in behalf of an officer elected especially to control them is insufferable." And added to all this criticism, he said, was the fact that "liquor was bought by white

51. *Ibid.*, June 1 (2, 3), 1864.
52. *Ibid.*, January 14 (3, 3), 1863; Hull, *Annals of Athens*, 286.
53. *Southern Watchman*, March 18 (3, 4), 1863.
54. *Ibid.*, April 13 (2, 1), 1864; *Southern Banner*, April 20 (3, 5), 1864.

men, upon the occasion, and freely dispensed to the assembled negroes upon public streets." [55] It was strictly against town ordinances and state laws to allow Negroes to have liquor, and the grand jury of Clarke County had called attention to the fact that many persons had "been Trading & furnishing slaves with Spirituous Liquors and that too by a class of persons who exercise no salutary moral influence in the community, but on the contrary, corrupt and ruin our slave property and undermine the structure of all moral law." [56]

The council ordered an investigation, but no report ever was submitted; or if it was, it was not recorded in the minutes. Christy in his *Watchman*, however, called attention to the fact that about this time a group of slave musicians had given a concert in the town for the benefit of the Athens volunteers going to the Confederate Army, and he could not refrain from throwing out the question, "What do the invaders of our soil think of this?" [57]

The lynching took place about a mile from town. A slave was brought into Athens from a nearby plantation to be tried for an assault on the wife of the overseer. Justice of the Peace Kirkpatrick held a preliminary hearing and announced the verdict sentencing him to jail to await trial in the Superior Court. An enraged mob immediately seized the Negro and, placing a rope around his neck, led him down Broad Street and hanged him from a pine tree near the Georgia Railroad track. It was ascertained that the mob had feared that the owner of the slave might rescue him and sell him to someone where the crime was not known (the owner receiving no recompense for executed slave property), or that the court might delay the trial and make possible his escape. Christy, who had no prejudices favorable to Negroes, was prejudiced decidedly in favor of law and order, and admitting that "a negro guilty of the most revolting crime known to the law," as this one was, still should be tried and executed according to law. "There is no doubt about the justice of his punishment," said Christy, "but we are utterly opposed to the *manner* of his execution. There can be no rational liberty which is not regulated by law. A deep and abiding respect for, and a rigid enforcement of the laws of the land, are, therefore, the greatest safeguard of freedom." [58]

55. *Southern Watchman*, February 5 (3, 3), 1862.

56. Minutes of Superior Court, August, 1860, p. 51.

57. *Southern Watchman*, January 22 (3, 3), 1862. See also *ibid.*, January 8 (2, 4), 1862.

58. *Ibid.*, July 23 (2, 5), 1862; *Southern Banner*, July 23 (3, 1), 1862; Hull, *Annals of Athens*, 255–56.

Athens was not alone in Negroes seeming to take charge, for what happened in Athens was somewhat characteristic of many of the towns and cities of the Confederacy. Conditions in Richmond, the capital of the Confederacy, were worse than they were in Athens.

Negroes in Athens were not the only ones to create disturbances: white "Juvenile Depravity" burst forth now and then, as chronicled by Christy, the watchdog of Athens decorum:

> One day last week, some half dozen small boys, from ten to fourteen years of age, were committed to the calaboose for petty thieving and perhaps other misdemeanors. We are not surprised at this. Our only surprise is, that the number did not reach fifty! So long as parents permit little boys to spend their time in idleness, and more especially in the streets—so long as they teach them that taking fruit, watermelons, &c., is not stealing—so long as they permit them to pelt hogs, dogs and cows with rocks—to throw rocks and bricks into other people's enclosures—to pull down young shade trees along the sidewalks—to tear down handbills and pull pailings off fences—and the thousand and one acts of villiany they are in the daily habit of perpetrating, it need not be wondered at that occasionally half-a-dozen of them are bagged for stealing! We can furnish a list of from fifty to a hundred boys in this place [who] will go to the penitentiary within the next twenty years unless they are hanged sooner, or (what is not likely) unless their parents cause them to amend their ways.[59]

The conscience of the city council finally led to action. In July, 1863, it passed an ordinance declaring that any white boy throwing rocks or any other missiles "[through mischief or pastime] . . . at any other boy, negro or other thing" in the public streets should be fined from $1 to $10. And if the parent or guardian did not pay the fine, the boy should be lodged in the calaboose. Any Negro boy guilty of this offense should be whipped by the marshal "without being tried . . . not exceeding twenty stripes." [60]

The peace of Athens was to continue undisturbed throughout the war except for its local disorders. No enemy troops ever came nearer than a half-dozen miles, except as prisoners of war. In 1864 outriders of some of Sherman's cavalry brushed with Confederate troops in the vicinity and were badly crippled and some hundreds captured. They were brought through Athens on their way to the Andersonville prison and quartered on the university campus, near Phi Kappa Hall, and guarded by the "Thunderbolts." The main group of prisoners numbered about two

59. *Southern Watchman*, April 1 (3, 4), 1863.
60. *Ibid.*, July 8 (3, 4), 1863.

hundred, and for some days thereafter small groups of stragglers were brought through.[61]

Prisoners of war were not the only evidence that a war was going on, apart from high prices, scarcities, and local disorders. From the very beginning Athens had been a collecting point for volunteers throughout the surrounding country as well as providing all of her own able-bodied men. During the first two years of the war it was a familar sight to see companies marching through the streets, off for the war. Later the casualty lists came in to be published in the local newspapers, and many families were thrown into mourning. By 1864 one lady had lost her husband and three sons and a fourth was at home near death from the ravages of disease brought on by the rigors of army life.[62]

Refugees poured into Athens from invaded regions as far away as Mississippi, taking up all spare rooms in town and occupying the university dormitories, except for space allotted as a "Wayside Home" for soldiers passing through town. The university chapel was used for hospital purposes.[63]

Even so, Athens after three years of war had its dull spells, when no Negro boys were "whooping it up" on the streets and no white boys were throwing rocks at anything which moved, whether dog or hog or Negro boy. No one on horseback galloped headlong down any streets, for it had now been made illegal by the city council for anyone to do so unless he were a physician or going for one. Violation by a white person led to a fine of $15 and, if by a Negro, a whipping was in store for him.[64]

Editor Christy in early 1864 found nothing to complain about, and in a woebegone spirit wrote:

> Every thing has been so completely dried up by the war that we have not a syllable of local news—not a single incident worthy of a paragraph—this week. What is the matter? Will nothing happen to break the dull monotony? The boys have even abandoned their ancient amusement of running "stray dogs" down Broadway with tin-kettles appended to their caudal extremities. "Cat Alley" has dried up!—Cat Alley, which once could boast half-a-dozen *rows* per day. Even Cat Alley is quiet! Nothing disturbs the "solemn stillness" except now and

61. *Ibid.*, July–August, *passim*, September 14 (2, 1), 1864; Mary Ann Cobb, Athens, Ga., August 4, 1864, to Col. Wm. M. Browne (MS letter in possession of present writer). The "Thunderbolts" were a home guard of old and infirm men, who facetiously gave themselves this name.

62. *Ibid.*, May 18 (2, 1), 1864.

63. *Ibid.*, July 6 (2, 3); October 26 (2, 2), 1864; Hull, *Annals of Athens*, 295.

64. *Southern Watchman*, August 24 (3, 5), 1864.

then a rickety ox-cart whose unlubricated axels make melancholy music! Our great thoroughfare which once was crowded with country wagons laden with the rich products of a generous soil, is now bare and desolate—its stores closed—the noise of trade hushed—nothing to break the stillness, save now and then the voice of some descendants of Abraham "jewing" a country-woman, whose butter and eggs he considers too high at $3 per pound and $1.25 per dozen! [65]

The war was dragging out a slow course to its inevitable end—the destruction of the Confederacy. Ever since Gettysburg and Vicksburg, the two great tragedies for the Confederacy, both coming within the week of July 4, 1863, more and more people were realizing that the war was lost. But with some—and more than one might suspect—"the hope springs eternal" attitude of mind still dominated to the very last. The South could not lose, for Robert E. Lee was at the head of the Confederate armies. Despite the fact that news hardly could have been worse for the past six months, when it reached Athens on April 26, 1865, that Lee had surrendered two weeks earlier (April 9), it was considered incredible. But it was true, and Christy wrote, "Not a hero in that immortal band which composed the remnant of LEE's forces will ever be ashamed to acknowledge that he belonged to the 'Army of Northern Virginia.' " [66] Even a week later Christy had not regained his composure: "The writer is free to confess, that after an experience of twenty-five years in the newspaper business, he has never before been so completely   silenced—stunned—paralized—by   rapidly-occurring events. He knows not *what* to say." But he could say this: "Rumors are as plentiful as blackberries in July. Our exchanges are filled with rumors. The passengers on the cars bring hundreds of rumors. It is rumor! rumor! everywhere!" [67]

Very soon there was something more than rumors; the people of Athens would be confronted with some hard facts, now that the war was over. Returning soldiers passing through, and some equally needy whites and Negroes of the town seized the small Confederate commissary here and ransacked it.[68] Why should they not do so, rather than wait for invading Yankees to do it? And the waiting would not have been long, for by May 4 Brevet Brigadier-General William J. Palmer swept down out of the mountains of eastern Tennessee and western North Carolina, with the Fifteenth Pennsylvania Cavalry and other

65. *Ibid.*, January 27 (2, 1), 1864.
66. *Ibid.*, April 26 (2, 1), 1865; Hull, *Annals of Athens*, 297–298.
67. *Southern Watchman*, May 3 (2, 2), 1865.
68. Hull, *Annals of Athens*, 298; Athens *Weekly Banner-Watchman*, August 3 (1, 3), 1886.

troops, trying to cut off and capture Jefferson Davis in his flight south-ward. He marched down Milledge Avenue and took possession of the town. While he was asking Brevet Major-General Emory Upton at Augusta what he should do with the Athens armory, with its 250 workmen "(mustered into the Confederate service and having their arms concealed)," and what to do "with a large number of Confederate officers here, including several generals," [69] his men were out over town pillaging homes and robbing the citizens. One soldier saw Patrick H. Mell, one of the university professors, sitting on his porch. Spying Mell's watch chain, he asked him to come out, saying that he wanted to speak to him. When Mell appeared, the soldier pointed his gun at the professor's breast, demanding his watch. Mell in a firm and quiet manner replied: "You may shoot me, sir, but you shall never have any of my property if I can help it. I am defenseless so far as weapons are concerned, but I will not yield one inch to you, even though you murder me." The soldier suddenly grabbed Mell's watch and made off with it. Mell was able to recover it before Palmer left, by going to him and protesting.[70] The General, being more of a gentleman than his men, marched away a few days later without destroying the armory or interfering with the workmen or with any officers he found in town.

Palmer and his men had come "in suddenly and unexpectedly as if they had dropped from the clouds," and they "passed away gradually until not one" remained. But even before Palmer had come and after he had left there was excitement enough. Many paroled Confederate troops came through, including Basil Duke's Kentuckians and Tennesseans. "Fightin' Joe" Wheeler was not so fortunate; he came through as a prisoner. General William J. Hardee with his wagon train was in town for a day or two, and Admiral Raphael Semmes was seen riding down the street on horseback—but probably not as good a horseman as a seafighter.[71]

Most Athenians did not know that an important part of the Confederate archives had been kept in one of the classrooms of the university for a time, and that in the middle of June they were turned over to Brevet Major-General James H. Wilson, in command at Macon. These manuscripts were the journals and other records of the Provisional Congress

69. *The War of the Rebellion: A Compliation of the Official Records of the Union and Confederate Armies* (Washington, 1880–1901), Series I, Vol. XLIX, Pt. II, 615, 630; Hull, *Annals of Athens*, 299.

70. P. M. Mell, Jr., *Life of Patrick Hues Mell by His Son* (Louisville, Ky., 1895), 145–146.

71. *Southern Watchman*, May 17 (1, 1–2), 1865.

of the Confederate States, which were in the keeping of Howell Cobb, who had been the permanent president of that body. They were sent to Georgia, where copies were being made (since they were not to be printed), and they were in Atlanta when Sherman was on his invasion of the state. To keep them from being captured they were sent to various places, including points in Alabama and South Carolina. They were finally brought to Athens, where they must have been stored previously, for Howell Cobb's home was in this town. Whether for the purpose of being used in the trial of Jefferson Davis, who was now in prison, or for their preservation as important historical records, Cobb wisely turned them over to General Wilson, who sent them, with other Confederate archives which had been gathered up, to Washington in forty boxes.[72]

With deep regrets that the war had been lost and with the hard facts before them, there was nothing left for Athenians to do but submit with as much grace and sincerity as possible. Christy in his *Watchman* advised all to become reconciled and to obey the laws, adding, "We are aware that it is very difficult for human nature to forgive and forget such wrongs as have been inflicted upon us during this cruel war—it requires time to forget such things." [73] And a little later there was a mass meeting of citizens of the town and of Clarke and the surrounding counties, which might be considered their formal surrender. They recognized that the war was over, and they now submitted to the laws of the United States and its constitution "in good faith, as loyal and orderly citizens." [74]

Troops had been marching in and out of Athens since Lee's surrender, but no permanent occupying garrison had come until May 29, when Captain Alfred B. Cree of the 22nd Iowa Volunteers set up a provost marshal government, making his headquarters in Phi Kappa Hall, on the university campus, and instituting his "Watch on the Oconee." [75] Athens had been getting along governed by its intendant and council, with the last meeting of the council on June 3rd until it met again on September 3rd.[76] There had been no term of the Superior Court from the upset days of August, 1864, until February, 1866.[77] Whatever little civil

72. *Official Records of Union and Confederate Armies*, Ser. I, Vol. XLIX, Pt. II, 998, 999–1000, 1032–1033; Dallas D. Irvine, "The Fate of Confederate Archives," *American Historical Review*, XLIV (1938–39), 838–839; Hull, *Annals of Athens*, 307.

73. *Southern Watchman*, May 17 (1, 2), 1865.

74. *Ibid.*, June 28 (1, 4), 1865.

75. *Ibid.*, May 31 (1, 1); (2, 4), 1865.

76. *Ibid.*, September 13 (1, 3–4); November 8 (3, 1), 1865.

77. Minutes of Superior Court, 1864–68, pp. 22–26.

authority there was left did not clash with Cree's provost marshalship, for he was well received, since he had "urbane manners and polite and gentlemanly bearing." [78]

His duties were specifically to parole soldiers, to administer oaths of allegiance, to assist the civil government (but to be the final authority), to preserve order, and to set up whatever rules he deemed desirable. One of his first decrees was to order all paroled Confederate officers and soldiers not residents of the town to leave within twenty-four hours. Also anyone who was found wearing the Confederate uniform of an officer would be arrested and tried in the Provost Court; but anyone who could not procure civilian clothes might continue in his uniform if "all military buttons, trimmings or insignia of rank" were removed. Anyone having "fire-arms, powder and ammunition" was required to turn them over to the provost marshal.[79]

Captain Cree's urbanity caused him not to be looked upon with fear and trembling by the ordinary citizen or anyone else, and when he and his Iowans evacuated the town on June 19 there were those who were loath to see him go. He was succeeded by Major Euen and his command of the 156th New York Regiment.[80] By this time Athenians were becoming used to Yankee soldiers and seem not to have stood in awe of them or their officers. As a case in point, one day Major Euen drove up Broad Street in his buggy (which might seem unmilitary) and stopped for a moment to enter a store. Finding no hitching post, he remarked to a by-stander, "Watch my horse until I come out." A moment later a mischievous person clucked at the horse and started him off. When the Major came out and did not see his horse and buggy, he chided the man for not "watching his horse," and he got this answer in a slow drawl: "I did watch him until he went around the corner, and I couldn't see him anymore then." [81]

In October the guard again was changed in Athens. As Major Euen and his troops departed for the Georgia Railroad depot to entrain, they "presented a fine martial appearance marching down Broad Street, as they left." [82] Captain Beckwith and a part of the 13th Battalion of Connecticut Volunteers now took over the "Watch on the Oconee." Some of these troops endeared themselves to the Athenians by assisting in saving the town hall from burning, and to show its appreciation the coun-

78. *Southern Watchman*, June 7 (1, 3), 1865.
79. *Ibid.*, May 31 (2, 4), 1865. See also *ibid.* (1, 1), 1865.
80. *Ibid.*, June 21 (1, 1); 28 (1, 3), 1865.
81. Hull, *Annals of Athens*, 305–306.
82. *Southern Watchman*, October 25 (2, 1), 1865.

cil made a gift of $5 each to some of the soldiers and $2.50 to others.[83]

The military occupation of Athens, as such, came to an end before the year was out, when Lieutenant-Colonel H. B. Sprague of this Battalion on December 4 was appointed agent for the Freedmen's Bureau at this place.[84] Federal troops in Athens had not been considered a very great burden, and there was little friction between them and the townsmen, though on one occasion there was some shooting but no one was killed.[85] Still, when the military authorities asked the Athenians to participate in the celebration of the "Glorious Fourth," it was decided that it would be "inexpedient, in view of our recent humiliation, our great losses of property, and more especially of men, to attempt a celebration this year." [86]

Yet Athenians were not sorry to see Yankee troops march away, and the university was more than glad to get rid of the burden it had had to bear, for the troops had been quartered in the buildings on the campus, including the chapel, which was used for various purposes and was left in shambles, with the seats removed, rubbish scattered everywhere, and the columns in front chipped by bayonet jabs and the bullets from rifle practice.[87] On account of this occupation and for other reasons, perhaps, the university did not re-open after the war until January 3, 1866.

How had the Negroes worked into this picture of the war's ending and the military occupation; how had the white population come to regard slavery; and, indeed, how had the Negro himself come to regard it? As the war approached its end, it was pretty evident to all people who would stop to think that slavery was on its way out—it was only a matter of how abruptly it would end. Some whistled in the dark like the man passing through the graveyard; others like the ostrich buried their heads in the sands.

Lincoln's Preliminary Emancipation Proclamation of September 22, 1862, and his final one of January 1, 1863, created a furor among high Confederate officials in Richmond, but the man on the street paid little attention to it, and most slaves who heard about it did not get much excited. In Athens there was not a ripple. Yet some editors of Georgia newspapers by 1865 had begun to slant their thinking toward emancipation, which led unterrified Christy of the *Watchman* to say, "Five years ago the editor in Georgia who would have admitted into his columns an

83. *Proceedings* of City Council, II, 232.
84. *Southern Watchman*, December 13 (3, 2), 1865.
85. Hull, *Annals of Athens*, 306.
86. *Southern Watchman*, July 5 (1, 2), 1865.
87. Hull, *Annals of Athens*, 302.

article squinting toward the abolition of slavery, however remotely, would have been hung with a grapevine, or at the least 'tarred and feathered.' " [88] And after Lee's surrender he did not believe "that the Government or the people of the United States will attempt to reduce the 'rebellious states' to a colonial condition, or to force upon them the immediate emancipation of their slaves." [89] Disregarding entirely as of no effect Lincoln's Emancipation Proclamation, the city council even after the war had ended continued to charge a fee to Athenians for allowing their slaves to live off their lots.[90] They would wait to see whether the amendment then before the country, which would free the slaves, would be ratified. But General Q. A. Gilmore, with headquarters at Hilton Head, South Carolina, whose department embraced South Carolina, Georgia, and Florida, did not wait for the ratification of this amendment; on May 15 he announced "that the people of the black race are free citizens of the United States." [91] This was the first attempt to give effect in Athens to Lincoln's proclamation. In November (1865) Georgia wrote a new constitution for the state, and in it she abolished slavery. The next month the amendment (the Thirteenth) was declared ratified and to be a part of the U.S. Constitution, which legally put an end to slavery throughout the country.

Freeing the slave did not automatically make him equal to the white man either in intelligence or in his ability to assume all the obligations of citizenship. Of this fact Christy was very certain: "The different races of man, like different coins at a mint, were stamped at their true value by the Almighty in the beginning. No contact with each other—no amount of legislation or education—can convert the negro into a white man. Until that can be done—until you can take the kinks out of his wool and make his skull thinner—until all these things and abundantly more have been done, the negro cannot claim equality with the white race." [92] And if there was to be a meeting of the two races, it would have to be made in this fashion: "Although a negro cannot elevate himself to the white man's standards, a white man may very well lower himself to the negro level!" [93]

The slaves as they entered into their freedom were being given some good advice by all who wished to help them. General Gilmore, in an-

88. *Southern Watchman*, February (2, 5; 3; 1), 1865.
89. *Southern Watchman*, May 3 (2, 2), 1865.
90. *Ibid.*, May 24 (1, 2), 1865; *Proceedings* of City Council, II, 222.
91. *Southern Watchman*, May 31 (1, 3), 1865.
92. *Ibid.*, June 14 (1, 2), 1865.
93. *Ibid.*, June 21 (1, 1), 1865.

nouncing that slaves were free throughout his department, advised them to go to work and avoid idleness, and he firmly declared that neither "idleness nor vagrancy will be tolerated, and the government will not extend pecuniary aid to any persons, whether white or black, who are unwilling to help themselves." [94] And Christy in his *Watchman* seconded this program:

> Those who are able to work will now find it necessary to establish good characters for industry, sobriety, honesty and fidelity. When detected in his frequent delinquencies, Sambo will now have no "maussa" to step in between him and danger. The time has arrived when he must "tote his own skillet." This will be rather hard upon him at first, but when he gets used to it the thing may work better than most persons suppose. . . . Under the new system the planter will hire only such as are willing and able to work—and when we say work, we mean work in earnest, and not the half play and half work to which many of the slaves have been accustomed. That has "played out"—they will now have to work like white men.[95]

Many Athens freedmen found work with their former masters, but some despite all advice were determined to see if their freedom did not include freedom from work—and especially was this so for many who flocked into town from the surrounding country. When someone remarked to the cook in one of the Athens families, "Aunt Betty, don't you know you are free?" she quickly replied, "Mas' Henry ain't told me so yit." And Aunt Betty continued to cook for the family as long as she lived.[96]

Back in early May, when General Palmer had marched into Athens to stay for a few days, the country freedmen flocked into town in great numbers; but "as their reception was not altogether such as they had expected," they soon drifted back.[97] When a period of permanent occupation came with Captain Cree arriving with his troops, there was another hegira of freedmen from the country to town. The Captain took advantage of the situation to address the Negroes; he told them that loafing and idling around would do them no good, that they should go to work, and it would be best for them to work for their former masters, who knew best how to sympathize with them and their problems. If they did not work, they should not draw rations from the government. According to the *Watchman*, "This address had a salutary effect. Country negroes have been very scarce here since its delivery. We under-

94. *Ibid.*, May 31 (1, 3), 1865.
95. *Ibid.*, May 31 (1, 2), 1865.
96. Hull, *Annals of Athens*, 292.
97. *Southern Watchman*, May 17 (1, 1), 1865.

stand they were very much disappointed, and think their freedom don't amount to much. The negro idea of freedom at present is, immunity from labor, plenty to eat and wear, and a good hot fire!" [98]

It was too much to expect all Athens Negroes to take the advice that was being so freely offered to them. Almost daily threats were "uttered by negroes who, as slaves, were vile, worthless and unruly, and now, as 'freedmen,' have added largely to their former stock of impudence." The better class of Negroes was receiving the respect and sympathy of Athenians.[99] The juveniles who had given so much trouble during slave times were no better now. These "juvenile 'American citizens of de African scent' frequently amuse themselves in our most public thoroughfares by an indulgence in the most abominable, loud mouthed profanity"; so it was reported.[100]

Thievery was now as rampant, if not more so, than during the war: "Every thing—fruits and vegetables, cereals and livestock, money and provisions, all kinds of property, everything of value—is stolen from day to day." [101] During one week in early June, from 50 to 100 Negro thieves had been reported to Captain Cree, and it was estimated that from 1000 to 500 had not been reported. Cree's Provost Marshal government was doing all it could to stop thievery; and during one week 150 thieves were arrested.[102]

Captain Cree came and went, but thievery stayed for his successors to deal with. Various methods were used by the military authorities to contain it, but whipping, as a remnant of slavery, was not allowed. Maybe Negro thieves could be shamed out of their crimes. At least it was tried. Two Negro thieves were drummed out of town "for some *slight irregularities* in their behavior—both of them having taken a fancy to other people's horses." They suffered one side of their head to be clean shaven, "the wool on the other side left intact." They were then encased in barrels, with sleeve holes cut out for their arms, with these placards attached, "I am a horse-thief." A drum and fife corps led them down the street, playing the "rogue's march," accompanied by a detachment of soldiers, and "a hundred or so juvenile freedmen following constituted the 'guard of honor.' " [103] Another Negro who was caught stealing was escorted out of town by a drum and bayonet corps, with both sides of

98. *Ibid.*, June 7 (1, 3), 1865.
99. *Ibid.*, June 21 (1, 1), 1865.
100. *Ibid.*, June 5 (1, 1), 1865.
101. *Ibid.*, October 4 (2, 2), 1865.
102. *Ibid.*, June 14 (1, 1), 1865; Hull, *Annals of Athens*, 303.
103. *Southern Watchman*, August 30 (1, 1), 1865.

his head shaved clean "so as to leave a ridge of wool about an inch in width, extending from the *os frontis* to the *os occipitus*, and presenting the most ludicrus aspect." [104]

On rare occasions Negroes engaged in threats which might have led to bloody encounters with the law. In the summer of 1865 the military authorities in Athens gave the county sheriff permission to raise a posse to prevent a gang of Negroes from proceeding across a bridge at Princeton with a large supply of meat which they had got from slaughtering stolen animals. A clash took place in which thirty of the gang were arrested and the meat seized, but the thieves, assisted by other Negroes, broke loose and re-seized the meat.[105] Around Christmas time there was a big demand among the Negroes for firearms, which led to this question: "What do they want with them?" [106] To foil any incipient uprising, the city council authorized the employment of twenty extra policemen.[107]

Christmastime in 1865 was an anxious time for white people, because of rumors that had been going the rounds that the Negroes were to divide up among themselves the property of their former masters about the end of the year. By mid-summer rumors were being spread among the Negroes in Athens and the surrounding country that there was to be a free barbecue in town, that a great speech was to be made to them telling them about things, that there was to be a free distribution of land and other property; and their minds were being abused with other fantastic tales. As a remedy, it was suggested that the "scamps who get up such 'cock and bull stories' ought to be tied up by their thumbs a few days." [108] So it was that now and then Athens overflowed with country Negroes, which led to this observation: "Can any body tell where so many idle negroes come from? Like the frogs of Egypt, they seem to be every where and in every body's way." [109]

For the very laudable purposes of taking care of the destitute, the United States had set up the Freedmen's Bureau following the war. Brigadier General Davis Tilson, assistant commissioner, with headquarters at Augusta, in an order issued on October 3 warned Negroes that they must get jobs unless they were unable to do so or unable to work. He disabused their minds that there would be a distribution of land at

104. *Ibid.*, October 4 (2, 2), 1865.
105. *Ibid.*, July 12 (1, 1–2), 1865.
106. *Ibid.*, December 20 (2, 4), 1865.
107. *Ibid.*, December 20 (3, 1), 1865.
108. *Ibid.*, August 9 (1, 1); September 20 (1, 3), 1865.
109. *Ibid.*, July 26 (1, 1), 1865.

Christmas or at any other time. Country Negroes flocking to towns would not be allowed to stay unless they could support themselves by work or other honorable means. The Bureau was acting as a labor agency, listing all jobs available and taking the names of Negroes looking for work. Contracts between employers and their Negro workmen would be in writing, and all were expected to obey the terms of employment. General Tilson declared in his order that all should remember "that it is the chief object of the Bureau to do simple justice to all persons, white or black—to aid to the utmost in securing to the employer permanent and reliable labor; and in restoring the state to its former condition of peace and prosperity." [110] Lieutenant-Colonel Sprague, having being appointed the local Bureau agent for Athens two months later, reinforced General Tilson's order by announcing that all able-bodied freedmen "having no visible means of support" would not be allowed to go about in idleness, much less would they "be allowed to live by thieving." The Bureau always stood ready to find jobs for them.[111]

It took the Negroes a long time to learn what their freedom meant. Some of them never learned, but continued in a way of life that could have been in reality less satisfactory than the life they had led in servitude. True freedom was something which could not be given to them by law and decree, after all, it had to be earned. But for some generations thereafter designing men for their own ends and idealists to bring pleasure to themselves in thinking that they were doing good, were by their actions and advice indicating that responsibility and respectability need not be earned.

110. *Ibid.*, October 18 (2, 2–3), 1865.
111. *Ibid.*, December 13 (3, 2), 1865.

Robert C. Reinders

Slavery in New Orleans in the Decade before the Civil War

At all times slavery was an institution founded upon a contradiction. The slave was both chattel and human, an economic investment as well as a frequently beloved member of the family. This basic contradiction did not always occur as a result of the antagonism between each of these aspects of the peculiar institution. Sometimes affection for the dedicated slave prompted the master to allow him privileges well beyond the accepted protocol of southern society. At other times the economic prospects promised by hiring out talented slaves allowed them lives of semi-freedom.

Economic opportunity as well as economic diversification was most characteristic of urban life. Throughout the antebellum period the South's most vital urban center was New Orleans. Historians agree that the South's failure to urbanize is one of the fundamental reasons why its economic growth lagged behind the North's. They are far less unanimous about why the South did not urbanize. The following article may provide some answers.

The rapid growth of cities promised new outlets for slave labor which more enterprising and less traditional southern businessmen were quick to utilize. Economic opportunity for slaves meant additional profits for their masters. This group of masters and slaves helped erode the basic premise of the peculiar institution, which was to maintain and control an alien labor force. Their activities also inhibited the growth of an indigenous, skilled white labor force. White workers could not compete with slave labor, and many refused to work alongside blacks.

New Orleans is not typical of southern cities. What occurred there, however, may well indicate another dimension of the impasse Ulrich Bonnell Phillips described. The full utilization of Negro labor to achieve its maximum economic advantage subverted the stability of the regime and laid the bases for class and racial conflict. This is, of course, a far different problem from the one Phillips describes, where profit was sacrificed to stability and the affection

Reprinted with permission from *Mid-America*, XLIV, no. 4 (October, 1962), 211–221.

which existed between master and slave often inhibited the sale of surplus slaves. In either case, the contradictions of the system had begun to manifest themselves by the end of the antebellum period. The result of the South's commitment to slavery, if we may deduce from two so disparate cases, was to stifle its economic growth and to consign itself to a position of inferiority within the Union.

W ith the vast preponderance of slaves in the antebellum South residing on plantations, the existence and condition of slavery in urban centers has often been overlooked. There are relatively few studies of urban slavery, and most of these are either superficial or treat urban slavery only in passing.[1] Yet the variety of experiences available to the urban slave was infinitely wider than that afforded by the routine patterns of his plantation brother. The study of urban slavery assumes a greater significance when it is remembered that the prewar urban slave and the urban free Negro served during and after the Civil War as Negro leaders as well as formulators of Negro institutional patterns and socio-political goals.

There were two groups of slaves in New Orleans: slaves who were brought into the city and sold in slave auctions, and slaves who were owned by New Orleans residents.

As a slave-trading center New Orleans was the greatest in the South.[2] The bull market in slaves, which lasted all through the 1850's for the Southwest, made this one of the major "products from the interior" sold in the city.[3] Slaves were sold by auctioneers or by slave dealers. The former received a commission on the sale, while the latter generally purchased slaves in the upper South and transported them by sea, steamboat, or in overland coffles to the city.[4] If the slaves were from Loui-

1. See John Smith Kendall, "New Orleans 'Peculiar Institution,'" *Louisiana Historical Quarterly*, XXIII (July, 1940), 864–888; Werner A. Wegener, "Negro Slavery in New Orleans" (thesis, Tulane University, 1935); Ulrich Bonnell Phillips, "Slave Labor in the Charleston District," *Political Science Quarterly*, XXII (September, 1907), 416–439; Kenneth M. Stampp, *The Peculiar Institution: Slavery in the Ante-Bellum South* (New York, 1956), 60–67; Ulrich Bonnell Phillips, *Life and Labor in the Old South*, 2nd ed. (Boston, 1937), 216–217.

2. Frederic Bancroft, *Slave Trading in the Old South* (Baltimore, 1931), 315.

3. *Daily Picayune*, February 8, 1860. All newspapers cited in this article were published in New Orleans.

4. Charles H. Wesley, "Manifests of Slave Shipments along the Waterways, 1808–1864," *Journal of Negro History*, XXVII (April, 1942), 172–173. New Orleans was also a shipping port for slaves to Texas. Ship Manifests, (MS) Xavier University Library, New Orleans.

siana and spoke French, they would be designated "Creole Negro"; if
from the upper South, they would be advertised as "Virginia Negro" or
"American Negro."[5] There were also a smaller number of slaves
brought directly from Africa, smuggled into the Delta area and sold in
New Orleans.[6]

Slaves were kept in "jails" or "yards," that is, compounds open to
view for prospective buyers and containing quarters for the slaves.
There were at least twenty-five of these slave depots within a half mile
of the St. Charles Hotel, mostly on Gravier, Baronne, Magazine, and Es-
planade Streets. Sales were made at the depots or by bilingual auctioneers in the rotundas of the St. Charles and St. Louis Hotels.[7] There
was no disapprobation connected with being a slave auctioneer; indeed,
some, such as Joseph A. Beard, Julian Neville, C. F. Hatcher, Thomas
Foster, and N. Vignie, were community leaders.[8]

In the interest of the slave dealers, their charges were well fed and
well dressed. When up for sale they were attired in their "Sunday best."
Men wore good quality blue cloth suits, with vests, ties, white shirts,
well-shined shoes, and high beaver hats. Women were adorned in mul-
ti-colored calico dresses with bright silk bandanas.[9]

To the average traveler the slave jails and auctions were terrifying re-

5. See, for example, an advertisement in *Daily Picayune*, November 19, 1860.

6. Kendall, "New Orleans 'Peculiar Institution,' " 879; S. J. Peters to Capt. T. C.
Randolph, March 2, 1850; Thomas C. Porter to James Guthrie, February 25, 1857;
Franklin H. Clark to F. H. Hatch, May 5, 1857; F. H. Hatch to Howell Cobb,
March 12, 1859; P. E. Weldon to Lt. B. J. Kellsam, July 14, 1860, in "Excerpts
from Letter Books of the United States Custom House, New Orleans, Louisiana,
1834–1912," Women's and Professional Projects Division, Works Progress Administration, Survey of Federal Archives in Louisiana, Archives of the Howard-Tilton
Memorial Library, Tulane University, New Orleans; *Weekly Mirror*, May 14,
1859; Harvey Wish, "Revival of the African Slave Trade in the United States,
1856–1860," *Mississippi Valley Historical Review*, XXVII (March, 1941),
585–586.

7. Bancroft, *Slave Trading in the Old South*, 318–320; "New Orleans," *Chamber's Edinburgh Review*, n.s. XVIII (November 6, 1852), 314–315; Ebenezer Davies, *American Scenes and Christian Slavery: A Recent Tour of Four Thousand
Miles in the United States* (London, 1849), 57–58; Henry Ashworth, *A Tour in
the United States, Cuba, and Canada; a Course of Lectures Delivered befor the
Members of the Bolton Mechanics Institute* (London, n.d.), 81–82; Moritz Wagner and Carl Scherzer, *Reisen in Nordamerika in den Jähren und 1853* (Leip-
zig, 1854), 354.

8. Bancroft, *Slave Trading in the Old South*, 324–325.

9. "Slaves for Sale," *Illustrated London News*, XXXVII (April 6, 1861), 307;
"Slave Market of New Orleans," *Chamber's Edinburgh Review*, n.s. XVI (July 19,
1851), 47–48.

minders of the existence of slavery in the mid-nineteenth century.[10]
What is less well known was local criticism of the slave depots. One
newspaper reported:

> Scarcely anyone desires to pass such places; while to the ladies it is like
> running the gauntlet, to be exposed to the prying, peering gaze of
> lengthened lines of grinning negroes of both sexes ranked in Indian file;
> and who have nothing to occupy their attention stare 'out of counte-
> nance' with their very large and saucer eyes. . . . They hardly await the
> passing of persons before their extended lines, ere they commence mak-
> ing thir comments, and these eke out lengthened and amusing conversa-
> tion for each other.[11]

Aware of these nuisances, the city council passed an ordinance in
December, 1856, to control the slave marts. No future slave depot was
allowed in the city without common council approval. If the majority
of people in a four-block area of a slave depot protested its presence, the
mayor could force the removal of the depot. The depots had to meet
standards of health, cleanliness, and privacy. Negroes were not to be displayed on the streets or sidewalks in front of the slave pens.[12]

New Orleans was not merely a place for slave depots with transient
slaves and masters utilizing the city's auction and transportation services.
New Orleans was also an extensive slave-owning area in itself; in fact,
Orleans Parish was the third-highest slave-holding parish in the state. In
1850 there were 18,068 slaves in New Orleans, but by the next federal
census the total had dropped to 13,385. As in the free Negro population,
women outnumbered men—8,003 to 5,382. In contrast, however, to
the free Negroes, among slaves the number of blacks was significantly
higher than the number of mulattoes.[13]

10. See especially, Francis and Theresa Pulszky, *White, Red, Black, Sketches of
American Society in the United States during the Visit of Their Guests* (New
York, 1853), II, 96–97.

11. *Daily Orleanian,* January 20, 1852. See also "New Orleans by an American,"
Chamber's Edinburgh Review, n.s. XVIII (November 27, 1852), 342–344.

12. Ordinance 3148, December 17, 1856, in Common Council Ordinances and
Resolutions, 1856–66. This volume, and one for the period 1852–56, both found
in the City Hall Archives, New Orleans, are scrapbooks of clippings from newspapers of city ordinances and resolutions.

13. U.S. Census Office, Seventh Census, 1850, *Statistical View of the United
States . . . Being a Compendium of the Seventh Census,* by J. D. B. De Bow (Washington, 1854), 248; U.S. Census Office, Eighth Census, 1860, vol. [1]. *Population of
the United States in 1860; Compiled from the Original Returns of the Eighth Census, under the Direction of the Secretary of Interior,* by Joseph C. G. Kennedy,
(Washington, 1864), 195.

There were very few large slaveholders in New Orleans.

In 1860 there were in New Orleans 1,435 individuals who owned one slave each; 821 who owned two slaves each; 609 who owned three slaves each; 369 who owned four slaves each; 203 who owned six slaves each; and 128 who owned seven slaves each. After that the numbers in one column diminished sharply while they increased in the other. Thus there were but forty persons in the city who owned fifteen slaves each; three who owned forty each, and but two who counted one hundred slaves among their possessions. There was nobody who owned as much as two hundred slaves. The total of 14,484 slaves in New Orleans was distributed among 4,169 owners.[14]

As can be observed from above, holdings were small, with one-third of the slaveholders possessing only one slave, and half owning two or fewer.

The majority of slaveholders in New Orleans were whites. The exact figure of slaves owned by free people of color is unknown, but by 1860 it was probably somewhat lower than in 1830, when 749 free Negroes owned slaves.[15] Free Negroes customarily purchased relatives or close friends; because the conditions of manumission were often difficult to meet, and after 1857 impossible, the purchase of a slave would at least overcome the spirit of slavery if not the exact letter.[16] There were also free Negroes who purchased slaves as investments or as servants, and their relations toward these slaves probably did not differ vitally from those of whites toward their slaves.[17]

While the number of slaves declined in the city, the total assessed value increased from $3,852,700 in 1852 to $6,394,058 in 1859.[18] In this latter year slaves were valued at $585.90 each—far below the market price. An indication of the value of the slaves may be observed by comparing it to other taxable values in the city (1859).

14. Kendall, "New Orleans 'Peculiar Institution,'" 871. The census returns listed slaves held in depots as locally owned, so it is reasonable to assume that some of the large holdings listed above were not actually possessed by permanent residents of New Orleans.

15. Carter Woodson, *Free Negro Owners of Slaves in 1830, Together with Absentee Ownership of Slaves in the United States in 1830* (Washington, 1924), v.

16. *Ibid.;* Donald Edward Everett, "Free Persons of Color in New Orleans, 1803–1865" (dissertation, Tulane University, 1952), 209–210.

17. One free colored woman caused the death of her slave by overwork. *Daily Crescent,* April 22, 1858; *Daily Picayune,* May 8, 1858.

18. New Orleans Comptroller, *Report,* 1859 (New Orleans, 1859), 9, 11. After 1856 the city and state placed an assessed values on slaves aged 1–5 at $200, 5–10 at $300, 10–15 at $450, females 15–45 at $650, males 15–45 at $850, over 45 at $300. *Louisiana Acts,* 1856, 180 (No. 173).

Slaves	$ 6,394,085
Real estate	76,742,324
Income	4,420,000
Furniture	1,694,850
Horses, cows, carriages	1,155,930
Stocks in ships and corporations	788,825
Capital and money at interest	18,592,782
Total	$109,788,796

In other words, slaves provided one-eighteenth of the major property value in the city, and at the regular market prices the figure would be somewhat higher.[19]

Probably the major employment for slaves in the city was as house servants in the form of cooks, washerwomen, maids, valets, butlers, carriage drivers, hairdressers, gardeners, and general handymen. Slaves were also used by small businessmen as porters, laborers, and general unskilled workers. German and Irish immigrants occasionally invested in slaves to operate drays or hacks.[20]

There were several industries in New Orleans which were large employers of slaves, among which were the Leeds and the Amstrong foundries, the gas works, the Canal Banking Company, and several cotton presses.[21] The gasworks had a Negro compound with all facilities for the slaves' room and board. Even the overseer was a Negro slave.[22] It should be noted that an extensive use of slave labor in New Orleans industry never developed.

More commonly large slaveholders rented slaves to private individuals as servants or to various companies as laborers.[23] The cotton presses took large numbers every winter season, as did the steamboat lines for stevedores. One example of the slave rentier was Isaac Pipkin. He brought his slaves from Virginia to New Orleans, where he hired them out chiefly as levee workers, employing his nephew as overseer. After the elder Pipkin's death the nephew continued to employ the slaves in this manner.

19. Comptroller, *Report*, 1859, 11.

20. U.S. Eighth Census, 1860, manuscript returns of Schedule 2, "Slave inhabitants," for Orleans Parish (original in the National Archives, microfilm copy in the Library of the University of Texas).

21. These examples were found in the slave census of the First District. U.S. Eighth Census, 1860, manuscript returns of Schedule 2, "Slave Inhabitants," for Orleans Parish. The federal government also employed as many as seventeen slaves on construction of the customs house. *Daily Creole*, July 26, 1856; *Daily Picayune*, June 4, 1858; *Daily Crescent*, October 18, 1858.

22. Pulszky, *White, Red, Black*, II, 98.

23. Charges ranged from $20 to $25 a month. *Weekly Delta*, June 19, 1853.

He had twenty males, ten females, and nine children. By hiring an assistant overseer, collecting slave wages daily, and efficient management, T. J. Pipkin made a profit of $16,538 in two years.[24]

Like the free Negro in this decade, the slave saw his position become subject to more stringent legal bounds.[25] The state government declared that slaves accused of a capital crime in Orleans Parish were to be tried by a jury of six slaveholders.[26] The penalties for slave offenses were made stricter in 1855 and then even more elaborate in 1857.[27]

Various restrictions on the slaves' mobility were enacted during the decade. By state law slaves were not allowed out after 9 P.M., before dawn, or on Sunday. Even loitering in front of a tavern or a warehouse was a punishable crime.[28] City ordinances were more restrictive even than state laws. Along with free Negroes, slaves were not allowed either to congregate in numbers or to shoot fireworks. Slaves had to have the approval of the mayor for Sunday dances. They could not carry sticks or guns, could not ride in public vehicles without their master's approval, and could not play cards with whites or free people of color. They might not purchase any article over five dollars without written

24. *Succession of Isaac Pipkin—T. J. Pipkin, Executor on an Opposition, M. E. More et al.* (1852), 7 La., 617–620. According to census figures Pipkin had thirty slaves in 1860 (U.S. Eighth Census, 1860, manuscript returns of Schedule 2, "Slave Inhabitants," for Orleans Parish).

25. It should not be imagined that the courts were indifferent to the plight of the slaves. On one occasion the state supreme court requested district attorneys to be "humane" and represent slaves in cases of appeal. The State *v.* Henderson, a Slave (1858), 13 La., 489–494. In the case Eulalie and Her Children *v.* Long & Mabry (1854), 9 La., 9–11, the court protected a Negro woman and her family from illegal seizure, but insisted upon the principle that the "State has absolute control by its legislation over that class of persons. . . ." In Maille *v.* Blas (1860), 15 La., 100–102, the Supreme Court took the position that "Slaves not being devoid of reason, but having a will to control their actions, are not looked upon as inert matter which may sometimes be driven about by the elements, but as intelligent beings, who are responsible to the law for their unlawful acts." Less interested in abstract justice was the city official who once left a slave woman in jail for two years because the owner did not pay her fine. The common council then decided to sell the slave if the owner did not turn up in a few months. Resolution 1118, July 28, 1853, in Common Council Ordinances and Resolutions, 1852–56. Under a city ordinance of 1855 slaves and free Negroes who were arrested could be kept in prison and employed on public works almost indefinitely. Ordinance 2493, December 10, 1855, *ibid.*, 1852–56.

26. *Louisiana Acts*, 1855, 37–38 (No. 43).

27. *Ibid.*, 1855, 377–391 (No. 308); *ibid.*, 1857, 229–234 (No. 232).

28. *Ibid.*, 1857, 183–184 (No. 187).

permission from their master. And in addition to the above, the city fathers proclaimed: "All slaves are forbidden to quarrel, yell, curse or sing obscene songs, or in anywise disturb the public peace, or to gamble in the streets, roads or other public places, or on the levee." [29]

The slave who wished to escape his servitude had several recourses. The first and most obvious was by manumission. Since a slave in New Orleans could often earn money, the wherewithal for buying his freedom was not always lacking. There were also slaves who were freed in their masters' wills or by a personal act of some white or free Negro benefactor or relative.[30] Of sixty-four slaves brought before a New Orleans emancipation court between January 7, 1850, and August 28, 1851, sixteen were emancipated under the terms of estates (two of which had free Negro executors), thirty-three by requests brought by whites, and fifteen by free Negroes. In this same period manumission was denied in twenty cases.[31] Manumission was obtained also through a direct legislative enactment and through the instrumentality of a local branch of the American Colonization Society.[32] During the antebellum years 290 slaves were sent to Liberia from Louisiana under the auspices of this Society.[33] Of these, 121 had belonged to John McDonogh.[34]

As community prejudice against free Negroes increased, it became more difficult for slaves to be emancipated. By an act of 1852 manumis-

---

29. Resolution 500, December 18, 1852, in Common Council Ordinances and Resolutions, 1852–56; Ordinances 3203, January 7, 1857, *ibid.*, 1856–1866; Henry J. Leovy, comp., *The Laws and General Ordinances of the City of New Orleans Together with the Acts of the Legislature, Decisions of the Supreme Court, and Constitutional Provisions, Relating to the City Government, Revised and Digested, Pursuant to an Order of the Common Council* (New Orleans, 1857), 257–262.

30. Wills or legal statements allowing a slave emancipation at a future date created a group of *statu liberi* Negroes who remained under slavery but were governed by the code of the free Negro. Thomas Gibbs Morgan, ed., *Civil Code of Louisiana with the Statutory References to the Decisions of the Supreme Court of Louisiana to the Sixth Volume of Annual Reports* (New Orleans, 1861), 6.

31. New Orleans Emancipation Court, Docket of Cases, 1846–51, MS, New Orleans Public Library Archives. A study of manumission cases in the Third District between 1846 and 1851 revealed that 260 slaves were freed by 178 masters. Of the masters, 60 were free Negroes. Everett, "Free Persons of Color in New Orleans," 144.

32. Sterling C. Scott, "Aspects of the Liberian Colonization Movement in Louisiana" (thesis, Tulane University, 1952), 65. After John McDonogh's death in 1850 the militancy of the local branch appears to have dissipated.

33. *Forty-Third Annual Report of the American Colonization Society, with the Proceedings of the Board of Directors and of the Society, January 17, 1860* (Washington, 1860), 72.

34. Scott, "Aspects of the Liberian Colonization in Louisiana," 65.

sion was to be allowed only if the slave were to leave the country.[35] This act was repealed in 1855, and emancipation was allowed by a suit for freedom in the state courts. The appellate had to be of good character and have an unblemished past. If the court permitted the individual to remain in the state after manumission, he had to post a $1,000 bond that he would not become a public charge.[36] Finally, in 1857, in the shortest law on the statute books for the decade, the state closed the legal door of emancipation:"*Be it enacted by the Senate and House of Representatives* [*sic*] *of the State of Louisiana in General Assembly Convened,* That from and after the passage of this act no slave shall be emancipated in this state." [37] In almost equally terse manner the state supreme court upheld this law.[38]

A few New Orleans slaves attempted to escape their bondage by simply running away. The average runaway of course was uninterested in a thousand-mile trip to free territory. He probably intended merely to escape from some immediate task; or he preferred to live by his wits in the anonymity of the city. There were frequent notices in the police records of Negro runaways or of individuals harboring them.[39] But for a few Negroes at least freedom via the Underground Railroad beckoned. Cases of Northerners or free Negroes being arrested for enticing, secreting, or transporting slaves were common enough to indicate that New Orleans was a way-station for slaves seeking freedom. The *Picayune,* noting a case of two free Negro sailors who attempted to hide two slaves on board a ship, advised local police and slaveholders "to keep a bright look out for these colored cooks, stewards and crews of foreign vessels, who are but too often the instruments which abolition fanatics use to carry out their nefarious designs." [40]

35. *Weekly Delta,* July 25, 1852; Everett, "Free Persons of Color in New Orleans," 46–47.

36. *Louisiana Acts,* 1855, 371–390 (No. 308).

37. *Ibid.,* 1857, 55 (No. 69).

38. Delphine f.w.c. *v.* Mrs. Guillet, *et al.* (1857), 13 La., 248; Pelagie Brown f.m.c. *v.* Ursin Roby (1859), 14 La., 41.

39. According to lists of arrests published in the *Crescent,* there were between 40 and 80 runaways picked up monthly. The police often jailed Negroes who were not actual fugitives and claimed a $10 reward from the owner. Slaves wandering over into Jefferson Parish often faced arrest by reward-eager policemen. *Weekly Picayune,* June 2, 1856; entries for July 19, September 5, 1856, in Mayor's Office, Complaint Book, 1856–59, MS, New Orleans Public Library Archives.

40. *Weekly Picayune,* June 25, 1855. In July, 1858, two white men were arrested for trying to entice a gas company slave to flee to Canada (*Daily Crescent,* July 31, 1858). A month earlier a free Negro couple and a white man were caught attempting to smuggle a slave woman on board a steamer bound for Canada (*ibid.,*

A slave revolt was apparently suggested once in this decade. On June 14, 1853, a free Negro warned the police about an insurrection planned by local slaves. The police ignored the warning until they arrested a heavily armed slave. He declared that 2,500 city and country slaves, led by a white teacher from a free Negro school, were involved in a plot to attack New Orleans in three places. Rural slaves were to kill their masters and march on the city.[41] Always ready for such an emergency, a militia unit was called out and armed patrols were sent to arrest all slaves found on the streets. Twenty dazed Negroes were brought in and locked up.[42] The "revolt" turned out to be a "humbug," the product of the cerebral wanderings of an overly imaginative slave.[43] But the extent to which the fantastic cloak and dagger plot was believed indicated the fear prevalent in the city.

In practice the New Orleans slave was not always as restricted as the nature of slavery was thought to be. Negroes were often free to seek their own hire and even their own room and board; in return the master asked only a certain remuneration.[44] Slaves were often street or market peddlers or flower girls with little or no regulation over their conduct. Occasionally slaves served as prostitutes with the tacit knowledge or even the overt direction of the master.[45]

Laws to regulate the slaves were often unenforced. There were constant complaints of slaves congregating with free Negroes and whites. One newspaper deplored the fact that the corner of Perdido and Baronne was "continuously blocked up with a great number of impertinent negroes, mingled with the lowest class of white people male and female.

June 24, 1858). A few slaves attempted to escape alone. During the epidemic of 1853 several slaves, claiming to be servants, took up-river berths for the North (*Commercial Bulletin*, August 3, 1853). In another case a slave so light he could pass for white boarded a steamboat for the North and got as far as Memphis before he was apprehended (Samuel T. Williamson *v.* Alexander Norton, Master [1852], 7 La., 393–395). One slave sought freedom through the courts by bringing suit against her master on the grounds that she had resided in free territory (France). The court rejected her plea. Liza c.w. *v.* Dr. Puissant *et al.* (1852), 7 La., 80–83.

41. *Daily Crescent*, June 16, 1853; *Weekly Delta*, June 19, 1853.

42. *Daily Crescent*, June 17, 1853; *Weekly Delta*, June 19, 1853; *Propagateur Catholique*, June 18, 25, 1853.

43. *Daily Crescent*, June 17, 1853.

44. *Weekly Delta*, June 19, 1853; January 7, 1856; E. Boulin *v.* W. J. Maynard (1860), 15 La., 658–659.

45. *Daily Orleanian*, May 19, 1852; *Weekly Picayune*, July 9, 1855.

. . ." [46] Slaves gambled, drank, and went hunting, often with impunity —directly contrary to municipal and state laws.[47] Even the mysterious purlieu of the white woman's bedroom was not unknown to the male slave, as some elements at least of southern womanhood were willing to share their favors with Africa's sons.[48]

The slave was excluded, of course, from most of the community's social institutions. One of the few exceptions was the church. Most of the Protestant churches made some allowance for slaves either in special areas of the main church or in mission churches.[49] Slaves attended the African Methodist Episcopal churches in New Orleans from the church's formation in 1848 to its closing by city ordinance in 1858.[50] Ministers were free Negroes, but slaves were probably given some responsible church functions; one slave, Stephan Walter Rogers, who taught Sunday school, was the author of a book of religious meditations and Bible hymns.[51] The Roman Catholic Church did not sanction racial segregation within its churches or cemeteries, though separate religious fraternities were established.[52]

46. *Louisiana State Republican*, March 31, 1855. See also *Weekly Picayune*, December 24, 1855; *Daily Crescent*, March 22, 1858.

47. *Daily Orleanian*, January 15, 1852. In one evening the Second District police arrested 150 Negroes for illegal assemblage, drinking in cabarets, gambling, and blocking sidewalks (*Weekly Picayune*, December 8, 1856).

48. *Weekly Picayune*, June 18, July 23, August 27, 1855; *Daily Orleanian*, January 15, February 12, June 6, 1852.

49. Herman Cope Duncan, *The Diocese of Louisiana: Some of Its History, 1838–1888. Also Some of the History of Its Parishes and Missions, 1805–1888* (New Orleans, 1888), 59, 187; Charles F. Deems, *Annals of Southern Methodism for 1856* (Nashville, 1857), 221; *Semi-Weekly Creole*, October 27, 1855; Louis Voss, *Presbyterianism in New Orleans and Adjacent Points* (New Orleans, 1931), 85; W. E. Paxton, *A History of the Baptists of Louisiana from the Earliest Times to the Present* (St. Louis, 1888), 126. For a general view, see Robert C. Reinders, "The Churches and the Negro in New Orleans, 1850–1860," *Phylon: The Atlanta University Review of Race and Culture*, XXII (Fall, 1961), 241–248.

50. The African Methodist Episcopal Church *v.* The City of New Orleans (1860), 15 La., 441–447; Everett, "Free Persons of Color in New Orleans," 256.

51. Nathan Wiley, "Education of the Colored Population of Louisiana," *Harper's New Monthly Magazine*, XXXIII (July, 1866), 250.

52. Frederick Law Olmsted, *A Journey in the Seaboard Slave States* (New York, 1856), 582; T. L. Nichols, *Forty Years of American Life*, 2nd ed. (London, 1874), 130; Davies, *American Scenes and Christian Slavery*, 76–77; George Rose, *The Great Country; or, Impressions of America* (London, 1868), 191; John T. Gillard, *The Catholic Church and the American Negro* (Baltimore, 1929), 30–31; *Propagateur Catholique*, December 20, 1851.

There was no school system for slaves, but literate slaves were not unknown, as clandestine schools and private tutors offered the rudiments of learning to a handful of slaves. However, during the 1850's the number of educated slaves declined due to rigid enforcement of laws against such teaching and the difficulty of obtaining instructors who were willing to accept this pedagogical task.[53]

Though there is no source for the personal view of any slaves in New Orleans concerning their position, it can probably be concluded from their actions that they were, on the whole, contented; certainly the urban slave had more freedom and adventure than the plantation Negro. However, it might well be that the comparative tolerance the slave found in New Orleans only whetted his appetite for freedom. But in 1857 all possibility of freedom was legally ended by the state legislature. This could have produced an added resentment in the slave community toward the white society, which might account for the fact that the local slaves were more than unusually pleased to see the "Bluecoats" in 1862.[54]

53. Wiley, "Education of the Colored Population of Louisiana," 249.

54. James Parton, *General Butler in New Orleans, Being a History of the Administration of the Department of the Gulf in the Year 1862 with an Account of the Capture of New Orleans and a Sketch of the Previous Career of the General, Civil and Military* (New York, 1864), 73, 130–131.

William L. Richter

Slavery in Baton Rouge, 1820 - 60

Much changed in the South during the antebellum period. The older regions suffered serious soil erosion and a continuous loss of whites, who emigrated to the more fertile areas of Alabama, Mississippi, and Louisiana. Political power declined here, but political influence did not. The key to this curious situation is that deferential patterns existed long after the end of the specific economic arrangements which created them. The life style of the Old South during the Revolutionary period combined love of the land, paternalism toward slaves, and dedication to the principles of the Enlightenment. Of the three it was the last which changed most dramatically during the antebellum period and which signaled other more basic changes in the area's political economy. Nonetheless, the Old South remained the region's intellectual center though its ideas and social philosophy bore little relation to the social and economic organization of the New South. In a section noted for its absence of great thinkers or great universities, the Old South's intellectual activity contributed to its prestige.

We know that the patricians of the Old South viewed the nouveau riche planters of the New South with disdain, for they were frequently crude and unlettered men. The attitudes of the New South's planters were more complex. Though they aspired to be gentlemen, they bore a degree of anti-intellectualism typical of men whose power and status were determined largely by wealth. More important, however, the ambivalence of the New South's leaders toward those of the Old South lay in the knowledge that the future of the South rested in the hands of its planters and not its theoreticians. They recognized that the chief distinction between the Old South and the New was economic. The latter was prosperous; the former was not.

Both econometricians and economic historians have written about the commercial ties between the two regions. They argue that the Old South sold its surplus slaves to the New South. This argument merely underlines the real differences between the two regions. The new ones were able to employ their slaves and utilize their full market value, whereas the old ones could not. The older regions of the

Reprinted with permission from *Louisiana History*, X (Spring, 1969), 125–145.

South were also unable to compete qualitatively or quantitatively in
the production of the South's major staple, cotton. This inferiority
explains why economic diversification began in the Old South,
where soils had been most damaged by intensive one-crop agriculture. Insofar as "class" is an analytical term comprehensible only
within a well-defined system, economic diversification restructured
the Old South's traditional class arrangements. Economic diversification produced social dislocation and explains why the states least
likely to gain by secession became its most militant advocates.

The social attitude toward profit and economic activity is one of
the distinguishing factors between a pre-capitalist and a capitalist
society. Historians have long argued that continuous investment in
land and slaves was economically unwise, thwarted establishment of
manufacturing, and produced a dependence upon the North which
was not unobserved by Southerners themselves. Interest in manufacturing and freedom from northern merchants and bankers was far
stronger at the end of the antebellum period that at the beginning.
Recognition that these forms of economic activity were vital to
southern development indicates a significant difference in outlook
between the two periods. Agricultural diversification in the older
areas of the South confirms this change. Where hostility or perhaps
indifference to manufacturing did exist, it can be explained by the
extraordinary price of cotton during the 1850's.

One further indicator of this change in outlook, as well as the
difference between the Old and New South, is the behavior and attitude of the slaveholders themselves. The following article describes
slavery in Baton Rouge, Louisiana. A cursory glance will show that
Baton Rouge was neither an Athens, Georgia, nor a Charleston,
South Carolina. The impression one gains is of a far freer community, less stratified and more mobile. And since slaveholding was
evenly distributed, Baton Rouge was democratic, if by that term we
mean the equal access of all white members of the community to
the means of production, the slaves. Those enterprising Baton
Rouge merchants who sold liquor to slaves in their grog shops were
more interested in profit than in property, and whatever social scru-
ples they possessed seemed lost amid the rings of the cash register.

Our real understanding of the differences between the Old and
New South will come when we are able to compare not only urban
centers but also plantations. Nonetheless, Richter's article should
make the careful student of southern history ask if, amidst the political turmoil and the unending debate over slavery, we have erred in
assuming that slaveholding derived from and produced an identical
worldview.

In the middle 1830's, a traveler described the streets of the river towns
above New Orleans as "solitary" with "closed stores and deserted taverns" which added "to their loneliness." The river trip north was bor-

ing, with miles of cane fields, levees, and, most of all, monotonously flat land. When he saw the hills a hundred miles above New Orleans, they appeared to him "like an oasis in the desert." Located on those hills was the town of Baton Rouge, " a delightful residence," neat, well-built, of Spanish and French architecture, with streets parallel to the Mississippi River and forty feet above the water.[1]

Baton Rouge was founded about 1808, south of the United States fort on the bluffs.[2] The town was laid out in several sections named after the men who established them. Included were Gras, Duval, Leonard, Hickey-Duncan, Mather, and Beauregard towns, which were incorporated into Baton Rouge in 1817.

In 1837 the state penitentiary was completed east of Baton Rouge, and in 1849 the state capitol was moved to the city. The first bluff on the south end of Baton Rouge was donated to the state, and the new capitol was erected there. Admirers described the building as a "grand, gloomy, and peculiar . . . ancient castle" standing in "solitary majesty," with "stately minarets and towers." Mark Twain was perhaps more realistic in calling it a sham castle which epitomized the southern romanticism gleaned from the pages of Sir Walter Scott.[3]

For a state capital, Baton Rouge in 1860 was far from rich.[4] A cyclical economy rose and fell with the picking of cotton and cutting of cane. To alleviate the problem in part, Baton Rouge merchants concentrated on volume business in the peak periods. The achievement of this goal depended upon the road system on the east bank of the Mississippi and the envisioned Plank Road to Clinton to the north. To tap the west bank, the city sponsored the Baton Rouge and Grosse Tete Railroad in the 1850's. The railroad was designed to cut competition from Plaquemine and even Donaldsonville. The wharf at Baton Rouge was changed from the worst on the Mississippi to one of the best. The one problem

1. Joseph Holt Ingraham, *The Southwest* (New York, 1875), I, 251–252. J. W. Dorr, "A Tourist's Description of Louisiana, 1860," ed. Walter Prichard, *Louisiana Historical Quarterly*, XXI (October, 1938), 1133.

2. "Historical Collections of Louisiana: Baton Rouge—Its Past, Its Present, Its Future," *De Bow's Review*, XXVI (1859), 441. Alcée Fortier, *Louisiana: Comprising Sketches . . . In Cyclopedic Form* (Atlanta, 1909), I, 71, places a town on the bluffs in 1719. The hills had been fortified by several powers for many years. However, the town was not incorporated until 1817 (*ibid.*, 72), nor represented in the census until 1820.

3. C. P. Liter, "History of Baton Rouge," in Ellis A. Davis, ed., *The Historical Encyclopedia of Louisiana* (n.p., n.d.), I, 69; "Hist. Coll. of La.: Baton Rouge," 443; Samuel L. Clemens, *Life on the Mississippi* (New York, 1963), 195.

4. Dorr, "A Tourist's Description of Louisiana, 1860," 1133.

for the city merchants that was never completely solved was convincing the large planters that they should buy from Baton Rouge, because the majority of them bought directly from New Orleans and thus bypassed the local middleman.[5] In 1860 Baton Rouge was a typical medium-sized town in the South. Its 5,428 people, black and white, were "on the make"—eager to advance themselves and their town.

Negro slaves were an important minority of Baton Rouge's population. In total numbers, the slave population grew from 266 in 1820 to 1,247 in 1860.[6] The growth was steady, and lowed by the 1850's. Female chattels between the ages of twenty and fifty outnumbered bondsmen of the same ages after 1830, but after 1840 there were never over fifty-one more females than males of working age. The closeness of the figures for males and females was due to the demands of mechanics and industry for male slaves. Twenty percent of the slaves were mulatto in 1850. This figure rose to 29 percent in 1860.

The rise and fall of slave numbers in relation to the total population seemed to depend on the panic of 1837 and the increased numbers of whites who moved to the city in the 1850's. At the same time the increase in slave population tapered off because of the demand from the plantations, and because of the inability of townsmen to buy much more than one slave at a time. Most obvious, however, was the reshuffling of the existing slaves among increasing numbers of new slaveholders. Only 20 percent of the people owning slaves in 1850 can be found in the 1860 census. The number of new slaveholders rose in the 1850's faster than the number of slaves; the number of whites owning one slave doubled, whereas the number owning more than twenty chattels decreased by two-thirds. Such statistics indicate that there was an appreciable amount of mobility in the slave system.

5. Josephine G. Keller, "Early Roads in the Parishes of East and West Feliciana, and East Baton Rouge" (thesis, Louisiana State University, 1936); Frederick Stuart Allen, "A Social and Economic History of Baton Rouge, 1850–1860" (thesis, Louisiana State University, 1936), 6–9; Raleigh Anthony Suarez, Jr., "Rural Life in Louisiana, 1850–1860" (dissertation, Louisiana State University, 1954), 326, 332, 333, 346. For other sketches of Baton Rouge, see J. St. Clair Favrot, "Baton Rouge: The Historic Capitol of Louisiana," *Louisiana Historical Quarterly*, XII (October, 1929), 620–621; Muriel LeBrane Douglas, "Some Aspects of the Social History of Baton Rouge from 1830 to 1850" (thesis, Louisiana State University, 1955); and Milledge L. Bonham, Jr., "Baton Rouge's Municipal Centenary," *National Municipal Review* (1917), 502–504.

6. All the figures in this and the following paragraphs are based on the manuscript census of the United States taken between 1820 and 1860. All calculations were made by the author. See also the appendix, and below.

Although the percentage of slaves in the total population fluctuated in the antebellum years, the number of whites who owned slaves remained about one-third of the population after 1840. Ninety percent of the slaveholders held fewer than ten slaves; an average slaveholder owned five slaves. Only once, in 1850, did more than three persons hold more than twenty slaves. By 1860 two of the three had left town or died, two had sold half of their bondsmen, and two retained the same number of chattels. Almost all of the large slaveholders were "gentlemen" by occupation. Fifteen slaves were the property of free men of color in 1860, an increase of 50 percent from the 1830 figures. In only one case did it appear that a free colored slaveholder owned other than the members of his own family.[7]

Few Negroes were able to escape the toils of bondage in Baton Rouge, although there were several individual emancipations by benevolent masters.[8] Emancipation became more difficult, and in 1857 impossible to achieve, because of the beliefs of Southerners as to the true nature of the Negro. The attitude of white Baton Rouge was typical of the South. Baton Rouge citizens thought their chattels to be child-like, inherently inferior, incapable of living as free men, irresponsible, and in need of discipline.[9] Due to the proximity of the Sugar Islands, Louisianians were particularly sensitive to the Haitian revolt and British emancipation. Jamaica was a prime example of the maxim that to extinguish the civilizing force of slavery would cause the Negro to "relapse into the barbarism of his race." Negroes had been slaves since the beginning of time. The *Baton Rouge Gazette* pointed to the capture of black ant pupae by red ants as conclusive evidence that nature fitted any black species "for no other end than to fill the station of slavery."[10]

While burdened with a negative stereotype, slaves were very important to the economic life of the community. They provided a means of

---

7. Louise C. Lange had six slaves, twice the number owned by any other individual. She also had a free family listed, unlike the other colored slaveholders. The ages of the slaves were too varied for all of them to be her children, although they could have been fathered by her son.

8. For the laws, Elizabeth Ethel Kramer, "Slavery Legislation in Ante-Bellum Louisiana, 1803–1860" (thesis, Louisiana State University, 1944), 40, 124, 127. For emancipations, see *Baton Rouge Gazette*, September 29, October 27, November 10, 1827; January 26, 1828; Minute Book, Police Jury, East Baton Rouge Parish, No. 1, for the years 1848, 1849, 1851, 1852.

9. For the Sambo stereotype, see Stanley M. Elkins, *Slavery: A Problem in American Institutional and Intellectual Life* (New York, 1963), 82.

10. *Baton Rouge Gazette and Comet*, February 8, 14, 1858; *Baton Rouge Gazette*, April 18, 1840; November 12, 1842.

income for their owners in various ways, including sales, industrial work, hiring out, domestic services, and apprentice duties. Although there was no exact record, the sharp decline in demand for more male slaves in Baton Rouge during the decade of the 1850's, as well as the high prices in the surrounding parish for fieldhands, indicated a possibility of speculation in slave prices by the town dwellers. The 1860 census shows two men, a "trader" and a "speculator," with eleven and twelve slaves respectively. Neither of these men nor their occupations were listed in previous records. Bondsmen were being sold in the country for $1,800, and one "not likely" boy brought $1,600 on the block. Sales were so popular that the members of the state legislature were often missing from their seats. Projected prices by local authorities ranged from $2,000 to $2,500 for male chattels, causing widespread "negro fever." [11]

Despite the profits to be made in the sale of male slaves to the country, Baton Rouge developed an industrial demand for sawyers and foundrymen that seemed to offset some of the plantation demand. In fact, industry was attractive enough to cause Frederick Arbour to invest his money and thirty slaves in sawmilling. John Hill and William Markham had twenty-one slaves working in their foundry. In each case, slaves constituted over half of the workers in the industry.[12]

Slaveholders in Baton Rouge, as in other southern cities, hired out their slaves. The hiring-out system operated in two ways. Either the slave was bound over to another white, or the slave was allowed to hire his own time. In Baton Rouge there was no evidence of a central hiring place or use of identification badges.[13] In fact, the slaveholders probably would have rebelled against such laws. For example, one Louisiana law denied Negro slaves the right to hire their own time. The *Gazette* had called for its enforcement by the mayor, but when the mayor did enforce the law, the local populace brought pressure to bear, forcing a concession by the city government. The slave was allowed to hire his

11. *Gazette and Comet*, January 7, 1857; January 14, 1858.

12. *Manufactures of the United States in 1860* (Washington, 1865), 196. Arbour seems to have changed from farming in 1850, when he listed his occupation as "none."

13. The badges were licenses allowing the slave to be hired for work. See Richard C. Wade, *Slavery in the Cities: The South, 1820–1860* (New York, 1964), 40–54, for hiring. Also Clement Eaton, "Slave Hiring in the Upper South: A Step toward Freedom," *Mississippi Valley Historical Review*, XLVI (1959–60), 663–678. There were few hiring notices; see *Baton Rouge Gazette*, October 31, 1829; August 29, 1840; September 20, 1845; April 27, 1850; *Weekly Comet*, June 9, 1856. Request for a Negro to hire, *Gazette and Comet*, December, 1857, weekly.

own time for a one-week contract, but in all cases he had to have the master's written permission.[14]

Although hiring time was an important use of slave labor, most Baton Rougeans employed their own slaves in domestic or "apprentice" work.[15] Females were almost exclusively used in domestic work as cooks, maids, and nurses. Male slaves were most often general laborers or helpers for carpenters, bakers, butchers, painters, wagonmakers, or shoemakers.[16] When slaves were employed in other than menial tasks, they often met opposition in the form of law. Any shop that sold liquor was off limits to Negro clerks. Restaurants run by free men of color or slaves were closed as nuisances and gathering spots of potential trouble. Chattels were not permitted to sell any goods without written permission from their masters. The penalty was twenty-five lashes and forfeiture of the goods. The profits, however, must have balanced the risk of capture, for punishment and reiteration of the laws failed to stop the illicit trade.[17]

Although slaves were used in many skilled and menial tasks, the white mechanics of Baton Rouge felt little competition from them.[18] The major reason for lack of complaint may have been the fact that mechanics hired and owned large numbers of slaves. It was not uncommon for carpenters to employ from three to ten slaves. Instead of creating competition, the slaves actually enabled a white mechanic to handle more than one job at a time.[19] In this respect Baton Rouge differed from the larger cities in the South.[20]

14. For Louisiana laws, see Kramer, "Slavery Legislation," 77–78, 87. No hiring at all was permitted in the Florida parishes east of East Baton Rouge, probably due to white mechanics' opposition. Also *Baton Rouge Gazette*, September, 1841, and City Record Book "B," August 1, 1854, 174. Hiring out appeared to be popular with single, older women, many of whom owned large numbers of slaves.

15. At least 70 percent of the slaveholders had only one slave at each census.

16. Female slaves' occupations are evident in hiring ads; the male slaves' occupations from the trades of their masters listed in the census.

17. City Record Book "A," June 27, 1846; *ibid.*, "B," June 3, 1859, 346, and October 3, 1859, 372; Minute Book, Police Jury, East Baton Rouge Parish, No. 1, January 25, 1851, 128; *Weekly Comet*, February 22, 1853. The same problem existed throughout the South. Wade, *Slavery in the Cities*, 85–87, 146, 149–60.

18. Only one complaint of Negro competition came from the mechanics, and this came late in the antebellum period. *Gazette and Comet*, July 15, 1858.

19. This assessment is based on the lack of mechanic complaints from an active Mechanics Association, and the slaves owned by skilled laborers in the 1850 and 1860 censuses. However, this same situation in Charleston created trouble. William W. Freehling, *Prelude to Civil War* (New York, 1966), 41.

20. Wade, *Slavery in the Cities*, 273–275. Wade could be wrong in many of his

If slaves did not compete with the Baton Rouge mechanics, the skilled workers were far from happy because of the competition from the state penitentiary. Both black and white convicts were leased to a company which, in turn, had the right to hire out prisoners who were sentenced to hard labor.[21] The lessees, McHatton and Ward, made the prison into a profitable business venture in several ways. They had the prisoners working on their plantation, hiring out to various townsmen, operating the lessees' cotton and woolen factory, as well as operating the bagging and rope plant located on the penitentiary grounds. Twenty years of protest resulted only in closing the penitentiary store and ending the sale of prison goods in town establishments. From the investment of $4,000 for their lease, McHatton and Ward realized $7,000 profit in 1860 alone.[22] The alleged lowering of wages and prices was the mechanics' constant complaint against cheaper prison labor and goods.[23]

Contrary to the pattern found in large southern cities,[24] the free colored population was specifically exempted from the complaint against "Black Mechanics." The free men of color were a fair form of competition, for they too had "families to support and taxes to pay." [25] The reason for Baton Rouge's judicial attitude toward the free man of color was that he did not compete with the white mechanics in the town economy. The free colored worked as laborers and cigarmakers; by 1860 they had begun to take over the barbering trade. Another field open to them was that of managing Negro boarding houses.[26] The restrictions against the free Negro's operating groceries, restaurants, and grog shops

---

statements. For a critique of Wade, see Herman Charles Woessner III, "New Orleans, 1840–1860: A Study in Urban Slavery" (thesis, Louisiana State University, 1967), 3–17.

21. Kramer, "Slavery Legislation," 157.

22. *Baton Rouge Gazette*, January 4, 1845; March 13, 1852; "Statistical Collections of Louisiana," *De Bow's Review*, XII (1852), 25–26; *Manufactures of the United States in 1860*, 196.

23. For typical complaints, see *Baton Rouge Gazette*, April 11, 1840; March 5, 1842; March 8, 15, 1842; February 7, 1846; September 11, October 9, 1847; March 6, 1852; *Weekly Comet*, September 25, 1852. The mechanic population remained nearly static between 1850 and 1860, fluctuating from 251 to 235.

24. Wade, *Slavery in the Cities*, 250–251. The fact that Baton Rouge did not follow the southern pattern may be the reason why Charles Gayarre (Louisiana secretary of state, 1850) is quoted by Wade to believe the free Negroes are "sober and industrious mechanics, quite useful citizens who are susceptible of noble sentiments and virtues" (*ibid.*, 250).

25. *Baton Rouge Gazette*, July 15, 1858.

26. See U.S. Census for 1850 and 1860.

seemed more concerned with keeping liquor out of any Negro's hands than with overt job discrimination.[27]

The free colored persons were, however, only a small part of the Negro population of Baton Rouge. Their slave brethren constituted one-fourth of the total inhabitants of the town and were the subjects of a massive list of state and local laws. These laws required the slave to be mentally alert at all times so that he might not find himself in a compromising situation. For example, a slave had to use great care in suppressing emotion while around whites. The slightest word, quick movement of a hand or arm, or a wrong look could lead to chains, lashes, or even instant death from the offended townsman. Slaves were corrected occasionally for abusive language or actions; but the profanity and misbehavior of soldiers in town on leave from the fort created nearly as much concern.[28]

Insulting language was a trivial problem compared to the fear and potential destruction by fire in Baton Rouge. According to Kenneth Stampp, arson was believed to be one of the chattel's favorite devices for revenge,[29] but there was no overt suspicion of the slave population voiced during the fire outbreaks. Yet so great was the danger of fires to the town, and so common was their occurrence, that a $500 reward was posted for the arrest and conviction of arsonists. Shortly thereafter one Negro was arrested for firing the house of a white who had refused to allow "the boy" to stay with his bondswoman, but this appears to have been an isolated instance, after which there was no call for extra surveillance of the Negroes to prevent further incidents.[30]

Theft was often directly traceable to the colored population, even if fire was not. Negro slaves broke into stores at night, once robbed a white man in his hotel room, and often tried to break into houses. One loyal slave exchanged shots with two Negroes who were lurking in his mistress's back yard. A popular joke of the time was the conversation between two slaves over a new hat. When asked how much the prized article cost, the "owner" replied, "I don't know, *de shop keeper wasn't dar*." Any black was under suspicion. The town constable was in the habit of arresting colored persons on his "intuitive knowledge of their

27. Minute Book, Police Jury, East Baton Rouge Parish, January 13, 1857, 341.

28. *Baton Rouge Gazette*, August 30, 1845; December 5, 1846; July 10, 1847.

29. Kenneth M. Stampp, *The Peculiar Institution: Slavery in the Antebellum South* (New York, 1956), 127–128.

30. *Baton Rouge Gazette*, April 13, 1850; September 28, 1850. For the fire outbreaks see *ibid., passim*, 1840–1850. Cf. Freehling, *Prelude to Civil War*, 61.

intentions." Many of these arrests resulted in the return of stolen goods.[31] Of the fourteen court cases involving chattels between 1838 and 1842, eleven concerned theft—a fact which testified to the magnitude of the problem.[32]

Most crime, including arson and theft, occurred at night when the streets were deserted. To combat nightly lawbreakers Baton Rouge relied on an institution called the patrol. Established as early as 1822, the patrol had to be re-created seven times before 1860. Each time it failed to function correctly.[33] Public apathy was stifling. The only other local organization with less public support was the state militia.[34] In theory, the patrol was to serve from nine at night to five the next morning. More often than not, the patrols ended up in a local tavern after a few hours of work and later added to the revelry in the streets. In short, the Baton Rouge patrol was far from being "hated and feared" by anyone, black or white.[35] Reliance for protection from crime shifted instead to a system of street lights, which was set up in 1829. Twenty years later the lights were in general disrepair because no one had the responsibility for taking care of them.[36]

The lackadaisical attitude toward patrol responsibilities did not mean that slaves were not caught and punished. Although the records are scarce,[37] punishment for slave offenders was generally corporal, harsh,

31. *Baton Rouge Gazette,* May 9, November 21, 1829; November 19, 1842; *Weekly Morning Comet,* January 23, 1856; *Gazette and Comet,* August 19, 1857.

32. Parish Court, Record of Proceedings, March 26, 1838–October 6, 1842. Two cases concerned "vilint" language, and one murder. There was only one acquittal in fourteen cases.

33. City Record Book "A," October 29, 1839, 116; City Record Book "B," October 9, 1851, 31; August 1, 18, 1853, 126, 129; December 19, 1856, 251–253; *Gazette and Comet,* May 6, 1857.

34. *Baton Rouge Gazette,* June 7, 1828; City Record Book "A," October 29, 1839, 116; Parish Court, Record of Proceedings, March 26, 1838–October 6, 1842, for the militia cases.

35. Stampp, *Peculiar Institution,* 214–215, suggests that patrols were feared by slaves. This may have been so in some areas, but one could hardly fear an almost nonexistent institution like Baton Rouge's patrols.

36. *Baton Rouge Gazette,* November 28, 1829; *Gazette and Comet,* September 21, 1858.

37. The only trial records available at the East Baton Rouge Parish Courthouse were for a four-year period, 1838–42. A similar book found for the early 1850's had no Negro cases like the earlier one. It is possible a separate record was kept of Negro cases and has been lost or misplaced with the passage of time. It was only by a morning-long search through piles of mildewed volumes that the author found the 1838–42 records.

and thorough. The common penalty was twenty-five lashes and a fine to pay for court costs. If the master of a convicted slave did not pay the court costs, the slave could work off the debt at fifty cents per day. It is interesting to note that the jailer had an unlimited expense account for "cowhides." [38]

Punishment for the individual slave's crimes was determined by the slave courts.[39] Although only a brief record of court cases is available, these facts are evident. Out of nearly 800 cases over a four-year period, 45 concerned Negroes, but of those, only 14 concerned slaves. Also, both slaves and free colored received acquittals as well as convictions. Several tentative conclusions might evolve from this information. Either the slaves were punished more often privately by their masters than publicly by the state for criminal acts, or the chattels behaved well and stayed within the law.[40] Also, as poorly as they may have been staffed with legal minds, the slave courts did try to find justice rather than convict solely on the matter of race.[41] The idea that slaves were innately inferior and criminally inclined should no longer be accepted without reservations. But the opposite notion of the unjust southern white is no more satisfactory. In actuality, the truth lies somewhere in between.

Slaves convicted for lesser crimes and lodged in the parish jail were liable to employment on city and parish public works. If Public Works Commissioner G. N. Kent needed more than the seventeen slaves he owned and conveniently hired to the city, the vagrants in jail were available. At fifty cents credit per day to their fine (up to $150), vagrants became a popular and cheap source of labor for the town's board of se-

38. For typical punishments, see *Gazette and Comet*, December 14, 1858; Parish Court, Record of Proceedings, March 26, 1838–October 6, 1842, *passim*; City Record Book "A," July 29, 1847, 275, for the authority to work prisoners at fifty cents per day. Jailer's expense account, Minute Book, Police Jury, East Baton Rouge Parish, No. 1, special session, October 1856. Cf. Wade, *Slavery in the Cities*, 183–191.

39. See Kramer, "Slavery Legislation," 151–154, for the composition, conduct, and modifications of slave courts in Louisiana. Slaves sentenced to death or to life imprisonment were appraised, and the sum paid in equal proportion to the owner and the sufferer of the crime, or his heirs.

40. For the Negro's "innate" tendencies toward crime, see Ulrich Bonnell Phillips, *American Negro Slavery* (Baton Rouge, 1966), 454.

41. Stampp, *Peculiar Institution*, 234–237, for the "modern view." The present concern for civil rights has created as much prejudice as the older view of Negro inferiority. The elimination of white freeholders for the generally better educated planter in slave courts may have led to a more "reasonable" attempt at justice; see Clement Eaton, *Freedom-of-Thought Struggle in the Old South* (New York, 1964), 84, 86, 115.

lectmen. The jailer, J. J. Odum, averaged $60 a month for "state work."[42]

Interestingly enough, the slave population of Baton Rouge did not seem to fear jail as punishment. The jails had a reputation for good food, easier work hours than their usual jobs, and an inability to insure maximum security. A total of forty-nine slaves escaped from jail between 1828 and 1841. Authorities concluded that the problem was created by a wooden building which housed the jail. Better law officers and a new brick jail finally ended the rash of escapes.[43]

The large number of slaves in the Baton Rouge jail was traceable not to the lawlessness of the local colored population, but to the fact that Baton Rouge was the central holding pen for runaways in middle and east Louisiana.[44] Not only was the parish jail full of runaways, but the surrounding woods were full, too.[45] The anonymity of town life drew many runaways into Baton Rouge. In the city were food, friends, shelter. A smart slave could hide in relative comfort rather easily. One slave, who said he was from Franklin County, Mississippi, was found in the belfry of the Methodist Church. His hideout contained kitchen furniture, extra clothes, dried beef, a revolver, and a knife. The town felt there were, no doubt, "other runaways in the neighborhood, who take advantage of nighttime to prowl about town and commit depredations."[46] A bondswoman named Jane disappeared into the town's hideaways and was still at large two years later. Her master, a prominent citizen, believed she was receiving aid from unknown persons.[47]

Despite the large number of runaways lurking in and about town, the fear of an insurrection inside the town was negligible throughout the

42. City Record Book "A," March 2, 1843, 160; April 29, 1846, 244; July 29, 1847, 175; City Record Book "B," October 6, 1856, 247; August 3, 1858, 333; June 6, 1859, 362.

43. *Baton Rouge Gazette*, June 21, 28, September 20, 1828; October 31, December 31, 1829; April 11, August 1, December 5, 1840; February 27, 1841; June 6, 1846. Slaves feared jails in larger towns. Wade, *Slavery in the Cities*, 184.

44. The holding centers were New Orleans, Baton Rouge, and Alexandria. Later Shreveport, Opelousas, Plaquemine, and Covington were added to the list; see Kramer, "Slavery Legislation," 144.

45. *Baton Rouge Gazette*, August 22, 1840.

46. *Ibid.*, May 1, 1850.

47. *Ibid.*, October 15, 1842; May 18, June 15, 29, July 6, 20, 1844. Other examples of runaways hiding in Baton Rouge: *ibid.*, April 18, 1840; December 4, 1841; August 14, 1847; *Weekly Comet*, June 5, 1853. Runaways often left in cypress-cutting gangs, whose bosses were careless in checking freedom papers. *Baton Rouge Gazette*, May 31, 1828.

antebellum period. Partly because of the presence of the U.S. Army in the fort, Baton Rougeans felt rather safe. The real fear in their hearts was that an insurrection in the Felicianas might send a band of armed Negroes south on Plank Road. The town dwellers never expressed doubt of their servants and relied on the censorship laws and laws against slave education to keep their Negroes free from "evil" ideas; however, many masters taught their slaves to read and write anyway, and some learned by stealth.[48]

Although there were incidents that can be pointed to as criminal acts, more often the court reports in the newspapers mentioned "a dearth of interesting items in the Police Courts." [49] In 1857 the parish grand jury found only thirty-eight true bills; most of these were against whites for carrying concealed weapons.[50] A year earlier, the newspaper reported ninety-six cases, of which the entire Negro population could account for about half. Baton Rouge generally had few serious crimes.[51]

The law disobeyed most was the curfew. In response to complaints by citizens that Negroes "perambulate the streets freely at all hours of the night," the local officials passed a 9:00 curfew.[52] The signal was the ringing of the Catholic Church bell, or, in the event that the bell was not rung, the beating of tattoo at the fort. The penalty for violation of curfew was a night in jail, ten lashes for the slave, and a two-dollar fine for the slave's owner. In 1839, an amendment of the law provided for ringing the bell at noon, at eight every night, and at four in the afternoon on Sundays. Any town slave out after 8:00 bell received the usual penalty. Slaves not living in town who remained in the streets past four on Sunday received fifteen lashes.[53]

The law was exact and left no doubt as to intent. Seldom, however, was it enforced. It is probable that the bell was rung indiscriminately and that few people knew why it was rung. In 1858 one white man appealed to the local editor to inform the town of the purpose of the bell.

48. Kramer, "Slavery Legislation," 70–74; *Baton Rouge Gazette*, September 5, 19, October 31, November 4, 1840; July, 1841. Cf. Freehling, *Prelude to Civil War*, 64.

49. *Weekly Morning Comet*, November 26, 1856.

50. *Gazette and Comet*, November 20, December 11, 1857.

51. E.g., *Baton Rouge Gazette*, June 8, 1844; *Gazette and Comet*, January 8, 1857. The figure of half was arrived at by including "slaves punished" in the total. But this is unfair to the chattels, as many masters had slaves punished by the jailer for noncriminal acts. Wade, *Slavery in the Cities*, 94–95.

52. For the complaints, *Baton Rouge Gazette*, March 27, 1830; July 30, 1831. For the law, *ibid.*, August 27, 1831.

53. City Record Book "A," January 26, 1835, 39–40; November 20, 1839, 117.

He had heard it ring at eleven the night before and had thought a fire was in progress.[54]

Not only was the curfew haphazardly enforced, but also masters were not restrictive in their housing policy. No slave was to live in any house if a white or a free man of color was not living on the same lot to be responsible for the slave's actions. The penalty was the same as curfew violation. Landlords generally rented, however, to anyone who would pay, and slaves often lived without any supervision of their activities. The problem became so acute that in 1854 the law was amended. In addition to the night in jail, ten lashes, and a two-dollar fine, the new law provided for a ten- to twenty-five dollar fine of the landlord and the slave's master for allowing such offenses.[55]

The most scandalous of all housing code violations was cohabitation. This subject of "extreme delicacy" horrified all "right thinking" Southerners. "Is there anything more revolting to our notions of morality," inquired the *Weekly Comet*, than the "white men in this community who are openly living in public places with ebony colored members of a different race . . .?" The standard practice was to "hire" the slave woman at eight to ten dollars per month and to "force her to become his own wife" while the owner winked at the practice and acquired new wealth from the illegitimate children.[56]

In an attempt to test the *Comet's* story, the single white men living with Negro women were tabulated from the 1850 and 1860 censuses. In the 1850 census there are three cases of white men living with black or mulatto women, who had purely mulatto children. The 1860 census showed five such cases. In 1860 a Cecilia Barry was listed as a white woman from Italy. She had four mulatto children with her name. These cases are not conclusive. The Negro women could have been maids or could have been bought along with their children as a form of speculation. Cecilia Barry may have taken in four orphan children and given them her name. In any case, the practice apparently did exist, but it was extremely limited.

Although slavery was at times unjust and harsh, the town slave had many outlets for his spare time of which his country cousin could only

54. *Baton Rouge Gazette*, April 27, 1850; *Weekly Comet*, July 5, 1853; *Gazette and Comet*, June 11, 1858.

55. *Baton Rouge Gazette*, August 27, 1831; August 14, 1847, for examples of slave-renting contrary to law; City Record Book "B," July 3, 1854, 172–173. The constant reports of slaves visiting friends on their master's property leads one to the conclusion that the housing in Baton Rouge was not as restrictive after hours as Wade suggests. *Slavery in the Cities*, 62–75.

56. *Weekly Comet*, August 19, 1853.

dream. The availability of entertaining distractions did much to ameliorate the repressiveness of bondage and to make town slavery more benign. Technically, the law forbade any assemblage of slaves,[57] but as usual law and practice were far apart.

One of the most common of Negro gatherings was the "frolic," or slave dance. The Black Code of 1806, as well as the town ordinances of 1831, prohibited slave dances. Not only did the slaves ignore the laws, but their masters also encouraged infractions and brought pressure on the board of selectmen to change the law. Under the new city code in 1841 slave dances were permissible if the owner of the place in which the dance was to occur applied for a permit.[58]

Dances, like other slave gatherings, opened up the possibility for slave fights. A town ordinance ordered the immediate flogging on the spot of any slave caught in a fight, and the town constable rigidly enforced the measure. Many fights began as gambling arguments; consequently, to protect the slaveowner's investment from harm (knives were the slaves' favorite weapons), and to deter the temptation of a slave to steal in order to cover debts, the town prohibited gambling. Whites who encouraged Negro "games" were liable to a fine not exceeding $1,000 and one year in jail. The betting fever only increased, however, and reports of card games and of the rolling of ten-pins were common, especially near the steamboat landing.[59]

In addition to dancing and gambling, a Baton Rouge slave enjoyed showing off on Sunday afternoons by racing his master's horse down Third Street at a fast gallop. Negroes could not ride without permits, but the masters freely gave permission. By 1846 the Sunday exercises had become common enough to cause danger to pedestrians on the boardwalks. The town government cracked down on violators with hearty floggings. In a short burst of morality, the police jury even abolished track races on the course outside town in the fall of 1860.[60]

Of all diversions available to the slave population of Baton Rouge, the one that was most popular and caused the most trouble was drinking.

57. *Baton Rouge Gazette,* August 27, 1831.
58. Kramer, "Slavery Legislation," 78–79; City Record Book "A," February 27, 1841, 136; *Baton Rouge Gazette,* May 27, 1830; August 27, 1831.
59. For the numerous laws and incidents, see Kramer, "Slavery Legislation," 96; *Baton Rouge Gazette,* May 30, 1829; May 27, 1830; August 27, 1831; September 28, 1842; June 7, 1845; *Weekly Comet,* April 30, 1854; *Weekly Morning Comet,* August 29, 1856; *Gazette and Comet,* April 25, 1860.
60. Kramer, "Slavery Legislation," 52; *Baton Rouge Gazette,* July 4, 1840; City Record Book "A," April 20, 1846, 242; Minute Book, Police Jury, East Baton Rouge Parish, No. 1, September 4, 1860, 495.

The cries of innocence raised by the merchants matched the complaints by slaveowners; but the slaves were drunk on the streets, and often riotous, especially on weekends. One irate citizen reported that he saw a slave treat several Negroes at a local grog shop where the slave had a charge account. "It is really time to open our eyes to such abuses which ought not to be tolerated in an incorporated town," concluded another townsman. "Slaves are allowed here too much privilege." Two slaveholders offered ten dollars to anyone who would inform them where their slaves purchased liquor. The well-being of the chattels and the safety of their masters were said to be at stake.[61]

Again the law was explicit in the matter of dispensing liquor to slaves. Ignorance of the law or of the sale was *prima facie* evidence of guilt. Slaveowners had the right to sue in all cases; the state affixed penalties of up to $800 for offenders.[62] The strictness of the law and its high fine, however, caused juries not to convict. The parish police jury petitioned the legislature not only to lower the punishment, but also to dispense with jury trials.[63]

Both the city government and certain slaves tried to set a good example in restricting the use of liquor. The jail suspended its liquor ration to slave prisoners in 1839, and slaves organized at least two temperance societies. Unfortunately, the first of these societies believed in experiencing the evils caused by drink firsthand before abstaining and had to be abolished posthaste. An attempt by the police jury to make East Baton Rouge Parish dry failed in 1855.[64] The whites liked their liquor, too.

Naturally, after a week of gambling, hell-raising, and drinking, most slaves went to church on Sunday to expiate their sins. According to Wade, Negro churches were controversial in the South, for a separate church offered the slave another place to go free from direct white supervision.[65] There was no record, however, of distrust by the whites of

61. *Baton Rouge Gazette*, May 27, 1830; January 29, February 5, 12, 1842; October 10, 1846.

62. For a good summary of state liquor laws, see Kramer, "Slavery Legislation," 88–94.

63. Minute Book, Police Jury, East Baton Rouge Parish, No. 1, January 13, 1857, 157–158.

64. City Record Book "A," May 6, 1839, 111; *Baton Rouge Gazette*, September 21, 1842; *Daily Comet*, September 19, 1852; Minute Book, Police Jury, East Baton Rouge Parish, No. 1, January 11, 1855, 227.

65. See Wade, *Slavery in the Cities*, 271. It is possible that the coexistent religious organizations like schools, aid societies, and social groups had not yet had

Negro churches in Baton Rouge. Both races enthusiastically supported religious services, whether held jointly or separately by race. A majority of Baton Rougeans felt churches and preaching made their slaves "contented and happy" and would "ameliorate the moral condition of the colored population. . . ." Slaves and free colored were invited to attend white churches and encouraged to set up their own churches. In 1858 a colored church was established by the town government, on a petition from "many citizens." They engaged a Methodist free colored preacher, George Menard, to preach.[66] Although the townsmen condoned separate churches, they distrusted camp meetings, often led by Yankees, who slipped anti-slavery sentiments into their preaching.[67]

The ease of establishing colored churches in Baton Rouge underlined an obvious aspect of the town's "peculiar institution." Slavery in Baton Rouge was an informal system of restraint of one part of the town's population. The black code and the city ordinances were harsh and strict, but the custom and tradition of nonenforcement informalized and ameliorated the letter of the law.[68] The laws were, as Ulrich Bonnell Phillips put it, like pistols kept for an emergency, but "out of sight and out of mind in the daily routine of peaceful industry." [69]

In violation of the slave codes, Negroes roamed the streets, consumed large quantities of liquor, and lived away from their masters. When possible, masters exerted pressure to result in changes of the laws. One example was the revision of the dancing laws. When the laws could not be changed, people conveniently ignored them, as when a storekeeper sold liquor to slaves or bought from them goods that they had possibly stolen. The merchant considered only the color of one's money, not the color of one's skin.

When laws were violated and the culprits were apprehended, the master was apt to administer discipline on the spot. The small number of court cases available involving slave crime for the period also suggest the

time to develop the "independent society" complained about in larger cities. *Ibid.*, 160–172, 272–273.

66. *Baton Rouge Gazette*, May 15, 1847; *Weekly Comet*, May 28, 1853; City Record Book "B," February 1, 1858, 312. Menard's name was derived from the 1860 census manuscript. See also Douglas, "Social History of Baton Rouge from 1830 to 1850," 61–87; Allen, "Social and Economic History of Baton Rouge, 1850–1860," 41.

67. *Baton Rouge Gazette*, September 28, 1833; November 4, 21, 1840; January 9, 1841.

68. Eaton, *Freedom-of-Thought Struggle*, 115–116.

69. Phillips, *American Negro Slavery*, 484.

possibility that the slaves were well behaved. The slave courts in Baton Rouge were not necessarily summary institutions of the quick whip,[70] but were relatively fair in their application of the law. If slave courts decided on whim, they only reflected a problem brought on by the rise of the common man in the Jacksonian Era, when any jury decision was liable to be "decided by a throw of the dice" by illiterate jurors.[71]

One factor that may have been more than instrumental in assuring the slave a fair treatment in Baton Rouge was the lack of competition between skilled slaves and the white mechanics. Slaves and free men of color remained in the unskilled jobs classified as "nigger work." If a slave was skilled, he was an apprentice of a white mechanic. All of the free Negroes in Baton Rouge were unskilled day laborers, cigarmakers, barbers, or proprietors of colored rooming houses. The Negro thus provided needed services for the community by taking over occupations which whites did not want.

Baton Rouge, unlike larger southern cities, did not have a great discrepancy in the numbers of Negro males and females of working age.[72] After 1840 the number of male slaves and female slaves became approximately the same. The probable reason was the demand for male slaves by artisans and industry. Foundry work and sawmilling employed nearly fifty slaves by 1860. Most of this increase came during the decade of the 1850's, and, in spite of the high prices for fieldhands in the countryside around Baton Rouge, the male slave population remained stable in the town.

The close ratio between male and female slaves also affected the amount of overt miscegenation. Contrary to the picture drawn by Wade,[73] "amalgamation" was not more common in the city than on the plantation. Perhaps a small population that knew each other better was the explanation, or perhaps casual unions were kept secret from the prying newspapers. The increase in mulattoes in the 1850's was difficult to trace to miscegenation, and few open cases were apparent from the census or from editorial complaints.

While "amalgamation" was difficult to prove, so was its absolute counterpart, segregation. Surprisingly, there were few facilities in Baton Rouge for whites only. Segregation was an informal, and never a total, situation. Baton Rouge really had few facilities, such as street cars or

70. Stampp, *Peculiar Institution*, 221–227, draws an overly bleak picture of slave courts which the Baton Rouge records fail to bear out.
71. Eaton, *Freedom-of-Thought Struggle*, 84.
72. Wade, *Slavery in the Cities*, 120–121.
73. *Ibid.*, 122–124, 258–262.

public parks, to segregate in antebellum times. However, the slave and free man of color were not "expected" in taverns, restaurants, and theaters. Although the slave could not attend the local theater, he could always find some store owner who would allow him and his black friends to gather, play cards, drink, and enjoy themselves. Segregation was neither absolute nor extensive. In the case of housing, segregation was desired by the slaves to avoid white control.[74]

In Baton Rouge, the large slaveowners were corporations and industries, a fact which conforms to Wade's findings for the South's larger cities. Unlike Wade's cities, however, in absolute numbers Louisiana's capital had no loss of slaves by 1860. Slavery in the small and medium-sized towns, if it resembled slavery in Baton Rouge, could be described merely as a viable economic institution, growing with the town, and continually involving a stable one-third of the city's white breadwinners.[75]

74. *Ibid.*, 266–277. Wade finds segregation to be more extensive in the larger cities. Baton Rouge had no recorded attempts at "job busting" Negroes out of trades. Segregation was mostly informal and sanctioned by both parties as in housing.

75. This is a direct contradiction of *ibid.*, 21–23, 243–244. Wade dismisses the smaller towns too quickly to make the generalization, "there is no reason to believe they [small towns] would not have shared the same attrition [in slavery] as they expanded."

APPENDIX

I. POPULATION OF BATON ROUGE

Census year	White			Free colored		
	Male	Female	Total	Male	Female	Total
1820	384	361	745	1	5	6
1830	482	440	922	52	71	123
1840	860	651	1,511	75	104	179
1850	1,141	1,121	2,262	112	139	251
1860	2,009	1,684	3,693	257	231	488
Population increase						
1820/30	98	79	177	51	66	117
1830/40	378	211	589	23	33	56
1840/50	581	470	1,051	37	35	72
1850/60	868	563	1,431	145	92	237

I. Population of Baton Rouge (*Continued*)

Census year	Total free	Slave			Total free & slave	% of total population —slave
		Male	Female	Total		
1820	751	130	136	266	1,017	26
1830	1,045	166	244	410	1,455	28
1840	1,690	236	330	566	2,256	25
1850	2,513	528	514	1,042	3,555	29
1860	4,181	556	691	1,247	5,428	23
Population increase						
1820/30	294	36	108	144	438	
1830/40	645	70	86	156	801	
1840/50	1,123	292	184	476	1,599	
1850/60	1,668	28	177	205	1,873	

II. Slaveholders

	Slaveholding heads of families							Non-slave-holding heads of families
	Numbers of slaves held							
Census year	1	1–5	6–10	Total 1–10	11–15	16–20	21–up	Total
1820	13	34	4	38	3	2	1	44	46
1830	24	71	13	84	5	2	2	93	141
1840	23	88	26	114	5	0	2	121	238
1850	31	127	32	159	15	2	6	182	343
1860	66	184	47	231	20	6	3	260	529

	Slaveholding heads of families							% of total families holding slaves
	Percent of slaves held							
Census year	1	1–5	6–10	Total 1–10	11–15	16–20	21–up	
1820	30	77	9	86	7	5	2	49
1830 *	26	76	14	90	5	2	2	40
1840	19	73	21	94	4	0	2	34
1850	17	70	18	88	8	1	3	35
1860	25	71	18	89	8	2	1	33

* Total equals less than 100% due to rounding off of figures.

Terry L. Seip

Slaves and Free Negroes in Alexandria, 1850 - 60

Throughout the antebellum period all major southern cities, with the exception of New Orleans, declined both absolutely and relatively. The South's failure to sustain its urban centers is a complex phenomenon. For all Southerners regardless of class, the plantation remained a social ideal and propinquity to land a major determinant of status. A cursory glance at local records throughout the South shows that individuals in the professions and commerce almost always reinvested their capital in land and slaves. Equally important is the destructive effect of an urban environment on the stability of Negro slavery. The most careful study to date, Richard Wade's *Slavery in the Cities*, demonstrates that the institution underwent profound changes which affected racial interaction. Close contact between blacks and poor whites undermined the racial barriers which the slaveholding elite and its ideologues had so carefully constructed. Between middle-class whites in the skilled trades and equally skilled blacks whose masters hired them out, acrimony and conflict were frequent. Reluctance to labor with skilled slaves who worked for less than whites with comparable abilities was one of the chief reasons immigrants located in northern cities. Failure of the South to attract an equal number of immigrants hastened its political decline in the House of Representatives, where even the three-fifths clause of the Constitution could not mask its growing impotence.

The most astute of all southern politicians, John C. Calhoun, sensed the cumulative effect of these facts in the South's decline and urged southern independence to free the South of northern domination. Though Calhoun thought independence necessary to protect slavery in the South and the territories west of the Mississippi, historians have wondered whether this strategy was a correct one. Recent studies no longer ponder whether the institution needed to expand or die, but rather whether slave labor precluded economic diversification and growth. The most sophisticated of these works argue that slavery thwarted economic diversification, stifled agricultural innovation, and made urbanization impossible.

The region Seip describes differs from the cities of the South and

Reprinted with permission from *Louisiana History*, X (Spring, 1969), 147–165.

the older regions where soil erosion, an exodus of whites, and a surplus of blacks caused serious economic and social dislocation and
encouraged political demagoguery. Louisiana was very different
from other southern states. It alone had a sizeable Whig element
whose economic interests bound it to the Union. The vote for
secession was very close, and the election only superficially democratic. Most important, Louisiana (and particularly the area Seip describes) was less stable, more heterogeneous, and economically and
politically more diverse; the economic and social attitudes toward
slavery differed significantly from the older and less prosperous
areas of the South.

Insofar as size and economic diversification provide convenient
measurements, Alexandria was a town. But since this area of Louisiana was historically a young one, it is difficult to gauge whether
we are studying a stable phenomenon or a stage in the development
from town to city. Alexandria was part of the social and commercial relations which existed between town and plantation and therefore is comprehensible only as part of Rapides Parish. The absence
of antipathy between plantation and town signifies an important difference between this area and other parts of the South. Lack of friction, however, may simply mask dependence. Whether Alexandria
was capable of economic independence seems impossible to determine because of the paucity of source materials.

Scattered throughout the newer regions of the South are other
towns which in outline at least resemble Alexandria. Careful scrutiny of sources may allow us to construct a model of the antebellum
southern town. More information will also provide a more rigorous
definition of the difference between town and city and let us measure the extent of urbanization wherever it occurred. In turn we
shall then be able to ask more precise questions about these towns,
their effect upon Negro slavery, and their influence upon the economic development of the South. Lest these be thought separate and
unrelated questions, it should be emphasized that although slaveholding was a means of racial control and a model of social accomplishment, it was above all an economic venture. The New South
developed during an economic epoch distinctly different from that
of the Old South. Further information about towns like Alexandria
will demonstrate how great these differences were, and whether
slavery or the social attitudes toward it affected economic growth.

In dealing with American Negro slavery, historians have traditionally
emphasized the rural patterns of the institution, often neglecting the
small contingent of Negroes dwelling in southern towns and cities.[1] Re-

1. The general surveys of slavery by Ulrich Bonnell Phillips and Kenneth M.
Stampp and Joe Gray Taylor's *Negro Slavery in Louisiana* (Baton Rouge, 1963)
give only sketchy attention to the urban Negro. This neglect is understandable be-

cent studies of the institutional patterns of slavery in the large southern cities have indicated that urban bondage differed substantially from its rural counterpart. The ground-breaking work in this area appeared in 1964 with the publication of Richard C. Wade's *Slavery in the Cities: The South, 1820–1860.* Endeavoring "to find out what happened to slavery in an urban environment," Wade concluded that as a city grew, slavery grew; but that at some point the institution "began to lose ground in the metropolis, and though still present it played an increasingly less important role." [2] In other words, when the essentially rural institution was subjected to the urban environment, it proceeded through a cycle of easy growth followed by stagnation and eventual decline.

Wade confined his study of urban slavery to ten of the largest cities in the antebellum South on the assumption that in "small as well as large towns" slavery "was fundamentally the same wherever it existed, and that the similarities of urban life were more important to the institution than differences in settlement, region, or age." [3] The present study tests certain of Wade's general conclusions on the nature of urban slavery when applied to the institution in a small antebellum town.[4] Additional attention has been given to the status of free Negroes, a necessary element in any study of slavery. Too often the serious historian has either neglected to examine the characteristics of small-town slavery or has simply blended it into the rural system of slavery. Others have implied that the small-town institution was in a "pre-stage" of the developmental patterns which slavery followed in the larger city. A closer examination, however, suggests that, just as the small town varied in function from urban and rural areas, small-town slavery also deviated significantly

cause the South was predominantly rural. Stampp estimates that about 10 percent of the South's total slave population lived in cities and towns; *The Peculiar Institution* (New York, 1956), 31. C. Vann Woodward suggests that by 1860 only 2 percent of the total slave population were "involved in the urban experience"; *The Strange Career of Jim Crow* (New York, 1966), 17. The 1860 census schedules for Louisiana (at best, only a rough estimate) list approximately 8 percent of the state's slaves and about 70 percent of the state's free Negroes as living in cities and towns.

2. Richard C. Wade, *Slavery in the Cities: The South, 1820–1860* (New York, 1964), viii–ix, 26–27.

3. *Ibid.,* ix.

4. For the purposes of this paper, the "small town" ranged from a frontier village of a few inhabitants and fewer buildings to a thriving community of perhaps fifteen hundred. For an excellent description of small town life in antebellum Louisiana, see Raleigh Anthony Suarez, Jr., "Rural Life in Louisiana, 1850 to 1860" (dissertation, Louisiana State University, 1954), 326–398.

from both the rural and more highly urban patterns of the institution.

Neglect of this particular topic is largely due to an acute lack of adequate and relevant source material. A preliminary survey of several small antebellum towns revealed that most lacked available manuscript census returns or surviving newspapers. Nearly all had some deficiency in public records.[5] Obviously the best use of the available source material would be to draw a composite profile of slavery in several towns in which the resources of each supplement and complement the others. The scope of this paper, however, is limited to a sketch and a statistical profile of Alexandria's slave and free Negro population in the decade preceding the Civil War.

Alexandria is situated on the Red River in Rapides Parish near the geographic center of Louisiana. A series of rapids directly above the town constituted an impediment to river travel during the dry season that made the location the virtual head of navigation for at least six months of every year. Alexandria was laid out on this natural location sometime between 1805 and 1810 and received a charter from the state legislature in 1818.[6] From its founding, the town functioned as the seat of justice for Rapides Parish. According to one estimate pine hills and pine flats covered at least five-sixths of the land in the antebellum parish, with the remaining one-sixth located in the alluvial valley of the Red River and its tributaries.[7] The parish economy was almost evenly divided between the production of cotton and of sugarcane in the late antebellum period. By 1860 Rapides ranked sixth among Louisiana parishes in the production of sugar and fourth in the production of cotton. As one of the largest parishes, it ranked first in total number of landholdings (841), sixth in total number of free families without land (952), and first in total number of slave inhabitants (15,358).[8] The slave population,

5. As a case in point, a fire which gutted Alexandria when the occupying Union Army left in May, 1864, destroyed the courthouse records, newspaper files, and many private papers. For comment, see G. P. Whittington, "Rapides Parish, Louisiana: A History," *Louisiana Historical Quarterly*, XV (October, 1932), 567; XVIII (January, 1935), 22–39; and Sue Eakin and Joseph Logsdon, eds., *Twelve Years a Slave: Solomon Northup* (Baton Rouge, 1968), xvi, 75.

6. Whittington, "Rapides Parish," XVI, 437; Alcée Fortier, *Louisiana: Comprising Sketches . . . in Cyclopedic From* (n.p., 1914), I, 32; J. Fair Hardin, *Northwestern Louisiana: A History of the Watershed of the Red River, 1714–1937* (Louisville, Ky., and Shreveport, 1939), I, 421–429.

7. Whittington, "Rapides Parish," XV, 569.

8. Statistics are taken from Roger W. Shugg, *Origins of Class Struggle in Louisiana: A Social History of White Farmers and Laborers during Slavery and After, 1840–1875* (Baton Rouge, 1939), Table II, 317; Table V, 322. See also Wil-

however, had decreased from an extraordinary 74 percent of the total population in 1840 to 61 percent by 1860.[9]

A contemporary observer characterized Alexandria in 1860 as a well-built town of about 1,600 inhabitants with "a number of substantial brick stores and other buildings," including three hotels, one being new with steam heat, "water and gas in every room, bathrooms, etc."[10] Other facilities included a "well-conducted restaurant," a number of fine bar and billiard rooms, and a rosin gas works that distributed gas through the town "to those who wish[ed] it at ten dollars per thousand feet." The town also supported a sash and blind factory, a machine shop, an iron foundry, three churches, and a nearly completed courthouse. A big warehouse dominated the steamboat landing, and a horse railroad passed around the rapids. A railroad managed by a man who was a "bit hard on the public" ran to Bayou Boeuf. At that particular time a drought had stricken the town. Cisterns were going dry, and the "strong dry winds" made the dust and heat unbearable. The sun had baked the ground so hard "the wheels and horses' hoofs rattle[d] over it as if it were frozen ground."[11]

On the other hand, floods and other calamities periodically ravaged the town. A flood in 1823 had been especially hard on the town; as late as 1849, the river reportedly put Alexandria under five feet of water for "two or three months." An outbreak of yellow fever promptly followed each flood.[12] Fire consumed the business section and portions of the residential areas at least three times between 1848 and 1852.[13] Barring these calamities, however, the surrounding community was booming; and Alexandria, like other typical antebellum towns, existed to fulfill the de-

---

liam Edward Highsmith, "Social and Economic Conditions in Rapides Parish During Reconstruction" (thesis, Louisiana State University, 1947), 15–31.

9. Based on figures from the United States Sixth Census, 1840 (Washington, 1841), 260–261; and Joseph C. G. Kennedy, *Population of the United States in 1860* (Washington, 1864), 194.

10. Walter Prichard, ed., "A Tourist's Description of Louisiana in 1860," *Louisiana Historical Quarterly*, XXI (October, 1938), 1155. The tourist, J. W. Dorr, traveled through Louisiana as a reporter for the *New Orleans Crescent*.

11. *Ibid.*, 1156, 1157, 1153.

12. *Ibid.*, 1155. Alexandria was fully leveed during the 1850's, but this did not curtail the threat of yellow fever. Frederick Law Olmsted noted that Alexandria "contains, usually, about 1,000 inhabitants, but this summer [1853] has been entirely depopulated by yellow fever. Of 300 who remained, 120, we are told died." *A Journey Through Texas* (New York, 1857), 44.

13. Alexandria *Red River Republican*, October 21, 1848; June 10, 1850; August 28, 1852. Two "colored boys" received the editor's praise for saving a "square" of the town in the fire of 1850.

mands of the countryside. The black Alexandrian, slave and free, functioned as a part of the background for the scene of growth and prosperity in Alexandria during the 1850's.

TABLE I. WHITE, SLAVE, AND FREE COLORED POPULATION:
ALEXANDRIA AND RAPIDES PARISH, 1850–60 [14]

	Alexandria		Rapides Parish	
	1850	1860	1850	1860
Total population	588	1,425	16,561	25,360
White male	246	583	2,809	5,390
White female	148	397	2,228	4,321
White total	394	980	5,037	9,711
Percent of total population	67%	69%	30%	38%
Slave male	61	143	5,876	7,968
Slave female	107	171	5,464	7,390
Slave total	168	314	11,340	15,358
Percent of total population	29%	22%	69%	61%
Free colored male	9	55	78	128
Free colored female	17	76	106	163
Free colored total	26	131	184	291
Percent of total population	4%	9%	1%	1%

The first available population statistics for Alexandria list 588 inhabitants in 1850—a figure which more than doubled in the next decade. A comparative examination of the population schedules for 1850 and 1860 revealed that Alexandria's white population increased about 150 percent and the slave population increased 87 percent during the decade. Comparison of these figures to the population increase for the parish as a whole reveals several population trends. For example, the slave population increased at a rate only slightly higher than that for the par-

14. All population statistics in Table 1 and those cited in the tables and text hereafter have been compiled from U.S. Census Schedule I ("Free Inhabitants") and Schedule II ("Slave Inhabitants") for 1850 and for 1860 unless otherwise indicated. For printed returns see J. D. B. De Bow, *The Seventh Census of the United States: 1850* (Washington, 1853), 473–474; and Kennedy, *Population of the United States in 1860*, 194. Deviations from the official census count of slaves in Alexandria have been made in both 1850 and 1860. Two men in 1850 (M. Calhoun—42 slaves, and R. S. Smith—42 slaves) and three men in 1860 (S. K. Johnson—16 slaves, T. K. Smith—8 slaves, and R. S. Smith—12 slaves) were farmers living in Alexandria and had plantations outside the town limits. Therefore, their slaves have not been included in Alexandria's slave count for these respective years. The corrected figures in Table I form the basis for all computations and statistics used throughout this paper.

ish as a whole and significantly less than that for the white population in the parish as well as the town. The slower rate of growth in slave numbers on the parish level could have been the result of slave movement from the parish (a cause which seems unlikely at this time), a greater influx of whites, or a heavier mortality rate for the slaves [15] during the decade. The second and third explanations seem most probable.

The resulting proportional decline of slave numbers within Alexandria is more difficult to explain. Wade found that in most larger southern cities such a proportional decline forecast an absolute decline in slave numbers. According to his thesis, the institution in Alexandria would have been in a stage of stagnation at this time. It is debatable, however, whether slavery in Alexandria and other similar small towns fit into Wade's neat scheme of growth, stagnation, and decline in the larger cities. It appears more likely that the failure of Alexandria's slave population to keep pace with her expanding free population was attributable to the particular function of the small, quasi-frontier town.[16] The town's economy was still geared to serve as a marketplace, a shipping point for parish productions, and a center of goods and services of professional men and artisans—all for the benefit of the surrounding agrarian interests. One authority aptly referred to the towns in Rapides Parish as "merely community centers around which plantations clustered." [17] The close proximity of the undeveloped countryside dissipated incentive to

15. Brief references to birth and mortality rates for Rapides Parish can be found in De Bow, *Seventh Census*, 475; and the U.S. Eighth Census, 1860, "Social Statistics." In 1850, the census recorded 161 births for the white and free colored and 198 for the slave. The same table lists 45 deaths for the white and free colored and 235 for the slave. In 1860, 29 whites and free Negroes and 323 slaves died.

16. Numerous town brawls, shootings, and stabbings during the decade impart a frontier flavor to the town. A contemporary remarked that "people here are so excitable. . . . to be sure the people are bad enough for *anything*, but every one goes armed and any attempt of [robberies] would be met with certain death." Anonymous letter to Mrs. Sarah W. Simpson, February 10, 1851, in Miscellaneous file, Department of Archives and Manuscripts, Library, Louisiana State University, Baton Rouge. While nearby, Olmsted heard that in Alexandria "there was . . . much immorality without any morality at all." *A Journey into the Seaboard Slave States* (New York, 1956), 630.

17. Highsmith, "Social and Economic Conditions," 17. A glance at the newspapers of the period indicated how strongly the town catered to the needs of the planters and farmers. Advertisements offered the services of doctors, lawyers, blacksmiths, wheelwrights, butchers, tinners, and carpenters. The town had a wagon and plow shop, a machine shop, iron foundry, mill and gin builder, saddle and harness manufactory, and carriage maker. The merchants dealt in every type of Negro goods, and the druggists offered the latest remedies for illnesses.

initiate self-sustaining industry. The presence of virgin land offered any townsman slaveholder or potential slaveholder an opportunity to become involved in lucrative agricultural pursuits. Evidence indicates that many Alexandrians hoped to acquire sufficient capital and slaves to move into direct production of a staple crop. Perhaps the movement of master and bondsman in response to opportunities in the countryside better explains the proportional decline of Alexandrian slave numbers, rather than the decline being interpreted as an indication of institutional stagnation in the town. Certainly the close proximity of the rural areas adds a degree of complexity to any judgment, based on simple variation in slave numbers, which pertains to the future of the institution.

At both the beginning and the close of the decade, the census listed significantly more female than male slaves in Alexandria. The opposite was true for the parish as a whole. Wade found the same disparity in the larger cities of the South and concluded that the practice of urban slaveholders' selling their younger males to planters produced the preponderance of urban female slaves.[18] If Alexandrian slaveholders followed this policy, there should have been a conspicuous lack of male slaves of working age in the town. Such was not the case. In 1850, for example, the census recorded 36 percent of the aggregate slave population as males, and males constituted 37 percent of the aggregate slave population in selected working-age group (age 16 to 55). These figures suggest no proportional deficiency of working-age males. Ten years later males numbered 46 percent of the total slave population and 38 percent of the slave population in the working-age group, a slight proportional decrease in males of working age. An investigation of other age groups revealed that the percent disparity between the male and female slaves in varying age groups did not deviate significantly from the male-female ratio in the aggregate slave count. The percentage of male slaves and the percentage of female slaves in the working-age group were about equal in 1860. These stable percentages (varying from 53 to 56 percent) correspond to a like comparison at the parish level in 1850 and 1860.[19] A comparison of the percentage of aggregate slave population (disregarding sex) of working age in Alexandria with that of the parish yields a relatively stable set of figures, varying from 54 to 59 percent. In short, the evidence does not indicate any proportional deficiency of working-age males or any significant difference in the percentages of working-age slaves (regardless of sex) between Alexandria and the parish as a

18. Wade, *Slavery in the Cities*, 23.

19. In 1850, Alexandria's slave population deviated from these figures with 51 percent of the males and 63 percent of the females in the working-age group.

whole. In effect, Alexandria had a balanced male slave population char-acterized by a normal pattern of age grouping comparable to male and female patterns in the rural areas—a facet of the problem that Wade did not investigate.

Wade maintains that slavery grew as an antebellum city grew, but that at some point in the growth the incidence of slaveholding and the size of the holdings began to decrease.[20] An examination of incidence and size of slaveholdings in Alexandria revealed that in 1850, 37 individuals held 168 slaves, an average holding of 4.5 slaves. Ten years later 71 slaveholders owned 314 slaves, an average of 4.4 slaves. The percentage of total free population listed as slaveholders did decline from 8.8 percent in 1850 to 6.4 percent in 1860, but the absolute number of slaveholders doubled during the decade.[21] The slight change in size of slaveholdings and the figures in Table II do not indicate that the institution lost its vigor during the 1850's, nor do they offer any basis for predicting the ultimate demise of slavery in Alexandria.

TABLE II

	Total slaveholders	Two slaves or fewer	Five slaves or fewer	Ten slaves or fewer	Largest individual holding
1850	37	35%	68%	89%	13
1860	71	48%	75%	89%	18

An investigation of the occupations of Alexandrian slaveholders produced no startling new conclusions. The greatest incidence of slave-holding occurred among the attorneys, physicians, merchants, and lodging keepers. In addition, the census recorded a number of single or widowed women as slaveholders. The individuals in these five groups constituted 59 percent of the total slaveholding population in 1850 and 55 percent in 1860. They held 71 percent of Alexandria's slaves in 1850 and 63 percent in 1860. Despite the apparent concentration of slaveholders in these five groups, it seems to have been relatively easy for Alexandrians to acquire slaves. For example, of the thirty-seven slaveholders in 1850, fifteen continued to live in Alexandria as slaveholders in 1860; at least eight had moved into the planter class by 1860, and fourteen ei-

20. Wade, *Slavery in the Cities,* 25–26.
21. This decline is due in part to the influx of free Negroes into Alexandria in 1860. Few free Negroes held slaves in 1860, yet they were part of the free population, the basis for figuring the incidence of slaveholding.

ther had died or had left the parish. An additional eighteen inhabitants of Alexandria in 1850 had become slaveholders by 1860. The number of slaves and slaveholders almost doubled during the decade—another indication of the viability and flexibility of the institution in Alexandria.

Sufficient evidence does not exist to determine the use of these slaves. The individual holdings of four or fewer slaves predominantly female or aged probably worked as domestics. The greatest number of holdings fit into this category; but a substantial number of larger holdings remain, slaves that had to be hired out, used in their master's business, or worked at unidentifiable occupations. In regard to the last, Schedule I of the census (Free Inhabitants) lists a number of Alexandrian slaveholders in nonagricultural occupations who had considerable capital invested in unidentifiable real estate.[22] This real estate could have been an interest in a farm or plantation managed by some planter.[23] Either case would have justified the ownership of and provided a use for a substantial number of slaves by Alexandrian slaveholders listed in non-agricultural pursuits. A check of Schedule IV (Agriculture) for 1860 found that several of Alexandrian slaveholders who held varying amounts of real estate in 1850 had advanced by 1860 into the planter class. For example, a merchant with thirteen slaves, a grocer with nine slaves, and a tavernkeeper with four slaves in 1850 all became planters during the decade.[24] It seems plausible that the slaves held by these Alexandria men in 1850 were actually working on unidentifiable "sideline" farms that would become full-time operations for their masters by 1860. The capital invested in land and slaves and evidence of the moving of town slaveholders into agricultural endeavors suggest the necessity of considering the closeness of the lucrative rural areas when evaluating the institution in the small southern town.

Proving that Alexandrian slaveholders commonly hired out their slaves is equally difficult. The town's newspapers occasionally carried advertisements for Negro labor to work as axemen, ditch diggers, sugar

22. In Louisiana, real estate included slaves. See Stampp, *Peculiar Institution*, 197. The Alexandrians referred to in this instance, however, also owned real estate other than chattels. For example, in 1860, one lawyer owned sixteen slaves and had more than $400,000 invested in real estate; a physician owned eighteen slaves with $88,000 in real estate. The bondsmen could have been domestic servants, but it seems doubtful that a small-town doctor or lawyer would have a servant staff of this size.

23. The Census of Agriculture lists a number of farms and plantations under agents' names, suggesting absentee ownership.

24. The men were D. C. Goodwin, W. Fant, and A. M. Hollowell respectively. U.S. Seventh Census, 1850, Schedules I, II; Eighth Census, 1860, Agriculture.

harvesters, or for an unspecified task.[25] The advertisements did not specify a choice between slave or free labor. The parish governing body, the police jury, often let contracts to Alexandrians for levee, bridge, or road work, but it is only speculation that the Alexandrian Negro provided the labor for these tasks.[26] One interesting reference to a slave who hired himself out and paid his master wages involved a chattel of John Curtis named King who died leaving nearly $700 in gold and silver. Shortly before his death, the slave had made out a will bequeathing twenty dollars to his mother, fifty dollars to one of his sons, and eighty dollars to the other son. The editor of the *Republican* did not know what provision had been made for the rest of the money, "but the gentlemen who he got to make out his will for him and who he appointed his executor, will no doubt faithfully carry out its provisions." Although according to the law, whatever belonged to a slave also belonged to his master, the editor had never heard of a master's enforcing this provision except "in cases where third persons have attempted to wrong a negro. King paid his wages regularly, and what he made over them, he was as usual, allowed to retain and dispose of as he pleased." [27] The townspeople sporadically expressed concern at the practice of slaves being allowed to hire their own time. One Alexandrian complained that "the presence of a population half free, such as slaves hiring the time of their nominal masters, exercises an equally injurious effect upon the slaves proper." [28] Another directed his displeasure at the "great number of houses kept in town and presided over by quasi-free slaves, who being permitted to hire their own time, pay their daily wages by theft, cheap whisky, and gambling. . . ." [29]

25. See, for example, *Republican*, January 29, 1848; January 5, 12, 1850; April 12, 1851. Most advertisements requested labor for the period of one year. The wages varied from $150 per annum to $15 per month.

26. Alexandria's central location had led to its establishment in 1826 as one of three area depots for runaway slaves in Louisiana. State law required the town's sheriff to advertise the runaways; if their owners did not claim them within two years, he was authorized to sell them. In addition, the city corporation was authorized to employ the depot slaves in their public works. This new source of labor may have made it necessary for Alexandria to hire slaves and free Negroes from within its own limits. See Ethel Elizabeth Kramer, "Slavery Legislation in Ante-Bellum Louisiana, 1803–1860" (thesis, Louisiana State University, 1944), 143–144.

27. *Republican*, August 19, 1848. It is singularly important to note that the master allowed his bondsman to draw up a legal will.

28. *Alexandria Louisiana Democrat*, February 22, 1860.

29. *Ibid.*, April 18, 1860. A city ordinance stating that "it shall not be lawful for any slave or slaves to keep house, or reside off the premises where their owner re-

The various small industries in Alexandria could have employed slaves, but probably only a small number of slaves worked in manufacturing establishments, and even then in menial positions.[30] One indication was the employment practice in 1860 of a machine shop in Alexandria which used sixteen white laborers. The head machinist owned only two slaves, a male and a female, and there is no evidence that he hired any other Negro labor, slave or free. The only example found of Negro labor in manufacturing was a harness and band leather factory which in 1853 employed "some twenty white hands, as well as a number of negroes."[31] None of the carriage makers, tinners, saddlers, shoemakers, or brickmakers were listed as slaveholders in either 1850 or 1860.[32] This does not rule out the hiring of slaves, but considering the size of the white labor pool and the smallness of each enterprise, it seems unlikely that slave labor was used extensively in this area.

The free colored population of Alexandria increased about 500 percent in the decade before the Civil War. Of the total parish increase of 107 free Negroes in the 1850's, 105 lived in Alexandria in 1860. These figures strongly imply that the free person of color naturally gravitated to the town. Wade concluded that this movement was normal, as the free Negro had no resources to buy land and "without many others of his own kind his social life was sparse."[33] In 1850 the census listed 73 percent of the free Negroes as being mulatto; a decade later mulattoes numbered 77 percent. At the same time, mulattoes constituted only 21 percent of Alexandria's slave count in 1850 and 36 percent ten years later. Only about 12 percent of the parish slaves were mulattoes in 1860. Wade cautiously suggests that the environment of the city was more

---

sides" had been passed in 1854, repealed in 1858, and reenacted in 1860. The ordinance simply had not been enforced to the satisfaction of some of the townspeople.

30. *Manufactures of the United States in 1860* (Washington, 1865), 200, lists Rapides Parish as having thirteen "manufactories" which employed thirty-five laborers, but does not enumerate those factories in Alexandria, nor does it specify any employment of slave labor.

31. *Republican*, August 20, 1853.

32. Even the merchants, one of the larger slaveholding groups (seven of thirty-two had chattels), averaged only three slaves each. One of these periodically offered one or two of his Negroes for sale. Another, a prospective merchant, offered this advertisement: "the subscriber with a view of going into the mercantile business, offers for sale seven likely and valuable negroes. . . ." *Republican*, January 19, 1849. This implies that the merchants did not consider a larger number of bondsmen a real asset. It is quite possible that the bondsmen held by the merchants were simply domestic servants.

33. Wade, *Slavery in the Cities*, 248.

conducive to contact and mixing between the races.[34] The applicability of this conclusion to Alexandria remains debatable, as Alexandria plainly lacked the "urban" environment. Undoubtedly some miscegenation occurred in Alexandria, but it is difficult to document. An early "humorous" column written by one Junius (the editor of the *Louisiana Herald*) offered a solitary comment reflecting on the relationship between the races. Junius mentioned encountering an old friend: "Beau Billy lounged in . . . mentioned a pretty mulatter girl at Misers, made my mouth water; take a peep at her; told him to bring her in the back way; Beau spoke of having nicked a few of the bucks. . . ."[35]

The census did not list any free Negro slaveholders in 1850, but a decade later six free persons of color held a total of twelve slaves.[36] Eight of the slaves were under thirteen years of age; one was sixty years old, and the other three were females of ages eighteen, twenty-five, and twenty-eight, respectively. It seems doubtful that the free Negroes exploited their slaves for their labor value. Considering the age of these slaves, the fact that they were held by free Negroes, and the possibility that they were relatives of the slaveholder, it would seem likely that they would have been emancipated had it not been contrary to law.[37]

Notably, Alexandria had few free colored men of working age. In 1850 the census listed 33 percent of the free Negro males between the ages of sixteen and fifty-five, whereas 65 percent of the free Negro females fit into this age group. Ten years later the figures were 38 and 58 percent respectively.[38] Although the few free Negro men undoubtedly

34. *Ibid.*, 258–262. The listing of a Negro as being either black or mulatto depended upon the discretion of the census taker; therefore the figures are somewhat subjective.

35. *Alexandria Louisiana Herald*, February 11, 1820.

36. Interestingly, the census records one of the free Negro slaveholders, a forty-five-year-old black drayman, as being born in Africa, indicating that he came to Louisiana after the slave trade legally closed.

37. For discussion of Louisiana emancipation laws, see Kramer, "Slavery Legislation," 123–130. In July, 1852, the parish police jury allowed twelve slaveholders (two of whom were free Negroes) to manumit a total of thirty-one slaves. In response to this action a contemporary complained, "If the negro is to be free, then let him be colonized, for God knows we have free niggers enough among us now. . . ." *Republican*, August 14, 21, 1852; January 1, 1853. A stricter emancipation law passed the legislature in late 1852.

38. In contrast to the balance in the slave population, most of Alexandria's free colored males were under fourteen years of age. The topic has not been investigated, but it is possible that a deficiency of free Negro men of working age existed

formed the bottom of the laboring class,[39] their status alone suggests their advantages over the bondsmen. The free person of color could hold personal estate, real estate, and slaves. Perhaps more important, he had a sense of privacy, the opportunity for a family life, and comparative freedom of movement.[40]

According to Wade, the larger southern cities witnessed a growth of rudimentary patterns of segregation in the last years before the Civil War.[41] The 1860 census gives a fragmented picture of the physical relationship between Alexandria's free colored populace and the white community.[42] In 1860 the 131 Negroes lived in forty households; free Negroes held twenty-nine of these households,[43] and 107 of the 131 Negroes lived in Negro-held households. Twenty-seven of the Negro-held dwellings were all black; the other two contained a total of three white persons—a shoemaker, an overseer, and a clerk. The remaining twenty-four free Negroes lived in eleven white-held households. These households were individually owned by a postmaster, two mer-

---

throughout the antebellum South. Another possibility is documented by an instance in which a free colored female of Alexandria sold her thirteen-year-old son for $700 to a planter in Natchitoches Parish with a contractual stipulation "that so soon as the said boy, Amos, shall have completed his twenty-first year, his mother shall affranchise and emancipate him, or sooner, if it can be done." Conveyances, Book 21, Parish of Natchitoches, No. 1138, 335; quoted from Annie Lee West Stahl, "The Free Negro in Ante-Bellum Louisiana," *Louisiana Historical Quarterly*, XXV (April, 1942), 337.

39. In 1860, free Negro occupations included five day-laborers, three draymen, a shoemaker, a boatman, a clerk, a gardener, and a barber. Average daily wages for the day-laborer were one dollar; female domestics earned an average of three dollars a week. Census, 1850, 1860, "Social Statistics."

40. Two property transactions involving free Negroes who paid cash for lots in Alexandria have survived. See Stahl, "Free Negro," 324. In regard to the free Negroes' opportunity for a family life, it should be noted that Alexandria had few whole free Negro families during the decade. Free Negro women headed most households.

41. Wade, *Slavery in the Cities*, 266.

42. Schedule I of the Census is practically the only source of data on the free person of color in Alexandria. The returns of the 1860 Census are used primarily because there were a larger and therefore more representative number of free Negroes in Alexandria in 1860 than 1850. Moreover, J. D. B. De Bow, the superintendent of the Census in 1850, expressed doubt that the Census effectively delineated between urban and rural population. De Bow, *Statistical View of the United States* (Washington, 1854), 192. Nevertheless, with careful and discerning use the antebellum censuses remain a singularly valuable source.

43. This is based on the assumption that the census-taker was consistent in listing the head of the household first.

chants,[44] four carpenters, a brickmason, a dentist, and a boarding-house keeper. A free colored day laborer occupied the eleventh house with a twenty-eight-year-old white woman. In addition to a substantial number of integrated households, the order of the census listing offers no evidence that the solidly black residences were isolated in one particular part of the town. There is little reason to suspect that segregation of an individual or residential nature characterized Alexandrian race relations in the decade before the war.[45]

The available evidence will not support an adequate description of the social environment in which the Alexandria Negro lived during the 1850's. The newspapers are the only surviving source for such material, and even then it is remarkably sketchy. For example, the *Republican* gave dubious mention to the appointment of a minister to the "Alexandria Colored, Mission" Methodist Episcopal Church, but no church records have survived.[46] For an admission fee (usually half the adult white rate), "colored persons" and servants could attend the numerous circuses, exhibitions, and theatrical productions staged in Alexandria. One editor asserted that "every man, woman, child *and* nigger (for it is fashionable for all) in and about town, will be delighted to learn that there will soon be a circus here." [47] Economically speaking, the parish police jury occasionally extended the monthly pauper list to include a few free Negroes.[48]

44. One of the merchants, Pierre Bax, a fifty-eight-year-old Frenchman, lived with forty-one-year-old Louisiana Bax (black) and two mulatto children of the same name. Eighth Census, Schedule I, 1860.

45. Wade has been justly criticized for attaching too much significance to the development of segregation in the antebellum period. C. Vann Woodward suggests that "the urban contribution to racial segregation in the South would seem to be less impressive than the encouragement that city conditions gave to interracial contact, familiar association, and intimacy." Because such a small part of the southern population shared the urban experience, "it would be a mistake to place too much emphasis on the urban experience, either as evidence of segregation or the opposite tendency." Woodward, *Jim Crow*, 16.

46. *Republican*, January 12, 1850. For a brief mention of the "Alexandria Mission to Colored," see Robert Henry Harper, *Louisiana Methodism* (Washington, 1949), 74. The only surviving church records of antebellum Alexandria are those of the St. James Protestant Church (all white).

47. *Republican*, May 13, 1848. See also *ibid.*, November 23, 1850; January 10, 1852; *Democrat*, November 1, 1859; *Alexandria Constitutional*, January 26, 1861.

48. For example, "Resolved that Tenas, a f.m.c. be allowed two dollars per month for his support. . . . Resolved that Hester Carr (f.w.c.) be allowed the sum of $75 being in full compensation for the past, present, and future maintenance of a foundling." *Republican*, September 25, 1847; *Democrat*, January 11, 1860.

There is little evidence that the Negro, slave or free, caused much trouble in Alexandria. When the Alexandria board of trustees was not legislating against hogs and goats in the streets or issuing licenses to ten-pin alleys and barrooms, they occasionally passed an ordinance dealing with the slave. For example:

> Be it ordained, that it shall be the duty of the town constable, after the ringing of the nine o'clock bell, to strike every slave found off of his or her master's premises without a pass or something to indicate that he or she is on his or her master's business, 25 lashes.[49]

Or, twenty minutes after the ringing of the 9:00 bell every Sunday morning, "any slave not residing within the limits of said town, who shall be found there in . . . shall be arrested by the constable and placed in the Lock Up."[50] Actually, many Louisiana towns and cities received permission from the state legislature to govern the slaves in their jurisdiction. There is no indication that the legislature granted Alexandria this power; the same codes and regulations which applied to the rural areas more than likely governed the town's slaves and free Negroes.[51] Again, this suggests the ruralness of the town; there was probably little need for more effective regulation of its black population.

As the decade drew to a close, the Alexandrian newspapers, reflective of their constituency, became more defensive. Denunciations of the "Black Republican Conspiracy" dominated the editorial columns. Even the advertisements reassured Alexandrians. For instance, a notice promoting the Memphis Railroad pointed out that while "passing through slave territory, the Railroads from Memphis offer the advantage of no annoyance or risk in the conveyance of servants."[52] The fear of a slave uprising appears to have been constant.[53] Shortly after John Brown's raid at Harpers Ferry, an overseer was murdered by a slave on a planta-

49. *Republican*, January 6, 1849.

50. *Constitutional*, December 2, 1860. The slaves probably had little fear of being "placed in the Lock Up" or jail. Numerous prisoner escapes from the jail during the decade led the *Republican* editor to refer to it as "that rotten concern."

51. For an excellent account of the codes and regulations in effect at various times in Louisiana, see Kramer, "Slavery Legislation," *passim*.

52. *Democrat*, July 13, 1859.

53. Whittington concluded that "whenever a planter or overseer was killed, rumors floated widely that it was a premeditated plan to kill all the whites." Whittington, "Rapides Parish," XVII, 538. The town itself never experienced a slave rebellion. There seems to be no collaborating evidence for rumors that the quickly squelched uprising near Cheneyville had supporters among the black people of Alexandria. See *ibid.*, XVI, 636–637; *Niles Weekly Register*, LIII (October 28, 1837), 129.

tion near Alexandria. The authorities, believing it to be a plot, arrested and jailed "ten or more" slaves in Alexandria. The next morning the townspeople discovered that a mob had entered the jail during the night, "obtained these prisoners and without trial had hanged them to different projections around the jail." [54]

Unforeseen, the day of "jubilo" for the Alexandrian Negro was fast approaching. The editor of the *Constitutional* remarked that the "colored population seemed to enjoy themselves to an unusual degree" at Christmastime in 1860; two years later a contemporary exclaimed that "the arrival of the Yankees alone turned the negroes crazy . . . subordination and restraint are at an end." [55]

The foregoing statistical profile and sketch may or may not be representative of the position of the Negro, slave and free, in other small antebellum towns. A hesitancy to draw any absolute conclusions from a single case study stems from the limits and nature of the source material, but a few general observations should be offered. For instance, the statistical differences in population and sex ratios, size and incidence of slaveholding, and the type of work done by the slaves definitely indicate that slavery in Alexandria differed from slavery in the rural areas.

Greater difficulty arises in any attempt to isolate differences between small-town and urban slavery. The statistical trends do vary: for example, both the size and incidence of slaveholding maintained approximately the same percentages in Alexandria from 1850 to 1860; in the larger cities both size and incidence declined by 1860. Like the larger cities, Alexandria had a deficiency of slave and free colored males, but the male slave population remained balanced with no proportional lack of working-age males. In contrast to Wade's findings, race relations in Alexandria did not involve segregation or any unusual element of conflict. The small-town environment plainly lacked the disintegrating effect that the urban environment apparently had on slavery. [56]

54. Whittington, "Rapides Parish," XVII, 546. Whittington did not date the lynching, nor did he note his source.

55. *Constitutional*, December 29, 1860; G. P. Whittington, ed., "Concerning the Loyalty of Slaves in North Louisiana in 1863; Letters from John H. Ransdell to Governor Thomas O. Moore, Dated 1863," *Louisiana Historical Quarterly*, XIV (October, 1931), 491.

56. This comparison of slavery in Alexandria to the urban institution does not question Wade's conclusions for the cities he has investigated, but suggests only that many of his findings do not apply to slavery in Alexandria. For a case study critical of Wade's methods and conclusions, see Herman Charles Woessner III, "New Orleans, 1840–1860: A Study in Urban Slavery" (thesis, Louisiana State University, 1967), esp. 3–17. See also a review of Wade's *Slavery in the Cities* by Eugene

It is also misleading to imply that small-town slavery would "have shared in the same attrition" that afflicted the urban institution as the small town grew.[57] If Alexandria had developed to the size of Wade's selected cities, it is conceivable that the institution of slavery and race relations would have experienced similar problems. But the fact remains that Alexandria and many other southern towns were not of equal "settlement, region, or age" and that the pattern of slavery in Alexandria deviated from the urban pattern significantly enough to warrant separate study.

On the whole, the institution in Alexandria remained stable and flexible during the decade, but to say that slavery was profitably viable in the town itself is debatable. The absence of any dynamic opportunity involving slave labor within the town, coupled with the closeness of the expanding rural economy, probably limited the use of most town slaves to menial duties and domestic service. If this restricted the town's demand for slaves and hirelings, in good years the surrounding countryside offered opportunities for town slaveholders either to hire their slaves to planters and farmers or to move with their slaves into direct participation in the agrarian economy. The total impact of the rural areas on slavery in the small town, as well as in large cities, awaits fuller investigation.

In conclusion, it appears that slavery and race relations in the small town of Alexandria, although differing from the rural and the more highly urban systems, possessed some characteristics of both. As yet, the history of the slave and free Negro in the numerous small southern towns remains a neglected—but necessary—element of the history of the American Negro in the antebellum period.

D. Genovese, "One-Tenth in Urban Bondage," *Nation*, CC (January 11, 1965), 38–39.

57. See Wade, *Slavery in the Cities*, 244.

Theodore Hershberg

Free Blacks in Antebellum Philadelphia

After the American Revolution slavery gradually died away in the North. The blacks who remained were the descendants of those freed after the Civil War, or individuals who had somehow escaped southern slavery. During the antebellum period the plight of the free Negro was a difficult one. His presence contradicted the basic tenets of the pro-slavery argument and subverted the regimen masters attempted to impose upon their slaves. Because of the ideological and social threat he posed to the old regime, he was everywhere unwelcome. Fear of his presence can be gauged by the decline in the number of manumissions granted and the increase in legislation dedicated to his expulsion.

The North, however, proved no haven for these outcasts of American society. Even the anti-slavery movement had a distinctly racist cast. The following article demonstrates that institutionalized racism existed beyond the confines of slavery and was a national phenomenon. In an urban setting race was as important an ingredient in the poverty of the free Negro as it was in the more rural South.

The urban dynamics of nineteenth-century America, however, affected blacks as well as whites. Race distinguished free blacks from other lower-class groups. Their poverty resembles that of other ethnic groups such as the Irish and the Poles when they first came from Europe. It was race, however, which negated the hard work of the free Negroes and confined them to the most menial jobs. Race rather than nationality appears to be the crucial determinant,

© 1972 by Peter N. Stearns. Reprinted from the *Journal of Social History*, V, no. 2 (Winter 1971–72), by permission of the editor.

This essay was originally read at the Annual Meeting of the Association for the Study of Negro Life and History (Philadelphia: October, 1970) and was presented in a revised form at the Temple University "Conference on the History of the Peoples of Philadelphia" (Philadelphia: April, 1971). It was revised once again for publication. The essay has benefited from suggestions offered by many individuals. The author expresses his gratitude for this assistance. A special note of thanks must go to the Center for Metropolitan Problems of the National Institute of Mental Health. Their financial support (2R01 MH16621), which began in April, 1969, has made this research possible.

not only in the social position they occupied but also in their prospects for social mobility.

Hershberg's study focuses upon the free black community in Philadelphia, and his conclusions are important for the historian of the cities and of slavery. The relative success of the ex-slave indicates that slavery was not the closed society its most vehement critics have imagined. For the talented black opportunities still existed, and those who were able to overcome slavery and the social and psychological pressures it exerted were indeed exceptional. The measure of difference between the ex-slave and all other members of the free black community in Philadelphia thus must form the focus of any future social history of American slavery or of the black community in the nineteenth century. And, as this article will indicate, Hershberg's mode of analysis will be a most useful tool in those studies.

Afro-American history in general has received a great deal of attention from historians in the past decade. The same cannot be said about the history of black Americans who were free before the Civil War. Studies published since Leon Litwack's *North of Slavery* have considered racial discrimination in the legal tradition, the relationship between race and politics, the establishment of black utopian communities, and the role of blacks in the abolitionist movement.[1] With a few exceptions notable in the earlier studies of the free Negro by Luther P. Jackson and John Hope Franklin, the literature lacks a solid empirical base, a sophisticated methodological and theoretical approach, and a focus on the black community itself.[2] There exists an important need for

1. Leon Litwack, *North of Slavery* (Chicago, 1961); Arthur Zilversmit, *The First Emancipation* (Chicago, 1967); Eugene H. Berwanger, *The Frontier against Slavery: Western Anti-Negro Prejudice and the Slavery Extension Controversy* (Urbana, Ill., 1967); V. Jacques Voegeli, *Free but Not Equal: The Midwest and the Negro during the Civil War* (Chicago, 1969); James A. Rawley, *Race and Politics* (Philadelphia, 1969); Eric Foner, *Free Soil, Free Labor, Free Men* (New York, 1970); William and Jane Pease, *Black Utopia* (Wisconsin, 1963); Benjamin Quarles, *Black Abolitionists* (Oxford, 1969); Carleton Mabee, *Black Freedom: The Non-Violent Abolitionists, 1830 to the Civil War* (New York, 1970).

2. Luther P. Jackson, *Free Negro and Property Holding in Virginia 1830–1860* (New York, 1942) and John Hope Franklin, *The Free Negro in North Carolina, 1790–1860* (North Carolina, 1943). There are, of course, many other state and local studies: W. E. B. Du Bois, *The Philadelphia Negro* (Philadelphia, 1899); Edward R. Turner, *The Negro in Pennsylvania* (Washington, 1911); John Russell, *The Free Negro in Virginia, 1830–1860* (Baltimore, 1913); John Daniels, *In Freedom's Birthplace: A Study of Boston's Negroes* (Boston, 1914); James M. Wright, *The Free Negro in Maryland* (New York, 1921); Robert A. Warner, *New Haven*

new studies of the family and social structure, of the development of community institutions such as the church, school, and beneficial society, of migration and social mobility.[3]

Antebellum Philadelphia offers the historian an important opportunity to study each of these topics. The free black population of the city had its roots in the eighteenth century. Its free black population in 1860, more than 22,000, was the largest outside the South and second only to Baltimore. All-black churches, schools, and voluntary societies were numerous. The National Negro Convention Movement met for the first time in Philadelphia in 1830, and the city hosted such meetings frequently thereafter. Many of the leading black abolitionists such as James Forten, Robert Purvis, and William Still were Philadelphians. Most significantly for the historian, the data describing all facets of this history are extant. The black history collections and the papers of the Pennsylvania Abolition Society at the Historical Society of Pennsylvania and the Library Company of Philadelphia are even richer for the antebellum period than the Schomburg Collection of the New York Public Library.

Negroes (New Haven, 1940); Emma Lou Thornbrough, *The Negro in Indiana* (Indianapolis, 1957). Especially valuable articles include Carter Woodson, "The Negroes of Cincinnati Prior to the Civil War," *Journal of Negro History*, I (January, 1916); Charles S. Sydnor, "The Free Negro in Mississippi before the Civil War," *American Historical Review*, XXXII (July, 1927); E. Horace Fitchett, "The Origin and Growth of the Free Negro Population of Charleston, South Carolina," *Journal of Negro History*, XXVI (October, 1941); J. Merton England, "The Free-Negro in Ante Bellum Tennessee," *Journal of Southern History*, IX (February, 1943).

3. There are, of course, important beginnings. Among them are E. Franklin Frazier's *The Free Negro Family* (Nashville, 1932) and Carter G. Woodson's *The Education of the Negro prior to 1861* (Washington, 1915), *The History of Negro Church* (Washington, 1921), and *Free Negro Heads of Families in the United States* (Washington, 1925). Fortunately there are studies of the free Negro currently under way and others awaiting publication which will make important contributions to the literature. I am aware of the following studies: Ira Berlin, University of Illinois, Chicago Circle, on the free Negro in the upper South; Rhoda Freeman, Upsala College, on the free Negro in New York; Carol Ann George, Oswego State College, on the free Negro church; Laurence Glasco, University of Pittsburgh, on the free Negro in Buffalo and Pittsburgh; Floyd Miller, Hiram College, on Martin Delany and the colonization movement; Carl Oblinger, Johns Hopkins University, on free Negro communities in southeastern Pennsylvania towns; Armisted Robinson, University of Rochester, on free Negroes in Memphis; Harry Silcox, Temple University, on free Negro education in Philadelphia and Boston; Arthur O. White, University of Florida, on the free Negro in Boston; Marina Wikramanayaka, University of Texas, El Paso, on the free Negro in Charleston.

| Census: Pa. Abol. Soc. 1838 | Total households | | | | | | Male-headed households | | | |
| | | | | | | | Ex-slave HH's Ex-slave heads | | | |
Variables	All free-born	Ex-slave HH's	Ex-slave HH HD's	Ex-slave HH HD's bought selves	All free-born	All	Free HD's	All	Manumitted	Bought selves
Churchgoers										
Non-churchgoers	17.8%	9.3%	5.4%	3.2%	18.5%	10.5%	13.5%	4.8%	7.1%	3.7%
White churches	5.5%	5.1%	5.7%	7.5%	5.2%	4.3%	4.1%	4.6%	3.8%	5.1%
Baptist	8.7%	10.3%	11.4%	12.9%	8.1%	11.0%	10.0%	12.7%	13.9%	12.8%
Methodist	70.7%	76.5%	74.1%	76.3%	71.1%	75.1%	77.7%	70.6%	70.9%	75.6%
Episcopal	7.0%	4.8%	4.7%	2.2%	8.1%	4.6%	0.4%	5.1%	3.8%	2.6%
Presbyterian	7.6%	5.3%	6.7%	5.4%	7.8%	5.8%	4.7%	7.6%	7.6%	5.1%
Catholic	4.1%	1.1%	1.3%	1.1%	2.6%	1.3%	0.9%	2.0%	2.5%	1.3%
Misc.	1.9%	2.0%	1.7%	2.2%	2.3%	2.2%	2.4%	2.0%	1.3%	2.6%
School										
HH chld attnd	27.6%	29.2%	29.0%	35.4%	29.7%	35.9%	35.3%	37.2%	36.5%	38.3%
HH chld not attd	22.5%	25.4%	15.9%	22.9%	25.2%	28.3%	32.2%	20.1%	17.6%	24.7%
Chld attnd	55.0%	67.1%	71.7%	71.2%	54.9%	61.4%	55.7%	72.7%	75.0%	70.8%
Benevolent Society										
HH w/ members	56.4%	56.1%	60.8%	64.6%	52.0%	57.7%	53.8%	65.2%	62.3%	69.1%
Members	27.1%	27.0%	35.1%	32.4%	25.5%	26.2%	22.6%	34.5%	34.6%	33.0%
Occupational category										
White-collar	4.0%	5.4%	8.2%	4.9%	4.2%	5.4%	4.4%	7.0%	7.3%	5.1%
Skilled	17.6%	16.6%	18.8%	20.7%	17.5%	15.6%	14.2%	18.4%	17.1%	20.3%
Unskilled	78.4%	78.1%	73.1%	74.4%	78.3%	79.0%	81.4%	74.6%	75.6%	74.7%

In many ways this essay resembles a preliminary progress report.[4] Despite the research and analysis which remain to be done, it is appropriate to discuss several important themes which emerge early in the study of nineteenth-century black Philadelphians: the socio-economic deterioration of the antebellum black community, the condition of the ex-slaves in the population and the value of understanding the urban experience for the study of black history.

A CONTEXT OF DECLINE

The decision of the Pennsylvania Abolition Society in 1837 to take a census of Philadelphia's free Negro population was made for both a specific and a general purpose. The specific purpose was to defeat the

4. The data are derived from three distinct sources. First, the Population Manuscript Schedules of the U.S. Census for Philadelphia County, 1850–80. From these census records enumerated decennially by the federal government, information was taken describing each of approximately 500,000 black, Irish, German, and native white American inhabitants—that is, a large sample of native white American and all Irish and German males above the age of 17, a large sample of Irish, German, and native white American households including all members of each sample household, and all black men, women, and children. The major variables listed in these census schedules include name, age, sex, color, occupation, property, and place of birth.

The second data source is the Manufacturing Manuscript Schedules of the U.S. Census for Philadelphia County, 1850–80. All places of business in the county with an annual product of $500 or more were included in the census. In all, data describing over 24,000 individual firms, ranging from 4,700 in 1850 to 8,500 in 1880, have been recorded. Although the information included in the census varied slightly from year to year, each firm was described in terms of the following variables: company name, name of business or product, amount of capital, number of employees (males, females, youths), wages, source of power, machines, materials and product (the latter two in kinds, quantities, and value), the number of months per year in operation, etc.

The third data source consists of three unusually detailed household censuses of the entire free Negro population of antebellum Philadelphia taken in 1838 and 1856 by the Pennsylvania Abolition Society and in 1847 by the Society of Friends. These censuses describe 11,600 households and include, in addition to those variables listed in the U.S. Census of population, membership in specific church, beneficial, and temperance societies, income, education, school attendance, house, ground, and water rent, slave birth, how freedom was acquired, the amount of property brought to Pennsylvania, and marital status. Most of the analysis included in this essay is based on this source.

The data describing each individual, household, and firm were put into machine-readable form. When all the data are verified, a sophisticated linkage program will instruct the computer in tracing specific individuals, households, and firms from census to census and within each census. When identifications are

move, already underway in Harrisburg, to write into the new state constitution the complete disfranchisement of Pennsylvania blacks. The
general purpose was "to repel" those who denounced "the whole of the
free colored people as unworthy of any favor, asserting that they were
nuisances in the community fit only to fill alms houses and jails." [5]

The strategy employed to accomplish these ends reveals a good deal
about the faith which the abolitionists had in hard fact and reasoned argument. The data from the census were presented to the delegates at
Harrisburg and to the public at large in the form of a forty-page pamphlet summarizing the findings. [6]

The pamphlet argued that disfranchisement should be defeated because the free Negro population made a worthy contribution to the
well-being of the entire community. Blacks paid considerable taxes and
rents, owned property, were not disproportionately paupers and crimi-
nals, cared for their own underprivileged, and, finally, put money as
consumers into the income stream of the general economy. The facts
contained in the published pamphlet, therefore, "gave great satisfaction
affording the friends of the colored people strong and convincing arguments against those who were opposed to their enjoying the rights and
privileges of freemen." [7]

Although unsuccessful in the specific purpose—blacks were disfran-
chised in Pennsylvania until 1870, when the Fifteenth Amendment was
adopted—the Abolitionists and Quakers undertook further censuses
in 1847 and 1856. [8] As in 1838, these later censuses were followed with
printed pamphlets which duly noted the discrimination and problems
facing free Negroes and counseled patience to the "magnanimous suffer-
ers," as they referred to their Negro brethren. The general tone of the
pamphlets was optimistic and pointed to important gains made in past
decades. The overall optimism, however, proved unfounded when the
actual manuscript censuses were submitted to computer analysis.

---

made, it will be possible to proceed with analysis of the intra- and inter-genera-
tional aspects of the research.

5. Edward Needles, *Ten Years' Progress: A Comparison of the State and Condition of the Colored People in the City and County of Philadelphia from 1838 to
1847* (Philadelphia, 1849), 7–8.

6. Pennsylvania Abolition Society, *The Present State and Condition of the Free
People of Color of the City of Philadelphia and Adjoining Districts* (Philadelphia,
1838).

7. Needles, 7–8.

8. Society of Friends, *Statistical Inquiry into the Condition of the People of
Color of the City and Districts of Philadelphia* (Philadelphia, 1849); Benjamin
Bacon, *Statistics of the Colored People of Philadelphia* (Philadelphia, 1859).

The "friends of the colored people," unfortunately, had been carried away by their admirable purpose. It was one thing to document that free Negroes were not worthless, that they could indeed survive outside of the structured environment of slavery and even that they could create a community with their own churches, schools, and beneficial societies; but it was quite another thing to argue that the people and the institutions they created actually prospered in the face of overwhelming obstacles. It is not so much that the Abolitionists and Quakers were wrong as that they went too far. And in so doing they obscured a remarkable deterioration in the socio-economic condition of blacks from 1830 to the Civil War.

Beginning in 1829 and continuing through the ensuing two decades, Philadelphia Negroes were the victims of half a dozen major anti-black riots and many more minor mob actions. Negro churches, schools, homes, and even an orphanage were set on fire. Some blacks were killed, many beaten, and others run out of town.[9] Contemporaries attributed the small net loss in the Negro population between 1840 and 1850 in large part to riots.[10] In the same decade white population grew 63 percent. While it is important to maintain the perspective that the anti-black violence occurred within a larger context of anti-Catholic violence, this knowledge must have been small comfort to Philadelphia Negroes.

A victimized minority, one reasons, should organize and bring political pressure on local government officials. But black Philadelphians after 1838 were denied even this remedy. Disfranchisement of all Negroes, even those citizens who owned sufficient property to vote in all elections during the previous twenty-three years, was all the more tragic and ironic because, at the same time, all white males in Pennsylvania over the age of 21 were specifically given the right to vote.

In addition to the larger, less measurable forces such as race riots, population decline,[11] and disfranchisement, after 1838 black Philadelphians suffered a turn for the worse in wealth, residential segregation, family structure, and employment.

The antebellum black community was extremely poor. The total wealth—that is, the combined value of real and personal property holdings—for three out of every five households in both 1838 and

9. Sam Bass Warner, Jr., *The Private City* (Philadelphia, 1968), 125–157.

10. Society of Friends, 7.

11. There was also a net population loss for blacks of 0.17 percent between 1860 and 1870; the white population in the same decade, however, increased some 20 percent.

Variables	Total households (3,295) (12,084 persons)				Male-headed households (2,361) (9,609 persons)			Ex-slave HH's Ex-slave heads		
	All free-born	Ex-slave HH's	Ex-slave HH HD's	Ex-slave HH HD's bought selves	All free born	All	Free HD's	All	Manu-mitted	Bought selves
Total HH's	2489	806	314	96	1760	601	394	207	85	81
Total persons	8867	3217	1013	358	6966	2643	1852	791	312	327
Fam. size (w/o singles)	3.88	4.27	3.84	4.12	4.06	4.40	4.70	3.99	3.80	4.72
Two-par HH (%)	77.0	79.8	79.3	90.5	99% of all male-headed households with 2 or more persons were two-parent households.					
Wealth categories										
$0–20 (%)	23.9	19.6	17.5	10.4	21.8	16.3	19.0	11.1	16.5	6.2
$21–40 (%)	21.1	19.6	19.7	11.5	18.6	18.1	19.5	15.5	16.5	8.6
$41–90 (%)	17.8	15.1	14.6	11.5	16.7	14.0	14.7	12.6	12.9	11.1
$91–240 (%)	18.6	21.1	18.8	25.0	20.9	23.0	22.6	23.7	24.7	28.4
$241+ (%)	18.6	24.6	29.3	41.7	22.1	28.6	24.1	37.2	29.4	45.7
Ave. TW	$252	$268	$295	$388	$257	$317	$284	$380	$388	$409
Ave. PP* All HH's	$176	$175	$191	$223	$181	$204	$180	$249	$269	$252
Ave. RP All HH's	$76	$93	$105	$164	$69	$113	$103	$131	$119	$157
Ave. RP Owners only	$987	$730	$567	$527	$768	$770	$1017	$564	$776	$472
% RP owners	7.7	12.8	18.5	31.2	9.0	14.6	10.1	23.2	15.3	33.3
Ave. rent	$48	$50	$47	$53	$53	$55	$55	$54	$49	$56

TW=Total Wealth PP=Personal Property RP=Real Property HH=Household
* There is little observable difference between the ave. PP for all HH's and the ave. PP for owners only: 95%–100% of all HH's owned PP.

1847 amounted to sixty dollars or less. This fact precludes the use of simple economic class analysis in determining social stratification in the black community.[12] The distribution of wealth itself, moreover, was strikingly unequal within the black population. In both 1838 and 1847 the poorest half of the population owned only one-twentieth of the total wealth, while the wealthiest 10 percent of the population held 70 percent of the total wealth; at the very apex of the community, the wealthiest 1 percent accounted for fully 30 percent of the total wealth.[13]

Between 1838 and 1847 there was a 10 percent decrease in per capita value of personal property and a slight decrease in per capita total wealth among Philadelphia blacks. Although the number of households included in the 1847 census was 30 percent greater than in 1838, the number of real propertyholders fell from 294 to 280, and their respective percentages fell from 9 to 6. There was, in other words, despite a considerable increase in the number of households, both absolute and percentage decrease in the number of real propertyholders.

Another way of highlighting the decline is to create roughly equal population groups, rank them by wealth, and determine at what point in the rank order blacks ceased to include owners of real property. In 1838 owners of real property extended through the wealthiest 30 percent of the ranked population; in 1847 they extended less than half as far. In 1838, moreover, it required a total wealth holding of between two and three hundred dollars in order to own real property; by 1847 an individ-

12. Social distinctions indispensable to the study of social stratification do exist among this 60 percent of the household population; however, they do not emerge along economic lines. Households averaging $30 of total wealth are not distinctively different from households worth $20 or $50. Important social distinctions can be determined by using specific non-economic measures such as church affiliation or a more general non-economic measure such as lifestyle which, in turn, is described by a number of other variables: residence, family structure, education, occupation, etc.

13. The unequal distribution of wealth was not unique to the black population. Stuart Blumin, "Mobility and Change in Ante Bellum Philadelphia," in Stephan Thernstrom and Richard Sennett, eds., *Nineteenth Century Cities* (New Haven, 1969), found greater inequality among a sample of the entire Philadelphia population in the U.S. Census for 1860 than I did among all blacks in the Abolitionist and Quaker censuses in 1838 and 1847: the wealthiest 10 percent in 1860 owned 89 percent of the wealth, and the wealthiest 1 percent owned 50 percent of the wealth. Data describing the universe of black, Irish, and German propertyholders in the U.S. Census for Philadelphia in 1860, however, indicate that inequality was pronounced in all three groups: in each case the wealthiest 10 percent of the population owned about 88 percent of the wealth. The Lorenz measures for the blacks, Irish, and Germans were .95, .94, and .92 respectively.

ual required a total wealth holding twice as high before he could purchase land or own a home.

This statistic is complemented by a measurable rise in residential segregation over the decade. Disfranchisement (perhaps as valuable to us as a symptom of contemporary feelings about Negroes as it was a cause), a decade of race riots, and a general backlash against abolitionist activities all contributed to the creation of social atmosphere in which it was considerably more difficult for even the wealthiest of Negroes to acquire real property. It is tempting to conclude quite simply that rising racism meant that a far higher price had to be paid in order to induce a white man to sell land to a black man. Stating such a conclusion with complete confidence, however, requires further comparative research in order to determine if instead this phenomenon applied equally to all ethnic groups, i.e., a period of generally appreciating land values.

The actual measurement of residential segregation depends upon the use of a "grid square"—an area roughly 1¼ blocks square—and is a vast improvement over far larger geographical entities such as districts or wards. Each Negro household was located on detailed maps and its precise grid square recorded. All variables about each household, then, are observable and measurable in small, uniquely defined units.

Residential segregation is measured in two dimensions: (1) the *distribution* of the household population—that is, the number of grid squares in which Negro households were located; and (2) the *density* of the population—that is, the number of Negro households per grid. Residential segregation was rising in the decade before 1838, and it increased 13 percent in all grid squares inhabited by blacks; more important, the percentage of households occupying the most dense grid squares (those with more than a hundred black households) increased by almost 10 percent. Between 1850 and 1860 the average density changed very little, but the trend toward settlement in the more dense grids continued. By 1860 the number of households occupying the most dense grid squares reached more than one in four, an increase of 11 percent over the previous decade and the high point between 1838 and 1880. During the Civil War decade residential segregation fell off, but it rose again from 1870 to 1880 as migration from the South swelled the Negro population of Philadelphia to 31,700, an increase of 43 percent over both the 1860 and 1870 totals.

Data from the Abolitionist and Quaker censuses, the U.S. census of 1880, and W. E. B. Du Bois's study of the seventh ward in 1896–97 indicate, in each instance, that two-parent households were characteristic of 78 percent of black families. That statistical average, however, belies a grimmer reality for the poorest blacks. There was a decline in the percentage of two-parent households for the poorest fifth of the population from 70 percent in 1838 to 63 percent ten years later; and for the poorest half of the black population the decline was from 73 percent to 68 percent. In other words, among the poorest half of the community at mid-century, roughly one family in three was headed by a female.[14]

An unequal female-male sex ratio no doubt indirectly affected family building and stability. Between 1838 and 1860 the number of black females per 1,000 black males increased from 1,326 to 1,417. For whites in 1860 the corresponding figure was 1,088. Between 1860 and 1890 the sex ratio for blacks moved in the direction of parity: 1,360 in 1870, 1,263 in 1880, and 1,127 in 1890. The age and sex distribution throughout the period 1838 to 1890 indicates that the movement away from, and after 1860 back toward, equal distribution of the sexes was due to a change in the number of young black males in the 20 to 40 age bracket. Changes in this age bracket usually result from two related factors: occupational opportunities and in- and out-migration rates. The remarkably high excess of females over males throughout the period probably reflects poor employment opportunities for black men (while the demand for black female domestics remained high), accompanied by net out-migration of young black males. The gradual improvement of industrial opportunities for young black males after 1860, accompanied by net in-migration of increasing numbers of young black men, reduced the excess of black females. The sociological consequences of such an imbalance in the sex ratios are familiar: illegitimacy, delinquency, broken homes and such. In light of these statistics, it is surprising that the percentage of two-parent households was as high as it was.

More important for our purposes, however, is another measure of the condition of the entire black population often obscured by the debate over the matrifocality of the black family, focusing as it does on narrow statistical analysis of traditional household units. How many blacks were living outside black households? How many were inmates of public institutions? How many were forced not only to delay beginning families, but to make lives for themselves outside the black family unit, residing in boarding houses as transients or living in white homes as domestic servants?[15]

14. Ninety-nine percent of all male-headed households were two-parent households as well. Female-headed households in the Abolitionist and Quaker censuses were invariably one-parent households.

15. The data necessary to answer a series of important questions concerning the black men and women who lived and worked in white households as domestic ser-

The data indicate that there was a slow but steady rise in the percentage of black men and women who found themselves outside the black family. Between 1850 and 1880 their numbers nearly doubled. By 1880 6,000 persons—slightly less than one-third of the adult population (inmates, transients, and servants combined) were living outside the normal family structures. One out of every five adults lived and worked in a white household as a domestic servant. That so many Negroes took positions outside their traditional family units is testimony to the strength and pervasiveness of the job discrimination which existed at large in the economy; that this occurred within a context of widening occupational opportunities for whites, a benefit of increasing industrialization and the factory system, makes it even more significant. In 1847 less than half of 1 percent of the black male work force was employed in factories. And this came at a time, it should be remembered, when thousands of Irish immigrants were engaged in factory work.

Blacks were not only denied access to new jobs in the expanding factory system, but because of increasing job competition with the Irish they also lost their traditional predominance in many semi-skilled and unskilled jobs. The 1847 census identified 5 percent of the black male work force in the relatively well-paying occupations of hod-carrier and stevedore. The following letter to a city newspaper written in 1849 by "P.O." attests to the job displacement. "That there may be, and undoubtedly is, a direct competition between them (the blacks and Irish) as to labor we all know. The wharves and new buildings attest this fact, in the person of our stevedores and hod-carriers as does all places of labor; and when a few years ago we saw none but blacks, we now see nothing but Irish." [16]

"P.O." proved perceptive indeed. According to the 1850 U.S. census the percentage of black hod-carriers and stevedores in the black male

---

vants will soon be available. Their age structure, marital status, mobility, social status, and the possibility of their families living close by will be examined. It will be valuable to know whether live-in service was a short-term or long-term experience and to determine its effects on family-building, family structure, and child-rearing techniques. Perhaps the most important question, and one which relates this form of employment to the experience of other ethnic groups, is whether such employment was seen by blacks as severely limiting, demeaning, and poorly paying— engaged in only because there were no other occupational alternatives available to them—or if they embraced such work as their own domain, desirable and pleased by the standard of living it afforded them.

16. The *Daily Sun*, November 10, 1849. I am indebted to Bruce Laurie, who originally came across this letter in his rigorous research on ethnic divisions within the working class of antebellum Philadelphia.

work force fell in just three years from 5 percent to 1 percent. The 1850 census, moreover, reported occupations for the entire country and included 30 percent more black male occupations than the 1847 census; nevertheless, the absolute number of black hod-carriers fell sharply from 98 to 28 and stevedores from 58 to 27.

A similar pattern of increasing discrimination affected the ranks of the skilled. Blacks complained not only that it was "difficult for them to find places for their sons as apprentices to learn mechanical trades," [17] but also that those who had skills found it more difficult to practice them. The "Register of Trades of the Colored People," published in 1838 by the Pennsylvania Abolition Society to encourage white patronage of black artisans, noted that 23 percent of 656 skilled artisans did not practice their skills because of "prejudice against them." [18] The 1856 census recorded considerable deterioration among the ranks of the skilled. The percentage of skilled artisans not practicing their trades rose from 23 percent in 1838 to approximately 38 percent in 1856. Skilled black craftsmen were "compelled to abandon their trades on account of the unrelenting prejudice against their color." [19]

Job discrimination, then, was complete and growing: blacks were excluded from new areas of the economy, uprooted from many of their traditional unskilled jobs, denied apprenticeships for their sons, and prevented from practicing the skills they already possessed. All social indicators—race riots, population decrease, disfranchisement, residential segregation, per capita wealth, ownership of real property, family structure, and occupational opportunities—pointed toward socio-economic deterioration within Philadelphia's antebellum black community.

EX-SLAVE AND FREEBORN

Among the 3,300 households and 12,000 persons included in the 1838 census, about one household in four contained at least one person who, although free in 1838, had been born a slave. Living in these 806 households were some 1,141 ex-slaves, or 9 percent of the entire population.

What was the condition of the ex-slave relative to his freeborn brother? Were ex-slaves in any way responsible for the socio-economic

17. *Register of the Trades of the Colored People in the City of Philadelphia and Districts* (Philadelphia, 1838), 1–8.

18. Appendix to the *Memorial from the People of Color to the Legislature of Pennsylvania*, reprinted in *Hazard's Register*, IX (1832), 361.

19. Benjamin C. Bacon, *Statistics of the Colored People of Philadelphia* (Philadelphia, 1859), 13–15.

deterioration just described? Contemporaries perceived two very different effects of direct contact with slavery. "Upon feeble and common minds," according to one view, the slave experience was "withering" and induced "a listlessness and an indifference to the future." Even if the slave somehow managed to gain his freedom, "the vicious habits of slavery" remained, "worked into the very grain of his character." But for others "who resisted . . . and bought their own freedom with the hard-earned fruits of their own industry," the struggle for "liberty" resulted in "a desire for improvement" which "invigorated all their powers and gave energy and dignity to their character as freemen." [20] An analysis of the data permits us to determine whether both groups were found equally in antebellum Philadelphia or whether one was more representative of all ex-slaves than the other.

The richness of detail in the census schedules allows us to make several important distinctions in the data describing the ex-slave households. We know which of the 806 households were headed by ex-slaves themselves—314—and how these 40 percent of all ex-slave households were freed—if, for instance, they were "manumitted" or if, as they put it, they had "bought themselves."

We are dealing, then, with several ex-slave categories: (1) 493 households in which at least one ex-slave lived, but which had a freeborn household head; I shall refer to this group as free-headed, ex-slave households; (2) 314 households in which at least one ex-slave lived, but which had an ex-slave household head; I shall refer to this group as ex-slave-headed households. In this second group of ex-slave-headed households, I have selected two subgroups for analysis: (a) 146 ex-slave household heads who were manumitted, and (b) 96 ex-slave household heads who bought their own freedom.[21]

20. Needles, 2.
21. The data describing the ex-slaves and the freeborn, although comprehensive, are not complete; specific age, specific place of birth, and length of residence information are not included in the census. Such data will become available for a significant number of individuals only after linkage between censuses (especially between the Quaker census of 1847 and the U.S. Census of 1850) is accomplished, because the latter began in 1850 to list age and place of birth data for every individual. While no explicit data exist in any of the censuses describing the length of residence, linkage will provide approximations of this information, especially where in-migrants (those not listed in 1838 but found in ensuing censuses) are concerned.

David Gerber of Princeton University pointed out to me that the absence of such data in this essay may represent serious limitations, for "there may well be intervening variables which offer a better and very different interpretation of the

Cutting across all of these groups is the dimension of sex. The census identified household heads as males, females, and widows. There was a strong and direct relationship between family size, wealth, and male sex, so that the largest families had the most wealth and the greatest likelihood of being headed by a male. Because there was also a strong and direct relationship between sex and almost all other variables, with males enjoying by far the more fortunate circumstances, it is important to differentiate by sex in comparing the general condition of the ex-slave groups to that of the freeborn population. Ex-slaves differ from their freeborn neighbors in a variety of significant social indicators:

Family size. The family size of all ex-slave households was 10 percent larger than households all of whose members were freeborn: 4.27 persons as compared to 3.88. Families of ex-slave households headed by freeborn males and those families headed by males who bought their own freedom were 20 percent larger: 4.70. The instances in which freeborn families were larger occurred only where female and, to a lesser extent, widow ex-slave households were involved. (This, by the way, is the general pattern in more variables; in other words, ex-slave females and widows more closely resembled their freeborn counterparts than ex-slave males resembled freeborn males.)

Two-parent household. Two-parent households were generally more common among the ex-slaves. Taken together, two-parent households were found 80 percent of the time among ex-slaves, while the figure for the freeborn was 77 percent. A significant difference, however, was found in the case of ex-slave household heads who bought their own freedom. In this group 90 percent were two-parent households.

Church. For two basic reasons the all-black church has long been recognized as the key institution of the Negro community. First, an oppressed and downtrodden people used religion for spiritual sustenance and for its promise of a better life in the next world; second, with the

---

data than the simple fact of free-birth and ex-slave status." No doubt other variables such as age and length of residence will affect some of my conclusions; however, I am of the opinion that when such information is analyzed the essential findings will remain intact. The most significant differences between the ex-slave and the freeborn are found among a specific group of ex-slaves: those who purchased their own freedom. This information makes it clear that we are dealing not with children who left slavery before its mark was firmly implanted on them, but with adults who must have worked long and hard in order to save up the money necessary to secure their freedom. I do not believe that knowing their exact age or length of residence in the city would affect to a great degree their peculiarly high level of achievement in Philadelphia.

ability to participate in the political, social, and economic spheres of the larger white society in which they lived sharply curtailed, Negroes turned to the church for fulfillment of their secular needs.

Important in the twentieth century, the church was vital to blacks in the nineteenth. Philadelphia Negroes were so closed off from the benefits of white society that church affiliation became a fundamental prerequisite to a decent and, indeed, bearable existence.[22] For this reason, non-church affiliation, rather than poverty, was the distinguishing characteristic of the most disadvantaged group in the community. Non-churchgoers must have enjoyed few of the benefits and services which accrued to those who were affiliated with a church in some manner. The socio-economic profile of non-churchgoers is depressing. They fared considerably less well than their churchgoing neighbors in all significant social indicators: they had smaller families, fewer two-parent households, high residential density levels, and they were disproportionately poor. Their ratios for membership in beneficial societies and for the number of school-age children in school was one-fourth and one-half, respectively, that of the larger community. Occupationally they were decidedly overrepresented among the unskilled sectors of the work force.

In this sense, then, the percentage of households with no members attending church is a more valuable index of general social condition than any other. Eighteen percent of the freeborn households had no members attending church; for all ex-slave households the figure was half as great. Although ex-slave households were one in four in the community at large, they were less than one in ten among households with no members attending church. The ratios were even lower (one in twenty) for ex-slave-headed households and lowest (one in thirty) for ex-slaves who bought themselves.

About 150 households, or 5 percent of the churchgoing population of the entire community, attended 23 predominately white churches. These churches had only "token" integration, allowing a few Negroes to worship in pews set apart from the rest of the congregation. Ex-slaves of all groups attended white churches in approximately the same ratio as did the freeborn—one household in twenty.

The churchgoing population of the entire community consisted of 2,776 households distributed among five religious denominations: Meth-

22. The data describing church affiliation are derived from the Abolitionist and Quaker census categories "name of religious meeting you attend" and "number attend religious meeting." These terms and the very high percentage of positive respondents make it clear that we are not dealing here with formal, dues-paying church membership, but rather with a loose affiliation with a church.

odists (73 percent), Baptists (9 percent), Presbyterians (7 percent), Episcopalians (7 percent), and Catholics (3 percent). Methodists worshipped in eight and Baptists in four all-black congregations scattered throughout the city and districts. Together they accounted for more than eight of every ten churchgoers. The various ex-slave groups were found more frequently among Methodists and Baptists.

In any case, Methodists and Baptists differed little from each other, and to describe them is to characterize the entire community: poor and unskilled. Within each denomination, however, a single church—Union Methodist and Union Baptist—served as the social base for their respective elites. And while ex-slaves attended all of the community's all-black churches, it was in these two churches where the ex-slaves were most frequently found. The ex-slave members of these two churches shared the socio-economic and cultural characteristics of the community's elite denominations, the Episcopalians and the Presbyterians; and it should not be surprising, therefore, to find ex-slaves of all groups underrepresented in each of these last two denominations.

Beneficial society. Next to the church in value to the community were the all-black beneficial societies. These important institutions functioned as rudimentary insurance groups which provided their members with relief in sickness, aid during extreme poverty, and burial expenses at death.

There were over a hundred distinct societies in antebellum Philadelphia. They grew out of obvious need and were early manifestations of the philosophy of "self-help" which became so popular later in the nineteenth century. Almost always they were affiliated directly with one of the all-black churches. The first beneficial society, known as the Free African Society, was founded in 1787. A dozen societies existed by 1815, 50 by 1830, and 106 by 1847.

Slightly more than 50 percent of freeborn households were members of the various societies. Making good the philosophy of self-help half a century before Booker T. Washington, the societies found ex-slaves more eager to join their ranks than freeborn blacks. Each group of ex-slaves had a higher percentage of members, especially ex-slave-headed households (61 percent), ex-slaves who purchased their own freedom (65 percent), and the males among the latter group (70 percent).

Membership in beneficial societies varied significantly by wealth and status. Ranking the entire household population in thirty distinct wealth categories revealed that, beginning with the poorest, the percentage of membership rose with increasing wealth until the wealthiest six categories. For this top 11 percent of the population, however, membership in beneficial societies declined from 92 to 81 percent. Among the wealthiest, and this applied equally to ex-slaves, there was less need for membership in beneficial societies.

Education. One household in four among the freeborn population sent children to school. For ex-slave households the corresponding figure was more than one in three. Ex-slave households had slightly fewer children but sent a considerably greater percentage of their children to school. For freeborn households the percentage was 55 percent; for all ex-slave households, 67 percent; and for ex-slave-headed households the figure rose to 72 percent. To the extent that education was valuable to blacks, the ex-slaves were better off.

Location and density. Small groups of ex-slaves clustered disproportionately in the outlying districts of Kensington, Northern Liberties, and Spring Garden. Twenty-five percent of the entire black population of Philadelphia, they comprised about 35 percent of the black population in these areas. Most ex-slaves, however, lived in the same proportions and in the same blocks as did the freeborn population.

More interesting than the pattern of their distribution throughout the city, however, was the level of population density in which they lived, i.e., the number of black neighbors who lived close by. To calculate the number of black households in a grid square of approximately 1¼ blocks, three density levels were used: 1-20, 21-100, and in excess of 100 households per grid square.[23]

The less dense areas were characterized by larger families, greater presence of two-parent households, less imbalance between the sexes, and fewer families whose members were entirely non-natives of Pennsylvania. In these areas lived a disproportionately greater number of wealthy families, and among them a correspondingly overrepresented number of real propertyowners. Here white-collar and skilled workers lived in greater percentages than elsewhere in the city, and unskilled workers were decidedly few in both percentage and absolute number. The major exceptions to the distribution of wealth and skill came as the result of the necessity for shopkeepers and craftsmen to locate their homes and their businesses in the city's more densely populated sections.

Ex-slave households were more likely than freeborn households to be found in the least dense areas (one in four, as compared with one in five).

23. Admittedly crude at this stage of research, the population density technique of analysis nevertheless yields interesting and important information, and with refinement promises to be an invaluable tool for the study of neighborhood and its relation to social mobility, class ecology, and community structure.

Conversely, ex-slave households were less likely to be found in those areas with the greatest density of black population.

Wealth. The parameters of wealth for Negroes in antebellum Philadelphia have already been described. The community was impoverished. Poverty, nevertheless, did not touch all groups equally. In terms of average total wealth, including both real and personal property, free-headed ex-slave households differed little from the freeborn population. In considering the ex-slave-headed household, however, differences emerge. Average total wealth for this group was 20 percent greater; for males in this group, 53 percent greater; and for males who freed themselves, 63 percent greater.

By far the most significant differences in wealth occurred in real property holding. One household in thirteen, or slightly less than 8 percent among the freeborn, owned real property. For all ex-slave households the corresponding ratio was one in eight; for ex-slave-headed households, one in five; for males who were in this group, one in four; and most dramatically, for males who purchased their own freedom, one in three owned real property. To these ex-slaves, owning their own home or a piece of land must have provided something (perhaps a stake in society) of peculiarly personal significance. Distribution of wealth, to view the matter from a different perspective, was less unequal for ex-slave households, particularly ex-slave household heads. The poorest half of the freeborn and ex-slave-headed households owned 5 and 7 percent respectively of the total wealth; for the wealthiest quarter of each group, the corresponding figure was 86 and 73 percent; for the wealthiest tenth, 67 and 56 percent; and for the wealthiest one-hundredth, 30 and 21 percent. Overall wealth distribution, in other words, while still skewed toward pronounced inequality, was more equally distributed for ex-slave household heads in the middle and upper wealth categories.

Occupation. The final area of comparison between the ex-slaves and the freeborn is occupation.[24] Analysis of the data using the same classification schema for Negroes as for white ethnic groups confirms an earlier

24. The construction of meaningful occupational categories has thus far proven to be the most difficult part of the research. While constructing such categories for the Irish, German, and native white American work force (currently under way) is certainly complex, one at least has the benefit of considerable occupational differentiation which provides vertical distance, a prerequisite for the study of social mobility and social stratification. Some 13 vertical categories including white collar/skilled/unskilled, non-manual/manual, proprietary/non-proprietary, and combinations of these schemata, and 102 horizontal categories including building-construction, food, clothing, and domestic service were constructed for the study of the black occupational structure.

suspicion that, although such schemata are necessary in order to compare the Negro to white ethnic groups, they are entirely unsatisfactory tools of analysis when social stratification in the Negro community is the concern. Despite the fact that the Negroes who comprised the labor force of antebellum Philadelphia described themselves as engaged in 400 different occupations, a stark fact emerges from the analysis: there was almost no occupational differentiation!

Five occupations accounted for 70 percent of the entire male work force: laborers (38 percent), porters (11.5 percent), waiters (11.5 percent), seamen (5 percent), and carters (4 percent); another 10 percent were employed in miscellaneous laboring capacities. Taken together, eight out of every ten working men were unskilled laborers. Another 16 percent worked as skilled artisans, but fully half of this fortunate group were barbers and shoemakers; the other skilled craftsmen were scattered among the building-construction (3.2 percent), home-furnishing (1.3 percent), leather goods (1.2 percent) and metalwork (1.2 percent) trades. Less than half of 1 percent of Negroes, as pointed out in another context, found employment in the developing factory system. The remaining 4 percent of the labor force were engaged in white-collar professions. They were largely proprietors who sold food or second-hand clothing from vending carts, and should not be considered as "storeowners."

The occupational structure for females was even less differentiated than for males. More than eight out of every ten women were employed in day-work capacities (as opposed to those who lived and worked in white households) as domestic servants: washers (52 percent), day workers (22 percent), and miscellaneous domestics (6 percent). Fourteen percent worked as seamstresses, and they accounted for all the skilled workers among the female labor force. Finally, about 5 percent were engaged in white-collar work, which, like the males, meant vending capacities in clothing- and food-selling categories.

It should come as no surprise that there were few distinctions of significance in the occupational structure of the ex-slaves and freeborn work forces. The differences in vertical occupational categories find male ex-slave household heads more likely to be in white-collar positions (7 percent, as opposed to 4 percent for the freeborn), equally distributed in the skilled trades, and slightly less represented in the unskilled occupations (75 percent, as opposed to 78 percent). Within the horizontal categories there were few important differences. Male ex-slave household heads were more likely than the freeborn to be employed as porters, carpenters, blacksmiths, preachers, and clothes dealers.

In summary, then, we find the ex-slaves with larger families, greater likelihood of two-parent households, higher affiliation rates in church and beneficial societies, sending more of their children to school, living more frequently in the least dense areas of the county, generally wealthier, owning considerably more real property, and being slightly more fortunate in occupational differentiation. By almost every socio-economic measure the ex-slave fared better than his freeborn brother. While ex-slaves were distributed throughout the socio-economic scale, they were more likely to be part of the community's small middle class which reached into both the lower and upper strata, characterized more by their hard-working, conscientious, and God-fearing life style than by a concentration of wealth and power.

AN URBAN PERSPECTIVE

On the basis of the data presented it is possible to state two conclusions, offer a working hypothesis, and argue for the necessity of an urban perspective. First, the relatively better condition of the ex-slave, especially the ex-slave who was both a male and who bought his own freedom, confirms the speculations of a few historians that the slave-born Negro freed before the Civil War was exceptional: a uniquely gifted individual who succeeded in internalizing the ethic of deferred gratification in the face of enormous difficulties.[25] More striking was the fact that the socio-economic condition of the great majority of ex-slaves was not markedly inferior to that of the freeborn. That ex-slaves were generally better off than freeborn blacks, however, should not suggest anything more than relative superiority; it does not imply prosperity and should not obscure the generally impoverished and deteriorating condition of the black community. Second, because the remaining 91 percent of Philadelphia's antebellum black population was freeborn, the dismal and declining socio-economic circumstances of that population cannot be attributed to direct contact with the "slave experience." Direct contact with slavery was undoubtedly a sufficient cause of low status and decay; it most certainly was not a necessary cause.[26]

In a very important sense the first conclusion has little to do with the

25. See the discussion of the "hiring-out system," in Richard C. Wade, *Slavery in the Cities* (New York, 1964), 38–54. It is highly likely that many of the ex-slave household heads who bought their freedom had, in fact, experienced the hiring-out system first-hand and migrated to Philadelphia.

26. There is some reason to believe that the total number of ex-slaves (1,141, or one out of every five persons who migrated to Pennsylvania) is understated. 1838

second. The latter is not arrived at because those who had direct contact with slavery fared better in the city than those who were born free. The second conclusion is not based upon a recognition that slavery was less destructive or benign (although in some aspects it certainly could have been so), but rather that the antebellum northern city was destructive as well. It is significant to understand that slavery and the discrimination faced by free Negroes in the urban environment were both forms of racism which pervaded the institutions and informed the values of the larger white society.

The comparison of the freeborn and the ex-slave was undertaken in an effort to learn more about the question which students of the black experience want answered: what was the effect of slavery on the slaves? In the case of antebellum Philadelphia the ex-slaves may not be representative of the slave experience. If they were, however, our insight

---

was not too early for free blacks to fear being sent South illegally or legally as runaway slaves. It is understandable, therefore, that despite the fact that Philadelphia blacks were asked by their clergymen to cooperate with the two census-takers (a white Abolitionist, Benjamin Bacon, and the black minister of the First African Presbyterian Church, Charles Gardner), many blacks who had in fact been born slaves reported instead that they had been born free. Although it is impossible to determine whether those who were non-natives of Pennsylvania had been in fact slave-born or freeborn, the likelihood that ex-slaves are underestimated is further supported by the fact that 50 percent of the black population had been born outside of Pennsylvania.

Of course, the important consideration concerns the consequences of understanding the actual number of ex-slaves among the black population. If the socioeconomic condition of the ex-slaves who identified themselves as freeborn was significantly worse than the actual freeborn, and if their numbers were sufficiently large, the conclusions offered in this essay would to a certain extent be compromised. The problem, however, can be resolved.

Consider the following: for the same reasons that one suspects that the ex-slaves are underenumerated, it is unlikely that many blacks born free or slave in the free states migrated to Philadelphia. It is also unlikely that more than a few elderly Pennsylvania-born blacks who had once been slaves were included in the 1838 census: Pennsylvania's gradual emancipation law had been passed in 1780. When we speak of the ex-slaves, whether or not correctly identified in the census, therefore, we can be fairly certain that they were not natives of Pennsylvania, but had migrated from the upper South. When all freeborn migrants (read as including a significant number of unidentified ex-slaves) were compared to all freeborn natives, their socio-economic profile was strikingly similar to that of the identified ex-slaves. In other words, the one population cohort in which unidentified ex-slaves might be found was at least as well off as the freeborn native population and in some important respects was better off.

would necessarily be limited to the effect of the mildest slavery system as it was practiced in Maryland, Delaware, and Virginia.[27]

De-emphasizing direct contact with slavery does not imply that the institution of slavery, and the debasement and prejudice it generated, did not condition the larger context. The indirect effect of slavery cannot be underestimated. The pro-slavery propaganda provided the justification not only for the institution, but for the widespread discriminatory treatment of the free Negro both before and long after emancipation.

Yet, on the other hand, one must not allow this understanding, or an often overwhelming sense of moral outrage, to lead to a monolithic in-

27. To determine the effect of slavery on the slaves as compared to blacks who were born free or who won their freedom before the Civil War, we would have to look after 1865. No one has yet found any data for the post-Emancipation period which distinguishes the freedmen from the freeborn (or from those freed before the Civil War). We can make the assumption that because 94 percent of the blacks in the South were slaves in 1860, a significant percentage of the migrants from the South after the Civil War were ex-slaves. But even if we discount the fact that if the migrants came from Maryland, Delaware, or the District of Columbia, they were more likely to have been free before the Civil War (55 percent of all blacks in these areas were free in 1860), we are still left with the problem of representativeness. To put it another way, even if we had data which distinguished the freed men from the freeborn, we would still be left with only the typical migrant, not the typical ex-slave. There is every reason to believe that Carter Woodson was correct in his observation that the migrants who came to the cities of the North before the Great Migration was not typical at all, but representatives of the "Talented Tenth." The migrants who came after 1910, and especially after 1915, although not "typical" of the millions of southern blacks who did not migrate, were nevertheless far more representative of Southern blacks than those who migrated before them. They came to the North for different reasons than did those who left the South a generation earlier, say between 1875 and 1900. The "push and pull" factors (floods, drought, and the boll weevil, and the demand for industrial labor heightened by the end of immigration from Europe) which led to the Great Migration simply were not operative in the earlier period. Those who came before 1900 were probably motivated for different reasons; the problems they faced in the South and the opportunities they saw in the North, if not different in kind, were certainly different in degree.

The logic of the situation suggests that we examine a Northern city during the period of the Great Migration, which had a significantly large antebellum black community and which experienced migration from the South between 1865 and 1900, hoping to identify and study three distinct groups of blacks: natives of the city, migrants arriving before 1900 (the "Talented Tenth"), and migrants arriving after 1900 (the "typical" migrant). The problem with this approach is twofold: first, we would no longer be dealing with the "typical" ex-slave, but with his children; second, the data necessary to distinguish the three groups among the population are not available.

terpretation of the effects of the slave experience. Stanley Elkins's treatment of slavery may be in error, but few historians doubt that his urging of scholars to end the morality debate and to employ new methods and different disciplines in the study of slavery was correct and long overdue.

There is no historically valid reason to treat the slave experience as entirely destructive or entirely benign; nor, for that matter, does historical reality necessarily fall midway between the two. It may be more useful to study the problems which blacks faced at different times and in different places in their history and make the attempt to trace their historical origins rather than to begin with slavery and assume that it represented in all instances the historical root. Some of the problems faced by blacks may more accurately be traced to the processes of urbanization, industrialization, and immigration occurring in a setting of racial inequality, rather than to slavery.

One of the most significant contributions to black history and sociology in recent years presents data which suggest the post-slavery, possibly urban, origins of the matrifocal black family. In ground-breaking essays on the Negro family after the Civil War, Herbert Gutman has demonstrated convincingly that traditional interpretations of slavery and its effect on the black family are seriously misleading. Examining "the family patterns of those Negroes closest in time to actual chattel slavery," Gutman did not find "instability," "chaos," or "disorder." Instead, in fourteen varied southern cities and counties between 1865 and 1880 he found viable two-parent households ranging from 70 to 90 percent.[28]

It is significant to note that of the areas studied by Gutman the four lowest percentages of two-parent households were found in cities: Natchez and Beaufort, 70 percent; Richmond, 73 percent; and Mobile, 74 percent. The urban experience was in some way responsible for the weaker family structure and for a whole set of other negative socio-economic consequences, all of which are found in the Philadelphia data.

Yet the city is more than a locale. Slavery itself underwent major transformations in the urban setting.[29] Sustained advances in technology, transportation, and communication made the city the context for innovation; and the innovation, in turn, generated countless opportunities for upward mobility for those who could take advantage of them. And here

28. Herbert Gutman, "The Invisible Fact: Negro Family Structure before and after the Civil War," Paper read at the Association for the Study of Negro Life and History (Birmingham: October, 1969) and in a revised form at the Organization of American Historians (Los Angeles: April, 1970).

29. Richard Wade, "The Transformation of Slavery in the Cities," 243–282.

was the rub. Blacks, alone among city dwellers, were excluded not only from their fair share, but from almost any chance for improvement generated by the dynamics of the urban milieu. That the exclusion was not systematic, but by and large incidental, did not make it any less effective. The city provided an existence at once superior to and inferior to that of the countryside: for those who were free to pursue their fortunes, the city provided infinitely more opportunities and far greater rewards; for those who were denied access altogether (or for those who failed), the city provided scant advantages and comforts. There were few interstices.

The data presented in this essay point to the destructiveness of the urban experience for blacks in nineteenth-century Philadelphia.[30] To proceed, data comparing the black experience to that of other ethnic groups are necessary, and they are forthcoming. Although much research remains, it is possible to offer a hypothesis. The forces which shaped modern America—urbanization, industrialization, and immigration—operated for blacks within a framework of institutional racism and structural inequality. In the antebellum context, blacks were unable to compete on equal terms with either the native white American worker or the thousands of newly arrived Irish and German immigrants. Philadelphia Negroes suffered in the competition with the Irish and Germans and recovered somewhat during the Civil War and Reconstruction decades, only to suffer again, in much the same circumstances, in competition with the new immigrant groups, this time the Italians, Jews, Poles, and Slavs who began arriving in the 1880's. Best characterized as a low-status economic group early in the century, Philadelphia's blacks found themselves a deprived and degraded caste at its close.

Students of black history have not adequately appreciated the impact of the urban experience. In part this is due to several general problems: to the larger neglect of urban history; to unequal educational opportunities which prevented many potential black scholars from study and other students from publication; to difficulties inherent in writing his-

30. A major interest of my research is to develop and make explicit for the city the characteristics of an "urban component" which distinguishes the urban from the rural experience. There is certainly agreement that urban conditions differ from rural ones in significant dimensions: family structure, sex ratios, mortality, fertility, housing conditions, diet, educational and occupational opportunities, plus the intangibles of values and expectations. In future work, however, I hope to demonstrate that it is seriously misleading to treat these urban/rural differences monolithically. The racial discrimination and structural inequality of the city affected each ethnic group differently. The advantages of the city were never equally available for all.

tory "from the bottom up"; and to present reward mechanisms which place a high premium on quickly publishable materials involving either no new research or shoddy and careless efforts.

There are, however, other and more important considerations, with no little sense of irony. The moral revulsion to slavery prevented development of alternative explanations of low status and decay. In the immediate post-slavery decades and throughout the twentieth century blacks and then white allies took refuge in an explanation used by many abolitionists before them, namely, that slavery and not racial inferiority was responsible for the black condition. They were, of course, not wrong; it was rather that they did not go far enough. It was, and still is, much easier to lament the sins of one's forefathers than it is to confront the injustices in more contemporary socio-economic systems.

Although August Meier and Elliot Rudwick titled their well-known and widely used text *From Plantation to Ghetto*, and, with the little data available to them, subtly but suggestively wove the theme of the impact of urban environment through their pages, scholars have been slow to develop it in monographic studies.

The Philadelphia data from 1838 to 1880 enable one to examine this theme in minute detail. Although 90 percent of the nation's black population in 1880 was southern and overwhelmingly rural, the key to the twentieth century lies in understanding the consequences of the migration from the farm to the city. The experience of Philadelphia Negroes in the nineteenth century foreshadowed the fate of millions of black migrants who, seeking a better life, found different miseries in what E. Franklin Frazier called the "cities of destruction."

If we are to succeed in understanding the urban experience, we must dismiss simplistic explanations which attribute all present-day failings to "the legacy of slavery" or to "the problems of unacculturated rural migrants lacking the skills necessary to compete in an advanced technology." We must understand, instead, the social dynamics and consequences of competition and accommodation among different racial, ethnic, and religious groups, taking place in an urban context of racial discrimination and structural inequality.

Jerome H. Wood, Jr.

The Negro in Early Pennsylvania:
The Lancaster Experience, 1730 - 90

Indentured servitude was America's earliest means of fulfilling her unending need for labor. Though the system varied from colony to colony, usually it involved some contractual arrangement whereby the master paid his servant's passage from the Old World to the New. In return, the servant promised to work for a specified number of years. Sometimes it also included instruction in a trade or the grant of land after the expiration of the indenture. Even if the master promised no such reward, the abundance of land meant a prosperous future for the industrious ex-servant. Originally all men regardless of race who came to work in the New World were indentured servants. Then between 1640 and 1660, in the midst of an agricultural depression in Virginia, a dramatic change occurred. Indentured Negro servants became servants for life—that is, slaves. For all Negroes this was a momentous event. Its significance was, of course, greater in the South, where the numbers of Negroes now enslaved altered both its economy and its social geography.

The origins of this change were both economic and racial. A comparison of slave life in Lancaster, Pennsylvania, with that found in other areas of the South during the same period suggests that the primary motive was economic. The change from a system of indentured servitude to one of life-long slavery in the South produced a continuous supply of labor which would not, after the usual seven years, leave to establish its own plantations. The need for a well-trained and highly routinized number of laborers reflects the beginnings of commercial agriculture in the South. This change was paralleled in the North by disparate developments, each of which signified the decay of mercantilism.

Mercantilism was medieval in its origins and was dedicated to a stable, well-ordered economic system. Late or post-mercantile economics was based on competition and individual aggrandizement. The decay of classic mercantilism had begun centuries before and would continue well into the nineteenth century. In the South this occasioned the departure from indentured servitude to plantation slavery, a more efficient and for the time being a more profitable means of economic organization. It provided a life-long supply of inexpensive and continuous labor.

In the North this change saw the decline and abolition of slavery.
In Lancaster, as Wood indicates, slaves frequently worked as apprentices. The relation between the two harked back to the Middle
Ages. This was not a racial but an economic relationship. As competition replaced stability and late mercantilism became a victim of
its own contradictions, blacks in the South and North suffered as a
result. Race became a crucial factor in their market value, for there
was certain labor which whites would not do. Its accomplishment
was possible only by blacks. The outstanding example is plantation
work, and as the price of cotton spiraled in the 1850's, so did the
price of slaves. Race became synonymous with caste; or, viewed
from another perspective, class and ethnicity became identical. In
the South the economic sphere of black activity increasingly restricted itself to plantation labor; in the North, as the preceding article makes clear, free blacks were allowed only the most menial
work. The relatively sanguine picture of slavery which Wood
paints is not the result of an urban environment or an ethnically diverse milieu, but the product of a historical epoch in which racial
and economic tensions were far less acerbic than they would be in
the future.

T he history of the Negro in Pennsylvania is as old as the state itself
—older, in fact. There were blacks living in the regions adjacent to
the Delaware River even before the Quaker colony was founded, when
Dutchmen and Swedes were still in possession of the area. Their numbers merely increased once Penn established his commonwealth; blacks
were present in Philadelphia County as early as 1684, and in Chester
County by 1687. Even before the beginning of the eighteenth century,
Philadelphia merchants had made the importation of Negroes a regular
part of their trans-Atlantic commerce. There were somewhere between
2,500 and 5,000 blacks in the province in 1721; thirty years later the
number reportedly stood at 11,000, with Philadelphia accounting for
more than half of the total. The 1751 figure, though it may be somewhat exaggerated, represented the largest number of Negroes in Pennsylvania prior to the adoption of the federal Constitution.[1]

Most of the black men in colonial Pennsylvania were slaves. Although
the practice of binding some Negroes to service for life had emerged *de
facto* before the end of the seventeenth century, it was not until 1700
that the province recognized *de jure* the institution of slavery. From
that date a slave code gradually evolved. Black bondsmen were not to
be tried in regular courts, but in a special judicial assembly consisting of

1. Edward R. Turner, *The Negro in Pennsylvania: Slavery, Servitude, Freedom,
1639–1861* (New York, 1969), Ch. 1.

two justices of the peace and six freeholders. Murder, burglary, and rape were to be punished by death; attempted rape by castration; and robbing and stealing by whipping. Racial intermarriage was forbidden in 1726. Slaves were not to go more than ten miles from their masters' abode without a pass. They were not to be out after 9 P.M., and not more than four were ever to meet together.[2]

The institution of slavery in Pennsylvania never possessed the characteristics it exhibited in the staple-producing colonies to the south. There were few large holdings of slaves in this colony; the average slaveowner possessed only one or two such servants. Certainly, the plantation form of agricultural production did not emerge in Penn's province, which was overwhelmingly the land of small farmers ploughing ther own fields with the help of their own families and, perhaps, a hired hand or two at harvest time. There seems to be general agreement that the institution of slavery in Pennsylvania was mild in its operation, allowing the slaves a surprising degree of liberty. Despite the laws Negroes moved about freely, visiting each other at their pleasure and enjoying a social life of their own.[3] Even the mildness of the institution here, however, did not allay the objections of humanitarians, who were opposed to the enslavement of men altogether; the remonstrance of the Germantown Mennonites in 1688 and the efforts of the Society of Friends to end slaveowning by its members are well-known stages in the progress of humanity in North America.

Recent historians of slavery in America have stressed the tendency towards permissiveness which characterized the institution when it existed in an urban setting.[4] Whereas the plantation slave found himself in a very circumscribed environment, the slave who lived in a city or town enjoyed greater freedom of movement and association and wider experiences of life than his plantation counterpart. Richard Wade and others have demonstrated that in larger cities slavery failed as an instrument of race control, and other means—such as segreation ordinances—were devised to maintain the desired separation between whites and blacks. That is essentially a nineteenth-century development, however. Our aim here is to focus attention on the colonial period, on the colony of Pennsylvania, and on a town which was—by the era of the Revolutionary War—the largest inland settlement in British

2. *Ibid.*; John Hope Franklin, *From Slavery to Freedom: A History of American Negroes* (New York, 1961), 95–98.
3. Franklin, 97.
4. See, for example, Richard Wade, *Slavery in the Cities: the South, 1820–1860* (New York, 1964).

North America. The problems may be defined as that of ascertaining the characteristics of black existence in that town, and that of ascertaining the extent to which slavery in that community did or did not conform to some of the broader generalizations that have been made concerning the institution in Pennsylvania and in the urban setting.

Founded in 1730 at the outset of a new phase of urban expansion in the Quaker colony,[5] Lancaster was filled in the next three decades with a swarm of hopeful immigrants. Despite the lack of a navigable stream, the town thrived, thus providing an early American contradiction to the "doctrine of natural advantages" often stressed as the key factor in the growth of a successful town. Rather did Lancaster benefit, even at its founding, from certain artificial advantages: it was laid out as the seat for Lancaster County, and it was promoted by its resident leaders and the proprietors who owned the land on which the town was built. So rapidly did the town grow that it was awarded the status of a borough in 1742—a mere twelve years after its founding. In 1790, there were 3,772 persons residing in the town.[6] Lancaster's preeminence in its region is to be explained essentially by its economic function. It quickly became the paramount marketing and manufacturing center for the bountiful and deservedly famous agricultural area surrounding it; indeed, until the 1770's the town was an emporium for the wide hinterland embracing western Pennsylvania and Maryland, as well as the upper part of the valley of Virginia.[7] Timing, too, counted significantly in the town's success; for having established economic dominance over its immediate area and the backcountry before midcentury, it hindered the growth of rivals close at hand.[8]

Within twenty years after its founding Lancaster was characterized by a high degree of differentiation in occupational specialization. In the years analyzed here, the number of residents engaged in trading fluc-

5. James T. Lemon, "Urbanization and the Development of Eighteenth-Century Southeastern Pennsylvania and Adjacent Delaware," *The William and Mary Quarterly*, XXIV (October, 1967), 501–542.

6. For the founding and development of Lancaster, see Jerome H. Wood, Jr., "Conestoga Crossroads: The Rise of Lancaster, Pennsylvania, 1730–1789" (dissertation, Brown University, 1969). The town was built on land owned first by Andrew Hamilton, sometime speaker of the assembly and attorney general of the province of Pennsylvania, and his son, James, sometime governor of the province. The 1790 population is taken from the *First Census of the United States, Pennsylvania* (Washington: Government Printing Office, 1908), 10.

7. Wood, Prologue, Chs. 2, 6.

8. Lemon, 501–542.

tuated from between 4 and 7 percent of the heads of families. Most of these individuals were retailers and single proprietors who proffered a variety of dry goods. But there were always to be found a half-dozen or so large shopkeepers—frequently in partnership with Philadelphia mercantile houses and engaged in extensive wholesaling operations—who engrossed a large volume of "the custom" of town and country and enriched themselves in brisk trading. However, Lancaster was above all the haven of industrious artisans, representative of those "laborious Handicrafts" William Penn deemed so essential to a flourishing commonwealth, whose number between 1759 and 1788 fluctuated between 60 and 71 percent of the heads of families and who engaged in nearly half a hundred mysteries. Laborers, earning their livelihoods through day's work in the town and on surrounding farms at harvest seasons, constituted a group varying from between 11 and 20 percent of the heads of families whose occupations can be determined. Not numerous but accorded high status as individuals and because of their callings were the professional men of the community—lawyers, court officials, teachers, physicians, and ministers—who represented 4 percent of the heads of families in 1759 and 5 percent at the end of the period.[9]

In its population Lancaster mirrored the demographic variety characteristic of the province of Pennsylvania as a whole. The town was "mostly inhabited by Dutch people," as more than one visitor described and misnamed the German-speaking majority who comprised approximately 67 percent of the heads of families in 1759 and about 63 percent at the end of the period. British people constituted the largest minority ethnic group, but there were other ethnic and national elements as well. To be sure, not all of the German-speaking inhabitants came from Germany; some of them were "Swissers" from the German-language cantons of Switzerland. A few French families—probably all of them related to Canadian Indian traders active in the Pennsylvania backcountry before the French and Indian War—settled in the borough. Negroes added further to the variety of the population within the community.

A black population—small, but destined to increase somewhat over the years—appeared within twenty years of the settling of Lancaster.

9. The analysis of the occupational structure of Lancaster, 1730–90, is based on assessment and tax lists for the borough which are located in the Lancaster County Historical Society, Lancaster, Pa., and in the Historical Society of Pennsylvania, Philadelphia. See especially the lists for 1759, 1772, and 1788 in the former institution, and the list for 1764 in the Lancaster County collection, Miscellaneous Papers, 1772–1816, 135, at the latter.

Most of the Negroes who lived in the town before 1790 were slaves, but a few free persons of color resided in the community at one time or another.

In the summer of 1750, when the Quaker tanner Isaac Whitelock advertised the disappearance of "a Negro Man with an iron Collar about his Neck," there were at least seven slaves in the borough. Six years later there were thirteen black bondsmen there, and by 1764 there were twenty-eight such servants.[10] The number of slaves dropped to twenty-three by 1775.[11] But it was, ironically, precisely during the years in which Americans fought to gain recognition of the principle that "all men are created equal" that the number of slaves owned by Lancastrians increased dramatically. Indeed, the number more than doubled between 1775 and 1783; there were fifty-four in 1779 and sixty-three in 1782. To be sure, some of the slaves included in the town's black population in 1782 were brought there by and belonged to Philadelphians who fled to the borough during the war in an attempt to escape the depredations of the British forces in the east. But of the sixty-three slaves known to have been in the borough in 1782, at least fifty-seven were owned by residents of the town.[12] The depression which was felt throughout the new nation after the war appears to have led some Lancastrians to sell their slaves. Only thirty-six such servants were recorded for the borough in 1788.[13] But the return of prosperity in the late 1780's seems to have brought with it a significant increase in the number of slaves; for according to the first federal census of 1790, there were fifty-seven slaves in the town.[14] There is always the possibility, however, that the tax records for the 1780's do not accurately reflect the true number of slaves —which would account for the otherwise curious fluctuations. Throughout this period the number of slaves never amounted to more than about 1 percent of the total population.[15]

10. Lancaster Borough Return, ca. 1750, Lancaster County Courthouse, Prothonotary's Office; Borough Return, 1756, Manuscript Box 16, Lancaster County Historical Society; Lancaster Borough Assessment, ca. 1764, Lancaster County Miscellaneous Papers, 1772–1816, Historical Society of Pennsylvania.

11. Constable Return, Lancaster Borough, 1775, Lancaster County Historical Society.

12. Assessment Roll, 1782, Lancaster County Historical Society.

13. List of Taxables, Lancaster Borough, 1788, Lancaster County Historical Society.

14. *First Census of the United States, Pennsylvania,* 10. The heads of families in the Borough of Lancaster can be found between pp. 135 and 138.

15. In 1782, when there were reportedly 63 slaves in the borough, the total population was approximately 3,270. See the borough assessment list for 1782, Lancaster

Slaves constituted the base of the colonial social pyramid; and, as is the case with all lowly folk of past times, the extant literary evidence tells us little about them. What we do know is derived in great measure from quantitative data. It is most probable that Lancaster's slave population—like that of Pennsylvania as a whole—consisted of persons born in America rather than in Africa. Advertisements of the sale of slaves frequently mentioned that the servants to be vended were "Country-born." What else can we know about them? The tax and assessment lists for the borough not only provide the number of Negro bondsmen in any given year but also yield other suggestive demographic information, albeit very inconclusive. Down to the time of the Revolution, at least, Lancaster's slave population appears to have been a relatively youthful one. Ten of the fifteen slaves listed in 1759 were age 25 or younger.[16] Twelve of the twenty-three black servants noted in 1775 fell into the same category.[17] Some Lancastrians appear to have acquired as their slaves children whom they kept for a number of years. In 1764, for example, nine of the twenty-eight slaves were age 16 or under.[18] Three years earlier Ulrich Reigart, butcher, sold "a likely healthy Negro boy, about 14 Years of Age," who was described as having had the smallpox and measles, and was, moreover, "fit to wait on a Gentleman." [19]

The information contained on the tax and assessment lists for the town also indicates that the slave population consisted of a large number of females. Unfortunately, the earliest records do not indicate the sex of slaves, but in 1783 twenty-four of the fifty-five slaves were girls or women.[20]

Despite its paucity, this demographic evidence—joined with traditional literary documentation—is suggestive of the character of slavery as an institution in Lancaster. It was never a factor in the economic life of the town. Although a few slaves may have been craftsmen and labored in the establishments of local artisans, most of them were domestic

County Historical Society. The population estimate is arrived at by multiplying the total heads of families by six—which appears to have been the average family size according to the Census of 1790.

16. Borough Return, 1759, Lancaster County Historical Society.

17. Constable Return, Lancaster Borough, 1775, Lancaster County Historical Society.

18. Lancaster Borough Assessment Roll, ca. 1764, Miscellaneous Lancaster County Papers, 1772–1816, 135, Historical Society of Pennsylvania.

19. *The Pennsylvania Gazette*, May 21, 1761, 4.

20. Lancaster Borough Assessment Roll, 1783, Lancaster County Historical Society.

servants in the homes of wealthy townsmen—a testimony primarily to the financial and social success of their owners. Although prosperous storekeepers appear to have been the first possessors of human cattle in the borough, wealthy men of other occupations acquired similar servants. Among the townsmen who owned slaves in 1764 were four shopkeepers, four innkeepers, a lawyer, a blacksmith, a butcher, a carpenter, a physician, a brewer, a militia officer, a candlemaker, a coppersmith, and a saddletree maker. In most instances the slaveowners of Lancaster held only one lifetime servant. The men who owned more were almost invariably shopkeepers and innkeepers, who were generally the wealthiest occupational group in the town. The largest number of slaves known to have been owned by a single individual in Lancaster were the five belonging in 1782 to Matthias Slough, the German host of the White Swan Inn and a shopkeeper as well.[21]

Most of Lancaster's slaves were individuals who had to face the world alone, without the sustaining affections of parents, siblings, or consorts. One or two of them were married, it is true, but in only one case are a slave husband and wife known to have lived together in the same household. Joseph Simon, perhaps Lancaster's most enterprising merchant, attempted to send his "black Wench" to Fort Pitt, where he maintained a store, in 1772; she was, however, the wife of another slave in the town and was about four months pregnant. When informed that she was to be sent away, she "went on in Such a Manner and would not Stir from here, sayd she'd Sooner kill herself" than leave Lancaster.[22] Hannah, a slave belonging to Edward Shippen, recorder of the Court of Quarter Sessions and prothonotary of the Court of Common Pleas, had a husband who was a slave to a resident of Chester, Pennsylvania, about seventy miles away. The husband was allowed to visit his wife periodically, however, and on one such occasion Shippen, observing Hannah's joy on her husband's arrival "and her Grief in parting with him, not knowing whether she will ever see him again," was moved to reflect, "Blacks have natural affections as well as we have."[23] Hannah's fear was not un-

21. Lancaster Borough Assessment Roll, ca. 1764, Miscellaneous Lancaster County Papers, 135, Historical Society of Pennsylvania; Assessment Roll, 1782, Lancaster County Historical Society.

22. Joseph Simon to Michael Gratz, October 10, 1772, McAllister MSS No. 3, Library Company of Philadelphia. (The manuscript collections formerly housed in the Ridgeway Branch, Library Company of Philadelphia, have now been transferred to the Historical Society of Pennsylvania.)

23. Edward Shippen to the Rev. George Craig, January 9, 1769 (copy of a letter which was not sent); Edward Shippen Letterbooks, Library of the American Philosophical Society, Philadelphia, Pa.

founded, for hanging over every slave was the possibility of being sold, of being separated from familiar surroundings, relatives, and friends. Matthias Slough, mentioned earlier as proprietor of the White Swan Inn, once sold a slave woman without including her child in the offer.[24]

Some of the slaves of Lancaster had masters who were intent upon the proper Christian upbringing of their servants and who thus provided that they received proper instruction and baptism. There was "a Negro" among the children of the Lutheran school in 1750. In the preceding year the Moravian congregation held a "Taufe des Negerknaben" ("baptism of the Negro boys"). In April, 1784, the three slaves of the merchant Paul Zantzinger—Louise, Flavia, and James—were baptized in St. James Episcopal Church, where Sarah Parr, a slave belonging to the merchant John Parr, entered the Christian faith a year later. Among the students in the school which he opened in 1771, Joseph Rathell, the Anglican curate, had in his charge "several Negroes belonging to different Families of the congregation," whom he taught on Sunday evenings in the schoolhouse, using his "best Endeavours to instruct them in their Catochism and some of the plainest Duties of Religion and Morality, by which I hope these poor Creatures will be much benefitted." [25]

It is clear that some of Lancaster's black servants were of uncommon intelligence and skill. In an advertisement announcing the sale of "one Negro woman and two pretty children," Solomon Etting, merchant, mentioned that the woman could speak both German and English, and was "suitable for city or country work. She would prefer," he added, "being sold to a German farmer who lives near Lancaster." Dan, a black man who ran away from the tailor Christian Wertz, was also bilingual, could play a fiddle which he bowed with his left hand, could "work a little at the saddler's trade," and was withal "a shrewd, cunning fellow." [26]

Insofar as the force implied in the subjection of one human being to another can ever be said to be mild, the institution of slavery in Lancaster displayed little of the harshness associated with plantation bondage;

24. *The Pennsylvania Gazette*, April 23, 1761, 3.

25. Diary of the Moravian Minister Abraham Reinke, December 10, 1749, St. Andrew's Moravian Church, Lancaster, Pa.; William Egle, *Notes and Queries*, Annual Volume (1900), 204; H. M. J. Klein and William F. Diller, *The History of St. James' Church, 1744–1944* (Lancaster, 1944), 46.

26. *Neue Unparthyesche Lancastersche Zeitung*, October 1, 1788, 3; *The Pennsylvania Gazette*, September 15, 1779, 4.

indeed, it exhibited the mildness generally ascribed to that labor system in Pennsylvania. Moreover, as the institution developed in this borough, it exhibited some of the tendencies toward permissiveness which have been noted in other studies of urban slavery. Slaves moved freely about the town and were allowed to mingle freely with each other. Aside from the yoke of lifetime servitude which was theirs to bear exclusively, these bondsmen appear to have been treated in the same manner as indentured servants.

In at least one instance a Lancaster slave was allowed to operate his own business. Thomas, the husband of Edward Shippen's slave Hannah but who lived with his master in Chester, was allowed to move to the Shippen household in 1776 and to open his own copper's establishment. The casks he made there were doubtless a part of the tremendous quantity of war material produced in the borough as a part of the Revolutionary War effort. Shippen provided him with account books and appointed his law clerk to keep them for him "as if for myself." "I often saw him and Thomas together in my office," Shippen wrote to the slave's owner in Chester, "when people were charged for Casks &c., and the Latter seemed always well pleased with the entrys. However, one day as I was walking on my pavement and Thomas was passing by in the Yard pretty near me, I heard him speaking to himself in a grumbling manner, saying that he could never bring [the clerk] to Settle accounts with him." [27]

Lancaster's slaves had an opportunity to mingle not only among themselves, but also with the handful of free men of color settled there. Little information survives concerning these people, however. In 1754 a woman called "black Sall" apprenticed her five-year-old natural mulatto son, Annis McAdam, to the saddletree maker John Bowne until he reached his majority, at which time he would be free. Most of the town's free blacks appear to have been domestic servants like the majority of the slaves, or common laborers. Rachel, "a free Mullattoe Girl" with a child in Maryland, was employed for seven months in 1767 as a maid to the sister of the attorney Jasper Yeates. The wife of Christopher Marshall, a Quaker apothecary from Philadelphia who lived in Lancaster during the Revolutionary War, employed a free black woman to help her keep house; and Marshall himself hired a black man named Charles as a sort of handyman—until the day when Charles received his pay, got "a hankering" to go to Baltimore, and left his employer

27. Edward Shippen to the Rev. George Craig, July 13, 1778 (copy); Edward Shippen Letterbooks, Library of the American Philosophical Society.

"without saying farewell." There is reason to believe that the "George Smith, negro, and Margaret Manson, mullato," married in St. James Episcopal Church in 1785 were free people. "Negro Ben," who had probably also been released from bondage, received a small sum from the borough in 1788 "for cleaning the Fire Engine House" on several occasions. According to the federal census of 1790, there were three black families among the thirty-nine non-white free persons of Lancaster.[28]

Merely the briefest shreds of evidence hint that the black residents of the town—slave and free—enjoyed some "society" amongst themselves. When his slave, Dinah, died in 1778, Christopher Marshall invited "the Negros in Lancaster" to attend the funeral. There is a suggestion that the town's black residents found conviviality together and with some of the white residents in Adams Town, the poorest and most thickly settled section of the borough. Poll, another slave belonging to Christopher Marshall, frequently stayed out all night; and when she did, her master spent the following morning looking for her in that part of town where she was wont to go dancing.[29] By the late 1780's blacks held a special holiday of their own each year.[30]

Most white Lancastrians doubtless accepted slavery as a given part of their environment and regarded the black man with prejudice and scorn. There were, to be sure, some townsmen who were of tender conscience as to the morality of one person's owning another. Edward Shippen, who owned three slaves himself in 1773, confided in a letter to his son that he could not help but "Consider the Condition of these poor Slaves; indeed, Strictly speaking, I think none [of them] ought to be bound longer than for Seven years." [31] Shippen was at least willing, it would seem, to have unfree blacks treated as indentured servants, who served not *durante vita* but for a stated term of years. He does not appear to

28. Indenture of Annis McAdam to John Bowne, August 17, 1754. Miscellaneous Manuscripts (1743–63), Library of the American Philosophical Society; Jasper Yeates, Memorandum Book (1764–69), 39, 40, Historical Society of Pennsylvania; Jasper Yeates, Day Book, February 23, 1767; Christopher Marshall, Remembrancer, 1777–79, *passim*, Historical Society of Pennsylvania; Records, St. James Church, 1784–99, Lancaster, Pa.; Lancaster Corporation Book, September 13, 1788, Mayor's Office, Lancaster, Pa.

29. Christopher Marshall, Remembrancer, May 18, June 3, 1778, Historical Society of Pennsylvania.

30. *The Pennsylvania Magazine of History and Biography*, XXIX, 257.

31. Edward Shippen to James Burd, July 17, 1778, Shippen Family Papers, VIII (1777–1821), 35, Historical Society of Pennsylvania.

have acted on this sentiment himself, however, for the borough assessment list for 1782 indicates that he still possessed one slave.

The extent of anti-Negro prejudice in the town is suggested by two
entries in Christopher Marshall's diary. When his servant Dinah died,
Marshall spent a day in search of someone who would lay her out, "as
all the poor women here are rich in Imagination, so that it was with difficulty one could be procured at any rate." It took another day's search
to secure persons "for to put the Negro woman in her Coffin. O what a
wretched place is here," Marshall lamented in his diary, "full of Relli-
gious Professions but not a grain of Love or Charity, except in words, in
the generality of the German inhabitants." [32] Marshall's gratuitous in-
sult to the Germans was itself uncharitable, for the prejudice and super-
stition which characterized their attitude toward blacks was not
unique.

The black experience in eighteenth-century Lancaster was essentially that of the slave. Although this borough was never as large as the
port cities of the continent—Boston, New York, Philadelphia, and
Charleston—the institution of slavery there did display some of the
characteristics ascribed to the institution in the larger urban setting. Most
of the slaves were domestic servants who were a part of their masters'
households. They were never a factor in the economic life of the borough, nor did they ever constitute more than 1 percent of the town's
population. They served rather as advertisements of their owners' high
economic and social status. With the obvious exception of the peculiar
length of their service, they were treated about the same as white indentured servants. No ordinances restricted their movement about the
town; they were never a special subject of local legislation. Together
with the free people of color who found their way to the town, they
found some opportunities for conviviality and enjoyment of life's plea-
sures—to the extent that they can be enjoyed by a man who knows that he
is despised or that his life is not fully his own.

32. Christopher Marshall, Remembrancer, May 2, 3, 1778, Historical Society of
Pennsylvania.

Index